SECOND

TOXIC TORT LITIGATION

Arthur F. Foerster & Christine Gregorski Rolph, Editors

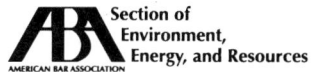

Cover design by Anthony Nuccio/ABA Publishing.

The materials contained herein represent the views of each chapter author in his or her individual capacity and should not be construed to be the views of the author's firms, employers, or clients, or of the editors or the other chapter authors, or of the American Bar Association or the Section of Environment, Energy, and Resources, unless adopted pursuant to the bylaws of the Association.

Nothing contained in this book is to be considered as the rendering of legal advice for specific cases, and readers are responsible for obtaining such advice from their own legal counsel. This book is intended for educational and informational purposes only.

© 2013 American Bar Association. All rights reserved.

No part of this publication may be reproduced, stored in a retrieval system, or transmitted in any form or by any means, electronic, mechanical, photocopying, recording, or otherwise, without the prior written permission of the publisher. For permission, complete the online form at http://www.americanbar.org/reprint.

Printed in the United States of America.

17 16 15 14 13 5 4 3 2 1

Library of Congress Cataloging-in-Publication Data

Toxic tort litigation / [edited] by Arthur F. Foerster and Christine Gregorski Rolph; Section of Environment, Energy and Resources, American Bar Association. — Second Edition.
    pages cm
  Previous edition (2007) edited by D. Alan Rudlin.
Includes bibliographical references and index.
ISBN 978-1-62722-127-6 (alk. paper)
1. Toxic torts—United States—Trial practice. 2. Toxic torts—United States. I. Foerster, Arthur F. II. Rolph, Christine Gregorski. III. American Bar Association. Section of Environment, Energy, and Resources.
KF8925.T69T69 2013
346.7303'8—dc23

2013026308

Discounts are available for books ordered in bulk. Special consideration is given to state bars, CLE programs, and other bar-related organizations. Inquire at ABA Publishing, American Bar Association, 321 N. Clark Street, Chicago, Illinois 60654-7598.

www.ShopABA.org

SUMMARY OF CONTENTS

Acknowledgments   xv
About the Editors   xvii
About the Contributors   xix

Part One: Elements of Toxic Tort Litigation

1. Introduction   3
L. Neal Ellis Jr.

2. Theories of Liability and Damages   9
Bruce Jones, Ryan T. Dunn, Courtney A. Lawrence, and Delmar R. Ehrich

3. Common Defenses   57
J Kevin Buster and Randy J. Butterfield

4. The Use of Scientific and Medical Evidence   121
William D. Dannelly, Rita A. Sheffey, Ashley Cummings, and Matthew F. Hanchey

5. Causation and the Use of Experts   139
Alan Rudlin, Alexandra Cunningham, and Thomas R. Waskom

6. Case Strategy and Trial Management   167
John P. Manard Jr., Steven J. Levine, S. Ault Hootsell III, J. Alan Harrell, Roy L. Bergeron Jr., and Evan Dicharry

7. Settlement Considerations 261
Brendan K. Collins

8. Emerging Areas of Litigation and Significant Legal Issues 279
Shawna Bligh and Chris Wendelbo

Part Two: Regional Standards for Causation

9. Western States 309
Karen R. Leviton, Michael G. Romey, and R. Peter Durning Jr.

10. Midwestern States 333
Andrew Holly and Colin Wicker

11. Southern States 363
Lisa Horvath Shub

12. Eastern States 405
Libretta Stennes

Table of Cases 435
Index 495

CONTENTS

Acknowledgments — xv
About the Editors — xvii
About the Contributors — xix

Part One: Elements of Toxic Tort Litigation

1. Introduction — 3
L. Neal Ellis Jr.
What Toxic Torts Are and What They Are Not — 3
The Legacy of Significant Actions — 4
Causation Is King — 4
The Evolution of Traditional Tort Theories — 5
Preview of the Following Chapters — 7

2. Theories of Liability and Damages — 9
Bruce Jones, Ryan T. Dunn, Courtney A. Lawrence, and Delmar R. Ehrich
Theories of Liability — 9
  Negligence — 9
  Trespass — 13
  Nuisance — 18
  Strict Liability and Absolute Liability — 21
  Statutory Liability — 26
  Former Landowner Liability — 28
  Other Liability Theories in the Toxic Tort Context — 30
Damages — 35
  Overview — 35
  Present Injury Requirement — 37
  Medical Monitoring — 40

Fear of Disease	43
Property Damage	45
Natural Resource Damages	47
Punitive Damages	50
Other Remedies: Injunctive Relief and Attorneys' Fees	53

3. Common Defenses — 57
J Kevin Buster and Randy J. Butterfield

Introduction	57
Common Toxic Tort Defenses	57
Statutes of Limitation	57
Statutes of Repose	70
Laches	72
Exhaustion of Administrative Remedies	73
Primary Jurisdiction	75
Preemption	76
Use and Applicability of Regulatory Safe Levels	88
Standing	90
Plaintiff's Culpable Conduct	93
Failure to Mitigate	95
Defenses to Nuisance Claims	97
Lack of Duty	101
Attacking Causation	107
State of the Art	113
Government Contractor Defense	116
Workers' Compensation Bar	118
Conclusion	119

4. The Use of Scientific and Medical Evidence — 121
William D. Dannelly, Rita A. Sheffey, Ashley Cummings, and Matthew F. Hanchey

Sampling and Analysis	121
Sampling Procedures	123
Quality Control	125
Calibration	126
Fate and Transport	127
Causation Analysis through Toxicology and Epidemiology	131
Toxicology	131
Epidemiology	133
Bradford Hill Criteria	136
Conclusion	137

5. Causation and the Use of Experts · 139
Alan Rudlin, Alexandra Cunningham, and Thomas R. Waskom

What Does Causation Mean in the Toxic Tort Context? · 140
   Exposure and Dose · 140
   General Causation · 140
   Specific Causation · 142
How Can You Prove (or Dispute) Causation in Toxic Tort Cases? · 143
   Establishing General Causation · 144
   Establishing Specific Causation · 148
Using Experts in Toxic Tort Cases · 157
   What Led to the Daubert *Decision?* · 159
   The Daubert *Trilogy: Defining the Trial Judge's Role* · 159
Conclusion · 164

6. Case Strategy and Trial Management · 167
John P. Manard Jr., Steven J. Levine, S. Ault Hootsell III,
J. Alan Harrell, Roy L. Bergeron Jr., and Evan Dicharry

Named Parties: Selection and Strategy · 168
   Joint and Several Liability/Comparative Fault · 168
   Market Share Liability · 170
   Parent/Successor Liability · 171
Alignment of Parties and Forums · 172
   Multidistrict Litigation · 172
   Joinder of Plaintiffs · 174
   Class Actions · 177
Discovery and Investigation Issues · 183
   Freedom of Information Act and Access to Government Information · 184
   Discovery of Environmental Audits · 186
   Discovery of Independent Researchers · 191
   Industry Experts · 192
   Discovery of Employees and Former Employees · 193
   Protective Orders · 198
   Analytical Testing and Site Access · 203
   Depositions of Environmental/Public Health Agency Employees · 207
   Identifying the Route of Exposure and Modeling Historical Exposure · 210
   Waste Stream Identification and Reconstruction · 212
   Preservation of Evidence · 214
Coordination with Parallel Regulatory Proceedings · 219
   Information Management · 222
Case Management and Case Management Orders · 224
Motion Practice (Other Than *Daubert*) · 229
   Venue · 229
   Vagueness or More Definite Statement · 230

        No Cause or Right of Action/Lack of Procedural Capacity/Failure to
            State a Claim 231
        Discovery Motions 232
        Evidentiary Motions 232
        Motions for Reconsideration 233
    Trial Issues 234
        Shaping the Case 234
        Admissibility of or Challenges to Lab Data 248
        Industry Codes 249
        Public Records and Reports 249
        Violations of Statutory or Regulatory Environmental Provisions 250
        Structuring the Multiplaintiff Trial 250
        Postinjury Evidence Concerning the Defendant's Culpability 256

7. Settlement Considerations   261
Brendan K. Collins

    Case Valuation: The First Step toward Settlement 261
        Assessing the Strengths and Vulnerabilities of Your Case 262
        Assessing Strengths and Vulnerabilities of Your Client 264
        Unique Considerations in Environmental Toxic Torts 266
    Settlement Methods and Alternative Dispute Resolution 267
        Negotiation 268
        Mediation 268
        Arbitration 268
        Summary Jury Trial 270
        Other Variations and Less Common Methods 270
    Class Settlements under Federal Rule of Civil Procedure 23 271
        U.S. Supreme Court's Views 271
        Lower Court Decisions 274
        State Court Settlement Class Certification 277
        Fairness Hearings 277
    Conclusion 278

8. Emerging Areas of Litigation and Significant Legal Issues   279
Shawna Bligh and Chris Wendelbo

    Emerging or Evolving Areas of Toxic Tort Litigation 279
        Hydraulic Fracturing 279
        Groundwater and Subsurface Contamination 282
        Climate Change–Based Nuisance Actions 287
        Workplace Exposure 293
    Significant Legal Issues in Toxic Tort Litigation 295
        Class Actions 295
        Experts 300

Medical Monitoring	304
Risk Assessments to Prove Causation	305

Part Two: Regional Standards for Causation

9. Western States — 309
Karen R. Leviton, Michael G. Romey, and R. Peter Durning Jr.

Alaska	310
Overall Standard for Causation	310
General and Specific Causation	310
Arizona	311
Overall Standard for Causation	311
General and Specific Causation	311
Arizona Federal Cases	313
California	314
Overall Standard for Causation	314
General and Specific Causation	315
Colorado	316
Overall Standard for Causation	316
Colorado Federal Cases	317
Hawaii	318
Overall Standard for Causation	318
General and Specific Causation	318
Hawaii Federal Cases	320
Idaho	320
Overall Standard for Causation	320
General and Specific Causation	320
Montana	322
Overall Standard for Causation	322
General and Specific Causation	322
Nevada	323
Overall Standard for Causation	323
Nevada Federal Cases	325
New Mexico	325
Overall Standard for Causation	325
General and Specific Causation	326
Oregon	327
Overall Standard for Causation	327
Standard of Proof and Expert Testimony	328
Utah	328
Overall Standard for Causation	328
General and Specific Causation	329

Washington | 329
   Overall Standard for Causation | 329
   General and Specific Causation | 330
Wyoming | 331
   Overall Standard for Causation | 331
   General and Specific Causation | 331

10. Midwestern States 333
Andrew Holly and Colin Wicker

Illinois | 333
   Overall Standard for Causation | 333
   General and Specific Causation | 335
Indiana | 336
   Overall Standard for Causation | 336
   General and Specific Causation | 336
Iowa | 337
   Overall Standard for Causation | 337
   General Causation | 337
   Specific Causation | 338
Kansas | 339
   Overall Standard for Causation | 339
   General and Specific Causation | 340
Michigan | 341
   Overall Standard for Causation | 341
   General Causation | 343
   Specific Causation | 344
Minnesota | 346
   Overall Standard for Causation | 346
   General Causation | 346
   Specific Causation | 346
Missouri | 347
   Overall Standard for Causation | 347
   General Causation | 348
   Specific Causation | 349
Nebraska | 350
   Overall Standard for Causation | 350
   General Causation | 350
   Specific Causation | 351
North Dakota | 352
   Overall Standard for Causation | 352
   General Causation | 353
   Specific Causation | 353

Ohio	354
Overall Standard for Causation	354
General Causation	355
Specific Causation	356
Oklahoma	358
Overall Standard for Causation	358
General Causation	359
Specific Causation	360
South Dakota	361
Overall Standard for Causation	361
General Causation	361
Specific Causation	362

11. Southern States   363
Lisa Horvath Shub

Alabama	363
Overall Standard for Causation	363
General and Specific Causation	365
Arkansas	366
Overall Standard for Causation	366
General Causation	367
Specific Causation	368
Florida	371
Overall Standard for Causation	371
General Causation	373
Specific Causation	375
Georgia	376
Overall Standard for Causation	376
General and Specific Causation	378
Kentucky	379
Overall Standard for Causation	379
General Causation	380
Specific Causation	380
Louisiana	382
Overall Standard for Causation	382
General Causation	382
Specific Causation	384
Mississippi	385
Overall Standard for Causation	385
General and Specific Causation	386
North Carolina	387
Overall Standard for Causation	387
General and Specific Causation	389

South Carolina	391
Overall Standard for Causation	391
General and Specific Causation	392
Tennessee	393
Overall Standard for Causation	393
Texas	396
Overall Standard for Causation	396
General Causation	396
Specific Causation	398
Virginia	399
Overall Standard for Causation	399
General Causation	400
Specific Causation 7	400
West Virginia	402
Overall Standard for Causation	402
General and Specific Causation	403
General Causation	403
Specific Causation	404

12. Eastern States   405

Libretta Stennes

Connecticut	405
Overall Standard for Causation	405
General and Specific Causation	406
Delaware	408
Overall Standard for Causation	408
General Causation	408
Specific Causation	409
District of Columbia	409
Overall Standard for Causation	409
General and Specific Causation	410
Maine	411
Overall Standard for Causation	411
General and Specific Causation	412
Maryland	412
Overall Standard for Causation	412
General and Specific Causation	413
Massachusetts	414
Overall Standard for Causation	414
General Causation	415
Specific Causation	416
New Hampshire	417
Overall Standard for Causation	417

New Jersey	418
Overall Standard for Causation	418
General Causation	420
Specific Causation	421
New York	422
Overall Standard for Causation	422
General Causation	423
Specific Causation	425
Pennsylvania	427
Overall Standard for Causation	427
General Causation	428
Specific Causation	429
Rhode Island	430
Overall Standard for Causation	430
Vermont	432
Overall Standard for Causation	432
General Causation	432
Specific Causation	432
Table of Cases	435
Index	495

ACKNOWLEDGMENTS

This being a multi-author book, the bulk of the effort for completing it was provided by the authors for each of the twelve chapters, not the editors who asked them to contribute. We deeply appreciate all the authors' significant efforts. We are well aware of the balancing acts faced from the competing demands on their time, and we thank the authors for their commitment.

Each of the chapters also received valuable peer review from toxic tort and environmental attorneys with years litigating these complex issues. These individuals include Roy Alan Cohen (Porzio, Bromberg & Newman P.C.); Timothy J. Coughlin (Thompson Hine LLP); Douglas A. Henderson (Troutman Sanders LLP); Professor Alexandra B. Klass (University of Minnesota Law School); Yancey A. McLeod III (Leath, Bouch & Seekings LLP); Amy Melvin (Leath, Bouch & Seekings LLP); Robert P. Scott (Blank Rome LLP); Michael R. Strom (Sieben Polk, P.A.); and Susan Paulsrud Welch (Abelson Herron Halpern LLP). We wish to extend our deep gratitude to each of these peer reviewers for their valuable contributions.

We also wish to thank Davon Collins, Jenna Gascoyne, J. Duane Gibson, Melissa Frankel, Will Kessler, Katherine McGrath, Hillary Steenberge, and Paul Vaglica now or formerly with Latham & Watkins LLP. It was no easy task to orchestrate the various chapters on the same schedule, to coordinate substantive topics to avoid duplication, and to achieve reasonable consistency in tone and format. Each of these individuals contributed invaluable assistance in some or all of these tasks. Additionally, we would express our great appreciation for our partners at Latham & Watkins LLP who offered their support and insightful assistance. We are thankful to be able to practice law at a firm where there is so much depth and breadth of experience to draw upon, and where people are so gracious about sharing their time.

Separately, Arthur Foerster wishes to give special thanks to his amazing wife, Rachelle, and his two energetic young sons, Quinn and Owen, for their unconditional love and support, and for his sons' never-ending patience with the fact that sometimes their jungle-gym has to go to work. Last, but not least, Arthur also wishes to thank his parents, Joan and George Foerster, who have always been there when needed.

Christine Rolph wishes to extend her sincere thanks and appreciation to her husband, Harold, and three children, McKayla, Brendan, and Katelyn, for their wonderful support and the boundless energy and enthusiasm for life they share with her every day. Christine also wishes to send a huge "thank you" to her parents, Stephen and Rosemary Gregorski, who constantly encouraged her dreams.

ABOUT THE EDITORS

Arthur F. Foerster is a partner in the Chicago office of Latham & Watkins LLP, where he has practiced environmental law and litigation since joining the firm in 2001. He is experienced in litigating matters involving toxic torts, products liability, contaminated sites, citizen suits, and the Clean Air Act. Mr. Foerster also litigates matters involving insurance coverage, industrial accidents, and other business contract and tort disputes. He is particularly experienced in litigation and trial work involving complex industrial processes and practices, complex issues of causation and damages, complex expert testimony, and complex regulatory programs. Mr. Foerster was recognized as a Rising Star by Law360 in 2013.

Mr. Foerster has lectured and published on topics including medical monitoring, workplace exposures, hydraulic fracturing, federal jurisdictional matters, and working with experts. He received his B.S. from Bradley University in 1996 and his J.D. from the UCLA School of Law in 1999. Mr. Foerster clerked for the Honorable Joe Billy McDade of the United States District Court for the Central District of Illinois.

Christine Gregorski Rolph serves as the Global Co-chair of Latham & Watkins's Product Liability, Mass Torts & Consumer Class Actions Practice and is a partner in the firm's Washington, D.C., office. She has been recognized as a Products Liability Litigation Star by Euromoney's Benchmark Institutions and also was named a leading attorney in both the Consumer Products and Mass Tort Defense areas by the Legal 500 US 2012. As a result of praise from clients and peers, Ms. Rolph was named in Benchmark Litigation's 2012 list of "local Litigation Stars" in Washington, D.C., for her products work. In 2012 and 2013, Benchmark also recognized Ms. Rolph as one of the "Top 250 Women in Litigation."

Ms. Rolph has extensive expertise in litigating toxic torts, consumer class actions, product liability/consumer fraud suits, and multiplaintiff matters. She has represented clients in various high-stakes environmental, chemical, and complex commercial matters in federal and state courts. Ms. Rolph graduated *summa cum laude* from Duke University (B.A. 1994) and from the University of Virginia School of Law (J.D. 1997).

ABOUT THE CONTRIBUTORS

Roy L. Bergeron Jr. is an associate in the Baton Rouge, Louisiana, office of Phelps Dunbar LLP. His practice focuses primarily on environmental litigation and regulatory counseling on state and federal environmental matters.

Shawna Bligh is a member of BW Law Group, LLC, a boutique firm in Kansas City, Missouri. Ms. Bligh focuses her practice on appellate law, complex civil litigation, and environmental law. Ms. Bligh's environmental practice includes litigation, including toxic tort litigation, permitting, and environmental issues related to business and real estate transactions. She is very active in the American Bar Association's Section of Environment, Energy, and Resources. Ms. Bligh serves on the editorial board for *Natural Resources & Environment* and the Section of Environment, Energy, and Resources's Book Publishing Board. She also serves as the American Bar Association's liaison to the Council for Agricultural Science and Technology. Ms. Bligh graduated from the University of Missouri–Kansas City School of Law and received her LL.M. in Environmental Law from Vermont Law School.

J Kevin Buster is a senior trial partner with King & Spalding LLP in Atlanta, Georgia, and serves as the head of the firm's Toxic Tort Litigation Practice Group. He has more than thirty years of courtroom experience in a wide variety of cases including toxic tort, product liability, environmental tort, criminal, antitrust, and commercial cases, although over the past twenty-five years he has focused on the various types of toxic tort litigation (environmental, product, and workplace). Mr. Buster's practice is nationwide, as he has litigated cases in both state and federal courts in more than thirty states. His toxic tort cases have involved a wide variety of chemical substances, including dioxins, polychlorinated biphenyls (PCBs), pesticides, metals, solvents, gases, odors, petroleum products, food products, pharmaceuticals, chemical warfare agents, asbestos, vinyl chloride, and others.

Randy J. Butterfield is of counsel in the Atlanta office of King & Spalding LLP where his practice focuses on environmental and toxic tort litigation matters. Over the past fourteen years, he has handled a wide variety of individual, mass joinder, and class action cases, both at the trial and appellate levels in state and federal court. Mr. Butterfield currently serves on the Board of the Environmental and Toxic Tort Section of the Atlanta Bar Association.

Brendan K. Collins is a litigation partner in the Philadelphia office of Ballard Spahr LLP, and a member of the Environment and Natural Resources Group and the Product Liability and Mass Tort Group. His work is focused on the energy sector, and he coordinates the firm's petroleum products practice, integrating litigation, environmental, real estate, and other disciplines to serve clients operating in this sector. Mr. Collins has represented clients in civil, criminal, and administrative matters at all levels of the state and federal judicial systems, including the U.S. Supreme Court and the Supreme Court of Pennsylvania. He currently serves as vice chair of the Toxic Torts and Environmental Law Committee of the American Bar Association (ABA) Tort Trial and Insurance Practice Section, and is a former chair of the Environmental Litigation and Toxic Torts Committee of the ABA Section of Environment, Energy, and Resources. Mr. Collins is listed in *Chambers USA: America's Leading Lawyers for Business* (2003–2012) and *The Best Lawyers in America* (2006–2013) for environmental law.

Ashley Cummings is a partner at Hunton & Williams LLP. Her practice focuses on class actions and other complex civil litigation, including financial services litigation, consumer fraud, and mass tort actions. She aids clients in assessing future litigation risks and strategic preparation for such risks. She also has significant experience with jury research and trial theme development. Ms. Cummings has served as second-chair in three nationwide class actions, and has played a central role in other large-scale class and collective actions. She also has significant experience in Georgia state and federal courts, including appellate practice before the Georgia Court of Appeals and the Eleventh Circuit Court of Appeals.

Alexandra Cunningham is a partner in the Richmond, Virginia, office of Hunton & Williams LLP, where she is a member of the National Business Torts and Product Liability team. She focuses her practice on complex tort claims, including class actions, multidistrict litigation, mass torts, and toxic and environmental exposure claims.

William D. Dannelly is a senior counsel at Hunton & Williams LLP. He has significant experience in litigation, other adversarial proceedings, transactions, compliance and regulatory affairs, including those involving toxic torts, Superfund, the Resource Conservation and Recovery Act (RCRA), water quality, brownfields, and related matters. Mr. Dannelly has appeared as lead counsel in numerous cases in state, federal, and administrative courts, handling both civil litigation and criminal investigations.

Evan Dicharry is an associate in Phelps Dunbar LLP's New Orleans office. He practices in the areas of tort and insurance litigation.

Ryan T. Dunn is an associate at Faegre Baker Daniels LLP in Minneapolis and focuses his practice on environmental and products liability litigation. He has worked on several toxic tort and product liability litigation and regulatory matters involving topics such as groundwater contamination, low- and no-injury toxic tort claims, and nuisance. Mr. Dunn is admitted in courts in Minnesota and California and served as a law clerk to two trial court judges in Los Angeles Superior Court after graduating from the UCLA School of Law.

R. Peter Durning Jr. is an associate in the Los Angeles office of Latham & Watkins LLP. Mr. Durning is active in a broad variety of litigation matters, and he is experienced in securities, mass tort, and insurance litigation. Mr. Durning is a graduate of Columbia Law School, where he was a Harlan Fiske Stone Scholar and an articles editor of the *Columbia Business Law Review*. He served as a judicial extern to the Honorable Robert D. Sack of the Second Circuit Court of Appeals. Mr. Durning completed undergraduate and graduate degrees at Stanford University, with honors.

Delmar R. Ehrich is a nationally recognized trial lawyer focusing his practice on complex environmental and natural resource damage litigation. He recently completed a five-month trial as lead counsel in one of the largest natural resource damage suits tried in the United States. Since joining Faegre Baker Daniels LLP in 1983, Mr. Ehrich has represented business clients in a wide variety of litigation and administrative proceedings involving all of the major federal environmental statutes. He has appeared in federal and state courts in every region of the country. Mr. Ehrich is a Fellow of the American College of Environmental Lawyers and ranked in *Chambers USA* in litigation.

L. Neal Ellis Jr. is a partner in the Ellis & Anthony LLP law firm of Wake Forest, North Carolina. Prior to joining Ellis & Anthony, Neal served for more than thirty years first as an associate, then as a partner, of the Hunton & Williams LLP law firm. His practice has concentrated on environmental, toxic tort, and products liability litigation. Mr. Ellis has served as a member of Council of the ABA's Tort Trial and Insurance Practice Section and chaired its Trial Techniques Committee. He has also served as a member of Council of the ABA's Judicial Division and chaired its Lawyers Conference. With the North Carolina Bar Association, Mr. Ellis served on the Board of Governors and as a member of its Executive Committee. He co-edited with Charles Case a treatise on toxic tort and hazardous substance litigation. Mr. Ellis is recognized in Best Lawyers in America (Bet the Company Litigation and Commercial Litigation), North Carolina Super Lawyers (Business Litigation), and Super Lawyers Corporate Counsel Edition (Business Litigation).

Matthew F. Hanchey is an associate at Hunton & Williams LLP. He represents clients on compliance with environmental laws. As part of his practice, Mr. Hanchey works with clients who are subject to enforcement at the state and federal levels and clients who are involved in corporate transactions involving brownfields or other properties with environmental law components. He also has a particular interest in advising clients on water allocation issues. Mr. Hanchey has experience working with owners of industrial facilities, particularly in the chemicals and energy industries, and real estate developers, among other clients.

J. Alan Harrell is a partner in the Baton Rouge, Louisiana, office of Phelps Dunbar LLP. His practice includes toxic tort and environmental litigation, class actions, and commercial litigation. He also advises clients on environmental regulatory compliance. Mr. Harrell regularly defends clients in class action and mass joinder litigation involving environmental and other theories of recovery.

Andrew Holly is a partner in the Minneapolis office of Dorsey & Whitney LLP. Mr. Holly is a member of the firm's Trial Department, and he represents clients in a variety of civil matters, including complex environmental litigation.

S. Ault Hootsell III is a partner in the New Orleans office of Phelps Dunbar LLP in the Commercial Litigation Section. Mr. Hootsell handles complex commercial and tort litigation matters, including client defense in class action and mass tort litigation. His class settlements include a settlement within the context of a bankruptcy reorganization of environmental claims allegedly related to an environmental waste disposal facility. Presently, Mr. Hootsell is working to resolve, through a mandatory limited fund settlement, all claims arising from Hurricane Katrina against the levee district in New Orleans.

Bruce Jones is a partner in the Product Liability and Environmental Group of Faegre Baker Daniels LLP, and is co-chair of the firm's Appellate Advocacy Practice. He frequently serves as the lead Law Team attorney in mass tort litigation, including environmental, toxic tort, consumer fraud, and drug and medical device litigation. Mr. Jones has prosecuted and defended scores of appeals in the state and federal appellate courts, and is listed in the Best Lawyers in America. He also has a Master of Fine Arts in Playwriting.

Courtney A. Lawrence is an associate in the Minneapolis office of Faegre Baker Daniels LLP, where she is a member of the Product Liability and Environmental Practice Group. She focuses her practice on litigation and regulatory matters within the food and agricultural industries. Ms. Lawrence graduated summa cum laude from William Mitchell College of Law in 2012, where she was an editor of the *William Mitchell Law Review*.

Steven J. Levine is a partner in the Baton Rouge, Louisiana, office of Phelps Dunbar LLP, where his environmental law practice includes litigation and regulatory counseling. Previously, he practiced in fisheries biology and estuarine ecology as a research associate at Louisiana State University's Center for Wetland Resources.

Karen R. Leviton is of counsel in the Los Angeles office of Latham & Watkins LLP and is a member of the Litigation Department. Her practice focuses primarily on mass tort and environmental litigation, complex business disputes in trial and appellate courts, and insurance coverage litigation on behalf of policyholders. In the mass tort area, she focuses on toxic torts, including the defense of multiplaintiff actions for alleged exposure to hazardous substances from airborne emissions or soil and groundwater contamination. Ms. Leviton graduated summa cum laude with high honors in English from Colgate University in 1974. She received her J.D., cum laude, from Georgetown University Law Center in 1978.

John P. Manard Jr. is a partner and practice coordinator of the Tort Litigation Group in Phelps Dunbar LLP's New Orleans office. His practice is exclusively litigation in the area of toxic torts, pharmaceutical, environmental, and class actions. Mr. Manard frequently speaks on tort and environmental law and has written several articles on that subject. He is currently on the Council of the Section of Environment, Energy, and Resources of the American Bar Association and a Fellow in the American College of Environmental Lawyers.

Michael G. Romey is a partner in the Los Angeles office of Latham & Watkins LLP and a member of both the Litigation and Environment, Land & Resources Departments. Mr. Romey has a broad range of litigation experience, with an emphasis on environmental litigation. He has represented clients in toxic tort, Superfund, cost recovery, Clean Air Act, Clean Water Act, RCRA, Proposition 65, and insurance coverage litigations. Since 1999, Mr. Romey has been an adjunct professor of environmental law at the University of Southern California School of Law where he teaches the Clean Air Act, the Clean Water Act, RCRA, the Endangered Species Act, Risk Assessment, and Climate Change. Mr. Romey graduated from Columbia University in 1985 and received his J.D. from the University of California, Berkeley, School of Law (Boalt Hall) in 1988.

Alan Rudlin is a partner in the Richmond, Virginia, office of Hunton & Williams LLP. He focuses his practice on complex commercial disputes, including class action, energy, environmental, and fiduciary litigation. Mr. Rudlin has been involved in numerous trials throughout the country. He has authored numerous books and articles, served on national editorial boards, and served as adjunct faculty at several law schools.

Rita A. Sheffey is a partner with Hunton & Williams LLP, where her practice focuses on complex litigation, primarily environmental, toxic tort, product liability, trademark infringement, and patent infringement litigation. She is very involved with the Atlanta pro bono community, the Atlanta Bar Association, and the State Bar of Georgia, among other organizations. Ms. Sheffey has been honored with numerous awards, including the Atlanta Bar Association's 2013 Charles E. Watkins, Jr., Award for Distinguished and Sustained Service, the Atlanta Bar Association's inaugural Rita A. Sheffey Public Interest Award and a POW! Award for Purposeful Women from Womenetics in 2012, a 2010 Emory School of Law Public Interest Committee's Unsung Devotion to Those Most in Need Award, the 2009 Atlanta Victim Assistance, Inc. Rachel Champagne Leadership Award, the Atlanta Bar Association Women in the Profession Section's 2005 Outstanding Woman in the Profession Achievement Award, and the 2004 State Bar of Georgia H. Sol Clark Pro Bono Award. Ms. Sheffey received her B.A. from University of Virginia in Chemistry, a Ph.D. in Chemistry from Duke University, and a J.D. from the Boston College Law School, cum laude.

Lisa Horvath Shub is a litigation partner with Fulbright & Jaworski LLP in San Antonio, Texas. Her practice includes mass tort, toxic tort, pharmaceutical, and environmental matters, with a focus on disputes surrounding the reliability and admissibility of scientific expert testimony. Ms. Shub also has significant experience handling commercial, energy, products liability, fiduciary duty, and contractual disputes.

Libretta Stennes is a partner with Steptoe & Johnson LLP, where she is a member of the firm's Mass Tort, Toxic Tort and Environmental Practice. Ms. Stennes has successfully defended toxic tort matters alleging harm from perfluorinated compounds, 1,2,3-TCP, benzene, MTBE, solvents, fly ash, and other contaminants. As part of her extensive class action litigation experience, she has defeated class certification for medical monitoring and property damage claims.

Thomas R. Waskom is a senior associate in the Richmond, Virginia, office of Hunton & Williams LLP. His practice focuses on representing companies in class action and mass tort litigation. Mr. Waskom has been recognized as a Rising Star by *Virginia Super Lawyers* magazine.

Chris Wendelbo is a member of BW Law Group LLC, a boutique firm in Kansas City, Missouri. Mr. Wendelbo focuses his practice on appellate law, complex civil litigation, and environmental law. He has handled more than two hundred civil and criminal appeals and also specializes in complex environmental litigation, regulatory compliance, brownfields redevelopment, and environmental due diligence. Mr. Wendelbo has handled multiparty litigation for claims arising under Sections 107 and 113 of CERCLA at privately owned sites, as well as former military installations and federal facilities. He serves as Chair of the Missouri Bar's Solo and Small Firm Committee. Mr. Wendelbo received his law degree from the University of Oklahoma College of Law and his LL.M. in Environmental Law from George Washington University.

Colin Wicker is a Senior Attorney in the Minneapolis office of Dorsey & Whitney LLP, where he is a member of the firm's Regulatory Affairs Practice Group. He represents clients in litigation and provides regulatory counseling in a number of areas.

PART ONE

Elements of Toxic Tort Litigation

CHAPTER 1

Introduction

L. Neal Ellis Jr.

Even in the highly litigious society in which we live, toxic tort cases are viewed as one of the types of litigation with the highest stakes. Releases of toxic substances from a single incident, ingestion of toxins from the distribution of a single product, or long-term exposure to contaminated environmental media are often alleged to cause injuries and in some cases death to hundreds and even thousands of unsuspecting people. Toxic tort actions may threaten the financial ability of a company and even an entire industry. Announcements that companies and whole industries are teetering on the brink of bankruptcy from lawsuits arising out of toxic releases are now received without any measure of surprise. What is it that makes the litigation of toxic tort cases so critical yet so different from other forms of litigation? We need to start with what toxic torts are and what they are not.

What Toxic Torts Are and What They Are Not

Broadly defined, toxic torts involve some claim of harm, physical or psychological, caused by exposure to a hazardous substance. Often, toxic tort actions involve claims for both property damage (diminution in value) and personal injury (cancer) as a result of the exposure. Frequently, these actions are brought by large numbers of plaintiffs, either as a group by way of joinder or in the form of a class action. Whole communities allegedly impacted by airborne releases or groundwater contamination from nearby industrial facilities are the paradigm. Just as frequently, exposures to hazardous substances with long latency periods in the workplace have generated substantial litigation. But actions alleging serious injuries by single plaintiffs in isolated instances of exposure to toxic substances are not uncommon.

It is difficult to date with any certainty the inception of toxic tort litigation. Many would say that toxic tort law could not have proceeded without the English court precedent of

Rylands v. Fletcher[1] and cases from the early 1900s that adapted sometimes antiquated legal doctrines to the needs of the Industrial Revolution. But technological, scientific, and medical advances almost certainly would have compelled the law to make adjustments. As the modern era of scientific and technological advances surged forward, the byproducts of industry found their way into the streams, groundwater, and air. Many years later, hazards from historical operations have manifested themselves in sometimes catastrophic and deadly ways.

The Legacy of Significant Actions

Prior to Agent Orange, Love Canal, Dalkon Shield, Bhopal, Times Beach, and countless others, courts rarely dealt with the phenomenon that we now call "mass torts." Occasional mass disasters in the mid- to late twentieth century involving air crashes tested the ability of the courts and lawyers to resolve large numbers of personal injury and wrongful death cases arising out of the same incident.

The late twentieth century sensitized the public to mass tort litigation. These more recent mass tort cases have arisen largely out of exposure to toxic substances. Their history has not always been free from controversy. No doubt, many lawsuits have been brought for imagined harm, and some plaintiffs have filed lawsuits using the leverage of their numbers to extort settlements from innocent defendants seeking to avoid the crushing cost of mass tort litigation. On the other hand, some recalcitrant defendants with clear liability may have fought the litigation onslaught with all of their resources to avoid, or at least to delay, any finding of culpability. That is especially true in this era of copycat litigation when settlement with an initial group of plaintiffs can encourage the filing of new cases by others.

Causation Is King

Perhaps the overriding issue in all toxic tort cases is causation. While causation plays a significant and sometimes determinative role in other tort litigation, causation is a chief battleground in toxic tort cases. The plaintiff has the burden of demonstrating that he or she was exposed to a toxic substance, that he or she suffered physical harm, and most important, that there is a legally sufficient causal link between the exposure and the harm suffered (i.e., whether exposure to the hazardous substance could cause the alleged injury and whether it actually did so in this case). Carrying that burden, when exposures may not produce harm until years and sometimes decades later, can often prove to be

---

1. 3 L.R. 330 (H.L. 1868). When defendant's construction of a water reservoir caused water to flow through an abandoned mine and flood plaintiff's active mine, the trial court in *Rylands* exonerated the defendant on the ground that negligence could impose no liability on a defendant ignorant of the risky conditions. The appellate court reversed and was affirmed by the House of Lords, creating the doctrine of strict liability for otherwise lawful activities that pose an extraordinary risk of harm.

an insurmountable task. Further complicating the burden is the fact that in our modern society the plaintiff may have difficulty identifying with particularity the specific source of the harm or trace with clarity and certainty the injury to the harmful source. New comment *c* to Section 28 of the *Restatement (Third) of Torts* is likely to generate a great deal of debate on the requirements of causation proof for exposure, and for general and specific causation.[2]

The Evolution of Traditional Tort Theories

Perhaps in no other field of the law have traditional theories undergone such adaptation to rapid technological and scientific change. The reasons are at least twofold.

First, our understanding of "the nature and extent of harm created by toxins in our environment" continues to evolve.[3] Each day our major news media bring us startling claims of yet another product that if ingested over time is linked to cancer or some other horrible disease. It is not surprising that we either become leery of any exposure to new substances and new products or we grow numb to the seemingly endless parade of horribles and warnings of hazards lying in wait for us. But science and technology will not allow a respite from the task of identifying harmful substances in our environment, and our justice system will not allow unjustified harm to go unredressed.

Second, the traditional tort doctrines imposed obstacles to recovery because of requirements for proof, causation, and manifestation of injuries.[4] Over the years, toxic tort plaintiffs have relied upon numerous traditional theories including trespass, public and private nuisance, strict liability for abnormally dangerous activity, negligence, products liability, and intentional infliction of emotional distress, among others.[5] Those theories have sometimes been stretched and expanded to accommodate the harms occasioned by exposure to toxic substances.

Take, for instance, the venerable doctrine of trespass. Originally, trespass was based upon the unauthorized entry of a person upon the land of another. *Blackstone's Commentaries* declare that each such entry "carries necessarily along with it some damage or other; for, if no other special loss can be assigned . . . the words of the writ itself specify

---

2. RESTATEMENT (THIRD) OF TORTS: PHYS. & EMOT. HARM § 28, cmt. *c* (2010). Comment *c* is a noble effort to distill decades of precedent on causation in toxic tort cases into a manageable form. Among other things, its authors conclude that general and specific causation may be used as tools to inform a court's analysis but are not formal elements of a cause of action. *See generally* Joseph Sanders, *The Controversial Comment c: Factual Causation in Toxic-Substance and Disease Cases*, 44 WAKE FOREST L. REV. 1029 (2009); Steve C. Gold, *The "Reshapement" of the False Negative Asymmetry in Toxic Tort Cases*, 37 WM. MITCHELL L. REV. 1507 (2011).
3. Michael Axline, *Theories of Liability*, in 1 A GUIDE TO TOXIC TORTS § 3.01[1] (1993).
4. Robert Blomquist, *Emerging Themes and Dilemmas in American Toxic Tort Law*, 18 S. ILL. U. L.J. 1, 25 (1993).
5. *Id.* at 26; Danielle Conway-Jones, *Factual Causation in Toxic Tort Litigation*, 35 U. RICH. L. REV. 875, 881 n.31 (2002).

one general damage, viz.: the treading down and bruising [of] his herbage."[6] To evolve and accommodate an unauthorized entry of a physical object or substance that was not cast directly onto the injured party's property, the *Restatement (Second) of Torts* acknowledged that "it is not necessary that the foreign matter should be thrown directly and immediately upon the other's land. It is enough that an act is done with knowledge that it will to a substantial certainty result in the entry of the foreign matter."[7] And now many jurisdictions no longer require the entry of a visible, tangible object so that trespass may lie upon the authorized invasion of the property by invisible particles.[8]

Damage theories also have expanded in scope at times to accommodate the uniqueness of toxic tort actions. Injured parties have brought claims and sought damages based on post-traumatic stress disorder, decreased quality of life, property damage, emotional distress, increased risk, fear of injury, and medical surveillance/monitoring.[9] Consequently, certain courts have permitted plaintiffs to proceed on theories that only a decade ago were relatively unknown to tort litigation.[10]

Long latency periods can make it difficult for a plaintiff to establish a causal nexus between the harm suffered and the source of the harm. Because the plaintiff has the burden of proof, a toxic tort suit may flounder because documentary evidence no longer exists and witnesses have disappeared. At the same time, long latency periods may be equally detrimental to the defense of toxic tort cases when an accused company is unable to locate witnesses or produce documents that may defeat liability or reduce damages.[11] Additionally, where once plaintiffs were denied relief because the latency of a disease permitted the statute of limitations to expire, many courts have responded with the "discovery rule," which, in some jurisdictions, forestalls the running of the statute of limitations until the plaintiff knew or should have known of the injury or facts forming the basis of the plaintiff's claim.[12]

---

6. 2 WILLIAM BLACKSTONE, COMMENTARIES *210–11.
7. RESTATEMENT (SECOND) OF TORTS § 158, cmt. *i* (1965), *cited in* Philip E. Karmel & Peter R. Paden, *Trespass as a Toxic Tort*, 47 CHEM. WASTE LITIG. REP. 343 (Feb. 2004).
8. *Id.* at Reporters Notes; *see also* Martin v. Reynolds Metals Co., 342 P.2d 790 (Or. 1959) (a pivotal case holding that a trespass would lie where invisible particulates of fluoride emitted by defendant's plant invaded plaintiff's property).
9. Lisa Heinzerling & Cameron Powers Hoffman, *Tortious Toxics*, 26 WM. & MARY ENVTL. L. & POL'Y REV. 67, 69 (2001).
10. *Id.* Decisions early in the twentieth century broke ground for the most recent damages theories. For instance, in what must have been the earliest "cancerphobia" case, *Alley v. Charlotte Pipe & Foundry Co.*, the court held that the probability of developing cancer "must necessarily have a most depressing effect upon the injured person" and entitled the plaintiff suffering from burns to compensation for mental distress. 74 S.E. 885, 886 (N.C. 1912).
11. Conway-Jones, *supra* note 5, at 879.
12. *See, e.g.*, Brown v. Dow Chem. Co., 875 F.2d 197, 200 (8th Cir. 1989); Joseph v. Hess Oil, 867 F.2d 179, 181 (3d Cir. 1989); Cornell v. E.I. DuPont deNemours & Co., 841 F.2d 23, 24 (1st Cir. 1988); Hildebrandt v. Allied Corp., 839 F.2d 396, 398 (8th Cir. 1987); Blanton v. Cooper Indus., Inc., 99 F. Supp. 2d 797, 801 (E.D. Ky. 2000); Peterson v. Instapak Corp., 690 F. Supp. 697, 698 (N.D. Ill. 1988); Schiro v.

Preview of the Following Chapters

In chapter 2, "Theories of Liability and Damages," we explore both the traditional theories of liability in toxic tort actions as well as the new evolving theories of liability. Damages theories are covered, including personal injury, medical monitoring, fear of disease, punitive damages, as well as property damage theories such as stigma and diminution in value. In chapter 3, "Common Defenses," we consider the unique aspects of the statutes of limitation and repose in toxic tort cases, preemption, jurisdictional defenses, defenses to common law claims, government contractor and government agent, product identification, and a host of others. Chapter 4, "The Use of Scientific and Medical Evidence," is devoted to traditional and emerging science, medicine, and technology, including developments in geology, hydrology, meteorology, toxicology, and epidemiology, among others. Chapter 5, "Causation and the Use of Experts," addresses one of the most important elements of any toxic tort pretrial and trial. Chapter 6, "Case Strategy and Trial Management," describes the selection and strategies utilized in naming parties, forum selection, class actions, discovery, case management devices, motions, and the trial of toxic tort cases. In chapter 7, "Settlement Considerations," we cover the methods used to resolve toxic tort cases short of trial. In chapter 8, "Emerging Areas of Litigation and Significant Legal Issues," we hit the latest topics in the field including hydraulic fracturing, workplace exposures, climate-based actions, medical monitoring, and others. Finally, in chapters 9 to 12, we survey the law of causation in personal injury toxic tort cases by region and state covering the standards for general and specific causation as well as specific topics that impact causation analysis such as the use of animal evidence and risk assessments.

We hope you will find that this book helps you to fight the toxic tort wars and better serve your clients.

Am. Tobacco Co., 611 So. 2d 962, 965 (Miss. 1992); Raymond v. Eli Lilly & Co., 371 A.2d 170, 174 (N.H. 1977); Tarazi v. Exxon Corp., 703 N.Y.S.2d 205, 206 (N.Y. App. Div. 2000).

CHAPTER 2

Theories of Liability and Damages

Bruce Jones, Ryan T. Dunn, Courtney A. Lawrence, and Delmar R. Ehrich

The evolution of the modern technological society has brought with it an exponential increase in human and environmental exposure to potentially toxic elements, including industrial chemicals, fertilizers, pharmaceuticals, various kinds of waste, and radiation. With this increase has come a proliferation of lawsuits asserting what have come to be called "toxic torts"—specifically, torts in which the plaintiff seeks damages or injunctive relief based (in the simplest sense) on the presence of toxic materials where plaintiffs claim that they should not be (e.g., in the human body, in plants or animals, or in the environment). Such claims may allege injury to human health, the need for an environmental cleanup, or economic loss from the mere presence of chemicals. In some cases, plaintiffs may seek relief even in the absence of any present or reasonably certain future injury.

This chapter addresses both the theories of recovery and the remedies that have been pursued in this rapidly developing area of the law.

Theories of Liability

Out of the growing body of toxic tort litigation, a number of legal theories have come to the forefront, some familiar and some newly minted.

Negligence

Perhaps the most familiar legal theory common to many toxic tort claims is the classic tort theory of negligence. The elements of a negligence action are familiar to most lawyers:

(a) A duty or obligation, recognized by law, requiring a person to conform to a certain standard of conduct, for the protection of others against unreasonable risks;

(b) A breach of that duty, that is, a failure on the person's part to conform to the required standard;

(c) A reasonably close causal connection between the breach and the resulting injury;

(d) Actual injury, loss, or damage resulting to the interests of another.[1]

The claimed breach of duty—the failure to exercise reasonable care—may focus on any of a number of different areas of conduct by the defendant, including the handling of chemicals, the design of products, the investigation of dangers, and the warning of risks. For example, in *Hubbard-Hall Chemical Co. v. Silverman*, the survivors of two farm workers killed by exposure to a dangerous pesticide sued the product manufacturer for negligently failing to warn the decedents.[2] The court upheld the jury's finding of negligence, holding that the jury could reasonably have concluded that the defendant should have foreseen that its product would be used by workers with limited education and failed to use reasonable care in warning such workers of the product's dangers.[3] Similarly, in *Drayton v. Jiffee Chemical Corp.*, an infant who had been disfigured through accidental dousing with a drain cleaner sued the manufacturer alleging (among other theories) negligent design.[4] Following a bench trial, the court found for the plaintiff on the negligent design claim, concluding that the manufacturer's "use of such a highly caustic chemical as sodium hydroxide and in such concentration . . . constitutes a breach of defendant's duty to design its product so as to be reasonably safe for the purpose intended."[5]

The hurdle plaintiffs often face in asserting such claims is demonstrating that the defendant knew or should have known of the hazard at the time of the conduct or exposure at issue. For example, in *Western Greenhouses v. United States*, the owners of property adjacent to an Air Force base claimed that a chemical used as a degreaser at the base had contaminated their property and sought to hold the government liable based on (among other theories) negligent investigation.[6] The court rejected plaintiffs' negligent investigation claim, holding that the claim failed because base employees did not and could not have known during the relevant period that the use of the degreaser could lead to plaintiffs' damages.[7]

---

1. W. PAGE KEETON ET AL., PROSSER AND KEETON ON THE LAW OF TORTS, § 30, at 164–65 (5th ed. 1984); *see* O'Neal v. Dep't of the Army, 852 F. Supp. 327, 335 (M.D. Pa. 1994). Many jurisdictions use a shortened version of this rule, combining the third and fourth elements into one. *See* Olivo v. Exxon Mobil Corp., 872 A.2d 814, 817 (N.J. Super. 2005) (listing elements as "a duty of care, a breach of that duty, and that the breach proximately caused the harm."); Fox v. Cheminova, Inc., 387 F. Supp. 2d 160, 171 (E.D.N.Y. 2005) (same); Mann v. CSX Transp., Inc., No. 1:07-CV-3512, 2009 U.S. Dist. LEXIS 106433, at *8 (N.D. Ohio Nov. 10, 2009) (same).
2. 340 F.2d 402 (1st Cir. 1965).
3. *Id.* at 404–05.
4. 395 F. Supp. 1081, 1085–86 (N.D. Ohio 1975).
5. *Id.* at 1089–90.
6. 878 F. Supp. 917 (N.D. Tex. 1995).
7. *Id.* at 927 (applying Texas law).

Although negligence claims often impose more burdensome proof requirements than the strict liability or statutory claims discussed below, plaintiffs nevertheless usually allege negligence as one of their alternative theories of recovery. This inclusion is doubtless due to the relative breadth of the negligence theory. Whereas other toxic tort theories address narrow bands of conduct or damage (e.g., trespass addresses physical invasion of real property, battery addresses physical contact), the theory of negligence allows a plaintiff to paint more broadly to allege a defendant's failure to use reasonable care in a much broader range of human conduct.

Two subspecies of negligence also deserve particular attention in the toxic tort context: negligence per se and res ipsa loquitur.

Negligence Per Se

Under the doctrine of negligence per se, a statute, regulation, or ordinance defines the duty of care owed by the defendant to the plaintiff, meaning that the simple violation of the enactment constitutes negligence. The most generally accepted test for determining whether such a law or rule defines a defendant's duty for purposes of tort recovery is set out in Section 286 of the *Restatement (Second) of Torts*, which provides:

> The court may adopt as the standard of conduct for a reasonable man the requirements of a legislative enactment or an administrative regulation whose purpose is found to be exclusively or in part: (a) to protect a class of persons which includes the one whose interest is invaded, and (b) to protect the particular interest which is invaded, and (c) to protect that interest against the kind of harm which has resulted, and (d) to protect that interest against the particular hazard from which the harm results.[8]

Jurisdictions differ in the legal effect of the showing of the violation of a statute or other law. Although some states hold that proof of such a violation establishes the element of breach of duty as a matter of law,[9] other states hold that such a violation is merely evidence of negligence to be weighed by the jury.[10] Some courts have taken the view that

---

8. RESTATEMENT (SECOND) OF TORTS § 286 (1965); *see also* RESTATEMENT (THIRD) OF TORTS: PRODUCTS LIABILITY § 4 (1998) (addressing the effects of compliance and noncompliance with product safety statutes and regulations); Martin v. Shell Oil Co., 180 F. Supp. 2d 313, 324 (D. Conn. 2002) (listing elements required for negligence per se under Connecticut law as "that the defendant violate a statute, that the plaintiff be part of the class sought to be protected by that statute, and that the injury suffered by the plaintiff be of the type the statute was created to prevent"); Rudd v. Electrolux Corp., 982 F. Supp. 355, 365 (M.D.N.C. 1997).
9. *See* Gore v. People's Sav. Bank, 665 A.2d 1341, 1349 (Conn. 1995) ("To establish negligence, the jury in a negligence per se case . . . merely decide whether the relevant statute or regulation has been violated. If it has, the defendant was negligent as a matter of law.") (quoting Wendland v. Ridgefield Constr. Servs., Inc., 439 A.2d 954, 956 (1981)); deJesus v. Seaboard Coastline R.R. Co., 281 So. 2d 198, 201 (Fla. 1973).
10. *See* Brady v. Ralph M. Parsons Co., 572 A.2d 1115, 1125 (Md. Ct. Spec. App. 1990).

where a statute does not itself create a private cause of action for monetary damages, that omission preempts any claim for negligence per se based on violation of that statute.[11] (A defendant's breach of its own self-imposed rules or policies does not constitute negligence per se, but may serve as evidence of negligence.[12])

Negligence per se claims are often pled as separate causes of action, but are normally paired with claims for ordinary negligence. The plaintiff claims that certain conduct by a defendant constituted negligence both because the conduct violated a statute or regulation and because the conduct breached the defendant's duty of reasonable care.[13] Importantly, the establishment of per se negligence through a violation of law does not eliminate the need to prove causation. "The violation of a statute raises no liability for injury to another unless the injury was in some manner the result of such violation."[14]

Res Ipsa Loquitur

In asserting a negligence claim based on res ipsa loquitur, a plaintiff in essence alleges that the defendant's breach of the duty of reasonable care may be inferred from the simple fact that the plaintiff's injury occurred in the way it did; *res ipsa loquitur* literally means "the thing speaks for itself."[15] To prove a defendant's negligence with respect to a particular event under the doctrine of res ipsa loquitur, the plaintiff must generally establish:

1. The event must be of a kind that ordinarily does not occur in the absence of someone's negligence;
2. It must be caused by an agency or instrumentality within the exclusive control of the defendant; and
3. It must not have been due to any voluntary action or contribution on the part of the plaintiff.[16]

Some courts also require the plaintiff to demonstrate that the defendant has (compared to the plaintiff) superior knowledge of, or superior opportunity to determine, the cause of the accident.[17] For example, a court agreed that a plaintiff could not have foreseen

---

11. *See, e.g.*, Sanford St. Local Dev. v. Textron, Inc., 768 F. Supp. 1218 (W.D. Mich., 1991) (addressing negligence per se claim based on claimed violation of federal Toxic Substance Control Act).
12. *See* Frias v. Atl. Richfield Co., 999 S.W.2d 97, 106 (Tex. App. Houston 14th Dist. 1999).
13. *See* Rivera v. Fairbank Mgmt. Props., Inc., 703 A.2d 808, 813–16 (Conn. Super. Ct. 1997) (asserting claims for lead poisoning based on theories of both common law negligence and negligence per se).
14. Inland Steel v. Pequignot, 608 N.E.2d 1378, 1383 (Ind. Ct. App. 1993).
15. BLACK'S LAW DICTIONARY 1424 (9th ed. 2009); *see also* 57B AM. JUR. 2D *Negligence* § 1163 (2012) ("Res ipsa loquitur derives from the understanding that some events ordinarily do not occur in the absence of negligence.").
16. KEETON ET AL., *supra* note 1, § 39, at 244; *see also* RESTATEMENT (SECOND) OF TORTS § 328D(1); Bahrle v. Exxon Corp., 652 A.2d 178, 192 (N.J. Super. 1995).
17. KEETON ET AL., *supra* note 1, § 39 at 244; *see also* Shutt v. Kaufman's, Inc., 438 P.2d 501, 503 (Colo. 1968); Wilson v. Stilwill, 309 N.W.2d 898, 905 (Mich. 1981); Nutting v. Northern Energy, 874 P.2d

that sitting down on a shop chair would cause her to be struck by a falling shoe stand. Nevertheless, because the circumstances at hand would have permitted the plaintiff to establish the nature of the defendant's negligence (if any), the court held that the doctrine of res ipsa loquitur did not apply.[18]

Case law varies somewhat over the effect of the plaintiff's proving these requisite elements. The traditional view is that by proving these elements, the plaintiff will have provided circumstantial evidence of negligence, leaving it to the jury to determine whether to draw an inference of negligence from that evidence; in other words, allowing but not requiring a jury to find that the defendant was negligent.[19] Some other courts have held that on meeting the res ipsa loquitur requirements, the plaintiff creates a rebuttable presumption that the defendant was negligent, shifting the burden to the defendant.[20] The general trend, however, is away from holding that a showing of res ipsa loquitur shifts the burden to the defendant.

Trespass

Toxic tort actions involving environmental damage often assert claims for trespass, alleging that a chemical for which the defendant is responsible has "trespassed" on, over, or under the plaintiff's property. To establish a claim for trespass, a plaintiff must establish that:

1. The defendant actually interfered with the possessor's right of exclusive possession of real property, and
2. That interference was wrongful, meaning that the trespasser had no privilege to enter.[21]

482, 484 (Colo. App. 1994); Debusscher v. Sam's East, Inc., 505 F.3d 475, 481 (6th Cir. 2007) (citing Michigan law in premises liability case).

18. *Shutt*, 438 P.2d at 503.
19. KEETON ET AL., *supra* note 1, § 40, at 258–59; *see, e.g.*, Bahrle v. Exxon Corp., 652 A.2d 178, 192–93 (N.J. Super. Ct. App. Div. 1995) (holding that res ipsa loquitur "permits an inference of negligence from plaintiff's proofs" but finding that res ipsa loquitur did not apply to causation of VOC contamination of wells by underground storage tanks).
20. *See, e.g.*, Lewis v. Kinder Morgan Se. Terminals, LLC, No. 2:07CV47ks-MTP, 2008 U.S. Dist. LEXIS 61060 (S.D. Miss. Aug. 6, 2008) (in a gas spill case, stating that "[w]here all of the elements of Res Ipsa Loquitur [sic] are met, a rebuttable presumption of negligence is raised"); Weiss v. Axler, 328 P.2d 88, 96–97 (Colo. 1958) (affirming judgment for the plaintiff when plaintiff established presumption of negligence under res ipsa loquitur in the defendant's application of permanent cold wave at beauty salon).
21. *See, e.g.*, Johnson v. Paynesville Farmers Union Co-op. Oil Co., 817 N.W.2d 693, 701 (Minn. 2012); Bittner v. Huth, 876 A.2d 157, 161 (Md. Ct. Spec. App. 2005); Singleton v. Haywood Elec. Membership Corp., 588 S.E.2d 871, 874 (N.C. 2003) (listing three elements: (1) possession of the property by plaintiff when the alleged trespass was committed, (2) an unauthorized entry by defendant, and (3) damage to plaintiff (internal citation omitted)); *see also* RESTATEMENT (SECOND) OF TORTS § 329 (1965) (defining trespasser as "a person who enters or remains upon land in the possession of another without a privilege to do so created by the possessor's consent or otherwise").

Actual damages generally are not an element of trespass; in the absence of actual damages, a plaintiff may recover nominal damages.[22] However, some courts have held that certain "invasions" of property that have minimal "tangible" presence (e.g., light, gases, or microscopic particulate matter) may be actionable only if they cause actual damage.[23]

The Exclusive Possession Requirement

Because the tort of trespass aims to vindicate a possessor's interest in exclusive possession of real property,[24] a plaintiff must have a possessory interest in the real property at issue such that the plaintiff's consent or permission is required before another person may enter or use the property.[25] Stated differently, a plaintiff's rights in the property must include the right to exclude others from entering or using such property. Absent a right to exclude others from property, a party has no right to complain about the presence of another (or another's chemicals) on that property.[26]

Fee simple owners of real property obviously have the right of exclusive possession.[27] But anyone who has "actual and exclusive possession" of land can bring a trespass action.[28] For example, lessees generally have a sufficient possessory interest to support a trespass claim.[29]

In contrast, public property generally is not exclusively possessed by any one person or entity. Because public property is open to all, there is no right to exclude others. And state law often affirmatively expands such rights of access to include the taking and use of such resources. For example, under Oklahoma law, stream water is subject to appropriation for the benefit and welfare of the people as provided by law,[30] and "[a]ny person has the right to take water for domestic use from a stream to which he is riparian or to take stream water for domestic use from wells on his premises."[31] As a result, any claim of trespass to public property—land, water, or air—faces a hard uphill battle on the

---

22. *Paynesville Farmers Union Coop.*, 817 N.W.2d at 701.
23. *See* Martin v. Reynolds Metals Co., 342 P.2d 790, 794–95 (Or. 1959).
24. *See Martin*, 342 P.2d at 794; Wallace v. Lewis Cnty., 137 P.3d 101, 108 (Wash. Ct. App. 2006) (discussing intentional trespass); Rockwell Int'l Corp. v. Wilhite, 143 S.W.3d 604, 620 (Ky. App. 2003) ("Trespass is designed to protect against interference with exclusive possession, and not just mere entry.").
25. *See* Swearingen v. Long, 889 F. Supp. 587, 592 (N.D.N.Y. 1995) (dismissing minors' claim for trespass caused by exposure to dry cleaning chemicals for lack of possessory interest).
26. *See* KEETON ET AL., *supra* note 1, § 13, at 67 ("In the bundle of rights, privileges, powers, and immunities that are enjoyed by an owner of property, perhaps the most important is the right to exclusive 'use' of the realty."); New York State Energy Research & Dev. Authority v. Nuclear Fuel Servs., Inc., 561 F. Supp. 954, 970 (W.D.N.Y. 1983).
27. *See* State *ex rel.* Rhodes v. Simpson, 385 S.E.2d 329, 332 (N.C. 1989); Patel v. City of Everman, 179 S.W.3d 1, 16 (Tex. App. 2004).
28. *See* RESTATEMENT (SECOND) OF TORTS § 329 (1965); *cf.* New York State Energy Research & Dev. Authority v. Nuclear Fuel Servs., Inc., 561 F. Supp. 954, 967–68 (W.D.N.Y. 1983) (noting the general rule that only a party in possession of real property may sue for a trespass and that ownership does not suffice to confer standing in trespass absent an owner's personal injury).
29. Harrington v. Chavez, 196 P. 320, 321 (N.M. 1921); Bass v. Planned Mgmt. Servs., 761 P.2d 566, 569 (Utah 1988).
30. OKLA. STAT. tit. 82, § 105.1A (2012).
31. OKLA. STAT. tit. 82, § 105.2(A) (2012).

element of exclusive possession, even if the claim is asserted by the State itself.[32] Despite such limitations, however, some state plaintiffs have tried to assert trespass claims based on the parens patriae doctrine, discussed below.

Wrongful Entry

A trespass involves the wrongful entry on the property of another without the express or implied consent of the owner or possessor of the property.[33] The necessary corollary to this rule holds that "conduct which would otherwise constitute a trespass is not a trespass if it is privileged. Such a privilege may be derived from the consent of the possessor, or may be given by law because of the purpose for which the actor acts or refrains from acting."[34] For example, where cities consented to the use of lead paint on their property, they could not later assert a trespass claim against the paint manufacturers based on the presence of the paint, even if the cities did not know of the paint's dangerous propensities at the time of its use. The claimed lack of knowledge did not "vitiate their consent to the placement of the lead on their properties."[35]

The Physical Invasion Requirement

Under the common law, a trespass requires a physical invasion of real property by tangible things.[36] Smoke, odor, light, noise, and other invasions were not typically held to be trespasses because they involved little or no "tangible" physical invasion.[37] Consistent with this traditional view, the more common modern view holds that if an intangible invasion disrupts a plaintiff's use and enjoyment of real property, then the action is for nuisance, not for trespass.[38]

---

32. *See* New Mexico v. Gen. Elec. Co., 335 F. Supp. 2d 1185, 1235 (D.N.M. 2004) (holding state had no common-law claim for trespass absent pleading of exclusive possessory legal interest), *aff'd in relevant part*, 467 F.3d 1223, 1247 n.36 (10th Cir. 2006); Mathes v. Century Alumina Co., No. 2005/0062, 2008 U.S. Dist. LEXIS 90087, at *28 (D.V.I. 2008).
33. *See, e.g.*, Reasoner v. Chicago, R. I. & P. R. Co., 101 N.W.2d 739 (Iowa 1960).
34. RESTATEMENT (SECOND) OF TORTS § 158 cmt. *e* (1965) (internal citation omitted); *see, e.g.*, Walters v. Prairie Oil & Gas Co., 204 P. 906, 908 (Okla. 1922); Church of Christ in Hollywood v. Superior Court, 121 Cal. Rptr. 2d 810, 815–16 (Cal. Ct. App. 2002); Mitchell v. Baltimore Sun Co., 883 A.2d 1008, 1014 (Md. Ct. Spec. App. 2005).
35. Cnty. of Santa Clara v. Atl. Richfield Co., 40 Cal. Rptr. 3d 313, 333 (Cal. Ct. App. 2006) ("Where the owner of property voluntarily places a product on the property and the product turns out to be hazardous, the owner cannot prosecute a trespass cause of action . . . because the owner has consented to the entry of the product onto the land."); *see also* Fibreboard Corp. v. Hartford Accident & Indem. Co., 20 Cal. Rptr. 2d 376, 388 (Cal. Ct. App. 1993) (holding asbestos products voluntarily incorporated into building by plaintiff could not form basis for trespass claim).
36. Maddy v. Vulcan Materials Co., 737 F. Supp. 1528, 1539 (D. Kan. 1990).
37. *See* Wendinger v. Forst Farms, Inc., 662 N.W.2d 546, 550 (Minn. Ct. App. 2003) (noting that Minnesota has not adopted theory of trespass by particulate matter or odors).
38. *See* RESTATEMENT (SECOND) OF TORTS § 160 (1965) (referring to trespass as continued presence of "a structure, chattel, or other thing"); Maddy v. Vulcan Materials Co., 737 F. Supp. 1528, 1539 (D. Kan. 1990) (citing PROSSER & KEETON for point that introduction of intangibles to another's land is actionable as a nuisance, but noting modern trend for airborne pollution to be considered a trespass).

Some courts have taken more nuanced approaches to whether such "intangible" invasions constitute trespass, focusing on such issues as whether the intangible invasion is trifling or substantial, whether the possessory interest invaded is worthy of legal protection, or whether the invasion causes actual damage.[39]

The Intent Requirement

Most jurisdictions treat trespass as an intentional tort.[40] A defendant need not have a specific intent to harm the landowner,[41] but the defendant must intend the act that amounts to or produces the unlawful invasion, and the intrusion must be at least the immediate or inevitable consequence of that willful act.[42] For example, in *National Telephone Co-Op. Association v. Exxon Corp.*, the plaintiff owner of a building sued the owner of an adjacent service station based on the seepage of petroleum material through the plaintiff's basement walls, asserting a claim for trespass (among others).[43] In addressing the defendant's summary judgment motion, the court focused on the issue of intent, noting that the defendant's commission of some act that ultimately results in harm to property is not sufficient to ground liability; trespass requires volition, that is, "a conscious intent to do the act that constitutes the entry upon someone else's real or personal property."[44] Because the defendant undisputedly had not intended to place any chemicals on the plaintiff's property, the trespass claim failed as a matter of law.[45]

Some courts have held that as long as the act causing the invasion is willful, the trespasser cannot escape liability merely because he exercised reasonable care in committing the act.[46] Other courts have held that a defendant may be found liable for an unintentional trespass, even if the intrusion results from the defendant's willful act, only if the defendant is negligent or is engaged in an ultrahazardous activity.[47]

---

39. *See generally* Martin v. Reynolds Metals Co., 342 P.2d 790, 793–95 (Or. 1959).
40. Acosta Orellana v. CropLife Int'l, 711 F. Supp. 2d 81, 93 (D.D.C. 2010); Miller v. Nat'l Broad. Co., 232 Cal. Rptr. 668, 677 (Cal. Ct. App. 1986); Gen. Tel. Co. v. Bi-Co Pavers, Inc., 514 S.W.2d 168, 170 (Tex. App. 1974).
41. *See* Lee v. Stewart, 10 S.E.2d 804, 805 (N.C. 1940); *Acosta Orellana*, 711 F. Supp. 2d at 93; N.Y. State Energy Research & Dev. Authority v. Nuclear Fuel Services, Inc., 561 F. Supp. 954, 974 (W.D.N.Y. 1983) ("A trespasser, to be such, need not intend harm or unlawful interference with the other's property and may in good faith believe that he or she or it is in some way entitled to enter or remain upon the property.").
42. *See* Phillips v. Sun Oil Co., 121 N.E.2d 249, 250–51 (N.Y. 1954); Martin v. Shell Oil Co., 180 F. Supp. 2d 313, 326 (D. Conn. 2002) ("it is enough that an act is done with knowledge that it will to a substantial certainty result in the entry of the foreign matter [on the property]").
43. 38 F. Supp. 2d 1, 3–4 (D.D.C. 1998).
44. *Id.* at 12.
45. *Id.* at 13.
46. *See* JBG/Twinbrook Metro Ltd. P'ship v. Wheeler, 697 A.2d 898, 909 (Md. 1997).
47. *See* Hudson v. Peavey Oil Co., 566 P.2d 175, 177 (Or. 1977). *Cf.* Dickens v. Oxy Vinyls, LP, 631 F. Supp. 2d 859, 864 (W.D. Ky. 2009) (noting that in Kentucky, "actions for damages to real property caused by another's negligence sound in trespass, not negligence" (citations omitted)).

Under any of these standards, a trespasser may be held liable for the consequences of its trespass even if it did not intend those specific consequences.[48] Thus, a defendant that directed consumers to apply a chemical herbicide to soil was liable for trespass when the chemical was found in public wells where such contamination was a substantially certain result of the application.[49]

Continuing Trespass

Toxic tort law also recognizes a "continuing trespass," where the continued presence of "a structure, chattel, or other thing" on land creates a trespass for the entire time during which the thing is on the land.[50] This doctrine is particularly significant with respect to applying statutes of limitation, because under most statutes the plaintiff's claim does not begin to accrue until the tortious conduct has ceased.[51]

Illustrative Trespass Cases Involving Toxic Tort Claims

A pair of examples may be useful in understanding courts' approaches to trespass claims in the toxic tort arena. In *Scribner v. Summers*, the plaintiffs lost a sale of their property when a prospective buyer withdrew after learning that a neighboring landowner had been indicted on charges of improperly disposing of hazardous material.[52] The plaintiffs' property was found to have been contaminated by the disposal, and the plaintiffs brought suit against the adjacent landowner, asserting (among others) a trespass claim. The district court rejected the trespass claim, finding that the plaintiffs had not shown that the defendants intended the barium-containing water that was used in the defendants' steel-treating process to enter the plaintiffs' land, situated downhill from the defendants' land. The Second Circuit reversed, holding that under New York law, the test for trespass was whether the defendant intended the act that amounted to or produced the unlawful invasion and whether the defendant had good reason to know or expect that migration would occur. Because the defendant continued to demolish barium-containing furnaces outside its building and spray them down with water in close proximity to the plaintiffs' property, the Second Circuit found the defendant to have intended the acts that caused the invasion of the property and held the trespass claim viable.[53]

---

48. *Acosta Orellana*, 711 F. Supp. 2d at 93; Abbatiello v. Monsanto Co., 522 F. Supp. 2d 524, 541–42 (S.D.N.Y. 2007).
49. State v. Fermenta ASC Corp., 656 N.Y.S.2d 342, 346 (N.Y. App. Div. 1997).
50. RESTATEMENT (SECOND) OF TORTS § 161, cmt. *b* (1965); *see also* Hoery v. United States, 64 P.3d 214, 219 (Colo. 2003); Rockwell Int'l Corp. v. Wilhite, 143 S.W.3d 604, 608 n.9 (Ky. Ct. App. 2003) (citing PROSSER).
51. *Hoery*, 64 P.3d at 219.
52. 84 F.3d 554 (2d Cir. 1996).
53. *Id.* at 558.

The Connecticut Supreme Court reached a similar conclusion in *City of Bristol v. Tilcon Minerals, Inc.*[54] The city condemned a portion of a landowner's tract to remediate potentially contaminated groundwater migrating from the city's landfill. The landowner filed a claim against the city for continuous trespass, alleging that the plume of contamination extended beyond the tract the city had taken over, affected another area that the landowner intended for residential development, and forced the owner to find a substitute source of drinking water. The court agreed that these facts constituted a trespass because the city knew it was placing toxic substances in an unprotected landfill situated uphill from adjacent property, where it was likely to migrate.[55]

Nuisance

Nuisance claims almost always accompany trespass claims in toxic tort cases. The common law tort of nuisance "is a class of wrongs which arises from an unreasonable, unwarranted, or unlawful use by a person or entity of property lawfully possessed, but which works an obstruction or injury to the right of another."[56] The law generally recognizes two types of nuisances: public and private. A private nuisance claim alleges that the defendant has interfered with the use and enjoyment of a particular person's land, while a public nuisance claim asserts that the defendant has interfered with the rights of the community at large.[57] The proper defendant in a nuisance suit is generally the defendant in possession or control of the property containing the nuisance, although some states have held that anyone who participates in the creation or maintenance of the nuisance can be liable.[58]

Generally, nuisance protects the possessor's right of enjoyment or use of property.[59] Although some courts have recognized nuisance claims based on the public's mere

---

54. 931 A.2d 237 (Conn. 2007).
55. *Id.* at 258–59.
56. Briscoe v. Harper Oil Co., 702 P.2d 33, 36 (Okla. 1985); *see also* Dickens v. Oxy Vinyls, LP, 631 F. Supp. 2d 859, 865 (W.D. Ky. 2009) ("A nuisance 'arises from the unreasonable, unwarranted, or unlawful use by a person of his own property and produces such material annoyance, inconvenience, discomfort or hurt that the law will presume a consequent damage.'") (citations omitted).
57. *See* Butler v. Advanced Drainage Sys., 717 N.W.2d 760, 769 (Wis. 2006); Brown v. Petrolane, Inc., 162 Cal. Rptr. 551, 554 (Cal. Ct. App. 1980). *See generally* 58 Am. Jur. 2d *Nuisances* §§ 23–24 (2012).
58. *Compare* Clark v. Greenville Cnty., 437 S.E.2d 117, 119 (S.C. 1993) (dismissing nuisance suit against corporate defendants who deposited waste at landfill), *with* Cnty. of Santa Clara v. Atl. Richfield Co., 40 Cal. Rptr. 3d 313, 325 (Cal. Ct. App. 2006) (stating that "liability for nuisance does not hinge on whether the defendant owns, possesses or controls the property, nor on whether he is in a position to abate the nuisance; the critical question is whether the defendant created or assisted in the creation of the nuisance" and holding manufacturer of lead liable for public nuisance for concealing dangers in lead paint (quoting another source)).
59. *See* Ballenger v. Grand Saline, 276 S.W.2d 874, 875 (Tex. Civ. App. 1955); Jerry Harmon Motors, Inc. v. Farmers Union Grain Terminal Ass'n, 337 N.W.2d 427, 428 (N.D. 1983) (citing state statute on nuisance).

perception of contamination, even where that perception may be unfounded,[60] most courts have held that plaintiffs cannot recover based on unfounded fears.[61]

Depending on the jurisdiction, a nuisance claim may be based on intentional conduct or on negligent or other nonintentional conduct.[62] The legal standard for an "intentional invasion" constituting a nuisance is:

> An invasion of another's interest in the use and enjoyment of land or an interference with the public right, is intentional if the actor (a) acts for the purpose of causing it, or (b) knows that it is resulting or is substantially certain to result from his conduct.[63]

Statutory Nuisance

Many states have codified the common law tort of nuisance.[64] Iowa's statutes reflect a common formulation of nuisance in the toxic tort arena:

> 657.1 Nuisance—What Constitutes—Action to Abate
>
> 1. Whatever is injurious to health, indecent, or unreasonably offensive to the senses, or an obstruction to the free use of property, so as essentially to interfere unreasonably with the comfortable enjoyment of life or property, is a nuisance, and a civil action by ordinary proceedings may be brought to enjoin and abate the nuisance and to recover damages sustained on account of the nuisance.
>
> 657.2 What Deemed Nuisances
>
> The following are nuisances:
>
> 1. The erecting, continuing, or using any building or other place for the exercise of any trade, employment, or manufacture, which, by occasioning noxious exhalations, unreasonably offensive smells, or other annoyances,

---

60. *See* Allen v. Uni-First Corp., 558 A.2d 961, 963–65 (Vt. 1988) (nuisance claim for perception of contamination from dry cleaner).
61. *See* Adkins v. Thomas Solvent Co., 487 N.W.2d 715, 721 (Mich. 1992) (alleging nuisance from improper handling and storage of toxic chemicals and contaminated groundwater); Lamb v. Martin Marietta Energy Sys., 835 F. Supp. 959, 969 (W.D. Ky. 1993) (alleging groundwater contamination from government-owned uranium plant).
62. *See, e.g.*, Butler v. Advanced Drainage Sys., 717 N.W.2d 760, 769 (Wis. 2006); Hoery v. United States, 64 P.3d 214, 218 (Colo. 2003); Carter v. Monsanto Co., 575 S.E.2d 342, 346 (W. Va. 2002); Phillips Ranch, Inc. v. Banta, 543 P.2d 1035, 1039 (Or. 1975); Hostetler v. Ward, 704 P.2d 1193, 1202 (Wash. Ct. App. 1985).
63. RESTATEMENT (SECOND) OF TORTS § 825 (1979); *see, e.g.*, Bradley v. Am. Smelting & Ref. Co., 709 P.2d 782, 792 (Wash. 1985) (finding a cause of action for nuisance based on intentional conduct where defendant knew for decades that its smokestack emitted microscopic particulates and must have known that the particulates would land on the ground).
64. *See, e.g.*, CAL. CIV. CODE §§ 3479–3508.2 (West 2012); KY. REV. STAT. § 411.500–411.570 (2012); MINN. STAT. § 617.81 (2012); N.D. CENT. CODE § 42-01-02 (2012).

> becomes injurious and dangerous to the health, comfort, or property of individuals or the public. . . .
>
> 10. The emission of dense smoke, noxious fumes, or fly ash in cities is a nuisance and cities may provide the necessary rules for inspection, regulation and control.

Applying this statute, the Iowa Supreme Court held that "the use of property or structures in such a manner as to unreasonably interfere with another's reasonable use and enjoyment of his property or in such a manner as to injure another's health is a nuisance."[65] Most states have adopted similar general language, which makes the actual determination of whether specific conduct or a specific condition constitutes a nuisance a highly case-specific decision. As one court described the inquiry:

> Whether a lawful business is a nuisance depends on the reasonableness of conducting the business in the manner, at the place, and under the circumstances in question. Thus the existence of a nuisance does not depend on the intention of the party who created it. Rather, it depends on the following three factors: priority of location, the nature of the neighborhood, and the wrong complained of. . . .
>
> A fact finder uses the normal person standard to determine whether a nuisance involving personal discomfort or annoyance is significant enough to constitute a nuisance. The normal-person standard is an objective standard . . . :
>
>> If normal persons living in the community would regard the invasion in question as definitely offensive, seriously annoying or intolerable, then the invasion is significant.[66]

Priority of location refers to "whether the complaining party moved to the nuisance."[67] If the nuisance already existed and was known at the time the plaintiff acquired an interest in nearby property, the plaintiff's claims for relief are weakened considerably. Priority of location is examined as of the point in time just prior to the commencement of the nuisance-producing activity.[68]

---

65. Miller v. Rohling, 720 N.W.2d 562, 567 (Iowa 2006).
66. Weinhold v. Wolff, 555 N.W.2d 454, 459 (Iowa 1996) (quoting RESTATEMENT (SECOND) OF TORTS § 821F, other citations omitted); *see also* Gacke v. Pork Xtra, L.L.C., 684 N.W.2d 168, 179 (Iowa 2004). Kentucky includes illustrative factors in its nuisance statutes for courts to apply in considering the existence of a private nuisance. KY. REV. STAT. § 411.550; *see* Rockwell Int'l Corp. v. Wilhite, 143 S.W.2d 604, 626–27 (Ky. Ct. App. 2003).
67. *See* Perkins v. Madison Cnty. Livestock & Fair Ass'n, 613 N.W.2d 264, 271 (Iowa 2000) (emphasis omitted); W.G. Duncan Coal Co. v. Jones, 254 S.W.2d 720, 723 (Ky. Ct. App. 1953).
68. *Miller*, 720 N.W.2d at 568; *see also* O'Brien v. O'Fallon, 400 N.E.2d 456, 461 (Ill. Ct. App. 1980) (finding that nuisance from disposal of raw sewage into a lake had not manifested itself prior to date that plaintiffs acquired lots and built the houses on the lake).

The nature of the neighborhood is also a factor to be considered, but it is not dispositive. For example, a court found the operation of a grain storage facility to be a nuisance to neighboring residents despite finding that the area in question was a "commercial" neighborhood.[69] On the other hand, courts addressing nuisance complaints by rural residents have observed that such residents must expect to bear with the type of farm and livestock conditions normally found in the area.[70] Most states statutorily protect certain land uses that might otherwise constitute nuisances, including "right to farm" statutes that give immunity to agricultural operations and related land uses from nuisance suits.[71]

Strict Liability and Absolute Liability
Strict Liability for Abnormally Dangerous Activities

The common law recognizes that some activities pose such serious risks that the person responsible for the activity will be held liable for any damages caused by the activity without regard to due care or fault. The seminal case in this area is the 1868 British decision in *Rylands v. Fletcher*, an action against mill owners who had built a large reservoir for the collection of water. When the impoundment failed, the stored water flooded the plaintiff's neighboring mineshafts. The Court of the Exchequer Chamber found the mill owners liable, holding that one who introduces a hazardous condition upon his property that, upon its escape, causes harm to another is strictly liable to the injured person even if the first party was not negligent. The House of Lords affirmed, adding that strict liability should attach only if the use was "non-natural" to the land.[72]

American law has largely adopted this doctrine. The *Restatement (Second) of Torts* notes that strict liability may be imposed on one "who carries on an abnormally dangerous activity" causing harm to persons or property even if that person "has exercised the

---

69. *Miller*, 720 N.W.2d at 568–69.
70. *See* Johnson v. Knox Cnty. P'ship, 728 N.W.2d 101, 108–09 (Neb. 2007) (reversing summary judgment for defendant on private nuisance claim by rural neighbors of cattle confinement facility).
71. *See, e.g.*, Miss. Code Ann. § 95-3-29 (2012) (stating that proof of the existence of an "agricultural operation" for one year or more is an absolute defense to a public or private nuisance action); N.J. Stat. Ann. § 4:1C-10 (stating that "there shall exist an irrebuttable presumption that no commercial agricultural operation . . . shall constitute a public or private nuisance . . ."); R.I. Gen. Laws §§ 2-23-1 to 2-23-7 (stating "[n]o agricultural operation . . . is found to be a public or private nuisance, due to alleged objectionable: (1) Odor from livestock, manure, fertilizer, or feed, occasioned by generally accepted farming procedures; (2) Noise from livestock or farm equipment used in normal, generally accepted farming procedures; (3) Dust created during plowing or cultivation operations; (4) Use of pesticides, rodenticides, insecticides, herbicides, or fungicides."). These "right to farm" statutes typically provide agricultural operations immunity from nuisance suits only if they existed before the plaintiff arrived in the vicinity. *See* Wis. Stat. § 823.08 (requiring that the land be "in agricultural use without substantial interruption before the plaintiff began the use of property that the plaintiff alleges was interfered with by the agricultural use or agricultural practice"); Swedenberg v. Phillips, 562 So. 2d 170 (Ala. 1990) (statute not applicable because residents suing for nuisance arrived before chicken farm).
72. 3 L.R. 330 (H.L. 1868).

utmost care to prevent the harm."[73] Courts generally consider the following factors in evaluating whether an activity should be deemed abnormally dangerous:

- existence of a high degree of risk of some harm to the person, land, or chattels of others;
- the likelihood that the harm that results from it will be great;
- the inability to eliminate the risk by the exercise of reasonable care;
- the extent to which the activity is not a matter of common usage;
- the inappropriateness of the activity to the place where it is carried on; and
- the extent to which the activity's value to the community is outweighed by its dangerous attributes.[74]

The states vary in their applications of the strict liability doctrine with respect to what activities are "abnormally dangerous," whether the judge or the jury decides whether an activity is abnormally dangerous, and even whether to recognize the doctrine at all.[75] Most courts hold that judges should determine whether an activity is abnormally dangerous as a matter of law,[76] but a minority permits a jury to determine the issue.[77] Some states still use the *First Restatement*'s standard of "ultrahazardous" (as opposed to "abnormally dangerous") activities, which imposes liability where an activity "necessarily involves a risk of serious harm which cannot be eliminated by the exercise of the utmost care" (as opposed to the "reasonable care" contemplated by the *Second Restatement*) and is "not a matter of common usage."[78]

---

73. RESTATEMENT (SECOND) OF TORTS § 519 (1977).
74. RESTATEMENT (SECOND) OF TORTS § 520 (1977); *see also* Grand Pier Ctr. LLC v. Tronox, LLC, No. 03 C 7767, 2008 U.S. Dist. LEXIS 88201, at *9 (N.D. Ill. 2008) (applying factors in determining whether disposal of mill tailings was abnormally dangerous).
75. *See* Hicks v. Humble Oil & Ref. Co., 970 S.W.2d 90, 97 (Tex. App. 1998) (noting that Texas has not adopted the portion of *Restatement* that calls for strict liability for abnormally dangerous activities); *In re* Derailment Cases, 416 F.3d 787, 796 (8th Cir. 2005) (noting that the Nebraska Supreme Court has consistently declined to reach the question of whether abnormally dangerous activities merit strict liability).
76. *See* Holder v. Enbridge Energy, L.P., No. 1:10-CV-752, 2011 U.S. Dist. LEXIS 99220 (W.D. Mich. Sept. 2, 2011); Berish v. Sw. Energy Prod. Co., 763 F. Supp. 2d 702, 705 (M.D. Pa. 2011); Liss v. Milford Partners, Inc., No. X07CV440251235, 2008 Conn. Super. LEXIS 2490 (Conn. Super. Ct. Sept. 29, 2008); *In re* Compl. of Weeks Marine, Inc., No. 04-494, 2005 U.S. Dist. LEXIS 30196, *17 (D.N.J. 2005); Apodaca v. AAA Gas Co., 73 P.3d 215, 223 (N.M. Ct. App. 2003).
77. *See* City of Neodesha v. BP Corp. N. America, 287 P.3d 214, 231 (Kan. 2012) (holding that when facts are undisputed, whether an activity is abnormally dangerous is a question of law; when facts are in dispute, determination is by jury); Harper v. Regency Dev. Co., 399 So. 2d 248, 254 (Ala. 1981) (noting that a jury determination of whether an activity is "abnormally dangerous" is "at odds with Comment (1) of the Restatement," but choosing to "adhere to the traditional rule of submitting both the issue of culpability and proximate cause to the jury except where no dispute of fact is presented on the issue by the evidence").
78. Parks Hiway Enters., LLC v. CEM Leasing, Inc., 995 P.2d 657, 665 & n.35 (Alaska 2000) (quoting Matomco Oil Co. v. Arctic Mech., Inc., 796 P.2d 1336, 1341–42 & n.13 (Alaska 1999)).

Some jurisdictions except common carriers from liability for transporting abnormally dangerous materials on public policy grounds, concluding that such carriers should not bear liability for faultlessly handling goods that they are legally required to transport.[79] Other jurisdictions have rejected such a common carrier exception, focusing on the superior position of the common carrier to distribute the loss among the public.[80]

Because of the strict liability imposed on those who undertake abnormally dangerous activities, courts have consciously limited the range of activities that come within the doctrine. The determination of whether an activity is abnormally dangerous is generally a fact-intensive inquiry,[81] although some states have broadly categorized certain types of activities as abnormally dangerous as a matter of law, such as the handling of explosives and certain dangerous chemicals.[82] Courts often look at whether the activity at issue could be made safe through the exercise of reasonable care and whether the activity is a matter of common usage.[83] Courts also give careful and case-specific consideration to the circumstances surrounding the particular activity at issue and the properties of the chemical at issue in toxic tort situations.[84] In cases concerning contamination by petroleum or other

---

79. E. Troy v. Soo Line R.R. Co., 409 F. Supp. 326, 330 (E.D. Wis. 1976) (citing seminal case of Actiesselskabet Ingrid v. Cent. R.R. Co. of New Jersey, 216 F. 72 (2d Cir. 1912)); Christ Church Parish v. Cadet Chem. Corp., 199 A.2d 707, 708 (Conn. Super. Ct. 1964).
80. Nat'l Steel Serv. Ctr. v. Gibbons, 319 N.W.2d 269, 273 (Iowa 1982); Chavez v. S. Pac. Transp. Co., 413 F. Supp. 1203, 1214 (E.D. Cal. 1976).
81. See Biniek v. Exxon Mobil Corp., 818 A.2d 330, 337 (N.J. Super. Ct. Law Div. 2002) (stating whether an activity is abnormally dangerous is determined on a case-by-case basis); Bella v. Aurora Air, Inc., 566 P.2d 489, 495 (Or. 1977) (holding that determination of whether an activity is abnormally dangerous is determined "in the locality and circumstances where it is done" in part by using a sliding scale comparing the seriousness of the harm and the chance of probability of harm).
82. See New Jersey v. Ventron Corp., 468 A.2d 150, 159–60 (N.J. 1983) (finding mercury and other toxic wastes abnormally dangerous and their disposal an abnormally dangerous activity); cf. Dickens v. Oxy Vinyls, LP, 631 F. Supp. 2d 859, 864 (W.D. Ky. 2009) (noting that "Kentucky does not categorically exclude any activity as being ultra hazardous, but it has only affirmatively recognized blasting activities and the pollution of a stream resulting in damage to a lower riparian landowner").
83. See In re Hanford Nuclear Reservation Litig., 350 F. Supp. 2d 871, 876 (E.D. Wash. 2004) (finding the chemical separation process in plutonium production was an abnormally dangerous activity because weapons grade plutonium production was not a matter of common usage and the risk of emissions of radioactive I-131 was unavoidable with due care); Arlington Forest Assoc. v. Exxon Corp., 774 F. Supp. 387, 390–91 (E.D. Va. 1991) (finding underground gasoline storage tanks not abnormally dangerous); Bloomington v. Westinghouse Elec. Corp., 891 F.2d 611, 616 (7th Cir. 1989) (citing ability of defendant to limit risks associated with PCBs through reasonable care as reason not to apply strict liability). In fact, whether the activity could be made safe through the exercise of reasonable care has been described as "at the core of" and "central to" the determination of whether an activity is abnormally dangerous for the purpose of imposing strict liability. Apodaca v. AAA Gas Co., 73 P.3d 215, 223 (N.M. Ct. App. 2003); Kis v. Amerigas Propane L.P., No. DV 98-359, 2000 Mont. Dist. LEXIS 1835, at *11 (Mont. Dist. Ct. 2000) (citing Erbrich Prods. Co. v. Wills, 509 N.E.2d 850, 857 n.3 (Ind. Ct. App. 1987)) (finding the application of herbicide not abnormally dangerous where the risk of harm could have been avoided by following the label directions).
84. See Ind. Harbor Belt R.R. Co. v. Am. Cyanamid Co., 916 F.2d 1174, 1175–82 (7th Cir. 1990) (finding that transportation of chemical used in manufacture of acrylics by rail car not an abnormally dangerous activity); Interfaith Cmty. Org. v. Honeywell Int'l, Inc., 263 F. Supp. 2d 796, 850–55 (D.N.J. 2003) (finding disposal and failure to remove chromium ore processing residue constitutes abnormally dangerous activity).

common fuels, courts have generally held that handling and disposing of these materials are not abnormally dangerous activities, often relying in part on the handlers' ability to ameliorate the risk through due care.[85] Courts have generally been cautious about extending the doctrine to cover new activities and emerging technologies such as hydraulic fracking, declining to rule on the issue in particular cases until discovery is completed and the *Second Restatement* factors can be applied.[86]

Strict Liability for Product Defects

Plaintiffs also can raise strict liability claims against manufacturers of products involved in toxic torts. Although the term *strict liability* is used in the contexts of both abnormally dangerous activities and products liability, the term applies to different substantive doctrines in the two contexts.

Strict liability claims in the product liability context generally follow Section 402A of the *Restatement (Second) of Torts*, which provides:

> 1. One who sells any product in a defective condition unreasonably dangerous to the user or consumer or to his property is subject to liability for physical harm thereby caused to the ultimate user or consumer, or to his property, if
>
> (a) the seller is engaged in the business of selling such a product, and
>
> (b) it is expected to and does reach the user or consumer without substantial change in the condition in which it is sold.
>
> 2. The rule stated [above] applies although
>
> (a) the seller has exercised all possible care in the preparation and sale of his product, and
>
> (b) the user or consumer has not bought the product from or entered into any contractual relation with the seller.[87]

---

85. *See* Parks Hiway Enters., LLC v. CEM Leasing, Inc., 995 P.2d 657, 665–66 (Alaska 2000); Henke v. Arco Midcon, LLC, 750 F. Supp. 2d 1052, 1059 (E.D. Mo. 2010); Nnadili v. Chevron U.S.A., Inc., 435 F. Supp. 2d 93, 101–02 (D.D.C. 2006) (relying in part on plaintiffs' lack of exposure to contaminants); Martin v. Shell Oil Co., 180 F. Supp. 2d 313, 325 (D. Conn. 2002). *But see* Yommer v. McKenzie, 257 A.2d 138, 141 (Md. 1969) (applying *Rylands* doctrine to "storage of large quantities of gasoline immediately adjacent to a private residence"); Branch v. W. Petroleum, Inc., 657 P.2d 267, 274 (Utah 1982) (finding that ponding of water created when drilling for oil in an area adjacent to wells was abnormally dangerous).
86. *See* Berish v. Sw. Energy Prod. Co., 763 F. Supp. 2d 702, 706 (M.D. Pa. 2011) (expressing opinion that it is likely that "fracking" will not be found abnormally dangerous); Holder v. Enbridge Energy, L.P., No. 1:10-CV-752, 2011 U.S. Dist. LEXIS 99220, at *11–12 (W.D. Mich. Sept. 2, 2011) (denying motion to dismiss strict liability claim based on transport of tar sands).
87. Restatement (Second) of Torts § 402A (1965).

This "defective condition unreasonably dangerous" to the consumer may take the form of a defect in the design of a product, a defect in the manufacture of a properly designed product, or a failure to provide adequate warnings and instructions for the safe use of the product.[88] For example, in *Elmore v. Owens-Illinois, Inc.*, the Missouri Supreme Court held that the plaintiffs could recover under a strict-liability defective-design theory simply by establishing that the product's design subjects people to unreasonable risks, without having to show that the defendant was "at fault."[89] In *Folsom v. Sears, Roebuck & Co.*, the court held that the plaintiff's testimony that she was burned when she inserted her hand into a microwave oven after operating it normally was sufficient circumstantial evidence to support a strict liability claim based on a manufacturing defect.[90] And in *Ford Motor Co. v. Ledesma*, the court emphasized that a strict-liability claim based on a manufacturing defect focuses on whether the product in question deviates from design specifications, holding that a jury charge that omitted the deviation requirement constituted reversible error and required a new trial.[91]

Despite the Restatement's apparent disclaimer of the exercise of reasonable care as a defense, most courts hold that a defendant cannot be held strictly liable for a design defect or a failure to warn unless the defendant could reasonably have anticipated the risk that caused the injury—essentially a negligence standard. For example, the Minnesota Supreme Court held that a chemical manufacturer's duty to warn under a strict liability theory extends to "reasonably foreseeable users" of the product.[92] As a result, the court found that jury's verdict that the defendant was not negligent could not be reconciled with its conclusion that the product was defective; if the product was defective, the defendant must have been negligent.[93] Some courts employ the "hindsight" test in strict-liability products-liability actions, holding that the danger of a product is unreasonable if the manufacturer would not have placed the product on the market if it had known of the danger.[94]

---

88. *See* Haddix v. Playtex Family Prods. Corp., 138 F.3d 681, 683 (7th Cir. 1998); Moe v. Springfield Milling Corp., 394 N.W.2d 582, 586 (Minn. Ct. App. 1986) (reversing summary judgment in favor of manufacturer of dioxin-contaminated feed supplement with regard to plaintiff's strict liability claims).
89. 673 S.W.2d 434, 437–38 (Mo. 1984); *see also* Stinson v. E.I. DuPont De Nemours and Co., 904 S.W.2d 428 (Mo. App. 1995) ("the burden of proving that a product's design is defective is satisfied when the product is proven unreasonably dangerous").
90. 329 S.E.2d 217, 218 (Ga. App. 1985).
91. 242 S.W.3d 32, 41–45 (Tex. 2007).
92. Hauenstein v. Loctite Corp., 347 N.W.2d 272, 275 (Minn. 1984); *see also* Anderson v. Owens-Corning Fiberglas Corp., 810 P.2d 549, 559 (Cal. 1991) (asbestos case); Owens-Ill., Inc. v. Zenobia, 601 A.2d 633, 641 (Md. 1992) (asbestos case). *But see* Johnson v. Raybestos-Manhattan, Inc., 740 P.2d 548, 549 (Haw. 1987) (referring to knowledge requirement for strict liability for failure to warn as "irrelevant" in asbestos case).
93. *Hauenstein*, 347 N.W.2d at 275.
94. *See* Wood v. Phillips Petroleum Co., 119 S.W.3d 870, 873 (Tex. App. 2003); Dart v. Wiebe Mfg., 709 P.2d 876, 881 (Ariz. 1985); Borel v. Fibreboard Paper Prods. Corp., 493 F.2d 1076, 1088 (5th Cir. 1973).

In contrast to the "abnormally dangerous" setting discussed above, courts in the product-liability setting have distinguished the concept of "absolute liability" from strict liability, generally agreeing that the law does not require a product manufacturer to be the insurer of its products.[95] As the Montana Supreme Court put it, "[f]rom the time we initially adopted strict products liability, we have reassured defendants that strict liability is not absolute liability."[96]

Statutory Liability

Congress and state legislatures have expanded and supplemented the traditional common-law theories of toxic tort liability through various statutory schemes, primarily the Comprehensive Environmental Response, Compensation, and Liability Act (also known as Superfund or CERCLA)[97] and the Resource Conservation and Recovery Act (RCRA).[98] A full discussion of these statutory schemes is beyond the scope of this chapter. Moreover, because these statutes are often at the heart of complex and lengthy litigation involving dozens of parties and millions of dollars, courts have generated a great deal of case law interpreting both the federal and state versions.

In a nutshell, CERCLA permits private plaintiffs to recover certain costs they have incurred for the remediation of sites where releases of hazardous substances have occurred or are threatened.[99] A plaintiff must meet certain regulatory requirements in conducting the remediation;[100] once those requirements are met, the plaintiff may seek to recover its response costs from a broad array of parties, commonly called "potentially responsible parties" or PRPs, who have some relationship to the presence of hazardous substances at the

---

95. *See Anderson*, 810 P.2d at 555, 559; Fibreboard Corp. v. Fenton, 845 P.2d 1168, 1175 (Colo. 1993) ("Strict liability is not absolute liability and a manufacturer is not required to be the virtual insurer of its products.").
96. Sternhagen v. Dow Co., 935 P.2d 1139, 1143 (Mont. 1997) (noting that strict liability plaintiff must still prove existence of defect and causal link between defect and injury).
97. 42 U.S.C. §§ 9601–9657.
98. 42 U.S.C. §§ 6901–6992k.
99. 42 U.S.C. § 9607(a). CERCLA also permits certain parties to seek damages for injury to, destruction of, or loss of natural resources, as discussed in the text below.
100. Most important, the remediation undertaken by the plaintiff must be consistent with the federal government's national plan for such remediations, called the "national contingency plan." *See* 42 U.S.C. §§ 9605, 9607(a)(4)(B); Gen. Elec. Co. v. Litton Indus. Automation Sys., Inc., 920 F.2d 1415, 1418 (8th Cir. 1990).

site.[101] To recover response costs under CERCLA, a private party must generally establish four elements:

1. the site where the hazardous substance is found is a "facility" as defined by CERCLA;
2. there has been a release or threatened release of a hazardous substance from the facility;
3. the release or threatened release has caused private party to incur response costs that were necessary and consistent with national contingency plan; and
4. the defendants fall within one of the four classes of parties subject to liability under CERCLA.[102]

When multiple PRPs are involved, CERCLA imposes joint and several liability for response costs unless the parties can show a reasonable basis for apportionment of the harm.[103] In addition, CERCLA permits contribution actions by the responsible parties against other parties who are responsible for the contamination at issue.[104] CERCLA also allows the federal government to bring enforcement actions against these PRPs.[105]

Under CERCLA's broad liability provisions, a party that owned a site during the disposal of wastes or transported wastes to the site may be liable for the remediation costs incurred many years after the disposal.[106] CERCLA also contains provisions that protect parties who settle CERCLA claims with the federal government from further liability to other plaintiffs or potentially responsible parties.[107]

---

101. "Potentially responsible parties" include the current owner or operator of the site, any owner or operator of a site at the time of the disposal of the hazardous substance, any person who arranged for the disposal of the hazardous substance at the site, and any person who transported the hazardous substance to the site who also selected that site for the disposal. *See* 42 U.S.C. § 9607(a); Burlington N. & Santa Fe Ry. v. United States, 556 U.S. 599, 608–09 (2009).
102. *See, e.g.,* Bunger v. Hartman, 851 F. Supp. 461, 463 (S.D. Fla. 1994).
103. *Burlington N. & Santa Fe Ry.*, 556 U.S. at 614–15.
104. 42 U.S.C. § 9613(f). CERCLA provides no avenue for redressing claims of personal injury.
105. 42 U.S.C. § 9604(a); *see* Polcha v. AT&T Nassau Metals Corp., 837 F. Supp. 94, 96 (M.D. Pa. 1993).
106. *See* Axel Johnson, Inc. v. Carroll Carolina Oil Co., 191 F.3d 409, 414 (4th Cir. 1999) (liability under CERCLA includes liability for former owners or operators "so long as some hazardous substances were deposited at the facility during the period when the party did own or operate [the site] and the other requirements of the statute are met"); Sealy Conn., Inc. v. Litton Indus., Inc., 9 F. Supp. 2d 105, 107–09 (D. Conn. 1998) (denying summary judgment to company that owned site from 1912 to 1958 on CERCLA cost recovery claims); Am. Cyanamid Co. v. Capuano, 381 F.3d 6, 21–22 (1st Cir. 2004) (affirming transporter liability for company that transported waste to site in 1977).
107. *See, e.g.,* 42 U.S.C. §§ 9613(f)(2), 9622(f), 9622(h)(4); Farmland Indus., Inc. v. Morrison-Quirk Grain Corp., 54 F.3d 478, 482 (8th Cir. 1995).

Many states have passed statutory schemes similar to CERCLA, although most feature local variations. For example, Alaska has incorporated much of CERCLA's "potentially responsible parties" scheme into its own cleanup statute,[108] but its highest court has held that the scope of liability under the state statute is even broader than CERCLA.[109] Some states, like Minnesota, set out different standards for recovering cleanup expenses depending on whether the plaintiff is a government entity or a private party.[110] And in New Jersey, private parties may under certain circumstances seek treble damages from other responsible parties who refuse to comply with a directive from the state cleanup agency.[111]

In contrast to the remediation-oriented CERCLA, RCRA (which preceded CERCLA by several years) is a forward-looking statute regulating the management and disposal of "hazardous waste" (a different set of substances than CERCLA's "hazardous substances").[112] The federal government, through the Environmental Protection Agency (EPA), can assess civil penalties for violations of RCRA or issue orders requiring compliance immediately or within a specific time period.[113] Under RCRA, "any person" may bring an action for injunctive relief (but not to recover cleanup costs).[114] Most states have enacted laws and created regulations that are at least as stringent as the regulations on hazardous wastes in RCRA and provide similar grounds for injunctive relief.[115]

---

108. Alaska Stat. § 46.03.822(a)(1)–(a)(5) (2012).
109. Berg v. Popham, 113 P.3d 604, 609 (Alaska 2005).
110. See Minn. ex rel. N. Pac. Ctr., Inc. v. BNSF Ry. Co., 686 F.3d 567, 574–75 (8th Cir. 2012) (distinguishing liability to governmental entity from liability to private parties under state version of CERCLA and finding that costs private party sought were not "removal" costs and thus not allowed).
111. N.J. Stat. Ann. §§ 58:10-23.11f.a(2) to 58:10-23.11f.a(3).
112. See N.J. Dep't of Envtl. Prot. & Energy v. Gloucester Envtl. Mgmt. Servs., 821 F. Supp. 999, 1006 (D.N.J. 1993) (finding that exception for household waste in RCRA does not apply to CERCLA and noting that "RCRA is preventative; CERCLA is curative" (internal citation omitted)); see also United States v. Atlas Minerals & Chems., Inc., No. 91-5118, 1995 U.S. Dist. LEXIS 13097, at *290 (E.D. Pa. 1995) (noting that "one of the objectives of CERCLA's passage was to supplement RCRA's prospective regulation scheme").
113. 42 U.S.C. § 6928(a).
114. 42 U.S.C. § 6972(a)(1); Furrer v. Brown, 62 F.3d 1092, 1094 (8th Cir. 1995). Some courts have allowed plaintiffs seeking response costs under § 107 to include those costs incurred to comply with RCRA. See Mardan Corp. v. C.G.C. Music, Ltd., 600 F. Supp. 1049, 1053–54 (D. Ariz. 1984), aff'd, 804 F.2d 1454, 1462–63 (9th Cir. 1986)); see also United States v. Rohm & Haas Co., 2 F.3d 1265, 1272 (3d Cir. 1993) (noting that "RCRA itself does not authorize EPA recovery of the cost of oversight conducted under RCRA" but that CERCLA "imposes liability for removal actions 'notwithstanding any other provision or rule of law'"), overruled on other grounds by United States v. E.I. Du Pont de Nemours & Co., 432 F.3d 161 (3d Cir. 2005); Chem. Waste Mgmt., Inc. v. Armstrong World Indus., Inc., 669 F. Supp. 1285, 1290–91 (E.D. Pa. 1987) (holding that "RCRA and its regulations do not preclude a RCRA owner/operator from recovering CERCLA response costs").
115. See 42 U.S.C. § 6926(b) (authorizing states to "administer and enforce a hazardous waste ... program"); 42 U.S.C. § 6929 (explaining state authority for hazardous waste programs); Safety-Kleen, Inc. v. Wyche, 274 F.3d 846, 863 (4th Cir. 2001) ("RCRA sets a floor, not a ceiling, for state regulation of hazardous wastes," (internal citation omitted)).

Former Landowner Liability

Plaintiffs asserting toxic torts frequently file suit against former owners of sites where toxic chemicals were used, stored, or disposed of, seeking to hold such former owners responsible for the release of those chemicals into the environment or for personal injuries or property damage caused by such releases.

The success of such claims against former landowners often depends on the type of tort asserted. Some states have allowed a current owner to assert strict-liability claims for abnormally dangerous activities against a former owner,[116] but most jurisdictions have held that under *Rylands v. Fletcher* and the *Restatement (Second)*, the requirement of damage to another person's land defeats any such liability.[117] Similarly, in the nuisance setting, states differ on whether a succeeding landowner can sustain a claim for nuisance against a former landowner who created the nuisance on the property.[118]

Plaintiffs also sometimes invoke common-law theories of fraud and concealment to pursue former owners, claiming that the former owners failed to disclose information about the presence of toxic chemicals at these sites or made representations that were knowingly or negligently false.[119] State legislatures have sometimes insulated former landowners from liability for such misrepresentation claims by prescribing specific disclosures that are sufficient as a matter of law. For example, in response to a decision by the New Jersey Supreme Court that held a developer liable for fraud for failing to disclose that the plaintiffs' homes had been constructed near an abandoned dump,[120] the New Jersey legislature created a statutory scheme for disclosure duties for transferring property.[121] In California, sellers of residential real estate must make a disclosure when properties are within one mile of areas "once used for military training purposes which may contain potentially explosive munitions,"[122] or

---

116. *See, e.g.*, T & E Indus., Inc. v. Safety Light Corp., 587 A.2d 1249, 1257-58 (N.J. 1991) (rejecting argument that strict liability could only apply to cases where an adjacent landowner was affected).
117. *See* Wellesley Hills Realty Trust v. Mobil Oil Corp., 747 F. Supp. 93, 101-02 (D. Mass. 1990); *see also* Kennedy Bldg. Assocs. v. Viacom, Inc., 375 F.3d 731, 739 (8th Cir. 2004) (noting that a majority of courts have held strict liability should not be extended to cover claims by subsequent owner).
118. *Compare* Nielsen v. Sioux Tools, Inc., 870 F. Supp. 435, 442-43 (D. Conn. 1994) (holding that successor landowner lacked standing to assert nuisance claim based on previous landowner's disposal of hazardous substances and noting that a private nuisance claim in Connecticut "requires that the nuisance which is the subject of the plaintiff's suit must be located on, or emanate from, a neighboring parcel of land" (emphasis omitted) (internal citation omitted)), *with* Mangini v. Aerojet-Gen. Corp., 282 Cal. Rptr. 827, 834 (Cal. Ct. App. 1991) ("Nor is it material that defendant allegedly created the nuisance at some time in the past but does not currently have a possessory interest in the property.").
119. *See, e.g.*, Adams v. NVR Homes, Inc., 135 F. Supp. 2d 675, 691-92 (D. Md. 2001) (granting summary judgment for the defendant on the plaintiff homeowners' fraud claim of concealment of reclaimed quarry in subdivision based on lack of evidence of knowing concealment with intent to deceive); Keywell Corp. v. Weinstein, 33 F.3d 159, 163-64 (2d Cir. 1994) (reversing summary judgment for the defendants on fraud claim where the plaintiffs allegedly relied on representations that no hazardous materials had been released or disposed of at a metals recycling plant the plaintiffs purchased).
120. Strawn v. Canuso, 657 A.2d 420, 429-31 (N.J. 1995).
121. N.J. STAT. ANN. §§ 46:3C-2 to 46:3C-12 (2012); *see also* Nobrega v. Edison Glen Assocs., 772 A.2d 368, 373-74 (N.J. 2001).
122. CAL. CIV. CODE § 1102.15 (Deering 2012).

when properties are adjacent to certain industrial uses or affected by a nuisance created by such uses.[123] A California statute explicitly allows buyers to recover damages when sellers of property fail to satisfy the state disclosure rules.[124]

Federal and state statutes often provide more viable means of holding former landowners liable for cleanup of contaminated sites. As noted above, any person who owned a contaminated site during the time a hazardous substance was disposed of at the site may be liable under CERCLA,[125] and many state analogs of CERCLA likewise hold former owners liable or allow for contribution suits against them.[126] Courts are split on whether RCRA provides a viable remedy against former operators of hazardous waste sites.[127]

Other Liability Theories in the Toxic Tort Context

Beyond these common law and statutory liability theories, toxic tort plaintiffs may invoke many other legal theories depending on the unique factual circumstances of their case. Below we set forth a brief discussion of frequently pled additional liability theories.

Breach of Warranty

Where the injury in a toxic tort action arises from a product purchased from a merchant, a plaintiff may assert a claim for breach of an express or implied warranty. Under the Uniform Commercial Code, a seller may create an express warranty through "an affirmation of fact or promise" or a description or sample of the goods "which is made part of the basis of the bargain."[128] Generally, for a breach of express warranty claim, the plain-

---

123. CAL. CIV. CODE § 1102.17 (Deering 2012).
124. CAL. CIV. CODE § 1102.13 (Deering 2012); *see also* Coldwell Banker Residential Brokerage Co. v. Superior Court, 11 Cal. Rptr. 3d 564, 569–70 (Cal. Ct. App. 2004) (interpreting § 1102.13 and holding that duty of care to prospective buyer was owed only to purchasers, not purchasers' minor son who allegedly developed asthma caused by toxic mold).
125. *See* 42 U.S.C. § 9607(a)(2) (holding liable "any person who at the time of disposal of any hazardous substance owned or operated any facility at which such hazardous substances were disposed of" responsible for response costs); Axel Johnson, Inc. v. Carroll Carolina Oil Co., 191 F.3d 409, 414 (4th Cir. 1999) (holding that under CERCLA "a former owner or operator can be held liable for response costs caused by hazardous substances that were deposited at the facility at times when it did not own or operate the facility, so long as some hazardous substances were deposited at the facility during the period when the party did own or operate it and the other requirements of the statute are met").
126. *See, e.g.*, OR. REV. STAT. § 465.255(1)(a) (2011) (holding "any owner or operator at or during the time of the acts or omissions that resulted in the release" strictly liable for remedial action costs); Bonnie Blue, Inc. v. Reichenstein, 127 S.W.3d 366, 369 (Tex. App. 2004) (interpreting Texas statutes on cost recovery claims and contribution claims and reversing summary judgment for former owner who sold contaminated site "as is").
127. *Compare* Bd. of Cnty. Comm'rs of La Plata v. Brown Grp. Retail, Inc., 598 F. Supp. 2d 1185, 1200–01 (D. Colo. 2009) (holding that cause of action under § 6972(a)(1)(A) of RCRA "can only be brought against an owner or operator of a polluting property who is 'alleged to be in violation' of the RCRA at the time the suit is brought"), *with* Scarlett & Assocs. v. Briarcliff Ctr. Partners, LLC, No. 1:05-CV-0145-CC, 2009 U.S. Dist. LEXIS 90483, at *33–36 (N.D. Ga. 2009) (finding that "the continued presence of illegally dumped hazardous wastes may constitute a 'current violation' of a RCRA regulation or standard, despite the fact that the operator's conduct occurred in the past").
128. U.C.C. § 2-313 (2011). The seller may establish an express warranty without using "formal words such

tiff must establish that an actual warranty was made;[129] that the plaintiff relied on the warranty;[130] that the product did not perform as warranted; and that the breach caused injury or damage.[131] In the context of toxic torts, express warranties may also be governed by state products liability statutes.[132]

A toxic tort plaintiff may also seek recovery under an implied warranty theory. Under the Uniform Commercial Code, "a warranty that the goods shall be merchantable is implied in a contract for their sale if the seller is a merchant with respect to goods of that kind."[133] To prevail on an implied warranty claim, a plaintiff must establish that the product is not fit for the ordinary purpose for which it was intended.[134]

In most cases, breach-of-warranty claims are not as well suited to prosecuting toxic torts as product-liability theories or environmental tort theories.[135] For example, in *Fisher v. Monsanto Co.*, the plaintiff sued a manufacturer of chemicals for breach of warranty, claiming that her husband died of brain cancer after exposure.[136] The court dismissed the plaintiff's claims for breach of both express and implied warranties. No express warranty arose because "besides warranting good title and that [the chemical] conformed to [the

---

as 'warrant' or 'guarantee,'" but the seller's mere opinion or "affirmation . . . of the value of the goods" does not create a warranty. *Id.*

129. *See In re* FEMA Trailer Formaldehyde Prods. Liab. Litig., No. 07-1873, 2010 U.S. Dist. LEXIS 35976, at *6 (E.D. La. Apr. 12, 2010) (dismissing the breach of warranty claim because it failed to establish that an express warranty was made); *In re* Bisphenol-A (BPA) Polycarbonate Plastic Prods. Liab. Litig., 687 F. Supp. 2d 897, 905–06 (W.D. Mo. 2009) (dismissing breach of express warranty claim because there was an "absence of 'affirmation of fact or promise'").

130. *See* Johnson v. Philip Morris, Inc., 159 F. Supp. 2d 950, 952 (S.D. Tex. 2001) (discussing the elements the plaintiff must prove to succeed on an express breach of warranty claim under Texas law); Burt v. Fumigation Serv. & Supply, Inc., 926 F. Supp. 624, 632–33 (W.D. Mich. 1996) (denying summary judgment in part because the plaintiffs did not see any labeling on which they could have relied); Reece v. Good Samaritan Hosp., 953 P.2d 117 (Wash. Ct. App. 1998) (summary judgment was properly granted for manufacturer because the plaintiff did not prove she relied on the alleged express warranty that "women have trusted Tampax tampons for over 50 years"). Some jurisdictions read the element of "reliance" into the "made part of the basis of the bargain" language contained in U.C.C. § 2-313, as adopted by the jurisdiction's state statutes. *See, e.g., In re* Bisphenol-A (BPA) Polycarbonate Plastic Prods. Liab. Litig., 687 F. Supp. 2d at 906 (stating that "the effect [of the U.C.C. language] is the same [as reliance]: a representation cannot be part of the "bargain" if the other party to the bargain did not know the representation was made").

131. *See* Lowe v. Sporicidin Int'l, 47 F.3d 124, 132 (4th Cir. 1995) (granting summary judgment for defendants because plaintiff's counsel admitted "no breach of express warranty . . . caused [plaintiff's] alleged injuries").

132. *See, e.g.*, ALA. CODE § 6-5-521(a) (2012); LA. REV. STAT. ANN. § 9:2800.53(6) (2012).

133. U.C.C. § 2-314(1) (2011).

134. McCracken v. Exxon/Mobil Co., No. 08-2932, 2009 U.S. Dist. LEXIS 106930, at *17–18 (E.D. Pa. Nov. 12, 2009) (dismissing the plaintiff's breach of implied warranty claim because "plaintiff did not allege that the gasoline failed to operate normally").

135. In addition to the issues cited in the text, the requirement of contractual privity formerly impeded many toxic tort warranty claims by plaintiffs remote from the original purchase of the product. More recently, however, most jurisdictions have abolished the requirement of contractual privity in personal injury claims based on breach of warranty. *See, e.g.*, McCormack v. Hankscraft Co., 154 N.W.2d 488, 497–99 (Minn. 1967).

136. 863 F. Supp. 285 (W.D. Va. 1994).

plant's] specifications," the defendant had made no express warranties.[137] Further, there was no implied warranty because the defendant produced the chemical according to the decedent's employer's "own specifications" and the employer, a "sophisticated purchaser," did not rely on the defendant's "'skill or judgment to select or furnish suitable goods.'"[138] Finally, at the time of sale, the defendant expressly disclaimed any warranties, so the plaintiff's alternative argument that an implied warranty arose through Monsanto's alleged "course of conduct" failed.[139]

Battery and/or Assault

Toxic tort plaintiffs also have traditionally invoked battery and assault liability theories. To establish a prima facie case for battery, a plaintiff must show (1) that the defendant intended to cause a "harmful or offensive contact" or "an imminent apprehension of such a contact" and (2) that a "harmful or offensive contact" with the plaintiff resulted.[140] To establish a prima facie case for assault, a plaintiff must show (1) that the defendant "intend[ed] to cause a [battery], or an imminent apprehension of [a battery]," and (2) that the plaintiff was "thereby put in such imminent apprehension."[141] The intent element of both assault and battery is satisfied if the defendant either "desires to cause the consequences of his act" or "believes that the consequences are substantially certain to result from" the act.[142] For example, in *Plourde v. Gladstone*, the plaintiffs claimed that the defendants' herbicide spraying had drifted onto the plaintiffs' property, injuring plaintiffs and resulting in a battery.[143] The Second Circuit affirmed the district court's dismissal of

---

137. *Id.* at 289.
138. *Id.* (citing VA. CODE ANN. § 8.2-315). In many states, the sophistication of the purchaser does not bar a claim by a user or a third party unless the user or third party is also sophisticated in the use of the product. *See, e.g.*, Mozeke v. Int'l Paper Co., 933 F.2d 1293 (5th Cir. 1991) (applying Louisiana law).
139. 863 F. Supp. at 289 (citing VA. CODE ANN. §§ 8.2-314(1), (3)).
140. RESTATEMENT (SECOND) OF TORTS § 13 (1965). Aside from direct physical contact between the defendant and the plaintiff, this contact can also be indirect physical contact between the plaintiff and an instrumentality controlled by the defendant or a force put into motion by the defendant. *See id.* §§ 9, 18 cmt. *c*. In one case, the plaintiffs even satisfied the contact element by showing that the defendants required them to clean a room with PCB levels greater than the EPA accepted standards without wearing protective clothing. *See* Gulden v. Crown Zellerbach Corp., 890 F.2d 195 (9th Cir. 1989).
141. RESTATEMENT (SECOND) OF TORTS § 21 (1965). In the toxic tort context, plaintiffs have raised assault claims based on their possible exposure to chemicals. *See, e.g., In re* Marine Asbestos Cases, 265 F. 3d 861 (9th Cir. 2001) (claiming exposure to asbestos); Kelley v. Cowesett Hills Assocs., 768 A.2d 425, 431 (R.I. 2001) (same).
142. RESTATEMENT (SECOND) OF TORTS § 8A (1965); *see also* Rhodes v. E.I. Du Pont de Nemours & Co., 657 F. Supp. 2d 751, 773 (S.D. W. Va. 2009) (granting defendant's motion for summary judgment on plaintiffs' battery claim because "an actor must act with the intention of causing a harmful or offensive contact with a person, and . . . the mere presence and resultant inhalation of chemicals in the air does not constitute a harmful or offensive contact by the emitter" (quoting McClenathan v. Rhone-Poulenc, Inc., 926 F. Supp. 1272, 1274 (S.D. W. Va. 1996)) (internal quotation marks omitted)); Hennessy v. Comm. Edison Co., 764 F. Supp. 495, 507 (N.D. Ill. 1991) (granting summary judgment for the defendant on the plaintiff's battery claim where the plaintiff failed to offer any evidence showing the defendant intended to cause harm from exposure to radiation or that it was substantially likely to occur).
143. 69 Fed. App'x 485 (2d Cir. 2003).

the battery claim, holding that the plaintiffs had produced no evidence that the defendants were substantially certain that the sprayings would result in injury, noting in particular that the defendants had sprayed a more drift-prone herbicide the previous year with no ill effect to plaintiffs.[144]

Although courts have been strict in requiring toxic tort plaintiffs to show the intentional act of the defendant that led to the contact or apprehension of contact with the hazardous substance, assault and battery (like most intentional torts) do not require the plaintiff to show that the defendant intended the hazardous substance to cause the plaintiff's harm. For example, in *Field v. Philadelphia Electric Co.*, the court held that the plaintiff had properly stated a claim for battery by claiming that the defendant's personnel intentionally vented radioactive gases into a tunnel where the plaintiff was working.[145] The court rejected as immaterial the lack of any claim that the defendant's personnel intended to actually harm the plaintiff.[146]

Unjust Enrichment and Restitution

"A person who is unjustly enriched at the expense of another is subject to liability in restitution."[147] Because it seeks an equitable remedy, an unjust enrichment claim is generally precluded if there is remedy at law available to the plaintiff.[148] In the context of toxic torts, the most common claims of unjust enrichment and restitution arise when a plaintiff landowner or lessee incurs costs in cleaning up hazardous waste that was unknown at the time of purchase or lease and seeks restitution from the previous landowner or the lessor.[149] For example, in *Russell-Stanley Corp. v. Plant Industries, Inc.*, the state compelled the lessee of a commercial site to clean up hazardous contamination at the site even though the plaintiff did not cause or know about the contamination at the time of the lease.[150]

---

144. *Id.* at 488.
145. 565 A.2d 1170, 1772 (Pa. Super. Ct. 1989).
146. *Id.* at 1178 (citing Barber v. Pittsburgh Corning Corp., 529 A.2d 491 (Pa. Super. Ct. 1987), *rev'd on other grounds*, 555 A.2d 766 (Pa. 1989)).
147. RESTATEMENT (THIRD) OF RESTITUTION & UNJUST ENRICHMENT § 1 (2011). "The root principle of unjustified enrichment is that the plaintiff suffers an economic detriment for which he should not be responsible, while the defendant receives an economic benefit for which he has not paid." Coastal Envtl. Specialists, Inc. v. Chem-Lig Int'l, Inc., 818 So. 2d 12, 19 (La. Ct. App. 2001).
148. *See Coastal Envtl. Specialists, Inc.*, 818 So. 2d at 19 (affirming trial court's dismissal of plaintiff's unjust enrichment claim in an environmental cleanup case because plaintiff had an available contractual remedy already pending).
149. However, unjust enrichment claims based on state law in CERCLA cases are preempted by the federal law. *See, e.g., In re* Reading Co., 115 F.3d 1111 (3d Cir. 1997) (affirming district court's holding that the plaintiffs' claims under New Jersey common law for restitution were preempted by CERCLA and stating "[p]ermitting independent common law remedies would create a path around the statutory settlement scheme, raising an obstacle to the intent of Congress"); *see also* Lenox Inc. v. Reuben Smith Rubbish Removal, 91 F. Supp. 2d 743, 752 (D.N.J. 2000); Cont'l Title Co. v. Peoples Gas Light & Coke Co., No. 96 C 3257, 1999 U.S. Dist. LEXIS 22206 (N.D. Ill. Mar. 18, 1999). Each state still retains its right to use suits at common law, regulatory systems, or statutory schemes to regulate within its borders. *See* 33 U.S.C. § 1370.
150. 595 A.2d 534, 536–37 (N.J. Super. Ct. Ch. Div. 1991).

The lessee asserted an unjust enrichment claim against its landlord, the owner of the site, asserting that the defendant owner would unjustly benefit from the plaintiff's cleanup.[151] The court held that the plaintiff needed to establish two elements to prevail on its claim: (1) that defendant received a benefit, and (2) that "the retention of that benefit without payment would be unjust."[152]

Parens Patriae

A state may claim that it has standing to assert certain claims in toxic tort cases based on its parens patriae status. The parens patriae theory presumes that a state adequately represents the interests of its citizens in cases raising matters of sovereign interest, and therefore gives states standing in such cases.[153] In order to maintain an action based on parens patriae standing, the state must "articulate an interest apart from the interests of particular private parties" who can obtain complete relief through their own litigation.[154] A state must therefore "articulate an injury to the well-being of the state as a whole or to a sufficiently large segment of its population."[155]

---

151. *Id.* at 549. The costs of restoration or remediation are very expensive and may even exceed the fair market value of the property itself. Some courts have limited damages in these cases to avoid overcompensating the plaintiffs.
152. *Russell-Stanley Corp.*, 595 A.2d at 550 (citing Callano v. Oakwood Park Homes Corp., 219 A.2d 332 (N.J. Super. Ct. App. Div. 1966)). These elements may vary slightly by jurisdiction. For example, in Louisiana, the supreme court set forth five prerequisites to successfully invoke an action for unjust enrichment: "(1) an enrichment, (2) an impoverishment, (3) a connection between the enrichment and the impoverishment, (4) an absence of justification or cause for the enrichment and the impoverishment, and (5) no other remedy at law available to the impoverishee." *Coastal Envtl. Specialists, Inc.*, 818 So. 2d at 19.
153. *See* South Dakota v. Ubbelohde, 330 F.3d 1014, 1025 (8th Cir. 2003), *cert. denied*, 541 U.S. 987 (2004).
154. *See* LG Display Co. v. Madigan, 665 F.3d 768, 771 (7th Cir. 2011) (noting that a state has a quasi-sovereign interest in the health and well-being, both physical and economic, of its residents in general); People v. Peter & John's Pump House, Inc., 914 F. Supp. 809, 812 (N.D.N.Y. 1996). The state must express a sovereign interest that falls into one of two general categories: (1) the health and well-being of its residents in general, or (2) not being discriminatorily denied its rightful status within the federal system. *See* Alfred L. Snapp & Son, Inc. v. Puerto Rico *ex rel.* Barez, 458 U.S. 592, 601 (1982) (articulating the two general categories of sovereign interests falling under parens patriae); Connecticut v. Cahill, 217 F.3d 93, 99 (2d Cir. 2000) (same); Estados Unidos Mexicanos v. DeCoster, 229 F.3d 332, 336 (1st Cir. 2000) (same).
155. *See* 72 AM. JUR. 2D States, Etc. § 95 (2012). The United States Supreme Court has observed that:

> The Court has not attempted to draw any definitive limits on the proportion of the population of the State that must be adversely affected by the challenged behavior. Although more must be alleged than injury to an identifiable group of individual residents, the indirect effects of the injury must be considered as well in determining whether the State has alleged injury to a sufficiently substantial segment of its population. One helpful indication in determining whether an alleged injury to the health and welfare of its citizens suffices to give the State standing to sue as parens patriae is whether the injury is one that the State, if it could, would likely attempt to address through its sovereign lawmaking powers.

Alfred L. Snapp & Son, Inc., 458 U.S. at 607.

In the context of toxic torts, states often claim natural resources within their borders as "sovereign interests" and assert their parens patriae status to gain standing to assert claims based on damages to those resources.[156] Even assuming that the state's natural resources or the waters of the state are in some sense "public," however, a key question in such actions is whether the state has exclusive possession sufficient to sustain its substantive claims. For example, blanket claims of dominion over all water are inadequate to support a trespass action. In *New Mexico v. General Electric Co.*, the State of New Mexico asserted a claim for trespass to recover damages for allegedly contaminated groundwater.[157] The state claimed that its "'proprietary interests' in its natural resources" and "'its role as public trustee' . . . [made] it 'the proper party' . . . in bringing a trespass action for actual damage to the public's water supply."[158] The district court rejected this argument, holding that neither New Mexico's "sovereign" interest in public waters nor its more general parens patriae status was sufficient to give it standing to maintain a trespass claim.[159] The district court therefore held that without "an exclusive possessory legal interest pertaining to the groundwater in question . . . Plaintiffs cannot maintain a common-law cause of action for trespass."[160]

Damages
Overview

Courts have developed several theories of damages in response to difficulties inherent in toxic tort litigation. These difficulties include the long latency periods between exposure to a substance and the development of symptoms, as well as the difficulty of proving causation, particularly with respect to "emerging" chemicals that have not been extensively studied by medical science. Courts have also considered claims for increased risk of disease, for medical monitoring, and for various types of emotional distress, including fear of future disease.

Generally, plaintiffs in toxic tort actions may seek the traditional tort remedies of compensatory damages for such items as wage loss, medical expenses, and loss of consortium,

---

156. *See, e.g.*, Comm'r of the Dep't of Planning & Natural Res. v. Century Aluminum Co., No. 05-62, 2012 U.S. Dist. LEXIS 77128 (D.V.I. June 4, 2012) ("'In its parens patriae capacity the State has an interest independent of and behind the titles of its citizens, in all the earth and air within its domain. It has the last word as to whether its mountains shall be stripped of their forests and its inhabitants shall breathe pure air.'" (citing Georgia v. Tenn. Copper Co., 206 U.S. 230, 237 (1907)); South Carolina v. North Carolina, 558 U.S. 256 (2010) (involving state's sovereign interest in ensuring that it receives an equitable share of interstate river's water).
157. 335 F. Supp. 2d 1185 (D.N.M. 2004), *aff'd*, 467 F.3d 1223 (10th Cir. 2006).
158. *Id.* at 1232.
159. *Id.* at 1234–35 (stating that New Mexico's claimed "broader sovereign and public trust/*parens patriae* interests in protecting the public's right to the use of all of the waters of New Mexico . . . fall outside of the scope of the law's protection traditionally afforded to private landowners' right of exclusive possession by the law of trespass").
160. *Id.* at 1234 (emphasis omitted).

as well as punitive damages. Compensatory damages seek to restore plaintiffs to the position they would have been in but for the defendant's tortious conduct.[161] Courts recognize two types of compensatory damages: special damages (also called actual or pecuniary damages) and general damages.[162] Special damages may reflect past or future damages,[163] and consist of those damages that can be computed or estimated with a reasonable degree of certainty.[164] Special damages may include wage loss,[165] diminished or lost future earning capacity,[166] past and future medical expenses,[167] and other out-of-pocket expenses.[168] A plaintiff usually must plead these damages fully and specifically.[169]

In contrast, general damages reflect noneconomic losses[170] and cannot be computed with mathematical certainty.[171] General damages flow naturally from the defendant's

---

161. *See* McGee v. ACandS, Inc., 933 So. 2d 770, 774 (La. 2006); Gen. Cas. Co. v. Hills, 561 N.W.2d 718, 724 (Wis. 1997) ("[T]he cost of repairing and restoring damaged property and water to its original condition is a proper measure of compensatory damages." (emphasis omitted)).
162. RESTATEMENT (SECOND) OF TORTS § 904 (1979); *see also In re* Haw. Fed. Asbestos Cases, 734 F. Supp. 1563, 1567 (D. Haw. 1990).
163. *See* Mauro v. Raymark Indus., Inc., 561 A.2d 257, 260–61 (N.J. 1989) (discussing special damages as including those future consequences of an injury inflicted by a wrongdoer when such damages are reasonably certain); Askey v. Occidental Chem. Corp., 477 N.Y.S.2d 242, 247 (N.Y. App. Div. 1984) (characterizing medical monitoring caused by alleged discharge of toxic substances as "an element of consequential damage" and that a defendant is liable for reasonably anticipated consequential damages that may flow later from an initial exposure to toxins).
164. *See Mauro*, 561 A.2d at 260–61 (using "reasonable certainty" standard for assessing damages in case involving exposure to asbestos); *In re* Hawaii Fed. Asbestos Cases, 734 F. Supp. at 1567 (referring to specific damages as those that "compensate claimants for specific out-of-pocket financial expenses and losses").
165. *See McGee*, 933 So. 2d at 774; Sellers v. Breaux, 422 So. 2d 1231, 1236 (La. Ct. App. 1982) (awarding plaintiff past wages for injuries suffered from inhaling creosote fumes).
166. *See* Wisner v. Ill. Cent. Gulf R.R., 537 So. 2d 740, 751 (La. Ct. App. 1988) (granting award of lost future income to state trooper exposed to toxic chemical spill). *But see* Boren v. Burlington N. & Santa Fe Ry., 637 N.W.2d 910, 927–28 (Neb. Ct. App. 2002) (affirming FELA award for lost earning capacity to railroad worker exposed to various substances but characterizing award as element of general damages).
167. *See Sellers*, 422 So. 2d at 1237; Ayers v. Jackson, 525 A.2d 287, 312–13 (N.J. 1987) (affirming award for medical surveillance for future medical tests, but not enhanced risk of injury); Potter v. Firestone Tire & Rubber Co., 863 P.2d 795, 821 (Cal. 1993) (characterizing medical monitoring claim as one "to recover the cost of future periodic medical examinations intended to facilitate early detection and treatment of disease caused by a plaintiff's exposure to toxic substances" (citing *Ayers*, 525 A.2d at 308)).
168. *See* Italiano v. Jones Chems., Inc., 908 F. Supp. 904, 907 (M.D. Fla. 1995) (awarding damages for property rendered unmarketable, lost business opportunity, and response costs incurred due to contamination of soil and groundwater). Other out-of-pocket expenses considered special damages in the toxic tort context might include attorneys' fees. *See In re* "Agent Orange" Prod. Liab. Litig., 611 F. Supp. 1296 (E.D.N.Y. 1985), *aff'd in relevant part*, 818 F.2d 226 (2d Cir. 1987).
169. FED R. CIV. P. 9(g); *see also* McDonnell v. Falco, 784 A.2d 1051, 1057 (Conn. App. Ct. 2001); *Italiano*, 908 F. Supp. at 907.
170. *See, e.g.*, Exxon Mobil Corp. v. Ford, 40 A.3d 514, 549–50 (Md. Ct. App. 2012) (characterizing the plaintiffs' claims for emotional distress as noneconomic damages); *In re* Hawaii Fed. Asbestos Cases, 734 F. Supp. 1563, 1567 (D. Haw. 1990) (characterizing general damages as providing "compensation for pain, suffering and emotional distress").
171. *See Sellers*, 422 So. 2d at 1237 (stating that remainder of $5,000 award after subtracting for medical bills and lost wages was general damages where the plaintiff alleged injuries for inhaling creosote fumes); *Boren*, 637 N.W.2d at 928 (citing factors used in calculation of impairment of earning capacity, including "the plaintiff's age, life expectance, habits, occupation, talents, skill, experience, training and industry").

conduct,[172] and include pain and suffering,[173] emotional distress,[174] loss of consortium,[175] and loss of enjoyment of life (hedonic damages).[176] Some jurisdictions require a showing of physical injury or exposure to a toxin in order to allege emotional distress damages in the toxic tort setting.[177]

Present Injury Requirement

It is well-settled law that a plaintiff may bring a cause of action only when the plaintiff has a present injury.[178] This does not mean that all the damages need already have occurred; where a plaintiff can demonstrate a present physical injury, that plaintiff may recover future medical expenses or damages from risk of future harm.[179] But such future damages must be reasonably certain, and the jury cannot be allowed to speculate or guess as to future events.[180] The requirement of a present injury is essentially a screening device for tort claims, establishing a clear standard by which judges can determine which plaintiffs

---

172. *See McDonnell*, 784 A.2d at 1057.
173. *See* Hagerty v. L & L Marine Servs., Inc., 788 F.2d 315, 317 (5th Cir. 1986) (reversing grant of summary judgment for the defendant when the plaintiff was drenched with toxic chemical). *But see Ayers*, 525 A.2d at 294–97 (holding that emotional distress claims against municipality based on contamination of private wells barred by state tort claims act).
174. *See* Bahura v. S.E.W. Investors, 754 A.2d 928, 937–39 (D.C. Ct. App. 2000) (reversing dismissal of emotional distress claim in "sick building" case); Jackson v. Johns-Manville Sales Corp., 781 F.2d 394, 414 (5th Cir. 1986) (awarding emotional distress damages to plaintiff worker injured because of exposure to asbestos).
175. *See* Emery v. Owens-Corp., 813 So. 2d 441, 456–57 (La. Ct. App. 2001), *cert. denied*, 815 So. 2d 842 (La. 2002); Cleveland v. Johns-Manville Corp., 690 A.2d 1146, 1149 (Pa. 1997) (but reversing award for loss of consortium to wife who married injured party after injury), *overruled on other grounds*, Norfolk & W. Ry. v. Ayers, 538 U.S. 135 (2003).
176. *See McGee*, 933 So. 2d at 772–73 (awarding damages related to loss of enjoyment of life in asbestos exposure case); *Ayers*, 525 A.2d at 293–94 (affirming judgment for plaintiffs for "quality of life" damages arising from landfill's contamination of private wells).
177. *See* Isabel v. Velsicol Chem. Co., 327 F. Supp. 2d 915, 919–21 (W.D. Tenn. 2004); Potter v. Firestone Tire & Rubber Co., 863 P.2d 795, 816 (Cal. 1993) (damages for emotional distress caused by fear of cancer when (1) plaintiff's exposure to toxic substance that threatens cancer and (2) plaintiff's fear stems from knowledge, corroborated by scientific or medical opinion, that it is more likely than not that plaintiff will develop cancer in the future because of the exposure).
178. *See* KEETON ET AL., *supra* note 1, § 13, at 75 (stating that trespass cases traditionally required proof of actual damage); *id.* § 30, at 165 (listing "actual loss or damage resulting to the interests of another" as an element of a negligence claim and stating that "[t]he threat of future harm, not yet realized, is not enough"); Jarvill v. Porky's Equip., Inc., 189 P.3d 335, 339–40 (Alaska 2008) (holding that cause of action for negligence does not accrue when injury "remained a matter of speculation"); Paz v. Brush Engineered Metals, Inc., 949 So. 2d 1, 5 (Miss. 2007); Hinton v. Monsanto Co., 813 So. 2d 827, 829 (Ala. 2001) (holding that possibility of future injury was insufficient to support a tort claim).
179. *See* Blumenshine v. Baptiste, 869 P.2d 470, 473 (Alaska 1994); Patton v. Gen. Signal Corp., 984 F. Supp. 666, 673 (W.D.N.Y. 1997); Thomas v. FAG Bearings Corp., 846 F. Supp. 1400, 1410 (W.D. Mo. 1994); Betts v. Manville Personal Injury Settlement Trust, 588 N.E.2d 1193, 1204 (Ill. App. Ct. 1992).
180. *See* Pluid v. B.K., 948 P.2d 981, 984 (Alaska 1997) ("It is, of course, the law that the *fact* of [future medical] damages must be proven by a preponderance of the evidence." (emphasis in original)); Henry v. Dow Chem. Co., 701 N.W.2d 684, 688–89 (Mich. 2005) (stating that, in toxic tort context, "Michigan law requires more than a merely speculative injury"); Alsteen v. Wauleco, Inc., 802 N.W.2d 212, 215 (Wis. Ct. App. 2011) ("[T]he mere possibility of future harm does not constitute actual injury or damage." (internal citation omitted)).

have stated a valid claim and keeping the fact-finder from "wondering whether a plaintiff has in fact been harmed in some way, when nothing but a plaintiff's own allegations support his cause of action."[181]

The development of new technologies and the accompanying ability to detect minuscule amounts of contaminants or genetic changes has brought to the forefront of toxic tort cases the issue of what degree of change in a plaintiff's physical state or the environment is required to constitute an "injury." In the context of nuisance and trespass cases, some courts have used regulatory limits as baselines to determine whether property has suffered "damage"[182] and thus whether a plaintiff has standing to bring a claim.[183] An emerging view, adopted by some courts, is that as long as the presence of a contaminant in the environment has created a need to remediate, the plaintiffs have shown a present injury and thus have standing.[184] A very few courts have gone so far as to allow testimony that any contamination, even a single molecule, is enough to cause an injury in certain

---

181. *Henry*, 701 N.W.2d at 690–91.
182. When public entities assert claims for natural resource damages, federal regulations find injury where there is "a measurable adverse change, either long- or short-term, in the chemical or physical quality or the viability of a natural resource[.]" 43 C.F.R. § 11.14(v). Federal regulations also outline the natural resource damages assessment process and find injury to biological resources when a concentration of a substance is sufficient to "[c]ause the biological resource or its offspring to have undergone death, disease, behavior abnormalities, cancer, genetic mutations, physiological malfunctions, or physical deformations," among other things. 43 C.F.R. § 11.62(f)(1). Under these standards, an injury determination is based on the "establishment of a statistically significant difference in the biological response between samples from populations in the assessment area and the control area." 43 C.F.R. § 11.62(f)(3).
183. *See* Iberville Parish Waterworks Dist. No. 3 v. Novartis Crop Prot., Inc., 45 F. Supp. 2d 934, 941–42 (S.D. Ala. 1999) (finding no evidence of particularized and imminent injury-in-fact where water district was never in violation of EPA standards for atrazine and where upgrades to treatment system were intended to improve taste of water, not filter contaminants); Brooks v. E.I. Du Pont de Nemours & Co., 944 F. Supp. 448, 449 (E.D.N.C. 1996) (holding that plaintiff landowners had suffered no injury from contamination in their wells when level of contaminants in water did not exceed state standards); *In re* Wildewood Litig., 52 F.3d 499, 503 (4th Cir. 1995) (applying South Carolina law and affirming directed verdict for defendant on nuisance claim when TCE levels "did not rise to the level of toxicological concern").
184. *See* City of Greenville v. Syngenta Crop Prot., Inc., 756 F. Supp. 2d 1001, 1005–07 (S.D. Ill. 2010) (finding standing for plaintiff water provider when a defendant "creates a need (not just a desire) to monitor or remediate raw water for the particular contaminant that it would not otherwise monitor or remediate in order to satisfy its duty to the public"); *In re* Methyl Tertiary Butyl Ether (MTBE) Prods. Liab. Litig., 458 F. Supp. 2d 149, 154–58 (S.D.N.Y. 2006) (contamination considered sufficient injury whenever contamination affects the quality of water supplied or protected by plaintiff well owners, not when presence of contaminant in water exceeds regulatory limits).

settings.[185] The issue of whether a contaminant exceeds a regulatory limit is not dispositive, however, where a plaintiff alleges damage though a diminution in property value.[186]

In the personal injury context, a few courts have even gone so far as to hold that changes to DNA or other subclinical impacts may constitute a present physical injury.[187] For example, in *Werlein v. United States*, people who lived near a chemically contaminated site asserted claims for increased risk of future physical harm as a result of exposure.[188] The court denied defendants' summary judgment motion on the claim, relying on the plaintiffs' expert's testimony that the plaintiffs had suffered current (albeit subcellular) chromosomal, cardiovascular, and immune system damage.[189] Such a standard poses potential problems for plaintiffs. If a claim accrues at the time of subclinical changes, the statute of limitations may pass before the plaintiff has any symptoms to suggest that an injury has occurred. Conversely, commencing lawsuits to preserve such subclinical claims would burden the courts with litigation that may in the end prove unnecessary if no symptoms ever arise.

Whether because of such concerns or other factors, the majority of courts have continued to require more than cellular or subclinical changes, including objective evidence of physical harm or damage that rises to a level of medical concern.[190] For example, in *Parker v. Brush Wellman*, plaintiffs claimed a "substantially increased risk of catastrophic latent disease" as a result of exposure to beryllium as a result of defendants' conduct.[191] Applying Georgia law, the Eleventh Circuit held that subclinical and cellular damage caused by

---

185. *See* Peteet v. Dow Chem. Co., 868 F.2d 1428, 1433 (5th Cir. 1989) (allowing "one-hit" causation testimony from medical expert in case involving exposure to herbicide); *cf.* Greenville v. W.R. Grace & Co., 827 F.2d 975, 977–78 (4th Cir. 1987) (holding that South Carolina courts would allow negligence claim by building owner against asbestos manufacturer for damages resulting from installation of asbestos-containing insulation that led to the "contamination" of a building with "asbestos fibers" and threatened a "substantial and unreasonable risk of harm by releasing toxic substances into the environment"); Borland v. Sanders Lead Co., 369 So. 2d 523, 528–29 (Ala. 1979) (allowing trespass claim by landowner adjacent to lead smelting operation that emitted unknown quantities of lead particulates and sulfoxide gases, but discussing and rejecting trespass claims against passing motorists for trespass caused by exhaust emissions and noting that "the law does not concern itself with trifles"). *But see* Baker v. Chevron USA, Inc., 680 F. Supp. 2d 865, 878 n.9 (S.D. Ohio 2010) (noting that "one-hit" or "no threshold" theory has been rejected as a theory for causation under *Daubert*).
186. *See* Bentley v. Honeywell Int'l, Inc., 223 F.R.D. 471, 478 n.11 (N.D. Ohio 2004) (distinguishing diminution in property value claim from claim for personal injury damages from unsafe water on motion for class certification in groundwater contamination case).
187. *See* Brafford v. Susquehanna Corp., 586 F. Supp. 14, 17–18 (D. Colo. 1984) (denying summary judgment for defendant on increased cancer risk claim based on inference of damage and "reasonable degree of medical probability" that exposure to radiation from uranium mill caused chromosomal damage).
188. 746 F. Supp. 887 (D. Minn. 1990), *vacated in part on other grounds*, 793 F. Supp. 898 (D. Minn. 1992)
189. *Id.* at 901.
190. *See* Dodge v. Cotter Corp., 203 F.3d 1190, 1202 (10th Cir. 2000) (applying Colorado law and finding no physical injury caused by exposure to activities at uranium mine without "a chronic objective condition caused by their increased risk of developing cancer"), *rev'd on other grounds*, 90 P.3d 814 (Colo. 2004); *In re* Hawaii Fed. Asbestos Cases, 734 F. Supp. 1563, 1567 (D. Haw. 1990) (requiring asbestos plaintiffs to show "an objectively verifiable functional impairment").
191. 230 Fed. App'x 878, 880 (11th Cir. 2007), *partially vacated on other grounds*, 2008 U.S. Dist. LEXIS 51751 (N.D. Ga. July 7, 2008).

exposure to beryllium insufficient to create present injury; to be actionable, the exposure must result in an "identifiable physical disease, illness, or impairing symptoms."[192]

Two relatively new claims or personal injury theories in toxic tort cases test the bounds of what constitutes a legal "injury" and whether a present injury even is required at all: medical monitoring and fear of cancer. The starting point of the personal injury analysis is still whether there is a present physical injury. Where there is none, however, the more interesting issues of increased risk of disease arise. In such cases, the inquiry often relates not only to level of exposure and genuineness of the risk of disease, but also to whether there is, in fact, a way to monitor for specific conditions and whether those conditions, if found, can be treated.

Medical Monitoring

In recent years, toxic tort plaintiffs have frequently asserted claims for the costs of medical monitoring. In essence, a claim for medical monitoring alleges that the plaintiff is at a significant risk of developing a serious, latent disease (cancer, for example) because of exposure to some toxic substance, and should therefore be compensated for the future costs of specific tests to detect the potential future onset of a disease. Unlike a claim for the costs of future treatment of an already diagnosed condition, a medical monitoring claim seeks to recover the costs of future testing for the existence of the condition, regardless of whether such a diagnosis is ever made.

The majority of jurisdictions that have considered such medical-monitoring claims, including the U.S. Supreme Court, have rejected such claims as a matter of law. For example, in *Metro-North Commuter Railroad Co. v. Buckley*, the U.S. Supreme Court rejected claims for medical monitoring based on federal law absent proof of an actual present injury, citing three public-policy grounds.[193] First, the Court observed that medical-monitoring costs under such circumstances are extra costs, over and above those costs recommended by the medical community for treating diseases, so the identification of such costs would "pose special difficulties for judges and juries."[194] The Court explained that "[t]hose difficulties in part can reflect uncertainty among medical professionals about just which tests are most usefully administered and when," and commented that "in part those difficulties can reflect the fact that scientists will not always see a medical need to provide systematic *scientific* answers to . . . whether an exposure calls for *extra* [medical] monitoring."[195]

Second, human beings are exposed daily to a huge number of natural and artificial toxins, and attributing a particular disease to a particular toxin is virtually impossible in most circumstances. *Buckley* recognized this modern reality by noting that "contacts,

---

192. *Id.* at 882–83.
193. 521 U.S. 424, 438–44 (1997).
194. *Id.* at 441 (citation omitted).
195. *Id.* (emphasis in original).

even extensive contacts, with serious carcinogens are common."[196] As a result, "tens of millions of individuals may have suffered exposure to substances that might justify some form of substance-exposure-related medical monitoring." The Court remarked that the high number of potential medical-monitoring plaintiffs, coupled with the potentially large damage awards, "could threaten . . . a 'flood' of less important cases," draining economic resources away from plaintiffs who are actually, presently harmed.[197]

Third, the Supreme Court noted that allowing medical-monitoring claims without proof of present injury:

> would ignore the presence of existing alternative sources of payment, thereby leaving a court uncertain about how much of the potentially large recoveries would pay for otherwise unavailable medical testing and how much would accrue to plaintiffs for whom employers or other sources (say, insurance now or in the future) might provide monitoring in any event.[198]

Other courts have observed that a large percentage of medical-monitoring damages are pocketed by plaintiffs' lawyers, rather than being used for actual medical tests.[199]

Buckley alludes to another policy consideration that comes into play when an asymptomatic plaintiff seeks recovery in tort: the need for the judicial system to separate worthy claims from unworthy ones.[200] As Dean Prosser recognized:

> It does not lie within the power of any judicial system to remedy all human wrongs. The obvious limitations upon the time of the courts, the difficulty in many cases of ascertaining the real facts or of providing any effective remedy, have meant that there must be some selection of those more serious injuries which have the prior claim to redress and are dealt with more easily.[201]

The public-policy grounds identified in *Buckley* have led the overwhelming majority of courts to reject claims for medical monitoring in absence of a present injury.[202]

---

196. *Id.* at 434.
197. *Id.* at 442.
198. *Id.* at 442–43.
199. *See, e.g.*, Wood v. Wyeth-Ayerst Labs., 82 S.W.3d 849, 858 (Ky. 2002) ("[M]edical monitoring claims will potentially clog the courts as contingency fee lawyers use consumers as vehicles for enormous awards; furthermore, money awarded for the purpose of health care will go in large percentage to those same lawyers, not the exposure victims.").
200. *See* S. Alaska Carpenters Health & Sec. Trust Fund v. Jones, 177 P.3d 844, 856 (Alaska 2008) ("In part, the requirement of a pre-existing relationship [in tort cases] was imposed as a screening device in an effort to separate worthy claims for emotional damages from unworthy ones.").
201. KEETON ET AL., *supra* note 1, § 4, at 23.
202. *See, e.g.*, Henry v. Dow Chem. Co., 701 N.W.2d 684, 697 (Mich. 2005) ("We would be unwise, to say the least, to alter the common law [by recognizing a claim for medical monitoring] when it is unclear

Because only a few jurisdictions recognize a claim for medical monitoring, the elements of the claim are not uniformly defined.[203] Most courts that recognize the claim require the plaintiffs to prove the following elements, in one form or another:

(a) The plaintiff had significant exposure to a proven hazardous substance through the defendant's culpable conduct;
(b) As a proximate result of the exposure, the plaintiff has a significantly increased risk of contracting a specific serious latent disease or injury;
(c) That increased risk makes periodic medical examinations reasonably necessary and consistent with contemporary scientific principles; and
(d) Monitoring and testing procedures exist that make early detection of the disease possible.[204]

Logically, a plaintiff would also need to show that the early-detection benefits of the monitoring plan outweigh the harms from the test itself or from false positive findings that may lead to invasive treatments. (For example, CT scans may be a useful diagnostic tool, but they involve radiation that some have suggested may cause cancer.) Finally, a plaintiff may need to prove that the early identification of the condition will actually have some benefit; if the condition at issue is untreatable, early identification could not affect the treatment or the outcome and could only cause the victim greater anxiety.[205]

---

what the consequences of such a decision may be and when we have strong suspicions, shared by our nation's highest court, that they may well be disastrous."); *Wood*, 82 S.W.3d at 859 ("Thus, having weighed the few potential benefits against the many almost-certain problems of medical monitoring, we are convinced that this Court has little reason to allow such a remedy without a showing of present physical injury."); Lowe v. Philip Morris USA, Inc., 183 P.3d 181, 187 (Or. 2008) ("Following our precedents, we hold that negligent conduct that results only in a significantly increased risk of future injury that requires medical monitoring does not give rise to a claim for negligence."); Paz v. Brush Engineered Materials, Inc., 949 So. 2d 1, 5 (Miss. 2007) ("The possibility of a future injury is insufficient to maintain a tort claim. Recognizing a medical monitoring cause of action would be akin to recognizing a cause of action for fear of future illness.").

203. *See* Badillo v. Am. Brands, Inc., 16 P.3d 435, 441 (Nev. 2001).
204. *See, e.g.*, Ayers v. Township of Jackson, 525 A.2d 287, 312 (N.J. 1987); Redland Soccer Club, Inc. v. Dep't of the Army, 696 A.2d 137, 145–46 (Pa. 1997); *In re* Paoli R.R. Yard PCB Lit., 916 F.2d 829, 852 (3d Cir. 1990).
205. *See* Hansen v. Mountain Fuel Supply Co., 858 P.2d 970, 979–80 (Utah 1993) (determining that a plaintiff must prove that the periodic administration of an existing test would be beneficial as an element of a medical monitoring claim); Henry v. Dow Chem. Co., 701 N.W.2d 684, 695 n.14 (Mich. 2005) (citing law review article raising issues of false positives and emotional damage as part of rejection of medical monitoring claim); CAL. CIV. JURY INSTRUCTION 3903B (listing "the medical benefit of early detection and diagnosis" as a factor for a jury to consider when determining damages awarded on medical monitoring claim (citing Potter v. Firestone Tire & Rubber Co., 863 P.2d 795, 825 (Cal. 1993))). *But see* Bower v. Westinghouse Elec. Corp., 522 S.E.2d 424, 433–34 (W. Va. 1999) (holding that a plaintiff need not show that a treatment currently exist for the disease that is the subject of medical monitoring).

Fear of Disease

Many of the same public policy considerations raised by medical monitoring also come into play with respect to claims for damages for the fear of contracting a disease, usually cancer, caused by exposure to a toxin. As with medical monitoring, courts are not uniform in approaching such "fear of disease" claims, differing on whether the plaintiff must prove a current physical injury, what level of toxic exposure must be shown, how likely the actual occurrence of the disease must be, and how much emotional distress a plaintiff must suffer to sustain a claim.

In a separate discussion in its *Buckley* decision, the U.S. Supreme Court addressed the plaintiff's fear-of-disease claim under the Federal Employers Liability Act (FELA) in terms that echoed its comments on medical monitoring. The plaintiff claimed that his exposure to asbestos in the workplace and his attendance at an asbestos-awareness class offered by his employer led to his fear that he would develop cancer. His medical experts opined that his exposure had indeed created an added risk of cancer of 1 to 5 percent.[206]

Applying the specific statutory standard of FELA, the Court addressed whether the physical contact with asbestos was a "physical impact" that would permit the recovery of damages.[207] Finding that the plaintiff's contact with asbestos caused only a risk of future disease, not a current physical impact, the Court rejected the claim for emotional-distress damages. The Court also noted several public policy concerns that supported its conclusion, particularly the difficulty that judges and juries would have in separating valid claims from trivial ones, the threat of unlimited and unpredictable liability, and the potential for a flood of trivial claims.[208]

As noted above, the majority of jurisdictions require that a plaintiff seeking to recover for emotional distress first demonstrate a present physical injury. This is known generally as the "impact rule."[209] For example, the Texas Supreme Court rejected claims for emotional distress based solely on exposure to asbestos, holding that the mere exposure (inhalation of asbestos fibers) and reasonable fear of producing disease was not a sufficient injury to permit recovery.[210] Many states, however, have modified the "impact rule" in cases where its application would be unjust, such as where a plaintiff is only a bystander

---

206. *Buckley*, 521 U.S. at 427.
207. *Id.* at 428–29.
208. *Id.* at 432–433.
209. *See* Hagan v. Coca-Cola Bottling Co., 804 So. 2d 1234, 1236–37 (Fla. 2001); Simmons v. Pacor, Inc., 674 A.2d 232, 238 (Pa. 1996) (declining to adopt plaintiffs' view that pleural thickening caused by exposure to asbestos established a sufficient "impact" to warrant recovery for mental anguish).
210. Temple-Inland Prods. Corp. v. Carter, 993 S.W.2d 88, 91–92 (Tex. 1999); *see also Buckley*, 521 U.S. at 432–33 (collecting cases); Berish v. Sw. Energy Prod. Co., 763 F. Supp. 2d 702, 706 (M.D. Pa. 2011) (emotional distress claims for exposure to contamination caused by "fracking" requires physical injury under Pennsylvania law); Paz v. Brush Engineered Materials, Inc., 949 So. 2d 1, 4 (Miss. 2007) (allowing emotional distress claim where there is a physical illness, which can include medically cognizable and treatable emotional harm).

to an accident or where a defendant's conduct is willful, wanton, or malicious.[211] Other cases have found an injury to property sufficient to establish the injury necessary to bring an emotional distress claim.[212]

A minority of jurisdictions hold that a claim for emotional distress does not require a present physical injury, but impose other requirements of proof for such claims. For example, extending an existing line of cases, the West Virginia Supreme Court held that a plaintiff need not demonstrate physical injury from exposure to asbestos to assert a claim for negligent infliction of emotional distress based on that exposure.[213] The court did require, however, that a plaintiff offer facts sufficient to guarantee that the claim is not spurious and that the emotional distress is undoubtedly real and serious. In the context of exposure to toxins, the court held that a plaintiff must show actual exposure to the toxin and demonstrate that the emotional distress was reasonably foreseeable. A plaintiff also must demonstrate that the exposure raises a medically established possibility of contracting a disease and that the disease will produce death or substantial disability requiring prolonged treatment.[214]

California took a slightly different approach to "fear of disease" claims in *Potter v. Firestone Tire & Rubber Co.*[215] The *Potter* plaintiffs claimed that they feared they would develop disease from ingesting groundwater that had been contaminated by toxins the defendant deposited in a nearby landfill in violation of California law. The court rejected any requirement of physical injury, finding it to be a "hopelessly imprecise" method of determining which claims were valid.[216] The court did acknowledge, however, some of the same policy concerns raised by the U.S. Supreme Court in *Buckley*, including the frequency of most people's exposure to carcinogens and the risk of unreasonable claims based on mere exposure. In light of these policy considerations, the California court adopted a standard requiring that fear-of-disease plaintiffs must offer medical or scientific evidence that it is "more likely than not" that they will actually develop the disease in question.[217] In addition to addressing the *Buckley* concerns, the court noted that this standard would discourage claims against manufacturers of prescription drugs for late-discovered side effects, preserve available dollars for persons who can present legitimate claims, and

---

211. See, e.g., Montega Corp. v. Hazelrigs, 189 S.E.2d 421, 422 (Ga. 1972); see also First Nat'l Bank v. Langley, 314 So. 2d 324 (Miss. 1975) (discussing history of rule and exception).
212. See Barlow v. Gen. Motors Corp., 595 F. Supp. 2d 929, 942 (S.D. Ind. 2009) (holding that plaintiffs could claim emotional distress damages on trespass or nuisance cases but rejecting plaintiffs' emotional distress claim); Nnadili v. Chevron U.S.A., Inc., 435 F. Supp. 2d 93, 99 (D.D.C. 2006) (allowing emotional distress claim where the defendant trespassed on and contaminated the plaintiffs' property).
213. Marlin v. Bill Rich Constr., 482 S.E.2d 620 (W. Va. 1996).
214. See id. at 637–38; see also Roes v. FHP, Inc., 985 P.2d 661, 667–68 (Haw. 1999) (recognizing the plaintiffs' emotional distress claims without need to show injury when the plaintiffs were exposed to HIV-positive blood in the workplace).
215. 863 P.2d 795 (Cal. 1993).
216. Id. at 810.
217. Id. at 811–12.

keep such claims viable by limiting their scope and number.[218] The California rule permits a claim for fear of cancer where the plaintiff can establish that (1) the plaintiff was exposed to a carcinogenic toxic substance as a result of the defendant's culpable conduct, and (2) the plaintiff has a fear of cancer based on knowledge, corroborated by medical or scientific opinion, that it is more likely than not that the plaintiff will develop cancer in the future due to the toxic exposure. However, where the exposure was due to the defendant's malice, fraud, or oppression, a plaintiff need only show a reasonable fear and that the risk of cancer is "significant."[219]

Property Damage

Plaintiffs can collect several different types of property damages in toxic tort cases, all designed to put them in the position they were in prior to the tort or compensate them for the loss sustained.[220] Compensation for harm to land may consist of (1) the diminishment in the value of the property as a result of the contamination or the reasonable costs of restoration, (2) the value of any lost use or enjoyment of the property, and (3) damages for any discomfort or annoyance.[221] With respect to the first category, plaintiffs may generally recover the lesser of the loss of market value or the cost to restore the property.[222] Put another way, if the cost to restore a property to its pre-injury state exceeds the loss in market value, a plaintiff's recovery is limited to the diminution in value.[223] Some states, however, permit a plaintiff to recover the greater amount under certain circumstances, such as where the landowner can demonstrate a legitimate "personal reason" to restore the land. For example, some courts have permitted plaintiffs to recover the cost of groundwater remediation under their homes, even though that cost exceeded the diminution in market value, because "a personal residence represents the type of property in which the owner possesses a personal reason for repair."[224]

---

218. *Id.* at 811–14.
219. *Id.* at 816–18.
220. *See* Stenger v. Hope Natural Gas Co., 80 S.E.2d 889, 897 (W.V. 1954).
221. RESTATEMENT (SECOND) OF TORTS § 929(1) (1979); *see* Ayers v. Jackson, 525 A.2d 287, 294 (N.J. 1987).
222. *See* Dickens v. Oxy Vinyls, LP, 631 F. Supp. 2d 859, 866–67 (W.D. Ky. 2009) (holding that plaintiff must measure damage in nuisance case "by a material reduction in fair market value or rental value" and that such a showing generally requires expert opinion and rejecting plaintiffs' evidence of loss of value as speculative); Carson Harbor Vill., Ltd. v. Unocal Corp., 287 F. Supp. 2d 1118, 1201–02 (C.D. Cal. 2003) (citing California law).
223. *Stenger*, 80 S.E.2d at 898; *see also* Trimble v. Asarco, Inc., 232 F.3d 946, 964 (8th Cir. 2000) (holding that Nebraska would "likely limit plaintiffs' recoveries on state law claims alleging property damage to the market values of their properties"), *overruled in part by* Exxon Mobil Corp. v. Allapattah Servs., 545 U.S. 546 (2005).
224. Sunburst Sch. Dist. No. 2 v. Texaco, Inc., 165 P.3d 1079, 1088–89 (Mont. 2007). *Compare* Johansen v. Combustion Eng'g, Inc., 834 F. Supp. 404, 409 (S.D. Ga. 1993) (holding that "mere subjective preference" is not enough to justify "personal reason" restoration exception to normal property damage calculation rule), *vacated on other grounds*, 517 U.S. 1217 (1996), *with* Allgood v. Gen. Motors Corp., No. 1:02-CV-1077-DFH-TAB, 2006 U.S. Dist. LEXIS 70764, at *68–78 (S.D. Ind. Sept. 18, 2006) (holding that Indiana state courts would probably not apply rigid standard for damages in case involving

Damages for loss of use and enjoyment are a type of consequential damages that sometimes arise in the nuisance context. These damages are distinct from damage to property and generally include an award for discomfort and annoyance.[225] Such consequential damages may be recovered in addition to any diminution in value or restoration costs. For example, in *Rust v. Guinn*, the Indiana Court of Appeals held that a trial court had not erred in instructing the jury that it could award a plaintiff asserting a nuisance damages for diminution in value, for out-of-pocket expenses, and for injury to health.[226]

An emerging damage theory in toxic tort cases asserts an entitlement to damages for the stigma caused by contamination of a plaintiff's property or nearby properties. Such "stigma" damages, where recognized, are generally considered part of the calculation of the reduction in market value caused by a toxic tort.[227] In a seminal case, the Third Circuit held that the stigma associated with the prior presence of polychlorinated biphenyls (PCBs) on the plaintiffs' land represented a "permanent, irremediable damage to property" that allowed the plaintiffs to recover for diminution in value without proving the permanent physical damage usually required under Pennsylvania law.[228] Some courts have even allowed plaintiffs to pursue "proximity" stigma claims for reduction in the market value of their properties when nearby areas are contaminated.[229] However, courts generally are more open to claims of stigma damages when a plaintiff's land has sustained a physical

---

    PCB contamination, but instead the "flexible and reasonable" standards allowing for "personal reason" damages).

225.   *See* Barlow v. Gen. Motors Corp., 595 F. Supp. 2d 929, 939–41 (S.D. Ind. 2009) (denying the defendant's motion for summary judgment on loss of enjoyment damages allegedly caused by the defendant's releases of PCBs because of flexibility in law allowing for award of general damages related to "the emotional and physical burden of dealing" with contaminated property); Boughton v. Cotter Corp., 65 F.3d 823, 832–33 (10th Cir. 1995) (distinguishing property damages for annoyance and discomfort from damages for fear of cancer and disease under Colorado law); Ayers v. Jackson, 525 A.2d 287, 293–94 (N.J. 1987) (in nuisance action related to contamination caused by landfill, distinguishing injury to right to obtain potable running water from wells from personal injuries barred by state tort claims act).

226.   429 N.E.2d 299, 301–05 (Ind. Ct. App. 1981).

227.   *See* AVX Corp. v. Horry Land Co., 686 F. Supp. 2d 621, 626–28 (D.S.C. 2010) (collecting cases from other jurisdictions on claims for stigma damages and refusing to dismiss claim, in part for lack of guidance from South Carolina courts); Walker Drug Co. v. La Sal Oil Co., 972 P.2d 1238, 1246 (Utah 1998) ("Stigma damages are a facet of permanent damages, and recovery for stigma damages is compensation for a property's diminished market value in the absence of permanent 'physical' harm.").

228.   *In re* Paoli R.R. Yard PCB Litig., 35 F.3d 717, 796–97 (3d Cir. 1994). The *Paoli* court also listed three elements of a claim for stigma damages: (1) defendants cause some (temporary) physical damage to plaintiffs' property; (2) plaintiffs demonstrate that repair of the damage will not restore the value of the property to its prior level; and (3) plaintiffs show that there is some ongoing risk to their land. *Id.* at 798.

229.   *See* Lewis v. Gen. Elec. Co., 37 F. Supp. 2d 55, 61 (D. Mass. 1999) (allowing the plaintiff's claim for public nuisance caused by the defendant's contamination of area, which allegedly interfered with public health and environment and made the plaintiff unable to sell her property); Walker Drug Co. v. La Sal Oil Co., 972 P.2d 1238, 1246 n.10 (Utah 1998) (noting that "[a] minority of courts allow recovery for stigma damages regardless of any temporary physical harm to the property" and suggesting that stigma damages could be awarded even absent physical damage in an appropriate circumstance); Scheg v. Agway, Inc., 645 N.Y.S.2d 687, 688–89 (N.Y. App. Div. 1996) (recognizing cause of action for diminution in property value from stigma caused by proximity of property to hazardous waste landfill).

injury.[230] Thus, in *Wilson v. Amoco Corp.*, the court rejected a claim for stigmatization damages in the absence of physical injury, despite acknowledging that plaintiffs' facilities were "in close proximity" to the defendant's contaminated property.[231] Finally, some courts permit stigma damages only when the condition caused by the defendant's actions cannot be abated and is considered permanent.[232]

Natural Resource Damages

Several recent environmental disaster episodes, including the 2011 Gulf of Mexico oil spill, have sparked renewed interest among federal, state, and tribal governments seeking to recover damages for injuries to natural resources caused by hazardous substances or petroleum. At the federal level, the two primary statutes authorizing federal agencies to pursue recovery of natural resource damages (NRD) are CERCLA[233] and the Oil Pollution Act of 1990 (OPA).[234] Many states have enacted their own statutes modeled after CERCLA that authorize them to recover natural resource damages.[235]

Although these statutes do not permit suits by private parties to recover natural resource damages, they are nevertheless of broad interest for several reasons. First, although private parties may not be NRD plaintiffs under these statutes, the defendants in such statutory actions are nearly always private parties. Given that fact, and given the broad contribution

---

230. *See* Smith v. Kan. Gas Serv. Co., 169 P.3d 1052, 1062–63 (Kan. 2007) (in case involving stigma from escape of natural gas and fear of future explosions, holding that diminution in value for marketplace fear or stigma requires "that the property sustained a physical injury as a direct and proximate result of the negligent conduct"); Leaf River Forest Prods. v. Ferguson, 662 So. 2d 648, 664 (Miss. 1995) (holding that the plaintiffs could not recover for stigma when dioxin contamination was 80 miles away).
231. 33 F. Supp. 2d 981, 986 (D. Wyo. 1998) (applying Mississippi law, noting that "claims of stigma damages absent some other definable physical harm to the property are simply too speculative to warrant serious consideration").
232. *See* Santa Fe P'ship v. Arco Prods. Co., 54 Cal. Rptr. 2d 214, 223–24 (Cal. Ct. App. 1996) (discussing nature of stigma claims and holding that plaintiffs cannot seek stigma damages because of lack of remediation expenses, lack of loss of use or enjoyment, lack of permanent nuisance, and lack of threat of future injury); Rudd v. Electrolux Corp., 982 F. Supp. 355, 372 (M.D.N.C. 1997) (holding that North Carolina law bars recovery for stigma damages for "temporary or abatable nuisances" and noting that stigma can be used in determining market price and diminution in value); Bradley v. Armstrong Rubber Co., 130 F.3d 168, 175–76 (5th Cir. 1997) (holding that Mississippi law allows for diminution in value caused by stigma where permanent injury to property caused by release of petroleum naphtha occurred, but reversing verdict for plaintiffs for stigma for lack of supporting evidence). *But see* Walker Drug Co. v. La Sal Oil Co., 972 P.2d 1238, 1246 (Utah 1998) (noting that calculation of restoration damages caused by temporary nuisance or trespass can be inaccurate because it does not capture lost market value, and holding that stigma damages are recoverable when damages are temporary).
233. 42 U.S.C. §§ 9601–9675.
234. 33 U.S.C. §§ 2701 to 2761. Note that the Clean Water Act also addresses injury to natural resources. 33 U.S.C. § 1321(f)(5).
235. *See, e.g.,* ALASKA STAT. § 46.03.822(a) (2012) (authorizing the Alaska state and local governments to recover past and future cleanup costs and damages to the environment); Minnesota Environmental Response and Liability Act, MINN. STAT. §§ 115B.01–.241 (2011) (state may recover response costs and, as "trustee" for natural resources, may recover damages for "injury to, loss of or destruction to natural resources"); New Jersey Spill Compensation and Control Act, N.J. STAT. ANN. § 58:10-23.11g(a)(2) (West 2012).

claims permitted under these statutes, the chances of a toxic tort lawyer encountering some aspect of such a claim is not small. Second, because the issue of what public constitutes natural resources subject to suit under these statutes is fact-specific, there exists the possibility of overlap between damage to privately owned resources and natural resource damages actionable under CERCLA.[236] And finally, because EPA and other government agencies have established uniform and widely accepted methods of identifying and measuring natural resource damages in CERCLA and OPA cases, both plaintiff and defense attorneys frequently employ those methods in prosecuting and defending actions for private property damage. For these reasons, a basic understanding of these NRD statutes may be useful.

Under CERCLA, the United States, the states, and Native American tribes may compel a defendant to restore or pay monetary damages for injuries to natural resources resulting from the release of hazardous substances.[237] As with the remediation aspects of CERCLA discussed above, "covered persons" liable for NRD include the present owner or operator of a facility, the owner or operators of facilities at the time of a release of hazardous substances, and those who arrange for disposal or transport the hazardous substances for disposal.[238]

The OPA creates liability for discharges of oil into navigable waters or adjoining shorelines or into the exclusive economic zone of deep ocean waters.[239] Parties liable under the OPA include the owners, operators, and charterers of transport vessels, the owners and operators of onshore facilities or pipelines, and the lessees of offshore facilities or deepwater ports.[240] Public vessels and permitted discharges are excluded from OPA liability.[241] The OPA's definition of "natural resources" is substantially similar to the CERCLA definition.[242]

Under CERCLA or the OPA, the plaintiff government or agency must first establish standing by demonstrating that it was appointed as trustee for the natural resources that were allegedly injured or lost. The President has already designated the federal trustees and has appointed the Secretaries of Commerce and the Interior as "trustees of those resources subject to their respective management or control."[243]

---

236. *See, e.g.,* Barnes v. Century Aluminum Co., No. 05-62, 2012 U.S. Dist. LEXIS 73120, at *39 (D.V.I. May 24, 2012) (holding privately owned groundwater resources are within CERCLA NRD claim because of substantial degree of governmental regulation).
237. 42 U.S.C. §§ 9607(a), 9613(f). "Hazardous substances" are defined in 42 U.S.C. § 9601(14) and explicitly exclude "petroleum, including crude oil or any fraction thereof which is not otherwise specifically listed or designated."
238. 42 U.S.C. § 9607(a).
239. 33 U.S.C. § 2702(a).
240. 33 U.S.C. § 2701(32).
241. 33 U.S.C. § 2702(c).
242. *Compare* 33 U.S.C. § 2701(20), *with* 42 U.S.C. § 9601(16).
243. 40 C.F.R. § 300.600 (applies to OPA as well). According to the Department of Interior Department Manual, Part 207, Section 6, dated September 14, 1998, the Secretary of Interior has further delegated trustee authority to the Director of the U.S. Fish and Wildlife Service (USFWS). The USFWS has responsibility for the following trust resources: National Wildlife Refuges, endangered and threatened species,

A trustee has standing to assert NRD claims under CERCLA only if the federal, tribal, or state government for which the trustee serves owns, manages, holds in trust, or otherwise controls the natural resource at issue. This is because CERCLA defines "natural resources" to include:

> land, fish, wildlife, biota, air, water, ground water, drinking water supplies, and other such resources *belonging to, managed by, held in trust by, appertaining to, or otherwise controlled* by the United States . . .[244]

Where a plaintiff cannot demonstrate that the subject resources meet these tests, the natural resource damage claim under CERCLA must be dismissed.[245] Courts have held that "natural resources" do not encompass "purely private resources."[246] However, the federal government did not undertake to define these excluded private resources, leaving the courts to make that determination on a case-by-case basis.[247] In one recent case, a court determined that where groundwater resources under private ownership are subject to a substantial degree of governmental regulation, the groundwater is not a "purely private resource" but rather comes within the scope of natural resources subject to CERCLA.[248]

Under CERCLA, NRD are limited to the loss of, or injury to, natural resources, including the costs of assessing these losses. For purposes of assessing liability and damages, an injury means an observable adverse change in a natural resource that is either directly or indirectly the result of a discharge. A change "in the chemical or physical quality or the viability of a natural resource" qualifies as an adverse change under CERCLA.[249] The

---

migratory birds, wild horses and burros, and other natural resources. *See, e.g.,* U.S. FISH & WILDLIFE, available at http://contaminants.fws.gov/Issues/Restoration.cfm (last visited Oct. 18, 2012).

244. 42 U.S.C. § 9601(16) (emphasis added); *see also* 42 U.S.C. § 9607(f)(1) (providing that in the case of an injury to, destruction of, or loss of natural resources "liability shall be to the United States Government and to any State for natural resources within the State or belonging to, managed by, controlled by, or appertaining to such State and to any Indian tribe for natural resources belonging to, managed by, controlled by, or appertaining to such tribe, or held in trust for the benefit of such tribe, or belonging to a member of such tribe if such resources are subject to a trust restriction on alienation").

245. *Compare* Oklahoma v. Tyson Foods, Inc., 258 F.R.D. 472, 483 (N.D. Okla. 2009) (granting defendants' motion to dismiss all monetary claims under CERCLA and the common law for natural resource damages because of significant interest of the Cherokee Nation, a nonparty, in the land and waters of the Illinois River watershed in Oklahoma and Arkansas), *with* Arkansas ex rel. Bryan v. Dow Chem. Co., 981 F. Supp. 1170, 1174 (E.D. Ark. 1997) (finding state's natural resource claim viable because it was based on "important water source to rice growers and aquaculturists of south central Arkansas" and thus fell within CERCLA definition of "natural resources").

246. Ohio v. U.S. Dep't of the Interior, 880 F.2d 432, 461 (D.C. Cir. 1989); *see also* Nat'l Ass'n of Mfrs. v. U.S. Dep't of the Interior, 134 F.3d 1095 (D.C. Cir. 1998) (stating that CERCLA does not "allow public trustees to recover for damages to private property or other 'purely private interests'").

247. The U.S. Department of Interior defended its refusal to further define excluded private resources in response to comments on proposed natural resource damage assessment regulations required by CERCLA, noting the diversity of private and governmental interests. Natural Resource Damage Assessments, 59 Fed. Reg. 14,262, 14,268 (Dep't of Interior Mar. 25, 1994).

248. *See Barnes*, 2012 U.S. Dist. LEXIS 73120, at *39.

249. 43 C.F.R. § 11.14(v) (1998).

OPA regulations include impairment of natural resource services as a component of injury.[250] Injury to natural resources can be demonstrated by empirical evidence of an adverse change in baseline conditions or by demonstrating that other regulatory standards have been violated with respect to that resource (e.g., water quality standards).[251]

Once injury is established, damages must be measured. CERCLA provides that the measure of natural resource damages shall not be limited by the amount required to restore, replace, or acquire the equivalent of, such natural resources.[252] A plaintiff trustee may also recover the value of the lost use of the damaged natural resources pending restoration or recovery to a "baseline" condition (i.e., the condition of the resource absent exposure to the hazardous substance).[253]

Punitive Damages

Punitive damages (also called exemplary damages) are not intended to compensate the plaintiff for an injury, but instead to punish the defendant for endangering the life or safety of others through conduct that courts and statutes variously define as willful, wanton, reckless, or deliberate disregard of the rights and safety of others.[254] Punitive damages were recognized at common law, but many states now have statutes codifying the availability of punitive damages. In most states, a plaintiff must show malicious, outrageous, or willful behavior and must meet an elevated standard of proof—usually clear and convincing evidence—to prevail on a claim for punitive damages.[255] To recover punitive damages against a corporation, a plaintiff generally must show that a controlling manager or executive either engaged in the activity or knew of and condoned the activity that merits punitive

---

250. 15 C.F.R. § 990.30 (2002).
251. *See, e.g.*, Coeur d'Alene Tribe v. Asarco, Inc., 280 F. Supp. 2d 1094, 1122–24 (D. Idaho 2003); *In re* Acushnet River & New Bedford Harbor: Proceedings re Alleged PCB Pollution, 716 F. Supp. 676, 685 (D. Mass. 1989) (where PCB contamination exceeded FDA tolerance levels, government could seek damages associated with closing the Harbor).
252. 42 U.S.C. § 9607(f)(2); *see also* Idaho v. Bunker Hill Co., 635 F. Supp. 665, 676 (D. Idaho 1986).
253. 43 C.F.R. § 11.14(e).
254. *See, e.g.*, City of Greenville v. W.R. Grace & Co., 827 F.2d 975, 983 (4th Cir. 1987) (applying South Carolina law); Ross v. Conoco, Inc., 828 So. 2d 546 (La. 2002) (citing former La. Civ. Code Art. 2315.3) ("wanton or reckless disregard for public safety"); Rivera v. United Gas Pipeline Co., 697 So. 2d 327, 334 (La. Ct. App. 1997); Minn. Stat. § 549.20, subd. 1(a).
255. *See* Cal. Civ. Code § 3294(a) (Deering 2012) (holding that plaintiffs must show a defendant is guilty of "oppression, fraud, or malice" by clear and convincing evidence); Ga. Code. Ann. § 51-12-5.1(b) (2012) (plaintiff must show by clear and convincing evidence "that the defendant's actions showed willful misconduct, malice, fraud, wantonness, oppression, or that entire want of care which would raise the presumption of conscious indifference to consequences"); Linthicum v. Nationwide Life Ins. Co., 723 P.2d 675, 681 (Ariz. 1986); Masaki v. Gen. Motors Corp., 780 P.2d 566, 575 (Haw. 1989); Tuttle v. Raymond, 494 A.2d 1353, 1363 (Me. 1985).

damages.[256] Some states cap punitive damages under certain circumstances,[257] while others prohibit them altogether.[258]

An award of punitive damages generally requires a showing of actual injury or an award of compensatory damages. For example, in a case based in part on claims for medical monitoring, a court reduced a punitive damage award on the ground that the medical monitoring claims did not involve personal injury and, thus, lacked any compensable current harm.[259] Other courts have implied or held that punitive damages are available for medical monitoring claims, but these cases are in the clear minority.[260]

The states vary in the factors they consider in determining whether punitive damages are appropriate. For example, in Texas, courts consider (1) the nature of the wrong, (2) the character of the conduct involved, (3) the degree of culpability of the wrongdoer, (4) the situation and sensibilities of the parties concerned, and (5) the extent to which such conduct offends a public sense of justice and propriety.[261] In Wisconsin, courts have identified five factors in product liability settings: (1) the existence and magnitude in the product of a danger to the public; (2) the cost and feasibility of reducing the danger to an acceptable level; (3) the manufacturer's awareness of the danger, and of the availability of a feasible remedy; (4) the nature and duration of, and the reasons for, the manufacturer's failure to act appropriately to discover or to reduce the danger; and (5) the extent to which the manufacturer purposefully created the danger.[262]

With respect to the amount of punitive damages, all such awards are subject to the U.S. Supreme Court's constitutional limitations on excessive punitive damages. Beginning in the seminal case of *BMW of North America v. Gore*, the Supreme Court has examined

---

256. *See, e.g.*, Barrous v. BP P.L.C., No. 10-CV-02944-LHK, 2011 U.S. Dist. LEXIS 113597, at *48–56 (N.D. Cal. 2011) (denying defendant's motion for summary judgment on punitive damages claim based on evidence of managing agent's unlawful remediation of contamination at gas station, citing CAL. CIV. CODE § 3294(b)); Schenk v. HNA Holdings, Inc., 613 S.E.2d 503, 507 (N.C. Ct. App. 2005) (citing N.C. GEN. STAT. § 1D-15(c)).
257. *See* GA. CODE. ANN. § 51-12-5.1(g) (outlining the cap on punitive damages in Georgia of $250,000 in nonproduct-liability tort cases and cases where defendant acted or failed to act with a specific intent to cause harm); MINN. STAT. § 466.04, subd. 1(b) (prohibiting award of punitive damages on tort claims against municipality).
258. *See* Stewart v. Bader, 907 A.2d 931, 943 (N.H. 2006) (noting that punitive damages are outlawed in New Hampshire unless authorized by statute); Miller v. Kingsley, 230 N.W.2d 472, 474 (Neb. 1975) (citing "fundamental rule" that punitive damages are not allowed in Nebraska).
259. Perrine v. E.I. Du Pont de Nemours & Co., 694 S.E.2d 815, 880–81 (W. Va. 2010); *see also* Hess v. A.I. DuPont Hosp. for Children, No. 08-0229, 2009 U.S. Dist. LEXIS 19492, at *43 n.9 (E.D. Pa. Mar. 5, 2009).
260. *See* Carlough v. Amchem Prods., Inc., 834 F. Supp. 1437, 1460 (E.D. Pa. 1993) (allowing plaintiffs' claim for punitive damages to be included with their medical monitoring claim to satisfy amount in controversy requirement).
261. North Am. Refractory Co. v. Easter, 988 S.W.2d 904, 920 (Tex. App. 1999) (citing Alamo Nat'l Bank v. Kraus, 616 S.W.2d 908, 910 (Tex. 1981)).
262. Nigh v. Dow Chem. Co., 634 F. Supp. 1513, 1516 (W.D. Wis. 1986) (citing Walter v. Cessna Aircraft Co., 358 N.W.2d 816, 820 (Wis. Ct. App. 1984)); *see also* Boyette v. L.W. Looney & Son, 932 F. Supp. 1344, 1349 n.10 (D. Utah 1996) (punitive damages can be awarded for "conduct involving some element of outrage similar to that usually found in crime" (citing the RESTATEMENT (SECOND) OF TORTS § 908)).

the amounts of state punitive damages awards under the Due Process Clause of the Fourteenth Amendment.[263] Observing that such punitive damage awards are "civil penalties" based on culpable conduct, the Court held that the basic Constitutional protection against "grossly excessive" punishment applies to such damages awards.[264] In *Gore* and the cases that followed it, the Court established three guideposts for determining whether a punitive damages award is unconstitutionally excessive: (1) the degree of reprehensibility of the defendant's misconduct; (2) the disparity between actual and punitive damages; and (3) a comparison of the punitive damages awarded and other civil or criminal penalties that could be imposed for similar misconduct.[265] The most important of these guideposts is the reprehensibility of the defendant's conduct, and the Court instructed courts to look in particular at whether:

- the harm caused was physical as opposed to economic;
- the tortious conduct evinced an indifference to or a reckless disregard of the health or safety of others;
- the target of the conduct had financial vulnerability;
- the conduct involved repeated actions or was an isolated incident; and
- the harm was the result of intentional malice, trickery, or deceit, or mere accident.[266]

Beyond those Constitutional requirements, state standards vary. For example, California courts examine the nature of the defendant's wrongdoing, the actual harm to the plaintiff, and the defendant's wealth when considering whether an award of punitive damages is excessive.[267] In New Jersey, by statute, triers of fact must consider the profitability of the misconduct to the defendant, when the misconduct was terminated, and the financial condition of the defendant, as well as the facts supporting whether any punitive damage award should be levied at all.[268]

The factors courts consider in addressing punitive damage claims in the toxic tort arena are consistent with the issues raised in other types of tort cases. For example, in *Phillip Morris, Inc. v. Emerson*, the owner of a laboratory facility unearthed canisters containing chemicals that had been buried by a previous owner and hired a consultant to help dispose of the chemicals. During the testing process, employees and emergency personnel were exposed to an extremely toxic chemical when an employee of the consultant negligently

---

263. 517 U.S. 559 (1996). The *Gore* line of cases was foreshadowed by the Court's decision in TXO Prod. Corp. v. Alliance Res. Corp., 509 U.S. 443 (1993) (collecting cases from early 1900s).
264. Id. at 562, 575.
265. Id. at 574–75; State Farm Mut. Auto. Ins. Co. v. Campbell, 538 U.S. 408, 419 (2003).
266. *Campbell*, 538 U.S. at 419.
267. Bankhead v. ArvinMeritor Inc., 139 Cal. Rptr. 3d 849, 855–56 (Cal. Ct. App. 2012) (citing Neal v. Farmers Ins. Exch., 148 Cal. Rptr. 389 (Cal. 1978)).
268. N.J. STAT. ANN. § 2A:15-5.12(c) (2012).

released the chemical into the air.[269] The trial court awarded punitive damages against the current owner of the facility, the former owner who had buried the canisters, and the consultant company responsible for the investigation. The appeals court reversed in part, finding that the attempts of the current and former owners to neutralize and dispose of the contents of the cylinders safely did not rise to the level of willful and wanton conduct because they showed some concern for the safety of others. The appeals court affirmed the award of punitive damages against the consultant, however, finding that the company had completely failed to take any precautions in disposing of the chemical, making the consultant's behavior willful and wanton.[270]

In *Bankhead v. Arvinmeritor, Inc.*, the California Court of Appeals addressed the propriety of a $4.5 million punitive damage award against an asbestos defendant found 15 percent liable at trial.[271] The court found that the physical injury involved, the defendant's indifference to the health of its product users, the duration of the defendant's inaction and the malice that inaction implied, and the 2.4:1 ratio of punitive to compensatory damages met both California's standard for an award of punitive damages and the *Gore* Due Process guideposts.[272]

Other Remedies: Injunctive Relief and Attorneys' Fees
Injunctive Relief

In addition to the recovery of legal damages, a number of common law and statutory toxic tort theories permit a plaintiff to obtain injunctive relief, generally when a plaintiff alleges a nuisance or another ongoing harm.[273] Indeed, several statutes expressly authorize injunctive relief in contexts where no monetary relief is available.[274] Most injunctions in toxic tort cases are subject to the usual equity-based limitations applicable to injunctions generally: an injunction is an extraordinary equitable remedy, "not a remedy which issues as of course" or "to restrain an act the injurious consequences of which are merely

---

269. Philip Morris, Inc. v. Emerson, 368 S.E.2d 268, 274–75 (Va. 1988).
270. Id. at 283–84.
271. 139 Cal. Rptr. 3d 849 (Cal. Ct. App. 2012).
272. Id. at 862–67.
273. See 35 Pa. Cons. Stat. § 6021.1305(b) (2012) (allowing mandatory and special injunctions to abate nuisances where "the circumstances require it or the public health is endangered"); Iowa Code § 657.1(1) (2012); Minn. Stat. § 617.83 (2012).
274. See, e.g., 42 U.S.C. § 7604 (citizen suits under Clean Air Act and allowing courts to enforce emission standards or limitations, order the EPA to perform an act or duty, and compel agency action unreasonably delayed); Minn. Stat. § 116B.03(1) (allowing private actions for declaratory or injunctive relief "for the protection of the air, water, land, or other natural resources located within the state").

trifling."[275] An injunction should issue only if "intervention of a court of equity is essential in order effectually to protect property rights against injuries otherwise unremediable."[276]

In order to obtain a permanent injunction, a plaintiff generally must establish: (1) actual success on the merits; (2) that the plaintiff is likely to suffer irreparable harm in the absence of the injunctive relief; (3) that the balance of equities tips in the plaintiff's favor, and (4) that an injunction is in the public interest.[277] As these elements suggest, there is no specific formula for determining whether an injunction is proper or not; the issue will depend on balancing the facts and equities in each particular case.[278]

The available scope of an injunction in a toxic tort case will depend on the scope of the underlying common law or statutory cause of action. For example, Minnesota's statute authorizing injunctive relief for environmental harms permits only injunctions to prevent new pollution, not as a means for courts to order remediation of past releases.[279]

Attorneys' Fees

Most common law theories in toxic tort actions are subject to the American rule, under which each party to litigation is responsible for its own attorneys' fees and litigation costs.[280] Many state and federal environmental remediation statutes, however, authorize

---

275. Weinberger v. Romero-Barcelo, 456 U.S. 305, 312–13 (1982) (remanding for further proceedings because district court had authority to issue appropriate remedy less restrictive than an injunction in a Clean Water Act case (quoting Consol. Canal Co. v. Mesa Canal Co., 177 U.S. 296, 302 (1900))); *see also* Wilsonville v. SCA Servs., Inc., 426 N.E.2d 824, 835 (Ill. 1981) ("[T]rifling annoyances or inconveniences of an operation will not give the character of a nuisance to a business that is useful and necessary to society.").
276. *See Weinberger*, 456 U.S. at 312 (quoting Cavanaugh v. Looney, 248 U.S. 453, 456 (1919)); *see also* Weinhold v. Wolff, 555 N.W.2d 454, 467 (Iowa 1996) (holding that injunctive relief was unnecessary for plaintiffs alleging nuisance caused by nearby hog facility because of availability of special damages for diminution in market value).
277. Winter v. Natural Res. Def. Council, Inc., 555 U.S. 7, 20, 32 (2008); *see also* Hackwell v. United States, No. 04-CV-00827-EWN, 2008 U.S. Dist. LEXIS 56641, at *8–25 (D. Colo. 2008) (citing eBay Inc. v. MercExchange, LLC, 547 U.S. 388, 391 (2006) for elements of injunctive relief, applying slightly different factors, and issuing declaratory judgment against application of attorneys' fee provision of federal Radiation Exposure Compensation Act); *Weinhold*, 555 N.W.2d at 466–67 (listing factors for balancing test for determination of whether to grant injunctive relief to abate a nuisance, including (1) the character of the interest to be protected, (2) the relative adequacy to the plaintiff of injunction and other remedies, (3) plaintiff's delay in bringing suit, (4) plaintiff's misconduct, (5) the relative hardship likely to result to defendant if injunction is granted and to plaintiff if it is denied, (6) the interests of third persons and of the public, and (7) the practicality of framing and enforcing the order or judgment).
278. *Wilsonville*, 426 N.E.2d at 836–41 (affirming injunction against prospective nuisance presented by operation of industrial waste disposal site, finding that trial court properly balanced utility of the landfill against danger presented to public); *see also* Neal v. Darby, 318 S.E.2d 18, 24 (S.C. 1984) (affirming permanent injunction against company operating site that handled and stored hazardous chemicals but allowing company to later seek to have the injunction modified if it could show a change in the conditions of the site).
279. Kennedy Bldg. Assocs. v. Viacom, Inc., 375 F.3d 731, 747–48 (8th Cir. 2004) (injunction preventing ongoing releases of PCBs and chlorobenzenes into soil and groundwater from former transformer repair site).
280. *See, e.g.*, Kallok v. Medtronic, Inc., 573 N.W.2d 356, 363 (Minn. 1998); Key Tronic Corp. v. United States, 511 U.S. 809, 814–15 (1994) (quoting Runyon v. McCrary, 427 U.S. 160, 185 (1986)).

courts to award attorneys' fees to plaintiffs who prevail on claims under these statutes.[281] Sometimes such attorneys' fees are categorized as part of a plaintiff's substantive damages. Under CERCLA, for example, attorneys' fees that are "closely tied to the actual cleanup" (such as fees incurred in "tracking down other responsible solvent polluters") are considered "response costs" and are thus recoverable as damages. Other fees, including attorneys' fees incurred in the course of negotiations or for the purposes of defending a party against expected litigation, are not considered response costs and are not recoverable under CERCLA.[282]

More often, statutes provide that judges are to award attorneys' fees "when appropriate." Courts have generally interpreted such provisions to authorize an attorney's fee award when a plaintiff or citizens group prevails in some substantial way on a claim under the relevant statute.[283] Some jurisdictions have passed more explicit statutes providing for attorneys' fees when plaintiffs bring suits that affect the public interest in a broad sense.[284]

---

281. *See, e.g.*, 33 U.S.C. § 1365(d) (Clean Water Act); 42 U.S.C. § 7607(f) (Clean Air Act); 42 U.S.C. § 6972(e) (Solid Waste Disposal Act); 15 U.S.C. § 2619(c)(2) (Toxic Substances Control Act); FLA. STAT. ANN. §§ 376.205, 376.313(6) (LexisNexis 2012) (both statutes allowing attorneys' fees when awards would be "in the public interest"); MINN. STAT. § 115B.14 (2004) (stating a court "may award" attorneys' fees).

282. *See, e.g.*, BNSF Ry. Co. v. California, No. 2:08-CV-02225-JAM-JFM, 2009 U.S. Dist. LEXIS 2802, at *4–8 (E.D. Cal. Jan. 7, 2009) (denying recovery of certain attorneys' fees in CERCLA contribution action as not sufficiently closely tied to an actual cleanup (citing Key Tronic v. United States, 511 U.S. 809, 820 (1994))); Gussack Realty Co. v. Xerox Corp., 224 F.3d 85, 91–92 (2d Cir. 2000) (affirming district court opinion denying expert fee recovery when the plaintiff identified the defendant as a potentially responsible party without expert assistance).

283. *See* Ruckelshaus v. Sierra Club, 463 U.S. 680, 694 (1983) (holding that it is not "appropriate" for a federal court to award attorneys' fees under the Clean Air Act "absent some degree of success on the merits"); Stoddard v. W. Carolina Reg'l Sewer Auth., 784 F.2d 1200, 1209 (4th Cir. 1986) (affirming award of attorneys' fees for plaintiffs bringing citizen suit under Clean Water Act related to nuisance created by government-owned sewage treatment facility when plaintiffs' actions "will tend to ensure compliance with the [Clean Water Act]" and, thus, serve public interest); Atl. States Legal Found., Inc. v. Tyson Foods, Inc., 897 F.2d 1128, 1143 (11th Cir. 1990) (stating, in a Clean Water Act case, that the court "cannot conceive of any grounds that would justify a denial of fees and costs" when a citizens' group has prevailed on the merits); St. John's Organic Farm v. Gem Cnty. Mosquito Abatement Dist., 574 F.3d 1054, 1061–62 (9th Cir. 2009) (listing different standards circuits have adopted for "appropriateness" in Clean Water Act cases and adopting "special circumstances" rule for the Ninth Circuit); Pound v. Airosol Co., 498 F.3d 1089, 1101–03 (10th Cir. 2007) (interpreting Clean Air Act as allowing for fee awards to plaintiffs "who, by bringing an action against an alleged violator of the Act, minimize the amount of pollution in the atmosphere, and thus promote the Act's goal" and dismissing concerns that award would be inappropriate because of the plaintiff's monetary interests in the outcome).

284. *See, e.g.*, CAL. CIV. PROC. CODE § 1021.5 (Deering 2012) (permitting an award of fees when a plaintiff's action "has resulted in the enforcement of an important right affecting the public interest if: (a) a significant benefit, whether pecuniary or nonpecuniary, has been conferred on the general public or a large class of persons, (b) the necessity and financial burden of private enforcement, or of enforcement by one public entity against another public entity, are such as to make the award appropriate, and (c) such fees should not in the interest of justice be paid out of the recovery, if any"); *see also* Karuk Tribe of N. Cal. v. Cal. Reg'l Water Quality Control Bd., 108 Cal. Rptr. 3d 40, 66–69 (Cal. Ct. App. 2010) (describing § 1021.5 as providing for attorneys' fees only when a plaintiff was "demonstrably influential" in overturning, remedying, or prompting a change in affairs challenged by the lawsuit and reversing award of attorneys' fees where plaintiffs obtained only a remand of permit decision to state water control board for further hearings on water quality issue); Consumer Def. Grp. v. Rental Housing Indus. Members, 40 Cal. Rptr. 3d 832, 856 (Cal. Ct. App. 2006) (referring to "lack of any real public benefit" from lawsuit

In contrast, prevailing defendants generally can recover their attorneys' fees only where the plaintiff's action was frivolous or unreasonable.[285] If a plaintiff is successful on claims that provide for an award of attorneys' fees but not on others, courts will (to the extent possible) allocate the fees incurred between the claims.[286]

With respect to the amount of attorneys' fees that may be awarded, plaintiffs seeking fees under federal fee-shifting statutes are generally limited to the "lodestar" amount, that is, an amount equal to the product of a reasonable number of hours spent on the successful litigation and the market hourly rate.[287] Some states permit recovery of an amount greater than the lodestar amount if the plaintiff can establish certain additional elements, such as a substantial risk for the lawyer in taking the case or an unusually high degree of success.[288]

---

that resulted in notices such as those informing people of auto exhaust fumes in parking lots and reversing consent judgments that included awards of attorneys' fees arising out of state carcinogen-awareness law).

285. *See* George v. Reisdorf Bros., 410 Fed. App'x 382, 387 (2d Cir. 2011) (affirming trial court's decision not to award defendant attorneys' fees in Clean Water Act action, despite grant of summary judgment to defendant, noting lack of "totally baseless" claims and recognizing "good faith" of plaintiffs' litigation (citing Christiansburg v. EEOC, 434 U.S. 412, 418 (1978))); Simsbury-Avon Pres. Soc'y, LLC v. Metacon Gun Club, Inc., No. 3:04cv803, 2010 U.S. Dist. LEXIS 30159, at *6–7 (D. Conn. Mar. 29, 2010) (holding that prevailing defendants in RCRA and Clean Water Act actions are entitled to costs only when the plaintiff's action was "frivolous, unreasonable, or without foundation, even though not brought in subjective bad faith" (citing *Christiansburg*, 434 U.S. at 421)).

286. *See* Citizens Against Pollution v. Ohio Power Co., 484 F. Supp. 2d 800, 808–12 (S.D. Ohio 2007) (holding plaintiff's unsuccessful RCRA claim legally distinct from successful reporting claims under CERCLA and other federal law and excluding from fee award time spent on RCRA claim); Kennedy Bldg. Assocs. v. Viacom, Inc., 375 F.3d 731, 748–49 (8th Cir. 2004) (remanding to district court for deduction from attorneys' fee award of fees incurred for work on claim under statute that did not provide for attorneys' fees).

287. *See* Pennsylvania v. Del. Valley Citizens' Council for Clean Air, 478 U.S. 546, 565 (1986) (in Clean Air Act case, noting strong presumption that lodestar figure represents a reasonable fee under fee shifting statutes but also noting that upward modifications are available in "rare" and "exceptional" cases); City of Burlington v. Dague, 505 U.S. 557, 567 (1992) (in case involving Solid Waste Disposal Act and Clean Water Act, rejecting "enhancement" of attorneys' fees of 25 percent over lodestar).

288. *See* Standard Guar. Ins. Co. v. Quanstrom, 555 So. 2d 828, 833–34 (Fla. 1990) (listing twelve factors for judges to consider when determining reasonable attorneys' fees in "public policy enforcement" cases such as those presenting environmental issues and allowing multipliers up to 2.5 in tort cases); Krebs v. United Ref. Co., 893 A.2d 776, 791 (Pa. Super. Ct. 2006) (holding that method of determining reasonable fees under state statute to abate nuisance is lodestar, but allowing adjustment "in light of the degree of success, the potential public benefit achieved, and the potential inadequacy of the private fee arrangement").

CHAPTER 3

Common Defenses

J Kevin Buster and Randy J. Butterfield

Introduction

Broadly speaking, toxic tort litigation encompasses any case alleging personal injury or property damage from exposure to toxic substances. Toxic tort cases thus involve a wide range of potential claims, from product liability, to workplace exposure, to environmental contamination. Given the range of potential claims, it is only natural that the types of defenses that may be available in any given case will also vary widely. Nevertheless, despite these considerable differences, there are several overarching issues and defenses that tend to cut across these distinctions. This chapter focuses on several of the most significant defenses likely to arise in the toxic tort context. Rather than provide an exhaustive discussion of these defenses, the objective here is to highlight some of the most critical and vexing issues that toxic tort litigants are likely to encounter. As those with even a cursory familiarity with this area realize, the law here can be complicated, contradictory, and confusing (even confused) and will often vary in important ways from state to state. It is essential, therefore, to delve into the law of the specific jurisdiction in question, anticipating that clear answers are not always to be found.

Common Toxic Tort Defenses
Statutes of Limitation

Given the often lengthy period of time that may take place between the release of or exposure to a toxic substance and any resulting damage or injury, statutes of limitation frequently play an important role in defending toxic tort cases. Simply stated, statutes of

---

The authors wish to thank Emily Shingler, a former associate at King & Spalding LLP and a current Assistant U.S. Attorney for the Northern District of Georgia, and Elizabeth Lucente, an associate with King & Spalding LLP, for their helpful research assistance.

limitation require claimants to file suit within a certain period of time following either the occurrence of the tortious conduct or the occurrence of the harm caused by that conduct. In the toxic tort context, the applicable limitations period can vary widely but typically falls between one to six years, depending on the particular claim raised and which state's law applies.

Determining the point at which a claim begins to "accrue" is critical to any statute of limitations defense. Under the traditional rule, the limitations period commences at the point when the defendant committed the tortious act or the act caused harm to the claimant. In the toxic tort context, therefore, the claims would accrue on the day that the claimant was exposed to the toxin or the day the incident causing the harm occurred. Importantly, the statutory period under this "exposure or occurrence" rule would accrue regardless of whether the claimant knew or should have known of her injury. Thus, if a person's illness or injury did not manifest for several years following the exposure or occurrence in question, or if the contamination of her property was not readily apparent, her cause of action may be time-barred before she even becomes aware of it. As a result, most jurisdictions have crafted exceptions to the traditional exposure or occurrence rule, either through judicial decisionmaking or legislation.[1]

The Discovery Rule

For example, most, though not all, jurisdictions have adopted some version of the "discovery rule."[2] Under this rule, plaintiffs will not be considered "injured," and thus their tort claims will not begin to accrue, until "the accumulated effects of the deleterious substance manifest themselves."[3] Though the exact wording varies by jurisdiction, this discovery rule generally provides that a cause of action will accrue at the time the plaintiff discovered or through the exercise of reasonable diligence should have discovered that she may have a basis for an actionable claim. The policy reasons generally advanced in support of this rule are that "it is inequitable to bar someone who has no idea he has been harmed from seeking redress,"[4] and that the discovery rule better comports with the purposes of the

---

1. *See, e.g.*, Syms v. Olin Corp., 408 F.3d 95, 109–10 (2d Cir. 2005) (discussing under New York law the traditional rule and the evolution that led to the adoption of the current rule in toxic tort cases); Jensen v. Gen. Elec. Co., 623 N.E.2d 547, 549–53 (N.Y. 1993) (same); Griffin v. Unocal Corp., 990 So. 2d 291, 293, 299–314 (Ala. 2008) (discussing traditional exposure rule in Alabama and reasons for adopting the discovery rule going forward).
2. Georgia, for example, has adopted the discovery rule in the personal injury context but does not apply the discovery rule to property damage claims. Corp. of Mercer Univ. v. Nat'l Gypsum Co., 368 S.E.2d 732, 733 (Ga. 1988) (stating that the discovery rule applies only to cases involving bodily injury that develops over time and not to property damage claims); *see also* Mitchell v. Contractors Specialty Supply, Inc., 544 S.E.2d 533, 534 (Ga. Ct. App. 2001); Andel v. Getz Servs., Inc., 399 S.E.2d 226, 228 (Ga. Ct. App. 1990). As another example, the Alabama Supreme Court did not adopt the discovery rule until 2008 and does not apply the rule retroactively. *Griffin*, 990 So. 2d at 293.
3. Urie v. Thompson, 337 U.S. 163, 170 (1949) (citations omitted) (internal quotation marks omitted).
4. O'Connor v. Boeing N. Am., Inc., 311 F.3d 1139, 1147 (9th Cir. 2002) (citations omitted) (internal quotation marks omitted).

statute of limitations, which requires that claims be brought "within a specified period of time *after* notice of the invasion of legal rights."[5]

This is not to say, however, that the discovery rule will apply in all toxic tort cases. To the contrary, the discovery rule typically applies only where the injury is latent or not otherwise readily discernible.[6] For purposes of accrual, however, the claimant typically need only be "apprised of the general nature of the injury. Lack of knowledge of the injury's permanence, extent, and ramifications does not toll the statute."[7] Moreover, the discovery rule is an objective standard, meaning that the statute of limitations begins to run when a reasonably diligent person would have been put sufficiently on notice.[8] Once that occurs, the claimant must investigate her claim, consult any experts, obtain legal counsel, and file a claim within the applicable limitations period.[9] A claimant's lack of actual subjective knowledge by itself will not suffice to toll the limitations period.

Jurisdictions differ widely as to what exactly must be discovered to trigger accrual under the discovery rule. In some states, the discovery of the injury, in and of itself, is enough to begin the limitations clock.[10] In *Angle v. Koppers, Inc.*, for example, the Mississippi Supreme Court affirmed the trial court's grant of summary judgment for the defendant where the property owner claimed she had been injured by exposure to harmful levels of toxic chemicals released from railroad tank cars and a nearby wood-treatment facility.[11] Importantly, the plaintiff's injuries had all been diagnosed well before the three-year statute of limitations. The court accordingly upheld the dismissal of the plaintiff's claims,

---

5. *Urie*, 337 U.S. at 170 (emphasis added).
6. *See, e.g.*, Asher v. Unarco Material Handling, Inc., 596 F.3d 313, 321 (6th Cir. 2010) ("Kentucky law is clear that the new plaintiffs may invoke the discovery rule only if their injuries were latent."); Cannon v. United States, 338 F.3d 1183, 1190 (10th Cir. 2003) (holding in case involving the Federal Tort Claims Act that the discovery rule "applies only in the 'exceptional case' where a reasonably diligent plaintiff could not immediately know of the injury and its cause" (quoting Plaza Speedway Inc. v. United States, 311 F.3d 1262, 1268 (10th Cir. 2002))); Schneider Nat'l Carriers, Inc. v. Bates, 147 S.W.3d 264, 279 (Tex. 2004) (recognizing "the discovery rule as 'a very limited exception' to accrual when an injury is both inherently undiscoverable and objectively verifiable"); Manhattanville Coll. v. James John Romeo Consulting Eng'r, P.C., 774 N.Y.S.2d 542, 546 (N.Y. App. Div. 2004) (holding that property damage caused by carbon monoxide was not latent and thus did not trigger the toxic tort discovery rule under New York law). *But see* Jones v. Chemetron Corp., 212 F.3d 199, 206 (3d Cir. 2000) (finding that under Ohio law, the discovery rule may apply even when the plaintiff's injuries are not latent where the plaintiff lacks knowledge of causation, *i.e.*, plaintiff has not discovered the causal relationship between defendant's actions and her injuries).
7. *Cannon*, 338 F.3d at 1190 (quoting Gustavson v. United States, 655 F.2d 1034, 1036 (10th Cir. 1981)); *see also Asher*, 596 F.3d at 322 (holding under Kentucky law that "the statute of limitations begins to run on the date the injury is inflicted even where the injury is slight initially and its full extent is not known until years later").
8. *See, e.g.*, Arvayo v. United States, 766 F.2d 1416, 1422 (10th Cir. 1985) (federal law); *Plaza Speedway*, 311 F.3d at 1271 (federal law).
9. *See* United States v. Kubrick, 444 U.S. 111, 123–24 (1979); *Plaza Speedway*, 311 F.3d at 1271.
10. *See, e.g.*, Cooper Indus., LLC v. City of South Bend, 899 N.E.2d 1274, 1280 (Ind. 2009) ("Under Indiana's discovery rule, a cause of action accrues, and the limitation period begins to run, when a claimant knows or in the exercise of ordinary diligence should have known of the injury.").
11. 42 So. 3d 1, 7 (Miss. 2010).

explaining that "[n]ot all discovery rules are created equal," and that, under Mississippi law, claims involving latent injury or disease accrue "upon discovery of the injury, *not discovery of the injury and its cause*."[12]

By contrast, in other states, the discovery rule is tied not only to notice of the injury, but also to notice of its cause. In these jurisdictions, the statute of limitations begins to run when the "plaintiff knows, or reasonably should know, (1) that he has been injured, and (2) that his injury has been caused by another party's conduct."[13] This has also been the approach taken by federal courts when applying the discovery rule to federal tort claims.[14] By way of illustration, in *Plaza Speedway Inc. v. United States*, the U.S. Court of Appeals for the Tenth Circuit found that the Army had been contaminating the soil and groundwater at its airfield for many years, long before plaintiffs acquired the neighboring property.[15] The plaintiffs' injury thus first occurred as soon as "they took title to the polluted land." The court, however, tolled the accrual date under the discovery rule because the plaintiffs, though aware that the Army "was doing something on its property with some substances," did not know "the toxic effect of the conduct."[16] But this only tolled the date of accrual until the point the plaintiffs knew about the contamination on their own property (having been so informed by the state's geologist) and the likely cause of that contamination (activities on the neighboring Army base). Because the plaintiffs failed to bring their claims within the two-year limitations period, even after taking into account the discovery rule, the court found that the plaintiffs' claims were barred.[17]

In other jurisdictions, discovery of the injury, its cause, and the party or parties responsible are required to start the statute of limitations clock. Under Kentucky law, for example, the statute of limitations does not begin to run until the claimant both knows that she has been wronged and "by whom the wrong has been committed."[18] Other jurisdictions also require that the claimant discover the tortious nature of the defendant's conduct. Thus,

---

12. *Id.* (emphasis in original) (quoting Caves v. Yarbrough, 991 So. 2d 142, 154–55 (Miss. 2008)); *see also* Lincoln Elec. Co. v. McLemore, 54 So. 3d 833, 838 (Miss. 2010) ("[K]nowledge of the cause of an injury is irrelevant to the analysis."); Barnes v. Koppers, Inc., 534 F.3d 357, 360 (5th Cir. 2008) (noting the limited scope of Mississippi's latent discovery statute).
13. Mest v. Cabot Corp., 449 F.3d 502, 510 (3d Cir. 2006) (applying Pennsylvania law); *see also* Jones v. Chemetron Corp., 212 F.3d 199, 205–06 (3d Cir. 2000) (applying Ohio law); Vector-Springfield Props., Ltd. v. Cent. Ill. Light Co., 108 F.3d 806, 809 (7th Cir. 1997) (applying Illinois law).
14. *See, e.g.*, Avila v. Willits Envtl. Remediation Trust, 633 F.3d 828, 841 (9th Cir. 2011); Granfield v. CSX Transp., Inc., 597 F.3d 474, 482 (1st Cir. 2010); Cannon v. United States, 338 F.3d 1183, 1190, 1192 (10th Cir. 2003); Townley v. Norfolk & W. Ry. Co., 887 F.2d 498, 501 (4th Cir. 1989); Kichline v. Consol. Rail Corp., 800 F.2d 356, 358 (3d Cir. 1986).
15. 311 F.3d 1262, 1268 (10th Cir. 2002).
16. *Id.*
17. *Id.* at 1270–71; *see also* Bayless v. United States, No. 2:09CV495DAK, 2012 WL 1802390, at *3, *7, *20 (D. Utah May 17, 2012) (holding that the plaintiff's personal injury claim accrued no later than the point at which she stated she was "pretty sure" that the Army's testing and destruction of chemical or biological weapons of were a "potential cause of her neurological symptoms").
18. Michals v. Baxter Healthcare Corp., 289 F.3d 402, 406 (6th Cir. 2002).

under California law, "the accrual date of a cause of action is delayed until the plaintiff is aware of her injury and its negligent cause."[19]

Even these variations of the discovery rule, however, fail to fully account for the range of potential issues over which there can be disagreement. Questions also arise, for example, as to the degree of knowledge or understanding required to trigger accrual. In many states, as in the federal courts, the discovery rule is stated in terms of what the claimant "knew or should have known." In other states, however, a "suspicion" can be enough to trigger accrual and a claimant's duty to investigate or risk losing a claim.[20] However, while jurisdictions may vary as to what constitutes sufficient notice, courts generally are in agreement that notice will trigger a duty on the part of the prospective plaintiff to inquire further and take appropriate legal action within the limitations period.

Identifying what constitutes the required injury and when it arises can also be a point of dispute.[21] In *Lincoln Electric Co. v. McLemore*, the Mississippi Supreme Court reversed a $1,855,000 jury verdict in favor of a welder claiming that exposure to welding fumes caused his alleged manganism, a neurological disease caused by high exposure to manganese.[22] In overturning the verdict, the Mississippi Supreme Court held that the statute of limitations began to run on the date that the welder was informed by his doctor that he had a different neurological injury (Parkinsonism) and that the injury might have been related to welding.[23]

---

19. Jolly v. Eli Lilly & Co., 751 P.2d 923, 926–27 (Cal. 1988); *see also* Clark v. Baxter Healthcare Corp., 100 Cal. Rptr. 2d 223, 227 (Cal. Ct. App. 2000) ("Under the discovery rule, the statute of limitations begins to run when the plaintiff suspects or should suspect that her injury was caused by wrongdoing, that someone has done something wrong to her." (emphasis omitted)). *But see* United States v. Kubrick, 444 U.S. 111, 122 (1979) (rejecting under federal law the notion that for statute of limitations purposes, a plaintiff's "ignorance of his legal rights" should receive identical treatment to his "ignorance of the fact of his injury or its cause"); Dennis v. ICL, Inc., 957 F. Supp. 376, 379 (D. Conn. 1997) (holding that the focus is on the plaintiff's knowledge of facts, not the discovery of applicable legal theories).
20. O'Connor v. Boeing N. Am., Inc., 311 F.3d 1139, 1147 (9th Cir. 2002) ("Under California law, a plaintiff discovers a claim when the plaintiff 'suspects or should suspect that her injury was caused by wrongdoing.'" (quoting Jolly v. Eli Lilly & Co., 751 P.2d 923, 927 (Cal. 1988))); *see also id.* at 1148 (noting that "[s]everal federal courts have distinguished the federal knowledge standard from a standard that commences a limitations period when a plaintiff merely suspects the cause of injury, reasoning that the federal standard requires more than suspicion alone"); Avila v. Willits Envtl. Remediation Trust, 633 F.3d 828, 842–43 (9th Cir. 2011) (discussing growing publicity related to contamination from a chrome plating facility and the point at which "people with a reasonable degree of awareness should have known that contamination from [the defendant's facility] was a serious health concern and made further inquiry").
21. *See, e.g.*, Vector-Springfield Props., Ltd. v. Cent. Ill. Light Co., 108 F.3d 806, 810 n.3 (7th Cir. 1997) (noting that under Illinois law, knowledge of "possible" injury is sufficient to trigger the limitations period); Xavier v. Philip Morris USA Inc., 787 F. Supp. 2d 1075, 1087 (N.D. Cal. 2011) (holding that the limitations period did not begin to run until the smokers knew or should have known that smoking Marlboro cigarettes significantly increased their risk of lung cancer when compared to the risk of smoking safer cigarettes that the defendant could have, but chose not to, manufacture); Harrison v. Digital Equip. Corp., 465 S.E.2d 494, 495 (Ga. Ct. App. 1995) (holding that a specific diagnosis of an injury will start the statute of limitations but is not necessary).
22. 54 So. 3d 833, 833–34 (Miss. 2010).
23. *Id.* at 838.

Identifying the requisite injury can be further complicated when there may be separate injuries caused by the same exposure or incident that manifest themselves at different times.[24] The analysis can also vary depending on whether the injury complained of is the increased risk of disease as opposed to the actual occurrence of disease.[25]

In short, there is considerable variation in the specific rules and approaches to the discovery rule. These issues and considerations are often interrelated so that a court's more stringent view on one question may make it more likely to accept a more lenient approach on a related question (or vice versa) in an effort to balance competing interests. As a result, it is critical to fully investigate the legal nuances of the particular jurisdiction at issue.

CERCLA's Discovery Rule

In an attempt to eliminate some of this variability and to provide further protection for potential litigants, Congress adopted the Superfund Amendments and Reauthorization Act of 1986 (SARA)[26] to amend the Comprehensive Environmental Response, Compensation, and Liability Act (CERCLA)[27] and provide a federal discovery rule in certain types of personal injury and property damage cases. As amended, CERCLA now provides:

> In the case of any action brought under State law for personal injury, or property damages, which are caused or contributed to by exposure to any hazardous substance, or pollutant or contaminant, released into the environment from a facility, if the applicable limitations period for such action (as specified in the State statute of limitations or under common law) provides a commencement date which is earlier than the federally required commencement date, such period shall commence at the federally required commencement date in lieu of the date specified in such State statute.[28]

---

24. *See, e.g.*, Snyman v. W.A. Baum Co., Inc., 360 F. App'x 251, 253 n.1 (2d Cir. 2010) (discussing the "open" status of New York's two-injury rule, which provides that "manifestations of injuries in toxic tort cases that do not become apparent until many years of exposure may be actionable if they are separate and distinct from an earlier medical problem caused by the same problem, even if the statute of limitations on the previous injury has expired" (citations omitted) (internal quotation marks omitted)); Mest v. Cabot Corp., 449 F.3d 502, 514 (3d Cir. 2006) (stating that "a misdiagnosis does not relieve a patient of all responsibility in pursuing the cause of her symptoms, and continued reliance on a misdiagnosis in the face of contrary evidence may be unreasonable"); Debiec v. Cabot Corp., 352 F.3d 117, 132 (3d Cir. 2003) (holding that the statute of limitations may be tolled where a doctor ruled out the actual disease that would have implicated the defendant); Anderson v. Sybron Corp., 353 S.E.2d 816, 817–18 (Ga. Ct. App. 1983) (holding that the plaintiffs' knowledge that they suffered certain physical injuries as a result of exposure to ethylene oxide (ETO) did not bar claims for other injuries when plaintiffs did not know other injuries were caused by exposure to ETO).
25. Ball v. Union Carbide Corp., 385 F.3d 713, 723 (6th Cir. 2004) (explaining that when the injury claimed is increased risk of disease, the accrual threshold is lower).
26. Pub. L. No. 99-499, 100 Stat. 1613 (1986).
27. 42 U.S.C. §§ 9601–9675.
28. *Id.* § 9658(a)(1).

Under this provision, certain types of state law tort claims for personal injury and property damage will be tolled at least until the "federally required commencement date." If state law provides for a later accrual date, that later date would still apply.

CERCLA defines the term "federally required commencement date" to mean "the date the plaintiff knew (or reasonably should have known) that the personal injury or property damages referred to in subsection (a)(1) of this section were caused or contributed to by the hazardous substance or pollutant or contaminant concerned."[29] Thus, at least when the requirements of this provision are satisfied, the applicable limitations period will not begin to run "until the date 'that [a plaintiff] knows or reasonably should have known' of both the existence and the cause of the injury."[30] CERCLA thus purports to preempt state law and impose a national discovery rule, at least for certain types of toxic tort cases.[31] Because claimants who invoke this discovery rule are asserting federal preemption of state law, they necessarily bear the burden of persuasion.[32]

In evaluating the scope and application of CERCLA's discovery rule, courts have taken three different approaches. At least one court has held that CERCLA's discovery rule applies only to state tort claims "where there is an underlying CERCLA action providing for cleanup and remedial activities."[33] The court there reasoned that the discovery rule must be read in light of CERCLA as a whole, and that the statute does not suggest a broad application to all toxic tort cases. Rather, the court found that the wording of CERCLA's discovery rule indicates that it is "limited to application in the situation where a state cause of action exists in conjunction with a CERCLA cause of action."[34]

At the other extreme, some courts have found that CERCLA's discovery rule ought to be applied broadly to state toxic tort claims. The U.S. Court of Appeals for the Eleventh Circuit, for example, has stated that CERCLA provides for a "federally mandated 'discovery rule' for environmental torts brought under state law."[35] The court explained that the refusal to recognize this discovery rule "would run counter to the purpose of the relevant portions of CERCLA and its amendments, which was to deal with the inadequacies of many state tort systems regarding the delayed discovery of the effect of a release of a toxic substance."[36] As such, the Eleventh Circuit applied the discovery rule without a detailed consideration of what is required to bring a cause of action under CERCLA.

---

29. *Id.* § 9658(b)(4)(A).
30. Avila v. Willits Envtl. Remediation Trust, 633 F.3d 828, 841 (9th Cir. 2001) (quoting O'Connor v. Boeing N. Am., Inc., 311 F.3d 1139, 1147–48 (9th Cir. 2002)).
31. *See* Tucker v. Southern Wood Piedmont Co., 28 F.3d 1089, 1091–93 (11th Cir. 1994).
32. Barnes v. Koppers, Inc., 534 F.3d 357, 365 (5th Cir. 2008).
33. Knox v. AC&S, Inc., 690 F. Supp. 752, 757 (S.D. Ind. 1998).
34. *Id.* at 758. *But see O'Connor*, 311 F.3d at 1149 & n.5 (explicitly rejecting the reasoning in *Knox*, explaining that "Section 9658 applies to actions that assert state law claims without an accompanying CERCLA claim").
35. *Tucker*, 28 F.3d at 1091.
36. *Id.* at 1093.

An increasing number of courts have adopted a middle view, holding that CERCLA's discovery rule applies only when a plaintiff can show that the conditions for a CERCLA cleanup have been met. The U.S. Court of Appeals for the Fifth Circuit has explained that CERCLA's discovery rule includes several terms that are given precise, technical meanings, such as "environment," "facility," "release," and "hazardous substance."[37] "[B]ecause § 9658 is imbued with the terminology of CERCLA, and because we are to presume, absent manifest Congressional intent, that Congress did not intend broad preemption in the traditional field of state tort remedies, we conclude that § 9658 operates only where the conditions for CERCLA cleanup are satisfied."[38] Thus, to successfully invoke the CERCLA discovery rule, a claimant "must prove that her claims arose from a 'release' of 'hazardous substances' into the 'environment,' as well as other case-specific preconditions establishing that the defendant's 'facility' falls within CERCLA."[39] Applying this test, the Fifth Circuit found that the plaintiff in the case before it failed to establish that the defendant's emissions gave rise to CERCLA coverage and accordingly rejected application of CERCLA's discovery rule.[40]

Aside from the general scope and application of the statute, defendants have raised a number of other arguments in an effort to defeat application of CERCLA's discovery rule. Some have argued, for example, that the rule, which applies to a plaintiff's personal injury and property damage claims, should not apply to survival and wrongful death actions.[41] Defendants have also sought to challenge CERCLA's discovery rule on constitutional grounds under the Tenth Amendment and the Commerce Clause.[42] Despite the difficulties typically encountered in mounting these types of constitutional challenges, some courts have given indications of a willingness to entertain such an argument. For example, one panel of the U.S. Court of Appeals for the Second Circuit initially characterized Section 9658 as having "questionable constitutionality."[43] Subsequently, however, the Second

---

37. *Barnes*, 534 F.3d at 363; *see also* 42 U.S.C. § 9601 (defining these and numerous other terms).
38. *Barnes*, 534 F.3d at 365.
39. *Id.*
40. *Id.* at 359; *see also* C.L. Ritter Lumber Co. v. Consolidation Coal Co., No. 1:11cv00019, 2011 WL 3793320, at *18–20 (W.D. Va. Aug. 25, 2011) (applying CERCLA discovery rule where statutory elements of a CERCLA claim were satisfied); Angle v. Koppers, Inc., 42 So. 3d 1, 8 (Miss. 2010) (holding that to invoke CERCLA's discovery rule, a claimant must show: "(1) property damage and/or personal injury (2) caused or contributed to by (3) a hazardous substance or pollutant or contaminant (4) released (5) into the environment (6) from a facility").
41. *See* Lee v. CSX Transp., Inc., 958 So. 2d 578, 583–84 (Fl. Ct. App. 2007) (rejecting application of the discovery rule in wrongful death case). *But see* Freier v. Westinghouse Elec. Corp., 303 F.3d 176, 182 (2d Cir. 2002) (holding that CERCLA's discovery rule applies to state law survivor and wrongful death claims).
42. *See, e.g., Angle*, 42 So. 3d at 4 (noting the constitutionality argument raised by counsel but ruling on other grounds).
43. ABB Indus. Sys., Inc. v. Prime Tech., Inc., 120 F.3d 351, 360 n.5 (2d Cir. 1997).

Circuit explicitly considered and rejected that contention.[44] The Alabama Supreme Court also expressed reservations about the provision's constitutionality:

> The potential ability of CERCLA's discovery rule to retroactively revive state-law-based claims for harm to persons or property from hazardous waste, which claims had previously expired under otherwise controlling state statutes of limitations, would seem to create several federalism issues as state government and federal government clash over which has the prerogative to control various facets of environmental policy. The rebirth of federalism in *United States v. Lopez*, [514 U.S. 549 (1995)], may call into question the constitutionality of § 9658.[45]

To date, however, the few courts formally ruling on the issue have found in favor of the provision's constitutionality.[46]

Continuing Torts

In addition to the discovery rule, many jurisdictions, though again not all,[47] have invoked the doctrine of "continuing" torts to extend or otherwise avoid the limitations period.[48] The practical significance of the continuing tort doctrine is that for purposes of the statute of limitations, a claim will not begin to accrue until the tortious conduct has ceased. What qualifies as a continuing tort, however, is often far from clear and varies considerably from state to state, and sometimes even within the same state.[49]

Generally speaking, courts have applied three different tests[50] in deciding whether a toxic tort is continuing: (1) whether the activity or conduct that caused the harm or nuisance is ongoing (i.e., whether the emitting plant is still operating or the pipeline is still

---

44. *Freier*, 303 F.3d at 203–05 (rejecting constitutional challenges under the Tenth Amendment and the Commerce Clause).
45. Becton v. Rhone-Poulenc, Inc., 706 So. 2d 1134, 1142 (Ala. 1997) (citations omitted).
46. *Freier*, 303 F.3d at 203–05; Bolin v. Cessna Aircraft Co., 759 F. Supp. 692, 706–08 (N.D. Kan. 1991).
47. *See, e.g.*, Syms v. Olin Corp., 408 F.3d 95, 110 (2d Cir. 2005) (explaining that the New York legislature when adopting the discovery rule in latent injury cases chose to eliminate the continuing tort doctrine); Highland Indus. Park, Inc. v. BEI Def. Sys. Co., 357 F.3d 794, 797 (8th Cir. 2004) (holding that "the continuing-tort theory is not recognized in Arkansas").
48. Moreover, in some states, the discovery rule applies only in cases involving continuous torts. *See, e.g.*, M.H.D. v. Westminster Sch., 172 F.3d 797, 804–05 (11th Cir. 1999) (holding that "in Georgia the discovery rule only applies to cases involving 'continuous torts,' where the plaintiff's injury developed from prolonged exposure to the defendant's tortious conduct").
49. *See, e.g.*, Corp. of Mercer Univ. v. Nat'l Gypsum Co., 368 S.E.2d 732, 733 (Ga. 1988) ("The continuing tort theory expressed in *Everhart v. Rich's, Inc.*, 229 Ga. 798, 194 S.E.2d 425 (1972), is limited to cases in which personal injury is involved. It is not applicable to cases which involve only property damage."); Smith v. Branch, 487 S.E.2d 35, 38 (Ga. Ct. App. 1997) (distinguishing *Mercer* on grounds that it "did not involve hidden contamination").
50. *See* Burley v. Burlington N. & Santa Fe Ry. Co., 273 P.3d 825, 829 (Mont. 2012) (discussing each of these tests and the cases supporting them and further discussing the issues of the stabilization, migration, and abatability of contamination as they related to continuing torts).

leaking);[51] (2) whether the contamination is migrating;[52] and (3) whether the contamination remains present on plaintiff's property.[53] With a few exceptions, the third test largely has been disavowed by the courts.[54]

---

51. *See, e.g.*, State ex rel. Doner v. Zody, 958 N.E.2d 1235, 1244–45 (Ohio 2011) (quoting Sexton v. City of Mason, 883 N.E.2d 1013, 1020–21 (Ohio 2008) (holding that a continuing trespass occurs when there is some continuing or ongoing tortious activity attributable to the defendant)); Hogg v. Chevron USA, Inc., 45 So. 3d 991, 1006 (La. 2010) (holding that when "the operating cause of the injury—the damage-causing conduct—is not continuing, there is no continuing tort"); Village of Milford v. K-H Holding Corp., 390 F.3d 926, 933 (6th Cir. 2004) (holding under Michigan law that the migration of existing contamination is not a continuing tort); Cannon v. United States, 338 F.3d 1183, 1193 (10th Cir. 2003) ("Under Utah law, a continuous tort requires recurring tortious . . . *conduct* and is not established by the continuation of *harm* caused by previous but terminated tortious . . . conduct." (emphasis in original) (citations omitted) (internal quotation marks omitted)).

52. *See, e.g.*, Burley, 273 P.3d at 844 (holding that "migrating pollution" may constitute a continuing nuisance); Taygeta Corp. v. Varian Assocs., Inc., 763 N.E.2d 1053, 1065 (Mass. 2002) (finding a continuing nuisance "based on the continuing seepage of pollutants that is still occurring within the statute of limitations," even though the defendant's operations had long since ceased); *Smith*, 487 S.E.2d at 38 ("The cause of action for causing a continuing nuisance is limited to situations where contamination continues to spread.").

53. *See, e.g.*, Hoery v. United States, 64 P.3d 214, 220, 222 (Colo. 2003) (holding that "Colorado law recognizes the concepts of continuing trespass and nuisance for those property invasions where a defendant fails to *stop or remove* continuing, harmful physical conditions that are wrongfully placed on a plaintiff's land," and further specifying that the failure to remove the existing pollution, by itself, "constitutes a continuing property invasion for the entire time the contamination remains" (emphasis added)); Interfaith Cmty. Org. v. Honeywell Int'l, Inc., 263 F. Supp. 2d 796, 857 (D.N.J. 2003) (finding under New Jersey law that contamination would present a continuing tort until excavated and removed).

54. *See Burley*, 273 P.3d at 829 (noting that the Colorado Supreme Court in *Hoery* took the doctrine of continuing torts "to an extreme by tolling the statute of limitations until every drop of pollution has been removed from a party's property"); Marin v. Exxon Mobil Corp., 48 So. 3d 234, 254 (La. 2010) ("Simply because the contaminants may have continued to dissolve into, or move with, the groundwater with the passage of time does not turn this into a continuing tort."); Kling Realty Co., Inc. v. Chevron USA, Inc., 575 F.3d 510, 519 (5th Cir. 2009) (failure to clean up contamination of agricultural property was not a continuing tort under Louisiana law); Sexton v. City of Mason, 883 N.E.2d 1013, 1020–21 (Ohio 2008) (rejecting view that the mere existence of continuing damage constitutes a continuing tort under Ohio law); MacBride v. Pishvaian, 937 A.2d 233, 240 (Md. 2007) (holding that continuing torts require "continuing unlawful acts, . . . not merely the continuing effects of a single earlier act"); Alston v. Hormel Foods, Corp., 730 N.W.2d 376, 381 (Neb. 2007) (holding that the "'continuing tort doctrine' requires that a tortious act—not simply the continuing ill effects of prior tortious acts—fall within the limitation period," and that "the necessary tortious act [cannot] merely be the failure to right a wrong committed outside the statute of limitations"); Highland Indus. Park, Inc. v. BEI Def. Sys. Co., 357 F.3d 794, 797 (8th Cir. 2004) (stating that the plaintiff's contention that the statute of limitations should be tolled until the defendant's contamination is actually removed "makes no sense"); Taygeta Corp. v. Varian Assocs., Inc., 763 N.E.2d 1053, 1065 (Mass. 2002) (holding that "a continuing trespass or nuisance must be based on recurring tortious or unlawful conduct" and not merely "the continuation of harm caused by previous but terminated tortious or unlawful conduct"); Breiggar Props., L.C. v. H.E. Davis & Sons, Inc., 52 P.3d 1133, 1135–37 (Utah 2002) (holding that continued existence of waste on the plaintiff's property was irrelevant to question of continuing trespass; rather, in determining whether a trespass is continuing, Utah law looks "solely to the *act* constituting the trespass, and not to the *harm* resulting from the act" (emphasis in original)); Fed. Deposit Ins. Corp. v. Laidlaw Transit, Inc., 21 P.3d 344, 356 (Alaska 2001) (rejecting application of continuous tort doctrine where defendants were "not exacerbating the contamination that they allegedly caused during the late 1980s," explaining that "since they have lost their connection to the land, they cannot be characterized as maintaining an ongoing nuisance"); Suarez v. City of Tampa, 987 So. 2d 681, 686 (Fla. Ct. App. 2008) (holding that a "continuing tort is 'established by continual tortious *acts*, not by continual harmful effects from an original, completed act.'" (quoting Horvath v. Delida, 540 N.W.2d 760, 763 (Mich. Ct. App. 1995))); Davis Bros.,

Though these tests can be simply stated, their actual meaning in practical terms often is not at all obvious or explained. For example, under the first test, the types of activities that may contribute to a nuisance often change substantially over time. A factory that may have emitted significant amounts of a particular contaminant in the past may have radically curtailed those emissions after phasing in new technology, but it may continue to emit that same substance at lower, permissible, and even permitted, levels. Should this count as a continuing nuisance? Or what about a plant that sporadically but not infrequently emits a contaminant at levels above those permissible? Will a court consider each exceedance a separate tort or a single "continuing" one? Countless other real-world examples could be cited here.

The second test—based on determining whether contamination is migrating—has also proven difficult to apply in practice. Determining whether contamination is "moving" in any legally relevant sense is often far from clear, both as a matter of fact and law. After all, contamination in the environment is always moving, even if only on a microscopic level.

As a further complication, some courts conflate the concepts of continuing nuisance, abatement of a nuisance, temporary nuisance, and permanent nuisance as those concepts apply to the applicable statute of limitations and to the damages that may be recoverable.[55] In some states, temporary nuisance and continuing nuisance are synonymous and used interchangeably, even though conceptually they deal with different topics.[56] Similarly, abatability has relevance to the statute of limitations issue in some states,[57] while in others it is a concept that relates primarily to the allowable damages.[58] Often as not, the case law is unclear and inconsistent, providing fertile ground for advocacy.

Damages Period

Even when plaintiffs can establish that the underlying tort is continuing and not barred by the statute of limitations, a court must still address the question of what the relevant

---

Inc. v. Thornton Oil Co., 12 F. Supp. 2d 1333, 1338 (M.D. Ga. 1998) (stating that Georgia courts have "flatly rejected" the contention that "the continued existence of contamination constitutes a continuing trespass or nuisance").

55. *See* Beatty v. Wash. Metro. Area Transit Auth., 860 F.2d 1117, 1125 (D.C. Cir. 1988) (noting that "a nuisance may be classified as 'permanent' for the purpose of assessing damages, and as 'continuing' for statute of limitations purposes" (citing Harrisonville v. W.S. Dickey Clay Mfg. Co., 289 U.S. 334 (1933) (awarding permanent measure of damages in nuisance case involving the discharge of pollutants into a stream, but finding the nuisance not permanent for statute of limitations purposes))); Walker Drug Co. v. La Sal Oil Co., 972 P.2d 1238, 1246 n.9 (Utah 1998) (explaining that "[w]hether [a] trespass . . . is continuous or permanent is a different question from whether the resulting injury . . . is temporary or permanent"; "[a] continuing trespass . . . may cause either a permanent or a temporary injury"); *see also Burley*, 273 P.3d at 829–44 (attempting to unravel the "particularly impenetrable" legal jungle of permanent, temporary, continuing, and abatable nuisances).
56. *See, e.g.,* West Virginia *ex rel.* Smith v. Kermit Lumber & Pressure Treating Co., 488 S.E.2d 901, 923 n.26 (W. Va. 1997).
57. *See* Mangini v. Aerojet-Gen. Corp., 912 P.2d 1220, 1226–29 (Cal. 1996); Hedgepath v. AT&T Co., 559 S.E.2d 327, 337 (S.C. Ct. App. 2001).
58. *See* Schneider Nat'l Carriers, Inc. v. Bates, 147 S.W.3d 264, 283–88 (Tex. 2004).

damages period should be. This issue can have a substantial effect on the scope of any claim and the potential damages that may be recovered.[59] Plaintiffs generally advocate for application of the "pure" continuing tort theory,[60] under which a continuing tort tolls the statute of limitations such that plaintiffs can sue for the full extent of the harm caused by the contamination over time, even when that harm may stretch back decades.[61] Defendants, on the other hand, typically seek to apply a "modified" version of the continuing tort theory,[62] maintaining that while a continuing nuisance may toll the statute of limitations, a plaintiff may recover only those new and additional damages that occurred during the limitations period.[63] Thus, for example, in those situations where a nuisance

---

59. Alston v. Hormel Foods Corp., 730 N.W.2d 376, 382–83 (Neb. 2007) ("Thus, some courts hold that where a tort is 'continuing,' the plaintiff can reach back to the beginning even if it lies outside the statutory limitations period. But other courts have concluded, in various contexts, that even if claims based on tortious conduct outside the statutory limitations period are time barred, claims based on subsequent tortious activity are not." (footnote omitted)).

60. White v. Mercury Marine, Div. of Brunswick, Inc., 129 F.3d 1428, 1430 (11th Cir. 1997) ("Under the pure version of the continuing tort theory, a cause of action for any of the damages a plaintiff has suffered does not 'accrue' until the defendant's tortious conduct ceases. Under the pure continuing tort theory, a plaintiff may recover for all the harm he has suffered, not just that suffered during the limitations period." (citations omitted)); accord Alston, 730 N.W.2d at 382.

61. See, e.g., Heard v. Sheahan, 253 F.3d 316, 319 (7th Cir. 2001) (stating that for continuing violations, "a plaintiff can reach back to its beginning even if that beginning lies outside the statutory limitations period"); Page v. United States, 729 F.2d 818, 821–22 (D.C. Cir. 1984) ("Since usually no single incident in a continuous chain of tortious activity can 'fairly or realistically be identified as the cause of significant harm,' it seems proper to regard the cumulative effect of the conduct as actionable. Moreover, since 'one should not be allowed to acquire a right to continue the tortious conduct,' it follows logically that statutes of limitation should not run prior to its cessation." (internal footnotes omitted)); Taylor v. Meirick, 712 F.2d 1112, 1118–19 (7th Cir. 1983) (allowing damages for the entire period of continuing wrong in the business tort context); Meadows v. Union Carbide Corp., 710 F. Supp. 1163, 1166 (N.D. Ill. 1989) (holding that the failure of chemical manufacturers and suppliers to provide a safe product with adequate warnings was a continuing tort and that the plaintiff's claim thus accrued on the date when he last faced chemical exposure, even though he may have known or should have known earlier that his deteriorating physical condition was or could have been caused by exposure to the defendants' chemicals); Ambling Mgmt. Co. v. Purdy, 640 S.E.2d 620, 625–26 (Ga. Ct. App. 2006) (same).

62. White, 129 F.3d at 1430 (noting that "the modified version of [the continuing tort theory] allows recovery for only that part of the injury the plaintiff suffered during the limitations period"); accord Alston, 730 N.W.2d at 382.

63. See, e.g., Burlington N. & Santa Fe Ry. Co. v. Grant, 505 F.3d 1013, 1029 (10th Cir. 2007) (holding that a plaintiff may recover the cost of remediating contamination that migrated onto the plaintiff's property within the two-year limitations period but not the cost of the prior contamination); Hoery v. United States, 324 F.3d 1220, 1222 (10th Cir. 2003) (holding that recovery in continuing tort case under Colorado law was restricted to damages incurred during limitation period); Nieman v. NLO, Inc., 108 F.3d 1546, 1559 (6th Cir. 1997) (holding that damages in continuing trespass case under Ohio law were limited to those "incurred within the four years prior to filing the lawsuit"); Huffman v. United States, 82 F.3d 703, 705 (6th Cir. 1996) (holding under Kentucky law that while a temporary nuisance claim is not barred by the statute of limitations, "recovery would be limited to damages caused within the limitations period immediately preceding the initiation of the action"); Tucker v. S. Wood Piedmont Co., 28 F.3d 1089, 1091 (11th Cir. 1994) (holding under Georgia law that "the plaintiff in a continuing tort suit can recover for any damages that were suffered within four years prior to the filing of the suit"); Santiago v. Lykes Bros. S.S. Co., 986 F.2d 423, 428 (11th Cir. 1993) ("Under the continuing tort theory, a plaintiff can only recover damages for any increase in injury which occurred within the statutory period of limitations. . . ."); Alston, 730 N.W.2d at 383–84 (holding that "the plaintiff is only barred from recovering those damages that were ascertainable prior to the statutory period preceding

is determined to be continuing because the contamination is continuing to migrate, a plaintiff may recover only those additional damages caused by the migration that took place during the limitations period preceding the filing of the lawsuit. If this is found to be the case, the fact that the nuisance is continuing may prevent outright dismissal; however, the scope of potential damages that may be recovered could be quite limited, unless a plaintiff can show some discrete, additional harm caused during the limitations period.

Although the "vast majority of courts limits recovery to only those damages for injuries (or worsening of existing conditions) that have accrued within the [limitations period],"[64] the manner in which litigants and courts address this issue, as with many aspects of nuisance law, frequently falls short of consistency. Plaintiffs and defendants thus often will find support in the various decisions as to what the relevant damages period ought to be.

Other Tolling Theories

In addition to the discovery rule and the continuing tort doctrine, there is a variety of other legal theories that may be advanced to toll or otherwise extend the statute of limitations.[65] While an extensive discussion of these other tolling devices is beyond the scope of this chapter, a few bear some mention.

Toxic tort litigants, for example, often contend that the statute of limitations should be tolled due to the defendant's fraudulent concealment. The fraudulent concealment doctrine tolls the limitations period when, through fraud, the defendant causes the plaintiff to relax vigilance or deviate from the duty of inquiry.[66] Claimants in toxic tort cases frequently point to statements made by the defendant to the effect that its product, releases, or emissions were safe and did not or could not have caused the harm alleged. To successfully invoke the fraudulent concealment doctrine, however, plaintiffs must not only establish that those statements were false, but also that plaintiffs relied on the statements and that reliance was reasonable. As with the discovery rule, the fraudulent concealment doctrine will not toll the statute of limitations if the plaintiff knew or should have known of his claim despite the defendant's misrepresentations.[67] Further, a defendant's silence, without more, is generally insufficient to invoke the fraudulent concealment doctrine. Rather,

---

the lawsuit"); *see also* Hanover Shoe, Inc. v. United Shoe Mach. Corp., 392 U.S. 481, 502 & n.15 (1968) (holding that a plaintiff in a case involving continuing harm was authorized to seek damages during limitations period).

64. Chatham v. CSX Transp., Inc., 613 So. 2d 341, 345–46 (Ala. 1993).
65. Additional examples of tolling theories adopted by some jurisdictions include, among others, absence from the state; disability due to imprisonment; death of the plaintiff; death of the defendant; equitable estoppel and equitable tolling; refiling of claim previously dismissed without prejudice; natural calamities; and contra non valentem.
66. *See, e.g.*, Mest v. Cabot Corp., 449 F.3d 502, 516 (3d Cir. 2006).
67. *Id.* (citing Bohus v. Beloff, 950 F.2d 919, 925–26 (3d Cir. 1991)); *see also* Ball v. Union Carbide Corp., 385 F.3d 713, 723–24 (6th Cir. 2004) (noting that while governmental secrecy may make it difficult to collect necessary facts, the facility in question was well known to have engaged in nuclear weapons manufacturing resulting in the release of toxic materials that could be hazardous).

"[t]here must be an affirmative and independent act of concealment that would divert or mislead the plaintiff from discovering the injury."[68] Silence itself will usually only give rise to a claim for fraudulent concealment when there is an affirmative duty to disclose, such as where there is a fiduciary relationship between the parties or some similar relationship of trust.[69]

The statute of limitations also may be tolled by certain disabilities, such as age or insanity. As a general rule, the limitations period will not accrue until the disability is lifted, such as when a minor reaches the age of majority. If, therefore, a young child has been exposed to a toxic substance of some sort, the limitations period may not even begin to run for an extended period of time.[70]

Statutes of Repose

Closely related to statutes of limitation, statutes of repose also have been adopted by some states in an effort to limit potential liability. Statutes of repose serve as an absolute bar to potential claims, setting a specific period of time following the date of some event (such as the manufacture, sale, or delivery of a product) after which the defendants will no longer be liable for injuries that they or their products may have caused, regardless of when a legally cognizable injury may have taken place.[71] Statutes of repose are generally based solely on the passage of time and are not based on "concepts of accrual, notice, or discovery—concepts that are applicable to statutes of limitation."[72] Accordingly, the statute of repose can, depending on the circumstances, bar a plaintiff's claim before the applicable limitations period expires or even begins to run. Simply stated, the statute of repose "is not concerned with the plaintiff's diligence; it is concerned with the defendant's peace."[73]

For example, in *Hodge v. Harkey*, several neighboring landowners brought claims against an oil company and a gas station operator for contamination to their properties caused by leaking underground storage tanks.[74] The North Carolina statute of repose provided that "no cause of action shall accrue more than 10 years from the last act or omission of the defendant giving rise to the cause of action."[75] Because the defendants had removed the underground storage tanks before that time, the North Carolina Court of Appeals found that the plaintiffs' tort claims were barred.[76] In so ruling, the court rejected the plaintiffs'

---

68. *Id.* (citing *Bohus*, 950 F.2d at 925).
69. *Id.* (citing Chiarella v. United States, 445 U.S. 222, 227–28 (1980), as well as several other cases).
70. *See, e.g.*, Tate v. Eli Lilly & Co., 522 F. Supp. 1048, 1051 (M.D. Tenn. 1981) (holding that action against DES manufacturer accrued at time of the plaintiff's birth, though the statute was tolled until one year after plaintiff reached age of majority).
71. McDonald v. Sun Oil Co., 548 F.3d 774, 779 (9th Cir. 2008).
72. *See, e.g., Ex parte* Liberty Nat'l Life Ins. Co., 825 So. 2d 758, 763–64 (Ala. 2002).
73. *McDonald*, 548 F.3d at 780 (quoting Underwood Cotton Co. v. Hyundai, 288 F.3d 405, 409 (9th Cir. 2002)).
74. 631 S.E.2d 143 (N.C. Ct. App. 2006).
75. *Id.* at 145; *see also* Wilson v. McLeod Oil Co., 398 S.E.2d 586, 597 (N.C. 1990).
76. *Hodge*, 631 S.E.2d at 146.

argument that the defendants had an "ongoing responsibility for the contamination,"[77] and also rejected the contention that the installation of a replacement well served as the defendants' "last act" as opposed to the removal of the tanks. Finally, the court found that "[t]he fact [that] plaintiffs did not discover that their land was contaminated until after the statute of repose had expired does not extend their time for filing suit."[78]

By way of contrast, in *Jones v. United States*, the plaintiff sued the federal government under the Federal Tort Claims Act, alleging that exposure to chemicals in the drinking water at a Marine base caused her cancer.[79] Interpreting the same statute of repose at issue in *Hodge*, the U.S. District Court for the Eastern District of North Carolina found that the statute did not apply to latent diseases. As a result, the plaintiff was allowed to pursue her claim despite the fact that the defendant's culpable conduct had taken place well outside the statute's ten-year period. The court further found that a contrary reading of the statute would raise serious constitutional questions, noting that "[s]everal states have already found similar statutes of repose unconstitutional under their state right to open courts when they are used to bar suits before a plaintiff could have discovered their illness or injury."[80]

There has been some disagreement in the courts as to whether the CERCLA discovery rule ought to apply to statutes of repose. CERCLA itself refers explicitly and repeatedly to "statutes of limitations," never mentioning statutes of repose.[81] Based on this omission, a number of courts have relied on the statute's plain language in finding that CERCLA's discovery rule does not preempt statutes of repose.[82] Other courts, however, have reached the opposite conclusion.[83] In so ruling, the U.S. Court of Appeals for the Ninth Circuit found that the meaning of "statute of limitation" at the time the CERCLA discovery rule was adopted in 1986 was ambiguous as evidenced by the fact that several cases and treatises at that time did not recognize the difference between statutes of limitation and repose but instead confused the terms or used them interchangeably.[84] The court thus turned to the

---

77. *Id.* at 145.
78. *Id.* at 146; *see also* Lindsay v. Pub. Serv. Co., 725 F. Supp. 278, 282 (W.D.N.C. 1989) (subjecting failure-to-warn claim to six-year product liability statute of repose); Wilson v. Dake Corp., 497 F. Supp. 1339, 1339–40 (E.D. Tenn. 1980) (subjecting failure-to-warn claim to ten-year product liability statute of repose). *But see* Allison v. McGhan Med. Corp., 184 F.3d 1300, 1306–07 (11th Cir. 1999) (holding that strict liability failure-to-warn claim was outside scope of ten-year statute of repose); Sharp *ex rel.* Gordon v. Case Corp., 595 N.W.2d 380, 382 (Wis. 1999) (holding that the eight-year statute of repose does not apply to post-sale failure to warn).
79. 751 F. Supp. 2d 835, 836 (E.D.N.C. 2010).
80. *Id.* at 841 (citing various cases from Alabama, Arizona, Florida, Indiana, New Hampshire, Ohio, Rhode Island, and Utah).
81. 42 U.S.C. § 9658(a).
82. *See, e.g.*, Burlington N.& Santa Fe Ry. Co. v. Poole Chem. Co., 419 F.3d 355, 364 (5th Cir. 2005); First United Methodist Church of Hyattsville v. U.S. Gypsum Co., 882 F.2d 862, 867 (4th Cir. 1989); Waldburger v. CTS Corp., No.1:11CV39, 2012 WL 380053, at *2–3 (W.D.N.C. Feb. 6, 2012).
83. *See, e.g.*, McDonald v. Sun Oil Co., 548 F.3d 774, 783 (9th Cir. 2008); Abrams v. Ciba Specialty Chems. Corp., 659 F. Supp. 2d 1225, 1239 (S.D. Ala. 2009).
84. *McDonald*, 548 F.3d at 781 & nn.3–4 (citing several cases and law review articles).

available legislative history, concluding that Congress did in fact intend to preempt state statutes of repose that might cut off claimants' rights before they become aware of them.[85]

Laches

The equitable counterpart to the statute of limitations is the doctrine of laches. Laches will bar litigation when a potential plaintiff has slept on her rights. Because it is an equitable defense, laches will bar a plaintiff's claims only when the defendant can show that the delay was both unreasonable and prejudicial. Courts generally consider four factors in evaluating the defense: (1) knowledge of the plaintiff; (2) conduct of the defendant; (3) interests to be vindicated; and (4) resulting prejudice. Trial courts generally have a fair amount of discretion in deciding whether the circumstances justify application of laches in a given case.[86]

As a general rule, the laches defense tends to be unsuccessful in toxic tort cases. As one court has explained: "Because environmental damage does not inflict harm only on the plaintiff, laches is strongly disfavored in environmental cases. The use of laches should be restricted to avoid defeat of Congress'[s] environmental policy."[87] By way of example, the New Hampshire Supreme Court in a case involving an illegal junkyard held that the plaintiff's claims were not barred by laches despite a fourteen-year period during which the plaintiff did not inspect his property to determine whether the encroachment had been removed after his initial demand.[88]

Moreover, several U.S. Courts of Appeals have held that equitable defenses—including not only laches but also unclean hands, caveat emptor, and others—have no application

---

85. *Id.* at 783 ("Congress's primary concern in enacting § [9658] was to adopt the discovery rule in situations where a plaintiff may lose a cause of action before becoming aware of it. . . . This predicament can be caused by either statutes of limitation or statutes of repose, and is probably most likely to occur where statutes of repose operate. Thus, given the ambiguity of the term 'statute of limitations' at the time of the adoption of § [9658], taken alongside the only evidence of Congressional intent, it is evident that the term 'statute of limitations' in § [9658] was intended by Congress to include statutes of repose.").
86. *See generally* Mailloux v. Town of Londonderry, 864 A.2d 335, 341 (N.H. 2004); Save the Peaks Coalition v. U.S. Forest Serv., 669 F.3d 1025, 1031–33 (9th Cir. 2012); Nature Conservancy v. Wilder Corp. of Del., 656 F.3d 646, 649 (7th Cir. 2011).
87. *Save the Peaks Coalition*, 669 F.3d at 1031 (quoting Ocean Advocates v. U.S. Army Corps of Eng'rs, 402 F.3d 846, 862 (9th Cir. 2005)); *see also* City of Newburgh v. Sarna, 690 F. Supp. 2d 136, 172 (S.D.N.Y. 2010) (noting that "laches is only rarely invoked in environmental cases" (citation omitted) (internal quotation marks omitted)). This is likewise true as to other equitable defenses, such as unclean hands. *See, e.g.*, Idaho Rural Council v. Bosma, 143 F. Supp. 2d 1169, 1182–83 (D. Idaho 2001) (holding that courts should not apply the unclean hands doctrine if it would frustrate the purpose of a federal statute or contravene public policy, and further holding that allowing a defendant to escape liability for conduct in violation of the Clean Water Act because plaintiff has engaged in similar violations would frustrate the purpose of the Act at the expense of the public).
88. *Mailloux*, 864 A.2d at 342.

in CERCLA cases.[89] Rather, the statute provides that the only available defenses are those specifically listed.[90]

Exhaustion of Administrative Remedies

While the statutes of limitation and repose will bar claims that are brought too late, plaintiffs' claims may also be precluded if brought too soon. Courts, for example, may lack jurisdiction to address certain claims unless and until the claimant has pursued all available administrative remedies. This is particularly true with respect to claims brought pursuant to a citizen suit provision under various environmental laws.[91]

These environmental citizen suit provisions generally authorize two types of actions: (1) actions against those in violation of the statute's provisions or regulations, and (2) suits against EPA for failure to discharge mandatory statutory duties.[92] In addition, under the Resource Conservation and Recovery Act, a party may also bring a claim against those who have handled or disposed of "any solid or hazardous waste which may present an imminent and substantial endangerment to health or the environment."[93] Before any of these types of citizen suits may be brought, however, the plaintiff must first provide formal notice to the EPA, to the appropriate state authority, and to the defendant.[94] The purpose of these notice provisions is to give the relevant agencies as well as the defendant

---

89. *See* Western Props. Serv. Corp. v. Shell Oil Co., 358 F.3d 678, 692–93 (9th Cir. 2004) (laches), *abrogated on other grounds by* Cooper Indus., Inc. v. Aviall Servs., Inc., 543 U.S. 157 (2004); Blasland, Bouck & Lee, Inc. v. City of N. Miami, 283 F.3d 1286, 1303–04 (11th Cir. 2002) (equitable pay-when-paid clause); Johnson v. James Langley Operating Co., 226 F.3d 957, 963 (8th Cir. 2000) (unclean hands); Town of Munster v. Sherwin-Williams Co., 27 F.3d 1268, 1271–73 (7th Cir. 1994) (laches); Velsicol Chem. Corp. v. Enenco, Inc., 9 F.3d 524, 530 (6th Cir. 1993) (laches); Gen. Elect. Co. v. Litton Indus. Automation Sys., Inc., 920 F.2d 1415, 1418 (8th Cir. 1990) (unclean hands), *abrogated on other grounds by* Key Tronic Corp. v. United States, 511 U.S. 809, 814 (1994); Smith Land & Improvement Corp. v. Celotex Corp., 851 F.2d 86, 89–91 (3d Cir. 1998) (caveat emptor).
90. *Western Props. Serv. Corp.*, 358 F.3d at 693 & n.64 (listing these defenses as "acts of God, acts of war, and acts or omissions of third parties other than by employees, agents, or parties to a contractual relationship" (citing 42 U.S.C. § 9607(a)).
91. Congress adopted the first citizen suit provision in 1970 as part of the Clean Air Act. *See* 42 U.S.C. § 7604. Since that time, nearly every federal environmental statute adopted by Congress has included a citizen suit provision. *See* Act to Prevent Pollution From Ships, 33 U.S.C. § 1910; CERCLA, 42 U.S.C. § 9659; Deepwater Ports Act, 33 U.S.C. § 1515; Deep Seabed Hard Mineral Resources Act, 30 U.S.C. § 1427; Emergency Planning and Community Right-to-Know Act, 42 U.S.C. § 11046; Endangered Species Act, 16 U.S.C. § 1540(g); Energy Conservation Act, 42 U.S.C. § 6305; Federal Water Pollution Control Act, 33 U.S.C. § 1365; Marine Protection, Research, and Sanctuaries Act, 33 U.S.C. § 1415(g); Natural Forests Act, 15 U.S.C. § 544(m)(b); Natural Gas Pipeline Safety Act, 49 U.S.C. § 1686; Noise Control Act, 42 U.S.C. § 4911; Ocean Thermal Energy Conservation Act, 42 U.S.C. § 9124; Outer Continental Shelf Lands Act, 43 U.S.C. § 1349; Powerplant and Industrial Fuel Use Act, 42 U.S.C. § 8435; Resource Conservation and Recovery Act, 42 U.S.C. § 6972; Safe Drinking Water Act, 42 U.S.C. § 300j-8; Surface Mining Control and Reclamation Act, 30 U.S.C. § 1270; Toxic Substances Control Act, 15 U.S.C. § 2619.
92. *See, e.g.*, Resource Conservation and Recovery Act (RCRA), 42 U.S.C. § 6972(a)(1)(A), (a)(2).
93. 42 U.S.C. § 6972(a)(1)(B). While several environmental statutes authorize EPA to bring suit to abate imminent hazards, RCRA is the only environmental statute that extends this power to private citizens.
94. *See, e.g.*, 42 U.S.C. § 6972(b)–(c); *see also* Meghrig v. KFC Western, Inc., 516 U.S. 479, 486 (1996); Hallstrom v. Tillamook Cnty., 493 U.S. 20, 26 (1989).

an opportunity to address the concerns raised.[95] Indeed, if EPA or the state agency takes appropriate enforcement action, the plaintiff's citizen suit will be barred entirely.[96] Likewise, if the plaintiff fails to provide the required notice, her claim will similarly be precluded.[97]

Consistent with these requirements, the notice given by the plaintiff must "serve the purpose of giving the appropriate governmental agencies an opportunity to act and the alleged violator an opportunity to comply."[98] Failure to provide adequate notice (such as identifying the specific contaminants and misconduct at issue) will thus bar a plaintiff's claims.[99]

Exhaustion of administrative remedies is also required when bringing claims under the Federal Tort Claims Act (FTCA).[100] As a general rule, the FTCA provides that the federal government can be held liable for torts just as a private individual. The FTCA does limit, however, the types of damages that may be recovered. For instance, a party cannot recover punitive damages or prejudgment interest under the FTCA.[101] In addition, claims pursuant to the FTCA may be brought only in federal district court.[102] Beyond these requirements, a plaintiff must first present her claims to the appropriate federal agency: "An action shall not be instituted" under the FTCA "unless the claimant shall have first presented the claim to the appropriate Federal agency and his claim shall have been finally denied by the agency."[103] This administrative exhaustion requirement is a "prerequisite to the maintenance of a tort suit against the United States."[104] Accordingly, a plaintiff must affirmatively plead administrative exhaustion in an FTCA case.[105] Failure to comply with these exhaustion requirements will result in dismissal of the plaintiff's claim.[106]

---

95. *Hallstrom*, 493 U.S. at 29 (explaining that "notice allows Government agencies to take responsibility for enforcing environmental regulations" and also "gives the alleged violator 'an opportunity to bring itself into complete compliance with the Act'" (quoting Gwaltney of Smithfield, Inc. v. Chesapeake Bay Found., Inc., 484 U.S. 49, 60 (1987))).
96. *Meghrig*, 516 U.S. at 486.
97. *Hallstrom*, 493 U.S. at 31 (holding that RCRA's notice requirements "are mandatory conditions precedent to commencing suit under the RCRA citizen suit provision; a district court may not disregard these requirements at its discretion").
98. Brod v. Omya, Inc., 653 F.3d 156, 166 (2d Cir. 2011) (citations omitted) (internal quotation marks omitted); *see also* 40 C.F.R. § 254.3(a) (requiring RCRA notice of intent to include "sufficient information to permit the recipient to identify the specific permit, standard, regulation, condition, requirement, or order which has allegedly been violated, [and] the activity alleged to constitute a violation").
99. *Brod*, 653 F.3d at 168–69.
100. 28 U.S.C. §§ 2671–2680.
101. *Id.* § 2674.
102. *Id.* § 2679.
103. *Id.* § 2675(a).
104. GAF Corp. v. United States, 818 F.2d 901, 904 (D.C. Cir. 1987); *see also* Frey v. EPA, 270 F.3d 1129, 1136 (7th Cir. 2001).
105. FED. R. CIV. P. 8(a)(1) (requiring a plaintiff to plead "a short and plain statement of the grounds for the court's jurisdiction").
106. Ayers v. United States, 67 Fed. Cl. 776, 779 (2005); Colbert v. U.S. Postal Serv., 831 F. Supp. 2d 240, 243 (D.D.C. 2011); United States v. Green, 33 F. Supp. 2d 203, 219 (W.D.N.Y. 1998).

Primary Jurisdiction

Closely related to the exhaustion of administrative remedies requirement, the primary jurisdiction doctrine provides that courts should defer certain questions to the administrative agency with authority and expertise regarding those matters.[107] The purpose of this doctrine is to allow courts to benefit from an administrative agency's specialized knowledge and to promote uniformity of regulation. As noted by the U.S. Supreme Court, primary jurisdiction comes into play whenever a claim properly before the court "requires the resolution of issues which, under a regulatory scheme, have been placed within the special competence of an administrative body."[108] "[I]n such a case the judicial process is suspended pending referral of such issues to the administrative body for its views."[109]

Because the primary jurisdiction doctrine applies only when authority to address an issue lies both with the court and an administrative agency, the doctrine is not really "jurisdictional," at least in the traditional sense. Rather, it is a principle of judicial restraint and administration similar to abstention.[110] The distinction is important as it leaves trial courts with considerable discretion in deciding whether to defer to an administrative agency.[111] Likewise, in granting a primary jurisdiction motion, a trial court has discretion to retain jurisdiction (e.g., stay the case) or not (i.e., dismiss the action without prejudice).[112]

There is no fixed formula for courts to apply when deciding whether to defer consideration of an issue under the primary jurisdiction doctrine. Rather, the determination is largely fact-specific, driven by several factors, including: (1) whether the question at issue

---

107. *See, e.g.*, Far East Conference v. United States, 342 U.S. 570, 574 (1952); Massachusetts v. Blackstone Valley Elec. Co., 67 F.3d 981, 992 (1st Cir. 1995); Miss. Power & Light Co. v. United Gas Pipe Line Co., 532 F.2d 412, 420 (5th Cir. 1976). Some courts have questioned whether the doctrine is applicable where the claim is brought under federal law and the referral would be to a state agency. *See* Boyes v. Shell Oil Prods. Co., 199 F.3d 1260, 1265 n.11 (11th Cir. 2000); Cnty. of Suffolk v. Long Island Lighting Co., 907 F.2d 1295, 1310 (2d Cir. 1990). However, if a state agency operates pursuant to a federal legislative scheme, as is often the case in the environmental context, the "state agency may be entitled to the same treatment." *Cnty of Suffolk*, 907 F.2d at 1310 n.9.
108. United States v. W. Pac. R.R. Co., 352 U.S. 59, 64 (1956).
109. *Id.*
110. *See, e.g.*, Friends of Santa Fe Cnty. v. Lac Minerals, Inc., 892 F. Supp. 1333, 1349 (D.N.M. 1995) (noting that the doctrine exists "for the proper distribution of power between judicial and administrative bodies, and not for the convenience of the parties" (citations omitted) (internal quotation marks omitted)).
111. Raritan Baykeeper, Inc. v. NL Indus., Inc., 660 F.3d 686, 691 (3d Cir. 2011) (holding that primary jurisdiction did not require district court to abstain in case where claimant sought remediation of contaminated sediments in a river near the defendant's former facility); *see also* Chico Serv. Station, Inc. v. Sol Puerto Rico Ltd., 633 F.3d 20, 31–32 (1st Cir. 2011) ("While we are not prepared to rule out categorically the possibility of abstention in a RCRA citizen suit, we believe that the circumstances justifying abstention will be exceedingly rare."); U.S. Pub. Interest Research Grp. v. Atl. Salmon of Me., 339 F.3d 34, 34 (1st Cir. 2003) (upholding district court's refusal to abstain under primary jurisdiction doctrine in case against salmon farms alleged to be polluting state waters); Interfaith Cmty. Org. v. PPG Indus., Inc., 702 F. Supp. 2d 295, 316 (D.N.J. 2010) (finding that primary jurisdiction doctrine did not preclude claim that chromium waste presented imminent and substantial endangerment under RCRA).
112. Reiter v. Cooper, 507 U.S. 258, 269–70 (1993); Davel Commc'ns, Inc. v. Qwest Corp., 460 F.3d 1075, 1091 (9th Cir. 2006); Am. Auto. Mfrs. Ass'n v. Mass. Dep't of Envtl. Prot., 163 F.3d 74, 82 (1st Cir. 1998).

is within the conventional experience of judges or whether it involves technical or policy considerations within the agency's particular field of expertise; (2) whether the question is particularly within the agency's discretion; (3) whether there exists a substantial danger of inconsistent rulings; and (4) whether a prior application to the agency has been made.[113] The relief sought in any given case can also play a significant role in the analysis as courts generally are more likely to defer jurisdiction when the claimant seeks injunctive relief as opposed to merely seeking monetary damages.[114]

While the doctrine developed long before passage of modern-day environmental statutes,[115] courts frequently have relied on the doctrine of primary jurisdiction to defer adjudication of complex environmental disputes until after full consideration of the issues by the EPA or a corresponding state agency. For example, in *Schwartzman, Inc. v. Atchison, Topeka & Santa Fe Railway Co.*, the plaintiff filed suit under state nuisance law seeking an order requiring the adjacent landowner to investigate and remediate soil and groundwater contamination.[116] The defendant, however, previously had agreed to an administrative order with EPA and the state agency requiring a remedial investigation and feasibility study. Based on this ongoing regulatory work, the court deferred to the expertise of EPA and refused to entertain the plaintiff's prayers for injunctive relief.[117] The overriding considerations in such cases are whether the claims would require the determination of technical issues not within the conventional experience of the courts, and whether full consideration and development of those technical issues by the administrative agency would be beneficial.[118]

Preemption

While the primary jurisdiction doctrine provides courts with discretion to defer resolution of a plaintiff's claims, the doctrine of preemption may foreclose such claims in their entirety. Pursuant to the Supremacy Clause,[119] federal law[120] will override and take precedence over

---

113. *See, e.g., Raritan Baykeeper*, 660 F.3d at 691; *U.S. Pub. Interest Research Grp.*, 339 F.3d at 34.
114. *Friends of Santa Fe Cnty.*, 892 F. Supp. at 1350 ("Courts refuse to defer jurisdiction if the plaintiff is seeking damages for injury to property or person, as this is the type of relief courts routinely evaluate; however, if the plaintiff seeks injunctive relief, requiring scientific or technical expertise, the doctrine is more readily applicable.").
115. *See* Tex.& Pac. Ry. Co. v. Abilene Cotton Oil Co., 204 U.S. 426 (1907).
116. 857 F. Supp. 838 (D.N.M. 1994).
117. *Id.* at 844; *see also Friends of Santa Fe Cnty.*, 892 F. Supp. at 1350 (deferring remediation issues to state environmental agency, noting that it chose "not to pollute the scene with still more studies and standards" (internal citation omitted)); Flo-Sun, Inc. v. Kirk, 783 So. 2d 1029, 1039–40 (Fla. 2001) (suspending nuisance claim involving pollution from sugar cane cultivation pending agency review under primary jurisdiction doctrine).
118. *See* United States v. W. Pac. Ry. Co., 352 U.S.59, 64 (1956).
119. U.S. CONST. art. VI, cl.2 ("This Constitution, and the Laws of the United States which shall be made in Pursuance thereof . . . shall be the supreme Law of the Land . . . any Thing in the Constitution or Laws of any State to the Contrary notwithstanding.").
120. For purposes of preemption, federal law is defined broadly to include the United States Constitution, federal statutes, federal regulations promulgated by administrative agencies, and actions taken by federal

any and all conflicting state or local laws.[121] The U.S. Supreme Court has identified three primary ways in which state law can be preempted under the Supremacy Clause. First, Congress may preempt state law by so stating in express terms.[122] Second, Congress may indicate implicitly an intent to occupy an entire field of regulation.[123] Finally, when there is neither express nor implied preemption, a state law may still be preempted when it conflicts with federal law or stands as an obstacle to the accomplishment and execution of the full purposes and objectives of Congress.[124] When evaluating the question of preemption, the central issue is the intent and objective of Congress and the corresponding role, if any, for involvement by state and local government.[125]

Given the number and type of federal laws addressing toxic substances, it should come as no surprise that federal preemption is raised frequently as a defense in toxic tort cases. While private toxic tort claims can and often do exist independently from federal regulation, there is increasing overlap between the duties defined by the common law and those set out in federal legislation. In defining the scope of these respective spheres of regulation, courts begin with the assumption that Congress, barring an express statement to the contrary, does not intend to displace state law.[126] This presumption takes on added strength when the state or local regulation concerns health, safety, or environmental issues,[127] particularly where the federal legislation fails to provide a remedy.[128]

Even with these presumptions, however, there remain several fertile areas for toxic tort litigants to raise the issue of preemption. Examples of frequently invoked federal

---

agencies pursuant to Congressionally delegated authority. *See* Hillsborough Cnty. v. Automated Med. Lab., Inc., 471 U.S. 707, 713 (1985).
121. State law, for purposes of preemption, includes state statutes, state regulations, and common law tort actions. *See* Sperry v. Florida, 373 U.S. 379, 403 (1963); *see also* Riegel v. Medtronic, Inc., 552 U.S. 312, 324–25 (2008).
122. Cipollone v. Liggett Grp., Inc., 505 U.S. 504, 516 (1992); English v. Gen. Elec. Co., 496 U.S. 72, 78 (1990); *Hillsborough Cnty.*, 471 U.S. at 713.
123. *English*, 496 U.S. at 79; Cal. Fed. Sav. & Loan Ass'n v. Guerra, 479 U.S. 272, 280–81 (1987); Rice v. Santa Fe Elevator Corp., 331 U.S. 218, 230 (1947).
124. Williamson v. Mazda Motor of Am., Inc., 131 S. Ct. 1131, 1136 (2011); Sprietsma v. Mercury Marine, 537 U.S. 51, 64 (2002); Geier v. Am. Honda Motor Co., 529 U.S. 861, 899 (2000); Freightliner Corp. v. Myrick, 514 U.S. 280, 289–90 (1995); Fla. Lime & Avocado Growers, Inc. v. Paul, 373 U.S. 132, 142–43 (1963); Hines v. Davidowitz, 312 U.S. 52, 67 (1941).
125. Wyeth v. Levine, 555 U.S. 555, 565 (2009); Gade v. Nat'l Solid Wastes Mgmt. Ass'n, 505 U.S. 88, 96 (1992); *Cipollone*, 505 U.S. at 516; *English*, 496 U.S. at 78.
126. *Levine*, 555 U.S. at 565 ("In all pre-emption cases, and particularly in those in which Congress has 'legislated . . . in a field which the States have traditionally occupied,' . . . we 'start with the assumption that the historic police powers of the States were not to be superseded by the Federal Act unless that was the clear and manifest purpose of Congress.'" (quoting Medtronic, Inc. v. Lohr, 518 U.S. 470, 485 (1996))); *see also* Maryland v. Louisiana, 451 U.S. 725, 746–47 (1981).
127. *Hillsborough Cnty.*, 471 U.S. at 715 (noting the "presumption that state or local regulation of matters related to health and safety is not invalidated under the Supremacy Clause"); Oxygenated Fuels Ass'n Inc. v. Davis, 331 F.3d 665, 673 (9th Cir. 2003) ("Environmental regulation is an area of traditional state control."); *see also Lohr*, 518 U.S. at 475.
128. Silkwood v. Kerr-McGee Corp., 464 U.S. 238, 263–64 &n.7 (1984) (Blackmun, J., dissenting) ("The absence of federal regulation governing the compensation of nuclear accidents is strong evidence that Congress intended the matter to be left to the states.").

statutes, to list just a few, include CERCLA, the Resource Conservation and Recovery Act (RCRA), the Toxic Substances Control Act (TSCA), the Atomic Energy Act (AEA), the Price-Anderson Act (PAA), the Federal Insecticide, Fungicide, and Rodenticide Act (FIFRA), OSHA's Hazard Communication Standard (HazCom Standard), and the Food, Drug, and Cosmetic Act (FDCA), each of which are discussed briefly below.

CERCLA

Congress enacted CERCLA in 1980 in response to the dangers of uncontrolled hazardous waste sites.[129] As directed by statute, EPA has adopted extensive regulations governing the cleanup of these sites. Although CERCLA, by its own terms, does not expressly preempt state law,[130] there are several ways in which ongoing CERCLA or other regulatory activities at a contaminated site may preempt common law tort claims. In particular, state laws and claims pursuant to those laws that conflict with or obstruct the purposes or objectives of CERCLA are precluded.[131]

For example, CERCLA establishes a process for remediating Superfund sites that requires investigating the extent of contamination, evaluating appropriate remedies, developing a proposed remediation plan, and adopting a final remediation plan. Once EPA has initiated a remedial investigation and feasibility study, CERCLA prohibits any potentially responsible party from undertaking any remedial action at a site unless EPA has approved the action:

> When either the President, or a potentially responsible party pursuant to an administrative order or consent decree under this chapter, has initiated a remedial investigation and feasibility study for a particular facility under this chapter, no potentially responsible party may undertake any remedial action at the facility unless such remedial action has been authorized by the President.[132]

---

129. *See* National Priorities List for Uncontrolled Hazardous Waste Sites, 61 Fed. Reg. 30,510, 30,511 (June 17, 1996).
130. 42 U.S.C. § 9614(a) ("Nothing in this chapter shall be construed or interpreted as preempting any state from imposing any additional liability or requirements with respect to the release of hazardous substances within such state."); 42 U.S.C. § 9652(d) ("Nothing in this chapter shall affect or modify in any way the obligations or liabilities of any person under other Federal or State law, including common law, with respect to releases of hazardous substances or other pollutants or contaminants."); *see also* New Mexico v. Gen. Elec. Co., 467 F.3d 1223, 1244 (10th Cir. 2006) ("Given these savings clauses, as well as the spirit of cooperative federalism running throughout CERCLA and its regulations, we may safely say Congress did not intend CERCLA to completely preempt state laws related to hazardous waste contamination."); Feikema v. Texaco, Inc., 16 F.3d 1408, 1415 (4th Cir. 1994).
131. *See, e.g.*, Cannon v. Gates, 538 F.3d 1328, 1335–36 (10th Cir. 2008); *New Mexico v. Gen. Elec. Co.*, 467 F.3d at 1244; *In re* Reading Co., 115 F.3d 1111, 1117 (3d Cir. 1997), *abrogated on other grounds by* E.I. DuPont De Nemours & Co. v. United States, 460 F.3d 515, 522 (3d Cir. 2006); United States v. City & Cnty. of Denver, 100 F.3d 1509, 1512–13 (10th Cir. 1996).
132. 42 U.S.C. § 9622(e)(6).

CERCLA, therefore, precludes any requested relief that would require undertaking any non-approved remedial action at a "facility." The potential for conflict here is compounded when one considers that CERCLA defines "facility" not just to include a plant's physical property boundaries but "any site or area where a hazardous substance has been deposited, stored, disposed of, or placed, or otherwise come to be located."[133] In other words, a "site" is not necessarily "equal to nor confined by the boundaries of any specific property that may give the site its name."[134]

Moreover, to ensure that remediation of contaminated sites is not slowed or halted by litigation, CERCLA provides that "[n]o federal court shall have jurisdiction under Federal law . . . to review any challenges to removal or remedial action selected under section 9604 of this title, or to review any order issued under section 9606(a) of this title."[135] Citing this provision, courts have generally held that no one, not even other potentially responsible parties, can challenge a response action until such action has been completed.[136] Plaintiffs thus may not circumvent the CERCLA process through an independent lawsuit.[137]

In addition, CERCLA establishes a statutory right of contribution for recovery of response costs expended in remediating contaminated sites.[138] The statute expressly states that it provides the only method of contribution for those seeking to recover response costs incurred under CERCLA.[139] The U.S. Court of Appeals for the Second Circuit has explained that this provision "is intended to standardize the statutory right of contribution and, in doing so, avoid the possibility of fifty different state statutory schemes that regulate the duties and obligations of non-settling PRPs who might be viewed as tortfeasors under

---

133. 42 U.S.C. § 9601(9).
134. National Priorities List for Uncontrolled Hazardous Waste Sites, 61 Fed. Reg. 30,510, 30,511 (June 17, 1996).
135. 42 U.S.C. § 9613(h).
136. *See Gates*, 538 F.3d at 1335–36 (finding that "the Government's conduct constitutes an ongoing removal action, with which the Cannon's suit would undoubtedly interfere," and thus dismissing the Cannon's claim for injunctive relief); *New Mexico v. Gen. Elec. Co.*, 467 F.3d at 1249 (barring plaintiff's citizen suit to "prevent[] citizens from using ingenious means to skirt a clear statutory bar to suit"); *see also* Pollack v. U.S. Dep't of Def., 507 F.3d 522, 527 (7th Cir. 2007); Broward Gardens Tenants Ass'n v. EPA, 311 F.3d 1066, 1072 (11th Cir. 2002); Razore v. Tulalip Tribes of Wash., 66 F.3d 236, 239 (9th Cir. 1995); McClellan Ecological Seepage Situation v. Perry, 47 F.3d 325, 330 (9th Cir. 1995); Wheaton Indus. v. EPA, 781 F.2d 354, 356 (3d Cir. 1986).
137. The U.S. Court of Appeals for the Seventh Circuit has held, however, that EPA cannot merely study and investigate a site indefinitely, thereby effectively avoiding judicial review. Frey v. EPA, 403 F.3d 828, 834–36 (7th Cir. 2005) (rejecting the suggestion that EPA will take action "at some point before the sun becomes a red giant and melts the earth" is enough to avoid judicial review; instead, "there must be some objective indicator that allows for an external evaluation, with reasonable target completion dates, of the required work for a site"). Other courts, however, have expressly rejected this view in light of CERCLA's plain language. *See, e.g., Gates*, 538 F.3d at 1335 n.7 (acknowledging the concern about open-ended removal or remedial actions, but rejecting *Frey*'s analysis based on the plain language of the statute).
138. 42 U.S.C. § 9613(f).
139. 42 U.S.C. § 9613(f)(3)(C) ("Any contribution action brought under this paragraph shall be governed by Federal law.").

the law of any particular state."[140] As such, separate contribution claims under state law to recover CERCLA response costs conflict with CERCLA and therefore are preempted.[141]

As another example, CERCLA authorizes the federal government as well as the natural resource trustees of the several states to recover damages for harm to natural resources.[142] The statute, however, specifically restricts the use of these natural resource damages, requiring that they be used "only to restore, replace, or acquire the equivalent of such natural resources."[143] The U.S. Court of Appeals for the Tenth Circuit has thus held that "CERCLA's comprehensive [natural resource damages] scheme preempts any state remedy designed to achieve something other than the restoration, replacement, or acquisition of the equivalent of a contaminated natural resource."[144] Accordingly, the court in that case rejected the state's request for "an unrestricted award of money damages" resulting from the defendant's contamination of the groundwater.[145]

The Resource Conservation and Recovery Act (RCRA)

In 1976, Congress passed the Resource Conservation and Recovery Act[146] to provide for the comprehensive regulation of solid and hazardous waste "from cradle to grave."[147] While CERCLA is designed to remediate contaminated sites, RCRA instead is intended primarily to prevent the need for remediation in the first place. As with other environmental statutes, RCRA expressly contemplates a significant continuing role for state regulation. Indeed, while RCRA provides that "no state or political subdivision may impose any requirements less stringent" than RCRA's regulations, the statute likewise provides that "[n]othing in this chapter shall be construed to prohibit any State or political subdivision thereof from imposing any requirements . . . which are more stringent than those imposed by such regulations."[148] RCRA's comprehensiveness and specificity, however, raise potential arguments for both implied and conflict preemption. Indeed, several state and local regulations regarding the disposal of hazardous waste have been challenged on these grounds, in some cases successfully and in others not.[149]

---

140. Niagara Mohawk Power Corp. v. Chevron U.S.A., Inc., 596 F.3d 112, 138 (2d Cir. 2010).
141. *Id.*; *see also* PMC, Inc. v. Sherwin-Williams Co., 151 F.3d 610, 618 (7th Cir. 1998). It should be noted, however, that CERCLA does not preempt state contribution claims for costs not covered by CERCLA.
142. 42 U.S.C. § 9607(f).
143. *Id.* § 9607(f)(1).
144. New Mexico v. Gen. Elec. Co., 467 F.3d 1223, 1247 (10th Cir. 2006).
145. *Id.* at 1247–48.
146. 42 U.S.C. §§ 6901–6992k.
147. Chicago v. Envtl. Def. Fund, 511 U.S. 328, 331 (1994); C&A Carbone, Inc. v. Town of Clarkstown, 511 U.S. 383, 408 (1994); *see also* Meghrig v. KFC W., Inc., 516 U.S. 479, 483 (1996) ("RCRA is a comprehensive environmental statute that governs the treatment, storage, and disposal of solid and hazardous waste.").
148. 42 U.S.C. § 6929.
149. *See* Blue Circle Cement, Inc. v. Bd. of Cnty. Comm'rs, 27 F.3d 1499, 1504–09 (10th Cir. 1994) (discussing and attempting to harmonize many of the RCRA preemption decisions).

In *Boyes v. Shell Oil Products Co.*, for example, the U.S. Court of Appeals for the Eleventh Circuit found that RCRA preempted certain aspects of Florida's program for regulating underground storage tanks.[150] In particular, the court found that the state provision limiting a party's right to sue for remediation of petroleum contamination conflicted with RCRA's citizen suit provision and was thus preempted. And in *ENSCO, Inc. v. Dumas*, the Eighth Circuit found that a local ordinance prohibiting the storage, treatment, and disposal of acute hazardous waste was implicitly preempted, explaining that "[a] county cannot, by attaching the label 'more stringent requirements' . . . to an ordinance that in language and history defies such description, arrogate to itself the power to enact a measure that as a practical matter cannot function other than to subvert federal policies concerning the safe handling of hazardous waste."[151]

By way of contrast, in *LaFarge Corp. v. Campbell*, the U.S. District Court for the Western District of Texas held that a state statute prohibiting the burning of fuel in certain locations was not preempted by RCRA.[152] Likewise, in *North Haven Planning & Zoning Commission v. Upjohn Co.*, the U.S. District Court for the District of Connecticut held that local regulation of a sludge pile was not preempted by RCRA and that the more stringent local standards fell within RCRA's savings clause.[153] And in *Feikema v. Texaco, Inc.*, the U.S. Court of Appeals for the Fourth Circuit found that the plaintiffs' state common law claims were preempted to the extent they sought injunctive relief in conflict with a RCRA consent order entered with EPA but that plaintiffs' common law claims for damages were not preempted.[154]

The Toxic Substances Control Act (TSCA)

In 1976, Congress enacted the Toxic Substances Control Act[155] to regulate the manufacture, distribution, processing, use, and disposal of chemical substances and mixtures that may present an unreasonable risk of injury to human health or the environment.[156] TSCA

---

150. 199 F.3d 1260, 1269–70 (11th Cir. 2000).
151. 807 F.2d 743, 745 (8th Cir. 1986). For other cases finding RCRA preemption, see, for example, Ogden Envtl. Servs. v. City of San Diego, 687 F. Supp. 1436, 1446–47 (S.D. Cal. 1988); Hermes Consol., Inc. v. People, 849 P.2d 1302, 1311 (Wyo. 1993); Jacksonville v. Ark. Dep't of Pollution Control &Ecology, 824 S.W.2d 840, 842 (Ark. 1992); Rollins Envtl. Servs. of La. v. Iberville Parish Police Jury, 371 So. 2d 1127, 1132 (La. 1979).
152. 813 F. Supp. 501, 512 (W.D. Tex. 1993) (holding that state law creating a buffer zone requirement on the siting of hazardous waste burning kilns was not preempted by RCRA as it did not completely prohibit the burning of hazardous waste derived fuel and because the buffer zone was supported by a rational basis).
153. 753 F. Supp. 423, 431–32 (D. Conn. 1990), *aff'd*, 921 F.2d 27 (2d Cir. 1990). For other cases rejecting RCRA preemption, see, for example, Old Bridge Chems., Inc. v. N.J. Dep't of Envtl. Prot., 965 F.2d 1287, 1296 (3d Cir. 1992); Hunt v. Chem. Waste Mgmt., Inc., 584 So. 2d 1367, 1381–82 (Ala. 1991), *rev'd on other grounds*, 504 U.S. 334 (1992).
154. 16 F.3d 1408, 1416–18 (4th Cir. 1994).
155. 15 U.S.C. §§ 2601–2697.
156. 15 U.S.C. § 2601.

also directs EPA to promulgate rules governing the disposal and labeling of certain specific chemicals, such as polychlorinated biphenyls (PCBs) and mercury.[157] Expressly addressing the question of preemption, TSCA provides that when EPA regulates a chemical substance or mixture under Section 6 of the act, any state regulation applicable to that substance or mixture is preempted. TSCA, however, also provides an exemption from this preemption provision in cases where the state regulation (1) is identical to the federal rule, (2) has been adopted under authority of federal law, or (3) prohibits use of the substance in the state or political subdivision.[158] TSCA also exempts from preemption those regulations promulgated under Section 6(a)(6) of the act relating to the disposal of chemical substances.[159]

Addressing the preemption question in the context of state or local regulation of PCBs, courts have reached very different conclusions on similar facts. For example, the U.S. Court of Appeals for the Fifth Circuit in *Rollins Environmental Services (FS), Inc. v. Parish of St. James* held that a local ordinance was preempted where it amounted, for all practical purposes, to a ban on the disposal of PCBs.[160] Likewise, in two related cases, the U.S. District Court for the Eastern District of North Carolina found a county ordinance preempted where it prohibited the storage, dumping, or disposal of PCBs.[161] By contrast, in *SED, Inc. v. Dayton*, the U.S. District Court for the Southern District of Ohio found that a city ordinance prohibiting the storage of PCBs was not preempted.[162] And in *Chappell v. SCA Services., Inc.*, the U.S. District Court for the Central District of Illinois found that TCSA did not preempt plaintiffs' state nuisance claims stemming from the operation of a hazardous chemical waste landfill containing PCBs.[163] This stark disagreement of opinion led one court to exclaim that it could find "no way to reconcile the decisions rendered on this issue; to agree with one is necessarily to disagree with another."[164]

The Atomic Energy Act (AEA) and the Price-Anderson Act (PAA)

Congress enacted the Atomic Energy Act in 1954 to establish a comprehensive regulatory scheme for military and domestic nuclear energy.[165] Subsequent amendments gave

---

157. 15 U.S.C. § 2605(e)–(f).
158. 15 U.S.C. § 2617(a)(2)(B).
159. *Id.*; see also Chappell v. SCA Servs., Inc., 540 F. Supp. 1087, 1097–98 (D.C. Ill. 1982) (discussing preemption of TSCA regulations regarding disposal).
160. 775 F.2d 627, 634 (5th Cir. 1985).
161. Warren Cnty. v. North Carolina, 528 F. Supp. 276, 289–90 (E.D.N.C. 1981), *aff'd*, 696 F.2d 992 (4th Cir. 1982); Twitty v. North Carolina, 527 F. Supp. 778, 781 (E.D.N.C. 1981), *aff'd*, 696 F.2d 992 (4th Cir. 1982).
162. 519 F. Supp. 979, 988 (S.D. Ohio 1981); *see also* City of Chesapeake v. Sutton Enter., Inc., 138 F.R.D. 468, 477–78 (E.D. Va. 1990); Potomac Elec. Power Co. v. Sachs, 639 F. Supp. 856, 864 (D.C. Md. 1986), *rev'd on other grounds*, 802 F.2d 1527 (4th Cir. 1986), *vacated sub nom.* Potomac Elec. Power Co. v. Curran, 484 U.S. 1022 (1988).
163. 540 F. Supp. 1087, 1089, 1100 (C.D. Ill. 1982).
164. *City of Chesapeake*, 138 F.R.D. at 476 (further noting that "frequently it is difficult to reconcile these cases with themselves").
165. 42 U.S.C. §§ 2011 to 2297h-13.

the states some limited regulatory authority, but the Atomic Energy Commission (now the Nuclear Regulatory Commission), "retain[ed] exclusive regulatory authority over 'the disposal of such . . . byproduct, source, or special nuclear material.'"[166] The U.S. Supreme Court has thus held that "the federal government has occupied the entire field of nuclear safety concerns, except the limited powers expressly ceded to the states."[167] As a result, the AEA preempts state law where "the matter on which the state asserts the right to act is in any way regulated by the federal government."[168] Indeed, courts have not hesitated to strike down state efforts to intrude on this area of federal regulation. As one example, the U.S. Court of Appeals for the Ninth Circuit held that the AEA preempted Washington's Cleanup Priority Act, which had required cleanup of existing contamination at the Hanford nuclear reservation before any additional radioactive waste could be disposed of there and further provided for citizen suits to enforce its provisions.[169]

That states may not intrude on the federal regulation of nuclear material does not necessarily mean, however, that plaintiffs cannot recover damages in a tort action for injuries caused by radiological contamination. To the contrary, the U.S. Supreme Court has held that Congress had no intention of forbidding the states from providing remedies for those suffering injuries from radiological exposure.[170] As the Court explained:

> It may be that the award of damages based on the state law of negligence or strict liability is regulatory in the sense that a nuclear plant will be threatened with damages liability if it does not conform to state standards, but that regulatory consequence was something that Congress was quite willing to accept.[171]

Nevertheless, the duty of care that controls these types of tort claims has been a point of dispute in some courts. Based on the Price-Anderson Act,[172] which was enacted to amend the AEA, most courts have held that the standard of care and the duty owed must be based

---

166. Silkwood v. Kerr-McGee Corp., 464 U.S. 238, 250 (1984) (quoting 42 U.S.C. § 2021(c)(4)).
167. Pac. Gas & Elec. Co. v. State Energy Res. Conservation & Dev. Comm'n, 461 U.S. 190, 212 (1983).
168. *Id.* at 213 (quoting Rice v. Santa Fe Elevator Corp., 331 U.S. 218, 236 (1947)).
169. United States v. Manning, 527 F.3d 828, 840–41 (9th Cir. 2008) ("The CPA is preempted by the AEA because its purpose is to regulate AEA materials for safety purposes and because the CPA has a direct and substantial effect on the [Department of Energy's] ability to make decisions regarding the disposal of radioactive hazardous waste."); *see also* United States v. Kentucky, 252 F.3d 816, 823–24 (6th Cir. 2001) (invalidating state efforts to regulate the amount of radioactivity and radionuclides that the federal government could place in its landfill).
170. *Silkwood*, 464 U.S. at 251.
171. *Id.* at 256; *see also* Pa. Dep't of Envtl. Prot. v. Lockheed Martin Corp., 684 F. Supp. 2d 564, 588 (M.D. Pa. 2010) (holding that recovery of response costs incurred in remediation of radioactive contamination not preempted by the AEA). While the Court in *Silkwood* held that plaintiffs could even recover punitive damages in such a case, this aspect of the decision was overruled by subsequent legislative amendment. *See* 42 U.S.C. § 2210(s); *see also* O'Conner v. Commonwealth Edison Co., 13 F.3d 1090, 1105 n.13 (7th Cir. 1994).
172. Pub. L. No. 86-256, 71 Stat. 576 (1957) (codified as amended in scattered sections of 42 U.S.C.).

on federal rather than state law. As amended, the PAA creates a federal cause of action for "public liability actions" that arise from nuclear incidents. As a result, a claim growing out of any nuclear incident is now compensable under the terms of the PAA or not at all.[173] The statute provides that "the substantive rules for decision in such action shall be derived from the law of the State in which the nuclear incident involved occurs, unless such law is inconsistent with [the Act]."[174] Nevertheless, when it comes to the applicable standard of care in these actions, every federal circuit that has considered the issue has held that the federal safety regulations control and preempt any more restrictive state standards.[175] Despite this weight of authority, however, at least one federal district court has ruled otherwise, finding that "Congress did not intend for federal regulatory standards to preempt state law standards of care in Price-Anderson public liability actions."[176]

Federal Insecticide, Fungicide, and Rodenticide Act (FIFRA)

The Federal Insecticide, Fungicide, and Rodenticide Act is a comprehensive statute that regulates the use, sale, and labeling of pesticides.[177] The statute includes a preemption provision mandating that state law not "impose or continue in effect any requirements for labeling or packaging in addition to or different from those required under [the Act]."[178]

In *Bates v. Dow Agrosciences, LLC*, the U.S. Supreme Court considered whether this provision preempted state common law tort claims, including strict liability (both for defective design and defective manufacture), negligent testing, breach of express warranty, violation of the state deceptive trade practice act, fraud, and failure to warn.[179] The plaintiffs there consisted of several peanut farmers who alleged that their crops had been severely damaged by application of the defendant's pesticide. The label for the pesticide stated that it "is recommended in all areas where peanuts are grown."[180] The plaintiffs

---

173. *In re* TMI Litig. Cases Consol. II, 940 F.2d 832, 854 (3d Cir. 1991).
174. 42 U.S.C. § 2014(hh).
175. *See, e.g., In re* Hanford Nuclear Reservation Litig., 534 F.3d 986, 1003 (9th Cir. 2008) ("Every federal circuit that has considered the appropriate standard of care under the PAA has concluded that nuclear operators are not liable unless they breach federally-imposed dose limits."); Roberts v. Fla. Power & Light Co., 146 F.3d 1305, 1308 (11th Cir. 1998) (holding that "federal safety regulations conclusively establish the duty of care owed in a public liability action"); Nieman v. NLO, Inc., 108 F.3d 1546, 1553 (6th Cir. 1997) (finding that the Price-Anderson Act preempted the plaintiff's state law claims); O'Conner v. Commonwealth Edison Co., 13 F.3d 1090, 1105 (7th Cir. 1994) (stating that "the application of something other than the federal safety regulations as a standard of care is inconsistent with the Price-Anderson scheme"); *In re TMI Litig. Cases*, 940 F.2d at 859 (holding that "states are preempted from imposing a non-federal duty in tort, because any state duty would infringe upon pervasive federal regulation in the field of nuclear safety, and thus would conflict with federal law").
176. Cook v. Rockwell Int'l Corp., 273 F. Supp. 2d 1175, 1180 (D. Colo. 2003). *But see* Wilcox v. Homestake Mining Co., 401 F. Supp. 2d 1196, 1201 (D.N.M. 2005) (arguing that *Cook*'s reasoning is based on precedent that predates subsequent amendments to the Price-Anderson Act).
177. 7 U.S.C. §§ 136–136y.
178. *Id.* § 136v(b).
179. 544 U.S. 431, 442 n.15 (2005).
180. *Id.* at 435.

asserted, however, that the defendant knew or should have known that the pesticide would stunt the growth of peanuts in acidic soils. In response, the defendant asserted that FIFRA preempted any such claims.

The Supreme Court rejected this defense, holding that while common law rules governing strict liability, negligence, and breach of warranty may affect the choices that manufacturers make, they are not state "requirements" for labeling or packaging and thus are not preempted. Even though jury verdicts on these claims might create economic incentives to avoid a feared outcome, those incentives do not "require[] that manufacturers label or package their products in any particular way."[181] By contrast, the plaintiffs' claims for fraud and failure to warn "are premised on common-law rules that qualify as 'requirements for labeling or packaging.'"[182] Accordingly, these types of claims are preempted by FIFRA to the extent they impose requirements that are "in addition to or different from" FIFRA's misbranding standards.[183]

OSHA's Hazard Communication Standard (HazCom Standard)

In 1985, the Occupational Safety and Health Administration (OSHA) promulgated the Hazard Communication Standard.[184] This standard is designed to "ensure that the hazards of all chemicals produced or imported are classified, and that information concerning the classified hazards is transmitted to employers and employees."[185] Among other things, the HazCom Standard requires manufacturers (1) to distribute to all "downstream employers" a material safety data sheet (MSDS) listing the health hazards posed by the chemicals in their products, and (2) to label each product container with "appropriate hazard information."[186] Its purpose is to address "comprehensively" the issue of evaluating and communicating the potential hazards of chemicals to employees as well as "to preempt any legislative or regulatory enactments of a state, or political subdivision of a state, pertaining to this subject."[187]

---

181. *Id.* at 444.
182. *Id.* at 446.
183. *Id.* at 447. Because the Court could not determine on the record before it whether the state law claims for fraud and failure to warn were equivalent to FIFRA's requirements, the Court remanded the case for further proceedings. *Id.* at 454. The Court made it clear, however, that "a manufacturer should not be held liable under a state labeling requirement subject to § 136v(b) unless the manufacturer is also liable for misbranding as defined by FIFRA." *Id.* Following the decision in *Bates*, the U.S. Court of Appeals for the Third Circuit addressed similar questions under New Jersey law. *See* Indian Brand Farms, Inc. v. Novartis Crop Prot. Inc., 617 F.3d 207, 225, 228 (3d Cir. 2010) (finding that farmers' failure-to-warn and design defect claims were not preempted under the standard set in *Bates*); *see also* Arlandson v. Hartz Mountain Corp., 792 F. Supp. 2d 691 (D.N.J. 2011) (addressing FIFRA preemption in light of *Bates* as to a variety of state tort theories).
184. 29 C.F.R. § 1910.1200; *see also* Ohio Mfrs. Ass'n v. City of Akron, 801 F.2d 824, 827 (6th Cir. 1986) (discussing history of the HazCom Standard).
185. 29 C.F.R. § 1910.1200(a)(1).
186. *See generally id.* § 1910.1200(a)–(g).
187. *Id.* § 1910.1200(a)(2).

Based on this language, some have argued that the HazCom Standard regulates the entire field of chemical-product warnings and, thus, preempts state failure-to-warn tort claims. For example, in *In re Welding Fume Products Liability Litigation*, welders brought failure-to-warn claims against the manufacturers, suppliers, and distributors of welding rods, alleging that exposure to welding fumes caused neurological injuries and that the defendants failed to adequately warn of these health risks.[188] Certain defendants moved to dismiss these claims as preempted under the HazCom Standard, citing the language quoted above. The district court, however, held otherwise. The court explained that the Occupational Safety and Health Act (OSH Act)[189] contains one of the broadest savings clauses enacted by Congress, providing that nothing about the act "shall be construed . . . to enlarge or diminish or affect in any other manner the common law or statutory rights, duties, or liabilities of employers and employees under any law with respect to injuries, diseases, or death of employees arising out of, or in the course of, employment."[190] The district court found it "difficult to imagine a more explicit statement of Congressional intention to preserve and not pre-empt state common law."[191] Based on this language, the court found that the OSH Act "cannot expressly pre-empt common law claims for failure to warn." As for implied preemption, the court held that the "HazCom Standard directs the defendants to give their employees appropriate warnings. State common law duties requiring manufacturers and suppliers to warn the general public of known hazards do[] not pose an obstacle to compliance with this federal directive."[192]

While several courts have likewise rejected preemption under the HazCom Standard,[193] at least two have accepted the defense.[194] In 2011, however, OSHA issued a "Standards Interpretation" endorsing the view of those courts rejecting the defense, stating that the HazCom Standard "does not preempt a failure-to-warn state tort claim."[195] It remains to be seen whether future courts will defer to the agency's legal analysis on this point.

---

188. 364 F. Supp. 2d 669, 673 (N.D. Ohio 2005).
189. 29 U.S.C. §§ 651–678.
190. *In re Welding Fume Prods.*, 364 F. Supp. 2d at 674 (quoting 29 U.S.C. § 653(b)(4)).
191. *Id.* at 688.
192. *Id.* at 698.
193. *See, e.g., id.* at 693; Anderson v. Airco, Inc., No. 03-123-SLR, 2003 WL 21842085, at *6–7 (D. Del. July 28, 2003); York v. Union Carbide Corp., 586 N.E.2d 861, 866 (Ind. Ct. App. 1992); Fullen v. Philips Elecs. N. Am. Corp., 266 F. Supp. 2d 471, 476 (N.D. W. Va. 2002).
194. Bass v. Air Prods.& Chems., Inc., No. A-4542-03T3, 2006 WL 1419375, at *2–3 (N.J. Super. Ct. App. Div. 2006); Vettrus v. Ashland, No. C9-04-817 (Minn. 3d Jud. Dist. 2008).
195. U.S. Dep't of Labor, Occupational Safety & Health Admin., *Clarification of Hazcom Provision Intended to Preempt Conflicting State Regulatory Actions, but Not Tort Claims*, OSHA Std. Interp. 1910.1210, 2011 WL 5317312 (D.O.L. Oct. 18, 2011).

Food, Drug, and Cosmetic Act (FDCA)

In 1938, Congress enacted the Federal Food, Drug, and Cosmetic Act[196] to prohibit "[t]he introduction or delivery for introduction into interstate commerce of any food, drug, device, tobacco product, or cosmetic that is adulterated or misbranded."[197] Congress in turn provided the U.S. Food and Drug Administration (FDA) with exclusive authority to enforce the FDCA.[198] Courts have thus consistently held that private parties cannot sue to enforce the FDCA through private court actions.[199] In enacting the FDCA, however, Congress did not expressly preempt common law tort actions for failure to include an adequate warning on prescription drugs.[200] As a result, drug manufacturers were left to argue that such claims were impliedly preempted by the FDCA. This defense met with varying degrees of success in different courts throughout the country.

In 2009, however, the U.S. Supreme Court set out to resolve some of this inconsistency in *Wyeth v. Levine*.[201] In that case, the plaintiff (a musician) received several shots of Phenergan, a drug used to treat nausea and headaches. Due to the error of a physician's assistant, the medication was injected into the plaintiff's artery, resulting in gangrene and ultimately requiring amputation of her arm. The plaintiff sued Wyeth claiming that it had not adequately warned of this risk. Wyeth responded that such claims were preempted. The Supreme Court disagreed, holding that FDA's approval of a drug's labeling does not, by itself, preempt state law claims. In response to Wyeth's contention that it was impossible to comply with federal and state law, the Court noted that federal regulations allow a manufacturer to alter a drug's labeling after FDA approval under certain circumstances.[202] While federal law will preempt state tort claims when there is "clear evidence that the FDA would not have approved a change to [a drug's] label," Wyeth failed to provide such evidence, and "the mere fact that the FDA approved [the drug's] label does not establish that it would have prohibited such a change."[203] The Court further held that state tort law, rather than posing an obstacle to the federal regulation of drug labeling, may complement FDA's federal mandate.[204] The Court did acknowledge, however, that "some

---

196. 21 U.S.C. §§ 301–399d.
197. 21 U.S.C. § 331(a).
198. 21 U.S.C. § 337(a).
199. *See, e.g.*, Buckman Co. v. Plaintiffs' Legal Comm., 531 U.S. 341, 349 n.4 (2001); Sandoz Pharm. Corp. v. Richardson-Vicks, Inc., 902 F.2d 222, 231 (3d Cir. 1990).
200. Wyeth v. Levine, 555 U.S. 555, 574 (2009) (noting that Congress did not enact an express preemption provision for prescription drugs (citing Riegel v. Medtronic, Inc., 552 U.S. 312, 327 (2008) ("Congress could have applied the pre-emption clause to the entire FDCA. It did not do so, but instead wrote a preemption clause that applies only to medical devices."))).
201. 555 U.S. 555 (2009).
202. *Id.* at 569–71.
203. *Id.* at 571, 573.
204. *Id.* at 574; *see also id.* at 578–79 ("The FDA has limited resources to monitor the 11,000 drugs on the market, and manufacturers have superior access to information about their drugs, especially in the postmarketing phase as new risks emerge. State tort suits uncover unknown drug hazards and provide incentives for drug manufacturers to disclose safety risks promptly. They also serve a distinct compensatory

state-law claims might well frustrate the achievement of congressional objectives."[205] The Court did not explain further what type of claims would present such an obstacle. Thus, while the decision in *Levine* has substantially limited the defense of implied preemption in the context of prescription drugs, there remains some room for invoking the defense, particularly where there may be evidence that FDA would have rejected a stronger warning.

Use and Applicability of Regulatory Safe Levels

One of the central considerations underlying virtually every toxic tort case is identifying the point at which the presence of a chemical substance rises to the level of actionable harm. The relatively recent ability of scientists to detect the presence of substances in parts per billion, trillion, and below has only heightened the significance of this issue. With some exceptions, most courts have adopted a pragmatic approach to determining the level at which a chemical substance will support an actionable claim. Courts often rely on regulatory safe levels for soil, water, and air set by state and federal agencies charged by law with protecting human health and the environment as the level below which no legally cognizable claim exists. Many decisions across the country now recognize that levels of a chemical substance below the regulatory safe level cannot give rise to a tort claim.

For example, in *Brooks v. E.I. duPont de Nemours & Co.*,[206] the plaintiffs alleged that the defendant had contaminated their groundwater even though the levels of contamination were within North Carolina groundwater standards. The court noted that under the applicable environmental regulations, "the groundwater quality standards represent the 'maximum allowable . . . concentrations which may be tolerated without creating a threat to human health or which would otherwise render the groundwater unsuitable for its intended best usage.'"[207] The court thus found that "levels of contaminants which fall below the maximum allowable concentration do not pose a threat; rather, such levels pose an acceptable risk." Because the plaintiffs "failed to demonstrate even a prima facie showing that they have been damaged under North Carolina regulations," the court dismissed as a matter of law their nuisance, trespass, negligence, and strict liability claims.[208]

Other courts have come to similar conclusions under comparable facts. In *Allgood v. General Motors Corp.*, for example, the U.S. District Court for the Southern District of

---

function that may motivate injured persons to come forward with information. Failure-to-warn actions, in particular, lend force to the FDCA's premise that manufacturers, not the FDA, bear primary responsibility for their drug labeling at all times." (footnote omitted)).
205. *Id.* at 581.
206. 944 F. Supp. 448 (E.D.N.C. 1996).
207. *Id.* at 449 (quoting 15A N.C. ADMIN. CODE 2L.0202 (1994)).
208. *Id.*; *see also* Adams v. A.J. Ballard, Jr. Tire & Oil Co., Nos. 01 CVS 1271, 03 CVS 912 & 03 CVS 1124, 2006 WL 1875965, at *31–32 (N.C. Super. Ct. June 30, 2006) (following *Brooks* and further explaining that "[s]tate authorities responsible for protecting the state's water sources are in a better position than courts to set and reset standards based on new scientific information and changing standards of health").

Indiana granted partial summary judgment as to the plaintiffs' allegations of property damage where the levels of PCBs were below the remediation standard approved by EPA and the State of Indiana.[209] Similarly, the court in *Player v. Motiva Enterprises LLC* held that "contamination below the minimum level set by [the New Jersey Department of Environmental Protection] . . . typically is insufficient to establish injurious toxic exposure."[210] And in *City of Moses Lake v. United States*, the court dismissed the plaintiff's property injury claims for lack of injury where no groundwater wells exceeded the maximum contaminant level within the limitations period.[211] Numerous other courts have likewise relied on applicable regulatory safe levels to establish a necessary threshold that must be exceeded to support a toxic tort claim.[212]

Nevertheless, this approach has not been universally adopted. Some courts have found that regulatory safe levels do not define whether a plaintiff has been harmed. For example, in *In re Methyl Tertiary Butyl Ether (MTBE) Products Liability Litigation*, the defendants sought dismissal of groundwater contamination claims brought by municipal water providers and regulators where the levels in question were below the maximum contaminant level (MCL).[213] The district court rejected this contention on the facts before it, explain-

---

209. No. 1:02-cv-1077-DFH-TAB, 2006 WL 2669337, at *37 (S.D. Ind. Sept. 18, 2006).
210. No. 02-3216 (RBK), 2006 WL 166452, at *9 (D.N.J. Jan. 20, 2006) (internal citation omitted) (internal quotation marks omitted).
211. 430 F. Supp. 2d 1164, 1184–85 (E.D. Wash. 2006).
212. *See, e.g.*, Adams-Arapahoe Sch. Dist. No. 28-J v. U.S. Gypsum Co., 958 F.2d 381 (Table), 1992 WL 58963, at *1–2 (10th Cir. Mar. 23, 1992) (asbestos within the range considered safe by OSHA does not give building owner a tort action against manufacturer); New Mexico v. Gen. Elec. Co., 335 F. Supp. 2d 1185, 1212 (D.N.M. 2004), *aff'd*, 467 F.3d 1223 (10th Cir. 2006) (holding that "use for drinking water purposes depends upon whether applicable water quality standards are met, not whether the water yet remains in its primordial state, untouched by any of the chemical remnants of the modern age"); Rose v. Union Oil Co. of Cal., No. C 97-3808 FMS, 1999 WL 51819, at *6–7 (N.D. Cal. Feb. 1, 1999) (trace petroleum constituents in soil and groundwater below regulatory levels insufficient to establish injury); Lamb v. Martin Marietta Energy Sys., Inc., 835 F. Supp. 959, 970 (W.D. Ky. 1993) (claim for diminution in property value dismissed because levels were below federal standards); Kansas v. Marion Cnty. Landfill, Inc., 76 P.3d 1000, 1010–11 (Kan. 2003) (reversing judgment for plaintiff on nuisance claim because plaintiff failed to offer expert testimony establishing contamination levels in excess of state standards); Branch v. W. Petroleum, Inc., 657 P.2d 267, 277 (Utah 1982) (injury to plaintiffs was not the total amount of chemicals in their wells but "rather the amount of contaminants above the safe level of 500 parts per million" established by federal health standards); Ronald Holland's A-Plus Transmission & Auto., Inc. v. E-Z Mart Stores, Inc., 184 S.W.3d 749, 756 (Tex. Ct. App. 2005) (holding that "to bring a cause of action when proper clean-up measures have taken place in compliance with TNRCC requirements, a plaintiff must show that there are 'unreasonable levels' of contaminants, meaning levels *in excess* of actionable levels of contamination" (emphasis in original) (internal quotation marks omitted)); D & J Co. v. Stuart, 765 N.E.2d 368, 375–76 (Ohio Ct. App. 2001) (property cannot be said to have been used in unlawful manner where levels of contaminants are below state residential cleanup standards); Muralo Co. v. Employers Ins. of Wausau, 759 A.2d 348, 352–53 (N.J. Super. Ct. App. Div. 2000) ("[S]ince it is clear that no untreated groundwater is ever entirely pure, we are satisfied that DEP standards are the most reliable guide for determining whether contamination causing damage . . . has occurred."); *see also* Koronthaly v. L'Oreal USA, Inc., 374 F. App'x 257, 259 (3d Cir. Mar. 26, 2010) (purchasers of lipstick had no standing to sue lipstick manufacturer where lipstick lead content did not exceed safe levels as determined by Food and Drug Administration).
213. 458 F. Supp. 2d 149, 158 (S.D.N.Y. 2006).

ing that the governmental claimants were under a statutory duty to protect groundwater resources and to take action before contamination exceeds regulatory levels, and in fact had incurred specific expenses in carrying out these obligations as a result of the defendants' contamination.[214] The court further found that while the MCL "may serve as a convenient guidepost in determining that a particular level of contamination has likely caused an injury, the MCL does not define *whether* an injury has occurred."[215] And in *Mercer v. Rockwell International Corp.*, the court, while emphasizing that a plaintiff must prove some actual harm resulting from levels of contamination above background, nevertheless found that the regulatory cleanup standards set by the state and federal agencies were not determinative of this question.[216]

Standing

The significance of the mere presence of contaminants below regulatory safe levels can also come up in the context of standing. To satisfy the constitutional minimum requirements of standing, a plaintiff must show that (1) she has suffered an injury-in-fact—that is, an invasion of a legally protected interest that is both concrete and particularized and actual or imminent; (2) there is a causal connection between the injury and the conduct complained of, meaning that the injury is fairly traceable to the challenged action of the defendant; and (3) it is likely, rather than merely speculative, that the injury will be redressed by a favorable decision.[217]

Applied to the issue of regulatory safe levels, the standing question that most frequently arises is whether the plaintiff has suffered an injury-in-fact. In *Iberville Parish Waterworks District No. 3 v. Novartis Crop Protection, Inc.*, public water suppliers sued a herbicide manufacturer to recover additional water treatment costs allegedly needed to treat water to remove the chemical.[218] The defendant moved for summary judgment on grounds that the chemical levels found were below regulatory levels and hence did not constitute an injury-in-fact. The court agreed, explaining that because the plaintiffs were in compliance with drinking water standards, they had not suffered "any actual invasion of a legally protected interest."[219] Along similar lines, in *LaBauve v. Olin Corp.*, the district court

---

214. *Id.* at 155–56.
215. *Id.* at 156–58 (emphasis in original).
216. 24 F. Supp. 2d 735, 752 n.12 (W.D. Ky. 1998) ("This is not a regulatory case, so the remediation standards are not relevant."); *see also* Rhodes v. E.I. de Pont de Nemours & Co., 657 F. Supp. 2d 751, 764 (S.D. W.Va. 2009) (denying summary judgment on the plaintiffs' claims even though levels of PFOA were below EPA guidelines).
217. *See, e.g.,* Friends of the Earth, Inc. v. Laidlaw Envtl. Servs. (TOC), Inc., 528 U.S. 167, 180–81 (2000); Lujan v. Defenders of Wildlife, 504 U.S. 555, 560–61 (1992); Whitmore v. Arkansas, 495 U.S. 149, 155 (1990); Sierra Club v. Morton, 405 U.S. 727, 740–41 (1972).
218. 45 F. Supp. 2d 934, 936–37 (S.D. Ala. 1999), *aff'd*, 204 F.3d 1122 (11th Cir. 1999).
219. *Id.* at 942; *see also* Emerald Coast Utils. Auth. v. 3M Co., 746 F. Supp. 2d 1216, 1231–32 (N.D. Fla. 2010) (water utility lacked standing to bring action against chemical companies where levels of contaminates were below EPA provisional advisories); Rockwell Int'l Corp. v. Wilhite, 143 S.W.3d 604, 623 (Ky.

dismissed for lack of standing the claims of those plaintiffs whose properties had levels of mercury that were below background (i.e., after accounting for the natural presence of mercury in the soil and the release of mercury from other local and distant sources).[220]

The question of standing, of course, can also arise in a wide variety of other contexts. For example, in *In re Premcor Refining Group, Inc.*, the defendants sought a writ of mandamus from the Texas Court of Appeals, arguing that the trial court had improperly denied their motion to dismiss the plaintiffs' nuisance claims for lack of standing on grounds that they did not own the land in question at the time the injury to the property first occurred.[221] The appellate court agreed and accordingly ordered the case back to the trial court to dismiss those claims.[222] Similarly, in *Watters v. General Electric Co.*, the plaintiff alleged that a nearby manufacturing plant caused PCBs to be deposited on the area of his property bordering a creek.[223] Although the plant operated from 1953 to 1998, and used PCBs in the manufacturing process until April 1977, the plaintiff had only purchased his property in December 1997.[224] The court explained that to prevail on a trespass or property damage claim, the plaintiff must prove that he owned or possessed the land at the time of the alleged trespass or injury. Because a claim for trespass or nuisance does not run with the land (at least absent an express provision in the deed), the plaintiff was required to "prove that the trespass or nuisance—that is, at least a portion of the PCB contamination—occurred during the time that Plaintiff owned the property."[225] Under this defense, often referred to as the prior trespass or prior nuisance doctrine, the plaintiffs' claims are thus limited to the additional harm, if any, that may have incurred after the date on which they acquired the property.[226]

Ct. App. 2003) (landowners lacked standing to sue for damage to land contaminated by insignificant amounts of PCBs). *But see* Suffolk Cnty. Water Auth. v. Dow Chem. Co., 942 N.Y.S.2d 765, 771 (N.Y. Sup. Ct. 2012) (water authority had standing to bring claims where contaminant levels were below MCL); City of Greenville v. Syngenta Crop Prot., Inc., 756 F. Supp. 2d 1001, 1007 (S.D. Ill. 2010) (public water supplier need not wait until levels of contamination exceed regulatory threshold to bring suit).

220. 231 F.R.D. 632, 646–48 (S.D. Ala. 2005). *But see* Forest Park Nat'l Bank & Trust v. Ditchfield, 881 F. Supp. 2d 949, 963 (N.D. Ill. 2012) (finding that "[e]ven a small amount" of contaminant on the plaintiff's property would be sufficient to "establish[] the required injury for standing purposes").
221. 233 S.W.3d 904, 908 (Tex. Ct. App. 2007) ("*Premcor I*") (permanent nuisance).
222. *Id.* at 908–09; *see also In re* Premcor Refining Grp., Inc., 262 S.W.3d 475, 480 (Tex. Ct. App. 2008) ("*Premcor II*") (temporary nuisance); Gates *ex rel.* Triumph Mortg., Inc. v. Sprint Spectrum, L.P., 349 F. App'x 257, 259 (10th Cir. 2009) (following *Premcor I*).
223. No. 4:98-cv-0195-HLM (N.D. Ga. April 2, 2001).
224. *Id.* at 23–25.
225. *Id.* at 32–33 (emphasis added) (citations omitted); *see also* Outdoor Sys., Inc. v. Wood, 543 S.E.2d 414, 417 (2000) ("The law in Georgia is that a cause of action for trespass does not run with the land...."); Rome Kraft Co. v. J.L. Davis, 102 S.E.2d 571, 574 (Ga. 1958) (holding that "a trespass upon land simply gives to the owner a right of action for damages, which cannot be said to 'run with the land,' and therefore does not pass to a subsequent purchaser").
226. *But see* David v. Velsicol Chem. Corp., 49 So. 3d 997, 14–15 (La. Ct. App. 2010) (holding that although contamination to the plaintiffs' property occurred prior to their ownership, the plaintiffs still had standing to bring claims that they had been injured from exposure to high levels of arsenic in the groundwater they had ingested).

Questions of standing also frequently arise in cases involving alleged violations of statutory obligations under various environmental statutes. For example, in *Covington v. Jefferson County*, the U.S. Court of Appeals for the Ninth Circuit examined the plaintiffs' standing to bring claims against a county dump for violations of the Clean Air Act (CAA) and the Resource Conservation and Recovery Act (RCRA).[227] The court noted that the plaintiffs lived just across the street from the landfill and that the statutory violations alleged created risks of fires, explosions, excessive animals, and groundwater contamination.[228] The plaintiffs also submitted evidence that the alleged violations had caused them to suffer watering eyes and burning noses. Based on this evidence, the court found that the plaintiffs did in fact have standing to bring their claims.[229] By contrast, in *Pollack v. United States Department of Justice*, the plaintiffs sued the federal government on grounds that the discharge of bullets from a government gun range into Lake Michigan was contaminating the water in violation of several environmental laws and also causing a nuisance.[230] The U.S. Court of Appeals for the Seventh Circuit dismissed the claims for lack of standing, noting that the plaintiff's property was approximately 13 miles away from the gun range and drew water from a different section of Lake Michigan. The court further explained that "[t]aken to its extreme, [the plaintiff's] argument would permit any person living on or near Lake Michigan to assert that he has been harmed by the bullets, because the lead could potentially have been carried to every part of the lake."[231] Relying on the U.S. Supreme Court's decision in *Lujan v. National Wildlife Federation*, the court held that "when a vast environmental area is involved and the pollution affects one discrete area while a plaintiff intends to visit a different discrete area, that plaintiff does not have standing."[232]

---

227. 358 F.3d 626 (9th Cir. 2004).
228. *Id.* at 638.
229. *Id.* at 640–41; *see also* Parker v. Scrap Metal Processors, Inc., 386 F.3d 993, 1003–04 (11th Cir. 2004) (evidence that the plaintiff's land had been contaminated, that underground storage tanks on the defendant's property were leaking, and that waste had migrated to the plaintiff's property were sufficient to establish standing to bring RCRA claim); Interfaith Cmty. Org. v. Honeywell Int'l, Inc., 399 F.3d 248, 256 (3d Cir. 2005) (finding standing to bring RCRA claims where the plaintiffs alleged recreating near, next to, and along the river that runs adjacent to the defendant's site). *But see* Knaust v. City of Kingston, 193 F. Supp. 2d 536, 543 (N.D.N.Y. 2002) (holding that more than a "hypothetical threat" of contamination is required to establish standing).
230. 577 F.3d 736, 738 (7th Cir. 2009).
231. *Id.* at 742.
232. *Id.* (citing Lujan v. Nat'l Wildlife Fed'n, 497 U.S. 871 (1990)); *see also* Maine People's Alliance v. Mallinckrodt, Inc., 471 F.3d 277, 284 (1st Cir. 2006) ("To establish an injury in fact based on a probabilistic harm, a plaintiff must show that there is a substantial probability that the harm will occur." (internal citations omitted)); Fisher v. CIBA Specialty Chems. Corp., 238 F.R.D. 273, 298–99 (S.D. Ala. 2006) (finding that purported class representative lacked standing because there was no evidence of actual or imminent contamination of his property).

Plaintiff's Culpable Conduct

Under the traditional common law rule of contributory negligence, plaintiffs were precluded from any recovery whatsoever if their negligence causally contributed to the harm suffered, even if the defendant's negligence greatly exceeded that of the plaintiffs. All but a small handful of states have now abolished the doctrine of contributory negligence, either by judicial or legislative action, replacing it with some form of comparative negligence.[233] Rather than barring any and all recovery by negligent plaintiffs, the doctrine of comparative negligence instead reduces the plaintiffs' recovery in proportion to the plaintiffs' fault.

There are two primary forms of comparative negligence: pure and modified. Pure comparative negligence applies comparative fault in all cases regardless of the percentage of fault that may be attributable to the plaintiffs. Under this approach, no plaintiff is barred completely from recovery based on her contributory negligence; even a plaintiff 90 percent at fault would be entitled to some relief. Modified comparative negligence, on the other hand, incorporates a complete bar on recovery at some specific breakpoint. In some states, plaintiffs are barred from recovery if their negligence is 50 percent or greater than the total fault of all parties; in other states, plaintiffs are barred from recovery if their negligence exceeds 50 percent of parties' total fault (i.e., is greater than 50%).[234] Still other states follow a "slight/gross" system when applying comparative fault, meaning that for a plaintiff to recover, her negligence must be slight or minimal, while the defendant's must be gross by comparison.[235]

Similarly, defendants may argue that a plaintiff is barred from recovery because she "assumed the risk." In general, to establish this defense, a defendant must prove that the plaintiff knew about the danger, understood and appreciated the risk, and voluntarily proceeded despite that risk.[236] In light of the modern trend toward adopting a system of comparative negligence, most jurisdictions have simply merged assumption of the risk

---

233. Victor E. Schwartz & Evelyn F. Rowe, Comparative Negligence § 1.01 (5th ed. 2010) (noting that by 1994, comparative negligence had replaced contributory negligence as a complete defense in forty-six states). Alabama, Maryland, North Carolina, Virginia, and the District of Columbia remain the sole holdouts. Victor E. Schwartz et al., Prosser, Wade, and Schwartz's Torts: Cases and Materials 621 (12th ed. 2010).

234. *See generally* Schwartz & Rowe, *supra* note 233, § 2.01.

235. *See, e.g.*, Neb. Rev. Stat. § 25-21, 185 (providing that "the fact that the plaintiff may have been guilty of contributory negligence shall not bar a recovery when the contributory negligence of the plaintiff was slight and the negligence or act or omission giving rise to strict liability in tort of the defendant was gross in comparison").

236. *See, e.g.*, Restatement (Second) of Torts § 496A (1977) ("A plaintiff who voluntarily assumes a risk of harm arising from the negligent or reckless conduct of the defendant cannot recover for such harm."), § 496C(1) ("[A] plaintiff who fully understands a risk of harm to himself or his things caused by the defendant's conduct or by the condition of the defendant's land or chattels, and who nevertheless voluntarily chooses to enter or remain, or to permit his things to enter or remain within the area of that risk, under circumstances that manifest his willingness to accept it, is not entitled to recover for harm within that risk."), § 496D ("Except where he expressly so agrees, a plaintiff does not assume a risk of harm arising from the defendant's conduct unless he then knows of the existence of the risk and appreciates its unreasonable character.").

into the analysis of comparative fault.[237] Indeed, the *Restatement (Third) of Torts* explicitly rejects the argument as an absolute defense.[238] As a practical matter, assumption of the risk is now only a partial bar to recovery. As a corollary to assumption of the risk, a plaintiff may argue that the defendant should be held liable, despite the plaintiff's own negligence, when the defendant had the "last clear chance" to avoid the injury and failed to do so. Again, while states vary in their precise approach, the modern trend is to simply fold this doctrine into the broader comparative fault scheme.[239]

Of course, this basic summary and categorization greatly oversimplifies the myriad of ways in which different jurisdictions address the wide variety of issues implicated when attempting to allocate fault between the parties, particularly in the field of toxic torts. These complicating issues include, for example:

- the existence of multiple tortfeasors (e.g., whether plaintiff's fault should be compared to each defendant individually or to the defendants collectively);
- the imposition of joint and several liability;
- the potential for absent, unidentifiable, immune, or insolvent parties;
- differences between negligent, reckless, and intentional (or even criminal) tortious acts;
- application, if any, to strict liability, breach of warranty, and other tort claims;
- application, if any, when a defendant violates a statutory duty or obligation;
- the continuing validity of legal theories that arose prior to the adoption of comparative negligence (e.g., the last clear chance doctrine);
- potential claims for contribution and indemnity and the point at which they must be raised; and
- complications posed by settlements and releases.

Though well beyond the scope of this brief discussion, the rules adopted as to each of these issues have the potential to implicate the manner in which legal fault is ultimately apportioned, often in significant ways.

While sorting out the relative fault of the parties is often viewed by courts as a task best suited for a jury, there are instances where a court may take it upon itself to enter judgment as a matter of law. As an example, in *Kolesar v. United Agri Products, Inc.*, the

---

237. *See, e.g.*, Kenneth W. Simons, *Reflections on Assumption of Risk*, 50 UCLA L. Rev. 481, 482 (2002) ("The modern conventional wisdom is that assumption of risk should be completely merged or assimilated within comparative fault and abolished as a distinct doctrine."). Nevertheless, it is the case that some courts continue to recognize assumption of risk as a viable and distinct substantive doctrine. *See id.* at 483 n.8 (citing cases).
238. Restatement (Third) of Torts: Apportionment of Liability § 2 cmt. *i* (2000).
239. *See, e.g.*, David W. Robertson, *Love and Fury: Recent Radical Revisions to the Law of Comparative Fault*, 59 La. L. Rev. 175, 189 (1998) ("It is almost universally accepted that the last clear chance doctrine must disappear whenever a comparative fault regime . . . goes into effect.").

plaintiff brought an action arising from accidental exposure to toxic chemicals.[240] The plaintiff was in the process of delivering these chemicals to the defendants' facility when he accidentally was sprayed by them. Notably, the plaintiff was not wearing any protective gear at the time as he had been instructed by his employer. The plaintiff also failed to seek prompt medical treatment following the accident. The defendants moved for summary judgment on several grounds, including the plaintiff's own culpable conduct. The court, noting that a plaintiff may not recover under Wisconsin law when he is more negligent than the defendants, found that the "greatest cause for the spill and the greatest part of the fault is upon Plaintiff's shoulders."[241] Accordingly, the court granted summary judgment, finding in favor of the defendants as a matter of law.

Failure to Mitigate

Plaintiffs have an affirmative duty to take reasonable measures to mitigate any damages caused by a defendant. As stated in the *Restatement (Second) of Torts*, "one injured by the tort of another is not entitled to recover damages for any harm that he could have avoided by the use of reasonable effort or expenditure after the commission of the tort."[242] Tort victims must therefore do what is reasonable and prudent under the circumstances in order to mitigate their damages.[243] Should they fail to do so, they "cannot recover for losses which might have been prevented by reasonable efforts and expenditures on [their] part."[244]

Defendants, as a result, may be able to limit or even foreclose potential damages for personal injury or property damages by offering to protect plaintiffs from further injury or otherwise mitigating existing harm. When plaintiffs avail themselves of such offers, their damages may be lessened; and where such offers are refused, plaintiffs may have failed to mitigate damages. By way of example, in *Romeo v. Sherry*, the owner of waterfront property brought a tort action against defendants for abandoning several barges offshore

---

240. 412 F. Supp. 2d 686 (W.D. Mich. 2006).
241. *Id.* at 699.
242. RESTATEMENT (SECOND) OF TORTS § 918(1) (1977). The *Restatement*, however, notes an exception in the case of intentional or reckless torts: "One is not prevented from recovering damages for a particular harm resulting from a tort if the tortfeasor intended the harm or was aware of it and was recklessly disregardful of it, unless the injured person with knowledge of the danger of the harm intentionally or heedlessly failed to protect his own interests." *Id.* § 918(2).
243. *See* M.F. *ex rel.* Flowers v. Delaney, 830 N.Y.S.2d 412, 414 (N.Y. App. Div. 2007) (holding in a case involving lead paint exposure that minor plaintiffs had no duty to mitigate but that the defendant had raised a viable defense as to the plaintiff mother); Hill v. Metro. Dist. Comm'n, 787 N.E.2d 526, 534 (Mass. 2003) (stating that claimants in property damage cases seeking damages are required to "take reasonable action to limit or mitigate damages" (quoting *Guaranty-First Trust Co. v. Textron, Inc.*, 622 N.E.2d 597 (Mass. 1993))).
244. United States v. Sierra Pac. Indus., 879 F. Supp. 2d 1128, 1136 (E.D. Cal. 2012) (quoting Valencia v. Shell Oil Co., 147 P.2d 558, 560 (Cal. 1944)); Kocher v. Getz, 824 N.E.2d 671, 674–75 (Ind. 2005) (explaining that an unreasonable failure to mitigate damages is not to be considered in the assessment of fault under a comparative negligence scheme but instead limits any damages a plaintiff could have avoided through reasonable care).

near his property.[245] The defendants had agreed to remove the barges for free if the plaintiff would obtain the necessary permit to do so, but the plaintiff declined, explaining that he did not believe the offer to be genuine. The court held that the plaintiff's tort claims were barred for failure to mitigate damages, explaining that had he followed through on the offer, he would have had no damages.[246]

Courts, however, will not always require a plaintiff to agree to a defendant's offer to mitigate. For example, in *Moody v. Cummings*, a plaintiff brought a tort action for injuries to his knee, neck, and back resulting from a car crash.[247] A jury found in favor of the plaintiff. The defendants appealed, arguing that the plaintiff failed to mitigate his damages by refusing to undergo the recommended arthroscopic knee surgery and epidural cervical injections prior to trial and failing to take his medication as prescribed. The Louisiana Court of Appeals acknowledged that tort victims have a duty to mitigate, but noted that "the care and diligence required of him is the same as that which would be used by a person of ordinary prudence under the circumstances." The court further noted that "an injury victim does not fail to mitigate his damages when he refuses to undergo treatment which would not significantly alleviate his disability, carries risks of failure, when the treatment is painful, or when he is unable to pay for the treatment."[248] In light of these considerations, the court found that the plaintiff did not fail to mitigate his damages and accordingly upheld the jury verdict in the plaintiff's favor.[249]

---

245. 308 F. Supp. 2d 128 (E.D.N.Y. 2004).
246. *Id.* at 146; *see also* Abrams v. CIBA Specialty Chems. Corp., No. 08-0068-WSB, 2009 WL 3254443, at *5 & n.11 (S.D. Ala. Oct. 1, 2009) (allowing the defendants to present evidence that the plaintiffs failed to mitigate property contamination caused by DDT, describing the "simple steps that can be taken to reduce the level of contamination" as a "textbook application of the doctrine of failure to mitigate damages"). *But see* Eskenazi v. Mackoul, 905 N.Y.S.2d 169, 171–72 (N.Y. App. Div. 2010) (finding that the defendants failed to establish that the plaintiffs did not mitigate property contamination from a leaking underground storage tank); Oresta v. Romano Bros., 73 S.E.2d 622, 632 (W. Va. 1952) (finding that "a person whose property has been injured by the maintenance of a nuisance is not bound to prevent or reduce the damages, especially where the nuisance is in a place over which he has no control," and further finding evidence that the plaintiffs refused to allow the defendants to enter their land to remedy the problem was inadmissible).
247. 37 So. 3d 1054 (La. Ct. App. 2010).
248. *Id.* at 1063–64.
249. *Id.* at 1064; *see also* Flemings v. State, 19 So. 3d 1220, 1228–29 (La. Ct. App. 2009). *But see* Jackson v. Target Corp., No. 09-10867, 2011 WL 533600, at *5 (E.D. Mich. Feb. 15, 2011) (denying a plaintiff's motion to prohibit a defendant from raising mitigation defense in light of plaintiff's refusal to undergo medical treatment); Robinson v. United States, 330 F. Supp. 2d 261, 295 (W.D.N.Y. 2004) ("New York courts have long held that the plaintiff is bound to submit to treatment prescribed or recommended by his physician, unless it can be shown that a physician of ordinary skill would not adopt or sanction that treatment. The plaintiff's disinclination to receive treatment, or the fact that the treatment might cause acute physical discomfort, are not sufficient reasons to refuse the recommended treatment." (internal citation omitted)).

Defenses to Nuisance Claims
Coming to the Nuisance

As somewhat analogous to assumption of the risk in negligence cases, defendants may argue in nuisance cases that the plaintiff "came to the nuisance." Of course, most states long ago abolished coming to the nuisance as a complete defense,[250] though the defense has been reinstated by statute in some cases for agricultural activities.[251] Notwithstanding the abolition of the defense generally, the plaintiff's knowledge of the activities alleged to be a nuisance may still be a relevant consideration in determining whether an actionable claim exists and what the remedy (if any) should be.[252] As explained in the *Restatement (Second) of Torts*: "The fact that the plaintiff has acquired or improved his land after a nuisance interfering with it has come into existence is not in itself sufficient to bar his action, but it is a factor to be considered in determining whether the nuisance is actionable."[253] What is called the "priority of occupation" (i.e., who was on the property first) may be considered in determining whether the alleged tortfeasor's use of the property is reasonable.[254]

Government Authorization: Permitted, Licensed, and Regulated Activity

Courts also have expressed some reluctance to find tortious those activities that are specifically authorized by the government, at least in certain contexts.[255] The recent decision

---

250. *See, e.g.*, Darney v. Dragon Prods. Co., 771 F. Supp. 2d 91, 109 (D. Me. 2011) (noting the "well-established principle that 'coming to the nuisance' does not act as a bar to a suit for nuisance" (quoting Eaton v. Cormier, 748 A.2d 1006, 1008 (Me. 2000))); City of Lebanon v. Ga.-Pac. Corp., No. 02-6351-AA, 2004 WL 1078982, at *7–8 (D. Or. May 11, 2004) (same).
251. *See, e.g.*, TDM Farms, Inc. of N.C. v. Wilhoite Family Farm, LLC, 969 N.E.2d 97, 111 (Ind. Ct. App. 2012) (stating that the Indiana Right-to-Farm Act prohibits "nonagricultural land uses from being the basis of a nuisance suit against an established agricultural operation" (citing Ind. Code § 32-30-6-9(b))); Alexander v. Hulsey Envtl. Servs., Inc., 702 S.E.2d 435, 462–63 (Ga. Ct. App. 2010) (rejecting application of Georgia's Right-to-Farm statute to the defendant's waste disposal facility); Vicwood Meridian P'ship v. Skagit Sand & Gravel, 98 P.3d 1277, 1280–81 (Wash. Ct. App. 2004) (discussing the coming to the nuisance defense under the Washington Right-to-Farm Act). *But see* Bormann v. Bd. of Supervisors, 584 N.W.2d 309, 321–22 (Iowa 1998) (nuisance immunity statute held an unconstitutional taking).
252. *See Darney*, 771 F. Supp. 2d at 109 (stating that while coming to the nuisance is not a complete defense, "[n]either . . . is it wholly irrelevant to a determination of the appropriate remedy in a nuisance action" (quoting *Eaton*, 748 A.2d at 1008)); *see also* Jacques v. Pioneer Plastics, Inc., 676 A.2d 504, 508 (Me. 1996) (same).
253. RESTATEMENT (SECOND) OF TORTS § 840D (1977).
254. *See id.* § 840D cmt. c & illus. 2–4; *see also* W. PAGE KEETON ET AL., PROSSER AND KEETON ON TORTS 634–36 (5th ed. 1984).
255. New England Legal Found. v. Costle, 666 F.2d 30, 33 (1st Cir. 1981) (rejecting claim that a power plant created a nuisance by burning oil containing 2.2% sulfur where EPA had specifically authorized that use); *see also* Carson Harbor Vill., Ltd. v. Unocal Corp., 270 F.3d 863, 888 (9th Cir. 2001) (affirming dismissal of nuisance claims on grounds that state had issued National Pollutant Discharge Elimination System (NPDES) permits authorizing discharge of storm water containing pollutants); Joffer v. Cargill, Inc., No. 08-4198, 2010 WL 1409444, at *3–4 (D.S.D. Apr. 1, 2010) (dismissing nuisance claims in grain dust case when the defendant's grain warehouse was specifically authorized by law); Stanley v. Amalithone Realty, Inc., 921 N.Y.S.2d 491, 498 (N.Y. Sup. Ct. 2011) (holding in a case involving the health effects from radio frequency emissions that the defendants were "entitled to dismissal of the private nuisance claim as the operation of the cell phone tower is not unreasonable because it complies with all applicable laws and regulations"); Beal v. W. Farmers Elec. Coop., 228 P.3d 538, 542 (Okla. Civ.

by the U.S. Court of Appeals for the Fourth Circuit in *North Carolina v. Tennessee Valley Authority* serves as a helpful illustration.[256] In that case, the State of North Carolina filed suit against the Tennessee Valley Authority (TVA), which owns several coal-fired power plants in nearby states. Although the Clean Air Act (CAA) and its accompanying regulations extensively regulate the air emissions from these plants, North Carolina nonetheless filed suit against TVA alleging that the emissions created a public nuisance. After an extensive hearing, the district court granted an injunction as to four of TVA's power plants, ordering the installation of additional air control equipment and requiring that emissions be reduced on an accelerated schedule from what state and federal regulators had required.

The Fourth Circuit reversed, explaining that the ruling would "scuttle the nation's carefully created system for accommodating the need for energy production and the need for clean air," resulting in "a balkanization of clean air regulations and a confused patchwork of standards, to the detriment of industry and the environment alike."[257] The court further noted that "[i]t ill behooves the judiciary to set aside a congressionally sanctioned scheme of many years' duration—a scheme, moreover, that reflects the extensive application of scientific expertise and that has set in motion reliance interests and expectations on the part of those states and enterprises that have complied with its requirements."[258] Indeed, the court found it "difficult to understand how an activity expressly permitted and extensively regulated by both federal and state government could somehow constitute a public nuisance."[259] Replacing the air quality standards established under this regulatory scheme, the Fourth Circuit explained, with the uncertainty of common law nuisance litigation would leave states and industries "at sea and potentially expose them to a welter of conflicting court orders across the country."[260] Moreover, beyond "the prospect of multiplicitous decrees or vague and uncertain nuisance standards," the court found that North Carolina's public nuisance claim "would reorder the respective functions of courts and agencies." Congress in adopting the CAA "opted rather emphatically for the benefits of agency expertise in setting standards of emissions controls, especially in comparison

---

App. 2009) (dismissing the plaintiffs' nuisance claim regarding EMF emissions because power transmission lines had been authorized by the government); Neuse River Found., Inc. v. Smithfield Foods, Inc., 574 S.E.2d 48, 53, 54 (N.C. Ct. App. 2002) (holding that because the defendants' waste management systems "exist pursuant to express legislative authority," it is "not the role of the judicial branch" to enjoin that activity); S. Lake Worth Inlet Dist. v. Town of Ocean Ridge, 633 So. 2d 79, 87 (Fla. Ct. App. 1994) ("Because the plant is operated under DNR's regulation and the lawful permit issued under that authority, the operation in compliance with the permit conditions simply cannot, without more that is lacking here, be deemed a public nuisance.").

256. North Carolina v. Tenn. Valley Auth., 615 F.3d 291 (4th Cir. 2010).
257. *Id.*
258. *Id.* at 301; *see also In re* Groundwater Cases, 154 Cal. App. 4th 659, 681 (Cal. Ct. App. 2007) ("Permitting courts and juries to second-guess the carefully considered decisions of the regulatory agencies on technical water quality issues would flout the Legislature's policy choice to entrust such matters to DHS and the PUC. This we will not do.").
259. *Tenn. Valley Auth.*, 615 F.3d at 296.
260. *Id.* at 301.

with the judicially managed nuisance decrees."[261] "It is crucial therefore that courts in this highly technical arena respect the strengths of the agency processes on which Congress has placed its imprimatur."[262] For these and other reasons,[263] the Fourth Circuit remanded the case with instructions to dismiss the action in its entirety.[264]

In a similar case, the U.S. Supreme Court recently held that the CAA displaces federal common law as to public nuisance claims involving greenhouse gas emissions. The Court explained that "Congress delegated to EPA the decision whether and how to regulate carbon-dioxide emissions from power plants" and that this delegation "displaces federal common law."[265] Explaining the policy reasons supporting its finding, the Court noted:

> It is altogether fitting that Congress designated an expert agency, here, EPA, as best suited to serve as primary regulator of greenhouse gas emissions. The expert agency is surely better equipped to do the job than individual district judges issuing ad hoc, case-by-case injunctions. Federal judges lack the scientific, economic, and technological resources an agency can utilize in coping with issues of this order.[266]

The plaintiffs, notably, had also brought state court nuisance claims, but the Court declined to address whether these claims could stand as they had not been fully briefed and considered by the courts below, leaving that issue for further consideration on remand.

Nevertheless, despite these examples, courts have held that mere compliance with a governmental permit, license, or standard will not bar a nuisance action. For example, in *Darney v. Dragon Products Co., LLC*, the U.S. District Court for the District of Maine held in a case brought against a cement manufacturing facility involving air pollution, noise, and vibrations that the plaintiff's nuisance claim was not barred by the fact that the defendant's activities were licensed by the state.[267] Likewise, in *Hanna v. Motiva Enterprises, LLC*, the U.S. District Court for the Southern District of New York found that the defendants could not avoid a nuisance claim merely because the remediation system they were operating was authorized and overseen by the state.[268] And in *Jacobs Farm/Del Cabo*,

---

261. *Id.* at 304
262. *Id.* at 305–06.
263. The Fourth Circuit also found that the district court had improperly applied home state law extraterritorially in violation of the Supreme Court's decision in *International Paper Co. v. Ouellette*, 479 U.S. 481 (1987).
264. *Tenn. Valley Auth.*, 615 F.3d at 312.
265. Am. Elec. Power Co. v. Connecticut, 131 S. Ct. 2527, 2538 (2011).
266. *Id.* at 2539–40.
267. 771 F. Supp. 2d 91, 109 (D. Me. 2011) (citing Johnston v. Me. Energy Recovery Co., 997 A.2d 741, 745 (Me. 2010)); *see also* C.C. Carlton Indus., Ltd. v. Blanchard, 311 S.W.3d 654, 660 (Tex. Ct. App. 2010) (holding that "even if a commercial enterprise holds a valid permit to conduct a particular business, the manner in which it performs its activity may give rise to an action for nuisance").
268. 839 F. Supp. 2d 654, 676 (S.D.N.Y. 2012) (rejecting contention that simply "because the activity performed was done pursuant to government oversight the activity is not unreasonable, negligent, or reckless").

Inc. v. Western Farm Service, Inc., the California Court of Appeals, addressing a statutory provision providing that "[n]othing which is done or maintained under the express authority of a statute can be deemed a nuisance," found that a defendant could be held liable in nuisance when its pesticide spray drifted to a neighboring organic farm, despite the fact that government permits authorized application of the pesticides.[269]

Plaintiffs' Conduct and the Conduct of Others

Just as contributory negligence may be a defense (or at least a partial defense) to negligence claims, it may also be a defense in certain types of nuisance claims. Thus, when the defendant's negligent conduct is the basis for liability in nuisance, the plaintiff's contributory negligence may serve as a defense as in other negligence cases.[270] However, where the harm is intentional or the result of recklessness, as opposed to mere negligence, contributory negligence may not be a defense.[271] Further, in some states, when the nuisance results from an abnormally dangerous condition or activity, not an infrequent allegation in toxic tort cases, contributory negligence may only be a defense when the plaintiff has "voluntarily and unreasonably subjected himself to the risk of harm."[272] Notably, however, the fact that others may have contributed to a nuisance generally does not act as a complete defense as to the defendant's contribution to the nuisance.[273]

---

269. 119 Cal. Rptr. 3d 529, 549–51 (Cal. Ct. App. 2010) (internal citations omitted); *see also* McGuire v. Kenoma, LLC, 375 S.W.3d 157, 186 (Mo. Ct. App. 2012) ("Merely because an area may be zoned industrial (or business or commercial) does not justify the maintenance of a nuisance." (internal citations omitted) (internal quotation marks omitted)).

270. *See, e.g.,* Vogel v. Grant-Lafayette Elec. Co-op., 548 N.W.2d 829, 833–34 (Wis. 1996) (holding that when an unintentional nuisance results from negligent conduct, "the plaintiff's contributory negligence is a defense to the same extent as in other actions founded on negligence"); Wilhelm v. City of Great Falls, 732 P.2d 1315, 1318 (Mont. 1987) ("[M]ost courts hold that where a nuisance has its origin in negligence, as distinguished from an absolute nuisance, contributory negligence is a defense, and in jurisdictions in which it is recognized, the doctrine of comparative negligence may be applied." (quoting 58 AM. JUR. 2d *Nuisances* § 221 (1971))); Copart Indus., Inc. v. Consol. Edison Co of New York, Inc., 362 N.E.2d 968, 973 (N.Y. 1977) (holding that "contributory negligence may be a defense where the nuisance is based on negligent conduct"); *see also* RESTATEMENT (SECOND) OF TORTS § 840B(1) ("When a nuisance results from negligent conduct of the defendant, the contributory negligence of the plaintiff is a defense to the same extent as in other actions founded on negligence."). *But see* Branch v. Western Petroleum, Inc., 657 P.2d 267, 276 (Utah 1982) (holding that contributory negligence is not a defense to a nuisance action).

271. *See, e.g.,* BNT Co. v. Baker Precythe Dev. Co., 564 S.E.2d 891, (N.C. Ct. App. 2002) (noting that contributory negligence may be a defense to a nuisance action based upon negligence but not to nuisance action based on defendant's intentional misconduct); Sandifer Motors, Inc. v. City of Roeland Park, 628 P.2d 239, 317 (Kan. Ct. App. 1981) (stating that "contributory negligence is no defense to an intentional nuisance"); Gerzeski v. State, 268 N.W.2d 525, 529 (Mich. 1978) (noting that "contributory negligence, while a defense for negligent nuisances, is not an appropriate defense for either nuisances per se or intentional nuisances"); *see also* RESTATEMENT (SECOND) OF TORTS § 840B(2).

272. *See, e.g.,* Amland Props. Corp. v. Aluminum Co. of Am., 711 F. Supp. 784, 802–03 (D.N.J. 1989); Pulley v. Malek, 495 N.E.2d 402, 406 (Ohio 1986); *see also* RESTATEMENT (SECOND) OF TORTS § 840B(3).

273. *See, e.g.,* Adkins v. Thomas Solvent, 487 N.W.2d 715, 743 n.75 (Mich. 1992) ("Particularly in pollution cases, third parties' contributions to a nuisance do not exonerate the defendant."); N.A.A.C.P. v. AcuSport, Inc., 271 F. Supp. 2d 435, 493 (E.D.N.Y. 2003) ("Where multiple actors contribute to a public nuisance, equity can reach actors whose conduct standing alone might not be actionable."); *see also*

On these general points, different states not infrequently take different approaches. Some states, for example, include recklessness and intentional harm in calculations of comparative fault while others do not. And of course, matters become even further complicated when the other issues relating to comparative fault discussed above (such as the existence of multiple tortfeasors, the imposition of joint and several liability, the violation of statutory duties or obligations, etc.) are taken into account. As a result, as with most of the defenses discussed here, it is necessary to closely examine the law of the specific jurisdiction in question.

Lack of Duty

In any case alleging negligence, the plaintiff must establish that the defendant violated some duty of care owed to the plaintiff. A duty of care is an obligation owed by one person to act so as not to cause harm to another.[274] In most states, whether the defendant did in fact owe the plaintiff such a duty is a question of law for the court.[275]

Duty of Care

The nature of any duty and the identity of those to whom the duty is owed are determined by the specific circumstances surrounding the conduct of the individual. As a general rule, the duty of care arises out of circumstances where there is a reasonable likelihood that an act or omission will cause harm or injury.[276] Foreseeability, however, is not the only consideration. Rather, the existence and extent of any duty of care can be significantly affected by public policy considerations. As one court famously explained, "Experience has shown that . . . there are clear judicial days on which a court can foresee forever and thus determine liability but none on which that foresight alone provides a socially and judicially acceptable limit on recovery of damages for that injury."[277] The overall determination of a duty of care and the scope of any duty will thus take into consideration the relationship of the parties, the foreseeability of the harm, the nature of the risk, and the impact that such a duty would have on public policy.[278]

RESTATEMENT (SECOND) OF TORTS § 840E.
274. W. PAGE KEETON ET AL., PROSSER AND KEETON ON TORTS 356 (5th ed. 1984).
275. *See, e.g.*, Saline River Props., LLC v. Johnson Controls, Inc., 823 F. Supp. 2d 670, 676 (E.D. Mich. 2011); Dep't of Fish & Game v. Superior Court, 129 Cal Rptr. 3d 719, 747 (Cal. Ct. App. 2011); Price v. E.I. duPont de Nemours & Co., 26 A.3d 162, 166 (Del. Super. Ct. 2011).
276. *See, e.g.*, Palsgraf v. Long Island R.R. Co., 162 N.E. 99 (1928).
277. Thing v. La Chusa, 48 Cal. 3d 644, 668 (Cal. 1989).
278. *See, e.g., In re* Certified Question from Fourteenth Dist. Court of Appeals of Texas, 740 N.W.2d 206, 216 (Mich. 2007) ("[U]nder Michigan law, the ultimate inquiry in determining whether a legal duty should be imposed is whether the social benefits of imposing that duty outweigh the social costs of imposing a duty. The inquiry involves considering, among any other relevant considerations: the relationship of the parties, the foreseeability of the harm, the burden on the defendant, and the nature of the risk presented." (internal quotation marks and citation omitted)); Olivo v. Owens-Illinois, Inc., 895 A.2d 1143, 1147 (N.J. 2006) ("The imposition of a duty to exercise care to avoid a risk of harm to another involves considerations of fairness and public policy implicating many factors. The inquiry has been summarized

By way of example, in *Vaillancourt v. Town of Southington*, the plaintiffs sued an industrial manufacturer for allegedly negligently disposing of its waste in a municipal landfill near plaintiffs' home.[279] Addressing the existence of any duty owed to plaintiffs, the court considered "(1) whether an ordinary person in the defendant's position, knowing what the defendant knew or should have known, would anticipate that the harm of the general nature of that suffered by the plaintiff was likely to result; and (2) whether, on the basis of public policy, the defendant's responsibility for its negligent conduct should extend to the particular consequences or particular plaintiff in the case."[280] Given the facts before it, the court found the link between plaintiffs' alleged injuries and the manufacturer's conduct in using the landfill too attenuated to support a negligence claim. The court noted, for example, the lack of any evidence to support the conclusion that the manufacturer had any reason to anticipate that the municipality would not operate, maintain, or close the landfill in a safe and proper manner.[281]

As another example, in *Armstrong v. City of New York, Inc.*, several clammers and a clam wholesaler sued Con Edison for economic losses allegedly resulting from a massive blackout that caused New York City's wastewater treatment facilities to spill untreated sewage into the water and contaminate local shellfish beds.[282] The plaintiffs alleged that Con Edison negligently discontinued the supply of electricity to these facilities, thereby causing the spill and the resulting damages. The court, however, found that "the orbit of duty owed by utilities for service interruptions" under New York law does not extend to those who do not have a contractual relationship with the utility.[283] While damages to third parties caused by a blackout may be "conceivably foreseeable," New York restricts the scope of a utility's duty as a matter of policy "to avoid crushing exposure to the suits of millions of electricity consumers."[284] The court accordingly granted Con Edison's motion to dismiss.

By way of contrast, in *Curd v. Mosaic Fertilizer, LLC*, the Florida Supreme Court found that the owner of a fertilizer storage facility near a waterway leading to Tampa Bay owed a duty of care to commercial fisherman there.[285] The court noted that it was foreseeable that the defendant's storage of pollutants and hazardous substances would harm the environment if released into public waters, and that the commercial fisherman in the

---

succinctly as one that turns on whether the imposition of such a duty satisfies an abiding sense of basic fairness under all of the circumstances in light of considerations of public policy." (internal citations and quotation marks omitted)).
279. No. X03CV010510816S, 2002 WL 1293053, at *2 (Conn. Super. Ct. May 7, 2002).
280. *Id.* (citing Zamstein v. Marvasti, 692 A.2d 781 (Conn. 1997)).
281. *Id.* at 3–4.
282. No. 111725/04, 2005 WL 742432, at *1 (N.Y. Sup. Ct. Feb. 22, 2005).
283. *Id.* at *2.
284. *Id.* at *2–3 (internal quotation marks and citations omitted).
285. 39 So. 3d 1216, 1227 (Fla. 2010).

area had a special interest within that zone of risk. The defendant, therefore, had a duty "to exercise prudent foresight and take sufficient precautions to protect that interest."[286]

Duty to Warn

In cases involving failure-to-warn claims, three related defenses frequently arise that address the circumstances under which a warning may not be required: sophisticated user/intermediary, bulk supplier/raw materials supplier, and learned intermediary.[287] Different states and different courts define the scope and application of these defenses somewhat differently; some use the terms interchangeably while others use them to refer to distinct legal doctrines.[288]

Sophisticated User/Intermediary

Under the sophisticated user doctrine, as articulated by the California Supreme Court, a manufacturer need not warn members of a trade or profession (i.e., sophisticated users) about dangers generally known to that trade or profession.[289] The defense thus applies to those sophisticated users who knew or should have known about the product's potential dangers.[290] The sophisticated user doctrine exempts manufacturers from their normal obligation to provide product users with warnings about the product's potential hazards.[291] Indeed, at least under California law, a manufacturer is not liable to a sophisticated user for failure to warn, even if the warning is required by statute.[292] By way of example, under the sophisticated user doctrine, the supplier of hazardous chemicals would have no duty to warn of its dangerous propensities when those dangers were already known to the party using the chemical.[293]

As a related defense, in some jurisdictions, a manufacturer's duty to warn the end user may also be obviated by the sophistication of an intermediary, such as the end user's employer.[294] Indeed, the modern trend is to expand the sophisticated user defense to

---

286. *Id.* at 1228.
287. Victor E. Schwartz & Christopher E. Appel, *Effective Communication of Warnings in the Workplace: Avoiding Injuries in Working with Industrial Materials*, 73 Mo. L. Rev. 1, 19–24 (2008).
288. Gray v. Badger Mining Corp., 676 N.W.2d 268, 275–81 (Minn. 2004); Miss. Valley Silica Co. v. Eastman, 92 So. 3d 666, 671–73 (Miss. 2012); Nye v. Bayer Cropscience, Inc., 347 S.W.3d 686, 700 n.15 (Tenn. 2011); *In re* Welding Fume Prods. Liab. Litig., No. 1:03-CV-17000, MDL No. 1535, 2010 WL 7699456, at *10–11, 103–05 (N.D. Ohio June 4, 2010).
289. Johnson v. Am. Standard, Inc., 179 P.3d 905, 912 (Cal. 2008).
290. *Id.* at 910 (holding that "sophisticated users need not be warned about dangers of which they are already aware or should be aware"); *see also, e.g.,* Parker v. Schmiede Mach. & Tool Corp., 445 F. App'x 231, 234–35 (11th Cir. 2011); Taylor v. Am. Chemistry Council, 576 F.3d 16, 24–25 (1st Cir. 2009); *Gray*, 676 N.W.2d at 276–77.
291. *Johnson*, 179 P.3d at 910.
292. Johnson v. Honeywell Int'l Inc., 179 Cal. App. 4th 549, 556 (Cal. Ct. App. 2009).
293. *See, e.g., Gray*, 676 N.W.2d at 277 (citing Hill v. Wilmington Chem. Corp., 156 N.W.2d 898, 904 (Minn. 1968)).
294. *See id.* at 277–78 (recognizing disagreement between courts as to whether the sophisticated user defense should be extended to sophisticated intermediaries); *see also* Little v. Liquid Air Corp., 952 F.2d 841,

include sophisticated intermediaries who possess the same level of knowledge as sophisticated users.[295] Where recognized, the sophisticated intermediary doctrine provides an exception to the duty to warn when either of two situations exists: "(1) the end user's employer already has a full range of knowledge of the dangers, equal to that of the supplier or (2) the supplier makes the employer knowledgeable by providing adequate warnings and safety instructions to the employer."[296] In deciding whether to apply the doctrine in a given case, courts will also consider the likelihood of harm if the intermediary does not pass on the warning, the nature and degree of that harm, the probability that the intermediary will not pass on the warning, and the difficulty of the manufacturer providing the warning to the ultimate user.[297]

Courts have applied the sophisticated user/intermediary doctrine in a variety of toxic tort cases. For example, the U.S. Court of Appeals for the First Circuit in *Taylor v. American Chemistry Council* upheld summary judgment based on the sophisticated user/intermediary doctrine in a case involving the risks of vinyl chloride.[298] The court found there that plaintiff's employer became aware of the dangers of vinyl chloride at "roughly the same time" as the suppliers of vinyl chloride and thus held that requiring these suppliers to provide warnings to plaintiff's employer would have been "superfluous."[299] In *Bergfeld v. Unimin Corp.*, the U.S. Court of Appeals for the Eighth Circuit found that a silica sand supplier had no duty to warn a foundry or the foundry's employees about the risks of silicosis because the foundry was well aware of the dangers of silica and the applicable regulatory standards.[300] Similarly, in *Irrer v. Milacron, Inc.*, the U.S. District Court for the Eastern District of Michigan granted summary judgment in a case involving the health risks of metalworking fluids (MWFs) sold to an automobile manufacturer.[301] The court there noted that the automobile manufacturer was one of the largest users of MWFs in the world, had long investigated the potential health effects of MWFs, and had even contributed through its employees a chapter concerning MWF health and safety to the leading

---

851 (5th Cir. 1992), *rev'd en banc*, 37 F.3d 1069 (5th Cir. 1994); Donahue v. Phillips Petroleum Co., 866 F.2d 1008, 1012–13 (8th Cir. 1989).

295. Schwartz & Appel, *supra* note 287, at 21–22; *see also* Taylor v. Monsanto Co., 150 F.3d 806, 808–10 (7th Cir. 1998) (affirming summary judgment based on sophisticated intermediary defense given resources used by employer and its presence on federal and industry task forces concerning PCBs).

296. *Gray*, 676 N.W.2d at 277–78; *see also* First Nat'l Bank & Trust Corp. v. Am. Eurocopter Corp., 378 F.3d 682, 691 (7th Cir. 2004) (quoting *Taylor*, 150 F.3d at 808); Curtis v. M&S Petroleum, Inc., 174 F.3d 661, 676 (5th Cir. 1999) (stating that a product manufacturer can discharge its duty to warn by providing the necessary information to a third party who in turn can be reasonably relied upon to communicate the information to the ultimate users); Doane v. Givaudan Flavors Corp., 919 N.E.2d 290, 297 (Ohio Ct. App. 2009).

297. *First Nat'l Bank & Trust*, 378 F.3d at 691 (internal quotation marks and citation omitted).

298. 576 F.3d 16, 24–31 (1st Cir. 2009).

299. *Id.* at 30–31; *see also* Genereux v. Am. Beryllia Corp., 577 F.3d 350, 363–73 (1st Cir. 2009) (upholding summary judgment as to certain risks posed by beryllium but reversing summary judgment as to other risks based on the knowledge of plaintiffs' employer).

300. 319 F.3d 350, 353–54 (8th Cir. 2003).

301. 484 F. Supp. 2d 677, 679–94 (E.D. Mich. 2007).

textbook on MWFs. As another example, in *Triplett v. Minnesota Mining & Manufacturing Co.*, the U.S. District Court for the Western District of Kentucky granted summary judgment where the plaintiffs alleged that the manufacturer of respiratory protection masks failed to warn a manufacturing plant's employees that the masks did not provide protection from toxic dusts.[302] The court found that the manufacturing plant was required by law and did in fact have a program to help employees make informed decisions regarding the use of respiratory devices, and that plaintiffs' allegations that this program had not been properly implemented by the plant were insufficient to avoid the defense.[303]

Bulk Supplier/Raw Materials Supplier

The "bulk supplier" defense is essentially a specialized version of the sophisticated intermediary defense. Here, because of the difficulty in reaching the end user, courts recognize that the supplier of material that is delivered in bulk can discharge its duty to warn the end user by warning the buyer of the potential danger.[304] As noted by one court, this defense is consistent with the HazCom Standard (discussed above in the preemption context), which requires manufacturers of hazardous chemicals to provide warnings to purchasers.[305] Along similar lines, the *Restatement (Third) of Torts: Products Liability* recognizes a defense to suppliers of raw materials that are used in a component in a final product. This defense provides that "when a sophisticated buyer integrates a component into another product, the component seller owes no duty to warn either the immediate buyer or the ultimate consumers of dangers arising because the component is unsuited for the special purpose to which the buyer puts it."[306]

Learned Intermediary

Similarly, the "learned intermediary" doctrine is another specialized version of the sophisticated intermediary defense. The learned intermediary doctrine is most often raised by prescription drug manufacturers, which may discharge their duty to warn users of their prescription drugs by providing notice of the medication's hazards to the prescribing physician.[307] In those circumstances, the prescriber acts as a "learned intermediary" between

---

302. 422 F. Supp. 2d 779, 786–87 (W.D. Ky. 2006).
303. *Id.* at 786–87.
304. Gray v. Badger Mining Corp., 676 N.W.2d 268, 280 (Minn. 2004); Hoffman v. Houghton Chem. Corp., 751 N.E.2d 848, 854–55 (Mass. 2001).
305. *Gray*, 676 N.W.2d at 280 (citing 29 C.F.R. § 1910.1200(f)–(g)).
306. RESTATEMENT (THIRD) OF TORTS: PRODUCT LIABILITY § 5 cmt. *B* (1997); *see also* Cimino v. Raymark Indus., Inc., 151 F.3d 297, 335 (5th Cir. 1998) (applying defense where asbestos was supplied to a manufacturer who incorporated it into insulating sheets that were sold to end consumers); *In re* TMJ Implants Prods. Liab. Litig., 872 F. Supp. 1019, 1025 (D. Minn. 1995) (noting that "[t]o require manufacturers of such 'building block' materials to guarantee the safety of their products for each and every possible use would impose an unbearable burden on those manufacturers").
307. Pustejovsky v. PLIVA, Inc., 623 F.3d 271, 276 (5th Cir. 2010); Brooks v. Medtronic, Inc., 750 F.2d 1227, 1231 (4th Cir. 1984); Klasch v. Walgreen Co., 264 P.3d 1155, 1158–59 (Nev. 2011); Rite Aid Corp. v.

the manufacturer and consumer because she "is in the best position to understand the patient's needs and assess the risks and benefits of a particular course of treatment."[308] Accordingly, "a warning to the physician is deemed a warning to the patient."[309] Under the learned intermediary doctrine, therefore, a plaintiff bears the burden of proving that (1) the drug manufacturer's warning to the plaintiff's physician was inadequate, and (2) the failure to warn was a producing cause of the plaintiff's injury.[310]

Traditionally, the learned intermediary doctrine applied only in prescription drug cases.[311] Since then, some courts have extended this doctrine to medical devices and equipment prescribed by a physician.[312] Courts, however, have been reluctant to extend the "learned intermediary" doctrine beyond the medical context.[313] As recently stated by the Tennessee Supreme Court, "we find good reason not to extend the learned intermediary doctrine to products liability cases where an employee claims damages for injuries from a product containing asbestos or some other highly toxic substance purchased by the employer

---

Levy-Gray, 894 A.2d 563, 577 (Md. 2006); McCombs v. Synthes, 587 S.E.2d 594, 595 (Ga. 2003); Vitanza v. Upjohn Co., 778 A.2d 829, 835 (Conn. 2001). *But see* State *ex Rel.* Johnson & Johnson Corp. v. Karl, 647 S.E.2d 899, 907) (W. Va. 2007) (rejecting learned intermediary doctrine for prescription drug manufacturers).

308. *Brooks*, 750 F.2d at 1231; *see also* Larkin v. Pfizer, Inc., 153 S.W.3d 758, 763–64 (Ky. 2004) ("The first and best rationale is that the prescribing physician is in a superior position to impart the warning and can provide an independent medical decision as to whether use of the drug is appropriate for treatment of a particular patient.... The second rationale for the rule is that manufacturers lack effective means to communicate directly with each patient.... The third rationale for the rule is that imposing a duty to warn upon the manufacturer would unduly interfere with the physician-patient relationship.").

309. *In re* Prempro Prods. Liab. Litig., 514 F.3d 825, 830 (8th Cir. 2008) (quoting Ehlis v. Shire Richwood, Inc., 367 F.3d 1013, 1016 (8th Cir. 2004)). Courts have also applied the doctrine beyond doctors to any health care provider authorized to prescribe drugs. *See, e.g.*, Ellis v. C.R. Bard, Inc., 311 F.3d 1272, 1282 (11th Cir. 2002) (characterizing a nurse as a learned intermediary); Wyeth-Ayerst Labs. Co. v. Medrano, 28 S.W.3d 87, 93 (Tex. Ct. App. 2000).

310. *See* Porterfield v. Ethicon, Inc., 183 F.3d 464, 468 (5th Cir. 1999); *see also* Ebel v. Eli Lilly & Co., 321 F. App'x 350, 356–57 (5th Cir. 2009); Ackermann v. Wyeth Pharm., 526 F.3d 203, 208 (5th Cir. 2008).

311. *See* Schwartz & Appel, *supra* note 287, at 22 & n.116; Gray v. Badger Mining Corp., 676 N.W.2d 268, 276 (Minn. 2004) ("This learned intermediary defense has been recognized in other jurisdictions but has essentially been limited to pharmaceutical products.").

312. *See, e.g., Ellis*, 311 F.3d at 1280; *Larkin*, 153 S.W.3d at 762; Hansen v. Baxter Healthcare Corp., 764 N.E.2d 35, 42 (Ill. 2002); Moore v. Mem'l Hosp. of Gulfport, 825 So. 2d 658, 662 n.6 (Miss. 2002); Vaccariello v. Smith & Nephew Richards, Inc., 763 N.E.2d 160, 164–65 (Ohio 2002).

313. *See* Carole A. Cheney, Comment, *Not Just for Doctors: Applying the Learned Intermediary Doctrine to the Relationship between Chemical Manufacturers, Industrial Employers, and Employees*, 85 Nw. U. L. Rev. 562, 587–90 (1991) ("Chemical manufacturers have raised the learned intermediary doctrine as a defense in cases involving the duty to warn in the workplace with mixed success." (footnotes omitted)); *see also* Donahue v. Phillips Petroleum Co., 866 F.2d 1008, 1013 n.9 (8th Cir. 1989) (refusing to extend learned intermediary defense to case involving chemical supplier and purchaser, noting that "[w]hatever else [the intermediate purchaser] may be, it is not a 'learned intermediary' within the meaning of" that doctrine); Gracyalny v. Westinghouse Elec. Corp., 723 F.2d 1311, 1320–21 (7th Cir. 1983) (holding that a manufacturer cannot escape liability by merely warning a middleman or distributor); Hall v. Ashland Oil Co., 625 F. Supp. 1515, 1519 (D. Conn.1986) (explaining that medical context contains significant safeguards to ultimate user that are not present in industrial workplace); *Gray*, 676 N.W.2d at 276 & n.5 (declining to extend learned intermediary defense to the employer/employee relationship in the industrial context).

and used by the employee during the course of his or her employment."[314] As discussed above, however, many states reach similar results under the sophisticated user/intermediary doctrine.[315]

Even when limited to the pharmaceutical context, there are a number of recognized exceptions to the "learned intermediary" doctrine. For example, the *Restatement (Third) of Torts* provides that when a "manufacturer knows or has reason to know that healthcare providers will not be in a position to reduce the risks of harm in accordance with the instructions or warnings" then the manufacturer's duty to warn runs to the patient-consumer.[316] In addition, the Connecticut Supreme Court has listed six categories of pharmaceuticals or medical devices exempt from the doctrine: (1) vaccines; (2) oral contraceptives; (3) contraceptive devices; (4) drugs advertised directly to consumers; (5) overpromoted drugs; and (6) drugs withdrawn from the market.[317]

Attacking Causation

Causation poses a particularly important and unique problem in toxic tort litigation. The types of injuries alleged are often fundamentally different from the immediate or acute injuries seen in other tort cases, like those involving car crashes.[318] In particular, the toxic injuries alleged frequently are illnesses associated with lengthy latency periods, usually have a number of different potential causes, and often exist in any given population. Given the difficulty in drawing a direct connection between the defendant's product or activity and a plaintiff's illness, defendants frequently attempt to defend these types of cases by arguing that plaintiffs cannot satisfy their burden on causation. Indeed, given the significance of this issue, several chapters of this book are dedicated exclusively to the topic.[319]

---

314. Nye v. Bayer Cropscience, Inc., 347 S.W.3d 686, 704 (Tenn. 2011).
315. *See also Gray*, 676 N.W.2d at 278 (discussing distinction between the two doctrines, noting that "[a]lthough the sophisticated intermediary defense has characteristics similar to the learned intermediary defense, the sophisticated intermediary defense is generally only available where the supplier can show that it used reasonable care in relying upon the intermediary to give the warning to the end user"); Adams v. Union Carbide Corp., 737 F.2d 1453, 1457 (6th Cir. 1984) (concluding the manufacturer of the toxic chemical could reasonably rely upon the purchaser/employer to convey information about the chemical's hazardous properties to its employees).
316. Restatement (Third) of Torts: Product Liability § 6(d)(2) (1997).
317. Vitanza v. Upjohn Co., 778 A.2d 829, 846–47 (Conn. 2001).
318. *See, e.g., In re* Meridia Prods. Liab. Litig., 328 F. Supp. 2d 791, 798 (N.D. Ohio 2004) (contrasting causation factors in standard tort cases with those in toxic tort cases); Vassallo v. Am. Coding & Marking Ink Co., 784 A.2d 734, 739 (N.J. Super. Ct. App. Div. 2001) (noting that toxic tort cases are unique in that they often involve "(1) exposure of long duration, chronic and repeated; (2) exposure to multiple toxins; and (3) harm normally resulting from biochemical disruption or acute toxic substance as opposed to physical trauma").
319. *See* chapters 5 and 9–12. In addition, it is worth noting that the *Reference Manual on Scientific Evidence: Third Edition* (*RMSE*) was released in 2011. *See* Fed. Judicial Ctr., Reference Manual on Scientific Evidence: Third Edition (2011). This edition was prepared in conjunction with the National Research Council and the National Academy of Sciences. The *RMSE* is designed to assist judges and litigants in cases involving complex scientific and technical evidence. Courts have relied heavily on prior editions of the *RMSE* and are likely to continue to do so going forward.

Accordingly, this chapter will not discuss the defense in any great detail but instead will simply highlight some of the significant issues currently facing toxic tort litigants.

General and Specific Causation

In order to establish a prima facie case, plaintiffs must demonstrate both "general" and "specific" causation. "General" causation refers to the overarching question of whether exposure to a given substance or product *can* cause the plaintiff's claimed injuries.[320] "Specific" causation, on the other hand, concerns the question of whether the exposure *did in fact* cause the plaintiff's injuries in a particular case.[321] Thus, to prove causation in a toxic tort case, a plaintiff must show both that the alleged toxin is capable of causing injuries like that suffered by the plaintiff and that the toxin, and not something else, was in fact the cause of the plaintiff's injury.[322]

In those cases where the scientific community generally acknowledges that a given substance or product can cause a specific disease, extensive inquiry into general causation may not always be necessary.[323] In the toxic tort context, however, this is a rarity.[324] Moreover, even for those diseases where general causation may be generally accepted, other causes often exist, thereby necessitating a rigorous analysis of specific causation.[325] When, however, the toxicity of a substance or product is not generally accepted, more extensive analysis of expert testimony regarding general causation is typically needed.[326] To that end, toxic tort litigants frequently look to the fields of epidemiology and toxicology.

Epidemiology examines the incidence and distribution of disease in populations and the risk factors associated with particular diseases.[327] Courts are not uniform as to the types of epidemiological evidence sufficient to establish general causation. For example, some courts require that the findings of epidemiological studies be "statistically significant"

---

320. RESTATEMENT (THIRD) OF TORTS: LIABILITY FOR PHYSICAL & EMOTIONAL HARM § 28 cmt. c(3) (2010) (noting that general causation "exists when a substance is capable of causing a given disease").
321. *Id.* § 28 cmt. c(4) (explaining that specific causation "exists when exposure to an agent caused a particular plaintiff's disease").
322. Mattis v. Carlon Elec. Prods., 295 F.3d 856, 860 (8th Cir. 2002).
323. *See, e.g.*, McClain v. Metabolife Int'l, Inc., 401 F.3d 1233, 1239 (11th Cir. 2005) (noting examples of asbestos and silica).
324. Examples are sometimes said to include asbestos and mesothelioma; benzene and acute myelogenous leukemia; coal dust and pneumoconiosis (black lung); vinyl chloride and angiosarcoma of the liver; and silica and silicosis.
325. A common misperception among jurors, and even some judges, is to leap from general to specific causation. For example, when a given substance is generally agreed to be capable of causing a particular disease, some simply assume that the plaintiff's disease must have been caused by that substance. This often results from the use of the term "signature disease." This, of course, is incorrect, both legally and specifically. General and specific causation are distinct inquiries, both of which must be affirmatively proven. *See* FED. JUDICIAL CTR., REFERENCE MANUAL ON SCIENTIFIC EVIDENCE: THIRD EDITION 609 (2011).
326. *McClain*, 401 F.3d at 1239.
327. *See, e.g.*, Rider v. Sandoz Pharm. Corp., 295 F.3d 1194, 1198 (11th Cir. 2002); Merrell Dow Pharm., Inc. v. Havner, 953 S.W.2d 706, 715 (Tex. 1997).

(i.e., unlikely to have occurred by chance) before they may be admissible to prove general causation.[328] Other cases, however, have found that statistical significance is not necessarily required.[329] Moreover, some courts require a risk ratio of at least 2.0 (i.e., at least a doubling of the risk) to show that there is a causal connection.[330]

Even when evidence suggests that there may be an association between exposure to a substance and the development of a disease, courts will evaluate other factors in determining whether a study adequately demonstrates causation. These factors, often referred to as the Bradford Hill criteria, include: (1) temporal relationship; (2) strength of association; (3) dose-response relationship; (4) replication of results; (5) biological plausibility of association; (6) consideration of alternative explanations; (7) cessation of exposure; (8) specificity of association; and (9) consistency with other relevant knowledge.[331]

Disputes also exist with respect to toxicological evidence. Toxicology involves the study of adverse effects of chemicals on living organisms. Given the limits of such study on humans directly, this evidence usually involves animal studies. Courts often disagree, for example, about whether expert testimony regarding general causation may be based solely on animal data, with most courts being critical of the exclusive reliance on animal data,[332] while others may accept expert testimony relying on animal data.[333]

If a claimant cannot establish general causation, there is no need to proceed any further as the cause of action necessarily fails.[334] However, if the claimant does offer sufficient

---

328. *See, e.g.*, Gen. Elec. Co. v. Joiner, 522 U.S. 136, 145 (1997) (finding expert's methodology unreliable in part because one of the epidemiological studies relied on did not contain statistically significant results); Norris v. Baxter Healthcare Corp., 397 F.3d 878, 887 (10th Cir. 2005) ("We cannot allow the jury to speculate based on an expert's opinion which relies only on clinical experience in the absence of showing a consistent, statistically significant association. . . ."); Hollander v. Sandoz Pharm. Corp., 289 F.3d 1193, 1215 (10th Cir. 2002) (affirming exclusion of expert testimony based on studies finding no statistically significant association); Brock v. Merrell Dow Pharm., Inc., 874 F.2d 307, 313 (5th Cir. 1989), *amended*, 884 F.2d 167 (5th Cir. 1989); Dunn v. Sandoz Pharm. Corp., 275 F. Supp. 2d 672, 681 (M.D.N.C. 2003) ("Statistically insignificant results do not constitute proof that Parlodel causes stroke."); Good v. Fluor Daniel Corp., 222 F. Supp. 2d 1236, 1243 (E.D. Wash. 2002); Miller v. Pfizer Inc., 196 F. Supp. 2d 1062, 1080 (D. Kan. 2002), *aff'd*, 356 F.3d 1326 (10th Cir. 2004).
329. Milward v. Acuity Specialty Prods. Grp., Inc., 639 F.3d 11, 24–25 (1st Cir. 2011); Turpin v. Merrell Dow Pharm., Inc., 959 F.2d 1349, 1357 (6th Cir. 1992); *In re* Viagra Prods. Liab. Litig., 572 F. Supp. 2d 1071, 1081 (D. Minn. 2008); *In re* Ephedra Prods. Liab. Litig., 393 F. Supp. 2d 181, 186 (S.D.N.Y. 2005).
330. *See, e.g.*, Merrell Dow Pharm., Inc. v. Havner, 953 S.W.2d 706, 715 (Tex. 1997); Daubert v. Merrell Dow Pharms., Inc., 43 F.3d 1311, 1320 (9th Cir. 1995); Estate of George v. Vermont League of Cities and Towns, 993 A.2d 367, 377–78 (Vt. 2010); *In re* Breast Implant Litig., 11 F. Supp. 2d 1217, 1225–26 (D. Colo. 1998).
331. *See, e.g.*, McClellan v. I-Flow Corp., 710 F. Supp. 2d 1092, 1133 n.29 (D. Or. 2010). *See generally* FED. JUDICIAL CTR., REFERENCE MANUAL ON SCIENTIFIC EVIDENCE: THIRD EDITION 597–606 (2011).
332. *See, e.g.*, *Brock*, 874 F.2d at 313; Richardson v. Richardson-Merrell, Inc., 857 F.2d 823, 830 (D.C. Cir. 1988); Bell v. Swift Adhesives, Inc., 804 F. Supp. 1577, 1579–80 (S.D. Ga. 1992).
333. *See, e.g.*, Metabolife Int'l, Inc. v. Wornick, 264 F.3d 832, 842 (9th Cir. 2001) (finding that the district court should not have per se dismissed animal studies); *In re* Heparin Prods. Liab. Litig., No. 1:08HC60000, MDL No. 1953, 2011 WL 2971918, at *31–42 (N.D. Ohio July 21, 2011) (stating that animal toxicology when combined with other nonepidemiological evidence may be sufficient to establish causation); Ruff v. Ensign-Bickford Indus., Inc., 168 F. Supp. 2d 1271, 1281 (D. Utah 2011).
334. *See, e.g.*, Norris v. Baxter Healthcare Corp., 397 F.3d 878, 881 (10th Cir. 2005).

evidence of general causation, she must also prove specific causation—that is, that the defendant's product or activity did in fact cause the harm or injury.[335] In evaluating specific causation, parties and courts must consider the nature of the substance the plaintiff was exposed to; the dose that the plaintiff was exposed to and the duration of that exposure;[336] whether the plaintiff's injury arose prior to the exposure;[337] whether the alleged injury is consistent with injuries found to be associated with the substance; whether the plaintiff's exposure is similar in manner and degree to that of the population in which such an association has been found; and whether the plaintiff can rule out other possible causes of the injuries.[338] As in the case of general causation, to establish specific causation, plaintiffs must offer admissible expert testimony. Frequently, as part of this analysis, plaintiffs will offer expert opinion providing a "differential diagnosis" (more properly referred to as "differential etiology") identifying the possible causes of the disease or condition and then ruling out various potential causes until a final causation determination is reached.[339] Where the majority of potential causes for a particular condition are unknown, it may not be possible to rule out those unknown causes.[340]

---

335. *See, e.g.*, Merrell Dow Pharm., Inc. v. Havner, 953 S.W.2d 706, 715 (Tex. 1997) (holding that "epidemiological studies cannot establish that a given individual contracted a disease or condition due to exposure to a particular drug or agent").
336. *See, e.g.*, McClain v. Metabolife Int'l, Inc., 401 F.3d 1233, 1242 (11th Cir. 2005) ("Dose is the single most important factor to consider in evaluating whether an alleged exposure caused a specific adverse effect." (internal quotations omitted)).
337. *See, e.g.*, Westberry v. Gislaved Gummi AB, 178 F.3d 257, 265 (4th Cir. 1999) (noting that a "temporal relationship between exposure to a substance and the onset of a disease or a worsening of symptoms can provide compelling evidence of causation"); Reighard v. Yates, 285 P.3d 1168, 1181 (Utah 2012) (same); Guevara v. Ferrer, 247 S.W.3d 662, 667–68 (Tex. 2007) (holding that "[m]ost federal courts that have considered the issue after *Daubert* have concluded that temporal proximity alone does not meet standards of scientific reliability and does not, by itself, support an inference of medical causation" (internal citations omitted)); *McClain*, 401 F.3d at 1243 (temporal relationship does not, by itself, establish causation); Moore v. Ashland Chem. Inc., 151 F.3d 269, 278 (5th Cir. 1998) (same).
338. *See Havner*, 953 S.W.2d at 720.
339. In the medical field, differential diagnosis is typically defined as "diagnosis based on comparison of symptoms of two or more similar diseases to determine which the patient is suffering from." TABER'S CYCLOPEDIC MEDICAL DICTIONARY 404 (14th ed. 1981). Nevertheless, many courts use the term to refer not only to the process of distinguishing between different diseases but to also describe the process of differentiating between different possible causes of a single disease. *See, e.g.*, Baker v. Dalkon Shield Claimants Trust, 156 F.3d 248, 252–53 (1st Cir. 1998) (noting that differential diagnosis is "a standard scientific technique, widely used in medicine, of identifying a medical 'cause' by narrowing the more likely causes until the most likely culprit is isolated"); Cavallo v. Star Enter., 892 F. Supp. 756, 771 n.31 (E.D. Va. 1995) (defining differential diagnosis as "a process whereby medical doctors experienced in diagnostic techniques provide testimony countering other possible causes . . . of the injuries at issue"), *aff'd in part, rev'd in part, remanded*, 100 F.3d 1150 (4th Cir. 1996). Some courts recognize, however, that the legal use of the term is contrary to the medical usage and instead use the more accurate term "differential etiology." *See* Zuchowicz v. United States, 140 F.3d 381, 385 (2d Cir. 1998); Aurand v. Norfolk S. Ry. Co., 802 F. Supp. 2d 950, 963 (N.D. Ind. 2011). For a discussion of some of the problems with using "differential diagnosis" in the toxic tort context, see Joe G. Hollingsworth & Eric G. Lasker, *The Case against Differential Diagnosis: Daubert, Medical Causation Testimony, and the Scientific Method*, 37 J. HEALTH L. 85 (2004).
340. *See, e.g.*, Whiting v. Boston Edison Co., 891 F. Supp. 12, 21 n.41 (D. Mass. 1995) ("If 90 percent of the causes of a disease are unknown, it is impossible to eliminate an unknown disease as the efficient cause

Product Identification

Another causation issue that frequently arises in toxic tort cases is the question of product identification. In any action claiming injury from a particular product, the claimant must show a causal connection between the defendant manufacturer and that product. Failure to do so will generally result in the dismissal of the plaintiff's claims. Thus, in *Byers v. Lincoln Electric Co.*, the U.S. District Court for the Northern District of Ohio granted summary judgment in favor of six of nine welding rod manufacturers because the evidence that the plaintiff used the manufacturers' products was either speculative or so de minimis that no reasonable jury could find a causal link between the manufacturer's products and the plaintiff's alleged injuries.[341] Similarly, in *Bockrath v. Aldrich Chemical Co.*, the California Supreme Court found the plaintiff's allegations that the products of several different defendants caused his cancer were legally insufficient because he did not (1) allege that he was exposed to each of the toxic materials claimed to have caused the specific illness; (2) identify each product that allegedly caused the injury; (3) allege that as a result of the exposure the toxins entered his body; (4) allege that he suffers from a specific illness and that each toxin that entered his body was a substantial factor in causing, prolonging, or aggravating that illness; and (5) allege that each toxin he absorbed was manufactured or supplied by a named defendant.[342]

Failure-to-Warn Causation Defenses

Additional causation defenses may also be available in cases alleging failure to warn. It is not enough in failure-to-warn cases merely to establish that a warning was inadequate; rather, the inadequate warning must also be a proximate cause of the plaintiff's injuries.[343] The plaintiff, in other words, must establish that an adequate warning would have made a difference.[344]

For example, if the claimant (or a learned intermediary) has independent knowledge of a product's dangers, then a failure to adequately warn of the danger is irrelevant.[345] In

---

of a patient's illness.").
341. 607 F. Supp. 2d 840, 859–66 (N.D. Ohio 2009); *see also In re* Welding Fume Prods. Liab. Litig., 526 F. Supp. 2d 775, 796 (N.D. Ohio 2007).
342. 21 Cal. 4th 71, 80–81 (Cal. 1999).
343. Pustejovsky v. PLIVA, Inc., 623 F.3d 271, 276 (5th Cir. 2010) (citing McNeil v. Wyeth, 462 F.3d 364, 372 (5th Cir. 2006)).
344. Thomas v. Hoffman-LaRoche, Inc., 949 F.2d 806, 812 (5th Cir. 1992) (holding that "to create a jury question, the evidence introduced must be of sufficient weight to establish . . . some reasonable likelihood that an adequate warning would have prevented the plaintiff from receiving the drug"); *see also* Christopher v. Cutter Labs., 53 F.3d 1184, 1192 (11th Cir. 1995).
345. *In re* Prempro Prods. Liab. Litig., 514 F.3d 825, 830 (8th Cir. 2008); *see also* Ehlis v. Shire Richwood, Inc., 367 F.3d 1013, 1016 (8th Cir. 2004) (holding that a drug's inadequate warning is not a proximate cause if the prescriber had independent knowledge of the risk); Eck v. Parke, Davis & Co., 256 F.3d 1013, 1021 (10th Cir. 2001) (finding no causal link where prescribing physician had independent knowledge of risk); Crook v. Kaneb Pipe Line Operating P'ship, 231 F.3d 1098, 1103 (8th Cir. 2000) ("[I]f a user is already aware of the dangers, the lack of warning is not the proximate cause of the injury.").

addition, if the plaintiff or intermediary did not read the warning given, the defendant may assert that the plaintiff cannot establish causation because it would not matter what the warning said.[346] Moreover, even if the plaintiff did read the supplied warnings, the plaintiff must also show that she would have, in fact, altered her behavior if given a better warning. Further, in the learned intermediary context, the plaintiff must demonstrate that an adequate warning would have caused the intermediary to make a different choice. Thus, if a physician would have made the same prescribing decision with an adequate warning, the plaintiff will not be able to show that the inadequacy of the warning was a proximate cause of her injuries.[347] Importantly, in addressing these questions of causation, the issue "is not what an objective physician would decide, but rather what plaintiff's doctor would determine based on his knowledge of the drug in question and the plaintiff's risk factors."[348]

Addressing these sorts of defenses, some states have adopted what is known as a "heeding presumption."[349] The heeding presumption is essentially a burden-shifting mechanism designed to assist a plaintiff in establishing causation. In the pharmaceutical context, for example, the heeding presumption establishes a rebuttable presumption that the prescriber would have read the warning and acted in accordance with it to minimize any risks.[350]

---

346. *See, e.g.*, Motus v. Pfizer Inc., 358 F.3d 659, 661–62 (9th Cir. 2004) (finding no causal link when the prescribing physician did not read or rely upon the manufacturer's warnings); Plummer v. Lederle Labs., 819 F.2d 349, 358–59 (2d Cir. 1987); Demmler v. SmithKline Beecham Corp., 671 A.2d 1151, 1155–56 (Pa. Super. Ct. 1996) (holding that if a health care provider does not rely on a medication's label in prescribing that medication to patient, the label cannot be a proximate cause of an injury to the patient). Nevertheless, there still may be room for a plaintiff to argue otherwise, under proper circumstances. For example, a plaintiff might argue that she did not read the warning because of the warning's size and placement. *See, e.g.*, Boyd v. Lincoln Elec. Co., 902 N.E.2d 1023, 1032 (Ohio Ct. App. 2008) (holding that "if the display of warnings is inadequate, the failure to read the warnings does not always absolve a manufacturer of liability").

347. *See, e.g., Pustejovsky*, 623 F.3d at 277 (upholding summary judgment where plaintiff had no evidence that her prescribing doctor had read or otherwise learned of the warnings given); Dietz v. SmithKline Beecham Corp., 598 F.3d 812, 816 (11th Cir. 2010) (affirming summary judgment where doctor testified that he still would have prescribed Paxil for the plaintiff's depression, even if provided with the most current research and FDA warnings); Ackermann v. Wyeth Pharm., 526 F.3d 203, 208 (5th Cir. 2008); Odom v. G. D. Searle & Co., 979 F.2d 1001, 1002–03 (4th Cir. 1992) (finding no causal link when prescribing physician knew of risk and still would have prescribed device because it was the best product on the market).

348. Stafford v. Wyeth, 411 F. Supp. 2d 1318, 1322 (W.D. Okla. 2006); *see also* Fraley v. Am. Cyanamid Co., 589 F. Supp. 826, 828 (D. Colo. 1984) ("The acts of the treating physician, not the average or 'reasonable' physician, are the acts relevant to proximate cause.").

349. *See, e.g.*, Eck v. Parke, Davis & Co., 256 F.3d 1013, 1019 (10th Cir. 2001); Reyes v. Wyeth Labs., 498 F.2d 1264, 1281 (5th Cir. 1974). *But see Ackerman*, 526 F.3d at 212 n.15 ("Texas has not adopted the heeding presumption."); Sosna v. Am. Home Prods., 748 N.Y.S.2d 548, 549–50 (N.Y. App. Div. 2002) (holding in pharmaceutical case that "it remains plaintiff's burden to prove that defendant's failure to warn was a proximate cause of his injury . . . and this burden includes adducing proof that the user of a product would have read and heeded a warning had one been given" (internal citations omitted)); Kurer v. Parke, Davis & Co., 679 N.W.2d 867, 876 (Wis. Ct. App. 2004) ("Even in the event that a warning is inadequate, proximate cause is not presumed."); Demmler v. SmithKline Beecham Corp., 671 A.2d 1151, 1155 (Pa. Super. Ct. 1996) (same).

350. *See Eck*, 256 F.3d at 1018.

Of course, because it is generally only a presumption, defendants may defeat the heeding presumption by pointing to evidence that the prescriber would have acted in the same manner, regardless of the warning.[351] While the heeding presumption is most frequently discussed in the pharmaceutical context, many states also recognize the presumption more generally, while others do not recognize the presumption at all.[352]

State of the Art

Further, many courts recognize an affirmative defense when a defendant's product, warning, or conduct complies with the "state of the art." What constitutes state of the art, however, is not always clear.[353] Courts, for example, have used the term to refer to a number of different concepts, including: (1) the custom or common practice within an industry; (2) independent standards developed by organizations such as the American National Standards Institute (ANSI), the American Society of Mechanical Engineers (ASME), and the American Society for Testing and Materials (ASTM); (3) standards provided in state and federal statutes and regulations; and (4) the technical, mechanical, or scientific knowledge available at a particular point in time.[354] Each of these concepts is discussed briefly here.

To begin with, some courts define state-of-the-art evidence in terms of custom and practice in an industry.[355] Indeed, most courts hold that evidence of a custom or practice within an industry is admissible in a negligence action on the question of reasonable care, though compliance with such a custom or practice is not necessarily conclusive.[356] Courts

---

351. *See id.* at 1016.
352. *See, e.g.,* Moore v. Ford Motor Co., 332 S.W.3d 749, 759–60 & n.3 (Mo. 2011) (citing numerous cases); Coffman v. Keene Corp., 628 A.2d 710, 720 (N.J. 1993) (extending heeding presumption to all product-liability cases based on a failure to warn). *But see, e.g.,* Rivera v. Philip Morris, Inc., 209 P.3d 271, 276–77 (Nev. 2009) (rejecting heeding presumption in strict liability failure-to-warn cases and citing several cases from other jurisdictions doing the same).
353. *See, e.g.,* Potter v. Chicago Pneumatic Tool Co., 694 A.2d 1319, 1345 (Conn. 1997) (recognizing that "the term 'state of the art' has been the source of substantial confusion").
354. *See* Richard C. Ausness, *"Fasten Your Seat Belt, Orville!": Exploring the Relationship between State-of-the Art, Technological and Commercial Feasibility, and the Restatement's Reasonable Alternative Design Requirement,* 45 IND. L. REV. 669, 676 (2012); *see also* Carrecter v. Colson Equip. Co., 499 A.2d 326, 329 n.6 (Pa. Super. Ct. 1985).
355. *See, e.g.,* Smith v. Minster Mach. Co., 669 F.2d 628, 633 (10th Cir. 1982) (defining "state of the art . . . to mean simply the custom and practice in an industry"); Sturm, Ruger & Co. v. Day, 594 P.2d 38, 44 (Alaska 1979) (stating that "[g]enerally speaking, 'state of the art' refers to customary practice in the industry"); Suter v. San Angelo Foundry & Mach. Co., 406 A.2d 140, 151 (N.J. 1979) (noting that state of the art includes common practice and industry standards). *But see* George v. Celotex Corp., 914 F.2d 26, 28 (2d Cir. 1990) ("In fulfilling its duty, a manufacturer may not rest content with industry practice, for the industry may be lagging behind in its knowledge about a product, or in what, with the exercise of reasonable care, is knowable about a product.").
356. *See, e.g.,* Donaldson v. Cent. Ill. Pub. Serv. Co., 767 N.E.2d 314, 336 (Ill. 2002) (upholding jury verdict despite evidence offered by the defendant of industry remediation standards in 1939); Textron, Inc. v. Aetna Cas. & Sur. Co., 754 A.2d 742, 751 (R.I. 2000) (discussing evidence offered as to the state of the art in sealing a chemical neutralization pond); O'Neal v. Dep't of the Army, 852 F. Supp. 327, 335 (M.D. Pa. 1994) (noting defendant's compliance with industry standards regarding the handling of toxic chemicals in finding that the plaintiff failed to establish a lack of due care); United States v. Hooker Chemicals & Plastics Corp., 850 F. Supp. 993, 1048–58 (W.D.N.Y. 1994) (evaluating custom in chemical industry

are in less agreement when it comes to strict liability cases, with some courts allowing such evidence as a factor to consider, particularly when analyzing the reasonable expectations of the consumer or user, while other courts hold that industry custom is irrelevant because it diverts attention from the condition of the product to the reasonableness of the defendant's conduct.[357]

As with industry custom, evidence of compliance with independent standards developed by organizations such as ANSI, ASME, and ASTM is generally admitted in negligence cases to show that the manufacturer exercised reasonable care.[358] But again, courts are in some disagreement as to whether such standards are admissible in strict liability cases. Nevertheless, many courts allow evidence of compliance with such standards to support the contention that a product is not defective.[359]

Compliance with government standards may also serve as a measure of the state of the art.[360] Indeed, in the negligence context, failure to comply with a government standard often constitutes negligence per se, meaning that the defendant's conduct is deemed negligent as a matter of law.[361] As a general rule, however, regulatory compliance does not conclusively establish that the defendant exercised reasonable care but instead constitutes evidence of due care to be evaluated along with other considerations and applicable evidence.[362] Most courts take a similar approach as to strict liability claims, reasoning that government standards are relevant, but not necessarily conclusive, to the question of defectiveness.[363]

---

when disposing of waste products at the time of Love Canal landfill operations).

357. *See, e.g.*, Robinson v. Audi NSU Auto Union Aktiengesellschaft, 739 F.2d 1481, 1486 (10th Cir. 1984) (finding evidence of industry custom relevant in a strict liability case to determine the expectations of an ordinary consumer); Habecker v. Clark Equip. Co., 36 F.3d 278, 282–83 (3d Cir. 1994) (holding that the trial court improperly admitted evidence of industry custom in a products liability trial); Norton v. Snapper Power Equip., 806 F.2d 1545, 1549 (11th Cir. 1987) (discussing different approaches taken by courts); *In re* Cordis Corp. Pacemaker Prod. Liab. Litig., No. MDL 850, C-3-86-543, 1992 WL 754061, at *11 (S.D. Ohio Dec. 23, 1992) (same).
358. *See, e.g.*, Getty Petroleum Mktg., Inc., 391 F.3d 312, 326 (1st Cir. 2004) (citing several cases involving a variety of independently established industry standards).
359. *See, e.g.*, Covell v. Bell Sports, Inc., 651 F.3d 357, 365–66 (3d Cir. 2011) (upholding district court's admission of evidence as to defendant's compliance with U.S. Consumer Product Safety Commission standard in product liability action); Vermett v. Fred Christen & Sons Co., 741 N.E.2d 954, 971 (Ohio Ct. App. 2000) (upholding trial court's grant of summary judgment in favor of defendant based in part on the defendant's compliance with ANSI standard).
360. *See, e.g.*, Wolf by Wolf v. Procter & Gamble Co., 555 F. Supp. 613, 616–17 (D.N.J. 1982); *see also* Ausness, *supra* note 354, at 682–83.
361. *Getty Petroleum*, 391 F.3d at 327 (citing cases).
362. *Smith*, 669 F.3d at 633 (citing cases).
363. *See, e.g.*, Rader v. Teva Parental Medicines, Inc., 795 F. Supp. 2d 1143, 1149 (D. Nev. 2011) (allowing evidence of defendants' compliance with FDA regulations in response to plaintiff's strict liability claim); O'Neil v. Novartis Consumer Health, Inc., 147 Cal. App. 4th 1388, 1393–96 (Cal. Ct. App. 2007) (upholding trial court's refusal to instruct jury that compliance with governmental standards cannot be considered as a basis for assessing the safety of a product in a design defect claim); *Smith*, 669 F.3d at 633 (noting that under Illinois law, compliance with federal safety standards is admissible evidence in a defective design case); Bruce v. Martin-Marietta Corp., 544 F.2d 442, 447 (10th Cir. 1976) (finding compliance with government regulations relevant to the issue of defectiveness). *But see* Malcolm v.

Technological feasibility and the state of scientific knowledge at the time are generally considered to be the principal focus of the state-of-the-art defense.[364] Most basically, in claims involving negligence, plaintiffs must establish that the harm caused by the defendant was reasonably foreseeable, meaning that a person of ordinary prudence should have anticipated the damage to others caused by the defendant's allegedly negligent act.[365] As a result, defendants will generally not be liable where the evidence shows that they did not know and had no reason to know of the potential risk of harm given the then existing state of knowledge.[366] As to strict liability claims, jurisdictions once again differ. While some courts impose strict liability by imputing to the manufacturer knowledge of a product's propensity to injure, most jurisdictions require plaintiffs to prove that the defendant either knew or should have known of the danger.[367] Further, most courts allow parties,

---

Evenflo Co., Inc., 217 P.3d 514, 521–22 (Mont. 2009) (upholding trial court's exclusion of defendant's compliance with product safety regulations in defective design case).

364. See, e.g., In re Fosamax Prods. Liab. Litig., No. 06 MD 1789(JFK), 2011 WL 2566074, at *8 (S.D.N.Y. June 29, 2011) (noting that under Florida's state-of-the-art defense, the fact finder in a design defect case must "consider the state of the art of scientific and technical knowledge and other circumstances that existed at the time of the manufacture, not at the time of loss or injury" (quoting FLA. STAT. ANN. § 768.1257)); Falada v. Trinity Indus., Inc., 642 N.W.2d 247, 250 (Iowa 2002) ("Custom refers to what was being done in the industry; state of the art refers to what feasibly could have been done."); Cavanaugh v. Skil Corp., 751 A.2d 518, 520 (N.J. 2000) ("State-of-the-art refers to the existing level of technological expertise and scientific knowledge relevant to a particular industry at the time a product is designed" (quotation marks and citation omitted)); Anderson v. Owens-Corning Fiberglas Corp., 810 P.2d 549, 558 (Cal. 1991) ("The rules of strict liability require a plaintiff to prove only that the defendant did not adequately warn of a particular risk that was known or knowable in light of the generally recognized and prevailing best scientific and medical knowledge available at the time of manufacture and distribution."); Montgomery Ward & Co. v. Gregg, 554 N.E.2d 1145, 1155 (Ind. Ct. App. 1990) (construing state-of-the-art defense as requiring a showing that defendant conformed to the "generally recognized state of technological or scientific knowledge existing at the time of manufacture"); Brown v. Superior Court, 751 P.2d 470, 482–83 (Cal. 1988) (holding that a manufacturer of prescription drugs is not strictly liable for injuries caused by a prescription drug so long as it was properly prepared and accompanied by a warning of its dangerous propensities that were either known or reasonably scientifically knowable at the time of distribution).

365. See, e.g., Western Greenhouses v. United States, 878 F. Supp. 917, 927 (N.D. Tex. 1995).

366. Id. at 927 ("Given the state of knowledge and the standard of industry practice during the period between the 1940s and the 1970s, [defendant's] employees had no reason to know that their waste disposal or maintenance activities could lead to plaintiffs' damages."); see also Alcoa, Inc. v. Behringer, 235 S.W.3d 456, 462 (Tex. Ct. App. 2007) (reversing jury verdict in plaintiffs' favor on negligence claim because "the danger of non-occupational exposure to asbestos dust on workers' clothing was neither known nor reasonably foreseeable to Alcoa in the 1950s"); Bolinder Real Estate, LLC v. United States, No. 2:97-cv-0912C, 2002 WL 732155, at *9 (D. Utah Apr. 24, 2002) (noting that "neither industry nor the military were aware of the potential for TCE to contaminate groundwater in hazardous quantities until after the late 1970's and early 1980's."); Smith v. Hughes Aircraft Co., 22 F.3d 1432, 1440 (9th Cir. 1994) (declining to conclude that the defendant knew TCE was likely to cause harm given evidence that, at the time in question, TCE was not considered harmful in moderate amounts, that TCE was commonly used as an anesthetic and disinfectant and was used to extract hops, decaffeinate coffee, and prepare fish meal, that the FDA did not propose banning TCE as a food additive until 1977, and that EPA did not propose a nonbinding standard for TCE in drinking water until 1979).

367. See Olson v. Prosoco, Inc., 522 N.W.2d 284, 288 (Iowa 1994) (citing numerous cases for the two approaches); see also Powers v. Taser Int'l, Inc., 174 P.3d 777, 784 (Ariz. Ct. App. 2008) (holding that a majority of jurisdictions require manufacturers "to warn only of risks that were known or should have been known to a reasonable manufacturer"); Gourdine v. Crews, 955 A.2d 769, 781 (Md. Ct. App. 2008)

both plaintiffs and defendants, to raise the issue of technological feasibility in design defect cases, particularly where the case involves a determination of whether a product's risk for harm outweighs its usefulness, known as the risk-utility test. Although most courts have held that an alternative design must be technologically feasible to be considered state of the art, this does not necessarily mean that the alternative design actually existed at the time the product was marketed, only that the alternative design was technologically feasible at that time. While most courts examine only the technical aspects of feasibility, some also take into account the commercial aspects of technological development.[368]

Government Contractor Defense

The U.S. Supreme Court established the framework for the government contractor defense in *Boyle v. United Technologies Corp.*[369] There the Court held that the "uniquely federal interest[]" in "getting the Government's work done" requires, under certain circumstances, that a private contractor be protected from the tort liability associated with its performance of a government contract.[370] Addressing this defense in the manufacturing context, the Court found that liability under state law will be precluded when (1) the government approved reasonably precise specifications for the product alleged to have caused injury; (2) the product conformed to those specifications; and (3) the contractor warned the government about the dangers in the use of the product that were known to the contractor but not to the government.[371] In order to prevail on this defense, the defendant will need to establish that the government actively participated in discretionary design decisions as opposed to simply approving a design with a "rubber stamp" and without scrutiny.[372]

The federal circuit courts have extended this test to failure-to-warn claims, applying the defense where (1) the government exercised its discretion and approved certain warnings; (2) the contractor provided the warnings required by the government; and (3) the contractor warned the government about dangers in the product's use that were known to the contractor but not the government.[373] In this context, it is not necessary to show

---

(same); Vassallo v. Baxter Healthcare Corp., 696 N.E.2d 909, 922 (Mass. 1998) (same); Sternhagen v. Dow Chem. Co., 935 P.2d 1139, 1143 (Mont. 1997) (holding that "knowledge of a product's undiscovered or undiscoverable dangers shall be imputed to the manufacturer"); Beshada v. Johns-Manville Prods. Corp., 447 A.2d 539, 549 (N.J. 1982) (holding asbestos manufacturers strictly liable for dangers not known at the time the product was sold); Feldman v. Lederle Labs., 479 A.2d 374, 386–88 (N.J. 1984) (limiting *Beshada* to cases involving asbestos and upholding pharmaceutical manufacturer's use of the state-of-the-art defense).

368. Ausness, *supra* note 354, at 684–90.
369. 487 U.S. 500 (1988).
370. *Id.* at 504–05.
371. *Id.* at 512.
372. *See, e.g.*, Tate v. Boeing Helicopters, 55 F.3d 1150, 1154 (6th Cir. 1995); Landgraf v. McDonnell Douglas Helicopter Co., 993 F.2d 558, 560 (6th Cir. 1993); Harduvel v. Gen. Dynamics Corp., 878 F.2d 1311, 1316 (11th Cir. 1989).
373. *See, e.g.*, Getz v. Boeing Co., 654 F.3d 852, 866–67 (9th Cir. 2011); Tate v. Boeing Helicopters, 140 F.3d 654, 656–57 (6th Cir. 1998); Oliver v. Oshkosh Truck Corp., 96 F.3d 992, 1003–04 (7th Cir. 1996).

3. Common Defenses   117

that the government either expressly forbade or required a specific preferred warning. Instead, the contractor must show that government's warning requirements limited the contractor's ability to comply with its duty to warn under state law.[374]

One particularly important procedural aspect of the government contractor defense is that it can provide a basis for removing a case from state to federal court under the Federal Officer Removal Statute.[375] Indeed, to support removal to federal court, the assertion of the defense need only be "colorable" at the time of removal.[376] As the Supreme Court has explained: "The federal officer removal statute is not 'narrow' or 'limited.' At the very least, it is broad enough to cover all cases where federal officers can raise a colorable defense arising out of their duty to enforce federal law. . . . The officer need not win his case before he can have it removed."[377]

The government contractor defense has come up in a variety of contexts in toxic tort cases. For example, in *In re "Agent Orange" Product Liability Litigation*, the U.S. Court of Appeals for the Second Circuit addressed the defense in a case brought by military veterans and their families alleging injury from exposure to dioxin found in Agent Orange.[378] The plaintiffs argued that the presence of dioxin would have been eliminated had the defendant manufacturers used a lower temperature in the production process. The Second Circuit acknowledged that the government had no preference as to how Agent Orange was to be produced, and that there was no inherent conflict between using a lower temperature and the defendants' contractual obligations.[379] Nevertheless, the court found that the defense applied given that the government had evaluated the toxicity of Agent Orange and had determined that it posed "no unacceptable health hazard for the wartime uses for which it was intended."[380] Under such circumstances, the "imposition of liability under state law would constitute a significant conflict with the [g]overnment's decision."[381] By contrast, courts have rejected application of the defense to claims involving nuclear incidents,[382]

---

374. *Getz*, 654 F.3d at 866; *Tate*, 140 F.3d at 658; *Oliver*, 96 F.3d at 1004 n.8.
375. *See* 28 U.S.C. § 1442(a) (authorizing federal officers and agents to remove state law claims to federal court by asserting a federal defense).
376. Jefferson Cnty. v. Acker, 527 U.S. 423, 431 (1999); Mesa v. California, 489 U.S. 121, 129 (1989); *see also* Bennett v. MIS Corp., 607 F.3d 1076, 1084-85 (6th Cir. 2010) (upholding removal of personal injury claims brought against mold remediation firms hired by government); Isaacson v. Dow Chem. Co., 517 F.3d 129, 140 (2d Cir. 2008) (upholding removal of Agent Orange personal injury claims); Leite v. Crane Co., 868 F. Supp. 2d 1023, 1038-41 (D. Haw. 2012) (finding removal proper in asbestos case alleging failure to warn).
377. Willingham v. Morgan, 395 U.S. 402, 406-07 (1969) (internal citations omitted); *see also Bennett*, 607 F.3d at 1084-85 (quoting *Willingham*, 395 U.S. at 406-07).
378. 517 F.3d 76 (2d Cir. 2008).
379. *Id.* at 94.
380. *Id.* at 96-97.
381. *Id.* at 95 (quoting Lewis v. Babcock Indus., Inc., 985 F.2d 83, 89 (2d Cir. 1993)); *see also id.* at 94 (holding that the government contractor defense applies where the government gave considered attention to the precise defect alleged and subsequently re-ordered the product).
382. *In re* Hanford Nuclear Reservation Litig., 534 F.3d 986, 1002 (9th Cir. 2008) (holding that the Price-Anderson Act forecloses application of the government contractor defense to claims brought by victims

claims involving exposure to contaminants during operation of a water plant,[383] and claims involving the storage and disposal of hazardous substances.[384]

Workers' Compensation Bar

When an employee is injured as a result of an accident arising out of and during the course of her employment, the sole remedy generally available is the applicable state workers' compensation statute. Workers' compensation statutes essentially force a tradeoff. On the one hand, they guarantee injured employees prompt and automatic entitlement to certain benefits regardless of the employer's negligence. In exchange, employees give up the right to sue their employer for potentially larger damages in civil tort actions.[385]

Many states, however, provide an exception to the exclusivity provision of workers' compensation statutes when the employee is injured due to an employer's intentional misconduct.[386] Nevertheless, this exception is often very narrowly construed. Indeed, in some states, to qualify as an intentional tort, the employer's conduct must be undertaken with an actual "desire to bring about the consequences of the act."[387] In such cases, mere knowledge and appreciation of a particular risk is not considered an intent to cause injury.[388] In other states, however, the plaintiff can satisfy this exception by proving either (1) a conscious desire to cause the physical result of the act, regardless of the likelihood of that

---

of nuclear incidents).

383. Bixby v. KBR, Inc., 748 F. Supp. 2d 1224, 1242–43 (D. Or. 2010) (noting that the defendants were under no contractual obligation to put their employees or others into situations involving the risk of environmental harm without appropriate protective gear).

384. Anderson v. Hackett, 646 F. Supp. 2d 1041, 1052 (S.D. Ill. 2009) (holding that the defense did not apply to claims that the defendants produced, stored, and disposed of their products in a shoddy manner resulting in the leaks and spills of hazardous substances, explaining that the defendants could point "to no federal interest that is implicated by requiring them to handle and dispose of their products with care"); Arness v. Boeing N. Am., Inc., 997 F. Supp. 1268, 1275–76 (C.D. Cal. 1998) (holding that the defense did not apply where the government did not require or forbid that steps be taken to prevent the release of TCE).

385. *See, e.g.*, Allen v. Int'l Bus. Machs. Corp., 128 F. App'x 311, 313 (4th Cir. 2005) (toxic mold); Frank v. Shell Oil Co., 828 F. Supp. 2d 835, 846 (E.D. La. 2011) (benzene); Roney v. Gencorp, 431 F. Supp. 2d 622, 627–28 (S.D. W. Va. 2006) (vinyl chloride); Stebbins v. Doncasters, Inc., 819 A.2d 287, 288–89 (Conn. 2003) (respiration of airborne droplets of petroleum-based metalworking fluids); Millison v. E.I. du Pont de Nemours & Co., 501 A.2d 505, 509 (N.J. 1985) (asbestos); Gen. Dynamics Corp. v. Brottem, 53 So. 3d 334, 336 (Fla. Dist. Ct. App. 2010) (toxic pollution); Cameron v. Merisel, Inc., 593 S.E.2d 416, 420 (N.C. Ct. App. 2004) (mold).

386. *Allen*, 128 F. App'x at 313 (addressing intentional misconduct exception under North Carolina law); Pyle v. Dow Chem. Co., 728 F.2d 1129, 1131–32 (8th Cir. 1984) (finding lack of sufficient intent under Arkansas statute); Ruble v. Alcoa, Inc., No. 1:07CV3521, 2012 WL 774958, at *3, 6 (N.D. Ohio Mar. 7, 2012) (addressing intentional tort exception as discussed by the Ohio Supreme Court in *Kaminski v. Metal & Wire Prods. Co.*, 927 N.E.2d 1066, 1088 n.16 (Ohio 2010)); *Roney*, 431 F. Supp. 2d at 627–28 (discussing deliberate intention exception under West Virginia law); *Frank*, 828 F. Supp. 2d at 848–49 (discussing intentional tort exception under Louisiana law).

387. Acevedo v. Consol. Edison Co. of New York, 596 N.Y.S.2d 68, 71 (N.Y. App. Div. 1993) (quoting another source) (injuries resulting from remediating explosion site contaminated with friable asbestos); *see also* Pereira v. St. Joseph's Cemetery, 864 N.Y.S.2d 491, 492 (N.Y. App. Div. 2008); Cicogna v. City of New York, 801 N.Y.S.2d 231, *5 (N.Y. Sup. Ct. 2005).

388. *See, e.g.*, Lauria v. Donahue, 438 F. Supp. 2d 131, 141 (E.D.N.Y. 2006).

result happening, or (2) knowledge that the result is substantially certain to follow, whatever the desire may be as to that result.[389] Regardless, given the high hurdle imposed under any articulation of the test, courts generally tend to be reluctant to invoke the exception.[390]

In *Alexander v. Bozeman Motors, Inc.*, for example, two employees alleged that they had been injured from inhalation of propane and carbon monoxide fumes from their employer's propane stove while working in their office.[391] The first employee had complained about conditions in the office on several occasions and eventually left his job after losing consciousness one day from the fumes. Shortly afterward, the second employee began working in the office, but he too became sick from the fumes and could no longer work there. Both employees claimed serious injuries resulting from the exposures and filed suit. The trial court granted the defendant's motion for summary judgment, finding the claims were barred by the workers' compensation statute. On appeal, the Montana Supreme Court explained that to avoid the workers' compensation exclusivity provision, the plaintiffs were required to show (1) an intentional and deliberate act specifically and actually intended to cause injury; and (2) actual knowledge of the injury's certainty.[392] As to the first employee, the court noted that while the employer did not respond to prior complaints about the dangerous conditions in the office, the employer did not have "actual knowledge" that requiring the employee to work in the office would result in "certain injury."[393] Thus, as to the first employee, the court upheld summary judgment. The court reversed, however, as to the second employee, noting that the employer by that point did in fact have actual knowledge of the harm posed as evidenced by the injuries to the first employee.[394]

Conclusion

Of course, as to virtually all of the defenses discussed above, there are countless variations, nuances, and exceptions that exist across different jurisdictions. As a result, it is imperative that the law of the specific state at issue be thoroughly examined rather than relying on general legal theories and defenses discussed here. The foregoing should serve as a helpful guide, though, in spotting and understanding the issues that potentially arise in the toxic tort context.

---

389. *Frank*, 828 F. Supp. 2d at 849 (citing Bazley v. Tortorich, 397 So. 2d 475, 481 (La. 1981)).
390. *But see* Gulden v. Crown Zellerbach Corp., 890 F.2d 195, 196–97 (9th Cir. 1989) (finding Oregon's deliberate intention exception satisfied where workers were required to remediate PCBs without protective gear).
391. 234 P.3d 880, 883 (Mont. 2010) (exception for intentional and deliberate act).
392. *Id.* at 886.
393. *Id.*
394. *Id.* at 889.

CHAPTER 4

The Use of Scientific and Medical Evidence

William D. Dannelly, Rita A. Sheffey, Ashley Cummings, and Matthew F. Hanchey

There are two common denominators in all forms of toxic tort litigation: causation and the use of scientific and medical experts to establish causation. Chapter 5 provides an in-depth discussion of causation and the use of experts in toxic tort litigation. Chapters 9 through 12 provide surveys of causation jurisprudence in toxic tort litigation by region and state. This chapter presents a brief introduction to several areas of science that provide the underlying principles for the scientific and medical evidence that is typically presented in toxic tort and environmental litigation.[1]

The goal of this chapter is twofold: first, to provide the practitioner with sufficient background to identify and anticipate the various experts who may be retained to assist in the pursuit or defense of a claim; and second, to identify for the practitioner methodologies and practices that may lend support to or discredit an expert's conclusions. This chapter addresses the manner in which samples are collected and analyzed, how science is used to trace chemicals in the environment, and how the link between exposure and injury is established or refuted through toxicology and epidemiology.

Sampling and Analysis

A medium, such as air, water, soil, groundwater, or house dust, may be contaminated with a hazardous, noxious, odiferous, or otherwise undesirable contaminant or substance. The

---

1. It is beyond the purview of this chapter to discuss any of the science in great detail. Further, because the authors of this chapter are not practicing scientists, there is necessarily a limitation to the depth of their discussion of scientific issues. In addition, the scientists and legal practitioners must consider rapid changes that can occur in some areas of science. Just as legal practitioners must update their legal research with new cases relevant to the issues in current disputes, scientists working with issues related to toxic tort litigation must consider the developing body of information relevant to their discipline.

plaintiff, with the aid of appropriate consultants, must identify activities that may have exposed him or her to the suspected contaminated media. If the plaintiff can establish an exposure pathway, he or she may present medical evidence to claim that exposure to the contaminant caused a personal injury. A plaintiff claiming property damage will likewise identify the contaminant and offer evidence that the contaminant has damaged, is expected to damage, or has otherwise restricted the use and enjoyment of his or her property.

Typically, the presence of a hazardous substance in air, water, soil, groundwater, or house dust cannot be proved through eyewitness testimony.[2] Therefore, evidence of that claim is generally presented through the collection and analysis of representative samples of the suspected contaminated media.[3] It is essential that the sample be collected without cross-contamination from the activities of the sampler, other samples, or other media. Likewise, the sample must be handled, transported, and stored so that a qualified laboratory performs an analysis that determines the content of the media.[4]

---

2. Eyewitness testimony may provide proof of a chemical's identity when, for example, the eyewitness observed a material being removed from a labeled container and the label identified the container's contents. Also, in some cases, a human sample may be used to establish exposure without corresponding sampling of environmental media. For example, asbestos fibers may be detected in the human body long after the actual exposure.
3. There are several sources of formalized sampling and analysis protocols employed by experts when analyzing environmental media for contamination. The United States Environmental Protection Agency (EPA) promulgates methods for sampling and analyzing certain contaminants in particular media. *See* 40 C.F.R. § 136.3. In other cases, EPA regulations require that sampling and analysis be performed, but do not specify the protocols to be followed. In these cases, EPA may, however, publish detailed procedures that satisfy the regulatory requirements to complete sampling and analysis. *See* EPA Test Methods for Evaluating Solid Waste, Physical/Chemical Methods (SW-846). Where EPA has not published, by regulation or otherwise, a specific protocol to be followed, suitable procedures may be found in publications produced by standards development organizations, such as the American Conference of Governmental Industrial Hygienists (ACGIH), or ASTM International, originally known as the American Society for Testing and Materials. *See* ACGIH—Industrial Hygiene, Environmental, Occupational Health & Safety Resource, http://www.acgih.org and ASTM International Standards Worldwide, http://www.astm.org (visited May 11, 2012). Once sampling and analysis is complete, it is likely an expert will be needed to provide a link between the alleged exposure and damage and the sample.
4. *See, e.g.*, 40 C.F.R. § 136.3 (with respect to the collection and analysis of water samples as required by discharge permits issued pursuant to the Clean Water Act, specifying for each type of contaminant of interest the material from which the sample collection container should be composed, the maximum allowable holding period before the sample is analyzed, methods to preserve the samples, including transportation and storage temperatures, and any necessary additives); EPA Test Methods for Evaluating Solid Waste, Physical/Chemical Methods (SW-846), Method 0011: Sampling for Selected Aldehyde and Ketone Emissions for Stationary Sources (Dec. 1996) (one of the approved methods for evaluating solid waste in conformance with RCRA regulatory requirements, specifying the composition and type of sampling instruments to be used and identifying calibration method and acceptable temperature range for the sampling probe); EPA Test Methods for Evaluating Solid Waste, Physical/Chemical Methods (SW-846), Method 9132: Total Coliform: Membrane-Filter Technique (Sept. 1986) (another of the approved methods for evaluating solid waste in conformance with RCRA regulatory requirements, specifying that water samples collected for analysis of fecal coliform content must be analyzed as soon as possible after collection or, if not analyzed within one hour of collection, stored on ice for transport below 10o C for a maximum transport time of six hours).

There are certain procedures that must be satisfied by the sampler, the transporter, and the laboratory to provide the basis for an accurate report of the test results.[5]

It is no simple matter for laboratory scientists to prove the accuracy of test results. The chemical analysis of unknown substances is a difficult process, subject to estimation and the application of other types of scientific reasoning at several stages in the process.

The U.S. Environmental Protection Agency (EPA) has established standard testing methodologies to be applied by scientists testing for unknowns. These procedures are published in the Federal Register and in other EPA publications.[6] Laboratories performing analytical work for certain EPA projects—such as Clean Air Act, Clean Water Act, or CERCLA-related studies—are required to follow these methodologies.[7] Even when not required by regulations, EPA standard methodologies serve as examples of good laboratory practice and are generally accepted throughout the scientific community. In the context of a toxic tort suit, a laboratory scientist may claim that test results are reliable, even if the laboratory did not perform its testing in accordance with EPA's procedures. Failure to follow EPA procedure is not always conclusive on whether such results are admissible.[8] Nonetheless, this position is vulnerable to arguments that the data should not be admitted unless additional proof is offered to show that the analytical procedures used were those generally accepted by scientists in the field, especially if there is a more stringent EPA methodology available.

Issues to be considered in developing or criticizing data for use in court proceedings include whether sampling procedures are accurate and documented, whether the laboratory implemented sufficient quality control measures and properly calibrated its equipment, and whether the samples were analyzed in a timely manner. Each of these issues is discussed briefly below.

Sampling Procedures

To obtain a sample that provides an accurate picture of the medium being tested, the sample must be taken so as to avoid contamination, and it must be taken at an acceptable

---

5. *See, e.g.,* Muzzey v. Kerr-McGee Chem. Corp., 921 F. Supp. 511, 521 (N.D. Ill. 1996) (refusing to admit expert testimony that relied on laboratory test results but did not have a laboratory report for the test).
6. *See, e.g.,* 40 C.F.R. pt. 136, App. A (2011); *see also* EPA's Forum on Environmental Measurements, Test Method Collections, http://www.epa.gov/fem/methcollectns.htm (last visited May 11, 2012).
7. For illustration, we refer to 40 C.F.R. pt. 136, App. A, which sets forth methods for organic chemical analysis of municipal and industrial wastewater under the Clean Water Act, specifically Method 601 regarding purgeable halocarbons. 40 C.F.R. pt. 136, App. A, Method 601 (2011) ("Method 601"). Methods set forth in Title 40 typically include the following sections (using these subtitles or similar subtitles): Scope and Application; Summary of Method; Interferences; Safety; Apparatus and Materials; Reagents; Calibration; Quality Control; Sample Collection, Preservation and Handling; Procedure; Calculations; and Method Performance. *See, e.g.,id.; cf.* 40 C.F.R. pt. 60, App. A-8, Method 26 (2011).
8. *See, e.g.,* Sanchez v. Esso Std. Oil Co., No. 08-2151, 2010 U.S. Dist. LEXIS 9942, at *34 (D.P.R. Feb. 5, 2010) (refusing to exclude sampling data that was obtained using a method that was not an EPA-approved method).

location and time. On the first point, before a sample is delivered to the laboratory, the sample can be contaminated by collecting the sample using contaminated equipment or by storing the sample in contaminated containers (sample bottles should be sterile). Also, contamination may occur when a sample is transferred from one container to another, or during transportation and interim storage before delivery to the laboratory. Procedures, almost always based on established protocols, should be followed to prevent any such contamination. Often such protocols are kept in a field manual that marks site locations and defines the applicable sampling procedures.

EPA recommends that "field blanks" be taken to where the sample is drawn. For example, if samples of water are being collected, sterilized water is taken into the field, and the field blank container is filled, handled, and stored as if it were a real sample. These field blanks are kept with the subject sample in the field and the laboratory, and both are analyzed by the same method.[9] In theory, if the analysis of the field blanks shows no chemical other than water or additives introduced during the protocol, then the subject sample was not contaminated in the field or during transportation to the laboratory. Some EPA standard testing methodologies require that a minimum frequency of field blanks accompany samples collected at a given site (e.g., 1 field blank for every 10 field samples).[10]

On the second point, the sampling protocol must be designed to account for variation in both time and space.[11] A single sample or small sample set may not provide an accurate picture of the entire medium being sampled. Likewise, if the medium can change over time, sampling at a particular point in time may not represent the medium at earlier or later times. Whether or not this variability is important or relevant to a particular case will depend on what the party is seeking to prove. The sampling protocol must be designed with the use of the data in mind.

The procedures by which samples are collected, the notations and data recorded at the time of sampling, and whether a sufficient number of samples were collected are all factors that are considered in determining the reliability of the conclusions drawn from the

---

9. *See, e.g.*, Guidance for Implementation and Use of EPA Method 1631 for the Determination of Low-Level Mercury (40 C.F.R. pt. 136), EPA 821-R-01-023, at 2-4 & 5-6 (March 2001) ("Guidance for Implementation"); *see also* Bauer v. Bayer A.G., 564 F. Supp. 2d 365, 377–78 (M.D. Pa. 2008) (citing contamination in blank samples as a basis for excluding laboratory data).
10. Guidance for Implementation, *supra* note 9, at 5-7.
11. *See, e.g.*, Crane-McNab v. Cnty. of Merced, 773 F. Supp. 2d 861, 869 (E.D. Cal. 2011) (finding that "the location at which the sample was taken could only provide information for a small area of influence" rather than the area of influence asserted by the plaintiffs in the case); Textron Inc. v. Barber-Colman Co., 903 F. Supp. 1546, 1554–55 (W.D.N.C. 1995) (holding that a sample of wastewater from 1974 could not serve as a basis for an expert's testimony about wastewater from the same system in 1975 and 1976); Renaud v. Martin Marietta Corp., 749 F. Supp. 1545, 1552–53 (D. Colo. 1990) (where plaintiffs' experts relied on only one sample to formulate their conclusions, a court-appointed expert criticized these conclusions because "[i]t is unsound scientific practice to select one concentration measured at a single location and point in time and apply it to describe continuous releases of contaminants over an 11-year period").

samples. These are areas in which expert testimony may be called into question.[12] Therefore, sampling procedures should be followed carefully and documented.

Quality Control

Laboratories establish procedures to assure that their analytical results maintain a high degree of accuracy. These procedures are often quite detailed, but as a general proposition, EPA requires or recommends that its approved laboratories use each of the following quality control (QC) procedures:

Check Samples

EPA has QC check samples, which contain chemical concentrations already known. A laboratory tests these samples without knowing the contents. It then submits its analytical results and compares them to the known concentrations of the QC check samples. If the laboratory accurately identifies the chemical concentrations in the QC check samples, this result serves to demonstrate that the laboratory is equally able to accurately identify the chemical composition of the field sample.[13]

Surrogate Spikes

The laboratory prepares a surrogate, which is a known quantity of a pure analyte[14] that is extremely unlikely to be found in any sample. It adds surrogates to portions of each sample to be analyzed, a practice known as "spiking." Analytical results for the surrogate are compared with the laboratory's predetermined QC standard for that surrogate analyte.[15]

Duplicate Samples

A duplicate sample is identical to the subject sample. The duplicate is analyzed separately from the subject sample. The laboratory should obtain approximately the same analytical results from the duplicate sample as it does from the subject sample. The same laboratory may prepare and analyze the duplicate and subject samples, but a better QC procedure is to have someone independent of the laboratory prepare and analyze the duplicate and not disclose that information to the laboratory.[16]

---

12. *See, e.g.*, City of Wichita, Kan. v. Trustees of the Apco Oil Corp. Liquidating Trust, 306 F. Supp. 2d 1040, 1063–65 (D. Kan. 2003) (the defendants challenged expert testimony on the basis that expert did not use required sampling protocols, did not conduct data validation tests, and did not establish a chain of custody; court found that the expert's testimony was reliable because he sufficiently documented in field notations his analysis of samples from the site).
13. *See, e.g.*, Method 601, *supra* note , §§ 8.2.1–8.2.6.2 (requiring use of QC check samples).
14. An "analyte" is the substance to be analyzed in an experiment.
15. *See, e.g.*, Method 601, *supra* note , § 8.7 (discussing use of surrogate compounds).
16. *See, e.g., id.* § 8.6 (recommending use of field duplicates); *see also* Crane-McNab, 773 F. Supp. 2d at 868–69 (citing problems with duplicates as a basis for finding sampling data to be not credible).

Multiple Laboratories

In some situations, a sample is split in the field and submitted to two different, independent laboratories. Again, if both laboratories are accurate in testing their samples, this QC check should provide substantially similar results. Interlaboratory variability may, however, cause diverging analytical results.[17]

Ultimately, the goal of QC is to provide a reasonable assurance that the laboratory's analytical procedures are functioning accurately. When the QC checks are "out of control," it is reasonable to infer that the test results are unreliable. If this circumstance occurs, the laboratory should investigate to determine whether equipment, stock solutions, storage procedures, sampling procedures, human error, or some other problem is causing the laboratory's results to be inconsistent or unreliable. Of course, if a laboratory does not utilize QC procedures, it has no way to verify that its results are reliable. Thus, most scientists would not accept as valid the reports of a laboratory that does not incorporate QC procedures to support its analysis.

Calibration

Laboratories use sophisticated, sensitive equipment. A laboratory must calibrate its equipment—that is, it must tune or adjust the equipment in accordance with a standardized measurement.[18] Calibration is critical to ensure that the laboratory obtains reliable analytical results.[19] In addition, known quantities of subject chemicals, known as stock solutions, must be analyzed by the same equipment to establish a baseline for quantification. There are numerous ways in which calibration errors occur: the laboratory may fail to calibrate the equipment; it could allow a stock solution to become diluted, and thus the stock solution would not reflect the assumed concentration; or it may fail to calculate the calibration accurately.

Sample Preservation

EPA methodologies establish maximum retention times for samples—that is, the maximum length of time a sample may be held before it is tested. If held longer, the results are

---

17. Interlaboratory variability refers to the circumstance in which separate laboratories analyze material from the same sample source using the same protocols, but produce divergent results due to variations attributable to the laboratory itself, such as sample holding time, deviation from the protocol-specified temperature, test duration, analyst technique and experience and, where qualitative analysis is employed, analyst judgment. *See* Dwayne R.J. Moore et al., *Intra- and Intertreatment Variability in Reference Toxicant Tests: Implications for Whole Effluent Toxicity Testing Programs*, 19 ENVTL. TOXICOLOGY & CHEMISTRY 105 (2000); Robin A. Silva-Wilkinson et al., *Results of an Interlaboratory Evaluation of an Analytical Screening Method for Assessing Persistent Bioaccumulative Toxic Chemicals in Sediment Samples*, 19 ENVTL. TOXICOLOGY & CHEMISTRY 2218 (2000).
18. *See, e.g.*, Method 601, *supra* note , § 10.2 (requiring daily calibration); *see also* Bauer, 564 F. Supp. 2d at 370, 377 (refusing to allow an expert to rely on test results in part because the instrument used to the obtain the results had problems with calibration).
19. *See, e.g.*, Method 601, *supra* note , §§ 7.1–7.5.4 (setting forth calibration procedures).

no longer deemed accurate. For example, some chemical contaminants in samples may evaporate or degrade if the sample is held too long before testing. Additionally, some sampling protocols require samples to be stored at certain temperatures or provide that samples must be analyzed by the laboratory within a particular time frame.[20]

In summary, it is crucial that the data to be relied on in toxic tort litigation be based on accurate and precise sampling in accordance with applicable and generally accepted methodologies. Moreover, a laboratory's analysis of the samples is not reliable if the laboratory does not follow QC and calibration procedures, or if the laboratory's analysis is not timely. Each of these points may provide a basis to criticize or argue for the exclusion of the opposing party's expert testimony.

Fate and Transport

The phrase "fate and transport" typically is used to refer to "the nature and distribution of chemicals in the environment."[21] "Fate" addresses the changes that a contaminant may undergo over time, while "transport" concerns the movement of a contaminant between environmental media.[22]

In toxic tort litigation, fate and transport analysis is an essential element in proving that the defendant's activities caused human exposure to a chemical or chemical compound.[23] A personal injury claim may exist even if there is no current evidence of contamination. Some illnesses do not manifest until well after exposure to the toxin; therefore, evidence of exposure may involve reconstruction of the history of the defendant's activities, the plaintiff's activities, and the fate and transport of toxins.[24]

In property damage cases, fate and transport is an essential element in proving that the defendant's activities caused certain chemicals to infiltrate or impact the plaintiff's property.[25] Fate and transport analysis is important in proving or disproving the source

---

20. *See, e.g., id.* §§ 9.1 & 9.3 (requiring samples to be iced or refrigerated between collection and analysis, and requiring analysis within fourteen days of collection).
21. Ranjit J. Machado, *Fate and Transport*, 17 NAT. RESOURCES & ENV'T 235, 235 (Spring 2003).
22. *City of Wichita*, 306 F. Supp. 2d at 1133.
23. Machado, *supra* note , at 235; *see also, e.g.*, Abarca v. Franklin Cnty. Water Dist., 761 F. Supp. 2d 1007 (E.D. Cal. 2011) (discussing whether plaintiffs can establish exposure to contaminants via an "air pathway," a "groundwater pathway" or a "surface water pathway"); Renaud, 749 F. Supp. at 1548 ("The issue [on summary judgment] was whether a reasonable juror could conclude that contaminants from Martin reached plaintiffs' taps in quantities sufficient to cause the injuries they have alleged.").
24. *See, e.g.*, Bulot v. Intracoastal Tubular Servs., Inc., 888 So. 2d 1017, 1019–20 (La. Ct. App. 2004) (plaintiff's decedent suffered from "long-latency occupational disease," plaintiff's expert testified regarding dose reconstruction based on decedent's work history).
25. *See, e.g.*, New York v. Solvent Chem. Co., 685 F. Supp. 2d 357, 431 (W.D.N.Y. 2010) (stating that the court was "troubled by the failure of the parties' hydrogeological experts to provide a basis upon which a reasonably definitive conclusion can be drawn with respect to the fate and transport of contaminants in the bedrock groundwater zones" but holding that sufficient evidence had been produced to determine migration and property damage); Hatco Corp. v. W. R. Grace & Co., 836 F. Supp. 1049, 1061 (D.N.J. 1993) ("The use of chemical fate and transport analysis in the assessment of environmental property damage has been endorsed by the [EPA].").

of the contaminants. Also, fate and transport analysis is useful in proving or disproving the presence of chemical contamination on the plaintiff's property or that there is a risk of migration leading to future contamination, factors that are essential to establishing a basis for remediation or damages.

Moreover, fate and transport analysis may be used to distinguish among various sources of a contaminant. It may even be used to date the release of contaminants. Expert opinions on these subjects may be useful in allocating liability among potentially responsible parties.[26]

Fate and transport is an interdisciplinary concept that can involve ranging areas of expertise. Parties often find it necessary to retain multiple experts to testify regarding fate and transport. Geology, meteorology, hydrogeology, chemistry, and environmental engineering are the predominant scientific disciplines that are typically involved in fate and transport analysis.

Geology is the science that deals with the history of the earth and its physical structure. Some contaminants are man-made, while others are naturally occurring. Geologists, therefore, help to define and distinguish what chemical elements are present as a result of human activities.[27] Geologists also address the issue of how various compounds move within the environment and come to be located in house dust, soil, or groundwater. Often, geologists rely on environmental sampling, which tracks the presence of compounds at specific locations and dates. Using various techniques, scientists use existing data to develop opinions about the movement of chemicals through the environment over time.[28] Modeling the fate and transport of chemicals is often critical to this analysis.[29]

Statisticians have developed complex statistical equations to predict the fate and transport of chemicals. Computer models apply these equations to develop opinions about historical movement of chemicals through the environment and to predict the future paths

---

26. *See, e.g.*, Kalamazoo River Study Grp. v. Eaton Corp., 258 F. Supp. 2d 736, 756–57 (W.D. Mich. 2002) (fate and transport analysis supported conclusion that contamination did not originate upstream from the defendant's facility); *Hatco Corp.*, 836 F. Supp. at 1059, 1061 (noting that "[c]hemical fate and transport analysis is crucial to determining which of a number of activities contributed to the contamination at the site" and finding that "[a] number of variables distinguish the respective parties' uses of the Hatco site," including "[t]he migratory aspects of the contamination and the exclusive use of certain chemicals").

27. *See* Dodge v. Cotter Corp., 328 F.3d 1212, 1224 (10th Cir. 2003) (offering testimony of geologist to establish presence of harmful substances in levels exceeding the natural background in soil, water, and vegetation samples taken in and around plaintiffs' properties).

28. *See, e.g., City of Wichita*, 306 F. Supp. 2d at 1062–64 (experts collected and analyzed soil and groundwater samples to determine concentrations of the contaminants, considered current and historical uses of the property, and studied the direction of groundwater flow).

29. *Id.* at 1108 ("Computer modeling is an accepted and, in appropriate circumstances, reliable method for use in determining groundwater flow and containment transport in an aquifer, and to evaluate the effectiveness of remedial alternatives."); *see also* Machado, *supra* note 21, at 235. For detailed discussions of modeling efforts, see Solvent Chemical Co., 685 F. Supp. 2d at 377–78 (air emissions dispersion modeling) and *In re* Methyl Tertiary Butyl Ether (MTBE) Prods., 739 F. Supp. 2d 576, 586 (S.D.N.Y. 2010) (groundwater modeling).

those chemicals are likely to take.[30] But "a model is only an estimate" or approximation, the accuracy of which depends largely on the quality and reliability of the data selected for use in the model.[31] Thus, data collected from a site may be used to validate or invalidate a model's predictions.[32]

Meteorologists use weather records to establish wind patterns. They may try to establish the distribution of contaminants from factory smokestack emissions, for example, over the course of the operation of that smokestack. Air modeling allows a scientist to estimate the distribution of a chemical through that air emission source.[33] It also allows the scientist to estimate the concentration and likely dispersion of a chemical over a specified time period.[34]

Hydrologists and hydrogeologists analyze the movement of contaminants through water or groundwater over a period of time. They use weather records, rely on evidence of dissolved materials, and consider the movement of sediment and solid particles through rain and flood events.[35] Similarly, hydrogeologists study the occurrence, distribution, and movement of water through the soil.[36] In environmental cases, hydrogeologists address the subsurface movement of chemicals through the soil and into and through groundwater

---

30. Machado, *supra* note 21, at 236; *see also, e.g.*, Marmo v. IBP, Inc., No. 8:00 CV 527, 2005 WL 675810, at *1–2 (D. Neb. Feb. 4, 2005) (admitting expert testimony using a fate and transport model to determine the extent of contamination and average exposures to hydrogen sulfide in the community; noting that the modeling procedures "are relied upon by regulators and experts in the field, and can be tested and measured for accuracy").
31. *City of Wichita*, 306 F. Supp. 2d at 1108.
32. Machado, *supra* note 21, at 237.
33. *See, e.g., Abarca*, 761 F. Supp. 2d at 1022–40 (discussing the use of an air model); Solvent Chem. Co., 685 F. Supp. 2d at 377–78 (same).
34. *See, e.g.*, Boyd v. Allied Signal, Inc., 898 So. 2d 450, 460–63 (La. Ct. App. 2004) (in a class action involving a toxic gas leak from a tanker truck, the plaintiffs and the defendants each presented meteorologists, air modeling experts, and experts in atmospheric chemistry to testify regarding the thermodynamic and thermohydrolic behavior of the chemical, its threshold limit and concentration values, and the meteorological conditions present over the applicable time period; experts prepared computer models to analyze atmospheric dispersion data and to derive probable downwind concentrations of the chemical over time; court relied on expert testimony to define geographic boundaries to define the plaintiff class).
35. *See, e.g.*, Exxon Corp. v. Makofski, 116 S.W.3d 176, 179–80 (Tex. Ct. App. 2003) (plaintiffs retained an expert in hydrology to support their theory that oil and gas from the defendant's operations had leaked into an underground aquifer); San Francisco Baykeeper v. Cargill Salt Division, No. C 96-2161 SI, 2003 U.S. Dist. LEXIS 8247, at *21 (N.D. Cal. Apr. 29, 2003) (the defendants' experts concluded that there was no hydrologic connection between a pond and a neighboring marsh area, yet they conceded that under the right hydrologic conditions, water could flow between the pond and the marsh during high tide); Wood v. Picillo, 443 A.2d 1244, 1247 (R.I. 1982) (experts in soil mechanics and groundwater hydrology testified that the composition of soil at the dump site would "allow any liquid or chemical in . . . it to percolate down to the water table and travel with the ground water in a northerly" direction).
36. *See City of Wichita*, 306 F. Supp. 2d at 1129.

systems.[37] They may rely on models, applying groundwater flow direction to determine the amounts and concentrations of a contaminant that could reach the soil at a particular site.[38]

Chemists or geo-chemists analyze the fate of a contaminant. A contaminant may begin as one chemical or compound and, over time or under certain conditions, convert or break down into a different chemical or chemicals. The byproduct may be more or less harmful than the original contaminant.[39] This conversion or breakdown can, of course, impact the nature of a toxic tort plaintiff's exposure and the associated risks relating to that exposure.

In addition, fate and transport analysis may be used to define the scope or reach of a remediation site, as well as the extent of necessary remediation.[40] Environmental engineers, for example, consider fate and transport analysis when developing methods to deal with the source of a contaminant, remediating its effects and containing contaminant migration.[41] Also, fate and transport analysis is used in ecological risk assessment to predict the potential reach of a contaminant and its impacts on an ecological system.[42]

Each of these disciplines can impact a toxic tort or environmental case. A party to a litigation or a regulatory action should, as an initial priority, identify the expert testimony necessary to establish the fate and transport aspect of its claim or defense. It may be necessary to retain multiple experts, within the multiple disciplines, to properly and thoroughly analyze fate and transport issues.

37. *See, e.g.*, Rosato v. 2550 Corp., 894 N.Y.S.2d 513, 804–05 (N.Y. App. Div. 2010) (the defendant produced expert testimony of a hydrologist to establish that a contaminant plume could not have reached the plaintiff's workplace); Mejdrech v. Lockformer Co., No. 01 C 6107, 2003 U.S. Dist. LEXIS 15598, at *18 (N.D. Ill. Sept. 4, 2003) (the defendants presented expert testimony calling into question calculations and interpretation of hydrogeologic data that served as the basis for plaintiffs' expert's opinions and identifying another potential source of contamination, which was supported by groundwater flow); Interfaith Cmty. Org. v. Honeywell Int'l, Inc., 263 F. Supp. 2d 796, 805–08 (D.N.J. 2003) (the plaintiffs and the defendants presented experts in geochemistry and hydrogeology who testified regarding technical formulas used to determine water flow and concentrations of a contaminant from the site); Preferred Mut. Ins. Co. v. Gordon, No. 02-3147, 2003 Mass. Super. LEXIS 155, at *10, 18 (Mass. Super. Ct. May 13, 2003) (the plaintiffs' and the defendants' experts collected hydrogeological data regarding the direction of groundwater flow to determine whether the release of oil from an underground storage tank had migrated or threatened to migrate to neighboring property).
38. Machado, *supra* note 21, at 236–37. *See, e.g.*, City of Wichita, 306 F. Supp. 2d 1040, 1064–65 (experts studied groundwater flow direction and used modeling to determine amounts of contaminant that could reach soil at various sites).
39. *See* Rudd v. Electrolux Corp., 982 F. Supp. 355, 362–63 (M.D.N.C. 1997) (discussing that the defendant's storage tanks released a compound known as TCA, which is not a hazardous chemical, but has a breakdown product known as DCE, which is considered hazardous).
40. *See, e.g.*, New Mexico v. Gen. Elec. Co., 335 F. Supp. 2d 1266, 1278–79 (D.N.M. 2004) (expert gathered sample data and prepared groundwater flow models to predict geographic movement of contaminated groundwater over a period of time and to identify a "buffer zone" for containment efforts); T.H. Agric. & Nutrition, LLC v. U.S. Envtl. Prot. Agency, 119 F. Supp. 2d 1367, 1370 (M.D. Ga. 2000) (property owner introduced fate and transport studies to support its argument that the EPA had ordered greater clean-up levels than were necessary).
41. *See, e.g., Interfaith Cmty. Org.*, 263 F. Supp. 2d at 809–10, 829 (expert in geology and hydrogeology testified regarding the feasibility of a proposed form of remediation).
42. *See, e.g.*, Natural Res. Def. Council, Inc. v. Texaco Ref. & Mktg., Inc., 20 F. Supp. 2d 700, 704 (D. Del. 1998) (observing that the study of fate and transport "is necessary to determine the impact of noncomplying discharges on living systems because it defines the route of exposure").

Causation Analysis through Toxicology and Epidemiology

Toxicology and epidemiology address a chemical's toxicity and the relationship between exposure, dose, and response.[43] Information gleaned from toxicological and epidemiological studies is applied to evaluate and assess the potential risk of disease that arises when an individual or a population is exposed to a chemical.[44] That information is used to address these questions, which are central to toxic tort litigation: "was plaintiff exposed to the toxin, was plaintiff exposed to enough of the toxin to cause the alleged injury, and did the toxin in fact cause the injury?"[45]

Toxicology

Toxicology is "'the study of the adverse effects of chemical and physical agents on living organisms.'"[46] It involves many different subsciences, which are applied to study and explain the origins of diseases. Toxic substances include both synthetic and natural chemicals.[47] Indeed, virtually all substances can cause a toxic effect, depending on these factors:

- *Dose*: the amount of the substance that enters the body;
- *Route*: the manner in which the substance is ingested (i.e., swallowed, inhaled, dermal contact, or injection);
- *Duration*: the number of days, weeks, months, or years over which the subject was exposed to the substance; and
- *Frequency*: the number of times per day, week, month, or year that the subject was exposed to the substance.[48]

The goal of toxicology is to determine the relationship between dose and effect, also known as the "dose-response" relationship.[49] For many toxins, toxicologists believe most humans have a "threshold," below which they will not experience any adverse health effects from exposure.[50] Therefore, not all exposure to toxins will result in injury. Indeed, it is a central tenet of toxicology that "the dose makes the poison."[51]

---

43. JAMES W. CONRAD, JR., ENVIRONMENTAL SCIENCE DESKBOOK § 4:5 (2012) (*available at* Westlaw, ENVS-CIDB § 4:5).
44. Bernard D. Goldstein & Mary Sue Henifin, *Reference Guide on Toxicology*, *in* REFERENCE MANUAL ON SCIENTIFIC EVIDENCE 633, 637 (3d ed. 2011) (*available at* http://www.nap.edu/catalog.php?record_id=13163).
45. McClain v. Metabolife Int'l, Inc., 401 F.3d 1233, 1239 (11th Cir. 2005).
46. Goldstein & Henifin, *supra* note , at 636 (quoting CASARETT AND DOULL'S TOXICOLOGY: THE BASIC SCIENCE OF POISONS 13 (Curtis D. Klaassen ed., 7th ed. 2007)).
47. David L. Eaton, *Scientific Judgment and Toxic Torts — A Primer in Toxicology for Judges and Lawyers*, 12 J.L. & POL'Y 5, 9 (2003).
48. *Id.* at 10.
49. *Id.* at 15.
50. *Id.* at 16.
51. Goldstein & Henifin, *supra* note , at 651.

Most information about the human toxicity of a chemical is developed and evaluated through experimental toxicology—that is, studies of laboratory animals (in vivo research) or of human or animal cells and tissues (in vitro research).[52] Experimental toxicology usually involves exposing laboratory animals or cells to chemicals, monitoring the response, and then comparing the response to an unexposed control group or sample.[53] The response of laboratory animals to toxic substances is sometimes used to predict the human response to that toxic substance, although this method is the subject of some debate.[54] That is, even if the research establishes some relationship between a substance and a response in a laboratory animal, many scientists believe additional information is needed before those results have relevance for humans.[55] Because there are significant differences between humans and laboratory animals, there must be a credible scientific explanation why an animal study supports a causation hypothesis for an individual or human population.[56] Some courts have held that animal studies alone do not establish causation in humans.[57]

This debate is a question of external validity: whether the cause-and-effect relationship identified in a toxicological study can be generalized to a particular population, or to a particular setting or time frame.[58] In other words, just because a cause-and-effect relationship arises under one set of circumstances does not mean that it can be generalized to a different set of circumstances.[59] For this reason, questions of external validity have been the basis for challenging the admissibility of toxicological evidence.[60]

The use of toxicology to establish causation is commonly understood at two levels: first, whether the substance in question causes harm in the population generally (general causation); and second, whether the substance caused this particular individual's injuries (specific

---

52. *Id.* at 639; *see also* 1 Lawrence G. Cetrulo, Toxic Torts Litigation Guide § 5:86 (2011).
53. Goldstein & Henifin, *supra* note , at 639.
54. *Id.* There are five major differences between animals and humans: basal metabolic rates; anatomy and organ structure; physiology and cellular biology; distribution of chemicals in tissues; and metabolism, bioactivation and detoxification of chemicals and their metabolic intermediaries. Robert C. James, *Role of Toxicology in Toxic Tort Litigation: Establishing Causation*, 61 Def. Couns. J. 28, 30 (Jan. 1994). For this reason, most substances proven to be carcinogenic in animals are not harmful to humans. *Id.* at 32–33.
55. 3 David L. Faigman et al., Modern Scientific Evidence: The Law and Science of Expert Testimony § 22:5 (2011–2012 ed.) (*available at* Westlaw, 3 MODSCIEVID § 22:5); *see also, e.g.*, Goewey v. United States, 886 F. Supp. 1268, 1280–81 (D.S.C. 1995) (finding neurotoxic effects on chickens could not be extrapolated to humans), *aff'd*, 106 F.3d 390 (4th Cir. 1997).
56. Joe G. Hollingsworth & Eric G. Lasker, *The Case against Differential Diagnosis: Daubert, Medical Causation Testimony, and the Scientific Method*, 37 J. Health L. 85, 92–93 (2004).
57. *Id.* at 92 (citing Siharath v. Sandoz Pharm. Corp., 131 F. Supp. 2d 1347, 1367 (N.D. Ga. 2001) and Wade-Greaux v. Whitehall Labs., Inc., 874 F. Supp. 1441, 1483–84 (D.V.I. 1994)).
58. 3 Faigman et al., *supra* note 55, § 22:5.
59. *Id.*
60. *Id.*; *see also, e.g.*, Allison v. McGhan Med. Corp., 184 F.3d 1300, 1313–14 (11th Cir. 1999) (expert "failed to explain the correlation of the results of . . . rat studies in which the rats were directly injected with silicone to symptoms in a human patient where the inner lumen of the implants had remained intact").

causation).[61] Thus, in regulatory or class action litigation, toxicological evidence may be offered to address how exposure affects a population or group.[62] And in individual toxic tort cases, toxicological evidence is often offered to support or refute a plaintiff's claim that his or her disease or injury was caused by exposure to a chemical or compound.[63] Toxicological studies rarely offer direct evidence that exposure caused a particular individual to develop a disease. Instead, toxicological studies provide scientific information regarding how a chemical causes a disease, whether there is an increased risk of contracting a disease from a certain dose, and helps to rule out other risk factors for the disease.[64]

Epidemiology

Epidemiology is the study of incidence, distribution, and possible causes of disease in human populations.[65] It combines the disciplines of statistics, sociology, and demography to produce biological inferences about how chemicals cause disease in humans.[66] Through the use of such disciplines, epidemiologists uncover data to demonstrate when disease does not occur uniformly throughout the population. They also try to identify subgroups with disproportionate incidence of disease and use the data to determine why that subgroup is at greater risk of contracting a particular disease.[67] In the context of toxic tort litigation, epidemiologists use such statistical results to support or refute a conclusion that there is a causal relationship between exposure to a toxic agent and a particular disease.[68]

---

61. 3 FAIGMAN ET AL., *supra* note 55, § 22:5; *see also, e.g.,* McClain, 401 F.3d at 1237 ("To prove their toxic tort claims, Plaintiffs must prove the toxicity of the ephedrine/caffeine combination and that it had a toxic effect on them causing the injuries that they suffered. . . .").
62. 3 FAIGMAN ET AL., *supra* note 55, § 22:5; *see also, e.g.,* Troy Corp. v. Browner, 129 F.3d 1290, 1292 (D.C. Cir. 1997) (EPA's decision to identify chemical as toxic substance was supported by substantial evidence of animal studies demonstrating significant increases in pathology). *See, e.g.,* Boyd, 898 So. 2d at 459–62 (the plaintiffs and the defendant introduced testimony of toxicologists addressing potential for injuries in plaintiff class based on duration and amount of exposure attributable to release of toxic gas from tanker truck).
63. Goldstein & Henifin, *supra* note , at 667; *see also, e.g.,* Gen. Elec. Co. v. Joiner, 522 U.S. 136, 143–47 (1997); Daubert v. Merrell Dow Pharms., Inc., 509 U.S. 579, 582–85 (1993).
64. Goldstein & Henifin, *supra* note , at 637; *see also* Hall v. Baxter Healthcare Corp., 947 F. Supp. 1387, 1413 (D. Or. 1996) ("[T]he expert must 'rule in' the suspected cause as well as 'rule out' other possible causes."); *see, e.g.,* Bosch v. Sec'y of Dep't of Health & Human Servs., No. 95-0313V, 1997 WL 254218, at *7 (Fed. Cl. Apr. 25, 1997) (dismissing petition where plaintiffs offered no evidence of how the vaccination caused the death of plaintiffs' child); Migliori v. Boeing N. Am., Inc., 114 F. Supp. 2d 976, 980 (C.D. Cal. 2000) (study concerning exposure of Boeing employees to radiation indicated that workers who received relatively higher dose had an increased risk of developing cancer). *See generally* King v. Burlington N. Santa Fe Ry. Corp., 762 N.W.2d 24 (Neb. 2009) (providing an explanation of the use of toxicological studies for showing causation).
65. 1 CETRULO, *supra* note , § 5:25; Michael D. Green et al., *Reference Guide on Epidemiology, in* REFERENCE MANUAL ON SCIENTIFIC EVIDENCE, *supra* note , at 549, 551.
66. Jeffrey Dintzer & Jonathan Mosher, *Epidemiologic Evidence in Toxic Tort Cases*, 17 NAT. RESOURCES & ENV'T 222, 271 (2003); G. Marc Whitehead & Larry D. Espel, *Causation and Experts in Toxic Tort Litigation: How to Use and Defend against Epidemiology, Toxicology and Biostatistics*, 387 PLI/Lit 169, 175 (1990).
67. Green et al., *supra* note , at 551.
68. 1 CETRULO, *supra* note , § 5:25.

Litigants may rely on epidemiological studies as circumstantial evidence to prove or disprove causation. Indeed, one court has concluded that "epidemiology is the best evidence of causation in the mass torts context."[69]

The focus of epidemiology is on general causation (i.e., whether the substance is capable of causing a particular injury in the general population), rather than specific causation (i.e., whether the substance caused this particular individual's injury).[70] When combined with direct evidence of exposure and direct evidence and/or expert testimony to exclude alternative causes, an expert witness may rely on general causation to support his or her conclusion that a substance caused harm or illness in a particular plaintiff.[71]

Experimentation by exposing humans to known doses of chemical agents can involve serious ethical implications and is, therefore, extremely rare.[72] Most epidemiological evidence applied in toxic tort litigation is based on observational studies where the epidemiologists have observed and compared individuals who have been exposed to a potentially toxic agent with a control group of individuals who have not been exposed. There are two primary types of observational studies: cohort studies and case-control studies.[73]

In a cohort study, the investigator compares the incidence of disease among exposed groups with the incidence of disease in nonexposed groups.[74] In a case-control study, the

---

69. In re Breast Implant Litig., 11 F. Supp. 2d 1217, 1224 (D. Colo. 1998); see also, e.g., In re Agent Orange Prod. Liab. Litig., 611 F. Supp. 1223 (E.D.N.Y. 1985) (plaintiffs' evidence was insufficient because it lacked any admissible epidemiological studies to demonstrate a causal connection between their exposure to Agent Orange and their injuries), aff'd, 818 F.2d 187 (2d Cir. 1987).
70. Green et al., supra note , at 552; Magistrini v. One Hour Martinizing Dry Cleaning, 180 F. Supp. 2d 584, 590 (D.N.J. 2002), aff'd, 68 Fed. App. 356 (3d Cir. 2003).
71. See, e.g., DeLucca v. Merrell Dow Pharm., Inc., 911 F.2d 941, 953 (3d Cir. 1990); In re Breast Implant Litig., 11 F. Supp. 2d at 1224 (D. Colo. 1998). In such cases, it is not necessary that the testifying expert conduct the epidemiological study or studies that form the basis of his or her opinion. Green et al., supra note , at 551 n.2, citing DeLucca, 911 F.2d 941 at 953 (expert's credentials were sufficient to allow him to interpret and render an opinion based on epidemiological studies).
72. Goldstein & Henifin, supra note , at 639; Dintzer & Mosher, supra note 66, at 222; see also Magistrini, 180 F. Supp. 2d at 590 ("Experimental studies in the form of randomized trials, clinical trials or true experiments . . . involve . . . two groups, one of which is exposed to the agent in question. . . When an agent is suspected of being harmful, most epidemiological studies concerning that agent are observational.").
73. Dintzer & Mosher, supra note 66, at 222–23; Green et al., supra note , at 556–57; see also Magistrini, 180 F. Supp. 2d at 590–93 (discussing two types of observational studies in epidemiology); Knight v. Kirby Inland Marine, Inc., 482 F. 3d 347, 352–55 (5th Cir. 2007) (analyzing the admissibility of case-control and cohort studies).
74. Green et al., supra note , at 557–59; see also, e.g., In re Orthopedic Bone Screw Prods. Liab. Litig., No. 1014, 1997 WL 230818, at *1 (E.D. Pa. May 5, 1997) (discussing cohort study to "estimate the rates for success of spinal fusion using pedicle screws and to identify risks associated with pedicle screw use and their rates of occurrence"); Exxon Corp. v. Makofski, 116 S.W.3d 176, 183–84 & n.28 (Tex. Ct. App. 2003) (discussing cohort study of workers exposed to benzene in factories in China); Fredric Gerr et al., Neurological Effects of Environmental Exposure to Arsenic in Dust and Soil among Humans, 21 NEUROTOXICOLOGY 475 (2000) ("Gerr Study") (an epidemiologic study in which a portion of more than 600 plaintiffs constituted the study group); Kaye H. Kilburn, Visual and Neurobehavioral Impairment Associated with Polychlorinated Biphenyls, 21 NEUROTOXICOLOGY 489 (2000) ("Kilburn Study") (an epidemiologic study in which the study group comprised ninety-eight individuals, including seven plaintiffs); cf. Nelson v. Tennessee Gas Pipeline Co., 243 F.3d 244, 248, 254 (6th Cir. 2001) (affirming magistrate's exclusion of plaintiffs' expert testimony regarding the Kilburn Study "because it did not

investigator measures and compares the frequency and amount of exposure to the agent in the diseased group to the frequency and amount of exposure in the nondiseased group, weighing the odds of developing a disease when exposed to a chemical agent versus the odds of developing the disease without exposure.[75] In each type of study, the goal is to determine whether there is an association between exposure and disease and, if so, the strength of that association.[76]

The term *association* is used to describe the relationship between two events. Epidemiological studies investigate whether there is an association between exposure to a particular chemical agent and a disease—that is, do "they occur together more frequently than one would expect by chance."[77] If an association is observed, the epidemiologist "must assess the strength of the association as well as whether the reason for the observed association is due to bias, chance or real effect"[78]—that is, association does not equal causation.[79] An association can, however, support an inference that a chemical caused a disease.[80]

Epidemiological studies identify a "relative risk," which is a term commonly used to describe the association between a chemical agent and disease. It is the ratio between the incidence of disease in exposed individuals and the incidence of disease in unexposed individuals.[81] The relative risk indicates the increased or decreased likelihood of an individual developing a disease resulting from exposure to a toxin. For instance, if the relative risk is greater than 1.0, the risk in exposed individuals is greater than the risk in unexposed individuals.[82] When the relative risk of a study reaches 2.0, that study indicates that chemical exposure doubles the risk of illness. In a toxic tort case, the plaintiff must, of course, show that it is "more likely than not" that exposure to the chemical caused his or her illness. To meet that standard, some courts require a relative risk number greater than 2.0 to support an inference that the plaintiff's illness was more likely than not caused by the suspected toxin.[83]

---

meet the standards for admission of scientific evidence under *Daubert* and its progeny"); Hall v. Babcock & Wilcox Co., 69 F. Supp. 2d 716, 722–23 (W.D. Pa. 1999) (granting a new trial due to procedural error committed in admitting expert testimony based on data not previously provided to the defense and generated from an epidemiological study published by the Pennsylvania Department of Health in which the plaintiffs' community was used as the study group).

75. Green et al., *supra* note , at 559–60; *see also, e.g.*, Sharpnack v. Sec'y of the Dep't of Health & Human Servs., No. 90-983V, 1992 WL 167255, at *2 (Cl. Ct. June 29, 1992) (discussing case-control study of relationship between vaccine and disease, comparing children with illness to children in control group); Summar v. Sec'y of the Dep't of Health & Human Servs., No. 90-415V, 1991 WL 133607, at *3 n.8 (Cl. Ct. July 3, 1991) (noting that case-control studies are "scientifically much more valid" than cohort studies). At least one court has declined to admit a case-control study. *See Nelson*, 243 F.3d at 248, 254.
76. Green et al., *supra* note , at 557.
77. *Id.* at 566.
78. Magistrini, 180 F. Supp. 2d at 591.
79. Green et al., *supra* note , at 552.
80. *Id.* at 552 n.7.
81. *Id.* at 566.
82. *Id.* at 567.
83. *Id.* at 612; *see, e.g., DeLucca*, 911 F.2d at 959 ("A relative risk greater than '2' means that the disease

When evaluating the quality and strength of an epidemiological study, several factors should be considered:

- *Study size*: In most instances, the greater the number of participants in the study, the more valid the study.
- *Statistical significance*: This factor indicates the probability that the results of the study are not due to chance.[84]
- *Bias*: Bias may result from poor study design or implementation. Bias may arise based on an error in the manner in which subjects are selected (selection bias). Or it may occur based on problems with data collection (information bias) resulting from the subject's recall or how the interview was conducted. It may also occur if a subject is misclassified (e.g., placed in the exposed group when he or she is not, in fact, exposed).
- *Confounding factors*: A confounder is another factor that is associated with the exposure that independently affects the risk of developing the disease.

These factors may be used to call into question the reliability of an epidemiological study.[85]

Bradford Hill Criteria

When interpreting whether an association between chemical exposure and disease establishes causation, toxicologists and epidemiologists frequently consider the Bradford Hill criteria:[86]

- *Strength of association*: What is the relative risk?
- *Consistency*: Have different investigators reproduced this study and reached the same conclusions?

---

more likely than not was caused by the event."); Merrell Dow Pharms., Inc. v. Havner, 953 S.W.2d 706, 717 (Tex. 1997) (scientifically reliable epidemiological studies showing more than a doubling of the risk may establish a causation link). *But see In re* Lockheed Litigation Cases, 23 Cal. Rptr. 3d 762, 765 (Cal. Ct. App. 2005) ("We conclude that that conclusion was error and that a court cannot exclude an epidemiological study from consideration solely because the study shows a relative risk of less than 2.0."). *Contrast* Daubert v. Merrell Dow Pharms., Inc., 43 F.3d 1311, 1321 16 (9th Cir. 1995) *with In re* Joint E. & S. Dist. Asbestos Litig., 52 F.3d 1124, 1134 (2d Cir. 1995) (rejecting the assertion that standardized mortality rates of 1.5 are statistically insignificant as a matter of law and finding that "it would be far preferable for" any evidence indicating a relative risk of over 1.0 to be submitted to the jury to determine the proper weight to be given to that evidence).

84. The statistical analysis of chance is a significant component of the epidemiologist's work and beyond the scope of this chapter. In Magistrini, the court retained its own expert and provided a succinct layperson's discussion of the use of statistical significance and confidence intervals and their role in evaluating chance in epidemiological studies. 180 F. Supp. 2d at 592–93.
85. *See generally* Green et al., *supra* note , at 572–96.
86. Douglas L. Weed, *Causation: An Epidemiologic Perspective (In Five Parts)*, 12 J.L. & Pol'y 43, 45 (2003); *see also, e.g.*, King, 762 N.W.2d at 40–42 (discussing the use of Bradford Hill factors to establish general causation).

- *Specificity*: Does this specific chemical, at a specific dose and over a specific time, cause a specific outcome?
- *Temporality*: Does the exposure precede the disease?
- *Dose response*: As the dose of exposure increases, does the risk of disease increase?
- *Plausibility*: How likely is it that exposure causes the disease? Are there alternate explanations?
- *Coherence*: Is the finding consistent with the current body of scientific evidence?
- *Experiment*: Does experimental evidence support the hypothesis? Do human and animal studies support a similar conclusion?[87]

It is not necessary that all of these factors be present for a true causal relationship to exist; nor does the presence of some factors establish a causal relationship.[88] Ultimately, a scientist's Bradford Hill analysis "is only as reliable as the underlying data upon which it is based."[89]

Conclusion

Scientific evidence is a critical part of toxic tort and environmental litigation. Therefore, at the outset of a case, precautions should be taken to ensure that sampling and analysis of the suspected contaminated media is conducted according to generally accepted methodologies. Fate and transport analysis is central to establishing the presence of a contaminant and that the plaintiff or plaintiff class was exposed to the contaminant. Finally, toxicology and epidemiology support or disprove an allegation that the contaminant caused or is likely to cause the plaintiff or plaintiff class to develop a disease. These sciences provide the building blocks for establishing or defending against a toxic tort claim.

---

87. Irva Hertz-Picciotto, *How Scientists View Causality and Assess Evidence: A Study of the Institute of Medicine's Evaluation of Health Effects in Vietnam Veterans and Agent Orange*, 13 J.L. & Pol'y 553, 579–80 (2005).
88. *Id.* at 580; Green et al., *supra* note , at 600; *see also* Havner, 953 S.W.2d at 718–19 & n.2 (discussing the Bradford Hill criteria and noting that "[a]lthough epidemiologists do not consider it necessary that all these criteria be met before drawing inferences about causation, they are part of sound methodology generally accepted by the current scientific community").
89. *Knight*, 363 F. Supp. 2d at 864.

CHAPTER 5

Causation and the Use of Experts

Alan Rudlin, Alexandra Cunningham, and Thomas R. Waskom

Causation is the linchpin of nearly every tort case, and medical causation is the central inquiry of toxic tort litigation. Because of the nature of the injuries at issue, however, toxic tort causation often presents a far more difficult question than that found in other tort cases. The cause of an acute injury is usually readily discernible—for instance, a pedestrian hit by a car likely will not need an expert to show the cause of his broken leg. On the other hand, in toxic tort cases, plaintiffs are often seeking recovery for injuries with many possible causes, and alleging that exposures that occurred long ago caused some chemical or genetic change in their bodies that triggered a disease process. For that reason, toxic tort causation can be difficult to determine and prove, and almost always requires expert testimony.

Toxic tort litigation encompasses a variety of forms, claims, and backgrounds. The plaintiffs may be individuals, a group, or a putative class. They may claim exposure to naturally occurring substances, chemicals, man-made fibers, radiation, bacteria, or pathogens. The period of exposure may be a single instance, or continuous over an extended time. The extent of exposure can be at high or barely detectable levels. The injuries asserted may be those conventionally recognized in medicine such as cancer, or an array of claimed signs and symptoms for which the plaintiffs' expert has created a new syndrome label. Regardless of these variations, there are two common denominators in all forms of toxic tort litigation: (1) the issue of medical causation; and (2) the use of scientific and medical experts to establish such causation. Put colloquially, in all the various makes and models of toxic tort cases, medical causation is the engine that drives each case, and experts are the fuel to run it. One is critical to the other, and it is important to understand how they relate.

This chapter proceeds in three sections: (1) a brief foundation on the key principles of medical causation in a toxic tort case; (2) a discussion of the strategic concepts for counsel to consider in litigating the causation issue; and (3) the critically important issue of how to deal with experts' causation opinions in the context of *Daubert* (or *Frye*) challenges.

What Does *Causation* Mean in the Toxic Tort Context?

There are three fundamental components to the causation analysis in any toxic tort case: exposure and dose (i.e., the amount of the allegedly causative agent to which the plaintiff was exposed and the dose received); general causation (i.e., whether the agent is capable of causing the disease at issue); and specific causation (i.e., whether the agent caused the disease in the particular individual).[1] A weakness in any one of the three categories can be fatal to legally sufficient evidence of causation in a case.

Exposure and Dose

At the outset of the case, it is important for defense counsel to examine the nature of the exposure that allegedly caused the plaintiff's harm. A surprising number of cases begin in the form of pleadings alleging exposure (without regard to time or circumstance) to a laundry list of chemicals or toxins (without reference to the source of the exposure). The magnitude and duration of the exposure are critical, the former often being expressed in terms of concentration in air, water, or soil, and the latter being described as either acute (typically a one-time heavy exposure) or chronic (exposure occurring continually or continuously over time at specified levels).

Once the details of the exposure have been defined, it must be established whether the plaintiff received an actual dose, and if so, of what substance and at what level. Numerous studies have established the basic proposition that just because a person is exposed to something does not mean that he will actually have a dose in his body. The typical routes of exposure for people to receive a dose—inhalation, ingestion, or dermal absorption—all have their own separate biologic barriers to protect people from casual exposure to toxic substances. Thus, there is no "guilt by association" in the sense that an individual is presumed to have received a dose simply by virtue of being in the vicinity of a toxic substance.

General Causation

General causation answers the basic question, "Is exposure to substance X capable of causing condition Y in a human?" Generally accepted scientific knowledge about the causal relationship between a specific exposure and a specific medical condition has been the subject of methodological analysis since at least the development in 1850 of what were

---

1. This distinction between general causation and specific causation is widely recognized in court opinions. *See, e.g.*, Kelley v. Am. Heyer-Schulte Corp., 957 F. Supp. 873, 875–76 (W.D. Tex. 1997), *appeal dismissed*, 139 F.3d 899 (5th Cir. 1998); Cavallo v. Star Enter., 892 F. Supp. 756, 771 n.34 (E.D. Va. 1995), *aff'd in part and rev'd in part*, 100 F.3d 1150 (4th Cir. 1996), *cert. denied*, 522 U.S. 1044 (1998); Casey v. Ohio Med. Prods., 877 F. Supp. 1380, 1382 (N.D. Cal. 1995).

known as the Henle-Koch postulates used to determine the cause of infectious diseases from bacteria. In 1965, British scientist Sir Austin Bradford Hill elaborated further upon these causation criteria, as they had evolved over the previous century, and developed what are today the most widely accepted scientific criteria to evaluate the concept of general causation. These criteria are largely based on a critical evaluation of epidemiology, that is, what has been published in the scientific literature about an association between a particular exposure and a particular medical condition.

Often, the first step in the toxic tort case is to research the epidemiological literature to see what has been reported on the causal relationship between exposure to the agent at issue and the medical condition alleged. This general causation information must then be critically evaluated by applying Hill's criteria. A full discussion of those criteria is beyond the scope of this chapter[2], but the key concepts are as follows:

Strength of Association

Epidemiological studies are often referred to as showing a "strong" or "weak" association, which refers to the extent of findings of a condition (e.g., lung cancer) and an exposure (e.g., tobacco smoke) in the people studied (the "study group"), compared to an otherwise similarly situated, but unexposed, group (the "control group"). The strength of the observed association is quantitatively expressed using a statistical concept that can be described in a variety of ways, such as the concepts of "relative risk" or "confidence interval."[3] Although not free from dispute, most scientists would acknowledge that any association with a relative risk of less than 2.0 would be considered a weak association, and this factor would detract from the overall qualitative judgment that there was any causal relationship.

Consistency of Association

The concept of consistency of association refers to whether the same or similar outcome is reported in more than one study. It is not uncommon to see variations in the results of epidemiological studies of the same substance. Some studies may find a substance has an association with a deleterious effect, while other studies may suggest the lack of an association or even a health protective effect. Without consistency across similar studies, the causal hypothesis is significantly undercut.

Specificity of Association

This criterion addresses how well the epidemiological study evaluates a specifically diagnosed medical condition in relation to a specific exposure. Was the exposure carefully

---

2. For a full discussion of many of these criteria, see FEDERAL JUDICIAL CENTER, REFERENCE MANUAL ON SCIENTIFIC EVIDENCE (2d ed. 2000).
3. *See id.* at 336–38.

delineated? Was the medical condition crisply defined or stated in general or vague labels with names not generally used by treating doctors or clinicians? Have confounding factors and issues of bias been addressed?

Temporal Relationship
A fundamental concept of causation is that the plaintiff's alleged medical condition occur *after*, not *before*, the exposure. As importantly, and sometimes subtly, it is necessary to consider whether a scientifically rational minimum period of time has passed for the condition, as best as medicine understands its development, to manifest itself. For example, most forms of cancer have very long latency periods between the time of first exposure and the development of a diagnosable tumor. A claim of cancer after a dramatically short exposure period may not be a scientifically rational temporal relationship. For other chemicals with acute exposure risks, too much time may have passed between the exposure and the onset of the injury or symptoms.

Dose Response
Does the medical condition exacerbate with greater dosage? Dose response is fundamental to causation. All chemical substances, whether man-made or of natural origin, can cause harm if exposures are excessive. Many of the commonplace things that we use and treat as innocuous can be toxic if taken in high enough doses. Similarly, unless the incidence of the human response increases as the dose increases, the likelihood of causation is diminished.

Biologic Plausibility
Is the causal relationship claimed logical in terms of what science or medicine knows about how the chemical operates on the body's systems, how the disease process occurs, and what's been seen in toxicological studies? In other words, does it make scientific sense?

Specific Causation

Assuming general causation can be established, the next hurdle is specific causation. The fact that a chemical can intrinsically cause a disease does not establish that it was the cause of disease in the particular plaintiff at issue. Specific causation requires analysis of the details of the individual plaintiff's claims, once both the facts of exposure (how much of the substance was the plaintiff exposed to, and for how long) and scientific evidence of general causation (i.e., that the substance has been recognized in science to have the potential for causing the harm alleged) have been established. It is, in effect, a "drill down" on the precise facts that form the basis for the particular plaintiff's toxic tort claim.

Once a careful dissection of the specific basis for the plaintiff's individual exposure has been completed, the next step is to evaluate whether the potential dose was in an amount that was sufficient in magnitude and duration to be capable of producing the effect alleged, based on what has been established in the scientific literature. If the dose-response relationship appears to be scientifically plausible, then a careful evaluation of the plaintiff's alleged condition in relationship to the exposure must be considered to determine whether the temporal relationship is plausible.

Finally, and perhaps most important, the issue of alternative cause must be considered. In many cases, science has not yet determined the cause or causes of a particular disease or condition. Thus, discovery and careful evaluation must account for other potential significant causes of a plaintiff's medical condition, including exposure to other substances, lifestyle, workplace, and heredity. The failure to consider and rule out these alternative causes, if applicable, can be fatal to a causation conclusion.

How Can You Prove (or Dispute) Causation in Toxic Tort Cases?

Toxic tort plaintiffs and defendants alike share causation challenges. For the toxic tort plaintiff, the challenge is one of proving causation to a reasonable degree of medical or scientific certainty in areas where science may not be ready to provide definitive answers. On the other hand, although legal burdens of proof may suggest that "uncertainty" on causation issues is a toxic tort defendant's ally, as a practical matter, jurors often look to the toxic tort defendant to disprove causation. That is, if the toxic exposure at issue did not cause a plaintiff's injury, the toxic tort defendant effectively bears the burden of persuasion to the jury, which is often not satisfied by the answer of current scientific uncertainty on an issue. Rather, a jury instinctively wants to know what, if not the defendant's chemical, drug, or other contaminant, caused the plaintiff's injury? As a result, the defendant may choose to point to alternative causes—"here's the culprit"—rather than resting on the frequently applicable scientific "candor" that, in some cases, nobody knows with the requisite degree of legal, or medical, certainty what actually caused the plaintiff's injury.

The basic concept is that a substance will not cause harm unless it is taken into the body in a sufficiently large amount. The amount necessary to cause harm is a function of a variety of factors, such as the specific toxicity of the chemical and the pathway of exposure, and individual factors, such as the effectiveness of the body's clearing mechanisms and the individual's body mass and metabolism. The concept that "the dose makes the poison" is perhaps the central tenet of modern toxicology.[4] Thus, simply proving exposure to a toxic substance does not amount to causation.[5] Instead, plaintiffs must prove

---

4. *See generally* W. HAYES, THE TOXICOLOGY OF PESTICIDES § 1.1 (1975) (cited in A GUIDE TO TOXIC TORTS § 10.02[1][b][ii] (1996); FEDERAL JUDICIAL CENTER, *supra* note 2, at 403. The principle traces its roots to the work of sixteenth-century Swiss physician Paracelsus, who is reputed to have stated that "dosage alone determines poisoning."
5. *See* Lyons v. Garlock, Inc., 12 F. Supp. 2d 1226 (D. Kan. 1998); Wright v. Williamette Indus., Inc., 91 F.3d 1105 (8th Cir. 1996) (discussed *infra*). *But see* Mattis v. Carlon Elec. Prods., 114 F. Supp. 2d 888 (D.S.D. 2000) (holding that the plaintiff is not required to produce "a mathematically precise table equating the

that as a result of being exposed to high enough levels over a sufficient period of time, they received sufficient doses to cause harm.

Establishing General Causation

The first step in demonstrating a causal link in a toxic tort case is proving general causation—that is, the agent at issue is capable of causing the medical condition at issue. General causation will typically be in greater dispute in cases involving immature claims. It is rarely disputed, for instance, in claims linking asbestos exposure to asbestosis or mesothelioma.

The gold standard for general causation proof is epidemiological evidence. As the *Reference Manual on Scientific Evidence* states,

> Epidemiologic evidence identifies agents that are associated with an increased risk of disease in groups of individuals, quantifies the amount of excess disease that is associated with an agent, and provides a profile of the type of individual who is likely to contract a disease after being exposed to an agent. Epidemiology focuses on the question of general causation (i.e., is the agent capable of causing disease?) rather than that of specific causation (i.e., did it cause disease in a particular individual?).[6]

The *Restatement (Third) of Torts* elaborates:

> These studies proceed by comparing the incidence of disease in a group that has been exposed to the agent with the incidence of disease in a group of unexposed persons. The latter group's disease, thus, is attributable to causes other than the agent being studied.... Occasionally, biological-mechanism evidence is sufficiently developed to prove general causation. More frequently, however, the evidence consists of scientific studies comparing the incidence of disease in groups of individuals (epidemiologic evidence) or animals (toxicologic evidence) with different levels of exposure. When a study finds a difference in the incidence of disease in the exposed and unexposed groups, an "association" exists between exposure and disease. Another type of epidemiologic study compares the extent of exposure among those with and without the disease. These studies seek to identify potentially causal substances at the aggregate population level—by finding a higher incidence of a disease in a group exposed to the substance (an "association").[7]

---

levels of exposure with levels of harm, but there must be 'some evidence from which a reasonable person could conclude' that the fumes" from the producer caused the plaintiff's injuries); Quate v. American Standard, Inc., 818 A.2d 510, 511 (Pa. Super. Ct. 2003) (holding that because plaintiff suffered from several medical conditions that could account for his breathlessness, plaintiff could not establish link between symptoms and asbestos exposure).

6. FEDERAL JUDICIAL CENTER, *supra* note 2, at 335–36.
7. RESTATEMENT (THIRD) OF TORTS § 28 cmt. *(c)(3)* (2010).

Courts are often skeptical of causation experts who are unable to marshal any epidemiological evidence in support of their position. For instance, in *Burleson v. Texas Department of Criminal Justice*,[8] an inmate alleged that his throat and lung cancer were caused by radioactive thorium to which he was exposed while working as a welder in prison. The Fifth Circuit Court of Appeals affirmed the district court's exclusion of the plaintiff's toxicology and occupational medicine expert, in part because the expert presented no reliable evidence about the plaintiff's dose of radiation and identified no epidemiological studies demonstrating a statistically significant link between radioactive thorium and the plaintiff's disease.[9]

The Supreme Court of Texas set down an even more exacting standard for general causation evidence in *Merrell Dow Pharmaceuticals, Inc. v. Havner*.[10] In *Havner*, which involved injuries allegedly caused by the drug Bendectin, the court prescribed standards for the use of epidemiological studies as evidence of general causation. While a plaintiff should rely on "properly designed and executed epidemiological studies," such studies must demonstrate that exposure to the substance at issue presented more than a "doubling of the risk" that the plaintiff's alleged injury would occur, to make it more likely than not that the exposure was the cause of the injury.[11] This is widely known as the *Havner* 2.0 Standard.

In another case out of Texas, *Daniels v. Lyondell-Citgo Refining Co.*, the Texas Court of Appeals affirmed dismissal of a suit against a refinery owner, determining that there was no evidence indicating that benzene exposure caused a worker's fatal lung cancer.[12] The widow and daughter of a refinery worker had alleged gross negligence on the part of the defendant in failing to protect the worker from benzene exposure. In support of the argument that the decedent's exposure to benzene caused his cancer, the plaintiffs introduced a study showing increases in the lung cancer death rate of more than 15,000 benzene-exposed workers in China,[13] a study of Canadian refinery workers finding increases in lung cancer deaths, a study of British refinery workers finding increases in lung cancer deaths, and an animal study showing an increase in bronchoalveolar cancer in mice exposed to crude petroleum.

The defendant moved for summary judgment, arguing, among other things, that there was no evidence that any particular dose of benzene could cause lung cancer, no evidence that any dose sustained by the decedent caused his disease, and no evidence to rule out

---

8. 393 F.3d 577 (5th Cir. 2004).
9. *Id.* at 585–86.
10. 953 S.W.2d 706 (Tex. 1997).
11. *Id.* at 717. *Havner* also requires that epidemiological studies use a 95 percent significance level, and warned lower courts against permitting experts to rest causation opinions on lone epidemiological studies. *Id.* at 723–24.
12. 99 S.W.3d 722 (Tex. App.–Hous. [1st Dist.] 2003, no pet.).
13. S.N. Yin et al., *A Retrospective Cohort Study of Leukemia and Other Cancers in Benzene Workers*, 82 ENVTL. HEALTH PERSP. 207, 207–13 (1989).

smoking as an alternative cause of the cancer. The court agreed and granted summary judgment to the defendant.[14]

Similarly, in *Allen v. Pennsylvania Engineering Corp.*,[15] the plaintiff alleged that the decedent's exposure to the defendant's product caused his brain cancer. The Fifth Circuit again held that the district court did not err in excluding the plaintiff's expert's testimony on causation, because the expert's conclusions were based on animal studies and cell biology rather than generally accepted epidemiological studies.[16]

In *Norris v. Baxter Healthcare Corp.*,[17] a silicone gel breast implant case, the Tenth Circuit likewise emphasized the primacy of epidemiological evidence in the general causation analysis, albeit from a slightly different angle. The court held that the plaintiff's expert's general causation opinion was unreliable not because no relevant epidemiology existed, but rather because the expert had failed to account for the epidemiology that *did* exist: "Plaintiff's experts completely ignored or discounted without explanation the many epidemiological studies which found no medically reliable link between silicone breast implants and systemic disease."[18] And in *Vargas v. Lee*,[19] the Fifth Circuit held that the district court erred in admitting expert testimony that the plaintiff's fibromyalgia was caused by a motor vehicle accident where the expert's opinion was based only on two inconclusive studies and the expert's anecdotal experience.[20]

That is not to say that epidemiological support is a *sine qua non* of admissible expert testimony on general causation in all jurisdictions—it is not. As the Eight Circuit has stated, "there is no requirement that published epidemiological studies supporting an expert's opinion exist in order for the opinion to be admissible."[21] For instance, in *Pipitone v. Biomatrix, Inc.*,[22] the Fifth Circuit reversed a district court's exclusion of the plaintiff's physician's causation testimony that was unsupported by epidemiological evidence. The Fifth Circuit reasoned that medical literature such as epidemiological research will rarely be available when only one person has been affected by the relevant causative agent—by definition, epidemiology studies the incidence of disease across populations.[23] In those circumstances, an expert can properly base her opinions on personal observations, professional experience, education, and training.[24]

---

14. *Daniels*, 99 S.W.3d at 726.
15. 102 F.3d 194 (5th Cir. 1996).
16. *Id.* at 197.
17. 397 F.3d 878 (10th Cir. 2005).
18. *Id.* at 885.
19. 317 F.3d 498 (5th Cir. 2003).
20. *Id.* at 501–02.
21. Bonner v. ISP Techs., Inc., 259 F.3d 924, 929 (8th Cir. 2001).
22. 288 F.3d 239 (5th Cir. 2002).
23. *Id.* at 246–47.
24. *Id.*; *see also* Knight v. Kirby Inland Marine Inc., 482 F.3d 347, 355 (5th Cir. 2007) (stating that an expert need not base his opinion on published studies that unequivocally support his conclusions; where the opinion is otherwise based on sound methodology, lack of textual support goes to weight, not admissibility).

The Ninth Circuit has taken a similar position. In *Clausen v. M/V New Carissa*,[25] commercial oyster farmers brought an action against the owners of a vessel responsible for an oil spill, alleging that the oil caused the death of oysters in the vicinity of the spill. The plaintiffs' causation expert identified (and included in his differential diagnosis) the low-level toxic effects of oil as a possible cause of the oyster deaths, despite the lack of any supporting peer-reviewed literature specific to oysters.[26] The court held that even in the absence of such published studies, the expert could reasonably base his opinion on government reports showing the presence of the vessel's oil in the oyster beds and the oysters themselves, his survey of the oyster beds, his clinical examination of the oysters, the history of the oyster beds, and the fact that contact toxicity had occurred in every other animal system studied.[27] As the court put it:

> We do not believe that a medical expert must always cite published studies on general causation in order to reliably conclude that a particular object caused a particular illness. The first several victims of a new toxic tort should not be barred from having their day in court simply because the medical literature, which will eventually show the connection between the victims' condition and the toxic substance, has not yet been completed. If a properly qualified medical expert performs a reliable differential diagnosis through which, to a reasonable degree of medical certainty, all other possible causes of the victims' condition can be eliminated, leaving only the toxic substance as the cause, a causation opinion . . . should be admitted.[28]

Clausen can fairly be seen as pushing the limits of permissible general causation evidence with its supposition that medical literature tomorrow "will eventually show the connection" that the plaintiffs are charged with proving today. But as a marker of that outer limit, it is instructive for plaintiffs and defendants alike to recognize what might (and what should not) carry the burden of proof on the general causation prong of the toxic tort causation analysis.

To set up the specific causation analysis discussed below, experts also may be called upon to opine on the dose at which a particular agent becomes toxic. In recent years, it has come into vogue for plaintiffs' experts to testify that there is "no safe level of exposure" in order to avoid some of the more difficult steps that come later in the causation analysis. Not all courts have looked favorably upon such efforts. For instance, in *Newkirk v. ConAgra Foods, Inc.*,[29] a plaintiff claimed that by eating five to seven bags of microwave

---

25. 339 F.3d 1049 (9th Cir. 2003).
26. *Id.* at 1059.
27. *Id.*
28. *Id.* at 1060.
29. 727 F. Supp. 2d 1006 (E.D. Wash. 2010).

popcorn a day for over a decade, he contracted so-called popcorn lung, a disease found in popcorn factory workers that is caused by exposure to diacetyl, a chemical found in artificial butter. Notwithstanding his suspiciously high daily popcorn intake, the plaintiff still faced the problem that popcorn lung is typically only found in individuals exposed to occupational-type levels of diacetyl. Thus, the plaintiff proffered the opinions of an expert who testified that "[t]here is no known safe level of diacetyl exposure."[30] But the court rejected that opinion on the ground that the expert had purported to rely on published studies far removed from the subject matter of his opinions.[31]

Similar "no safe level of exposure" opinions have also recently drawn fire from courts in asbestos cases. For instance, in *Moeller v. Garlock Sealing Technologies, LLC*,[32] the Sixth Circuit rejected the opinions of plaintiffs' experts claiming that "any exposure" to "any fiber" could cause an asbestos-related illness. Likewise, in *Gregg v. V-J Auto Parts Co.*,[33] the Pennsylvania Supreme Court observed that although it was "common for plaintiffs to submit expert affidavits attesting that any exposure to asbestos, no matter how minimal, is a substantial contributing factor in asbestos disease," such opinions are "not couched within accepted scientific methodology."[34]

Thus, "the dose makes the poison" is an important concept to keep in mind in building a general causation case. It is often not enough to merely show that an agent can cause a disease at some dose. Many courts will require the plaintiff to show that the agent can cause the disease at the relevant dose. Only then will the general causation evidence be strong enough to permit a plaintiff to use dose and specific causation to connect the causal dots.

Establishing Specific Causation

General causation is only the first step in toxic tort causation analysis. "The plaintiff must establish not only that the defendant's agent is capable of causing disease but also that it did cause the plaintiff's disease."[35] Essentially, a plaintiff must draw a line connecting his own exposure and dose to the general causation evidence to show that the agent *could have* caused his disease, and that it is more likely than not that the agent *did* cause his disease. Most courts require a plaintiff to demonstrate that the agent was a "substantial factor" in causing his disease—but how a plaintiff must go about doing that varies widely.

The "Substantial Factor" Test(s)

Courts have developed a patchwork of requirements for the proof a plaintiff must adduce to link exposure and dose to specific causation. Perhaps the most widely cited standard

---

30. *Id.* at 1015.
31. *Id.* at 1016.
32. No. 09-5670, 2011 U.S. App. LEXIS 19987 (6th Cir. Sept. 28, 2011).
33. 943 A.2d 216 (Pa. 2007).
34. *Id.* at 226.
35. FEDERAL JUDICIAL CENTER, *supra* note 2, at 382.

for proving specific causation in toxic tort cases (especially asbestos cases) comes from *Lohrmann v. Pittsburgh Corning Corp.*[36] Courts following *Lohrmann* will require a plaintiff to adduce "evidence of exposure to a specific product on a regular basis over some extended period of time in proximity to where the plaintiff actually worked."[37] With this, the Fourth Circuit endorsed the "frequency, regularity and proximity" test that can serve as a type of soft, nonquantitative dose assessment sufficient to show that a particular product or chemical was a "substantial cause" of the plaintiff's disease. It is "essentially a test used to analyze the sufficiency of evidence needed to satisfy the substantial factor [causation] requirement."[38]

The *Lohrmann* test has gained a wide following in asbestos cases.[39] Many states have adopted it or something like it. For instance, in *Lyons v. Garlock, Inc.*,[40] the court determined that to prove that asbestos caused the illness, the plaintiff must show that he was exposed to the substance on a regular basis over an extended period of time, not merely that the product was in the plant. The fact that asbestos was present somewhere in the employer's building concurrently with the plaintiff's employment did not meet the burden of proving causation.

When there is solid epidemiological evidence supporting that injury only occurs at a certain dose, the plaintiff may be required to prove that he was exposed not only to the substance, but at the level necessary to cause harm. An Oklahoma court dismissed a wrongful death suit against Texaco based on the conclusion that the plaintiff failed to present evidence that a worker's benzene exposure could have caused his leukemia. In *Holstine v. Texaco Corp.*,[41] the plaintiff worked for a rock crusher in Stringtown, Ohio, for twenty-six years. One of his daily job duties included using solvents containing benzene to clean and repair engine parts. Every three months, he also used pure benzene for about one hour. He died at age seventy-two from acute myelocytic leukemia (AML). The defendants moved to exclude the plaintiff's expert testimony and for summary judgment.

Based on epidemiological studies and other reports, the parties' experts agreed that long-term exposure to high levels of benzene can cause AML. Yet, the plaintiff had shown only

---

36. 782 F.2d 1156 (4th Cir. 1986).
37. *Id.* at 1162–63.
38. Spaur v. Owens-Corning Fiberglas Corp., 510 N.W.2d 854, 859 (Iowa 1994) (citing Beeman v. Manville Corp. Asbestos Disease Comp. Fund, 496 N.W.2d 247, 254 (Iowa 1993)). While *Lohrmann*'s adoption has been urged in some quarters by defendants and in others by plaintiffs, it is not without its drawbacks. There is a decided lack of rigor to the "frequency, regularity and proximity" test. But in a tort system largely built on the reasonable man standard, the uncertainty such a test breeds could be considered by some a feature rather than a bug.
39. *See* Slaughter v. S. Talc Co., 949 F.2d 167, 171 (5th Cir. 1991) (noting that *Lohrmann* is "[t]he most frequently used test for causation in asbestos cases"); *see also, e.g.*, Nolan v. Weil-McClain, 910 N.E.2d 549 (Ill. 2009) (following *Lohrmann*); Monsanto Co. v. Hall, 912 So. 2d 134 (Miss. 2005) (adopting *Lohrmann*); Chavers v. Gen.l Motors Corp., 79 S.W.3d 361 (Ark. 2002) (adopting *Lohrmann*).
40. 12 F. Supp. 2d 1226 (D. Kan. 1998).
41. No. CJ-97-221, 2001 WL 605137 (Okla. Dist. Ct. Apr. 16, 2001).

that the decedent was exposed to benzene on a long-term, low-level dose. The plaintiff's expert failed, however, to provide any studies showing that long-term, low-level exposure to benzene also results in AML. Therefore, the court concluded that the plaintiff failed to provide evidence of causation.

In *Wright v. Willamette Industries, Inc.*,[42] the Eighth Circuit stated that "a plaintiff in a toxic tort case must prove[: (1)] the levels of exposure that are hazardous to human beings generally[; and (2)] the plaintiff's actual level of exposure to the defendant's toxic substance."[43] The plaintiffs, who lived in the vicinity of the defendant's fiberboard manufacturing plant, sought recovery for exposure to formaldehyde used in the defendant's manufacturing processes. The plaintiffs proved at trial that they were exposed to defendant's emissions and that wood fibers from the defendant's plant were in their sputum and urine. Notwithstanding proof of their exposure, the Eighth Circuit found that part of the plaintiffs' expert's evidence regarding the toxicity of the plaintiffs' exposure should have been excluded by the trial court under *Daubert*:

> It is true that [the expert] . . . testified that the [plaintiffs'] complaints were more probably than not related to exposure to formaldehyde, but that opinion was not based on any knowledge about what amounts of wood fibers impregnated with formaldehyde involve an appreciable risk of harm to human beings who breathe them. The trial court should therefore have excluded [the expert's] testimony, as [the defendant] requested it to do, because it was not based on scientific knowledge. . . . [The expert's] testimony regarding the probable cause of the [plaintiffs'] claimed injuries was simply speculation.[44]

The plaintiff in *Becton v. Rhone-Poulenc, Inc.*[45] similarly failed to carry his burden of producing legally sufficient evidence of exposure. The plaintiff alleged that he sustained various injuries as a result of continuous exposure to carbon disulfide used in his employer's manufacture of rayon. In opposition to the defendant's motion for summary judgment, the plaintiff submitted an affidavit stating that he had learned that his injuries were related to exposure to CS2 "inside and outside" the employer's facility. (This affidavit apparently was the plaintiff's only evidence of exposure.) The affidavit did not provide any facts as to the details of his exposure, offering "only conjecture as to some unspecified duration and/or degree of exposure to carbon disulfide."[46] Affirming the trial court's entry of summary

---

42. 91 F.3d 1105 (8th Cir. 1996).
43. *Id.* at 1106.
44. *Id.* at 1108 (citations omitted). The remainder of the plaintiffs' expert evidence on this point was legally insufficient because it related to a different manner of exposure (gaseous formaldehyde) than that claimed by the plaintiffs (wood fibers impregnated with formaldehyde).
45. 706 So. 2d 1134 (Ala. 1997).
46. *Id.* at 1141.

judgment for the defendant, the Alabama Supreme Court ruled that this conjecture was insufficient to create a fact question as to the issue of the plaintiff's exposure.[47]

Perhaps the most rigorous specific causation test is that set out by the Supreme Court of Texas in *Borg-Warner Corp. v. Flores*.[48] In *Flores*, the plaintiff claimed that he had developed asbestosis (which typically requires a large dose of asbestos exposure) from his work with brake pads manufactured by Borg-Warner. As in *Lohrmann*, the plaintiff was called upon to demonstrate that exposure to asbestos released from the defendant's product was a substantial cause of his disease. But the court went beyond what many others have required, rejecting the premise that "if there is sufficient evidence that the defendant supplied *any* of the asbestos to which the plaintiff was exposed, then the plaintiff has met the burden of proof."[49]

Instead, in Texas state courts post-*Flores*, a plaintiff must show (1) quantitative evidence of the approximate dose to which the plaintiff was exposed, (2) evidence of the percentage of the dose attributable to the particular defendant, and (3) evidence that the defendant-specific dose by itself is sufficient to cause the alleged injury.[50] Thus, *Flores* requires plaintiffs to present expert testimony regarding retrospective dose reconstruction and then compare that dose to data from epidemiological studies that satisfy the *Havner* 2.0 standard.[51]

The Problem of Multiple Causative Agents

The "substantial factor" test was developed as a remedy for an issue endemic to toxic torts—the problem of many causes for a single indivisible injury. Many courts have followed *Lohrmann*'s lead in requiring a plaintiff to link his disease to a *particular defendant's* agent—not just the agent in general. For instance, in *Anglado v. Leaf River Forest Products, Inc.*,[52] the court dismissed the plaintiffs' claim for stigma and property damages because the plaintiffs failed to show that the dioxin present on their land matched that released from the defendant's mill.[53]

The Ninth Circuit has addressed the thorny issue of multiple causes of long latency disease. In *Kennedy v. Southern California Edison Co.*,[54] the court found that the evi-

---

47. *See id.*
48. 232 S.W.3d 765 (Tex. 2007).
49. *Id.* at 773 (emphasis in original).
50. *Id.* at 771–73.
51. Dose reconstruction can itself become a battleground for experts. *See, e.g.*, Green v. George's Farms, Inc., No. 10-26, 2011 WL 553916 (Ark. Feb. 17, 2011) (affirming trial court's decision to exclude plaintiff's expert's report purporting to quantify dose of fertilizer to which child had been exposed on ground that it was methodologically unsound).
52. 716 So. 2d 543 (Miss. 1998).
53. *Id.* at 544.
54. 268 F.3d 763 (9th Cir. 2001). The procedural history is unusual. The Ninth Circuit withdrew its prior opinion in the case, reported at 219 F.3d 988 (9th Cir. 2000), in which the court had determined that the *Rutherford* instruction, *see* Rutherford v. Owens-Ill., Inc., 941 P.2d 1203 (Cal. 1997), was applicable in a single-defendant case. The new opinion concluded that failure to give a *Rutherford* instruction was harmless error.

dence at trial did not support a finding that microscopic particles of radioactive material that the plaintiff's husband carried home on his work clothes were a substantial factor in causing her leukemia. Interpreting California law, the Ninth Circuit defined substantial as something more than "negligible" or "infinitesimal" or "theoretical."[55]

Exposure to a variety of chemicals may also pose difficulties to the plaintiff in establishing his burden of proof on causation. Many jurisdictions require the plaintiff to link the defendant's product to the disease suffered. In *Chism v. W.R. Grace & Co.*,[56] the Eighth Circuit affirmed the district court's summary judgment for the defendant because the plaintiff could not establish that the manufacturer's chemical caused her husband's disease. It was established that the deceased had been exposed to both raw asbestos and the manufacturer's chemical, Zonolite. Nevertheless, because the plaintiff could not prove that the Zonolite directly contributed to the harm suffered, the court granted summary judgment.[57]

Circumstantial Evidence

In some cases, courts have held that a toxic tort plaintiff could prove causation through mere circumstantial evidence. In *Aguilar v. Citgo Refining & Chemicals Co.*,[58] the plaintiffs claimed they suffered respiratory, gastrointestinal, and other illnesses as a result of the release of hydrogen sulfide during an explosion and fire at Citgo's Corpus Christi, Texas, facility. Because the plaintiffs' experts could not positively link the plaintiffs' injuries to the Citgo release of hydrogen sulfide, the plaintiffs withdrew the experts. The plaintiffs theorized that the jury did not need an expert to determine whether the acute, immediate health effects were caused by the release of hydrogen sulfide from the Citgo facility. The judge agreed to let the jury decide.[59]

The plaintiffs did offer evidence of exposure to the chemical, through their own testimony about the fire, explosion, and aliments they suffered shortly thereafter. The defendants, however, presented expert testimony undermining the plaintiffs' allegations that the injuries were a result of the release of hydrogen sulfide. The experts testified that the plants around the facility—which are much more sensitive than humans to hydrogen fluoride—suffered no harmful effects. Because the plants showed no damage from a release of hydrogen fluoride, the expert concluded that the release was insufficient to affect human health. The jury returned a verdict exonerating the defendants.[60]

But a plaintiff who prosecutes a toxic tort claim without sufficient support does so at his own risk, as dismissal of the case for lack of causation evidence may not be the only

---

55. *Id.* at 770–71.
56. 158 F.3d 988 (8th Cir. 1998).
57. *Id.*
58. No. C-97-279 (S.D. Tex. Nov. 3, 1998), *reported in* 13 Tox. L. Rptr. 810 (BNA) (Nov. 25, 1998).
59. *Id.*
60. *Id.*

setback when the critical causation element is lacking. In *Jandrt v. Jerome Foods, Inc.*,[61] a law firm filed suit on behalf of three children with birth defects, claiming that the defects were caused by the mother's exposure during pregnancy to chemicals at the defendant's facility. Nine months later, the plaintiffs offered to dismiss the action because the causal connection could only be demonstrated through epidemiological studies that the plaintiffs did not want to undertake. The defendant then filed a motion seeking sanctions for commencing and continuing a frivolous suit.

Because the plaintiffs' counsel had failed to make a reasonable inquiry into causation before or after filing its complaint, the trial court found both the commencement and the continuation of the action were frivolous. The Wisconsin Supreme Court did not agree that the commencement of the suit was frivolous. Rather, the court determined that while it may have been good practice to consult an expert prior to filing suit, it was not required. The court did agree, however, that the continuation of the suit without investigating causation was frivolous. The plaintiffs' counsel made no efforts outside of discovery to establish the necessary causal nexus. Even when experts were contacted, they were not provided with information obtained by the plaintiffs during discovery. For these reasons, the court determined the continuation of the action was frivolous and awarded reasonable attorneys' fees and costs starting from the time when, six weeks after filing the action, the plaintiffs' counsel served the defendant a request for documents that caused the defendants to incur substantial expense.[62]

On the other hand, the Eighth Circuit has ruled that a plaintiff's strong temporal relationship between exposure to a toxic chemical and symptoms, along with evidence that the exposure was at an "unsafe" level, was sufficient to prove causation.[63] In *Bonner v. ISP Technologies, Inc.*,[64] the Eighth Circuit recognized that to prove causation in a toxic tort case, the plaintiff must show both that the toxin is capable of causing injuries like those suffered by the plaintiff when an individual is exposed to the same level of toxin as the plaintiff and that the toxin actually caused the plaintiff's injury. Yet the court determined that the temporal relationship between the plaintiff's exposure and the injuries—the plaintiff immediately experienced the symptoms listed on the material safety data sheet (MSDS)—was powerful evidence of causation. Although the court determined that the plaintiff need not present "'a mathematically precise table equating levels of exposure with levels of harm in order to show' she was exposed to a toxic level," the court noted the importance of proving exposure to a quantity of the toxin that exceeded safe levels.[65]

---

61. 601 N.W.2d 650 (Wis. 1999).
62. *Id.* at 653.
63. Bonner v. ISP Techs., Inc., 259 F.3d 924, 931 (8th Cir. 2001).
64. 259 F.3d 924.
65. *Id.* at 928.

Differential Diagnosis

Differential diagnosis, or differential etiology, is considered a type of circumstantial evidence. It "is a standard scientific technique of identifying the cause of a medical problem by eliminating the likely causes until the most probable one is isolated."[66] Perhaps the pithiest formulation of the method comes from Sherlock Holmes: "Eliminate all other factors, and the one which remains must be the truth."[67]

Some courts have permitted treating physicians or medical experts to base a causation opinion on differential diagnosis. For instance, in *Hall v. Babcock & Wilcox*, the plaintiffs' expert employed the differential diagnosis methodology in his determination that radiation from a specific facility was the most likely cause of their illnesses.[68] The defendants argued that the expert's testimony was unreliable for several reasons, including that he did not personally perform the medical examinations. The court noted that differential diagnosis is a technique that has enjoyed widespread acceptance in the medical community, has been subject to peer review, and does not frequently lead to incorrect results. The court then held that the reliability of expert testimony is not diminished because the physician performing a differential diagnosis did not personally perform the medical examinations, and stated that a doctor's evaluation of a patient's medical records, as compared to the doctor's actual examination of the patient, can be a reliable method of concluding that the patient is ill.

The Sixth Circuit has articulated a test for the admissibility of a differential diagnosis.[69] A medical expert's causation opinion based on differential diagnosis is reliable and admissible where the expert (1) objectively ascertains the nature of the plaintiff's injury, (2) "rules in" one or more causes of the injury using a valid methodology, and (3) uses standard diagnostic techniques to rule out alternative causes, thereby reaching a conclusion as to the most likely cause.[70] Other courts have used similar frameworks. For instance, in *Guinn v. AstraZeneca Pharmaceuticals LP*,[71] the Eleventh Circuit affirmed a trial court's decision to strike a medical opinion based on differential diagnosis where the expert had failed to adequately consider and exclude possible alternative causes of the plaintiff's injury. The Fourth Circuit likewise has held that a "differential diagnosis that fails to take serious account of other potential causes may be so lacking that it cannot provide a

---

66. Lennon v. Norfolk and W. Ry. Co., 123 F. Supp. 2d 1143, 1153 (N.D. Ind. 2000) (citing Baker v. Dalkon Shield Claimants Trust, 156 F.3d 248 (1st Cir. 1998)).
67. ARTHUR CONAN DOYLE, THE SIGN OF THE FOUR 13 (1890).
68. 69 F. Supp. 2d 716 (W.D. Pa. 1999).
69. Best v. Lowe's Home Ctrs., Inc., 563 F.3d 171 (6th Cir. 2009).
70. *Id.* at 179.
71. 602 F.3d 1245 (11th Cir. 2010).

reliable basis for an opinion on causation."[72] And in *Ruggiero v. Warner-Lambert Co.*,[73] the Second Circuit emphasized that "[w]here an expert employs differential diagnosis to 'rule out' other potential causes for the injury at issue, he must also 'rule in' the suspected cause, and do so using 'scientifically valid methodology.'"[74]

That last point is crucial. While in certain circumstances differential diagnosis can serve as evidence of *specific* causation, it does not relieve a plaintiff of the burden of producing other, reliable evidence of *general* causation. Differential diagnosis cannot prove general causation. As the Tenth Circuit has held:

> Plaintiff's experts completely ignored or discounted without explanation the many epidemiological studies which found no medically reliable link between silicone breast implants and systemic disease. . . . Plaintiff's experts relied solely on differential diagnosis and case studies to support their belief that silicone gel breast implants can cause systemic disease. Their reliance on differential diagnosis without supporting epidemiological evidence is misplaced and demonstrates the unreliable nature of the testimony.[75]

Differential diagnosis can be a useful and reliable methodology, but only for the purposes for which it is intended. Parties and experts who try to stretch its application beyond its appropriate limits do so at their peril.

The Role of Governmental Standards and Risk Assessments

In response to some courts' lenient standards for admissibility of causation evidence, and in addition to *Daubert*, discussed below, defendants in several cases have been able to foreclose plaintiffs' recovery through the use of governmental standards relating to exposure levels. In these cases, defendants argue that if the exposures incurred by actual individuals do not exceed overly protective regulatory levels, it would be appropriate to conclude that their disease or injury was not caused by exposure to the substance in question.

In *Thompson v. Southern Pacific Transportation Co.*,[76] the plaintiffs brought an action for injuries allegedly caused by the contamination of drinking wells with trichloroethane. The court found that the testimony of the plaintiffs' expert was insufficient to prove

---

72. Westberry v. Gislaved Gummi AB, 178 F.3d 257, 265 (4th Cir. 1999); see also *In re* Paoli R.R. Yard PCB Litig., 35 F.3d 717, 759 (3d Cir. 1994) ("[A]t the core of differential diagnosis is a requirement that experts at least consider alternative causes—this almost has to be true of any technique that tries to find a cause of something.").
73. 424 F.3d 249 (2d Cir. 2005).
74. *Id.* at 254; *see also* Pluck v. BP Oil Pipeline Co., 640 F.3d 671 (6th Cir. 2011) (affirming exclusion of plaintiff's expert's differential diagnosis opinion because expert failed to reliably rule in benzene exposure as a potential cause of plaintiff's cancer and failed to rule out some other potential exposures).
75. Norris v. Baxter Healthcare Corp., 397 F.3d 878, 884–85 (10th Cir. 2005).
76. 809 F.2d 1167 (5th Cir.), *cert. denied*, 484 U.S. 819 (1987).

causation of adverse health effects from concentrations of 8 ppb where the EPA recommended maximum contaminant level was 200 ppb.[77]

The plaintiffs in *Brooks v. E. I. du Pont de Nemours & Co.*[78] faced a similar result. The court ruled that contamination that meets state groundwater quality standards is not actionable. It dismissed two suits against the former owner of a machine parts cleaning facility upon the former owner's motion for summary judgment. Under the state's administrative code, the groundwater quality standards represented the "maximum allowable . . . concentrations which may be tolerated without creating a threat to human health or which would otherwise render the groundwater unsuitable for its intended best usage."[79] Finding that the standards embodied the legislature's finding that contaminant levels below the maximum allowable concentration do not pose a threat, but merely an acceptable risk, the court granted the defendant's summary judgment motion.[80]

Plaintiffs also may attempt to use regulatory levels or governmental risk assessments as proof of causation, arguing that if an individual is exposed to a chemical above a regulatory limit, it is evidence that his disease was caused by exposure. However, most often, these levels are derived to provide safe levels of exposure, and provide a high degree of confidence that even the most sensitive members of a large population will be protected from exposure to a chemical. Such protective criteria are not useful in evaluating harm to specific individuals—they are intended to apply to generic populations having individual and high sensitivities to chemical toxicity. As the *Reference Manual on Scientific Evidence* states, "Particularly problematic are generalizations made in personal injury litigation from regulatory positions."[81]

By and large, courts have rejected the use of risk assessments as evidence of causation. For instance, in *Gates v. Rohm & Haas Co.*,[82] the Third Circuit affirmed a district court's ruling that the plaintiffs "would be unable to prove a concentration of vinyl chloride that would create a significant risk of contracting a serious latent disease for all class members."[83] The court found that a governmental risk assessment could not stand in as a proxy for causation on a classwide basis: "Although the positions of regulatory policymakers are relevant, their risk assessments are not necessarily conclusive in determining what risk exposure presents to specified individuals."[84]

---

77. *Id.* at 1169.
78. 944 F. Supp. 448 (E.D.N.C. 1996).
79. *Id.* at 449.
80. *Id.* at 450; *see also* Pichowicz v. Atlantic Richfield Co, 37 F. Supp. 2d 98 (D.N.H. 1997) (affirming dismissal of claims where plaintiffs relied on state environmental statutes as standard of care for negligence claims, but failed to allege violation of statutes as cause of damages).
81. FEDERAL JUDICIAL CENTER, *supra* note 2, at 423.
82. 655 F.3d 255 (3d Cir. 2011).
83. *Id.* at 267.
84. *Id.* at 268.

Other courts have taken an even harder line on the use of risk assessments, reasoning that the agencies developing them are addressing fundamentally different issues than those faced by courts. As the Fifth Circuit said in *Allen v. Pennsylvania Engineering Corp.*,[85] regulatory agencies "assess the carcinogenicity of various substances" using a "threshold of proof [that] is reasonably lower than that appropriate in tort law, which 'traditionally makes more particularized inquiries into cause and effect' and requires a plaintiff to prove 'that it is more likely than not that another individual has caused him or her harm.'"[86]

In short, risk assessments and government regulations are typically a poor fit for causation analysis in a toxic tort case—and, as explained *infra*, that poor fit precludes them from forming the basis of an admissible expert opinion on causation.

Using Experts in Toxic Tort Cases

With rare exceptions, courts require expert testimony in toxic tort cases, because the cause of medical conditions is beyond the ken of most jurors.[87] Thus, in toxic tort litigation, admissibility of expert testimony will be perhaps the most important issue for the parties and the court, and will often serve, in practical terms, as a summary judgment decision.

For several decades, the admissibility of expert testimony in federal courts turned on the *Frye* standard.[88] *Frye* established the "general acceptance" test:

---

85. 102 F.3d 194 (5th Cir. 1996).
86. *Id.* at 198; *see also* Glastetter v. Novartis Pharm. Corp., 252 F.3d 986, 991 (8th Cir. 2001) ("The FDA's 1994 decision that Parlodel can cause strokes is unreliable proof of medical causation in the present case because the FDA employs a reduced standard (vis-a-vis tort liability) for gauging causation when it decides to rescind drug approval."); Abarca v. Franklin Cnty. Water Dist., 761 F. Supp. 2d 1007, 1041–42 (E.D. Cal. 2011) ("[T]he express purpose of the [Risk Assessment] was to provide a regulatory body . . . with conservative estimates of risk and provide a wide margin of protection for human health. It does not establish general exposure. It is not particularized. . . . Plaintiffs do not address [how] the Risk Assessment is relevant to prove actual causation."); Rhodes v. E.I. DuPont de Nemours & Co., 253 F.R.D. 365, 377–78 (S.D.W. Va. 2008) ("[A] risk assessment is of limited utility in a toxic tort case, especially for the issue of causation, because of the risk assessment's distinct purpose. Risk assessments have largely been developed for regulatory purposes and thus serve a protection function in providing a level below which there is no appreciable risk to the general population. They do not provide information about actual risk or causation. . . . Because a risk assessment overstates the risk to a population to achieve its protective and generalized goals, it is impossible to conclude with reasonable certainty that any one person exposed to a substance above the criterion established by the risk assessment has suffered a significantly increased risk."); Sutera v. Perrier Group of Am. Inc., 986 F. Supp. 655, 664 (D. Mass. 1997) ("However, a regulatory standard, rather than being a measure of causation, is a public-health exposure level that an agency determines pursuant to statutory standards set by Congress.").
87. *See, e.g.*, Korte v. ExxonMobil Coal USA, Inc., 164 Fed. App'x 553, 556 (7th Cir. 2006) ("Expert testimony is needed to establish causation in cases alleging an adverse health effect when the 'medical effects [of exposure to the toxin] are not within the ken of the ordinary person.'") (quoting Goffman v. Gross, 59 F.3d 668, 672 (7th Cir. 1995)). *But see* Gass v. Marriott Hotel Servs., Inc., 558 F.3d 419 (6th Cir. 2009) (plaintiff not required to present expert testimony that variety of symptoms were caused by exposure to pesticides because defendant failed to present its own expert testimony on the issue). *Gass* is best viewed as an outlier, but remains good law.
88. Frye v. United States, 293 F. 1013 (D.C. Cir. 1923).

Just when a scientific principle or discovery crosses the line between the experimental and demonstrable stages is difficult to define. Somewhere in this twilight zone the evidential force of the principle must be recognized, and while courts will go a long way in admitting expert testimony deduced from a well-recognized scientific principle or discovery, the thing from which the deduction is made must be sufficiently established to have gained general acceptance in the particular field in which it belongs.[89]

The abandonment of this standard in *Daubert v. Merrell Dow Pharmaceuticals, Inc.*[90] was a watershed moment in federal litigation.[91]

No single case in the last twenty-five years may have had as broad an impact on federal civil litigation as *Daubert*.[92] Before 1993, federal judges typically had a liberal admissibility attitude toward expert testimony, and let it in for the jury to sort out.[93] Today, as a result of *Daubert* and the U.S. Supreme Court's subsequent holdings in *General Electric Co. v. Joiner*[94] and *Kumho Tire Co. v. Carmichael*,[95] federal trial judges play an active role in deciding what expert testimony goes to the jury. Trial lawyers must, from the outset of a case, have a carefully developed strategy in preparation for the almost certain *Daubert* hearing that likely will determine if the case is viable.

The purpose of this section of the chapter is, after briefly reviewing what led to the Supreme Court's *Daubert-Joiner-Kumho* trilogy of directives to the district courts, (1) to identify the *types* of expert testimony to which *Daubert* challenges are now properly made; (2) to discuss a remaining gray area still resolved in the lower federal courts on how *Daubert* applies; and (3) by reference to three recent federal court decisions applying *Daubert*, to illustrate how critical the pretrial *Daubert* challenge process has become in the federal litigation process. Later chapters of this book address how *Daubert*, *Frye*, and other expert admissibility standards have been adopted and adapted in individual states.

---

89. *Id.* at 1014.
90. 509 U.S. 579 (1993).
91. Some state courts have incorporated the *Daubert* framework into their jurisprudence *in toto*. Several, however, have "confirmed allegiance to the 'germinal' *Frye* decision." People v. Leahy, 882 P.2d 321, 325 (Cal. 1994). The approaches taken by individual states are addressed in later chapters.
92. Some commentators have questioned the substantive effect of the shift to *Daubert*. *See* Edward K. Cheng & Albert H. Yoon, *Does* Frye *or* Daubert *Matter? A Study of Scientific Admissibility Standards*, 91 Va. L. Rev. 471 (2005) (suggesting that a jurisdiction's choice of admissibility standard has little impact on admissibility determinations in tort cases).
93. As Fifth Circuit Judge Patrick E. Higginbotham cautioned in a pre-*Daubert* decision, appellate judges should review "with a sharp eye" the trial court's admission of expert testimony where "the decision to receive expert testimony was simply tossed off to the jury under a 'let it all in' philosophy." *In re* Air Crash Disaster at New Orleans, La., 795 F.2d 1230, 1234 (5th Cir. 1986).
94. 522 U.S. 136 (1997).
95. 526 U.S. 137 (1999).

What Led to the *Daubert* Decision?

In *Daubert v. Merrell Dow Pharmaceuticals, Inc.*,[96] the U.S. Supreme Court rose to address the issue, and in a landmark ruling in federal evidentiary law, set out both a detailed framework of analysis and an explicitly active role for the trial judge in handling expert testimony. Since that decision giving federal trial judges their explicit assignment as gatekeepers of what expert testimony is permitted to go to a jury, subsequent decisions, both by the Supreme Court and lower federal courts, have interpreted *Daubert* and provided a fairly clear topographical map of the terrain to be covered in the battlefield of expert testimony in federal court. Post-*Daubert* cases have clarified more precisely the significantly expanded role the Supreme Court assigned to federal trial judges in handling expert testimony. Today's large body of opinions by federal, appellate, and trial courts makes plain how profoundly important the *Daubert* motion and hearing are in any federal case involving expert testimony. This makes it imperative for all federal trial lawyers to have more than passing familiarity with the current law on *Daubert*.

The *Daubert* Trilogy: Defining the Trial Judge's Role

In *Daubert*, a case concerning the effects of an antinausea drug on the developing fetus, the U.S. Supreme Court held that scientific expert testimony is admissible only if it is both reliable and relevant. Citing a distinguished federal trial judge and expert on federal evidentiary issues, the Court explicitly noted the danger of expert witnesses before a jury was that their testimony had the potential to "be both powerful and quite misleading because of the difficulty in evaluating it."[97]

The Court in *Daubert* identified four factors to consider when determining the reliability of a particular scientific theory or technique: (1) the "testability" of the scientific theory or technique, that is, whether the hypothesis is capable of repetition and verification; (2) whether the scientific opinion has been published after being subjected to peer review, that is, an independent editing analysis of the scientific data and conclusions by unbiased professional peers; (3) the known or potential error rate of the technique; and (4) whether the opinion has been generally accepted in the relevant scientific community.[98] The Court emphasized that trial judges have the role of "gatekeeper" in ensuring

---

96. 509 U.S. 579 (1993).
97. *Id.* at 595 (citing Judge Weinstein, 138 F.R.D. 632 (1991)).
98. *Id.* at 593–94. The legal basis for the Court's review in *Daubert* was to review the continued validity of the so-called common law *Frye* rule holding that expert opinion based on a scientific technique is inadmissible unless the technique is generally accepted in the relevant scientific community. *See* Frye v. United States, 293 F. 1013 (1923). The trial court, as affirmed by the Court of Appeals, granted summary judgment to defendant on the basis that the plaintiffs' eight experts' opinions did not meet the *Frye* standard. The Supreme Court granted certification to clarify the divisions in the lower courts as to whether the *Frye* "general acceptance" test had been superseded by the Federal Rules of Evidence on the admissibility of expert evidence. Interestingly, in holding that *Frye* had been superseded, the Court's more detailed four-step approach appears to be more demanding than the *Frye* rule. Indeed, careful observers will readily note that *Daubert*'s fourth factor incorporates the *Frye*-rule concept.

that these requirements are satisfied, and counseled trial judges against abdicating their responsibility to screen scientific evidence by simply ruling that novel expert opinion testimony is a matter of weight for the jury.[99] Instead, the Court stressed that the issue is one of threshold admissibility to be determined by trial judges.[100]

In short, the Court in *Daubert* put meat on the bare bones of the duties that Rule 702 imposes on a trial judge. It did so by explicating in detail what the responsibility entailed and how a court should go about discharging its duty.[101]

In *Joiner*, the Supreme Court, resolving a split among the federal circuits, underscored the wide discretion afforded federal trial courts in exercising their gatekeeping function by holding that trial court decisions applying *Daubert* are to be reviewed under a permissive abuse of discretion standard.[102] The *Joiner* decision also made clear that in determining the reliability of expert evidence, the trial court need not limit its analysis to the expert's *methodologies* used to reach a conclusion but may also consider the actual *conclusions* themselves drawn by the experts.[103]

In *Joiner*, the plaintiff electrician alleged he contracted lung cancer as a result of exposure to polychlorinated biphenyls (PCBs).[104] The district court granted the defendant's motion for summary judgment, ruling that the plaintiffs' evidence on the issue of causation was inadmissible under Federal Rule of Evidence 702 and *Daubert*. Specifically, plaintiffs' experts relied on studies of infant mice purporting to establish a link between PCBs and small-cell lung cancer in humans.[105] In addition to the animal studies, plaintiffs also pointed to several publications that they contended supported their experts' opinions.[106]

The district court made short work of the infant mice studies, taking note of various concessions from plaintiffs' own expert, including the facts that (1) the studies were preliminary in nature; (2) the lung cancer in the rodents was not the same as the plaintiff-electrician's (small-cell carcinoma); (3) the tumors were dose-related; and (4) the mice first had been given a known initiating carcinogen and then injected with pure PCBs directly into their stomachs.[107] With respect to the publications relied on by the plaintiffs as supportive of their experts, the court excluded them either because they were based upon

---

99. *Id.* at 589.
100. *Id.* at 592.
101. As the majority opinion said in rejoinder to Chief Justice Rehnquist's concurring and dissenting opinion: "The Chief Justice 'do[es] not doubt that Rule 702 confides to the judge some gatekeeping responsibility,' *post*, at 600, but would neither say how it does so nor explain what that role entails. We believe the better course is to note the nature and source of the duty." 509 U.S. at 589 n.7.
102. Prior to *Joiner*, the circuits were divided three ways on the standard of review for trial courts' *Daubert* rulings: (a) "manifestly erroneous;" (b) "abuse of discretion;" and (c) the "stringent, non-deferential" or "hard look" standard.
103. 522 U.S. at 146.
104. Joiner v. Gen. Elec. Co., 864 F. Supp. 1310, 1312 (N.D. Ga. 1994).
105. *Id.* at 1322–23.
106. *Id.* at 1324–26.
107. *Id.* at 1322–24.

epidemiological studies of statistically insignificant numbers of cases, did not address PCBs, or had not been subject to peer review.[108]

The Eleventh Circuit reversed. According to the Circuit, the district court erred in excluding the plaintiffs' expert evidence because the opinions expressed by the plaintiffs' experts were based on scientifically reliable methodologies.[109] The Eleventh Circuit criticized the district court for supposedly overstepping its authority under *Daubert*—that of evaluating the *reliability* of principles and methodology—by going beyond to evaluate the reliability of the *conclusions* drawn by plaintiffs' experts. In its decision, the Eleventh Circuit applied "a particularly stringent standard of review" based upon what the court characterized as the preference of the *Federal Rules of Evidence* for the admissibility of expert testimony.[110]

The U.S. Supreme Court reversed the decision of the Eleventh Circuit.[111] As a threshold matter, the Court held that the Eleventh Circuit's "particularly stringent" standard of review impermissibly deviated from the abuse of discretion standard ordinarily applicable to the review of evidentiary rulings.[112] The Court next held that it was not an abuse of discretion for the district court to have excluded plaintiffs' expert evidence. Addressing the Eleventh Circuit's emphasis on the distinction between the conclusions and methodologies of experts, the Court noted that:

> [C]onclusions and methodology are not entirely distinct from one another. Trained experts commonly extrapolate from existing data. But nothing in either *Daubert* or the Federal Rules of Evidence requires a district court to admit opinion evidence which is connected to existing data only by the ipse dixit of the expert. A court may conclude that there is simply too great an analytical gap between the data and the opinion proffered.[113]

Joiner thus underscores—in three important respects—the wide discretion afforded federal trial courts in exercising their "gatekeeping" function under *Daubert*. First, their review of the reliability of expert evidence may extend beyond the *methodologies* used and reach the *conclusions* drawn by experts. Second, the decisions made by district courts in this area are to be afforded considerable deference by the courts of appeal. And finally, instead of a bias favoring admission of expert testimony, the trial judge, when in doubt or equipoise on a close case, may reasonably decide to exclude it.[114]

---

108. *Id.* at 1324–25. Moreover, one of the publications actually concluded that there were no grounds for associating lung cancer deaths with the decedents' exposure to PCBs in a capacitor manufacturing plant.
109. Joiner v. Gen. Elec. Co., 78 F.3d 524, 531 (11th Cir. 1996).
110. *Id.* at 529.
111. Gen. Elec. Co. v. Joiner, 522 U.S. 136 (1997).
112. *Id.* at 141.
113. *Id.* at 146.
114. In one of the most significant passages in the *Daubert* majority opinion, the Court expounds on the distinction between the "quest for truth" in the courtroom versus the scientific arena, and holds that the

Kumho Tire v. Carmichael arose out of a vehicle accident caused by a tire blowout. In their products liability suit against the tire's maker and distributor, the plaintiffs depended in significant part on deposition testimony provided by an expert in tire failure analysis.[115] The expert testified based on a visual and tactile inspection of the tire and on the theory that in the absence of at least two of four specific symptoms indicating tire abuse, tire failure of the sort that occurred was caused by a defect.[116] At the district court level, the defendants successfully moved to exclude the expert's testimony and for summary judgment.[117]

The Eleventh Circuit reversed, asserting that a *Daubert* analysis applies only where an expert "relies on the application of scientific principles, rather than on skill- or experience-based observation."[118] The Supreme Court granted certiorari to determine whether the *Daubert* gatekeeping obligation applies only to scientific testimony or to all expert testimony.

As a starting point, the Supreme Court looked to the language of Federal Rule of Evidence 702, which provides for the admission of expert testimony if "scientific, technical, or other specialized knowledge will help the trier of fact."[119] The Court emphasized that Rule 702 does not distinguish between scientific, technical, or other specialized knowledge.[120] Accordingly, the Court determined that the relevance and reliability standard set forth in *Daubert* applies to all scientific, technical, or other specialized knowledge, noting that the *Daubert* opinion referred to scientific testimony simply because that was the nature of the expertise at issue in that case.[121]

---

trial judge's gatekeeping role and the Federal Rules of Evidence envision occasional exclusion of novel albeit "authentic" scientific views:

> Petitioners . . . suggest that recognition of a screening role for the judge that allows for the exclusion of "invalid" evidence will sanction a stifling and repressive scientific orthodoxy and will be inimical to the search for truth. It is true that open debate is an essential part of both legal and scientific analyses. Yet there are important differences between the quest for truth in the courtroom and the quest for truth in the laboratory. Scientific conclusions are subject to perpetual revision. Law, on the other hand, must resolve disputes finally and quickly. The scientific project is advanced by broad and wide-ranging consideration of a multitude of hypotheses, for those that are incorrect will eventually be shown to be so, and that in itself is an advance. Conjectures that are probably wrong are of little use, however, in the project of reaching a quick, final, and binding legal judgment—often of great consequence—about a particular set of events in the past. *We recognize that, in practice, a gatekeeping role for the judge, no matter how flexible, inevitably on occasion will prevent the jury from learning of authentic insights and innovations.* That, nevertheless, is the balance that is struck by Rules of Evidence designed not for the exhaustive search for cosmic understanding but for the particularized resolution of legal disputes.

509 U.S. at 596–97 (citations omitted, emphasis added).
115. 526 U.S. at 142.
116. *Id.* at 143–44.
117. *Id.* at 145.
118. Carmichael v. Samyang Tire, Inc., 131 F.3d 1433, 1435 (11th Cir. 1997).
119. 526 U.S. at 147.
120. *Id.* at 148.
121. *Id.* at 147.

Additionally, the Court explained that it would be difficult, if not impossible, for a trial judge to distinguish between scientific knowledge and other types of knowledge.[122] Thus, the Court concluded that the principles enumerated in *Daubert* apply whether the expert testimony reflects scientific, technical, or other specialized knowledge. "[W]here such testimony's factual basis, data, principles, methods, or their application are called sufficiently into question . . . the trial judge must determine whether the testimony has 'a reliable basis in the knowledge and experience of [the relevant] discipline.'"[123]

Another significant element of the Court's decision in *Kumho* was holding that a trial judge *may* (but is not required to) consider all four specific *Daubert* factors (testing, peer review, error rates, and general acceptance) if doing so will help determine the testimony's reliability.[124] Stressing the flexible nature of the inquiry, the Court explained that in other cases, the relevant reliability concerns may focus upon an expert's personal knowledge or experience.[125]

Having established the broad discretion the trial judge has in applying the *Daubert* "four-factor" test to any particular expert testimony situation, the Court made equally clear that many different types of expert testimony are subject to a *Daubert* analysis.[126] The Court held that expert testimony subject to *Daubert* can address a wide range of topics, and cited land valuation, agricultural practices, railroad procedures, and attorney's fee valuation as examples of expert testimony under Federal Rule of Evidence 702.[127] Because expert testimony is so varied, the Court stressed that the trial court must have wide latitude both in deciding *how* to test an expert's reliability (e.g., by applying the four *Daubert* factors or by some other method) as well as *which type* of expert testimony is subject to that reliability analysis.[128]

The Court concluded that Rule 702 grants the district judge the discretionary authority, reviewable only for abuse, to determine reliability in light of the particular facts and circumstances of the particular case.[129] After reviewing the methodology used by the tire expert and its application to the particular matter at issue—whether a defect caused the blowout—the Court reversed the Eleventh Circuit's judgment.[130] Practically speaking, the end result was that the testimony was excluded and the defendants were granted summary judgment.[131]

---

122. *Id.* at 148.
123. *Kumho*, 526 U.S. at 149 (citing *Daubert*, 509 U.S. at 592).
124. *Id.* at 153.
125. *Id.*
126. *Id.* at 150–51.
127. For example, the Court noted a "perfume tester able to distinguish among 140 odors at a sniff" as an expert witness to whom the *Daubert* analysis would apply. *Id.* at 151.
128. *Id.*
129. *Id.* at 158.
130. *Id.*
131. *Id.*

Conclusion

Medical causation is often the determinative issue in toxic tort cases. After *Daubert*, questions of medical causation, such as the impact of breast implants on the body or whether a drug like Bendectin causes birth defects, should first be addressed by the judge evaluating what hard scientific research has shown, not what an expert is willing to testify to in a courtroom and perhaps persuade a jury to accept based on a sympathetic plaintiff. The *Daubert* analysis is now also applied to expert testimony grounded primarily on skill- or experience-based observations.

Federal Rule of Evidence 702 was amended on December 1, 2000. Now, an expert witness may testify only if three new requirements are met: (1) the testimony must be based upon sufficient facts or data; (2) the testimony is the product of reliable principles and methods; and (3) the witness has applied the principles and methods reliably to the facts of the case. Of course, these new requirements are straight from *Daubert*.

Many state courts have adopted *Daubert* or codified its principles. It is clear that most courts take their gatekeeping responsibility seriously and that there is at least the potential for the *Daubert* analysis to be applied in an even wider variety of cases. Although a survey of cases decided after *Kumho* indicates that the *Daubert* analysis is most often applied to scientific testimony, there is a noticeable trend toward a broad application of *Daubert* to all types of expert testimony, whether based on scientific, technical, or "other specialized" knowledge. Moreover, courts have not been reluctant to exclude an expert's testimony after conducting the *Daubert* analysis. In fact, according to a study conducted by the Federal Judicial Center, judges are increasingly likely to exclude expert testimony in civil trials than they were in the past.[132] The courts, relying on *Daubert* and its progeny, will exclude experts' opinions not only in the absence of reliable support from hard data and accepted methodologies, but also where the subject of the opinion is unsettled and a matter of substantial scientific debate.[133]

In summary, the *Daubert* hearing and ruling have effectively become virtually as case-outcome determinative as a class certification hearing and ruling. *Daubert* hearings are often every bit as case dispositive, practically speaking, as a summary judgment hearing. Thus, lawyers whose cases rely in any material way on expert testimony must familiarize themselves with the "algorithm" of how federal trial courts evaluate *Daubert* challenges,

---

132. Mark Hansen, *Admissions Tests: Fewer Post-Daubert Federal Judges Allow Experts to Testify without Limitation in Civil Trials, Study Finds*, 87 A.B.A.J. 28 (2001). The study concluded that judges "are responding to the Supreme Court's invitation to examine the basis of expert testimony under the new standards and exclude evidence that doesn't meet those standards." *Id.*

133. One innovative approach to the scientific debate issue is the court's empanelling of its own expert panel. Former Chief Judge Sam C. Pointer of the U.S. District Court for the Northern District of Alabama appointed an expert panel in 1996 to assist him in assessing scientific evidence in a multidistrict litigation action involving the health effects of silicone breast implants. The expert panel issued a report denying any link between silicone breast implants and immune disorders. *In re Silicone Gel Breast Implant Litig.*, MDL No. 926 (N.D. Ala. Nov. 30, 1998), *reported in* 26 PRODUCT LIABILITY REP. 1194 (Dec. 4, 1998).

and be prepared for a full-blown "trial within a trial" that the *Daubert* hearing often becomes. Following the plain encouragement of the Supreme Court in *Daubert*, *Joiner*, and *Kumho Tire*, the federal trial courts are vigorously pursuing their role as gatekeepers to ensure that speculative and scientifically conjectural expert testimony does not infect a jury trial. And, some, but not all, state courts are following their lead.

CHAPTER 6

Case Strategy and Trial Management

John P. Manard Jr., Steven J. Levine, S. Ault Hootsell III, J. Alan Harrell, Roy L. Bergeron Jr., and Evan Dicharry

Toxic tort litigation is complex, fluid, and rarely cookie cutter in its ultimate evolution. Often times the "litigation" commences within hours after an incident and runs through the moment when final documents are exchanged between parties and courts, typically years later. This chapter takes you from that beginning through that end, along the way tackling each of the principal topic areas that are likely to confront you.

The complexity lies in the multiple track nature and large scale of these cases. It is not uncommon for such cases to involve multiple parallel tracks, involving governmental regulatory action, civil actions, and sometimes criminal issues. More often than not, such cases involve many plaintiffs, a substantial number of defendants, state and federal courts, and seriously disputed issues of fact and science. Because of their ultimate significance, procedural battles are frequently hard fought, making resort to appellate courts on an interlocutory basis common. Cases almost always involve complicated issues of science and the handling of evidence, while at the same time presenting, through the sheer volume of plaintiffs, less esoteric but equally important case management issues and requirements.

The nature of toxic tort trials reflects this complexity, with the core issue in many cases being how to reduce such complexity to an understandable level for a jury. Accomplishing that is no easy task.

This chapter covers an enormous area in a relatively concise number of pages. It will help you identify in advance some of the key issues on which you will want to focus, suggests to you lines of reasoning to consider, and places in your hands good starting points for research and evaluation. While no book can cover all of this territory in complete detail, as many of these issues are ultimately are driven by state laws that vary widely, toxic tort cases do tend to present similar issues and dynamics, the most common of which are addressed here.

Named Parties: Selection and Strategy

While identifying and naming the proper defendant(s) is an initial concern in every action, this determination can carry even greater ramifications in toxic tort litigation.[1] Because alleged injuries sometimes manifest themselves years after exposure, simply identifying the proper defendant(s) can be problematic. The corporate entity that existed at the time of manufacture or exposure may, through merger, acquisition, bankruptcy, or simply the passage of time, have undergone such an organizational identity change that it is difficult to recognize, if the entity is not altogether defunct. In addition, even if the proper defendant(s) can be located, there remain substantive legal considerations that bear directly upon a plaintiff's ability to recover from parent, successor, and joint defendants.

At the outset, plaintiffs' counsel should conduct a thorough investigation of the corporate history of the prospective defendants. Particularly where there is a considerable latency between exposure and the onset of illness, obtaining factual information concerning predecessors, successors, and parent companies can uncover potentially viable avenues for the imposition of successor liability[2] or parent liability.[3] In addition, other "nontraditional" liability theories, such as alternative liability, concert of action or conspiracy, enterprise liability, and market share liability may be available depending on the chosen jurisdiction and specific facts of the case.[4]

Joint and Several Liability/Comparative Fault

The doctrine of joint and several liability has substantially eroded in the wake of recent tort reform and with the rise of comparative fault.[5] Addressing joint and several liability for tortfeasors who cause indivisible injury, the *Restatement (Third) of Torts* acknowledges that it is "difficult to make a compelling argument for either a pure rule of joint and several liability or a pure rule of several liability once comparative responsibility is in place."[6] That said, pure joint and several liability still exists in certain jurisdictions.[7]

---

1. While the considerations that should be taken into account in selecting plaintiffs is equally important, that topic is addressed more fully in the section "Alignment of Parties and Forums."
2. *See, e.g.*, Pfohl Bros. Landfill Site Steering Comm. v. Allied Waste Sys., 255 F. Supp. 2d 134, 159–63 (W.D.N.Y. 2003) (purchaser of rubber waste processor was subject to CERCLA liability as corporate successor).
3. *See, e.g.*, United States v. Bestfoods, 524 U.S. 51, 61–73 (1998) (under certain circumstances, parent corporation may be charged with CERCLA liability for its subsidiary's actions).
4. *See, e.g.*, City of Philadelphia v. Lead Indus. Ass'n., 994 F.2d 112, 123–29 (3d Cir. 1993) (rejecting market share liability, alternative liability, and enterprise liability against manufacturer of lead paint pigment).
5. *See* Richard Cupp, Jr., *Asbestos Litigation and Bankruptcy: A Case Study for Ad Hoc Public Policy Limitations on Joint and Several Liability*, 31 Pepp. L. Rev. 203, 211–14 (2003) (fifteen jurisdictions have abolished (or virtually abolished) joint and several liability, and most other jurisdictions have in some significant way acted to limit the doctrine).
6. Restatement (Third) of Torts: Apportionment of Liability § 10, cmt. *a* (1999).
7. *See id.* § 17, reps. note, cmt. *a* (table). The plaintiffs' bar maintains that these jurisdictions are Alabama, Arkansas, Delaware, District of Columbia, Maine, Maryland, Massachusetts, Minnesota, North Carolina, Pennsylvania, Rhode Island, South Carolina, South Dakota, Virginia, and (with certain medical malpractice exceptions) West Virginia.

The perceived significance of the doctrine is that plaintiffs can sue as few or as many responsible defendants as they wish, leaving to the defendants the task of seeking indemnity or contribution from unnamed parties.[8] Thus, identifying all of the defendants may not be a major concern. However, the current trend toward comparative fault renders the foregoing reasoning somewhat antiquated. In light of the significant statutory modifications in the many states of the liability of multiple tortfeasors, it is imperative to review the law of the state in which the action lies before naming the parties.[9] It is no longer advisable, if it ever was, to simply rely upon the concept of joint and several liability as an alternative to investigating all potentially culpable parties.

Of course, the naming of the parties simply sets the process in motion. Throughout the litigation, parties will jockey for position with regard to what factors are most important in placing the greatest degree of fault and exposure on particular defendants. The plaintiffs, in general, will want to ensure that the principal responsibility is placed upon the defendant(s) who have the necessary assets to pay the judgment, are most easily demonstrated to be at fault, and whose conduct is most likely to inflame a jury's passions, thus driving up compensatory damages and, where recoverable, increasing punitive damage exposure. The defendants, on the other hand, each have independent interests in minimizing the importance of their own conduct (if any) and, either by direct efforts or implication, increasing the role of the other defendants.

In a toxic exposure case, the science will focus on key elements of toxicity, dose, and duration of exposure. In cases where multiple toxic substances—whether individual products or constituents within products—are involved, the parties are presented with multiple ways to argue who is most at fault on a comparative fault basis. While the actual science plays a role in that, limiting or expanding a party's likelihood of being persuasive, often the self-interest of the individual parties simply drives them to the positions they take on what importance to accord to such factors as toxicity, duration of exposure, dose, sophistication of the defendant in connection with the product and its handling, alternative sources of exposure to the same or similar toxins, plaintiff conduct, and a myriad other similar factors.

Accordingly, each party, from the very outset, must consider how it intends to approach the issue of comparative fault. As experts are retained and the evidence develops, much of what is done and how it is pursued is driven by a particular party's theory of fault. While a party must react and realign its thinking to conform to the evidence that is developed during the course of the case, it is never too early to formulate a basic initial theory and

---

8. *See id.* A18, cmt. *a.*
9. *See generally* James v. Bessemer Processing Co., 714 A.2d 898, 915–16 (N.J. 1998) (joint and several liability preserved by New Jersey's Comparative Negligence Act for environmental tort actions except in cases where the extent of negligence or fault can be apportioned). It should be noted that federal environmental claims under CERCLA do enjoy a joint and several liability scheme. *See* 42 U.S.C. §§ 9607, 9613.

strategy regarding how your party's position on comparative fault should be proposed to the jury.

Market Share Liability

Like other theories of collective liability, market share liability targets a group of defendants rather than a single causative defendant. The theory applies where a plaintiff is unable to identify the particular defendant manufacturer that caused the injury. The market share theory predicates liability (typically products liability) on a defendant's creation of risk, placing the burden of proof upon the defendant to exculpate itself from the probability that its product actually caused the harm.[10] Absent exculpatory proof, the manufacturer is held liable in proportion to its market share of the injurious product.[11]

The theory of market share liability emerged in the context of the drug Diethylstilbestrol (DES), where, due to the fungibility of the various brands of the drug and the long interval between its sale and illness, the plaintiffs were unable to specifically identify the company that produced the particular DES that was ingested.[12] The theory has limited applications beyond DES cases,[13] for instance, the Wisconsin Supreme Court has applied it in the context of lead paint exposure;[14] however, there is no nationwide consensus that market share liability should even be embraced.[15] Compounding the incongruous application is the frequent absence in toxic tort cases of the very elements that make the rationale for market share liability compelling.[16]

Nevertheless, should a toxic tort case arise in a jurisdiction that recognizes market share liability,[17] the potential application of the theory to the facts of the case should be

---

10. See Brenner v. American Cyanamid Co., 263 A.D.2d 165, 168–73 (N.Y. App. Div. 1999) (rejecting market share liability in lead paint action and noting that it is a "seldom used exception to the general rule in products liability actions that a plaintiff 'must establish by competent proof . . . that it was the defendant who manufactured and placed in the stream of commerce the injury-causing defective product.'" (quoting Healey v. Firestone Tire & Rubber Co., 87 N.Y.2d 596, 601 (N.Y. 1996)).
11. See City of Philadelphia v. Lead Indus. Ass'n., 994 F.2d 112, 123–29 (3d Cir. 1993) (noting that "as between an innocent plaintiff and negligent defendants, the latter should bear the cost of the injury" (quoting Sindell v. Abbott Laboratories, 607 P.2d 924 (Cal. 1980))).
12. See City of Philadelphia, 994 F.2d at 123–24.
13. See Brenner, 263 A.D.2d at 170 (noting the New York courts have refused to extend the market share liability theory beyond cases involving DES); see also Hamilton v. Beretta U.S.A. Corp., 750 N.E.2d 1055, 1068 (N.Y. 2001) (rejecting market share liability in gun manufacturer case). But see Hamilton v. Beretta U.S.A. Corp., 222 F.2d 36, 46 (2d Cir. 2000) (identifying courts that have applied market share liability in non-DES cases).
14. See Thomas ex rel. Gramling v. Mallett, 285 Wis. 2d 236, 289–93 (2005) (applying market share liability to lead paint exposure).
15. See City of Philadelphia, 994 F.2d at 125–26.
16. See Brenner, 263 A.D.2d at 171–73 (inability to define an appropriate national market and narrow time period in which to apply it, no identical and generic market product, lack of exclusive manufacturer control, and no signature injuries distinguished lead paint case from DES cases making exceptional remedy of market share liability inapplicable).
17. "The highest state courts in six states, Hawaii, New York, Wisconsin, Washington, Florida, and California, have adopted varying versions of market share liability." City of Philadelphia, 994 F.2d at 124, n.10.

considered when selecting defendants. Under certain extraordinary circumstances, market share liability may provide an appropriate remedy for those plaintiffs who cannot identify the defendant responsible for causing the harm.[18]

Parent/Successor Liability

Unlike joint and several liability and market share liability, parent and successor liability is frequently encountered in toxic tort litigation because toxic injuries often do not manifest themselves until long after exposure. During these lengthy latency periods, the corporate structure of the offending party may change dramatically. This poses two fundamental problems for plaintiffs: (1) identifying the proper party to name as a defendant, and (2) attributing liability to the predecessor or successor company once it has been identified.

These problems are not wholly unrelated. The selection and strategy of naming defendants should involve researching both the facts of the case as well as the applicable law to determine whether, and to what extent, successor liability and corporate veil piercing may be available as a viable means of recovery. As a general rule, a successor corporation is not responsible for the liabilities of its predecessor.[19] Likewise, a parent corporation is generally not liable for the acts of its subsidiaries.[20] However, there are exceptions to both rules.

> [A] corporation acquiring the assets of another corporation only takes on its liabilities if any of the following apply: (1) the successor expressly or impliedly agrees to assume them; (2) the transaction may be viewed as a de facto merger or consolidation; (3) the successor is a "mere continuation" of the predecessor; (4) or the transaction is fraudulent.[21]

In addition, some courts have adopted a fifth exception to the rule of nonliability for successor corporations, called the "product line" liability theory.[22] This theory, only followed in a small minority of courts, is applicable when the original manufacturer has been acquired by a successor company. In such circumstances, liability may be found when (1) the original manufacturer no longer exists as a separate entity, thereby destroying the injured party's remedy against them; (2) the successor has the ability to assume the original manufacturer's risk-spreading role; and (3) the successor company is enjoying the good will of the original manufacturer in the continued operation of the business.

---

18. *See Brenner*, 263 A.D.2d at 170.
19. *See, e.g.*, Pfohl Bros. Landfill Site Steering Comm. v. Allied Waste Sys., 255 F. Supp. 2d 134, 162 (W.D.N.Y. 2003).
20. *See, e.g.*, United States v. Bestfoods, 524 U.S. 51, 61 (1998).
21. *Allied Waste Systems*, 255 F. Supp. 2d at 162 (quoting B.F. Goodrich v. Betkoski, 99 F.3d 505, 519 (2d Cir. 1996)).
22. *See* Leo v. Kerr-McGee Chem. Corp., 37 F.3d 96, 99 (3d Cir. 1994) (quoting Ramirez v. Amsted Indus., Inc., 431 A.2d 811 (N.J. 1981) (product line liability applies where successor purchases all of the selling corporation's assets and continues the same line of business and selling corporation dissolves shortly thereafter).

However, product line liability is not widely accepted, and at least one court has refused to extend the theory to a successor in a toxic tort case.[23]

Distinct from successor liability, but equally relevant when selecting defendants, is the concept of parent liability. In a CERCLA suit for costs associated with cleaning up industrial waste generated by a chemical plant, the U.S. Supreme Court in *United States v. Bestfoods* held that CERCLA does not bar a parent corporation from direct liability for its own actions, nor does it operate to reject well-settled derivative liability concepts like corporate veil piercing.[24] This contemplates a situation where the facility at issue in the CERCLA claim is, at least on paper, operated by a subsidiary. The parent (so-called because of control through ownership of another corporation's stock) can be held liable under CERCLA, but only if the facts support a claim that the parent has actually exerted direct force in the operation of the facility. The focus is on which party can be said to "operate" the facility—an analysis based on the facts concerning the operation of the facility itself, not simply the type of veil piercing that comes up in any number of respects in the non-CERCLA world. These important factual and legal considerations should be taken into account at the outset of the case when developing case strategy and prior to the selection of parties.

Alignment of Parties and Forums

Toxic tort cases involve multiple plaintiffs and defendants. Such litigation often traverses multiple jurisdictions, both state and federal. If not coordinated in some fashion, these complexities would render the cases unmanageable. Accordingly, over the years, the courts have developed several mechanisms for handling such situations, including multidistrict litigation, class actions, and various means of handling mass joinder of parties.

Multidistrict Litigation

Toxic tort cases, as well as a number of other types of cases, when pending in federal courts can be transferred and consolidated into a single proceeding before one district court known as multidistrict litigation (MDL). This process is established by 28 U.S.C. § 1407. The purpose is to take civil actions "involving one or more common questions of fact" that are pending in different districts and transferring them for consolidation in a single district in a proceeding that "will be for the convenience of the parties and witnesses and will promote the just and efficient conduct of such actions."[25]

One important aspect of MDL, which separates it from other procedural devices, is the fact that MDL does not take the case all the way through to its conclusion. Instead,

---

23. *See id.* at 99–101 (rationale of product line successor liability not as compelling in toxic tort setting).
24. 524 U.S. 51 (1998) (when, but only when, the corporate veil may be pierced, a parent corporation may be charged with derivative CERCLA liability for its subsidiary's actions in operating a polluting facility).
25. 28 U.S.C. § 1407.

the transferee court can only take the proceeding through pretrial stages.[26] Typically, that involves taking the cases through pretrial discovery and many pretrial motions, including *Daubert*[27] hearings and rulings. In *Lexecon, Inc. v. Milberg Weiss Bershad Hynes & Lerach*, the Supreme Court dealt with a case arising out of the Lincoln Savings & Loan failure. A number of suits were brought together in the United States District Court for the District of Arizona by the Judicial Panel on Multidistrict Litigation. After all other issues had been resolved, a claim by Lexecon against the attorneys for two law firms involved in the case, alleging defamation, remained. Lexecon moved to have its remaining claim sent back to the court where it was originally filed, namely the Northern District of Illinois. The law firms moved to have the District of Arizona transfer the claim to itself, which it did. The U.S. Supreme Court took up the issue. The transfer by the District of Arizona to itself was invalidated by the U.S. Supreme Court, which held that a transfer back to the original transferor courts was required. However, note that *In re Carbon Dioxide Industry Anti-Trust Litigation* held that the parties could voluntarily elect to have the transferee court try the case to conclusion, even after the MDL process had come to a conclusion at the end of the pretrial stages.

In mass torts cases, the MDL device tends to draw together efforts of the parties concerning general causation discovery and the resulting qualification or disqualification of key experts. The MDL process oftentimes furnishes the parties with a means to get cases, or large portions of them, settled, as the resolution of the *Daubert* process in many instances is a strong indicator of how the case is likely to progress in the future even if transferred back to the original districts in which the claims were filed.

The entire process is directed by the Judicial Panel on Multi-District Litigation (JPML), seven judges designated by the Chief Justice of the United States, not more than one of whom can be from a single circuit. Their administrative offices are in Washington, D.C., and are staffed by administrators, clerks, and lawyers. The panel itself sits in various places around the country, moving east to west and north to south.

Interested parties seeking to have MDL established may file a motion with the panel. The JPML then decides whether that will be done and if so, where. The location is based upon a variety of factors, including expertise and availability of an appropriate judge (the statute permits the appointment of either a district court judge or a circuit judge), the convenience of the parties and witnesses (easy availability of the forum by airlines is, in fact, an important factor), and any case-specific issues (if there is a central location for case-related events, a concentration of witnesses, etc.). There is some overlap between

---

26. *See* Lexecon, Inc. v. Milberg Weiss Bershad Hynes & Lerach, 523 U.S. 26 (1998); *see also* Case Comment, Lexecon, Inc. v. Milberg Weiss Bershad Hynes & Lerach: *Respecting the Plaintiff's Choice of Forum* 74 NOTRE DAME L. REV. 1337 (1999). For discussion of the implications of *Lexecon*, albeit in distinguishable circumstances, *see* Florida v. Liquid Air Corp. (*In re* Carbon Dioxide Indus. Antitrust Litig.), 229 F.3d 1321 (11th Cir. 2000), *cert. denied*, 532 U.S. 920 (2001).
27.. 509 U.S. 579 (1993).

what one might more commonly call "products liability" cases and the types of "toxic tort" cases addressed in this book. But, there are a number of truly toxic tort cases that have, over the years, been the subject of MDLs.[28]

Once the decision is made to transfer the cases, a process commences in the various district courts to identify those cases that should be transferred. The parties in those cases can oppose the transfer, which is decided by the JPML. In the event a party wishes to engage in oral argument before the JPML, an interesting rule is generally in place that limits oral argument to one minute. The process before the JPML is governed by the Rules of Procedure, Panel on Multi-District Litigation.[29] Of course, new cases may continue to be filed in district courts after the initial wave of transfers and once an MDL has been established. Those later filed cases, once identified as being potentially susceptible to transfer, are identified as "tagalong" cases, typically by the parties to the litigation who wish to have them brought to the MDL. Those tagalong cases are identified to the JPML, and the transfer process, including the right to object, is triggered.

Until they are transferred back to the transferor court, the transferee court (commonly referred to as the MDL court) has exclusive jurisdiction. Appeals from rulings of the MDL court are made to the circuit court in the circuit in which the MDL court sits.

The JPML has a useful Web site, www.jpml.uscourts.gov. Additionally, for more detailed information on the operation of MDLs, there are good summary materials available to the practitioner.[30]

Joinder of Plaintiffs

Federal Rule of Civil Procedure 20 governs permissive joinder. If a question of law or fact is common to all the plaintiffs and if all the plaintiffs assert some claim to relief based

---

28. See, e.g., In re Union Carbide Corp. Gas Plant, 601 F. Supp. 1035 (J.P.M.L. 1985) (eighteen actions in seven districts concerning the December 1984 methyl isocyanate gas release in Bhopal, India, which were centralized in the Southern District of New York before Judge Keenan and were dismissed on forum non conveniens grounds); In re Union Carbide Corp. Gas Plant Disaster at Bhopal, 634 F. Supp. 842 (S.D.N.Y. 1986), order aff'd as modified, 809 F.2d 195 (2d Cir. 1987); In re Liquid Carbonic Truck Drivers Chem. Poisoning Litig., 423 F. Supp. 937 (J.P.M.L. 1976) (thirty-five actions from three districts concerning chemical poisoning by liquid carbon monoxide of truck drivers were consolidated in the Eastern District of Louisiana); In re Radiation Incident at Washington, 400 F. Supp. 1404 (J.P.M.L. 1975) (six actions concerning exposure to radioactive materials carried on Delta Airlines were centralized in the District of Columbia).
29. These Rules are promulgated by the JPML pursuant to the authority in 28 U.S.C. § 1407 and 28 U.S.C. § 2112, and they can be found on the website of the JPML at www.jpml.uscourts.gov.
30. See Manual for Complex Litigation (Fourth) § 2013 (2004); Desmond T. Barry, Jr., A Practical Guide to the Ins and Outs of Multi-District Litigation, 64 Def. Couns. J. 58 (1997); Patricia D. Howard, A Guide to Multi-District Litigation, 124 F.R.D. 479 (1989); Earle F. Kyle, IV, The Mechanics of Motion Practice before the Judicial Panel on Multi-District Litigation, 175 F.R.D. 589 (1998); Note, The Judicial Panel and the Conduct of Multi-District Litigation, 87 Harv. L. Rev. 1001 (1974); see also Gregory Hansel, Extreme Litigation: An Interview with Judge Wm. Terrell Hodges, Chairman of the Judicial Panel on Multidistrict Litigation, 19 Maine Bar J. 16 (2004) (interesting interview with the current chairman of the JPML, Judge William Terrell Hodges).

upon the same transaction or occurrence or series of transactions or occurrences, joinder is permitted.[31]

Depending upon the circumstances, joinder, and perhaps consolidation,[32] should be considered and their benefits compared with other procedural devices.[33] In some instances, consolidation is sometimes favored by toxic tort plaintiffs. While the benefit of convenience is considerable, so too can be the risk of prejudice to the defendant, especially where the time frame to be considered by the jury spans decades and plaintiffs' individual exposures, diseases, and damages vary.[34]

Prejudice arising out of likely juror confusion in a chemical exposure action led the Texas Supreme Court to reverse the consolidation of twenty plaintiffs' claims against nine defendants.[35] Due to the varying lengths of time of exposure and the varying types and mixtures of chemicals to which plaintiffs were allegedly exposed, the court held: "Whatever advantage may be gained in judicial economy or avoidance of repetitive costs is overwhelmed by the greater danger an unfair trial would pose to the integrity of the judicial process."[36]

Whether the combination of plaintiffs in one proceeding is accomplished by means of joinder or consolidation, the court and the parties often will confront the task of selecting individual cases for trial. That task begs the question of what the objectives of that selection process are. There is no paradigm that fits all mass tort cases that present a variety of permutations and combinations of considerations such as exposure, causation, and injury type. It can fairly be said that the goal of selecting individual cases for trial is to find the method that is the fairest and most practicable; one that is designed to provide a representative picture of the universe of the plaintiffs' claims.

Quite often, the parties, left to their own devices, will present the court with a group of the "best" and the "worst" of the universe of their "favorite" plaintiffs. The Fifth Circuit Court of Appeals has criticized this process severely, endorsing instead the use of a stratified random sampling as a means of fostering settlement.[37] The court observed as follows:

> [T]he reasons for acceptance by bench and bar are apparent. If a representative group of claimants are tried to verdict, the results of such trials can be beneficial for litigants

---

31. *See* FED. R. CIV. P. 20; *see also* WRIGHT & MILLER FEDERAL PRACTICE & PROCEDURE § 76; 28 U.S.C. § 1407 (2012) (MDL procedure).
32. *See* FED. R. CIV. P. 42; D. Alan Rudlin & Christopher R. Graham, *Toxic Torts: A Primer*, 17 NAT. RESOURCES AND ENV'T 210 (2003) (hereinafter "Rudlin & Graham"); Richard L. Marcus, *Confronting the Consolidation Conundrum*, 1995 BYU L. REV. 879 (1995); Charles Silver, *Comparing Class Actions and Consolidations*, 10 REV. LITIG. 495 (1991).
33. *See* Roger H. Trangsrud, *Joinder Alternatives in Mass Tort Litigation*, 70 CORNELL L. REV. 779 (1985).
34. Malcolm v. Nat'l Gypsum Co., 995 F.2d 346, 351–52 (2d Cir. 1993); Thomas E. Willging, *Mass Tort Problems and Proposals: A Report to the Mass Tort Working Group*, 187 F.R.D. 328, 354 (1999).
35. *In re* Van Waters & Rogers, Inc., 145 S.W.3d 203 (Tex. 2004).
36. *Id.* at 211.
37. *In re* Chevron, USA, 109 F.3d 1016 (5th Cir. 1997).

who desire to settle such claims by providing information on the value of the cases as reflected by the jury verdicts.[38]

In fact, the process of the selection of trial plaintiffs, often called "bellwether" plaintiffs, can fall wide of the mark of selecting representative plaintiffs. Accordingly, whatever method is ultimately chosen, it is fair to expect that the court will want the parties to agree to a plan that allows the parties some latitude but only within the confines of an approach that assures the subset of plaintiffs ultimately selected is representative of the plaintiffs as a whole.

With that in mind, what parameters might be expected to govern that selection? At a glance, it occurs to formulate a plan that selects the plaintiffs on the basis of the type of injury. The problem with that process, however, is that in a mass joinder situation, just as in a class action situation, the plaintiffs' injuries fall across a wide severity spectrum, ranging anywhere from mere fear and fright to death. In a matter where only 5 percent of the universe of plaintiffs died, a "bellwether" group of only dead or severely injured people, but that excludes representatives of the majority of plaintiffs who were merely scared, is not representative at all. Likewise, a defendant's selection process that selects only the plaintiffs who were afraid, but excludes the more seriously hurt plaintiffs, is subject to the same criticism. Accordingly, composing the subset of plaintiffs merely on the basis of an injury is not helpful. The plaintiffs chosen should be representative and proportionate in number to the group of plaintiffs as a whole.

Moreover, such a linear approach, even if it does produce a representative variety of injuries, does not incorporate the important parameters of exposure and causation. Again, since fact situations can vary widely, no formulaic approach can be applied in all cases. Suffice it to say, however, that an approach that not only accounts for injuries on a representative basis, but also selects plaintiffs on the basis of an appropriate gridding, taking into account proximity and intensity of exposure, and intensity in terms of the duration of exposure, particularly in long-term exposure cases, will be superior.

There are few legal limits on the criteria methodology to be used in selecting trial plaintiffs, and there is no reason why the court could not take it upon itself to pick the plaintiffs from a gridded system prepared by the parties; and in that situation, the court could decide to give or not to give the parties strikes of the plaintiffs it would select. Discretion is the watchword.

---

38. *Id.* at 1019.

Class Actions

In-depth treatment of mass tort class actions is found elsewhere.[39] Most mass torts certified as class actions are based upon Federal Rule of Civil Procedure 23(b)(3) or some state law equivalent. Under that rule, before a class action can be certified, the party seeking certification must demonstrate first under Rule 23(a) that:

(1) the class is so numerous that joinder of all members is impracticable,

(2) there are questions of law or fact common to the class,

(3) the claims or defenses of the representative parties are typical of the claims or defenses of the class, and

(4) the representative parties will fairly and adequately protect the interests of the class.[40]

Second, the proposed class must satisfy the requirements listed in Rule 23(b)(3), which states that a class may be maintained where "questions of law or fact common to class members predominate over any questions affecting only individual members," and a class action would be "superior to other available methods for fairly and efficiently adjudicating the controversy."[41]

While it is difficult, if not impossible, to generalize, most would agree that Rule 23(b)(3) class action treatment is often disfavored by courts where the individuality of multiple issues such as exposure, causation, injuries, and alternative explanations for the injuries pertain.[42]

---

39. See LAWRENCE G. CETRULO, TOXIC TORTS LITIGATION GUIDE §§ 14:43, 14:44 (2011); Debra Lyn Bassett, *When Reform Is Not Enough: Assuring More Than Merely "Adequate" Representation in Class Actions*, 38 GA. L. REV. 927 (2004); Samantha Y. Warshauer, *When Futures Fight Back: For Long-Latency Injury Claimants in Mass Tort Class Actions, Are Asymptomatic Sub-Classes the Cure to the Disease?* 72 FORDHAM L. REV. 1219 (2004); Elizabeth Cabraser, *New Developments in Mass Torts and Class Actions: "Issues" Certification; Mass Torts Top 10 of 2003; Rule 23's New Provision and Action Trial Plans; and the FJC "New Plain Language" Class Notice*, SJ035 ALI-ABA 997 (2004); Richard D. Freer, *The Cauldron Boils: Supplemental Jurisdiction, Amount in Controversy, and Diversity of Citizenship Class Actions*, 53 EMORY L. J. 504 (2004); Thomas D. Rowe, Jr., *Shift Happens: Pressure on Foreign Attorney-Fee Paradigms from Class Actions*, 13 DUKE J. COMP. & INT'L L. 125 (2003); David Rosenberg, *Decoupling Deterrence and Compensation Functions in Mass Tort Class Actions for Future Loss*, 88 VA. L. REV. 1871 (2002); Paul D. Rheingold, *Mass Tort Litigation* (2004); David F. Hare, *Annotated Manual for Complex Litigation* (2004); Charles W. Schwarz & Lewis C. Sutherland, *Class Certification for Environmental and Toxic Tort Claims*, S.E. 73 ALI-ABA 85 (2000); Frances McGovern, *Class Actions and Social Issues in the Gulf South*, 74 TUL. L. REV. 1655 (2000); Elizabeth Cabraser, *Class Action Update 2001: Mass Tort Trends, Choice of Law, Rule 23(f) Appeals and Proposed Amendments to Rule 23*, CF 42 ALI-ABA 757 (2001); John C. Coffee, Jr., *Class Wars: The Dilemma of the Mass Tort Class Action*, 95 COLUM. L. REV. 1343 (1995); Patrick Woolley, *The Availability of Collateral Attack for Inadequate Representation in Class Suits*, 79 TEX. L. REV. 383 (2000); Howard M. Erichson, *Mass Tort Litigation and Inquisitorial Justice*, 87 GEO. L. J. 1983 (1999).
40. FED. R. CIV. P. 23(a) (paragraph breaks added).
41. FED. R. CIV. P. 23(b)(3).
42. Castano v. Am. Tobacco Co., 84 F.3d 734 (5th Cir. 1996). *But see* Olden v. LaFarge Corp., 383 F.3d 495 (6th Cir. 2004).

An important recent class action decision is *Wal-Mart Stores, Inc. v. Dukes*.[43] Although an employment discrimination case brought under Rule 23(b)(2)[44] rather than Rule 23(b)(3), its application of the Rule 23(a) certification factors will impact toxic tort cases. That includes most particularly the court's treatment of the commonality element (Rule 23(a)(2)) as requiring a common question capable of classwide resolution.

In *Wal-Mart Stores*, the Supreme Court confirmed that the commonality requirement in Rule 23(a)(2) requires not only that there be "a common contention" upon which the class claim depends, but such contention must be "of such a nature that it is capable of classwide resolution—which means that determination of its truth or falsity will resolve an issue that is central to the validity of each one of the claims in one stroke."[45] It is not merely a matter of raising common questions, but "'rather the capacity of a classwide proceeding to generate common *answers* apt to drive the resolution of the litigation. Dissimilarities within the proposed class are what have the potential to impede the generation of common answers.'"[46]

The Supreme Court confirmed that "Rule 23 does not set forth a mere pleading standard. A party seeking class certification must affirmatively demonstrate his compliance with the Rule—that is, he must be prepared to prove that there are *in fact* sufficiently numerous parties, common questions of law or fact, etc."[47] Further, the Court made plain both that certification is proper "only if 'the trial court is satisfied, after a rigorous analysis, that the prerequisites of Rule 23(a) have been satisfied,'" and that such "'rigorous analysis' will entail some overlap with the merits of the plaintiff's underlying claim."[48]

In *Wal-Mart Stores*, the Supreme Court concluded that "[w]ithout some glue holding the alleged *reasons* for all [allegedly discriminatory decisions by Wal-Mart's managers nationwide] together, it will be impossible to say that examination of all the class members' claims for relief will produce a common answer to the crucial question *why was I disfavored*."[49]

In one toxic tort case applying *Wal-Mart Stores*, the Louisiana Supreme Court reversed certification of a proposed class of persons seeking property damages associated with contamination from a facility producing creosote-treated railroad ties.[50] Relying in part on *Wal-Mart Stores*, the court stated that to establish a common issue the plaintiffs must pres-

---

43. 131 S. Ct. 2541 (2011).
44. Rule 23(b)(2) applies when "the party opposing the class has acted or refused to act on grounds that apply generally to the class, so that final injunctive relief or corresponding declaratory relief is appropriate respecting the class as a whole."
45. *Wal-Mart Stores*, 131 S. Ct. at 2551.
46. *Id.* (citing Nagareda, *Class Certification in the Age of Aggregate Proof*, 84 N.Y.U. L. Rev. 97, 132 (2009) (emphasis in original)).
47. *Id.*
48. *Id.* (citing Gen. Tel. Co. of Sw. v. Falcon, 457 U.S. 147, 160, 102 S. Ct. 2364 (1982)).
49. *Id.* at 2552 (emphasis in original).
50. Price v. Martin, 79 So. 3d 960 (La. 2011).

ent evidence not simply that emissions occurred, but that emissions resulted in depositing unreasonably elevated levels of toxic chemicals on the plaintiffs' property, which must be capable of resolution for all class members based on common evidence. The plaintiffs had to prove they could show with common evidence that the substances found on the properties of class members derived from the defendant's facility. As to causation, the court concluded that the plaintiffs did not present sufficient evidence to prove the existence of a common thread that held the claims together.[51]

One technique that had been employed by plaintiffs to wire around this legal problem was to seek only medical monitoring remedies. Recent decisions have not been receptive to this approach. In *Gates v. Rohm & Haas Co.*, the Third Circuit Court of Appeal, relying on *Wal-Mart Stores*, declined to certify a class seeking medical monitoring and property damage.[52] To the extent the plaintiffs sought certification under Rule 23(b)(2), the court's rationale was based in part on failure to demonstrate the necessary cohesiveness. Individual issues were significant to certain elements of the medical monitoring claim under state law, such as potential variations in proving exposure, a significantly increased risk of a serious latent disease, and the reasonable necessity of the monitoring regime. The court also held that the plaintiffs could not substitute evidence of exposure to actual class members with evidence regarding hypothetical, composite persons to gain class certification.[53] Particular caution is also warranted where the substantive law controlling the plaintiffs' claims comes from multiple states.[54]

Merely restricting the damages claimed to property damages does not necessarily make class certification any more appropriate than it would be in a case where the damages included both property damage and also personal injuries. Even within a pure property damage case, the court must make a Rule 23(b)(3) determination that individual issues predominate over individual ones. An instructive case in point is *Oullette v. International Paper Co.*[55] In *Oullette*, the court certified a class of lakefront property owners whose properties were damaged by the defendant's activities polluting the waters of Lake Champlain. Factors in a particular case that would distinguish *Oullette*, and thus make class certification a more complicated legal task, would include factors such as the method of exposure, for example, air or water; the type of property involved, for example, all residential, or a mix of residential, industrial, and agricultural; the type of property damages claimed, for example, loss of use of the property and stigma damages. The more the individual property claims are alike, obviously, the more likely certification. The more the individual claims

---

51. *Id.* at 969–72.
52. Gates v. Rohm & Haas Co., 655 F.3d, 255 (3d Cir. 2011).
53. *See also* Wall v. Sunoco, Inc., 211 F.R.D. 272 (M.D. Pa. 2002), and Perez v. Metabolife Int'l Inc., 218 F.R.D. 262 (S.D. Fla. 2003), in which plaintiffs' motions for certification of medical monitoring class actions were denied.
54. Spence v. Glock, 227 F.3d 308 (5th Cir. 2000).
55. 96 F.R.D. 476 (D. Vt. 1980).

vary along parameters such as those listed above, the more likely a court is to determine that individual issues predominate and, accordingly, class certification is inappropriate.

Finally, the precise details of the Class Action Fairness Act of 2005 (CAFA) have been described at length elsewhere and so do not need repeating here.[56] Perhaps the most significant change wrought by the legislation is a dramatic expansion of federal diversity and removal jurisdiction. For putative class actions where the number of class members exceeds 100 and the aggregated claims of the class exceed $5 million, CAFA eschews the centuries-old complete diversity requirement.[57] Only one member of the plaintiff class need be from a state different from any defendant for federal diversity jurisdiction to lie.[58]

CAFA makes this change meaningful by removing ready loopholes. First, CAFA applies not only to state class actions, but also to state cases joining multiple plaintiffs for trial. Such mass joinders for trial are denoted as "mass actions" under CAFA. This label is defined as any action joining for trial more than 100 plaintiffs, each of whom raises a claim in excess of $75,000. The "mass action" provision contains a number of important exceptions and is focused more narrowly on the problem of joinder abuse. While intended to prevent plaintiffs in certain cases from avoiding federal jurisdiction through crafty pleading, courts have recognized that the language of the statute may not apply to all circumstances. In *Tanoh v. Dow Chemical Co.*, for example, the Ninth Circuit upheld a *sua sponte* remand to state court of seven actions involving allegations of exposure to pollutants while working on banana and pineapple plantations.[59] Although no single action had 100 or more plaintiffs, the combined cases did. The court rejected the defendant's argument that plaintiffs should not be permitted to evade CAFA's "mass joinder" provisions by artificially structuring their suit to avoid removal.[60]

Second, CAFA removes easily manipulated barriers to the removal of class actions. For any class action that originally could have been brought in federal court, there is no one-year limitation, no requirement for unanimous consent of defendants, and no prohibition against removal where one of the defendants is a citizen of the forum state.[61]

Importantly, CAFA carves out exceptions to the jurisdiction-expanding provisions. In addition to exempting securities class actions and suits against states and state officials who would enjoy Eleventh Amendment immunity in federal court, CAFA contains a "Local Controversy Exception"[62] and a "Home State Exception."[63] The Local Controversy

---

56. John Beisner & Jessica Davidson Miller, *For: The Class Action Fairness Act: Cleaning Up the Class Action Mess*, 6 BNA CLASS ACTION LITIG. REPORT 104 (Feb. 11, 2005).
57. Strawbridge v. Curtiss, 7 U.S. (3 Cranch) 267 (1806).
58. *See* 28 U.S.C. § 1332(d)(2)(A).
59. 561 F.3d 945 (9th Cir. 2009).
60. *See also* 28 U.S.C. § 1332(d)(11)(B)(ii)(IV) (CAFA provision regarding claims "consolidated or coordinated solely for pretrial proceedings").
61. *See* 28 U.S.C. § 1453(b).
62. *See* 28 U.S.C. § 1332(d)(4)(A).
63. *See* 28 U.S.C. § 1332(d)(4)(B).

Exception requires remand where in-state plaintiffs comprise more than two-thirds of the class, at least one "significant" defendant is from the forum state, the injuries were incurred in the forum state, and no parallel class actions were filed during the preceding three years. The Home State Exception somewhat redundantly mandates remand where in-state plaintiffs comprise greater than two-thirds of the class and all of the "primary defendants" are from the forum state.[64]

These exceptions set up some interesting questions in the context of tort litigation. The Rudlin and Sibley article includes two examples to illustrate important points. The first involves a toxic release:

> One recurring type of state court class action is the localized toxic release case. Consider, for example, a case involving the one-time release from a railcar of a large quantity of hazardous material in a populated area. Local residents file a class action in state court against a small local company that was handling the railcar and a large out-of-state petroleum company that owned the hazardous substances involved. Assume that there are greater than 100 members of the class and that their aggregated claims exceed $5 million.

CAFA's applicability in this example is not clear-cut, and the case likely remains in state court. While all of the requirements of Section 1332(d)(2) are satisfied, application of the Local Controversy Exception likely leads to remand. Here is how the carve-outs operate.

Assuming the plaintiff is able to satisfy its burden of proof,[65] the Local Controversy Exception is probably applicable because more than two-thirds of the class members and a "significant" defendant are both from the forum state.[66] The Home State Exception is likely inapplicable because one of the "primary defendants"—the large petroleum company—is an out-of-state company.[67]

The Local Controversy Exception's two-thirds rule—which mandates remand where at least one defendant from whom "significant relief" is sought and whose alleged conduct forms a "significant basis" for the claims asserted is a citizen of the forum state[68]—does

---

64. D. Alan Rudlin & George P. Sibley, III, CAFA 2005: The Early Return 1–2 (adapted from an article entitled *CAFA 2005: New Vintage or Same Old Wine in a New Bottle?*, originally published in 6, no. 5 CLASS ACTION LITIG. REPORT 185, (Mar. 11, 2005); *see also* Frazier v. Pioneer Americas LLC, 445 F.3d 542 (5th Cir. 2006), interpreting "primary defendants" as used in CAFA to mean all primary defendants.
65. For example, in *Anthony v. Small Tube Mfg. Corp.*, 535 Fed. Supp. 2d 506 (E.D. Pa. 2007), plaintiffs sought remand to state court, arguing that CAFA's home-state controversy exception applied. Because plaintiffs failed to satisfy their burden under that exception of demonstrating that two-thirds of the class members were Pennsylvania citizens and because the four primary defendants were from the forum state, the court denied their motion to remand.
66. 28 U.S.C. § 1332(d)(4)(A).
67. *See* 28 U.S.C. § 1332(d)(4)(B) (mandating remand where, inter alia, "the primary defendants . . . are citizens of the State in which the action was originally filed").
68. 28 U.S.C. § 1332(d)(4)(A).

raise questions as to how much relief is "significant relief" and at what point does a defendant's conduct constitute a "significant basis" for the claims asserted?

In this example, it seems likely that the claims against the local company would satisfy both of these requirements. While the terms "significant basis" and "significant relief" are empty statutory vessels to be filled in by court definitions, they likely will apply to a defendant like our local company from whose property the spill emanated. Moreover, the interaction between CAFA and substantive law (at least in states that do not recognize joint and several liability) drives both plaintiffs and out-of-state defendants to amplify the role of arguably culpable local parties.

What CAFA attempts to foreclose in cases such as this is the manipulation of the system to keep truly "diverse" cases in state court. If the local company has been joined purely to defeat removal, the out-of-state defendants will be able to remove without having to satisfy the high bar of proving fraudulent joinder.[69]

But a slight alteration in the facts of the hypothetical reveals a perhaps unforeseen consequence:

> Instead of a single-release toxic spill, consider instead a chronic exposure scenario where a factory (owned by a corporation that is not a citizen of the forum state) emits pollutants that allegedly have harmed over the years nearby citizens, some of whom have moved out of state. Plaintiffs sue only the factory owner and no other parties. Assume further that these out-of-state parties may or may not constitute greater than one-third of the putative class, depending on how plaintiffs define the class.

A more forgiving nonmandatory exception allows the federal court discretion to maintain jurisdiction over the case where greater than one-third but less than two-thirds of the members of all proposed plaintiff classes in the aggregate and the primary defendants are forum state citizens. Of the six factors that the district court is required to consider under the discretionary exception contained in Section 1332(d)(3), five seem to counsel in favor of remand.[70]

The second example in the Rudlin and Sibley article addresses a products liability situation:

---

69. The burden for establishing fraudulent joinder is quite high. *See, e.g.,* Coyne v. American Tobacco Co., 183 F.3d 488, 493 (6th Cir. 1999) ("[I]f there is a colorable basis for predicting that a plaintiff may recover against non-diverse defendants, [the federal court] must remand the action to state court" (emphasis added)).
70. The claims do not involve a matter of national interest (§ 1332(d)(3)(A)); the laws of the forum state are likely to govern (§ 1332(d)(3)(B)); there is a distinct nexus between the forum and the cause of action (§ 1332(d)(3)(C)); there is a predominance of plaintiffs from the forum state (§ 1332(d)(3)(E)); and there have been no "copy-cat" actions filed (§ 1332(d)(3)(F)).

The final category is a class action where a large number of plaintiffs have been harmed by a single product. This category would include most products liability and occupational exposure class actions. As one example, consider a putative class action on behalf of all people nationwide who owned a certain model of automobile tires, alleging product liability, breach of warranty, and other claims. The defendants consist of a local dealer of the tires, and the out-of-state manufacturer of the tires. Members of the putative class exceed 100, their aggregated claims exceed $5 million, and less than one-third are from the forum state.

CAFA pushes this type of case to federal court. All of the prima facie requirements are satisfied, and none of the exceptions apply.

Again, CAFA proponents achieve their goals. This nationwide class action involving allegations of nationwide import with a significant impact on interstate commerce will be litigated in federal court. Moreover, CAFA will eliminate the practice of plaintiffs' lawyers in these types of cases of seeking nationwide class certification by filing copy-cat suits in courts around the country.[71] All such cases will be removable, and once removed, they likely will be consolidated under 28 U.S.C. § 1407. One district judge can then make a class certification determination, subject to interlocutory review under Rule 23(f) that has binding effect nationwide.

Opponents' economies-of-scale critique of CAFA falls flat here. In comparison to the consumer fraud example, the injuries in this product liability example are significant. Removal in this context may deny some parties their home-state forum for adjudicating injuries occurring in-state, but only if they attempt to pursue a nationwide class—or do not opt out. A statewide class of one form or another would likely satisfy the Home State Exception's two-thirds rule for the same reasons identified with respect to the "toxic spill" example discussed above.[72]

Discovery and Investigation Issues

Typically, toxic tort cases involve relatively complex issues of science and fact, multiple parties, and activities that have stretched over a number of years. Whether the focus of a particular case is on the plaintiffs trying to develop some evidence from the defendants' records and witnesses in support of generalized allegations, the defendants trying to expose what they contend is junk science, the defendants trying to separate out unmeritorious individual claims, the defendants jockeying for positions of lesser liability among one another, or other dynamics, the process of investigation and discovery will be central to the

---

71. Judge Easterbrook recently described how and why the pre-CAFA rules allowed this to happen. *See In re* Bridgestone/Firestone, Inc. Tires Prods. Liab. Litig., 333 F. 3d 763, 766–67 (7th Cir. 2003).
72. Rudlin & Sibley, *supra* note 64, at 6.

ultimate disposition of the case. Here are some aspects of discovery and investigation that have important and sometimes unique characteristics in the context of toxic tort litigation.

Freedom of Information Act and Access to Government Information

A substantial amount of information is available through federal and state governments. Some is accessed by formal request through the Freedom of Information Act (FOIA), state open records laws, and related agency regulations, while some is simply accessed directly from Web sites and government publications. The information held by the government can be very helpful to a litigator. Over time, more and more of that information has become readily available, both at the state and federal level. Information that in previous years could only be obtained by virtue of time-consuming FOIA requests now is often directly available to a litigant. Consequently, toxic tort litigators now need to know not only how to write an FOIA letter, but also how to access information that is already readily available to them.

Fortunately, the ABA Section of Environment, Energy and Resources has published a book that directly addresses, in detail, this entire subject area.[73] This chapter's overview is limited to FOIA.[74] The act requires prompt production of records that the requesting party "reasonably describes," subject to nine exemptions. The nine exemptions are (1) state secrets relating to national defense or foreign policy; (2) internal personnel rules; (3) documents exempted by another statute; (4) trade secrets and other confidential commercial or financial information; (5) inter-agency or intra-agency memoranda and correspondence that would not be available by law to a party in litigation with the agency;[75] (6) personnel and medical files; (7) investigatory records compiled for law enforcement purposes; (8) documents arising out of the supervision of financial institutions; and (9) geological and geophysical data.[76]

"There is no magic formula for making a successful FOIA request. Instead, obtaining the records you are after requires an understanding of the rules of the game, knowledge of the agency and its operations and records keeping, patience, persistence and sometimes a little luck."[77] The various agencies of the federal government publish regulations with respect to

---

73. Accordingly, to understand and explore the options available, critical processes and issues, and the best way to obtain information, *see* P. STEPHEN GIDIERE III, FEDERAL INFORMATION MANUAL: HOW THE FEDERAL GOVERNMENT COLLECTS, MANAGES, AND DISCLOSES INFORMATION UNDER FOIA AND OTHER STATUTES (ABA 2006). Important topics covered include: (1) An Overview of Information Disputes; (2) Agency Collection of Information; (3) Agency Records Management; (4) Access to Federal Records; (5) Electronic Records and Federal Public Web Sites; (6) Making a Successful FOIA Request; (7) Reasons for Agency NonDisclosure; (8) Confidential Business Information; (9) Litigating to Compel Disclosure of Agency Records; (10) Homeland Security; (11) Classified Information; and (12) Constitutional Considerations.
74. *See* 5 U.S.C. § 552. Many states have similar open records laws.
75. For a good discussion on this topic, see *NLRB v. Sears, Roebuck & Co.*, 421 U.S. 132 (1975).
76. 5 U.S.C. § 5522(b).
77. GIDIERE, *supra* note 73, § 7.1.

FOIA requests and have FOIA officers designated throughout their organizations. There are a number of key issues in making a successful FOIA request. First, you should obtain the agency's regulations and work carefully with them. Second, you must consider where to direct the request. It is the agency's obligation to determine where the relevant records are. However, where an agency, in its regulations, specifies that it need only search in the office to which the request is made, that limitation might be upheld.[78] Consequently, one strategy is to send a request to the headquarters of the agency, perhaps also sending it to the regional or other office at the same time. Third, it is important to clearly define the records sought, unless the real objective is to have the government declare that it has no records (perhaps of tactical significance in some cases). Records must be identified with "reasonable specificity." Fourth, it is important to send the request in a fashion that gives the requesting party proof of receipt by the government. The government initially has twenty days to produce the records, and that twenty days is triggered by receipt. Note, however, that a number of agencies now allow requests to be made by e-mail or through agency Web sites. Indeed, DOJ guidance encourages that process.[79]

The government has a duty to undertake a reasonable search, with reasonableness assessed on a case-by-case basis.[80] FOIA does not require agencies to answer questions, but only to produce records.[81] However, the Electronic Freedom of Information Act Amendments of 1996 (EFOIA) require that "an agency shall make reasonable efforts to search for the records in electronic form or format, except when such efforts would significantly interfere with the operation of the agency's automated information system."[82] The courts have made it difficult for the government to limit its efforts in this regard, holding that developing a search program and producing a subset of data from larger databases is not creating "new records."[83] Courts have found that searches requiring 185 hours and 51 hours to assemble information do not qualify for the "significantly interfere with operation of the agency's automated information system" exemption.[84]

---

78. *See, e.g.,* Church of Scientology v. IRS, 792 F.2d 146, 150 (D.C. Cir. 1986); *see also* Domingues v. FBI., 229 F.3d 1151 (Table), 2000 WL 1140594, at *1 (6th Cir. 2000); Moayedi v. U.S. Customs & Border Prot., 510 F. Supp. 2d 73, 81 (D.D.C. 2007); Gabel v. IRS., 1998 WL 817758 at *5 (N.D. Cal. June 25, 1998).
79. *See* FOIA Update XIX vol. 1 (Winter 1998).
80. *See* Weisburg v. U.S. Dep't of Justice, 705 F.2d 1344, 1351 (D.C. Cir. 1983); Lechliter v. Dep't of Def., 371 F. Supp. 2d 589, 593 (D. Del. 2005); Tota v. United States, 2000 WL 1160477, at *2 n.1 (W.D.N.Y. July 31, 2000).
81. *See* Stuler v. IRS., 216 F. App'x 240, 242 (3d Cir. 2007); Zemansky v. U.S. EPA, 767 F.2d 569, 574 (9th Cir. 1985); Di Viaio v. Kelley, 571 F.2d 538, 542–43 (10th Cir. 1978); Harrison v. Fed. Bureau of Prisons, 681 F. Supp. 2d 76, 83 (D.D.C. 2010); Lamb v. IRS, 871 F. Supp. 301, 304 (E.D. Mich. 1994).
82. 5 U.S.C. § 552(a)(3)(C).
83. People for Am. Way Found. v. U.S. Dep't of Justice, 451 F. Supp. 2d 6 (D.D.C. 2006); Schladetsch v. United States HUD., No. 99-0175, 2000 WL 33372125 (D.D.C. Apr. 4, 2000) (Memorandum Opinion).
84. *Schladetsch*, 2000 WL 33372125 at *4; *see also* Dayton Newspapers, Inc. v. Dep't of the Air Force, 35 F. Supp. 2d 1033 (S.D. Ohio 1998), *on reconsideration*, 107 F. Supp. 2d 912 (S.D. Ohio 1999).

Twenty days, however, may not always prove to be the time limit for production. In "unusual circumstances" the government may unilaterally extend the twenty-day limit, giving notice to the requestor prior to the expiration of the twenty days. That said, unusual circumstances are limited to searching other offices, voluminous amounts of material, and the need by the government for consultation, and only give the government an additional ten days per the terms of the statute.[85] If the agency simply fails to act at that point, the requestor can proceed to federal court. However, the federal court will not necessarily immediately force action. Instead, the judge will have the option to grant the agency additional time while still retaining jurisdiction, a process referred to as an "*Open America* Stay of Proceedings."[86] Oftentimes, therefore, the most practical thing to do is to work with the agency to determine why there is a delay and to seek to shorten it.

Additionally, one should not always assume that his or her request is being handled on a first-come, first-served basis. The agencies, by regulation, may establish multiple tracks for handling requests, with the easier requests being put on a faster track and more complicated ones being put on a separate track. Within a particular track they are typically handled on a first-come, first-served basis. But, the tracks will not necessarily proceed at equal pace.

You can also anticipate paying fees, which could include charges for search time, review, and copying. There are various schedules established, largely dependent upon the type of party making the request and the intended use of the information. If the amount is to exceed $25, the agency is obligated to advise the requestor in advance of the cost.

An agency is required in its response to state whether the agency has located any responsive records and, if so, whether the agency is releasing or withholding the records.[87] If it withholds records, the agency must state why it is withholding them, give an estimate of the volume of information being withheld, and identify those people involved in making the decision to withhold.[88] The requesting party is given a right of appeal. The agency has twenty days within which to rule on the appeal, judged from receipt.[89] Unlike the original request, the time limitations for appeals are not subject to an "*Open America*" stay of proceedings. The individual agencies establish their own procedures for appeal.

Discovery of Environmental Audits

States vary in their laws on the protectability of environmental audits. An important facet of this issue is how EPA views discoverability of audits. Overall, EPA is not supportive of a self-audit privilege. What follows in this section is drawn, often verbatim and with

---

85. 5 U.S.C. § 552(a)(6)(B).
86. *See* Open Am. v. Watergate Special Prosecution Force, 547 F.2d 605 (D.C. Cir. 1976).
87. 40 C.F.R. § 2.104(f).
88. 40 C.F.R. § 2.104(h).
89. 40 C.F.R. § 2.104(k).

permission of the authors and publishers, from an excellent earlier work on this topic, *Toxic Tort and Hazardous Substance Litigation*, by L. Neal Ellis Jr. and Charles D. Case.[90]

Over a decade ago, in 1995, EPA adopted an interim policy with respect to the agency's use of environmental audits in enforcement proceedings.[91] This interim policy voices a strong opposition to the developing case law and state legislation establishing a privilege against the disclosure of environmental audits. According to EPA, an environmental audit privilege "could be misused to shield bad actors or to frustrate access to crucial factual information."[92] This interim policy further states that EPA will closely scrutinize local environmental enforcement efforts in states that have adopted such a privilege.

Under EPA's 1995 interim policy, the agency will not routinely request audit reports prior to the commencement of enforcement proceedings. The interim policy provides:

> EPA will not request a voluntary environmental audit report to trigger a civil or criminal investigation. For example, EPA will not request an audit in routine inspections. Once the agency has reason to believe a violation has been committed, EPA may seek through an investigation or enforcement action any information relevant to identifying violations or determining liability or extent of harm.[93]

The interim policy further provides that the agency may reduce civil penalties if the following conditions are met:

1. Voluntary self-policing. The regulated entity discovers a violation through a voluntary environmental audit or voluntary self-evaluation appropriate to the size and nature of the regulated entity; and
2. Voluntary disclosure. The regulated entity fully and voluntarily discloses the violation in writing to all appropriate federal, state and local agencies as soon as it is discovered (including a reasonable time to determine that a violation exists), and prior to (1) the commencement of a federal, state or local agency inspection, investigation or information request; (2) notice of a citizen suit; (3) legal complaint by a third party; or (4) the regulated entity's knowledge that the discovery of the violation by a regulatory agency or third party was imminent; and
3. Prompt correction. The regulated entity corrects the violation either within 60 days of discovering the violation or, if more time is needed, as expeditiously as practicable; and

---

90. L. NEAL ELLIS, JR. & CHARLES D. CASE, TOXIC TORT AND HAZARDOUS SUBSTANCE LITIGATION (Michie Butterworth 1995).
91. *See* Voluntary Environmental Self-Policing and Self-Disclosure Interim Policy Statement, 60 Fed. Reg. 16,875 (Apr. 3, 1995).
92. *Id.* at 16,878.
93. *Id.*

4. Remediation of imminent and substantial endangerment. The regulated entity expeditiously remedies any condition that has created or may create an imminent and substantial endangerment to human health or the environment; and
5. Remediation of harm and prevention of repeat violations. The regulated entity implements appropriate measures to remedy any environmental harm due to the violation and to prevent a recurrence of the violation; and
6. No lack of appropriate preventive measures. The violation does not indicate that the regulated entity has failed to take appropriate steps to avoid repeat or recurring violations; and
7. Cooperation. The regulated entity cooperates as required by EPA and provides such information as is reasonably necessary and required by EPA to determine applicability of this policy. Cooperation may include providing all requested documents and access to employees and assistance in any further investigations into the violation.[94]

Additionally, EPA will not recommend criminal charges if these conditions are met and if the violation does not involve "(1) a prevalent corporate management philosophy or practice that concealed or condoned environmental violations; (2) high-level corporate officials' or managers' conscious involvement in or willful blindness to the violation; or (3) serious actual harm to human health or the environment."[95]

The summary above applies to government enforcement actions. In private party cases, federal courts are split on the issue of whether environmental audits may fall within a self-critical analysis privilege. These cases also vary on when an environmental audit will fall within the scope of the attorney-client privilege.

In *Reichhold Chemicals v. Textron*, a Florida district court adopted the self-critical analysis privilege in the context of environmental litigation. The court explained the rationale as follows:

> The self-critical analysis privilege has been recognized as a qualified privilege which protects from discovery certain critical self-appraisals. It allows individuals or businesses to candidly assess their compliance with regulatory and legal requirements without creating evidence that may be used against them by their opponents in future litigation. The rationale for the doctrine is that such critical self-evaluation fosters the compelling public interest in observance of the law. The privilege protects an organization or individual from the Hobson's choice of aggressively investigating accidents or possible regulatory violations, ascertaining the causes and results, and correcting any violations

---

94. *Id.* at 16,877.
95. *Id.* at 16,877–78.

or dangerous conditions, but thereby creating a self-incriminating record that may be evidence of liability, or deliberately avoiding making a record on the subject (and possibly leaving the public exposed to danger) in order to lessen the risk of civil liability. The self-critical analysis privilege is analogous to, and based on the same public policy considerations as, Rule 407, Federal Rules of Evidence, which excludes evidence of subsequent remedial measures.[96]

The court noted that four criteria must be met in order for information to fall within the scope of this privilege: (1) the information must arise from a self-analysis conducted by the party claiming the privilege; (2) a strong public policy must exist in favor of performing the type of self-analysis at issue; (3) the information is of a type that would likely be curtailed if the privilege were not recognized; and (4) any document embodying the self-analysis must have been prepared with the expectation that it would be kept confidential and such documents must in fact be kept in confidence. The court noted, however, that the privilege is "qualified" and production of the documents would be required "if one or more of the defendants can demonstrate extraordinary circumstances or special need."[97]

Environmental audits may also be protected from discovery by the general attorney-client privilege. In *Olen Properties Corp. v. Sheldahl, Inc.*, the court concluded that an audit prepared for the purpose of assisting counsel in evaluating a company's compliance with environmental laws is protected by the attorney-client privilege.[98] Because the audit was conducted for the purpose of obtaining an opinion of law from an attorney and the

---

96. 157 F.R.D. 522, 524 (N.D. Fla. 1994) (citations omitted).
97. *Id.* at 527. Other courts have rejected the self-critical evaluation privilege in the environmental context. *See, e.g.,* Andritz Sprout-Bauer, Inc. v. Beazer East, Inc., 174 F.R.D. 609, 635 (M.D. Pa. 1997) ("There is no authority before us which suggests that Pennsylvania or Virginia has adopted the self-critical analysis test. We are not persuaded that either would follow the limited number of jurisdictions which have recognized such a privilege."); United States v. Dexter Corp., 132 F.R.D. 8 (D. Conn. 1990) (self-critical analysis privilege inapplicable in enforcement proceeding under the Clean Water Act); CPC Int'l, Inc. v. Hartford Accident & Indem. Co., 262 N.J. Super. 191, 202, 620 A.2d 462, 467 (N.J. Super. 1992) ("[T]his Court finds that the public need for disclosure of documents relating to environmental pollution and the circumstances of such pollution outweighs the public's need for confidentiality in such documents."); State *ex rel.* Celebrezze v. CECOS Int'l Inc., 583 N.E.2d 1118, 1121 (Ohio Ct. App. 12 Dist. 1990) (internal performance evaluations prepared by hazardous waste generator do not fall within the scope of the self-critical evaluation privilege due to "clear legislative directive that the hazardous waste industry be subject to public scrutiny"); *cf.* Warren v. Legg Mason Wood Walker, Inc., 896 F. Supp. 540 (E.D.N.C. 1995) (refusing to hold self-critical analysis privilege applicable to audit report); Reich v. Hercules, Inc., 857 F. Supp. 367, 371 (D.N.J. 1994) (safety audit not within scope of privilege due to public interest in allowing the government to freely investigate potential OSHA violations). The self-critical evaluation privilege has been the subject of heated debate among commentators. *Compare* James F. Flanagan, *Rejecting a General Privilege for Self-Critical Analysis*, 51 Geo. Wash. L. Rev. 551 (1983) *and* S. Kay McNab, Note, *Criticizing the Self-Criticism Privilege*, 1987 U. Ill. L. Rev. 675 (1987) *with* Robert J. Bush, *Stimulating Corporate Self-Regulation—The Corporate Self-Evaluative Privilege: Paradigmatic Preferentialism or Pragmatic Panacea*, 87 Nw. U. L. Rev. 597 (1993) *and* Note, *The Privilege of Self-Critical Analysis*, 96 Harv. L. Rev. 1083 (1983).
98. 1994 U.S. Dist. LEXIS 7125 (C.D. Cal. 1994).

confidentiality of the audit memoranda had been maintained, the audit was deemed to be protected by the attorney-client privilege.

In contrast to *Olen Properties*, the court in *United States v. Chevron U.S.A., Inc.* rejected the defendant's argument that an environmental audit fell within the scope of the attorney-client privilege.[99] In *Chevron*, the defendant conducted an audit of one of its refineries for purposes of determining the facility's compliance with environmental laws and regulations. The defendant's in-house counsel was a member of the audit team that conducted this review. The court, however, concluded that this alone is not sufficient to establish a claim of privilege. For the attorney-client privilege to apply, the communication must be between the client and his attorney in his capacity as an attorney, and the purpose of the communication must be to provide legal advice. The court found that the mere presence of the defendant's attorney did not make the audit privileged if the attorney acted only as a business advisor.

Although environmental audits may be subject to protection from discovery under certain circumstances, documents prepared by an environmental consultant with respect to the remediation and assessment of a site are less likely to be protected. In *United States Postal Service v. Phelps Dodge Refining Corp.*, the defendants claimed as privileged numerous documents that were exchanged between environmental consultants performing remediation at a site and the defendants' counsel.[100] The court emphasized that the role of the consultants was not to assist with providing legal advice to the defendants. The court noted the consultants "were hired by defendants to formulate a remediation plan acceptable to [the state] and to oversee remedial work at the Property. Their function was not to put information gained from defendants into usable form for their attorneys to render legal advice. . . ."[101] The court, accordingly, concluded that the attorney-client privilege did not protect the consultant documents.

Notably, the court also found that documents containing notations of the defendants' attorneys concerning the reports were not substantive and, therefore, did not fall within the attorney-client privilege. The court concluded the documents did not fall within the work product doctrine, because the defendants had failed to demonstrate that litigation was contemplated.[102]

Questions and limitations on the discoverability of environmental self-audits do not always inhibit companies from conducting them. Indeed, it is common in some states for regulatory agencies to suggest or order a company to conduct a multimedia self-audit in connection with the resolution of an enforcement action. The practitioner must always

---

99. Civ. A. No. 88-6681, 1989 WL 121616 (E.D. Pa. Oct. 16, 1989).
100. 852 F. Supp. 156 (E.D.N.Y. 1994).
101. *Id.* at 161.
102. *See id.* at 162 n. 4. *But see* Vermont Gas Sys. v. United States Fid. & Guar. Co., 151 F.R.D. 268, 275–76 (D. Vt. 1993) (work product claim may be asserted with respect to documents generated after receipt of information request from EPA).

advise his or her client to take the necessary steps that maximize the opportunity to assert a privilege over the audit report, an argument which is least likely to succeed when the audit is part of or associated with a public record. In state court, one needs to know whether a self-audit privilege exists under state law and, if so, the framework of that protection. In federal court, in the absence of binding circuit court precedent in the jurisdiction of the case at bar, the only prudent pathway is to ensure that the audit is conducted by third-party consultants engaged for the client by outside counsel and that the audit report is provided by that counsel to the client in response to a documented request by the client for legal advice.

Discovery of Independent Researchers

Particularly within the realm of toxic tort litigation, where causation is oftentimes the dispositive issue, independent research conducted by one who is skilled, learned, or experienced in a particular field can be a valuable source of information for both the plaintiffs and the defendants. Discovery of this information is not without its complications, however. Because independent researchers are not afforded the same discovery protections under the Federal Rules as expert witnesses and nontestifying retained experts, federal courts are especially sensitive to the production burdens placed upon nonparty, involuntary, and otherwise disinterested academicians possessing research and data sought by litigants.[103]

"However, non-retained or involuntary experts or researchers do not have any federal statutory, case law or common law privilege which protects against their having to involuntarily share their expertise with the parties in the litigation."[104] In cases that have declined to force an independent researcher to turn over confidential or expert information, there has typically been a concomitant finding that the need for the information was not compelling under the circumstances or that its production would be unduly burdensome.[105] This determination is made by balancing the relevance and need of the

---

103. *See In re* Snyder, 115 F.R.D. 211, 214–15 (D. Ariz. 1987) ("The protections of Fed. R. Civ. P. 26(b)(4) do not extend to an expert who has not consented to participate in a lawsuit, because the rule applies only to facts known to and opinions held by experts that were acquired or developed in anticipation of litigation or for trial."); *see also* Virginia G. Maurer, *Compelling the Expert Witness: Fairness and Utility under the Federal Rules of Civil Procedure*, 19 GA. L. REV. 71, 75–104 (1984) (reviewing legal distinction between Rule 26(b)(4) experts and independent researchers, or "pure" experts).
104. Anker v. G.D. Searle & Co., 126 F.R.D. 515, 519 (M.D.N.C. 1989).
105. *See* Farnsworth v. Proctor & Gamble Co., 758 F.2d 1545, 1547–48 (11th Cir. 1985) (affirming order to quash manufacturer's subpoena against Center for Disease Control to divulge names and addresses of women who participated in research on toxic shock syndrome); Deitchman v. E.R. Squibb & Sons, Inc., 740 F.2d 556, 560–66 (7th Cir. 1984) (remanding case to district court to fashion protective order allowing defendant "the least necessary amount of information to avoid a miscarriage of justice" without doing harm to the independent researcher); Buchanan v. Am. Motors Corp., 697 F.2d 151, 152 (6th Cir. 1983) (affirming order to quash on ground of burdensomeness); Dow Chem. Co. v. Allen, 672 F.2d 1262, 1270–73 (7th Cir. 1982) (recognizing vital public interest in promoting research in balancing interests of party seeking discovery and independent researcher); *In re* Yasmin & Yaz (Drospirenone) Mktg., Sales Practices & Prods. Liab. Litig., MDL 2100, 2011 WL 5547133 (S.D. Ill. Nov. 15, 2011); *In re* Fosamax Prods. Liab. Litig., MDL 1789, 2009 WL 2395899 (S.D.N.Y. Aug. 4, 2009); *In re* Snyder,

information (taking into consideration whether such information is reasonably available from an alternate and less burdensome source) against the burden and prejudice to the nonparty, involuntary expert.[106] Even if granted, district courts have great discretionary power to fashion protective orders that can lessen the burden and prejudice to the independent researcher in any number of ways.[107]

Included within the balancing test employed by some courts is the potential harm that may come to a researcher's publication prospects.[108] Obviously, this "qualified protection" would not apply in instances where the results of the research have already been published.[109] However, a party is typically restricted to seeking only historical opinions or data and is precluded from requesting the nonparty to analyze or re-analyze data and form a new opinion.[110]

Industry Experts

The toxic tort litigant may find it helpful to retain an expert with knowledge of industry practices and standards of care.[111] To the extent that such an expert intends to testify as to scientific, technical, or other specialized knowledge, the admissibility of that testimony is generally governed by the *Daubert* analysis discussed elsewhere in this book.[112]

However, *Daubert*'s focus on scientific reliability may not always apply to the admissibility of an industry expert's testimony; in some cases, "the relevant reliability concerns

---

115 F.R.D. 211, 214–15 (D. Ariz. 1987) (noting that the potential for burdensome repetition and the lack of finality can create serious problems for a researcher whose work is relevant to many actions); *Anker*, 126 F.R.D. at 521 (relevance and need for the information did not outweigh the burden and prejudice to the nonparty independent researcher).

106. See *Anker*, 126 F.R.D. at 521.
107. See *In re Fosamax*, 2009 WL 2395899 at *5 (noting that courts have great discretion to craft protective orders); Wright v. Jeep Corp., 547 F. Supp. 871, 877 (E.D. Mich. 1982) (ordering parties to submit proposals to the court to lessen the burden of independent researcher and compensate him adequately for his evidence); *Deitchman*, 740 F.2d at 565–66 (remanding case to district court to fashion protective order); *Anker*, 126 F.R.D. at 521 (noting that such protection could entail requiring that the party who conducts the deposition retain such records and make them available to subsequent requesters).
108. *Compare* Dow Chem. Co. v. Allen, 672 F.2d 1262, 1272–73 (7th Cir. 1982) (finding that immediate public access to the requested material would deprive researchers of both the opportunity to have their results published by prestigious peer-reviewed journals, as well as the professional benefits accompanying this achievement) *and In re Yasmin*, 2011 WL 5547133 at *2 (noting the importance of confidentiality in the peer review process), *with* Burka v. U.S. Health & Human Servs., 87 F.3d 508, 521 (D.C. Cir. 1996) (unwilling to say that there is an established or well-settled practice of protecting research data in the realm of civil discovery on the grounds that disclosure would harm a researcher's publication prospects).
109. See *In re* Am. Tobacco Co., 880 F.2d 1520, 1530 (2d Cir. 1989); Sw. Ctr. for Biological Diversity v. USDA, 170 F. Supp. 2d 931, 942–43 (D. Ariz. 2000).
110. See *Anker*, 126 F.R.D. at 520 (citing Annotation, *Expert Testimony Refusal*, 50 A.L.R. 4th 680 (1986)).
111. *See, e.g.*, United States v. Leo, 941 F.2d 181, 196–97 (3d Cir. 1991) (allowing testimony of expert regarding the customs and practices of the defense contracting industry); United States v. Schiff, 538 F. Supp. 2d 818, 846 (D.N.J. 2008), *aff'd*, 602 F.3d 152 (3d Cir. 2010) (admitting the defendant's expert's testimony regarding the complex pharmaceutical distribution system).
112. Kumho Tire Co. v. Carmichael, 526 U.S. 137 (1999) (holding that the *Daubert* analysis applies not only to scientific testimony, but to all expert testimony under Fed. R. of Evid. 702).

may focus upon personal knowledge or experience."[113] This standard can open the door to testimony from individuals regarding important, but nonscientific, matters. For example, plaintiff's counsel may find that an industry expert can be used to establish industry standards in existence at the time of an injury, thereby strengthening his argument that the defendant was negligent in failing to comply with these standards.[114] The testimony of such an expert may also allow a plaintiff to survive a motion for summary judgment.[115] On the other hand, defense counsel may wish to retain an industry expert to explain his client's complex industry in simple, layperson's terms for the jury.[116] For these reasons, practitioners should consider retaining an expert with experience in a complex field, but who may not otherwise have the scientific training to qualify as a technical expert under *Daubert*.

Discovery of Employees and Former Employees

It is elementary that in toxic tort litigation involving corporate and other juridical entities, the voices of these entities come from the entity's employees and ex-employees. Identifying the correct people, getting access to documents associated with them, and doing the most effective job of ascertaining what their testimony will be is a key part of discovery in toxic tort litigation. Here, we briefly summarize some of the issues that arise in this area.

Employee witnesses fall into several categories. They can be present employees of a party, past employees of a party, or present or past employees of a nonparty involved in the circumstances and transaction of litigation. In certain instances, as described elsewhere, an employee can himself be a party, either because the plaintiff's counsel believes that there is some independent liability on the part of that employee, or the more likely motive, naming an employee of a defendant can interfere with or prevent removal to federal court based on diversity of citizenship.

---

113. *Kumho Tire*, 526 U.S. at 150; *see also* L.S. v. Scarano, 2011 WL 4948099 at *4 (S.D. Ohio Oct. 18, 2011) (finding that "expert opinion may be based only on experience," and that trucking industry expert's opinion was therefore admissible despite no foundation in scientific methodology); United States Fid. & Guar. Co. v. Sulco, Inc., 171 F.R.D. 305, 308 (D. Kan. 1997) (finding that challenge to insurance industry expert's testimony based on experience of expert went to weight, not admissibility, of testimony); Fillingane v. Siemens Energy & Automation, Inc., 809 So. 2d 737, 740 (Miss. Ct. App. 2002) (applying Mississippi evidence rules and finding that expert could not testify as to industry standards from twenty-five years prior when he did not have personal knowledge of such standards).
114. McGowan v. Cooper Indus., 863 F.2d 1266, 1273 (6th Cir. 1988) (allowing expert to testify as to industry custom for purposes of establishing the defendant's duty, but not allowing testimony regarding an opinion on breach of that duty); Bartlett v. Mut. Pharm. Co., 742 F. Supp. 2d 182, 189 (D.N.H. 2010) (permitting testimony regarding standard of care in the pharmaceutical industry).
115. In re Asbestos Prods. Liab. Litig. (No. VI), MDL 875, 2011 WL 3925419 at*4 (E.D. Pa. July 27, 2011) report and recommendation adopted, MDL 875, 2011 WL 4001031 (E.D. Pa. Sept. 6, 2011) (granting defendant's motion for summary judgment after noting that plaintiff did not provide testimony of an industry expert to establish that cables in question would have contained asbestos).
116. *See, e.g., Schiff*, 538 F. Supp. 2d at 846.

Employee Named to Defeat Diversity

While the details of removal procedure and jurisprudence are treated in detail elsewhere in this subsection, it bears mentioning that the "summary proceeding," which characterizes a court's adjudication of a motion to remand for fraudulent or improper joinder of a company employee, does not involve the testimony of witnesses or the review of documents.[117]

Other Employees

The first step for counsel in discovery is to identify present and former employees who do (or may) have information and documents pertinent to the case. This process, while often initiated by propounding written discovery, in practical terms nearly always involves a search-and-find process both on the part of the adversarial party seeking the information and the party required to provide it. Identification of the people will occur along with identification of the documents associated with those people. An attendant process will be the review of those documents, the potential for creation of a bates-numbered scannable database for those documents, and an evaluation of whether the documents are protected from discovery under the attorney-client privilege or the work product doctrine.

Whether the person is a present or former employee, counsel for the defendant will, once the person is identified, need to promptly establish contact, advise him or her of the pendency of litigation, and begin the process of ascertaining what the person knows and what kind of witness this person is likely to be. Often this process will occur within the structure of a corporate deposition under Federal Rule of Civil Procedure 30(b)(6) or an analogous state law. In that case, the focus is upon designating a present (or a former) employee or employees with sufficient knowledge of the areas of inquiry contained in the corporate deposition notice to satisfy the requirements for a diligent inquiry and the designation of a knowledgeable corporate representative.

A corporation is not relieved of its duty to designate an individual to testify even though the tortious event occurred decades prior to the lawsuit and any employees with knowledge are either retired or deceased.[118] In *United States v. J.M. Taylor*, the court ruled that such institutional memory problems related to long-ago events "do not relieve a corporation from preparing its Rule 30(b)(6) designee to the extent matters are reasonably available, whether from documents, past employees, or other sources."[119] According to the district court, Rule 30(b)(6) explicitly requires the corporation to designate persons, even former employees, to testify on its behalf as to matters known or reasonably known. In addition, the court interpreted Rule 30(b)(6) to implicitly require that the designated person adequately prepare for the deposition by reviewing all historical information reasonably

---

117. *See* 14B WRIGHT & MILLER, FEDERAL PRACTICE AND PROCEDURE § 3723.
118. For thorough discussion see, 8A WRIGHT, MILLER & MARCUS, FEDERAL PRACTICE AND PROCEDURE: CIVIL 2d § 2103 and § 2110.
119. 166 F.R.D. 356, 361 (M.D. N.C. 1996).

available. To interpret Rule 30(b)(6) otherwise would allow the "'sandbagging' of an opponent by conducting a half-hearted inquiry before the deposition but a thorough and vigorous one at trial."[120]

For example, a corporation might retain its former industrial hygienist, long ago retired, to testify regarding safety measures instituted by the corporation in the 1960s to protect its employees from asbestos exposure. In addition to relying upon his own memory, the former industrial hygienist would prepare for the deposition by reviewing the historical (often archived) documents and interviewing others who may have knowledge. Since a former employee usually expects compensation for his efforts, the corporation might retain the former employee as a paid consultant for purposes of litigation. By so doing, the corporation not only benefits from the individual's personal knowledge of long-ago events but also prevents opposing counsel from communicating, ex parte, with this former employee who has become a current paid consultant.[121]

Sometimes a corporate deposition will be the only discovery experience for a corporate employee or former employee. In other cases, there may be a corporate deposition and a deposition where the same employee also appears as an individual witness.

The ability of counsel to directly contact employee witnesses varies with the status of that employee. Ethical rules may prohibit contact by a lawyer or his representative with a present employee of a represented party in litigation about matters that are within the scope of the litigation.[122] ABA Model Rule 4.2 prohibits opposing counsel from communicating with "a person the lawyer knows to be represented by another lawyer in the matter, unless the lawyer has the consent of the other lawyer or is authorized to do so by law or a court order." In the case of a represented corporation, Comment 7 of ABA Model Rule 4.2 prohibits contact with a current "constituent" of the corporation who "supervises, directs or regularly consults with the organization's lawyer concerning the matter or has authority to obligate the organization with respect to the matter or whose act or omission in connection with the matter may be imputed to the organization for purposes of civil or criminal liability." As to a former employee, Comment 7 simply states that "[c]onsent of the organization's lawyer is not required for communication." The rules governing contact with corporate employees, both current and former, vary from state to state.[123] The practitioner should proceed cautiously in this area and, at the outset, must carefully review the rules of professional conduct for his particular state.

---

120. *Id.* at 362.
121. *See* MODEL RULES OF PROF'L CONDUCT R. 4.2, cmt. 7, which prohibits *ex parte* communications with "a constituent of the organization who supervises, directs or *regularly consults with the organization's lawyer* concerning the matter. . . ." (emphasis added).
122. *See* MODEL RULES OF PROF'L CONDUCT R. 4.2.
123. *See* Ellen J. Messing & James S. Weliky, *Contacting Employees of An Adverse Party: A Plaintiff's Attorney's View*, 2 Ann. 2004 ATLA-CLE 1785 (2004) (wherein the authors discuss and cite within footnotes the differences between the states' model rules governing communications with a represented person).

As to current employees, depending upon the jurisdiction, some or all of the employees may fall within the scope of ABA Model Rule 4.2. Accordingly, practitioners must ascertain which current employees are within the purview of Rule 4.2 or the state's equivalent ethical provision.[124] In interpreting Rule 4.2, courts have adopted a variety of tests and rules that determine which employees may not be contacted ex parte by opposing counsel.[125] A number of possibilities exist, among those that a court may adopt are: (1) a blanket rule that allows contact with all current employees;[126] (2) a blanket rule that forbids contact with all current employees;[127] (3) a case-by-case balancing test;[128] (4) a control group test;[129] (5) a litigation control group test;[130] (6) a managing-speaking agent test;[131] (7) an alter ego test;[132] and (8) a test based on the comments to Rule 4.2 prior to the 2002 amendments.[133]

---

124. For in-depth treatment of the issues implicated in this section, see SUSAN J. BECKER, DISCOVERY FROM CURRENT AND FORMER EMPLOYEES (ABA 2005).
125. See Palmer v. Pioneer Inn Assocs., LTD., 59 P.3d 1237 (Nev. 2002) (providing an extensive discussion of differing tests that courts have adopted in response to Rule 4.2).
126. See, e.g., Public Serv. Elec. & Gas Co. v. Assoc. Elec. & Gas Ins. Servs., Ltd., 745 F. Supp. 1037, 1042 (D.N.J. 1990) (concluding that current and former employees could not be investigated through *ex parte* contact by opposing counsel). *But see* Klier v. Sordoni Skanska Constr. Co., 766 A.2d 761, 769 (N.J. 2001) (applying a litigation control group test and stating that *Public Service Electric* had been superseded by amendments to the ethical rules).
127. See, e.g., Chambers v. Capital Cities/ABC, 159 F.R.D. 441 (S.D.N.Y. 1995) (upholding the decision of magistrate court to prohibit plaintiff's counsel from having *ex parte* contact with current corporate employees).
128. See, e.g., Morrison v. Brandeis Univ., 125 F.R.D. 14, 18 (D. Mass. 1989). In *Morrison*, the court found that a case-by-case approach would allow it to strike the appropriate balance based upon the particular needs of the case.
129. See, e.g., Fair Auto. Repair, Inc. v. Car-X Serv. Sys., 471 N.E.2d 554, 560 (Ill. App. Ct. 1984). The control group is generally defined as persons who are at the top level of management in the corporation and have the authority to make final decisions. The control group may also include those whose advisory role is integral to the making of final decisions.
130. A variation of the control group test is the litigation control group test. Also called the "legal position test," this test focuses on whether the employee has significant involvement or control on the legal positions the corporation takes in litigation. *See* Andrews v. Goodyear Tire & Rubber Co., 191 F.R.D. 59, 75 (D.N.J. 2000).
131. The managing-speaking test restricts *ex parte* contact with those employees who have "speaking authority" for the corporation. *See, e.g.,* Wright v. Group Health Hosp., 691 P.2d 564, 569 (Wash. 1984).
132. Also called a binding admissions test, this rule was articulated in Niesig v. Team I, 558 N.E.2d 1030 (N.Y. 1990) and has similarities to the managing-speaking agent test and litigation control group test. The alter ego test prohibits *ex parte* contact with those people who are in effect the "alter ego" of the corporation. This group includes "those officials, but only those, who have the legal power to bind the corporation in the matter or who are responsible for implementing the advice of the corporation's lawyer, or any member of the organization whose own interests are directly at stake in the representation." *Id.* at 1035. *Accord* Cole v. Appalachian Power Co., 903 F. Supp. 975, 977 (S.D. W.Va. 1995).
133. Prior to the 2002 amendments to Model Rule 4.2, the comments to Rule 4.2 state that the rule prohibits:

> communications by a lawyer for one party concerning the matter in representation with persons having a managerial responsibility on behalf of the organization, and with any other person whose act or omission in connection with that matter may be imputed to the organization for purposes of civil or criminal liability, or whose statement may constitute an admission on the part of the organization.

Unlike the situation with current employees, both the case law and Comment 7 generally permit ex parte communication with former employees. However, one federal case has restricted communication with a former employee when the corporation "continues to have a vital interest in the employee's knowledge of privileged information and its potential release to opposing counsel in litigation after the employee leaves."[134] Indeed, Comment 7 states that "[i]n communicating with a current or former constituent of an organization, a lawyer must not use methods of obtaining evidence that violate the legal rights of the organization," such as inquiries within the scope of the corporation's attorney-client privilege. Moreover, some courts may restrict opposing counsel's contact with former corporate employees.[135]

Because an unrepresented former employee of the corporation may unwittingly waive a preexisting attorney-client privilege, corporate counsel should consider notifying certain former employees of their right to seek legal counsel if approached by opposing parties and as a reminder that privilege protection continues even postemployment.[136] The opposing party who contacts a former employee, ex parte, should be careful to avoid any impropriety by fully identifying himself and the purpose of the interview, by advising the former employee of his right to decline the interview, and by not seeking disclosure of privileged information. The former employee, unless he or she is under subpoena, is free to refuse to communicate with counsel.

Often, a particular subject matter will generate knowledge that is shared by a number of employees or a party or nonparty. It is crucial for counsel to learn the seniority and responsibility hierarchy present within the organization that employs these people. It may be necessary to evaluate whose deposition should be taken first. When a top-down hierarchy exists, counsel may be well advised to start at the bottom—that is, to take the lowest-ranking person's deposition first, working to the most highly ranked employee. If the top-ranking person is deposed first, there is an opportunity for counsel of that party to disseminate that deposition among subordinate employees with the corresponding chance

---

See Becker, *supra* note 124, at 38 (explaining that the pre-2002 comments suggest three categories of persons that the no-contact rule is applicable to). Some courts have adopted those categories; *see, e.g.*, State *ex rel.* Pitts v. Roberts, 857 S.W.2d 200, 202 (Mo. 1993).

134. Rentclub, Inc. v. Transamerica Rental Fin. Corp., 811 F. Supp. 651, 658 (M.D. Fla. 1992); *see also* Messing & Weliky, *supra* note 123, for a short discussion of other cases prohibiting ex parte contact with a former employee for various reasons.

135. *See* Bryant v. Yorktowne Cabinetry, Inc., 538 F. Supp. 2d 948, 950 (W.D. Va. 2008) (noting a substantial disagreement by some courts with a blanket ban on *ex parte* communications with former employees, but providing guidelines to counsel who contact those parties); Curley v. Cumberland Farms, Inc., 134 F.R.D. 77, 82 (D.N.J 1991) (rejecting a complete bar of all *ex parte* contact with former employees but recognizing that in some instances such a prohibition of such contact would be appropriate); *see also* Benjamin J. Vernia, *Right of Attorney to Conduct Ex Parte Interviews with Former Corporate Employees*, 57 A.L.R. 5th 633 (2003) (providing extensive treatment of state and federal decisions regarding Rule 4.2 and former employees).

136. *See* Frank G. Usseglio, *How to Limit Opposing Counsel's Access to Former Employees*, PROD. LIAB. L. & STRATEGY 15 (6), 1 (Dec. 1996) for a discussion of other practice tips.

that their testimony may be unnaturally consistent with the testimony of the person at the top, even if that person has the least real personal knowledge of the circumstances of the case. It may be more effective to depose the more hands-on person actually involved in the matters at hand (such as the driver of the truck that released the chemical, etc.) than the person who is on paper responsible for these activities, but who in reality had nothing to do with them.

Protective Orders

It is common in toxic tort litigation for defendant companies to be asked to produce sensitive internal documents. Often, those documents contain trade secrets or other confidential research, development, or commercial information, as well as self-critical internal analysis. Consequently there inherently is a tension with respect to whether such documents must be produced and, if so, what protection against dissemination will be put in place by agreement between the parties and/or by court order.

In recent years, an additional and important dynamic has emerged—the public's right to gain access to such documents. A significant body of analysis and jurisprudence has begun to emerge in this area, and is still developing at this writing. Before turning to those issues, it is important to first examine the mechanics of protective orders as commonly used in toxic tort and other litigation.

As a general proposition, protective orders are to serve the purpose of protecting a producing party from "annoyance, embarrassment, oppression, or undue burden or expense."[137] Traditionally, two approaches to protective orders have been taken: (1) the "umbrella" protective order; and (2) the particularized protective order.[138]

Umbrella Protective Orders

The umbrella protective order is typically the product of a stipulation between parties at the outset of the litigation that certain designated documents are subject to the protections of Rule 26(c).[139] The effect of such a blanket designation is to allow a party to

---

137. FED. R. CIV. P. 26(c); *see also* Baker v. Liggett Group, Inc., 132 F.R.D. 123, 125–26 (D. Mass. 1990) (defendants failed to demonstrate that absence of blanket protective order prohibiting dissemination of both confidential and nonconfidential documents would lead to adverse pretrial publicity and embarrassment impairing fairness of trial process). The laws of the individual states, of course, govern proceedings in those states' courts. FED. R. CIV. P. 26(c), however, has been replicated in one fashion or another in many states and serves as a good example for these overview purposes.
138. *See* Cipollone v. Liggett Group, Inc., 113 F.R.D. 86, 93–94 (D.N.J. 1986) (holding that the burden of proof is the same under either approach). *See generally* ANNOTATED MANUAL FOR COMPLEX LITIGATION (FOURTH) § 11.432 (2004).
139. *See* Bond v. Utreras, 585 F.3d 1061, 1067 (7th Cir. 2009) (noting that parties often stipulate to protective orders when discovery commences); Chicago Tribune Co. v. Bridgestone/Firestone, Inc., 263 F.3d 1304, 1307 (11th Cir. 2001) (noting that umbrella method replaces need to litigate claim to protection document by document until confidential designation is challenged); *In re* Se. Milk Antitrust Litig., 666 F. Supp. 2d 908, 913 (E.D. Tenn. 2009) (stipulated protective orders have become increasingly common in complex litigation).

temporarily enjoy the protections of Rule 26(c) without first requiring a particularized showing of confidentiality on a document-by-document basis. In this way, the stipulation is thought to jump-start the discovery process by avoiding the delays and expense associated with document-specific adjudication.[140] The parties' ability to craft such an order is broad, permitting many unique protections such as "attorney-eyes only" designation for highly sensitive documents.

An umbrella protective order, while making designated documents presumptively confidential, does not, however, dispense with the requirement that there be an adjudication of good cause whenever the order is challenged.[141] Rather, it simply postpones an individualized showing until a particular challenge has been made.[142]

Moreover, the umbrella order does not shift the burden under Rule 26(c) from the party seeking protection to the party challenging it. "A plain reading of the language of Rule 26(c) demonstrates that the party seeking a protective order has the burden of showing that good cause exists for issuance of that order."[143] Federal courts have superimposed a "balancing of interests approach" to the good cause requirement.[144] This standard requires the district court to balance one party's interest in accessing documents with the other party's interest in keeping the information confidential.[145] General allegations of harm, unsubstantiated by specific examples or articulated reasoning, do not satisfy this test.[146] When challenged, the burden of justifying the confidentiality of each and every document sought to be covered by a protective order remains on the party seeking the protective order regardless of whether the parties initially, and without a particularized showing, stipulated to umbrella protection.[147]

---

140. *See In re* Alexander Grant & Co. Litig., 820 F.2d 352, 356–57 (11th Cir. 1987). *But see* John Does I-VI v. Yogi, 110 F.R.D. 629, 632 (D.D.C. 1986) (blanket orders create more problems than they solve).
141. *See* Leucadia, Inc. v. Applied Extrusion Tech., Inc., 998 F.2d 157, 166–67 (3d Cir. 1993) (when parties' initial confidentiality designations under umbrella protective order are subsequently challenged, party seeking protection must make a particularized showing for the need for continued secrecy).
142. *See In re* Parmalat Sec. Litig., 258 F.R.D. 236, 243 (S.D.N.Y. 2009) (recognizing that protective orders postpone the showing of good cause until a party or intervenor challenges the confidential treatment of documents); *Yogi*, 110 F.R.D. at 632 ("Blanket orders only postpone, rather than prevent, the need for the Court to closely scrutinize discovery materials to see if the seal is justified.").
143. *In re* "Agent Orange" Prod. Liab. Litig., 821 F.2d 139, 145 (2d Cir. 1987); *see also In re* Terrorist Attacks on September 11, 2001, 454 F. Supp. 2d 220, 221 (S.D.N.Y. 2006) (noting that requiring the party seeking a protective order to demonstrate good cause protects a litigant's First Amendment right to speak and the public's right of access to the courts).
144. *See In re* Eli Lilly & Co., 142 F.R.D. 454, 456–57 (S.D. Ind. 1992) (citing Farnsworth v. Proctor & Gamble Co., 758 F.2d 1545, 1547 (11th. Cir. 1985)).
145. See Chicago Tribune Co. v. Bridgestone/Firestone, Inc., 263 F.3d 1304, 1313 (11th Cir. 2001).
146. *See Leucadia, Inc.*, 998 F.2d at 166.
147. *See id.* (noting that any other conclusion would turn Rule 26(c) on its head); *see also* Cipollone v. Liggett Group, Inc., 113 F.R.D. 86, 93–94 (D.N.J. 1986) (district court erred when it concluded that umbrella order shifted burden of proof to plaintiffs).

Particularized Protective Orders

In the absence of an umbrella order, any person from whom discovery is sought may, under Rule 26(c), move for a protective order limiting disclosure of and/or imparting confidentiality to designated information. Protective orders are typically requested to avoid public disclosure of confidential information relating to company trade secrets, manufacturing processes, or other sensitive commercial information.[148] Like umbrella orders, the burden of proof is on the party seeking protection.[149]

"Where a business is the party seeking protection, it will have to show that disclosure would cause significant harm to its competitive and financial position. That showing requires specific demonstrations of fact, supported where possible by affidavits and concrete examples, rather than broad, conclusory allegations of potential harm."[150] Note, however, that a party's interest in preventing disclosure of information that may ultimately be shared with other litigants in other tort claims is not "good cause" for a protective order.[151]

Concepts Applicable to Both

Because public disclosure of discovery material is subject to the discretion of the trial court under Rule 26(c), confidential materials filed in connection with pretrial discovery remain protected so long as "good cause" has been shown.[152] Discovery materials filed in connection with motions like a summary judgment, however, are subject to the common law right of access and may potentially lose confidential status when filed or introduced

---

148. *See, e.g., In re* Eli Lilly & Co., 142 F.R.D. at 459; Deford v. Schmid Prod. Co., Div. of Schmid Labs., Inc., 120 F.R.D. 648, 653 (D. Md. 1987); *see also* Humboldt Baykeeper v. Union Pac. R.R., 244 F.R.D. 560 (N.D. Cal. 2007) (denying developer's motion for protective order to prevent plaintiffs from disclosing results of testing on contaminated site).

149. *See In re* Eli Lilly & Co., 142 F.R.D. at 459–60.

> [A]nalysis of protective orders under Rule 26(c)(7) requires three lines of inquiry. First, is the matter sought to be protected "a trade secret or other confidential research, development, or commercial information" which should be protected? Second, would disclosure of such information cause a cognizable harm sufficient to warrant a protective order? Third, has the party seeking protection shown "good cause" for invoking the court's protection?

> *Id.* at 459 (quoting Zenith Radio Corp. v. Matsushita Elec. Indus. Co., 529 F. Supp. 866, 889 (E.D. Pa. 1981)); *see also Deford*, 120 F.R.D. at 653 (setting forth six factors for determining whether information is a trade secret).

150. *Deford*, 120 F.R.D. at 653 (citing Cipollone v. Liggett Group, Inc., 785 F.2d 1108, 1121 (3d Cir. 1986)) (speculative allegations of injury from the disclosure of years-old information are not sufficient to warrant issuance of a protective order); *see also* Foltz v. State Farm Mut. Auto. Ins. Co., 331 F.3d 1122, 1130 (9th Cir. 2003); Waterkeeper Alliance, Inc. v. Alan & Kristin Hudson Farm, 278 F.R.D. 136, 140 (D. Md. 2011); Tinman v. Blue Cross & Blue Shield, 176 F. Supp. 2d 743, 745 (E.D. Mich. 2001).

151. *See Deford*, 120 F.R.D. at 654 ("sharing discovery materials may be particularly appropriate where multiple individual plaintiffs assert essentially the same alleged wrongs against a national manufacturer of a consumer product").

152. *See* Chicago Tribune Co. v. Bridgestone/Firestone, Inc., 263 F.3d 1304, 1310 (11th Cir. 2001) (citing Seattle Times Co. v. Rhinehart, 467 U.S. 20, 36–37 (1984)) (where discovery materials are concerned, constitutional right of access standard is identical to Rule 26(c) balancing test); Flagg *ex rel.* Bond v. City of Detroit, 268 F.R.D. 279, 293–94 (E.D. Mich. 2010), reconsideration denied (June 24, 2010).

at trial.[153] Courts often give greater scrutiny to materials the parties seek to file "under seal" than simply the exchange of information between parties.

A protective order, whether it be umbrella or particularized, always remains subject to modification by the parties, the court, or as previously mentioned, by intervention of nonparty persons or agencies seeking access to protected information.[154] When information is sought for use in related litigation, "the court should balance the continuing need for protection against the efficacy and judicial economy that may result from release."[155]

Nonparty Rights

While applications for umbrella orders are usually presented to the court by stipulation of the parties,[156] in some cases, particularly in high-profile litigation, nonparties (often the media and/or special interest groups) may intervene in a pending or even settled tort suit for the limited purpose of challenging the stipulated order.[157] In such a situation, which often occurs when parties have filed materials "under seal" in the public record, it is within the discretion of the district court to vacate the umbrella order and permit access by the intervener to certain discovery materials subject to the individualized showing of good cause, just as if a party had made the challenge.[158] The district court must balance the party's interests in keeping information confidential against the contention that disclosure serves the public's legitimate interest.[159]

For a good overview of the issues and a source of additional authorities, see *Estate of Frankl v. Goodyear Tire & Rubber Co.*[160] *Estate of Frankl* involved a tire separation and subsequent automobile accident. The parties entered into an umbrella protective order. The plaintiffs challenged "confidential" designations of certain documents by Goodyear, a challenge that was not resolved by the time the case was settled (at which time the plaintiffs abandoned their challenge). In the meantime, the media and advocacy groups had intervened, arguing that important public safety information was contained in the withheld documents and should be produced to them. The case was decided adversely to

---

153. See *Bridgestone/Firestone*, 263 F.3d at 1311–13; *see also* Leucadia, Inc. v. Applied Extrusion Tech., Inc., 998 F.2d 157, 163–66 (3d Cir. 1993).
154. See *In re "Agent Orange" Prod. Liab. Litig.*, 821 F.2d 139, 147–48 (2d Cir. 1987) ("[T]here is no question that a Rule 26(c) protective order is subject to modification. Whether to lift or modify a protective order is a decision committed to the sound discretion of the trial court."); *In re* Ethylene Propylene Diene Monomer (EPDM) Antitrust Litig., 255 F.R.D. 308, 316–17 (D. Conn. 2009); *In re* Linerboard Antitrust Litig., 333 F. Supp. 2d 333 (E.D. Pa. 2004).
155. Annotated Manual for Complex Litigation (Fourth) § 11.432 (2004) (setting forth considerations to be taken into account by a court when making this determination).
156. *Id.*
157. *See generally* Jessup v. Luther, 277 F.3d 926 (7th Cir. 2006); *Bridgestone/Firestone, Inc.* 263 F.3d 1304; *Leucadia, Inc.*, 998 F.2d 157; *In re EPDM*, 255 F.R.D. 308.
158. See *Bridgestone/Firestone*, 263 F.3d at 1310; *Leucadia, Inc.*, 998 F.2d at 166–67.
159. See *Jessup*, 277 F.3d at 927–28; *Bridgestone/Firestone*, 263 F.3d at 1314–15.
160. 853 A.2d 880 (2004).

the intervenors on the basis of the state court rule that closely followed Federal Rule of Civil Procedure 26(c).

Estate of Frankl raises several interesting points of interest, worth considering when dealing with sensitive documents and protective orders. First, depending upon a state's rule, challenge an umbrella protective order on the basis that the court enter the order without any showing that there is a legal or factual foundation for the protection it is affording to the defendants, albeit a protection the plaintiffs in the case retain a right to challenge. Second, there is the legal question of whether nonparties have any rights, regardless of the balancing of interests, with respect to documents that are not filed in the court record. Third, if the analysis in a particular court progresses to this point, there ultimately is a balancing of the interests of the parties, which *Estate of Frankl* summarizes well.

Some of the arguments for a presumption of public access are as follows: (1) it would advance important societal interests, primarily those of public health, safety, and the administration of public office, which are often not represented by parties in the litigation; (2) it would improve the judicial system's overall efficiency by avoiding duplication of discovery efforts; and (3) it would eliminate the conflicts created by the current system whereby a lawyer must agree to confidentiality for the current client's benefit despite the result that potentially harmful information that would benefit the public will be withheld.[161]

Arguments against a presumption of public access include points that access would: (1) invade the privacy of litigants and nonparties; (2) jeopardize a litigant's right to the exclusive use of private property, including trade secrets and other competitive commercial information; (3) unjustly harm reputation, profitability, and even the viability of socially beneficial ventures; (4) undermine the confidentiality and hence the investment value of important research and development; and (5) limit judicial discretion necessary to advance discovery and litigation generally.

Before such balancing, however, the threshold legal question is whether such nonparties have rights with respect to documents that have not been filed into the court record. That becomes particularly important, from a practical perspective, because of Federal Rule of Civil Procedure 5(d) and similar state court rules, which provide that documents produced in discovery, until they are used in motion or trial practice, may not be filed in the record. In *Estate of Frankl*, the court ultimately ruled that unfiled documents were not subject to any such rights of nonparties, noting the following:

> Despite the academic debate and state-by-state efforts by the Association of Trial Lawyers of America to obliterate the distinction between filed and unfiled documents in discovery, the distinction remains intact across the nation. Furthermore, the 2000 Amendment to Federal Rule of Civil Procedure 5(d), setting forth that discovery must *not* be filed until

---

161. *Id.* at 886.

it is "used in the proceeding," bolsters the distinction between filed and unfiled documents and supports the conclusion that unfiled discovery is not meant to be accessible to nonparties.[162]

This is not likely to be a static area of law. Additional decisions by courts and activity by state legislatures can be anticipated. It is an area to be mindful of when considering protective orders in such litigation.

Analytical Testing and Site Access

As noted abundantly elsewhere, one of the continuing issues in toxic tort litigation is the prevalence and the role of scientific data. Data are evidence and the building blocks of the regulatory framework. The outcome of litigation and the resolution or path to closure of a site under state or federal governmental authority both are tightly linked to, if not controlled by, evidence.[163] In many instances, there may be existing data; issues pertaining to existing data sets are covered elsewhere.[164] Here, we discuss the issues surrounding the collection, analysis, dissemination, protectability, and site access that arise when lawyers in toxic tort cases decide that analytical testing needs to be done.[165]

Data as Evidence

Scientific data assume such a prominent role in toxic tort litigation because without admissible evidence, persuasive to the finder of fact, that describes the environmental condition at issue, there can be no adjudication. Claims for diminution of property value, personal injury, punitive damages, or business loss are all founded upon the judge and jury accepting the plaintiff's or the defendant's views on, for instance, whether the site is contaminated, what is the nature of the contamination, and in many cases, how that contamination came to exist.

Counsel involved in toxic tort litigation will need to make an initial decision on whether to conduct analytical testing at all, and if so, whether to conduct such testing via a consulting expert, which may allow the results and conclusions to remain outside the scope of discovery,[166] or via a testifying expert, whose documents and conclusions will be fully

---

162. *Id.* at 886–87 (citing Arthur Miller, *Confidentiality, Protective Orders, and Public Access to the Courts*, 105 HARV. L. REV. 427 (1991)).
163. For a comprehensive discussion of the evidentiary issues surrounding analytical testing, sampling, and data, see R. Vinal, *Admissibility and Reliability of Laboratory Analysis of Soil, Water and Air Samples in Environmental Litigation*, 24 AM. JUR. 3D *Proof of Facts* 609 (2004), and the cases cited therein.
164. *See infra* section titled "Preservation of Evidence."
165. *See In re* E.I. DuPont De Nemours & Co.—Benlate Litig., 99 F.3d 363 (11th Cir. 1996) (dealing with discovery disputes that arise when a party undertakes analytical testing and is subjected to sanctions for failure to share results of testing).
166. *See* FED. R. CIV. P. 26(b)(3) and (4).

available to all parties.[167] Opportunity and risk affect the distinct roles of testifying and consulting expert—especially if there is any question about site conditions involving groundwater or subsurface soil. For example, a consulting expert could develop opinions with regulatory consequences going beyond the litigation, opinions that may or may not need to be incorporated into testimony.

A consulting expert can be retained by counsel for the client. Such an expert can evaluate data, develop opinions, and provide advice to counsel and client in confidence.[168] This serves to preserve options in the face of uncertainty about site issues (opportunity); however, once the consulting expert has developed information, risk enters the picture. Whether the information is favorable or unfavorable, issues of discoverability, admissibility, and persuasiveness arise.[169] If a testifying expert has been retained, it will not be easy to replace that person with your consulting expert. The court is unlikely to allow two experts in the same discipline to testify on behalf of a party.[170] It may well be that a consulting expert does not possess the tools to testify. Depending upon the jurisdiction, once any of the consulting expert's materials are provided to the testifying expert, all of the consultant's materials may be discoverable and the consultant could be deposed.[171] Further, a testifying expert whose opinions are wholly or partly based upon those of a consulting expert may not be perceived favorably by the jury.

Regardless of the tactical and strategic decisions connected with this process, there are certain fundamentals that must always be followed. First and foremost, analytical testing must be conducted in a scientifically acceptable and rigorous fashion. This is to ensure reliable results, and to maximize counsel's opportunity to get the data admitted as evidence in a case. Regardless of whether the testing is designed to be confidential or discoverable, reputable, reliable, independent environmental consultants must be retained and provided sufficient budget to ensure their work is sound. This same fundamental extends to the choice of an analytical laboratory, and in most cases also means that final analytical data should be validated by a second independent third-party validator to ensure reliability and maximize the chance of admissibility.

---

167. *See* FED. R. CIV. P. 26(a)(2).
168. FED. R. CIV. P. 26(b)(4); *see also* David H. Marion & Christopher Pushaw, *Expert Witnesses: Pitfalls Posed by the Discovery Process*, 3 SEDONA CONF. J. 199 (Fall 2002).
169. For example, under the Federal Rules of Civil Procedure, any facts or data considered by an expert in forming his opinion are not protected from discovery. FED. R. CIV. P. 26(a)(2)(B)(iii). Additionally, regulatory requirements may make certain data public and therefore not protectable.
170. Federal courts commonly issue pretrial orders limiting each side to only one testifying expert in any given field. *See, e.g.*, Riley v. Dow Chem. Co., 123 F.R.D. 639, 640 (N.D. Cal. 1989) (citing Ruud v. United States, 256 F.2d 460 (9th Cir.), *cert. denied*, 358 U.S. 817 (1958)) (noting that it is the usual practice of that court to limit parties to one expert for each discipline, citing as authority FED. R. CIV. P. 16, which gives the court the power to take action at a pretrial conference to avoid unnecessary proof and cumulative evidence).
171. See thorough discussion in Bruce R. Parker, *Pitfalls of Testing Products in Design Defect Actions*, 60 DEF. COUNS. J. 37 (Jan. 1993).

In certain cases, there may not exist an immediately obvious, acceptable analytical methodology for the lab to use because of unique qualities of constituents detected at the site or other problems. When this occurs, it is essential that a competent chemist advise counsel on the most scientifically valid and acceptable methodology. An example would be when a site is impacted by two chemically similar constituents, one of regulatory and toxicological concern, and the other of no such concern (or lesser concern). In seeking to define the "footprint" of contamination at the site, the defendant would benefit from the ability to distinguish between those two compounds (in other words, "speciate them"), because this could allow for a finding that a smaller and shallower area has been contaminated. However, the plaintiff in this circumstance would probably prefer that the finder of fact rely on an unspeciated analysis because this would create a larger footprint, resulting in a more extensive claim and greater remedial cost and other damages. The prudent defense counsel will be very careful in this situation to ensure that any analytical method designed to speciate these compounds can be validly executed by the lab and will yield reliable results. Otherwise, unreliable evidence will be vulnerable to attack by the plaintiffs, will put the defendant's credibility at risk, and will greatly complicate any accompanying regulatory cleanup regime.

Sharing Data

Litigation involving scientific evidence is easier to present to the finder of fact when it is simplified to the maximum extent possible. Nearly all judges and jurors (and many lawyers) have little or no scientific background. The technical nature and jargon connected with scientific data do not, without a great deal of effort, lend themselves to a smooth, streamlined, simple, and persuasive presentation. For these reasons (leaving aside the rare cases where there is an actual viable dispute over the objective physical condition of the soil, groundwater, surface water, or air at issue in the case) both sides in toxic tort litigation should expend the maximum amount of effort to produce a single set of data for presentation to the court. This can only be done if data are shared, samples are split, and analytical results are exchanged. This does not in any sense mean that the parties are not free to dispute vigorously the meaning, significance, impact, or any other relation to the issues that the data may present. Instead, counsel are advised that given the limited time and resources available in almost every court, state or federal, the adjudication of toxic tort cases proceeds much more smoothly when counsel have worked effectively to present a clear picture to the finder of fact of the data in the case.

Often, the judge will sign an order early in the case requiring that analytical testing be carried out only after prior written notice to all parties who are provided the opportunity to attend, observe, and collect split samples.[172] The order may also require that all analyti-

---

172. *See* 2 Michael Dore, Law of Toxic Torts § 22:3 (2004).

cal data be available for exchange between the parties. This is the sort of transparency that tends to simplify issues and to prevent credibility-damaging battles over unavailable data, lost data, distorted data, and unreliable data. The technical foundation for this notion is the fact that in most cases, the environmental condition of a site, including the extent and level of contamination in its groundwater, is an available, objectively demonstrable set of facts rather than a completely nuanced, opinion-based matter. Whether the finder of fact is a judge or a jury, that finder of fact wants to know what the reliable scientific picture is. Asking the finder of fact to choose between competing databases purporting to measure the exact same aquifer, area of soil, or stretch of surface water is counterproductive, inefficient, and inconsistent with the type of effective and forceful presentation required for successful adjudication in toxic tort litigation.

Again, we stress that even in a cooperative environment as discussed above, there are numerous opportunities in toxic tort litigation for motions in limine, *Daubert* attacks, and other adversarial scenarios involving data. However, in nearly every case, counsel will find that the path to persuasion lies through a streamlined, simplified, accurate depiction of the environmental facts.

Site Access

Site access is not always a problem. If the site at issue is already under a state or federal regulatory regime, there may be sufficient data available in a preexisting form to eliminate the need for further analytical testing at all. Where this is not the case, and sampling needs to be done, issues of site access generally turn upon the legal status and ownership of the site for which access is needed. If the defendant owns or controls the site, the plaintiff's access may be gained by agreement or through orthodox discovery measures, such as obtaining an order for entry and inspection.[173] The same is true with regard to the defendant's access to the plaintiff's property. While disputes over access are an unfortunate common feature of toxic tort litigation, ideally there is nothing to be gained by the plaintiff or the defendant unreasonably obstructing or limiting the other side's access to property for analytical testing. Such sampling, and access associated with it, can be subject to variability arising from several sources. If the site is subject to a regulatory proceeding, access issues are likely to be different than if the site is subject only to a private damages claim.

One issue that is a continuing feature of mass tort or class action toxic tort litigation arises when residential or commercial property needs to be sampled. In these circumstances, counsel and their third-party consultants should be aware of state rules prohibiting ex parte communications with a represented party, although the technical rules on contact of represented parties usually require only that such parties not be contacted by the opposing side on matters related to the litigation. It is usually safest to presume that contact

---

173. *See* FED. R. CIV. P. 34.

of any kind with anyone who is or may be represented by counsel should be initiated by contact with that counsel.[174] This is the best way to avoid needless adversarial activities arising from contact with represented parties by consultants, counsel, and/or paralegals.

Analytical testing may lead to obligations to report the results to the state or federal agencies. Whether or not the site at issue is also subject to a parallel regulatory proceeding, the collection and generation of data may trigger reporting obligations under state or federal statutes.[175] If there is a parallel regulatory framework in place, the issue is somewhat more subtle because the regulator will already be aware that the site is contaminated and may in fact have a history with the site stretching back for decades with voluminous existing public record data. This does not mean, however, that analytical testing conducted during toxic tort litigation is not capable of generating a requirement to supplement any existing reporting situation. If new constituents are discovered, if new environmental media are found to be contaminated, if a previously undiscovered groundwater contamination situation is found to have a relationship to surface water, the owner or operator or responsible party of the site at issue needs to evaluate carefully whether reporting obligations have been triggered and how to deal with them. This issue is presented differently when there is no existing parallel regulatory proceeding. If the plaintiff owns or controls the property and has analytical testing conducted on that property for litigation purposes, the data generated from this exercise may well trigger a duty under state or federal law to report the results in a timely fashion and manner to the regulatory bodies. This is the case whether or not the testing is carried out by a confidential consultant working under attorney-client privilege. If a plaintiff provides site access to the defendant's consultants, and the defendant's consultants generate data that may trigger a reporting obligation, the plaintiff may not incur the obligation if the data are not provided to the plaintiff by the defendant's experts. Because the consequences of reporting issues range from the triggering of a parallel regulatory proceeding to civil and criminal penalties for inadequate disclosure or failure to report, these issues must be given careful consideration.

Depositions of Environmental/Public Health Agency Employees

State and federal environmental and public health agencies have jurisdiction over environmental matters, drinking water matters, and other related types of issues, and as such their employees often can be important witnesses in toxic tort cases. Among the host of potential hypothetical examples, some worth mentioning include the following: state police explosive expert who carried out controlled detonation of railroad tank cars involved in multicar, multichemical train derailment; state environmental groundwater administrator

---

174. For discussion of problems that arise when counsel has *ex parte* communications with employees or consultants of the opposing party, *see* Olson v. Snap Prods., Inc., 183 F.R.D. 539 (D. Minn. 1998).
175. For a survey of reporting requirements under the laws of every state as well as under federal law, *see* Morgan, Lewis & Bockius LLP, Environmental Spill Reporting Handbook (2003).

in toxic tort case involving allegation of actual or potential contamination of aquifer used as municipality's sole source of drinking water; and EPA Superfund administrator in case involving multigenerator, multiparty waste site. The public employee's involvement may be direct as in the first example above, may be primarily regulatory and compliance-driven as in the second example given above, or may be a mixture of the two as in the example of the EPA Superfund administrator. In all cases, these public employees will possess information and familiarity with documents that could play a significant role for the plaintiffs and the defendants in toxic tort cases. This section will briefly describe the mechanics of setting up their depositions, and some of the strategy and tactical issues that arise when public employees in these categories are witnesses in toxic tort litigation. As will be seen below, the mechanics and the strategy/tactics often converge.

Although there are some specific rules that govern the role of agency employees in discovery,[176] there is no broad general immunity of federal or state environmental employees from the discovery process. Similarly, with certain limitations, the public records laws make available to any member of the public all of the file documents in the custody of the agency for which the employee works. In some cases, the public agency itself may be a party. State environmental agencies sometimes are sued as defendants to defeat diversity of citizenship jurisdiction or to co-opt the credibility of the agency if the plaintiff believes that the agency's testimony would tend to favor the defendant. In some instances, state agencies may have a statutory right to intervene in private toxic tort litigation.[177] In instances where the agency is a party, the role of its employees in discovery will, of course, differ from the instances where the agency is not a party.

Agency a Party

When the agency is a party litigant, other parties may notice the agency's deposition pursuant to Federal Rule of Civil Procedure 30, which specifically provides for the deposition of a governmental agency. The deposition may be achieved without the necessity of a subpoena. The party need only issue a formal notice that describes with particularity the matters to be covered by the deposition, and the agency is then responsible for designating the proper employees to testify regarding such matters.[178] Because the agency is a party, it is subject to the general discovery rules including sanctions for failure to appear for deposition or to otherwise cooperate in the discovery process.

Agency Not a Party

As a nonparty, an agency is not obligated to respond to a mere notice of deposition. Instead, a subpoena must be served upon the agency pursuant to Rule 45 of the Federal Rules of

---

176. *See infra* section titled "Issues Regarding the Role of Agency Employees in Litigation."
177. *See, e.g.*, La. R.S. 30:2015.1 (2012).
178. *See* Fed. R. Civ. P. 30(b)(6).

Civil Procedure. However, the issuance of a subpoena does not guarantee the agency's cooperation. The agency may successfully challenge the subpoena on a motion to quash.[179] For example, EPA need not comply with requests for voluntary testimony (as a nonparty) unless it determines that the testimony will be in the interests of the agency.[180]

Issues Regarding the Role of Agency Employees in Litigation

The relationship between environmental and public health agencies (state and federal) and private toxic tort litigation is, at best, uneasy. As described elsewhere, the goals and applicable standards of such agencies often differ materially from the agendas of the parties and their counsel in toxic tort litigation. Because this frequently is expressed that state or federal remedial and risk-based cleanup standards are arguably minimalist standards insufficient to address the overall interest of the private property owner or the private person, agencies often find themselves and their work exploited or disparaged in private toxic tort litigation. This, plus the awareness on the part of the agencies and their employees that they are being pulled into a private dispute in which an award of money damages is the ultimate goal, tends to create an atmosphere in which the agency and its employees make an effort to avoid close involvement in toxic tort litigation. Furthermore, state and federal governmental policy typically aims to avoid allowing private parties in toxic tort litigation to obtain "free expert testimony," and there are limitations on the admissibility of the opinions (but not the facts) contained in conclusions reached by many state and federal governmental employees.[181] This is particularly difficult, because in most instances, the testimony of governmental employees will, in terms of its technical content and complexity, often be equivalent to testimony provided by experts retained by the parties. In some jurisdictions, this testimony may come in as "lay opinion giver" testimony.[182]

It is crucial for the practitioner to evaluate how the testimony of the governmental employees will be used in the case at hand. If counsel believes that the finder of fact will give credibility to such testimony and if the testimony appears to be favorable, then obviously counsel will want to give such testimony a role (potentially prominent) in the case. Given the probable discomfort of the agency and its employees with this role, and the fact that participation in private litigation is a considerable imposition upon state or federal governmental employees, counsel is well advised to avoid the tactic of simply issuing deposition subpoenas to such employees. Instead, once it is confirmed that agency employees are not otherwise prohibited from testifying under applicable regulations,

---

179. *See* Dravo Corp. v. Liberty Mut. Ins. Co., Civ. A. No. 95-MC-229-GTV, 1995 WL 519959 (D. Kan. Aug. 21, 1995) (wherein the court granted EPA's motion to quash a deposition subpoena).
180. *See* 40 C.F.R. § 2.401 *et seq.*
181. *See, e.g.*, 5 C.F.R. § 2635.805 (prohibiting federal executive branch employees from testifying as expert witnesses, but not fact witnesses, in federal court litigation in which the United States is a party or has a direct interest).
182. *See, e.g.*, Young v. United States, 181 F.R.D. 344, 346 (W.D. Tex. 1997).

counsel for the agency should be contacted in advance, and much courtesy extended to the agency's employees in scheduling matters and the other attendant mechanics of the depositions. If, on the other hand, counsel sees the agency as an adversary, it may be in the client's interest to treat the agency's employee as a hostile witness, thereby permitting the use of leading questions on direct examination. In some states, where there may be a prevailing view that environmental agencies are not adequately protecting the public from environmental risk, the adversarial use of state employees may be an appropriate tactic for certain parties.

It also is crucial for counsel to realize that testimony of agency employees will be compared against testimony of retained experts. Therefore, it is necessary to carefully assess whether the employee's testimony will be consistent or inconsistent with the testimony of experts. In many instances, depositions of agency employees may lead to the conclusion that it is unnecessary or unwise to call these people as witnesses. Assuming that all the pertinent documents exist and are discoverable, a party's retained expert may do a more effective job of advocating a particular position, without the potentially confounding influence of either a friendly or an adversarial agency employee in the courtroom.

Identifying the Route of Exposure and Modeling Historical Exposure

Toxic tort cases, whether they involve personal injury claims, property damage claims, or both, often involve the issue of exposure. There is tremendous existing literature on the science and the legal issues pertaining to the exposure of human beings and other organisms to environmental contamination.[183] Here, we will summarize these issues in the litigation context.

The fundamental tenets of toxicology are transferable to legal actions. The core toxicology concept, as described by Paracelsus, is that "the dose makes the poison."[184] That ancient phrase is shorthand for the principle that toxic constituents, whether in the soil, water, groundwater, or air, do not present a risk to living things absent a route of exposure through which a toxicologically significant dose can be shown to have occurred. As demonstrated elsewhere, this risk is handled quite differently in a regulatory proceeding than in litigation, where issues of damages rather than issues of site remediation predominate. As is so often the case in this area of practice, the job of the advocate is to develop reliable, persuasive, scientific information that becomes evidence for the finder of fact. There is no way to do this without the services of third-party experts. In most cases, sev-

---

183. For thorough discussion regarding methods of scientific proof in regard to exposure and causation issues, *see* 2–3 MICHAEL DORE, LAW OF TOXIC TORTS ch. 27 (2004).
184. *See In re* Zicam Cold Remedy Mktg., Sales Practices, and Prods. Liab. Litig., 797 F. Supp. 2d 940, 943 (D. Ariz. 2011) (citing Fed. Judicial Ctr., *Reference Manual on Scientific Evidence* at 403 (2d ed. 2000)); *In re* Rezulin Prods. Liab. Litig., 369 F. Supp. 2d 398, 430 (S.D.N.Y. 2005); Nat'l Bank of Commerce v. Dow Chem. Corp., 965 F. Supp. 1490 (E.D. Ark. 1996) (the court relied on the Paracelsus principle that "the dose makes the poison.").

eral disciplines of scientific experts will be required. Practitioners in hydrogeology and related fields will be hired to collect and submit to laboratories for analysis samples of soil, groundwater, surface water, air, and like. Once these data are generated, finalized, and validated, they are submitted to toxicologists and/or medical doctors who will develop opinions upon whether site conditions are such that a complete exposure pathway does or does not exist for particular constituents.

As noted above, these issues are not limited to personal injury cases. While the connection is certainly more direct when people claim that they are ill or fear that they will become ill because of exposure to environmental contamination, the risk posed by such contamination also has a direct connection to issues of property damage, diminution of property, and business losses, because of the potential negative perception that contamination of property creates in the marketplace.[185] Therefore, defense counsel should not rule out being confronted with these issues outside of the personal injury context, nor should the plaintiff's counsel overlook this category of evidence.

Modeling v. Actual Data

Modeling is the art and science of simulating environmental conditions where 100 percent of the actual data required to reach certain conclusions is unavailable.[186] For example, in a groundwater case, the horizontal and vertical boundaries of the contamination may be well understood. Further, the rate of movement in the groundwater and the contaminants in the groundwater with respect to speed and direction may also be well understood. Likewise, the characteristics of the aquifer and its composition may be well understood. However, what may not be known is how long it will take for certain concentrations of constituents to reach areas currently unaffected by the contamination. Similarly, in a case involving an accident such as an industrial release or a railroad derailment, data may exist on the quantities released, the duration of any fires or explosions producing releases to the atmosphere, and the like. However, the fate and transport and concentrations of released constituents to the atmosphere over a period of time may not have actually been measured. In cases such as these, modeling may be used to provide a scientifically reliable predictor of the behavior of these contaminants through time and space.

As in any form of science, the practitioner's goal is to provide the finder of fact with accurate, simple, understandable, and persuasive evidence. Modeling is a highly technical, computer-driven activity, which, unlike the actual collection and laboratory analysis of

---

185. *See, e.g.*, AVX Corp. v. Horry Land Co., 686 F. Supp. 2d 621, 627–28 n.3 (D. S.C. 2010) (identifying jurisdictions that have explicitly or implicitly recognized a right to recover such "stigma damages").
186. *See* discussion of modeling in City of Wichita v. Trs. of APCO Oil Corp Liquidating Trust., 306 F. Supp. 2d 1040, 1106 (D. Kan. 2003); *see also* Abarca v. Franklin Cnty. Water Dist., 761 F. Supp. 2d 1007 (E.D. Cal. 2011).

samples of soil or groundwater, is capable of great subjectivity and variability depending upon the skill of the modeler and the agenda of the people who hire him.[187]

The modeler must use an accepted and correct model for data entry. More than that, however, the modeler must also obtain reliable input data for the model. In the case of an air modeling exercise, the modeler needs to obtain the most accurate meteorological information, the most accurate and complete information about the constituents at issue and the circumstances of their release, whether that evidence includes real-time monitoring data collected at the site, photographic or videographic evidence, or interviews with witnesses. The choices made during the modeling process can produce tremendous variation in the models or results generated by experts hired by the plaintiffs and the defendants. In light of the potential *Daubert* issues, and the practicalities of persuading laypersons that modeling evidence is reliable, we suggest that great care be employed when hiring and managing modelers.

Waste Stream Identification and Reconstruction

Toxic tort cases that involve wastes, as opposed to products, impose particular issues on the practitioner. Essentially, all data-related issues are more complicated when the case involves wastes. That is because it is frequently more difficult to clearly identify waste compounds, to understand what their impact will be on the environment or upon living things, and to rule in or rule out a particular party's involvement (or the magnitude of) a site that contains commingled wastes.[188] For these reasons, the identification and reconstruction of waste streams may assume a prominent role.

Pre- and Postregulatory Scenarios

Prior to RCRA in 1970, there was no uniform, accepted, or mandatory set of standards for the management of waste. As a result, there are many sites in the United States at which industrial wastes have been generated and disposed of with no reference to modern scientific or regulatory standards. Often, the practitioner will need to develop evidence demonstrating to the trier of fact what role each party had with respect to contributions of waste to the particular site, at which the wastes are completely and miscellaneously commingled.

After the enactment of the Resource Conservation and Recovery Act (RCRA) and its state analogs, the existence of a cradle-to-grave system of documentation of responsibility for management of wastes came into being.[189] This means that in the ordinary course of

---

187. *See City of Wichita*, 306 F. Supp. 2d. at 1107 (wherein the court discusses the conflicting conclusions reached by different models).
188. For example, problems posed by commingled waste were faced by courts in United States v. Odabashian, 1999 WL 33944059 (W.D. Tenn. May 18, 1999); United States v. Vertac Chem. Corp., 966 F. Supp. 1491 (E.D. Ark. 1997) and United States v. Atlas Minerals & Chems., 41 ERC 1417 (E.D. Pa. 1995).
189. *See* 42 U.S.C. § 6901 *et seq.*

business, when a chemical waste is generated, it must be managed in a particular way from the point of generation to the point of disposal. A whole series of specialized documents created under environmental regulations is designed to create a paper trail of manifests that, ideally, will allow any member of the public to ascertain exactly the composition, quantity, point of generation, method of transport, and method and place of disposal of waste. This system is a great aid to toxic tort litigation practitioners when the required documentation is present and in order. It is litigation involving older sites that predates the enactment of the modern waste management system that provides the greatest issues and that deserves a more detailed treatment here.

Analytical Data

Analytical data developed from samples will depict what constituents are present, at what levels, and in which media. In certain instances, particular chemicals may be sufficiently unique such that their mere presence will overwhelmingly tie them to a particular entity. However, in most circumstances, a commingled preregulatory waste site will contain a mixture of petroleum hydrocarbons and/or chlorinated solvent-type compounds bearing no particular lineage. When this is the case, the practitioner must reconstruct and identify processes and circumstances at the point of generation of each party's waste in order to determine exposure of that party in the litigation.

This is a forensic process that contains both documentary and human elements. The first step is to review available data showing the chemical composition of the waste at issue. The rest of the process is one of reconstructing the past. Here, counsel needs to identify and interview (or engage in discovery with respect to) present and former employees and other witnesses who may have worked at the plant, driven trucks to the waste site, lived near the waste site, or otherwise come into contact with events that could aid not only in the identification of the waste material, but also in the connection of particular waste material to particular parties. Statements can be taken from present and former employees, regulatory personnel who may be working on a parallel regulatory proceeding at the site, third-party consultants hired in connection with such work, site residents, or any other individual with personal knowledge of facts pertinent to the case.[190] Additionally, numerous forms of documentary evidence may exist to aid in the reconstruction and identification of waste streams. These include engineering log books, purchasing records, process flow diagrams, and annual or quarterly reports.

One of the most useful sources of information for preregulatory sites are the so-called Eckardt reports or other reports generated as a result of the enactment of modern environmental legislation. Under CERCLA, reports were generated by a statutory deadline of

---

190. For discussion of persons and documents with relevant information, *see* 2 MICHAEL DORE, LAW OF TOXIC TORTS ch. 27 (2004).

June 1981 in order to provide EPA with the best available evidence of where companies may have disposed of waste prior to the enactment of modern regulatory statutes.[191] These reports are public record and are available via FOIA[192] and also usually can be found in company records maintained during the normal course of business. The process of generating these reports was an onerous one and usually would have been accompanied by notes, memoranda, and other communications that can shed nearly as much light on the process as the report itself. These documents, as opposed to the public reports, may be confidential, privileged, or no longer in existence.

Another class of documents of particular interest in this type of case might have been generated by local governmental bodies. In many instances, preregulatory commingled waste sites were nothing more than the city, town, or county dump, which, prior to the enactment of modern standards, may have been used for the disposal both of ordinary household garbage and chemical waste. Counsel should attempt to locate, if in existence, the minutes of meetings of local governmental bodies discussing the selection, creation, or operation of dump-sites and the employment of people to run these sites. These minutes potentially can shed a great deal of light on the operation of early sites and therefore can be of aid in the identification and reconstruction of waste streams.

Preservation of Evidence

The preservation of evidence can play a critical role in toxic tort litigation. That role encompasses the actual physical process of preserving evidence, the tactical and strategic choices made during that process, and the legal standards that bear upon this issue. This section will touch upon all three of these facets.

At the outset, it is essential to note that for any practitioner the critical time for meaningful decisions and actions on the preservation of evidence is as soon as possible after the evidence is created or found. A wrong decision may be irrevocable physically, since evidence that is not preserved can cease to exist or, at minimum, may prove to be inadmissible. A wrong decision may expose counsel and client to fatal problems of liability for spoliation of evidence, in addition to a loss of credibility affecting the working relationships between lawyers in a case and the ability of a lawyer to be a persuasive advocate for a client. For this reason, the fundamental core tenet is to be aware of the very early need to deal with evidence preparation issues and be attuned to the opportunities that may be created if your opponent does not share the same concern.

---

191. *See* 42 U.S.C. § 9603(c).
192. 5 U.S.C. § 552.

Examples of Evidence in Toxic Tort Litigation

Toxic tort litigation involves a wide range of potential settings. Evidentiary preservation issues will vary in physical scope and in the nature of their occurrence in a case along with the type of setting involved.

For example, a case arising from alleged contamination of subsurface soil and groundwater of a neighborhood adjoining a chemical manufacturing plant will often involve events that occurred gradually over an extended period of time and often long ago. This type of case may feature documentary evidence in the form of a wide variety of company records ranging from ancient log books to modern environmental memoranda and analyses. It also may involve physical evidence in the form of, for example, soil and groundwater samples that are often collected during the actual pendency of the case. By contrast, a case arising from an accident such as a train derailment will have the documentary and the physical evidence mentioned above, but it will also have another category of physical evidence: railcars, cargo from railcars, and track components. Regardless of the type of case, the need to recognize and successfully manage evidence preservation is the same, even if the actions related to that management will necessarily differ. Also, the goals are always the same: to maximize the opportunity to prosecute or defend your case using high-quality, admissible, persuasive evidence, and to avoid the significant ethical and professional problems connected with being on the wrong side of a spoliation of evidence claim.

Medical examination reports and test results of the plaintiff are another example of evidence. In a typical asbestos exposure case, defense counsel might request that the plaintiff be examined by an independent physician to determine whether, and to what extent, the plaintiff's lungs have been damaged. The examination would include lung x-rays and a pulmonary function test, the results of which might later be introduced into evidence at trial.

Federal Rule of Civil Procedure 35 sets forth the procedure for requesting an independent medical examination (IME) of a plaintiff as follows: "When the mental or physical condition of a party . . . is in controversy, the court in which the action is pending may order the party to submit to a physical or mental examination by a suitably licensed or certified examiner." Rule 35 further provides that a court's order for an IME may be issued "only on motion for good cause shown." The defendant requesting the IME must bear the costs of the examination, while the party being examined usually pays the cost of his own transportation, although some cases have required the defendant to bear costs of transportation.[193] Defendants are generally allowed to choose the medical examiner who will conduct the IME of the plaintiff. However, the plaintiff is not required to accept the defendant's choice of examiner when a valid objection is raised.[194] While most states

---

193. *See* Mark E. Weinstein, *Rights of a Plaintiff When an Independent Medical Examination Is Ordered*, 10 EMP. L. STRATEGIST 1 (Oct. 2002) (wherein the author discusses authority supporting a plaintiff's claim for the defendant to bear the costs of transportation and incidental expenses).
194. WRIGHT, MILLER & MARCUS, *supra* note 118, at 485.

have adopted IME provisions modeled after the federal rule, the state procedural rules do vary and the practitioner must be aware of these differences.[195]

While defendants have no entitlement to an IME of the plaintiff and must make a showing of "good cause," the U.S. Supreme Court has held that in the typical negligence case the plaintiff's pleadings alone are sufficient to constitute good cause. The Court explained that "[a] plaintiff in a negligence action who asserts mental or physical injury . . . places that mental or physical injury clearly in controversy and provides the defendant with good cause for an examination to determine the existence and extent of such asserted injury."[196] It is unclear whether a defendant is entitled to a mental examination of the plaintiff when the complaint alleges fear of future disease.[197]

In determining whether to request an IME, defense counsel must consider the possibility that the medical examiner will reach conclusions that favor the other side. In such a case, plaintiff's counsel may attempt to use the defendant's retained examiner to plaintiff's advantage by calling the expert to testify at trial or introducing into evidence the favorable IME reports.[198]

Spoliation of Evidence

"Spoliation of evidence," generally defined as the negligent or intentional destruction of evidence by a party or its counsel in anticipation of or during the existence of litigation, is to be avoided by all lawyers, staff, and client personnel. The law of spoliation of evidence varies by jurisdiction when it comes to the details, but in every state, spoliation of evidence is an offense that can lead to professional sanctions and the inability to introduce evidence needed in a case. In federal courts, the law of spoliation comes within the rubric of discovery sanctions pursuant to Federal Rule of Civil Procedure 37(b)(2), which can be very detrimental.[199]

For these reasons, it is essential that at the moment litigation is reasonably anticipated, a defense attorney must effectively advise his client that all paper and electronic documents

---

195. *Id.* at 467.
196. Schlagenhauf v. Holder, 379 U.S. 104, 119 (1964).
197. In an automobile accident case, one court granted the defendant's request for a psychiatric IME based on the plaintiff's allegation that he suffered "excruciating and agonizing aches, pains, mental anguish, suffering, emotional distress, humiliation, [and] inconvenience." Womack v. Stevens Transp., Inc., 205 F.R.D. 445, 447 (E.D. Pa. 2001).
198. *See* Jay P. Mayesh, et al., *Can Your Opponent Take Advantage of Your Independent Medical Examiner?*, Prod. Liab. L. & Strategy 19 (2), 1 (Aug. 2000).
199. *See* Shepherd v. Am. Broadcasting Cos. Inc., 62 F.3d 1469, 1476 (D.C. Cir. 1995) (the court has the inherent power to sanction a party that destroys relevant and discoverable evidence); Dillon v. Nissan Motor Co., Ltd., 986 F.2d 263, 268 (8th Cir. 1993) (the decision to impose sanctions, as well as the appropriate sanction to be fashioned, lies within the sound discretion of the trial court); Victor Stanley, Inc. v. Creative Pipe, Inc., 269 F.R.D. 497, 540–41 (D. Md. 2010) (ordering defendant to serve two years in jail unless and until he paid plaintiff's attorneys' fees and costs incurred in filing motion and proving defendant's spoliation efforts); Shaffer v. RWP Group, 169 F.R.D. 19 (E.D.N.Y. 1996) (party's destruction of relevant evidence warranted an adverse inference jury instruction at trial).

bearing any palpable relationship to the subject matter of the anticipated or pending litigation must be preserved until further notice. This might mean that company-standard document destruction polices must be overridden. Such steps often are cumbersome, at best, and the cause of questions and even hostility, at worst, to a client. Counsel needs to be prepared not simply to mandate preservation, but also he must be prepared to explain to the key personnel why the process is necessary, and be prepared with an organized system to assist in the process.

It is not sufficient to allow original documents to be destroyed and copies to be made and retained. The originals must be kept. In cases where there is physical evidence, spoliation is avoided by promptly and securely segregating that evidence. For example, in the train derailment case mentioned above, it may be necessary to set aside a sizeable area (fenced and environmentally secure) within which to store, for a lengthy period of time, railcars, railcar components, and track components. If the case involves third-party contractors such as analytical laboratories, these entities must also be instructed to keep all paper and electronic documents, along with all existing samples, even if doing so causes samples to be kept past their retention time.

The practitioner must be aware of the unique and evolving issues surrounding electronic data discovery and preservation.[200] Electronic data are discoverable, regardless of the form in which they are stored, as long as deemed relevant.[201] Federal Rule of Civil Procedure 34 specifically includes "electronic data compilations" as discoverable. Litigants must demonstrate good faith efforts to identify discoverable electronic data and inform the other party when data are available for production in electronic form.[202] A party's failure to fully investigate the existence of such data and make proper disclosures during the discovery phase of litigation can result in harsh sanctions.[203]

As to content, electronic data include e-mails, instant messaging, word processing files, and computer databases. Storage devices may include hard drives, networks, backup tapes,

---

200. For thorough treatment of electronic data problems and issues encountered in discovery, see *Ten Tips for Electronic Discovery [A Special Interview with Judge Shira A. Scheindlin]*, ACC DOCKET 23 (1) 56 (Jan. 2005) and Virginia Llewellyn, *Electronic Discovery Best Practices*, 10 RICH. J.L. & TECH. 19 (2004).
201. FED. R. CIV. P. 16(b)(3)(B)(iii) (requiring district court to issue scheduling order that provides for disclosure or discovery of electronically stored information); FED. R. CIV. P. 26(a)(1(A)(ii) (requiring parties to include within their initial disclosures a copy or description of all electronically stored information that may be used to support a party's claims or defenses); FED. R. CIV. P. 34 (providing for production of electronically stored information).
202. FED. R. CIV. P. 16(b)(3)(B)(iii); *Electronic Discovery Best Practices*, *supra* note 200.
203. *See, e.g., In re* Delta/AirTran Baggage Fee Antitrust Litig., 846 F. Supp. 2d 1335 (N.D. Ga. 2012); Nacco Materials Handling Group, Inc. v. Lilly Co., 278 F.R.D. 395 (W.D. Tenn. 2011); Rimkus Consulting Group, Inc. v. Cammarata, 688 F. Supp. 2d 598 (S.D. Tex. 2010); *In re* NTL, Inc. Sec. Litig., 244 F.R.D. 179 (S.D.N.Y. 2007). *But see* FED. R. CIV. P. 37(e) (providing that sanctions may not be imposed for failing to produce electronically stored information lost as a result of routine, good-faith operation of an electronic information system). For more on sanctions for spoliation of electronic information, see T. McKee, *Avoiding the Scarlet "S": Attorneys Must Be Proactive to Avoid Sanctions for Spoliation of Electronic Evidence*, TRIAL ADVOC. Q. 30 (1), 9 (Winter 2011).

laptops, disks, and optical disks. Once litigation has commenced or is anticipated, the duty to preserve all relevant electronic data attaches and the party must take affirmative steps to preserve potential electronic evidence that might otherwise be destroyed in the usual course of business. According to the federal court in *Zubulake v. UBS Warburg, LLC*, a party's preservation obligation may extend even to backup tapes as follows:

> Once a party reasonably anticipates litigation, it must suspend its routine document retention/destruction policy and put in place a litigation hold to ensure the preservation of relevant documents. As a general rule, that litigation hold does not apply to inaccessible backup tapes, for example, typically maintained solely for the purpose of disaster recovery, which may continue to be recycled on the schedule set forth in the company's policy. On the other hand, if the backup tapes are accessible, namely they are actively used for information retrieval, then such tapes would likely be subject to the litigation hold. However . . . if a company can identify where particular employee documents are stored on backup tapes, then the tapes storing the documents of key players to the existing or threatened litigation should be preserved if the information contained on those tapes is not otherwise available. This exception applies to all backup tapes.[204]

Failure to properly preserve can result in a spoliation claim and justify a negative inference instruction.[205] In all cases, a detailed record of the steps taken to preserve evidence must be kept. This will serve both to organize the database of evidence and to provide an antidote to any later claims (which often will follow a Federal Rule of Civil Procedure 30(b)(6) corporate deposition) that evidence was not preserved. Additionally, such a record will help in the compilation of a privilege log.[206]

---

204. 220 F.R.D. 212, 218 (S.D.N.Y. 2003).
205. *See* Talavera v. Shah, 638 F.3d 303, 311 (D.C. Cir. 2011); Levy v. Remington Arms Co., 836 F.2d 1104 (8th Cir. 1988).
206. This subject is ubiquitous in the literature, and the law is developing at a fast pace. *See* Thomas Allman, *Conducting E-Discovery after the Amendments: The Second Wave*, 10 SEDONA CONF. J. 215 (2009); Thomas Allman, *The "Two-Tiered" Approach to E-Discovery: Has Rule 26(b)(2)(b) Fulfilled Its Promise?*, 14 RICH. J.L. & TECH. 7 (2008); Hon. John M. Facciola et al., *Sanctions in Electronic Discovery Cases: Views from the Judges*, 78 FORDHAM L. REV. 1 (2009); David K. Isom, *Electronic Discovery Primer for Judges*, 2005 FED. CTS. L. REV. 1 (2005); Michael R. Nelson & Mark H. Rosenberg, *Duty Everlasting: The Perils of Applying Traditional Doctrines of Spoliation to Electronic Discovery*, 12 RICH. J. L. & TECH. 14 (2006); Mafe Rajul, "*I Didn't Know My Client Wasn't Complying!" The Heightened Obligation Lawyers Have to Ensure Clients Follow Court Orders in Litigation Matters*, 2 SHIDLER J. L. COM. & TECH. 9 (2005); Douglas L. Rogers, *A Search for Balance in the Discovery of ESI since December 1, 2006*, 14 RICH. J.L. & TECH. 8 (2008); Lloyd S. van Oostenrijk, *Paper or Plastic? Electronic Discovery and Spoliation in the Digital Age*, 42 HOUS. L. REV. 1163 (2005); Burke T. Ward, et al., *Electronic Discovery: Rules for a Digital Age*, 18 B.U. J. SCI. & TECH. L. 150 (2012).

Court Orders to Preserve Evidence and for Splitting of Samples

It is common in toxic tort litigation for a court, either on its own motion or by a party, to issue an order specifically requiring the preservation of evidence.[207] An order of this type, in a case that involves sampling and the generation of analytical data, often will also require any samples collected to be offered for splitting amongst the parties, and for any sampling exercises to be announced ahead of time so that any party who so wishes can attend and observe the activities. The splitting of samples requires the professionals collecting the samples to be told ahead of time of the circumstances so that sufficient quantities of sample are taken to allow for division amongst the parties and so that all who wish to obtain splits have the appropriate sample containers and means to transport the sample to their retained analytical laboratory.

Certain types of samples, such as the bodies of animals, for one, are much harder to split than would be, for example, a soil sample. Cooperation between the parties and their third-party contractors is a necessity.

Evidence Preservation and Advocacy

Toxic tort litigation involves the difficult process of turning data into evidence. Expert testimony plays a significant role, and the underlying goal of the lawyers, which is to persuade the fact finder that their positions have merit, always will turn on whether the fact finder understands and accepts how the evidence relates to the claims and defenses in the case. This states the obvious, but usefully so, because the preservation of evidence is key to the process. On one level, evidence that does not exist or that is inadmissible is a problem. On another level, the credibility of a party is never enhanced if the judge and jury suspect or know that documents, samples, or other things were mishandled, lost, or kept out of the effective reach of a party to a case (leaving aside the potential penalties for spoliation).

Coordination with Parallel Regulatory Proceedings

Representing clients in environmental matters frequently involves both regulatory and litigation issues. No rules expressly control what happens when regulatory and litigation interests meet at the same site. Site investigation and remediation are law- and regulation-based iterative processes, executed by the client, directed by counsel and specialized consultants, and involving technical subcontractors such as laboratories.[208] Oversight is

---

207. *See* Capricorn Power Co., Inc. v. Siemens Westinghouse Power Corp., 220 F.R.D. 429 (W.D. Pa. 2004) (wherein the court discussed at length factors to be considered in deciding whether to issue order to preserve documents, things, and land).
208. *See, e.g.*, Louisiana Risk Evaluation and Corrective Action Program (RECAP) adopted by the state Department of Environmental Quality pursuant to statutory authority and LA. ADMIN. CODE tit. 33, part XI, §1307, *available at* http://www.deq.louisiana.gov/portal/DIVISIONS/UndergroundStorageTank-andRemediationDivision/RemediationServices/RECAP.aspx (last visited Oct. 9, 2012).

by state or federal regulatory personnel. The work is public and the goal is cleanup.[209] The design and execution of a remedial plan is generally an exercise in consensus building. Usually (and this is the source of critical divergence between cleanup and tort defense), the work is centered on the site of the release and the area of immediate impact.

In tort litigation, the audience is different and the client's goals likely differ. The case will include both the area subject to the cleanup and points well beyond. This arena is adversarial—a win-or-lose effort, not investigation or remediation. While counsel, consultants, and subcontractors may remain the same, the tort audience includes lay juries lacking technical training and/or judges, many of whom are elected officials. The involvement of insurance for cleanup, tort liability, or defense costs can further complicate the management of the litigation defense.

While the particular circumstances of a hazardous substance release and the resulting response will vary, the typical focus of the regulator and the responsible party is the source of the release and the area measurably (regarding applicable risk-based standards) impacted by the release. It is rare—but not unheard of, particularly in the Superfund context—for a site cleanup and any accompanying risk assessments to extend over a significant geographic area. This is a consequence of ordinary practicality and the recognition under risk-based closure regulation that in most instances it is infeasible and unnecessary to delineate and remove every last molecule of a release from the environment.[210]

In the investigatory/remedial arena, there are substantial practical limitations on attorney-client privilege and work-product protection.[211] Counsel, consultants, subcontractors, and the client should recognize that most factual information and data will be public record. Regulators will not allow litigation considerations (such as the party's desire for privacy) to interfere with the administration of a cleanup. Despite this, a crucial tenet in the investigation/remediation arena is: Do not allow the litigation to affect the science applied to the cleanup.

On the tort litigation side, the corollary is: Do not let the science inhibit your ability to be an advocate. The government is not the audience. Rather, the audience has several facets. First are the claimants and their lawyers. Their goal is to maximize recovery. A second constituency comprises state or federal judges and juries. Many have little technical background.[212]

---

209. *See* Louisiana Const., Art. 9, § 1; James G. Wilkins & Michael Wascom, *The Public Trust Doctrine in Louisiana*, 52 LA. L. REV. 861 (1992).
210. *See* closure requirements under Louisiana RECAP standards, *supra* note 176.
211. *See* Vermont Gas Sys. v. U.S. Fid. & Guar. Co., 151 F.R.D. 268 (D. Vt. 1993) and other cases cited *supra* "Environmental Audits."
212. Some federal courts allow for "blue-ribbon jury venire" comprising, for example, only persons who have attained high school diploma or higher. *See, e.g.*, DEL. CODE ANN. tit. 10, § 4506 (2012) (providing for a "special jury" in a complex civil case upon the application of any party); *In re* Richardson-Merrell "Bendectin" Prods. Liab. Litig., 624 F. Supp. 1212 (S.D. Ohio 1985), *aff'd sub nom. In re* Bendectin Litig., 857 F.2d 290 (6th Cir. 1988) (judge offered to impanel a jury only of individuals knowledgeable in the

Tort-law standards, governing when and how much the plaintiffs can recover, are totally different from the risk-based corrective action standards applicable to cleanups. For example, while the state may be willing to issue a no further action letter when contaminants remain in the soil and groundwater at levels deemed to represent no threat under risk-based health standards, this same scenario can remain a threat for a tort defendant.[213] Plaintiffs may still pursue claims on any level of contaminants, even one-molecule. As such, defense counsel must create and manage a body of evidence that allows for the defense against claims, many of which are utterly unscientific. Privilege and work-product protection must be maintained to the extent possible despite the fact that the factual substrate of the case will be public record.

Earlier, we noted that investigation and remediation work usually occurs within a geographic scope related to, and limited by, scientifically significant impacts to the environment. In tort litigation, particularly when the case is a class action or multiparty case, the opposite is true. Here, the geographic focus may include many square miles. Claims will include personal injury and property damage arising from the alleged or actual presence of unknown, often unnamed compounds thought to result from the combustion or the breakdown of chlorinated compounds in soil and groundwater. These compounds have risk exposure implications, are persistent in the environment, and are often difficult to assess and remediate. When the case involves fires and explosions, claims will involve the physical effects of the deposition via air of dust and soot containing PAHs (polycyclic aromatic hydrocarbons), semi-volatile compounds, dioxins, and furans. Some of these classes of compounds are the source of risk, many are not, especially at the concentrations likely to occur miles from a release. At the same time, these compounds are ubiquitous in modern society and every house, yard, and garden is likely to contain them at some level, even in the absence of a recognized release.[214]

One legitimate goal of site cleanup is to perform a cost-effective remediation, which may mean meeting the minimum regulatory standards as quickly as possible. Tort litigation often renders that goal infeasible or unwise. A defendant may deem it necessary to oversample and overanalyze in order to develop a defensible record. When insurance is involved, tasks and costs that go beyond the regulatory minimums may raise questions from the insurers.

In cases involving claims of long-term exposure on private property, a reliable way to address whether the area at issue is "safe" is to conduct a background study.[215] This

---

field or with the highest levels of education, but noted that such an offer was separate and apart from the rules of the United States District Courts and the local court); *see also* discussion in *Developments in the Law: Confronting the New Challenges of Scientific Evidence*, 108 HARV. L. REV. 1481, 1583 (1995).
213. *See, e.g.*, Magnolia Coal Terminal v. Phillips Oil Co., 576 So. 2d 475 (La. 1991).
214. *See, e.g.*, Carroll v. Litton Sys., No. B-C-88-253, 1990 WL 312969 at *35–36 (W.D. N.C. Oct. 29, 1990).
215. For case involving a "background study," *see* Eagle-Pitcher Indus. v. U.S. EPA, 822 F.2d 132 (D.C. Cir. 1987).

requires sampling at a number of locations similar to the one at issue (but unimpacted by the incident) for the constituents of concern. The average juror or judge may not realize that no house, business, or property is "non-detect" for PAHs, dioxin furans, semi-volatiles, and other hazardous chemicals. Therefore, he or she may be reluctant to accept the argument that there is no risk, even when provided with accurate data, if the result is anything above "non-detect." However, if it can be shown that an unimpacted area also has chemicals present in concentrations not significantly different from the area at issue, and if it is explained why certain compounds are ubiquitous, a persuasive argument can be made, but the cost can be substantial, and the methodology and conclusions will likely be attacked by opposing counsel. Counsel should be prepared to guide the client through the cost-benefit analysis on the need for background testing.

Information Management

Site investigation/remediation following appropriate scientific and agency procedures is always the standard. Even when a site is the subject of tort litigation, consultants should be retained to design and implement a remedy that protects human health and the environment under applicable regulatory standards. Although remediation consultants may prefer not to be bothered by litigation considerations, the fact is that the substantial interface with the litigation arena must be addressed. Consultants must be prepared in a specific manner when there is tort litigation arising from circumstances at the site. All subcontractors working with consultants, particularly laboratories, must also understand that litigation is involved. The managerial personnel at consulting firms and the laboratories should be furnished with copies of primary pleadings, and face-to-face contact should assure they understand the basics about the parties and the issues.

Further, whether or not required by state or federal regulators, all laboratory data should be "validated."[216] Data validation is a process in which laboratory procedures and data are reviewed to ensure that the data are supportable; that is, the data can be used for their intended purpose. Validation confirms that the procedures used meet the criteria established by the laboratory method, by EPA, and by any pertinent work plans. Whether performed internally at the laboratory or by third parties, validation is expensive.

Consultants and subcontractors must be prepared for press contacts and for discovery.[217] These people will be subpoenaed as witnesses for deposition and/or trial. Corporate deposition and document subpoenas will be served upon the companies involved in the cleanup. To that end, it is essential that all documents generated are captured, reviewed, and preserved for each consultant and lab used. Consultants and subcontractors must be trained to minimize the generation of undisciplined and unprotectable memoranda, field

---

216. See Vinal, *supra* note 163, and the cases cited therein.
217. For general discussion of this subject area, *see* 2 MICHAEL DORE, LAW OF TOXIC TORTS, chs. 16, 23, and 24 (2004).

book entries, diary and calendar entries, and e-mails. This is particularly difficult in the early stages of an investigation or immediately after an accident. Areas of disagreement among consultant personnel, regulators, and the client can generate harmful documents to be exploited in litigation. If an insurance company is being asked to pay for the environmental work, documents such as invoices, chains-of-custody, logbooks, and manifests must be well organized from the outset, or reimbursement problems will occur.

Finally, remediation consultants must be prepared to work constructively with testifying expert witnesses. Some of these experts will be in the same disciplines as the cleanup consultants and others (such as air modelers) may not be, but all will need access to the people and the documents involved at the cleanup level in order to render their opinions. This is another area where parochial self-protection is counterproductive. There must be open communication in order to assess the true strengths and weaknesses in the client's position in the litigation.

Tort liability is not necessarily determined by regulatory standards. Frequently, winning or losing a tort case is unrelated to standard science. Defense of tort claims may require going well beyond regulatory minimums. As noted, a background study may be needed. Because so much of the work that is done during investigation and remediation is not protectable, one must retain consulting experts for privileged technical work, in addition to testifying experts.[218]

Issues of admissibility and scientific validity are key.[219] Junk science must be challenged, and counsel must be able to defend its expert opinions against attack by the plaintiffs. In technical cases, some federal courts will use "blue-ribbon" juries comprising people with at least a high school education.[220] However, in most instances, the jury will consist of a cross-section of the lay public. They may be unfamiliar with environmental science, toxicology, air modeling, and the other disciplines that find their way into tort litigation.

A prudent step under these circumstances is to hire a data quality testifying expert. This is a specialist (usually a chemist) who provides opinions on the technical and scientific validity of all of the data in the case. Such an individual should be equally hard on defense data as on that of the plaintiffs. This adds to the need for care in the selection of laboratories and other subcontractors. When laboratories are asked to handle a large volume of data quickly and when they are asked to conduct analyses of compounds or combinations of compounds for which no standard methods are available, problems can arise, ranging from substandard documentation to erroneous results to vulnerability under the principles of *Daubert*.

---

218. *See* FED. R. CIV. P. 26(b)(3) and (4)(B). However, even when an expert has been retained, the facts or data considered by the expert in forming his opinion are not protected. *See* FED. R. CIV. P. 26(a)(2)(B) and (C).
219. *See* A. Dallas Wait, *Environmental Forensic Chemistry and Sound Science in the Courtroom*, 12 FORDHAM ENVTL. L.J. 293 (2001).
220. Regarding "blue-ribbon" jury, *see supra* note 212.

The eventual use of data as evidence illuminates the essential dichotomy of the regulatory/remediation-litigation relationship. In a remediation, there is a benefit in keeping sampling/testing to a minimum and sharing all the resulting data with the audience. The regulatory audience has the expertise to evaluate the data. Litigation turns this "formula" on its head. In litigation there may be a benefit in oversampling and overtesting, in that extensive sampling is helpful to establish backgrounds, to counter arguments that testing was insufficient and selective, and to validate data. While all this information is subject to discovery, it would be unwise to present this mass of data to the ultimate audience—the judge and/or jury. The data must be carefully prepared and only a minimal amount of highly relevant data will become evidence at trial.

Another potential point of divergence between remediation and litigation is in the area of insurance coverage. Particularly in a catastrophic accident scenario, the involvement of one or more insurers introduces yet another "master" with a legitimate interest in the response to the accident and in the amount of money spent on remediation.[221]

Counsel should also be aware that the costs of remediation may ultimately be paid out of several different pockets. For example, damages to the client's own equipment and property may be covered by one policy, while damages to other property may be covered by another policy or by different terms of the same policy. The different policies may have different coverages, deductibles, and exclusions.[222]

A party conducting site investigation and cleanup must meet all technical requirements, satisfy the state and federal government, meet budget considerations, and protect human health and environment while investigating and remediating a site. At the same time, a body of evidence is created that may be used in tort claims. In contrast to remedial activities, litigated claims will be presented to an audience that is not technical. The claims may not be scientifically grounded. There are many phases in this process. Most have narrowly focused responsibilities—thin slices in the two arenas. Only a few people will have responsibility for both arenas. Environmental counsel often find themselves with this dual responsibility and should be prepared to deal with the issues inherent in the intersection.

Case Management and Case Management Orders

A comprehensive case management order (CMO) is critical to the effective management and satisfactory disposition of toxic tort cases.[223] CMOs govern areas of case administra-

---

221. For a thorough discussion of the role of insurance in toxic tort litigation, see 4 MICHAEL DORE, LAW OF TOXIC TORTS ch. 31 (2004) and numerous cases cited therein.
222. See id. § 31:23–31:64.
223. Indeed, the opening sentence in the current version of the *Manual for Complex Litigation* reads: "Fair and efficient resolution of complex litigation requires at least that (1) the court exercise early and effective supervision (and, where necessary, control); (2) counsel act cooperatively and professionally; and (3) the judge and counsel collaborate to develop and carry out a comprehensive plan for the conduct of pre-trial and trial proceedings." MANUAL FOR COMPLEX LITIGATION (FOURTH) § 10. For an overview on this area and why CMOs are important, *see* Joseph F. Madonia & Anthony G. Hopp, *Case Management*

tion (lead counsel and committees, fee and cost issues for plaintiffs' counsel, mechanics of filings, electronic communications, and similar matters), discovery and motions (sequencing, document management, stays relative to some aspects while moving forward with others, and the all-important gatekeeper process—the *Daubert* issues—relative to experts), and disposition (bellwether trials, bifurcation, reverse bifurcation, trifurcation, and other techniques). Though there certainly are single-plaintiff toxic tort cases, most—and those addressed here—involve many plaintiffs and oftentimes several defendants. Cases involving multiple parties, complicated discovery, numerous experts, and high stakes cannot proceed to disposition without effective case management. Indeed, it is common for a CMO to be put in place early in a case, followed by multiple revisions over the life of the case, generally in sequentially numbered CMOs, as the issues and needs of the case come more sharply into focus and change.[224]

The courts have continued to refine the management techniques that are memorialized in CMOs, hence many good examples are available.[225] But notwithstanding years of developed experience with CMOs, it remains true that effective CMOs must be tailored on a case-by-case basis. Accordingly, every party is advantaged by putting considerable thought and effort into how the initial CMO and any amendments are written.

Federal Rule of Civil Procedure 16(c)(12) provides the court with authority to require "special procedures for managing potentially difficult or protracted actions that may involve complex issues, multiple parties, difficult legal questions or unusual proof problems."[226] Most states have adopted some procedural authority or approaches to allow trial judges to meaningfully exercise their inherent authority to control litigation, including the formulation of CMOs.

This topic is too broad to address in mere summary fashion here. However, one particularly good source to turn to is the *Manual for Complex Litigation*.[227] A second strong

---

Techniques in Complex Tort Litigation, NAT. RESOURCES & ENV'T 238 (Spring 2003). And, for a recent overview on this topic, set in the context of a good overview discussion of toxic tort litigation, *see* Rudlin & Graham, *supra* note 32.

224. *See* MANUAL FOR COMPLEX LITIGATION (FOURTH) § 22.63, addressing the variety of issues that oftentimes require such supplemental or amended CMOs, including adding parties, issues with respect to pleadings and motions, deferred docketing (used in long latency exposure cases), issue identification and development, and electronic communications issues.

225. Twenty years of experience in the courts have led to a considerable reservoir of knowledge on the topic. In 1986 Francis E. McGovern, early a recognized authority on the topic, wrote: "The managerial horse is out of the judicial barn. Federal Judicial Center and National Judicial College Programs, the Federal Rules of Civil Procedure, and the *Manual for Complex Litigation, Second* illustrate the significant commitment made by academics and leaders of the judiciary in encouraging judges to become more active litigation managers." Francis E. McGovern, *Toward a Functional Approach for Managing Complex Litigation*, 53 U. CHI. L. REV. 440 (1986).

226. FED. R. CIV. P. 16(c)(2)(L); *see also* FED. R. CIV. P. 16, 26, 37, 42, and 83 for additional relevant authority.

227. *See also* Ronald J. Hedges, *Latest Developments in Complex Civil Litigation: An Analysis of the Federal Judicial Center's New Manual for Complex Litigation, Fourth*, ALI-ABA Course of Study (Dec. 11–13, 2003), sponsored with the cooperation of the Federal Judicial Center, SJ070 ALI-ABA 1. Additionally, though focused on insurance coverage disputes, for some good thoughts on what the issues will be and

source of useful discussion and authorities on this topic can be found in D. Alan Rudlin, et al., *Environmental and Toxic Tort Matters: Updates and Trends, Case Management and Health Claims in Toxic Tort Litigation*.[228]

Every lawyer and judge in such circumstances is in search of good examples of what has been done in other cases. One good resource to look to in that regard is *Manual for Complex Litigation, Fourth*, § 40. It not only contains a series of forms, but it also directs the reader to two other valuable sources of additional information, namely (1) other compilations of such forms and (2) various Internet sites created for complex cases, which include their CMOs.[229]

The first aspect of any CMO is to get the lawyers, the court, and the clerk of court organized. Though this certainly sounds like mundane activity, over the life of a case it can be of great significance. Often times, such cases are characterized by substantial volumes of paper, the potential for contentious interaction between lawyers, substantial sums of money being at issue in terms of fees, and an ongoing need to bring matters, both large and small, to the court for resolution in an orderly and streamlined fashion. A CMO can address much of that activity and can be tailored to the particulars of a case.

Organizing the lawyers is a critical first step. Typically, courts and counsel agree on drawing the large groupings of both plaintiff and defense lawyers into more manageable situations. The techniques include using "liaison counsel" (principally tasked with administrative coordination amongst the lawyers on either side), "lead counsel" (tasked with taking the lead for either side on substantive topics), "trial counsel" (principal trial lead for either side), and "committees of counsel" (covering specific topics involved in particular cases, commonly under the coordination of liaison or lead counsel). The CMO will set forth the powers and responsibilities of such lawyers. In establishing such responsibility for some of the lawyers, the court typically will also take into account how those lawyers should be compensated with regard to such activities for the common benefit and how they must keep records concerning time and costs.[230]

Important to the effective management of cases today are issues related to the electronic transmission of information. That can run the gamut from such simple things as required communications amongst counsel on scheduling matters to filings, service, and even the required establishment of Web sites for particularly complex multiparty matters.[231]

---

some sample language, *see* Patricia B. Santelle & Michael E. DiFebbo, *Use of Case Management Orders to Shape the Case for Resolution*, Practicing Law Institute, Litigation and Administrative Practice Course Handbook Series (Feb. 17–18, 2004), 702 PLI/Lit 143.

228. 11th Annual Advanced ALI-ABA Course of Study (March 27–28, 2008), SN082 ALIABA 25, see particularly § II(B).
229. *See* Manual for Complex Litigation (Fourth) § 40, at 727–29.
230. *See id.* §§ 10.22, 14.215, and 14.216.
231. *See id.* § 22635.

Next come sections regarding discovery and motions. Controlling the conduct of discovery and motion practice is central to any effective CMO. The issues include:

- scheduling;
- protective orders;
- mechanisms for dispute resolution;
- document management (including document repositories);
- depositions and the manner in which they are conducted;
- specific limitations on the use of interrogatories;
- required stipulations;
- stays with regard to some aspects of a case while other aspects proceed forward; and
- conduct of the entire gatekeeper process from the furnishing of expert reports to the court's rulings on admissibility.

There are many potential variations in how each of these topics can be regulated in a CMO. In many respects, a CMO governs how the lawyers conduct their daily lives in such cases for months and years. And many cases are settled before they get much beyond the discovery stage, making it particularly important.

One important aspect of the discovery and motion process is the elimination of unmeritorious claims. If a case is ultimately tried to conclusion, such elimination has obvious benefits. But more often its real use is in laying the groundwork for settlement. Weeding out the unmeritorious claims oftentimes facilitates that process. One mechanism for accomplishing this is the "*Lone Pine*" order,[232] whether standing alone as a form of CMO or incorporated within a broader CMO. The *Lone Pine* order requires that the plaintiffs establish a prima facie case with regard to causation and damages before allowing the case to go forward at all.[233] This device is particularly useful in cases involving many plaintiffs and only vague allegations as to product identification, causation, and damages on an individual basis. In *Acuna v. Brown and Root, Inc.*, the court was dealing with approximately 1,600 plaintiffs suing more than 100 defendants.[234] The *Lone Pine* order in that case required the plaintiffs to supplement vague allegations in their complaints with affidavits containing specifics. Those that failed to furnish the specifics had their cases dismissed. The court stated: "In the federal courts, such orders are issued under the

---

232. Lore v. Lone Pine, Inc., No. L-33606-85, 1986 WL 637507 (N.J. Super. Ct. Nov. 18, 1986).
233. Whether precisely following the *Lone Pine* model or proceeding to consider the same issue concerning the merits of the claims, courts have fashioned means to weed out unmeritorious claims. *See, e.g.*, Renaud v. Martin Marietta Corp., 749 F. Supp. 1545 (D. Colo. 1990), *aff'd*, 972 F.2d 304 (10th Cir. 1992); Grant v. E.I. DuPont de Nemours and Co., Civ. A. No. 91-55-CIV-4H, 1993 WL 146634 (E.D.N.C. 1993); Able Supply Co. v. Moye, 898 S.W.2d 766 (Tex. 1995); Hannan v. Pest Control Servs., 734 N.E.2d 674 (Ind. Ct. App. 2000) (a dismissal on summary judgment of inadequate scientific evidence).
234. 200 F.3d 335, 340 (5th Cir. 2000).

wide discretion afforded district judges over the management of discovery under Fed. R. Civ. P. 16."[235] The court, denying the plaintiffs' claim that the *Lone Pine* order imposed too high a burden for the early stages of litigation, held that the order merely "required that information which plaintiffs should have had before filing their claims pursuant to Federal Rule of Civil Procedure 11(b)(3)."[236] A similar argument might be made based upon Federal Rule of Civil Procedure 8(a),[237] perhaps also referencing Federal Rule of Civil Procedure 12(e) (more definite statement). However, courts have sometimes looked unfavorably upon *Lone Pine* orders and opted for alternative methods of case management. In *Morgan v. Ford Motor Co.*, the court reasoned that a *Lone Pine* order would create an unfair imbalance in discovery, burdening plaintiffs while acting as "what amounts to a summary judgment motion without first allowing the party opposing the motion a chance to conduct discovery."[238] As an alternative, the court required each plaintiff to supply a simpler statement identifying the "nature and extent of injuries suffered" pursuant to Federal Rule of Civil Procedure 26(a)(1) and for the designation of bellwether plaintiffs.[239]

Ferreting out claims that have no foundation is but one of the problems *Lone Pine* or similar orders can address. Other issues include aligning specific individual plaintiffs with particular allegations and particular defendants. That has implications with respect to both managing the cases and, in some jurisdictions and situations, with respect to misjoinder.[240]

Typically, this type of requirement by the court would be embodied in a CMO, and the CMO would require the individual plaintiffs to furnish basic limited information in claim forms designed for that purpose (typically done under oath) or affidavits, within a relatively short period of time. The penalty for failing to do so ordinarily is dismissal. Depending upon the circumstances of the case, this may prove to be a satisfactory step in and of itself. However, in other cases, it may be appropriate for the defendants to then also seek a required amendment to the original complaint to bring it into compliance

---

235. Id.
236. Id.; see also Grant v. E.I. DuPont de Nemours & Co., Civ. A. No. 91-55-CIV-4H, 1993 WL 146634 (E.D.N.C. 1993); Eggar v. Burlington N. R.R., Nos. CV 89-159-BLG-JFB, CV 89-170-BLG-JFB, CV 89-179-BLG-JFB, CV 89-181-BLG-JFB, CV 89-236-BLG-JFB, and CV 89-291-BLG-JFB, 1991 WL 315487 (D. Mont. Dec. 18 1991); Cottle v. Superior Court, 3 Cal. App. 4th 1367 (Cal. App. 2d Dist. 1992); Atwood v. Warner Elec. Brake & Clutch Co., 605 N.E.2d 1032 (Ill. App. Ct. 1992); *In re* Love Canal Actions, 547 N.Y.S. 2d 174 (N.Y. Sup. Ct. 1989), *modified* 555 N.Y.S. 2d 519 (N.Y. App. Div. 4th Dep't 1990).
237. See Frederick v. Koziol, 727 F. Supp. 1019 (E.D. Va. 1990).
238. Morgan v. Ford Motor Co., Civ. A. No. 06-1080, 2007 WL 1456154 at *7–8 (D.N.J. May 17, 2007).
239. Id. at *9.
240. It is not uncommon for there to be large numbers of plaintiffs in particular toxic tort cases. Similarly, it is not uncommon for there to be multiple defendants in the same case. Depending upon the nature of the underlying event or events, there can be substantial issues with respect to whether there has been a misjoinder of plaintiffs and/or a misjoinder of defendants. Those joinder issues can have implications with respect to removal and remand in the context of a fraudulent joinder contention. Obviously, it is important to the defendants to consider that issue early on, while removal is still an option. *See* Tapscott v. MS Dealer Serv. Corp., 77 F.3d 1353 (11th Cir. 1996); *In re* Benjamin Moore & Co., 309 F.3d 296 (5th Cir. 2002).

with the other pleading rules noted herein. That is something for individual consideration in individual cases.

Disposition of a multiparty toxic tort case often does not occur in a traditional single trial, followed by a single appeal. Oftentimes, a process is established with settlement in mind as the ultimate objective. Coupled with that is an equally compelling objective, presenting individual juries with only the amount of information that they are able to process at any given time—not presenting them with so many plaintiffs that justice is accorded to none and settlements do not result from their findings.

As to the sequencing of the proceeding, the principal techniques that have emerged are bifurcation (of liability and damages) and reverse bifurcation[241] (where damages are tried first in the hope that by defining the damages a settlement can be reached without the necessity of the liability trial) and trifurcation (liability, damages, and punitive damages, in varying sequences).[242] A related issue is managing the number of plaintiffs and issues that are put before a single jury at a single time. Bellwether or representative plaintiffs furnish both the courts and the parties a good opportunity to manage this particular problem.[243]

Motion Practice (Other Than *Daubert*)

As noted above, toxic tort litigation, as it progresses from the filing of suit to resolution, is largely a matter of case management. While courts will exercise their power to manage the procedural and logistical facets of the case, via case management orders and the like, counsel have the opportunity to manage parties, claims, defenses, and evidence via motion practice. With the exception of summary judgment, which is discussed elsewhere, this section summarizes motions particularly pertinent to toxic tort cases.[244]

Venue

An initial consideration for a toxic tort defendant is whether the plaintiffs filed suit in the proper venue. If not, the defendant may file a motion to dismiss or transfer to a proper venue.[245] An objection to improper venue must be raised at the time the defendant files the answer or other motions, or else the objection to venue is waived.[246]

In addition to the dismissal or transfer of a suit filed in an improper venue, a defendant also has a potential remedy even if the suit was filed in a proper venue. In such a case, the defendant can file a motion to request a transfer to a more convenient venue.[247] Unlike

---

241. *See infra* section titled "Bifurcation and Reverse Bifurcation."
242. *See infra* section titled "Trifurcation."
243. *See infra* section titled "Test Plaintiffs." For a discussion on bellwether trials, *see In re* Chevron USA., Inc., 109 F.3d 1016, 1019 (5th Cir. 1997); MANUAL FOR COMPLEX LITIGATION (FOURTH) § 22315.
244. Note that *Daubert* issues are covered in chapter 5.
245. FED. R. CIV. P. 12(b)(3); 28 U.S.C. § 1406.
246. FED. R. CIV. P. 12(b).
247. 28 U.S.C. § 1404 (1996).

the motion to dismiss for improper venue under 28 U.S.C. § 1406(a), a transfer based on the inconvenience of the forum is not waived by failure to raise it prior to filing the answer or other motions.[248] In determining whether to grant a motion to transfer based on the inconvenience of the forum, a court will consider the convenience of the parties, the witnesses, and the interest of justice.[249]

A defendant can particularly benefit from this transfer if the lawsuit is filed in a jurisdiction with a limited or biased jury pool that will make it difficult for the defendant to obtain a fair trial. For instance, such a transfer can allow the defendant to transfer the case away from a small town, where the injuries occurred and where it would be difficult to find an unbiased pool, to a more neutral environment. However, some courts hold that the plaintiff's choice of forum is to be given deference in ruling on a motion to transfer.[250] In these jurisdictions, if the plaintiff files in a proper forum, the defendant will have to fight an uphill battle to convince the court that another forum is more convenient for all parties, witnesses, and the court.

Vagueness or More Definite Statement

While toxic tort litigation may arise in a complex context involving multiple plaintiffs and defendants, as well as a technical factual legal setting, it is common for a petition or complaint (whether in a fact pleading or a notice pleading jurisdiction) to lack specificity. This can be due to a hasty filing, a lack of knowledge, or the choice of a strategy to keep the defendants off balance. Whatever the cause, an excessively vague pleading will not adequately inform the defendant of the nature and thrust of the claims asserted against it and will inhibit intelligent responsive pleading. This is a situation for a motion, filed prior to the answer, asking the court to order the plaintiff to revise the petition or complaint such that it adequately informs the defendant of the claims against it.[251]

---

248. *See, e.g.*, Andrade v. Chase Home Fin., LLC, No. 04 C 8229, 2005 WL 3436400 at *2 (N.D. Ill. Dec. 12, 2005) (noting that a motion to transfer under § 1404 may be filed at any time); Bankers Life & Cas. Co. v. Case, No. 05 C 6532, 2005 WL 3542523 (N.D. Ill. Dec. 23, 2005) (defendant's motion to transfer under § 1404 was granted after it filed motion to dismiss). *But see* Miller v. Batesville Casket Co., 219 F.R.D. 56 (E.D.N.Y. 2003) (finding that under Fed. R. Civ. P. 12(h), a failure to raise a defense of improper venue in the answer is a waiver of that defense, whether it is brought under Rule 12 or under § 1404).
249. 28 U.S.C. § 1404(a); *see also* Blane v. Am. Inventors Corp., 934 F. Supp. 903, 907 (M.D. Tenn. 1996) (citing Walker v. Consumers Power Co., 1990 U.S. App. LEXIS 2575(6th Cir. 1990), *cert. denied*, 498 U.S. 815 (1990)) (the court will consider (1) the location of willing and unwilling witnesses, (2) the residence of the parties, (3) the location of sources of proof, and (4) the location of the events that gave rise to the dispute).
250. *See* Kroll v. Lieberman, 244 F. Supp. 2d 100, 102–03 (E.D.N.Y. 2003); Asbury v. A.W. Chesterton Co., 2010 WL 1280470 (R.I. Super. Marr. 29, 2010). *But see* Acceleron, LLC v. Egenera, Inc., 634 F. Supp. 2d 758, 764 (E.D. Tex. 2009) (noting that plaintiff's choice of forum is not a factor in the transfer analysis).
251. *See* FED. R. CIV. P. 12(e).

Such a motion is often disfavored in other types of litigation.[252] Lawyers (and judges) often believe that this type of motion is merely a stall tactic, that discovery will fill in any gaps in the allegations, and that filing a vagueness motion may even irritate the judge early in the case. These tactical/prudential factors are not to be taken lightly in a toxic tort case, but they need to be weighed against the need for specificity that this kind of case brings into play.

For example, if a plaintiff in a case alleging property damage from oil field activities does not clearly set forth what his claimed interest in the affected tract is, the defendants may be denied the ability to contest standing or to evaluate whether the plaintiff has failed to state a claim against a defendant. Similarly, if a multiparty complaint arising from a waste disposal site does not specify whether defendants are generators, transporters, or disposers of what particular compounds, intelligent responsive pleading is impossible. For these reasons, counsel must consider while drafting or responding to a lawsuit whether the allegations are specific enough to withstand initial scrutiny.

No Cause or Right of Action/Lack of Procedural Capacity/Failure to State a Claim

Assuming that the lawsuit is not defectively vague, counsel will need to determine whether the allegations, as written and taken as true, set forth a viable claim for relief. In state and federal courts, this motion, filed prior to or along with the answer, can be used to narrow the issues, create a record on appeal, or to develop settlement leverage.[253] Either a particular claim or claims or the entire case, depending upon the details of the lawsuit, can be the subject of this motion.

As noted above, this motion does not involve the offering of evidence or the opportunity for the court to evaluate witness credibility. Likewise, discovery and expert opinions are not part of the adjudication of this motion. If counsel offers any matter outside the pleadings, the court will treat it as a motion for summary judgment.[254]

Numerous defenses in toxic tort litigation can be asserted with this motion, such as statute of limitations, failure to have sent jurisdictionally required notice/demand letters,

---

252. Mitchell v. E-Z Way Towers, Inc., 269 F.2d 126 (5th Cir. 1959); Country Classics at Morgan Hill Homeowners' Ass'n v. Country Classics at Morgan Hill, LLC, 780 F. Supp. 2d 367, 371 (E.D. Pa. 2011) ("Because Federal Rule of Civil Procedure 8 requires only a short and plain statement of the claim, motions for a more definite statement are 'highly disfavored.'"); Patterson v. Anderson, 2010 WL 5092769 (M.D. Tenn. Dec. 7, 2010) (noting that information sought by motion for a more definite statement was better obtained through discovery); BB In Tech. Co. v. JAF, LLC, 242 F.R.D. 632, 640 (S.D. Fla. 2007) ("Federal Courts disfavor motions for a more definite statement, in view of the liberal pleading and discovery requirements set forth in the Federal Rules of Civil Procedure.").
253. *See* FED. R. CIV. P. 12(b)(6).
254. *See* FED. R. CIV. P. 12(b).

and lack of procedural capacity to sue.[255] These defenses also can be raised later in the case with evidence via summary judgment if the court denies them.[256]

Discovery Motions

As discussed elsewhere, toxic tort litigation can involve discovery of facts involving evidence from witnesses, documents, things, and the physical environment. Efforts to obtain information via depositions and written discovery often will lead to disputes about the appropriate scope and timing of these efforts. Information may be privileged or commercially sensitive. Property of parties or third parties may need to be entered and/or sampled. Discovery response deadlines may require adjustment. When the parties cannot agree on these issues, or when a record must be made, counsel will seek participation by the court.

In all cases, counsel will need to be familiar with local and court rules on how and when discovery motions can be filed. The conventional wisdom is that these motions are a last resort; courts usually conclude that when a discovery motion has been filed: (1) unreasonable requests or responses have been made, and (2) the parties have not worked well enough with each other to avoid bringing the court into the problem.

Evidentiary Motions

Daubert and the admissibility of expert opinions are the subject of another chapter. Toxic tort cases generate other evidentiary issues that relate to whether the court should admit particular evidence. The motion *in limine* is the vehicle for seeking a court decision on admissibility of evidence.[257] While the general context is whether the evidence under the pertinent state or federal rules of evidence is relevant, these issues can arise from a wide range of sources.

For example, in a suit alleging soil and groundwater contamination and resulting property damage, the plaintiff may have discovered evidence on how the defendant handled waste in settings distinct from that of the case at bar. The evidence may, to the plaintiff, shed light on the validity of the defendant's assertion that it was unaware of the dangers posed by the compounds at issue or that the releases at issue were caused by the *ultra vires* conduct of renegade employees, rather than deliberate corporate conduct. The defendant may see the same evidence as unfairly prejudicing it in the eyes of the jury while having no connection to the core question of whether its actions at the site at issue were wrongful. The court, in deciding the motion, will evaluate these issues and will consider how the evidence will affect the consumption of judicial resources. The range of outcomes

---

255. *See* 5B and 5C WRIGHT & MILLER, FEDERAL PRACTICE AND PROCEDURE: Civil 3d § 1357 and § 1360 (and cases cited therein).
256. *See* FED. R. CIV. P. 12(b) and (h)(2).
257. *See* FED. R. CIV. P. 16 and FED. R. EVID. 103. For a thorough discussion of the *Motion in Limine*, *see* 21 WRIGHT, MILLER & COOPER, FEDERAL PRACTICE AND PROCEDURE §§ 5037, 5037.1, and 5040.

includes excluding all the evidence, admitting all the evidence, controlling how much is admitted, or advising counsel to make their objections at trial.

Motions for Reconsideration

There are times when a ruling on a motion is either not appealable (as in a granting of a motion to remand) or when an appealable ruling needs to be attacked immediately and in the trial court. Counsel may believe that the court's focus was misdirected or may have located probative additional evidence. New precedential jurisprudence may have emerged. Under these circumstances, asking the court to reconsider its previous ruling is a potential tool.[258] Usually, a motion to reconsider needs to be filed expeditiously after receipt of the adverse ruling or of obtaining new information that calls the previous court order into question.[259]

This motion can be of substantial import in toxic tort cases, especially class actions. If, for example, the trial judge certifies a class with boundaries that are excessive because they are not well enough connected with the undisputed extent and migration path of the groundwater plume being sued upon, the remainder of the case could be significantly affected. Even though a class certification ruling is appealable,[260] and even though class boundaries can be adjusted postcertification by the court,[261] it may be best to seek an immediate change in the ruling. The area certified might contain sensitive populations (such as an elementary school) and once the "bell is rung" that such an area is within the class, profound consequences could follow. For these reasons, counsel on the losing end of a ruling on a motion should keep in mind the prospect of seeking reconsideration.[262] Motions to reconsider, however, should be filed with circumspect. Judges generally do not appreciate parties who simply seek to rehash the same points. Where a true error was made, or where new information is uncovered, a motion may be necessary but should be weighed within the context of the entire case.

---

258. *See* 28 U.S.C. § 59; *see also* 11 WRIGHT, MILLER & KANE, FEDERAL PRACTICE AND PROCEDURE: CIVIL 2d § 2804 and § 2812.
259. *See* 28 U.S.C. § 59; *see also* Standard Quimica De Venez. v. Central Hispano Int'l., Inc., 189 F.R.D. 202 (D.P.R. 1999) (wherein the court explained that generally a motion for reconsideration should be filed no later than ten days after entry of judgment pursuant to Rule 59(b), but that this statutory deadline does not apply to the reconsideration of an interlocutory judgment, and the timeliness of such a motion for reconsideration rests solely on whether or not the motion was filed unreasonably late).
260. *See* 28 U.S.C. § 23(f).
261. *See* 28 U.S.C. § 23(c)(1)(C).
262. *See Class Actions—Certification Ruling–Reconsideration Motion*, FED. LITIG. 16 (6), 157 (June 2001).

Trial Issues
Shaping the Case
What Is a Trial Really About?

Recognize the essential human quality of trial; it is not a mechanical exercise. The question for the advocate is how best to structure the case during opening and at trial, so as to link the underlying dispute to a morality play and thereby unite the very different members of the final jury to one's cause.

A similar view is that trials are not about "objective truth" but about something much more subjective, "justice":

> Trials are not about truth. Trials are about justice. The jurors listen to the evidence and try to determine which side of the courtroom is good and which side is bad; which side is right and which side is wrong; which side is just and which side is unjust. That is the best that they can do. It is not about truth. It is about justice.[263]

Another practical assessment of the process underlines the essential humanistic quality of a trial and the importance that a trial lawyer recognize it:

> The civil jury trial is very much a people process. Therein lies the uncertainty. How individual jurors think, feel, act, and make decisions is as important to the outcome as the rules of evidence and procedure. The attitudes, values, and life experiences that a juror brings to a trial will play a greater role in how your client's case is perceived than your most compelling closing argument. Jurors perceive information differently based on a variety of factors, including their individual values, ethnicity, education, cultural orientation, religion, and upbringing. Understanding the background of your jurors and how they make decisions is the trial lawyer's responsibility.[264]

What core values are at stake in your case? Being on time? Personal responsibility? Doing a job diligently? Taking care of your own business and not meddling in the affairs of another? Following the rules? Caring about your fellow man as much as you care about yourself? Keeping a proper lookout? Following the checklist? Putting safety first? Truth-telling? You need to know what these values are before you rise to address the venire. Indeed, you need to think about the trial themes beginning the day you take the case. As discussed below, themes help you design the lexicon of the case. Themes shape your expert testimony, and they help you choose the jury.

---

263. Sidney K. Kanazawa, *Apologies and Lunch*, FOR THE DEFENSE 46 (7), 32 (July 2004).
264. John C. Childs, *Cats, Dogs and Hammer Handles: The Predictive Value of Research*, 28 LITIG. 36, 36 (2002).

You need to know the personal context in which the jurors will hear your case. They are not lawyers (usually), and they don't think like lawyers. They will process the evidence and arguments through their own framework, their own definition of the "issues" and values.[265] How will your client measure up to those values? What kind of juror will be receptive to your client's case? Are you really ready to pick the jurors most likely to see things your way?

Simple Common Sense

Know the audience. Your audience, the jury, has not prepared for trial. Accordingly, every case, especially a mass tort case, needs to be simplified. Jargon needs to be avoided, and things need to be explained in commonsense terms. Kanner's book begins with emphasis on the "role of simplicity," where he refers to the lawyer as a builder, a sculptor.[266] The more subtle point Kanner makes is that the lawyer is a balancer whose goal is to find the sweet spot between "information and presentability." In support of this, he cites Einstein: "Everything should be made as simple as possible, but not simpler."[267]

Jury Selection

As you contemplate how best to pick a jury, regardless of whether you represent the plaintiff or defendant, whether you are a veteran or a neophyte, you are not alone. You can find pertinent, helpful, and scholarly articles and books on all aspects of the task. For example, in the *Toxic Torts Litigation Guide*,[268] you will find discussion of and thorough citations to articles on jury selection addressing the intuitive and empirical considerations. *Environmental and Toxic Tort Trials* is another excellent and thorough discussion of jury selection principles.[269] You will be challenged to find enough time to absorb all of the discussion and advice in those two works and the many sources cited therein.

Use of Jury Consultants

"[J]ury selection, whether good or bad, will determine the result of your trial."[270] Kanner emphasizes the venerability of this principle, well recognized before the advent of jury consultants:

> Indeed how could anything be more important than the selection of the men who are to decide the case? It matters not how thorough one may have been in preparation; it

---
265. *See id.*
266. Allan Kanner, Environmental and Toxic Tort Trials § 1.00 (2003).
267. *Id.*
268. Lawrence G. Cetrulo, Toxic Torts Litigation Guide §§ 15.2 and 15.3 (2011).
269. Kanner, *supra* note 266, §§ 2.00–2.07.
270. *Id.* § 2.01, at 2-2.

matters not how good a case one may have—unless he selects the proper kind of men to decide it, he is bound to have a mistrial or a defeat.[271]

The wide variety of case facts, venues, and lawyers' skill sets combine to confound any attempt to generalize about technique in selecting a jury in a mass tort case. Good old-fashioned intuition is arguably a trial lawyer's sharpest tool.[272] It should never be ignored. The use of intuition alone, however, is "unreliable and illogical."[273] "Some lawyers say it borders on malpractice not to use a jury consultant if financially practicable."[274] Whether that is so or not, if the resources are there, it is worth consideration in mass tort cases that present huge economic risks to the defendant and hold the promise of huge rewards for the plaintiffs.[275]

Many experts are happy to help. Veteran members of the plaintiff and defense bars and the most sophisticated corporations have experience with these experts, and if you do not, you should check with your colleagues in those groups. As the *Toxic Torts Litigation Guide* points out,[276] these experts come in varying stripes, including psychologists, sociologists, communications researchers, psychics, lawyers, marketing specialists, handwriting experts,[277] face readers, and body language readers.[278]

How you use them is another matter. Many options are available, ranging from a full mock trial to a more limited and easily executed focus group exercise designed to test reactions to witnesses or story lines. Even within the mock trial category, there are variations on the theme.[279] Some of the options are discussed and reviewed broadly in the *Toxic*

---

271. Francis L. Wellman, Day In Court or the Subtle Arts of Great Advocates 111 (1931). Kanner provides a brief but intriguing bibliography of cases and articles on the subject of toxic torts dating back to the year 1306. Kanner, *supra* note 266, § 1.01 n.3.
272. "Talk to people, partners, support staff. And, please, do something that you don't do at home: Listen to them. You're just not as cool as you think. You don't know the music, the TV shows, the movies of the 20- or 30-somethings. If your kids call you a dork, you are. Discuss the facts of your case—look and listen to reactions. Determine what strategy works, and then go with it. But do not substitute research for insight. You might just be right." Kenneth P. Nolan, *Tilting the Playing Field*, 29 Litig. 6, 62 (2003).
273. Cetrulo, *supra* note 268, § 15:2, at 15-5 and nn.4 & 5.
274. Leonard Post, *The Dollars Involved in "Voodoo" Focus Groups*, Broward Daily Bus. Rev. (April 21, 2004).
275. Cetrulo, *supra* note 268, § 15:2, at 15-5 and -6, nn.5 & 6.
276. Cetrulo, *supra* note 268, § 15:8.
277. "[I]f a person prints precisely rather than in a free-flowing style and has not been trained to do that by way of his profession, it may indicate that the individual leans toward seeing things very black and white." Kelly Lucas, *Movie Runs Away from Reality*, The Indiana Lawyer (Nov. 19, 2003) (quoting trial psychologist Nina Miller and citing V. Hale Starr & Mark McCormick, Jury Selection, § 15A.2, 172 (3d ed. 1991).
278. Tom McCann, *Jury Consultants Try to Turn Voir Dire into a Science*, Chicago Lawyer (Aug. 2004) (referring to Gene Hackman's character in "Runaway Jury") ("Contrary to their Hollywood image, jury consultants do not lurk around wearing dark glasses and hidden earpieces, tracking down potential jurors with a vast array of spy gadgetry.").
279. *See* Barry Richard, *Mock Jury Exercises*, Nat'l L. J. (Mar. 1, 2004) (noting the differences between "adversarial" and "nonadversarial" mock trials).

Torts Litigation Guide and authorities cited therein:[280] juror questionnaires,[281] community attitude assessments, focus groups, mock trials, shadow juries, credibility studies of counsel and of chief witnesses, and suggested *voir dire* questions.[282]

There are differing views on the value to be had from a consultant:

> There's not much empirical research about the efficacy of jury consulting. . . . That's because a lot of them are not very visible. . . . A lot of their work is proprietary. They don't want to be tipping their hands. The competition is intense.[283]

As is the case in the courtroom, the trial lawyer makes all the difference between a good and a bad experience with a jury consultant. Indeed, the "garbage-in-garbage-out" principle has no finer application than in the context of using jury consultants. The consultant is only as good as the information he or she receives. It is one thing to win the mock trial. It's another to win the case. You need to be frank with the consultant and let him or her know about all the good and all the bad points in your case. Your client will receive optimal value from using a consultant only if you have a clear vision of the case and a clear objective in mind for the consultant and are candid about all the potential problems.

Planning and participating in the exercise, whether by a full mock trial or a focus group, will sharpen your thoughts about the case because it requires you to lift your attention up from the day-to-day work of litigation and to put the case together, to make it simple. Many a veteran trial lawyer has made his case as simple as he thought it could be only to find out that the jury was confused about one point or another. A consultant can help avoid that result.

Reputable consultants are trained by way of academic study and clinical experience in sociological considerations important to the task of persuading people. They can help you refine your objectives (indeed your whole approach to the case) and help you design the mock trial–focus group exercise, no matter how simple or complicated it might be. Listen to the consultant.[284] The same listening skill that empowers an effective cross-examiner will serve that lawyer well as he meets with the jury consultant. He knows things you don't. Your initial plan, for example, a full mock trial on all issues in the case, might be

---

280. See CETRULO, *supra* note 268, §§ 15:8, 15:25.
281. See id. § 15:10. "[A] jury questionnaire is a valuable tool for attorneys because a juror will answer voir dire questions in a way that is socially acceptable—not necessarily truthful. In a public setting, most people feel the need to say the proper thing, or at least the 'politically correct' thing. The privately conducted questionnaire permits more candid and accurate attitudes." Rodney R. Nordstrom, *Discovering Which Way Jurors Might Be Leaning*, CHICAGO DAILY L. BULL. 5 (Mar. 24, 2004) (agreeing with PAUL M. LISNEK, THE HIDDEN JURY: AND OTHER TACTICS LAWYERS USE TO WIN (Sourcebooks 2003); see also Childs, *supra* note 264.
282. See id. §§ 15:11–15:16.
283. McCann, *supra* note 278, quoting Steven Penrod, professor at New York's John Jay College of Criminal Justice.
284. See generally Richard, *supra* note 279.

too complicated to be achieved in one day. You might learn that your theory of the case is too convoluted and full of jargon.

You and the consultant must be on the same page. You might have heard the one about the actuary, whose client asked him what 2 plus 2 equals, and who then closed the blinds and asked, "What do you want it to be?" Likewise, the jury consultant needs to know and share your goals and objectives.

The fruit of that meeting of the minds will be clear objectives, for example, get a prediction of findings of fact on selected issues; test juror willingness to find for the defendant even though the plaintiff is badly injured; test quantum; test credibility of an expert; provoke discussion and deliberations with a view toward formulating lines of direct and cross-examination. The scope of your project can be as broad or as narrow as time and money permit.

You must guard against trying to do too much. You must prioritize the issues because you probably will have to cram the entire experience into one day.[285] In the mass tort case, where you have many issues, you must be highly selective in choosing which issues and topics to test. It is unlikely that you validly can test in one day all of the issues to be presented in a trial that will last weeks or months. For example, in one day can you mock try all the following: the cause-in-fact of the incident, the negligence of one or more defendants, the plaintiff's negligence, the existence of damages (e.g., increased risk of future disease), the cause of damages, and quantum? Perhaps so, but not likely. You must choose carefully and be prepared to make some difficult choices. The consultant can help you judge how best to design an exercise of value to you and your client.

Recognize the variables influencing each issue. For example, if the case turns on the question of causation of damages, and if—as is often the case—the issue will be decided on the basis of a duel of experts, how can you incorporate into the design a test of the experts' credibility? Will you get an accurate prediction of the real jury's assessment of the causation issue at trial? Can you? Do you have video deposition transcripts of the actual witnesses? If not, do you really think you can replicate their personalities and design into the exercise, a component that accounts for the sometimes all-important subjective aspect of credibility?[286] If not, perhaps you should consider a more modest objective, such as testing key words and phrases and the impact of demonstrative evidence.[287] Use the exercise to find the appropriate balance of information and presentability.[288]

---

285. *See* Lisnek, *supra* note 281 (focus group less expensive than mock trials and a good source of information on themes and story lines); Tamara Loomis, *Jurors; Post-Enron Distrust Crosses Class, Race Lines Study: Stacking Juries with White Men No Longer Safe Bet*, CONN. L. TRIBUNE (October 28, 2002).
286. *See infra* at note 303 (discussion of then candidate Ronald Reagan's famous line in a debate with President Carter, "There you go again.").
287. *See* discussion of hyperbole, *infra*.
288. *See* KANNER, *supra* note 266.

Consultants bring practical perspective to the process. Perhaps you should acknowledge that you cannot reasonably design a *voir dire* to pick the jurors best suited to your case. Maybe you should lower your sights and be satisfied if you can eliminate the worst of the venire.

> [A]ttorneys shouldn't focus on picking ideal jurors but on eliminating the most dangerous ones. Your jury pool is the luck of the draw, so you have to find the very worst possible and eliminate them. You'll always have fewer strikes than jurors you want to get rid of.[289]

Quite separate and apart from designing and executing a mock trial or focus group, consultants can provide other kinds of advice. For example, use the consultant to comment on and evaluate demonstrative evidence. Color and size deserve study, and most lawyers have not been educated in such nuances.

Consultants can be very useful in trial as well. Many lawyers will admit they don't try as many cases as they used to, and most will confess they haven't tried a large number of mass tort trials:

> Most attorneys do just one or two trials a year, if they're lucky. But a good consultant has studied hundreds of juries and knows which behaviors and characteristics to look out for.... [C]onsultants serve as an extra set of eyes and ears for the lawyer. When an attorney is questioning a potential juror, a third party can do a better job of observing their rapport and checking out the jurors' reactions.[290]

A jury consultant can educate the client. Clients who are defendants, like lawyers, have intuition and experience; most can evaluate a case. Clients, like lawyers, however, should not rely solely on intuition, especially where the stakes are as high as they usually are in mass tort cases. Clients, like lawyers, can get too close to a case, losing objectivity about the matter. Jury consultants can broaden and objectify case evaluations. Especially on the defense side, where the client is likely to be savvy and experienced, client involvement in the design phase can be very important and helpful:

> Watching a mock jury deliberate the facts of your case—and observing how your case themes can be marshaled by some jurors to persuade others—can help clients become true believers.[291]

---

289. McCann, *supra* note 278, quoting trial consultant Patricia McEvoy.
290. *See id.* (quoting Daniel Wolfe, trial consultant with Trial Graphix in Chicago and former president of the American Society of Trial Consultants).
291. Childs, *supra* note 264.

Postpresentation sessions can be formatted to suit your objectives and can range from a self-directed "jury" deliberation to a moderator-led discussion of the issues. This is the payoff, so you want to have plenty of time for these sessions. They usually are videotaped and analyzed by the consultant. Jury deliberations and focus groups can tell you much about the clarity of your presentation and the marketability of your themes. The predictive value of such a jury deliberation not led by a moderator must be evaluated skeptically, however, because, as is the case in any deliberation, the force and influence of leaders and group dynamics can vary widely from group to group, compromising the ability to predict a trial's outcome based on a given mock jury verdict. The moderator-led discussion better assures coverage of the issues you care about, and you have a better chance of getting feedback from all participants. There is no right or wrong way to debrief the mock jury or focus group participants. Discuss the options with the consultant and recognize that the postpresentation session is where you get real value from the exercise.

You might be concerned about the discoverability of a consultant's opinions. That is a valid concern, but full treatment is beyond the scope of this effort. Suffice it to say that, except in extraordinary circumstances, the work product doctrine extends to consultants as it is expected that the communication between counsel and a consultant will reflect the mental impressions, opinions, conclusions, and legal theories of counsel.[292]

Let's now turn our attention to technique considerations, style, and language, when picking a jury.

Jurors Are People, Too
The veteran trial lawyer realizes that the task of picking the final twelve jurors who will find the facts and persuading them to see the case in her or his client's favor is most likely accomplished by following a few basic rules. The process often begins with facing a venire of thirty or forty people: (a) in all shapes and sizes; (b) some wearing three-piece suits, some wearing t-shirts; (c) some with college degrees, some who did not finish high school (some of whom are smarter than the ones with degrees); (d) who have been cooped up in a windowless room for several days or weeks, who have endured multiple *voir dire* presentations in varying degrees of quality, who could recite from memory the lawyers' perfunctory speeches about pure intentions and lack of interest in personal details (when that is exactly their interest); and (e) who know nothing about and who probably do not care much about the controversy at hand. Of course, that controversy has dominated the lawyer's time and his or her client's time, and which may well put at risk tens or hundreds of millions of dollars. They may be basic, but the lawyer knows that he or she ignores them at his or her client's peril: keeping it simple without being patronizing (discussed above), using common sense (also discussed above), breaking the case into its components and

---
292. *See In re* Cendant Corp. Sec Litig., 343 F.3d 658 (3d Cir. 2003).

recognizing where one ends and the other begins (coming), and using all the elements of persuasion to maximum advantage (also coming).

Since most mass tort cases take a long time, you are going to be with your jury for several weeks or more, much more. *Voir dire* is your first chance to convey your personal thoughts and sensitivities. You will not have an opportunity to talk directly to these people on a personal level again for a long time, not until closing argument, so do not blow this opportunity. Tell the venire you realize those chosen will have to make a significant personal sacrifice of time and energy. Acknowledge that sacrifice and, where permitted, thank them in advance.

The challenge, of course, is to do so without pandering. That is in large part a matter of personal style, well beyond the scope of this section. This can be done, however, in a way that is not apologetic or that blunts their interest in the case. Indeed, you must interest them in the case; otherwise you will never persuade them. The point is, you have a better chance of persuading jurors who believe you have their interests at heart. The tension between being candid about the upcoming time and energy commitment on one hand and interesting them in your client's case is unavoidable. Do not ignore this tension; use it:

> Mrs. Jones, I know you [examples: have three school-age children, own your own business, do not have your own transportation], so I recognize that serving on this jury will present a hardship. If you serve on the jury, however, you will hear a very important case about many different subjects such as exactly what chemicals and things are in smoke, what causes cancer, and how long does it take to develop. The point is that my client is very sympathetic about Mr. Smith's (plaintiff) having cancer, but we believe the evidence will show that [examples: the fire, the explosion, the leak] did not cause that cancer. It is important that people on the jury not be put in a position where they will not be able to tend to their personal affairs and still be asked to pay careful attention to the case. Will you be able to manage your [children's needs, work, transportation needs] in a way that will allow you to take care of your personal obligations and, at the same time, concentrate on the case and make important decisions?

This approach allows you to connect on a personal level and, at the same time, to educate and condition the whole panel. In the process you acknowledge the reality of the situation from their point of view. By confronting the tension, you can reach out to them personally, sympathize with their situations, and commence the persuasion process.

Aristotle explained the three components of persuasion theory: (1) pathos, emotional and moral considerations; (2) logos, the force of objective facts and logic; and (3) ethos, the credibility of the speaker.[293] In a toxic tort trial, the odds are that emotional and moral

---

293. Aristotle, *Rhetoric*.

considerations are in the plaintiff's favor, at least insofar as liability is concerned (chemical releases are bad). As plaintiff's counsel, you want to capitalize on this in *voir dire* and look for emotional jurors. If you represent the defendant, recognize this feature of the climate and find other aspects of the case where the pathos edge is less in the plaintiff's favor—maybe even in the defense's favor, such as causation and the lack of serious damages (opportunism is bad). Look for jurors who can make the distinction between liability and damages and are able to set emotions aside. Regardless of your representation, plaintiff or defendant, find your strong points and look for jurors open to your case—or find and eliminate as many hostile ones as possible.

The credibility of every speaker at trial, witness and lawyer alike, must be taken into account. As the trial lawyer, your credibility will rise and fall not only on the basis of your innate abilities and presentation style, but also on your ability to manipulate all elements of persuasion, the emotional or moral justifications at play, the force of logic and objective evidence, and the power of personality and credibility. Recognizing and distinguishing between the good and the bad parts of your case; making concessions where you must to be credible; recognizing where pathos is in your favor, for example, liability if plaintiff, causation if defendant; knowing when and how you must explain the complicated if arcane aspects of your case (logos); and recognizing the variability of witnesses' and lawyers' credibility (ethos) will help you plan your presentation at every step of the trial.

Hyperbole v. Explanation
The lexicon of the trial should be the product of deliberate language choices by the trial lawyers. *Environmental and Toxic Tort Trials*[294] and the *Toxic Torts Litigation Guide*[295] explore and discuss the linguistic principles involved here. Hyperbole and explanation each has its place. Kanner, in the context of opening statements, points to the importance of a lawyer's selection of "a unifying theme as well as . . . any sub-themes in the case."[296] He also points to the value of couching the presentation in part through the use of "key words, phrases, and images."[297] For example, the plaintiff lawyer uses highly charged words and phrases like "poison" and "dangerous, cancer-causing chemical," while the defense lawyer must seize every reasonable opportunity to demystify the substance and defuse the hyperbole, using less charged words and phrases such as "common solvent," all in an effort to explain and to put the case on a less emotional level.[298] The plaintiff's "multibillion dollar defendant" is the defendant's "underdog."[299] All of this is to say that words can trigger emotion, and they can control it.

---

294. KANNER, *supra* note 266, § 2.05.
295. CETRULO, *supra* note 268, § 15:6.
296. KANNER, *supra* note 266, §§ 3.02, 3.04.
297. Id.
298. Id. §§ 3.02, 3.04, and 3.05.
299. Kanazawa, *supra* note 263.

For instance, the use of highly charged key words and phrases comes naturally in a chlorine release case involving many deaths. Words and phrases such as "poison" and "risk of immediate death" and images of skulls and crossbones come from the defendant's product or process literature and material safety data sheets. In contrast, hyperbole or conscious exaggeration are devices to be used by the plaintiff's attorney in a mass tort case involving the release of an innocuous chemical. Even in those cases, so the argument goes, there should not have been a release/explosion/fire, and in any mass tort case, including even those involving a relatively benign chemical or a tiny amount of a more dangerous one, the sheer number of people evacuated, the frightful nature of the occurrence, and the community-wide scope of the outrage provide an open invitation to the plaintiff to present a case of outrage—to use hyperbole.[300]

As defense counsel, the goal is to calm the emotions and explain. Explain the process. Explain the chemical. If it is a dangerous chemical, you will not be able to minimize its hazard per se, but you might be able to prove that exposures were below symptom levels. Explain the "symptom level" concept. Explain the toxicological rule that the poison is the dose and give examples using everyday items. Explain the care and attention your client brought to the process, design, and operation. Point out the fact that the defendant's employees work in the plant and would no more put the community at risk than they would put themselves at risk. Take a lesson from Madison Avenue and politicians:

> If you are a politician, perhaps nothing is more important than defining yourself before the opposition does, and one way you do so is with the words you choose . . . . [I]f voters find it strange that talk among Republicans in the presidential race changes from "drilling for oil" to "exploring for oil," they will have focus groups to thank. Similarly, phrases like "climate change" and "death tax" entered into the public discourse only after the careful scrutiny of social scientists.[301]

Business interests arguably learned this lesson first:

> Focus groups, like many other modern political tools, have their origins on Madison Avenue. For decades, advertising copywriters have used them to vet slogans for products like laundry detergents, and Hollywood executives have relied on them to select endings for summer beach busters.[302]

Polls and focus groups have their place, but in the end there is no substitute for personality and credibility:

---
300. *See* CETRULO, *supra* note 268, § 15:4, at 15-13.
301. Alex Williams, *The Alchemy of a Political Slogan*, N.Y. TIMES, Aug. 22, 2004, at 9.
302. *Id.* (e.g., "tax relief" better than "tax cut"; "climate change" more persuasive than "global warming").

If you took a focus group and told them that Jimmy Carter was going to attack Reagan on Social Security, and Reagan was going to respond, 'There you go again,' you probably would have assumed he'd lose . . . . But you couldn't have tested the way Reagan was going to say it, the tone of voice, the look on his face.[303]

This tells us that while you can learn from focus groups, in the end, the credibility of witnesses and lawyers may make the difference regardless of the words.[304]

Pick Your Spots

Decide what part of your case is most important and look for jurors receptive to it. Some, but not all, jurors who are disposed to think in the plaintiff's favor with regard to liability may be disposed in the defendant's favor in terms of causation and damages because they do not like an opportunistic, overreaching plaintiff. To state the obvious, the defense lawyer may look for such jurors and try to get them in the box. Likewise, identify the jurors who are unable to make the liability-causation distinction and challenge them. Here, the jury consultant can help you identify those people most able to distinguish between liability and damages.

Plaintiff's counsel likely will prefer emotional jurors, those who will be unlikely to compartmentalize emotions and process objective evidence (e.g., it is deplorable that the defendant had an aniline release, but the plaintiff should not be compensated for her fear of cancer because aniline is not a carcinogen).

The force of objective evidence and logic also must be employed. In a case where there is little dispute as to fault for the release of a chemical but a hot dispute as to the existence of damages and causation, the defense lawyer will rely heavily on the logic and force of the evidence as presented through experts. As discussed above, in a mass tort case, there is a special premium on the defense's ability to explain and demystify. Most jurors will not find for the defendant in a case where the plaintiff is not badly injured if they do not fully understand the concept of "symptom level" or "dose," or, where the plaintiff is badly injured, if they do not understand the defendant's product or process.

For example, in a dose case, tell them that acrylic acid goes into their child's diapers and the masking tape they used to seal the box full of Christmas presents. Tell them that without methyl chloride, they would have no air conditioning. If there were no 1, 2-dichloropropane or Lexane, they would not have the paint stripper or rubber cement that made last weekend's project easy. If it weren't for dicyclopentadine, they would not enjoy the plastic products that are ubiquitous in the home. Will they know, if you don't tell them, that phenol was in last night's fried chicken or their morning's mouthwash?

---

303. *Id., quoting* Kenneth L. Khachigian, Republican speechwriter.
304. Aristotle, *Rhetoric* (ethos).

The jurors want to do justice. They want to find the right side of the morality play, but they cannot vote for a defendant unless that defendant has explained the chemicals in a clear, nonpatronizing fashion.

Get the Sting Out Early

By their nature, toxic tort trials, more so than conventional litigation, last a long time and involve more complicated issues of fact. If the determination of a fact issue in the case, whether it be the fault of the defendant, causation, or damages, is going to be reached only after sorting through competing and often contradictory evidence, no single part of which is determinative, the defendant is well advised to be the one to tell the jury about the bad parts of the case in opening and, in the process, put them in context.[305] This approach will take some of the sting out of the plaintiff's case. In other words, bringing out the bad news in *voir dire* and the opening statement, if it is certain to come out during trial, where it has not been brought out by the plaintiff in opening, is a way for the defendant to preempt the sting, and if not inoculate his client, soften the blow of hurtful evidence. In the process, your credibility (ethos) and, vicariously, your client's, will benefit.

Demonize v. Personalize

The plaintiff typically will want to demonize the defendant. Sometimes the target is a given employee of the defendant; sometimes an expert offered by the defendant will be the surrogate target of that attack. The defendant must anticipate and counteract the demonization effort. The best way to blunt an attempt to demonize is to personalize the defendant. This can be done if you have a personable witness or witnesses to tell the company's story. You should look for them as early as possible in the representation.

John C. Childs gives a real-world example from a lender liability case, which provokes thought and suggests that the defense lawyer in mass tort cases needs to put the client in a good light, telling the good-company story:

> An equally important part of the strategy was to call numerous bank employees, to personalize the bank. The image of a lender had to be recast as that of a responsible protector of the jurors' hard-earned monies. What does a bank do with monies deposited in savings accounts? It lends that money so it can pay the saver interest. It puts that money to work in the local community. The bank's customer and the bank work together to grow the customer's interest. Consequently, when a loan is not repaid, it is the bank customer's money that the bank seeks to protect through foreclosure. By describing the basic

---

305. See Cetrulo, *supra* note 268, § 15:3, at 15-7.

business relationship, we could defuse jurors' hostility toward banks, thereby allowing the jurors to hear and agree with the defense.[306]

Prove the Cleanup—or Take Advantage of Failure to Cleanup

As defendant, your ability to persuade the jury that you are on the right side of the courtroom will be bolstered by proof that your client cleaned up, or is cleaning up, the mess.[307] At the risk of overemphasizing the defense sensibilities, but consistent with an acknowledgment that every persuasive case has a pathos element, take all relevant opportunities to show that the toxic release has been remediated. Show photographs of the site all cleaned up. Tell them how many millions of pounds of contaminated soil was hauled away to demonstrate how much time, effort, and money was spent on the cleanup.

Recognizing that jurors will think it good that a mess has been cleaned up, optimize the proof, in terms of quantity and quality, of your client's efforts to remediate following the release. Doing so gives the jury, which seeks to do right, which seeks justice, which follows a moral imperative, the confidence to find for the defendant or to keep damages at a reasonable level. Of course, the plaintiff attorney on a case where the mess was not cleaned up has special opportunities to inflame the jurors and maximize damages.

Demonstrative Evidence—Technology in the Courtroom

Gone are the days when the trial lawyer can afford to ignore technology. The rapid pace of its development means that arguments can today be made in ways more efficient and memorable than ever before. Further, as society has adopted modern technology through now ubiquitous devices like smartphones and tablets, jurors have become increasingly sophisticated in their own right and expect a certain pace, interactivity, and graphical nature to information.[308] The failure of a lawyer to bolster his arguments with such modern aids can often mean the difference between capturing the jury's attention and being largely ignored.

Judicious use of modern tools such as presentations made with Microsoft's PowerPoint or Apple's Keynote software, maps, graphs, interactive timelines, and video clips can all be put to use to help simplify complex issues, particularly those that abound in mass tort cases. Additionally, efficient use of animation and color can help ensure the full attention of the jury. To facilitate this trend, most courts are integrating technology into the courtroom, such as sound systems, projectors, and TV monitors for the court, counsel, and jury, while cutting-edge lawyers are storing exhibits on and presenting from tablet computers

---

306. Childs, *supra* note 264.
307. See Kanazawa, *supra* note 263.
308. See Noah Wick & R. Craig Smith, *Jurors Are Tech Savvy; Now, It's Your Turn*, 53 ORANGE CNTY. LAW. 18 (June 2011).

like the iPad.[309] More can be written on the rapidly expanding influence of technology at trial than this effort is intended to address.[310]

Closing Argument

In closing argument, the trial lawyer brings together the themes and key words in the context of all the evidence and the law. The issues that provided the framework for the opening statement should provide the framework for closing argument as well. A corollary principle is that the lawyer will seize upon any failure of his opponent to deliver evidence as promised in opening.

Here, the lawyer treads the fine line between arguing the case and instructing the jury. Argument in its most powerful form will/must incorporate reference to the controlling legal principles. Some courts will permit you to blow up charges for use during argument; some won't. All will permit argument based on the legal principles to be explained in the charge. If you don't know how your judge runs closing argument, find lawyers who do know, or talk to the law clerk.

If you were successful throughout the trial in persuading the jurors of your personal credibility, here you will reap the rewards. Concede facts when you must to maintain credibility. For example, you might have to concede a share of fault in order to credibly argue that the plaintiff was not exposed enough to be injured. Don't think you have to win on every issue. Ideally, your theme and case story will reflect a plan to circumnavigate problem areas and permit a favorable verdict even though you can't win on every fact. This can be done via a theme that minimizes the importance of fact issues you cannot win.

Technology can be a real asset here. When you argue that the opponent's expert should not carry the day, insert key portions of his video testimony or highlight key portions of his report. If the case has been in trial for months, a picture of the witness can be very helpful whether in support or attack. Move quickly from exhibit to exhibit; use all the tools. Keep the jury's interest and focus. There is an entertainment component that cannot be ignored.

Weave all three elements of persuasion (emotions, logic, and personal credibility) into a tight fabric of a case. In closing argument, where the defense trial attorney believes he has a strong case that the chemical in question does not cause cancer, the lawyer should not talk solely about the empirical, toxicological, and epidemiological proof put forward by his experts. This is not to say that all appropriate arguments on the evidence should not be made. That lawyer should go farther and recognize the pathos opportunity lying

---

309. Lit Software, LLC's TrialPad for iPad is one such popular tool for lawyers to have quick access to documents and images in a small package.
310. *See* James O'Connor Gentry, Jr., *Effective Use of Technology in the Courtroom*, 11 U. PITT. J. TECH. L. & POL'Y 1 (2011); J. Bradley Ponder, *But Look Over There: How the Use of Technology at Trial Mesmerizes Jurors and Secures Verdicts*, 29 LAW & PSYCHOL. REV. 289 (Spring 2009).

therein. Instead of merely pointing out how thorough and more complete the defense expert was in his analysis of the causation question, point out the relief that should accompany the recognition that this chemical does not cause cancer. The plaintiff's fears about the occurrence, while legitimate in the information vacuum immediately following the event, are not warranted, and, of course, no compensation is due. This approach recognizes the morality play aspect of the toxic tort trial. It recognizes that the jury seeks to do justice, not merely to find an objective truth, and it might make all the difference in the verdict.

Admissibility of or Challenges to Lab Data

Without a proper foundation, evidence of environmental contamination or the lack thereof[311] may be subject to exclusion as hearsay under Federal Rule of Evidence 803.[312] When soil, water, or air samples are at issue,[313] that foundation may consist of testimony establishing the following:

- The sample taken accurately represents the larger body;[314]
- Proper sampling procedures were followed;[315]
- The equipment's sterility and accuracy have been validated;
- Chain of custody procedures were followed to ensure the sample was not confused with others;
- The witnesses were competent; and
- The testing methodology was appropriate.[316]

---

311. *See* Hickman v. Thomas C. Thompson Co., 644 F. Supp. 1531, 1537 (D. Colo. 1986) (refusing to suppress a laboratory testing report showing compliance with an applicable code).
312. This section addresses lab data collected and analyzed by private entities. The admissibility of data collected and analyzed by governmental agencies is addressed in the section titled "Public Records and Reports" *infra*. If the lab report is one kept in the ordinary course of the preparer's business, it may be admissible on that basis as another exception to the hearsay rule. *See* Fortier v. Dona Anna Plaza Partners, 747 F.2d 1324, 1332 (10th Cir. 1984).
313. The U.S. EPA's regulations address approved collection, preservation, and analysis methodologies for soil, water, and air samples. 40 C.F.R. §§ 260–270; 40 C.F.R. § 136; 40 C.F.R. §§ 60–61, Appendices A and B; Adams v. Consolidated Rail Corp., 591 S.E.2d 269, 276 (W. Va. 2003); Anna M. Michalak, *Environmental Contamination with Multiple Potential Sources and the Common Law: Current Approaches and Emerging Opportunities*, 14 FORDHAM ENVTL. L. J. 147 (2002).
314. Renaud v. Martin Marietta Corp., 749 F. Supp. 1545, 1552–53 (D. Colo. 1990), *aff'd*, 972 F.2d 304 (10th Cir. 1992) (noting "no one has any idea of whether this sample is representative of the 'normal' contaminant's concentration.").
315. *See* Grine v. Coombs, 214 F.R.D. 312, 322, n. 6 (W.D. Pa. 2003), *aff'd*, 2004 WL 1179349 (3d Cir. 2004).
316. This last requirement almost inevitably involves the question of the admissibility of expert testimony under *Daubert*, an issue beyond the scope of this work. However, expert testimony may not always be needed. As explained by the Fifth Circuit:

   > When applicable law mandates the use of a particular test, the proponent of the test's results should not have to establish its reliability. Even if the opponent could prove that it is unreliable, it would be unfair to the proponent to exclude his expert evidence based on the mandated technique. Rather, its reliability irrefutably should be presented. Any other rule would place the testimony's proponent in the untenable position of being unable to prove compliance with applicable law because he could not introduce the results of the test mandated by that same law.

Industry Codes

Most decisions allow the introduction into evidence of industry standards or codes.[317] Just as evidence of custom is admissible, "bearing on the standard of care in determining negligence,"[318] evidence of industry codes is relevant and admissible to prove the reasonableness of certain conduct.[319]

Public Records and Reports

Federal Rule of Evidence 803(8) similarly deems public records, reports, or data compilations in any form made by governmental entities admissible unless a lack of trustworthiness is indicated by the circumstances.[320] Although many courts may instinctively believe a government agency's report is trustworthy, some courts have found factors indicating untrustworthiness and therefore have excluded the evidence.[321] For example, government reports have been excluded due to untrustworthiness where the preparer lacked the expertise needed to write the report,[322] an investigator failed to follow up,[323] or when inadequate hearing procedures were employed.[324]

Violations of Statutory or Regulatory Environmental Provisions

Many courts hold the defendant's violation of an environmental statute or regulation is evidence of negligence per se in a damages suit based upon state law.[325] Others, analyzing

---

Rushing v. Kansas City S. Ry., 185 F.3d 496, 507 (5th Cir. 1999), *cert. denied*, 528 U.S. 1160, (2000). Note also that, per Cutting Underwater Techs. USA, Inc. v. Eni United States Operating Co., 671 F.3d 512 (5th Cir. 2012), which superseded *Rushing*, and FED. R. CIV. P. 56(c)(1)(a), the burden of challenging an expert's affidavit has been lowered from a required motion to strike to merely objecting to the material.

317. *See, e.g.*, Elledge v. Richland/Lexington Sch. Dist. Five, 573 S.E.2d 789 (S.C. 2002); Demos v. Ferris-Shell Oil Co., 740 N.E.2d 9 (Ill. App. Ct. 2000); Brown v. Nat'l Football League, 219 F. Supp. 2d 372, (S.D.N.Y. 2002).
318. Muncie Aviation Corp. v. Party Doll Fleet, Inc., 519 F.2d 1178, 1180 (5th Cir. 1975).
319. *See* Woodbury v. CH2M Hill, Inc., 76 P.3d 131 (Or. Ct. App. 2003); *see also* CHRISTOPHER B. MUELLER & LAIRD C. KIRKPATRICK, FEDERAL EVIDENCE § 89 (2d ed.); Daniel E. Feld, *Admissibility in Evidence, on Issue of Negligence, of Codes or Standards of Safety Issued or Sponsored by Governmental Body or by Voluntary Association*, 58 A.L.R.3d 148 (2004).
320. *See generally* 30C WRIGHT & MILLER, FEDERAL PRACTICE AND PROCEDURE § 7049; Fred Warren Bennett, *Federal Rule of Evidence, 803(8): The Use of Public Records in Civil and Criminal Cases*, 21 AM. J. TRIAL ADVOC. 229 (1997); James E. Robinson, *Challenging Admissibility and Use of Government Investigative Reports*, 38 TORT TRIAL & INS. PRAC. L. J. 887 (2003); Kurtis A. Kemper, *Admissibility, under Rule 803(8)(c) of Federal Rules of Evidence of "Factual Findings Resulting from Investigation Made Pursuant to Authority Granted by Law*," 180 A.L.R. Fed. 61 (2004).
321. *See* Robinson, *supra* note 320, at 887, 890–903 (discussing methods of "establishing 'enough negative factors to persuade a court that a report should not be admitted'") (citing *In re* Nautilus Motor Tanker Co., 85 F.3d 105, 113 (3d Cir. 1996)).
322. *See* Matthews v. Ashland Chem. Inc., 770 F.2d 1303, 1309–10 (5th Cir. 1985).
323. *See* Moss v. Ole South Real Estate, Inc., 933 F.2d 1300, 1310 (5th Cir. 1991).
324. *See* CHRISTOPHER B. MUELLER & LAIRD C. KIRKPATRICK, EVIDENCE 601 (1995).
325. Because federal environmental statutes generally do not allow recovery of damages, plaintiffs offer evidence of defendant's statutory/regulatory violation as evidence of their negligence claims based upon state law. The following decisions are representative of those that have concluded these environmental violations are evidence of negligence per se: Gill v. LDI, 19 F. Supp. 2d 1188 (W.D. Wash. 1998);

the issue under the *Restatement (Second) of Torts*,[326] conclude a negligence per se claim cannot be based upon violation of a statute enacted for the benefit of the general public rather than to protect individual interests from harm.[327] Still others hold violations of environmental statutes and regulations should be considered by the jury as nonconclusive evidence of negligence.[328]

Structuring the Multiplaintiff Trial
Bifurcation and Reverse Bifurcation

Since 1938, federal judges have been authorized to try issues separately.[329] Given the complexity of mass tort cases, bifurcation in one form or another must be considered. The process has provoked strong reactions from both sides of the proposition.[330]

In *Simon v. Philip Morris*, Senior District Judge Weinstein's opinion provided a comprehensive survey of the law beginning with English practice.[331] Judge Weinstein then turned his attention to a review of early American practice and modern authority, to include Federal Rules of Civil Procedure 42(b), 16, and 23(c)(4)(a). The court then comprehensively analyzed bifurcation in a Seventh Amendment context and specifically discussed a trial court's broad discretion to sever issues for trial in mass tort cases. In his summary, Judge Weinstein observed the context in which these decisions must be made:

> As previously noted in its related tobacco decisions . . . , this Court, in deciding how to structure *Simon II*, cannot ignore two fundamentals: (1) It is dealing with human institutions that, unlike the precise machinery of atomic physicists with variances approaching

---

Bernbach v. Timex Corp., 989 F. Supp. 403 (D. Conn. 1996). *See also* cases collected in Rudlin & Graham, *supra* note 32; Kenneth S. Abraham, *The Relation between Civil Liability and Environmental Regulation: An Analytical Overview*, 41 WASHBURN L.J. 379 (2002); Sheila G. Bush, *Can You Get There from Here?:Noncompliance with Environmental Regulations as Negligence Per Se in Tort Cases*, 25 IDAHO L. REV. 469 (1989); Roger Meiners & Bruce Yandle, *Common Law and the Conceit of Modern Environmental Policy*, 7 GEO. MASON L. REV. 923 (1999); Ellen Relkin, *The Sword or the Shield: Use of Governmental Regulations, Exposure Standards and Toxicological Data in Toxic Tort Litigation*, 6 DICK. J. ENVTL. L. & POL'Y 1 (1997).

326. RESTATEMENT (SECOND) OF TORTS §§ 286, 288.
327. *See, e.g.*, 325–343 E. 56th Street Corp. v. Mobile Oil Corp., 906 F. Supp. 669 (D.D.C. 1995) and commentary noted above.
328. *See, e.g.*, NutraSweet Co. v. X-L Eng'g Corp., 926 F. Supp. 767 (N.D. Ill. 1997) and commentary noted above.
329. *See* FED. R. CIV. P. 42(b).
330. *Compare* Steven S. Gensler, *Bifurcation Unbound*, 75 WASH. L. REV. 705 (2000) (discussing virtues of bifurcation) *with* Jennifer M. Granholm & William J. Richards, *Bifurcated Justice: How Trial-Splitting Devices Defeat the Jury's Role*, 26 U. TOL. L. REV. 505 (1995) (surveying and discussing reasons why bifurcation, severance, forced stipulations, and special verdicts should be eliminated in all but narrowly defined circumstances).
331. "[T]he court or judge may, in any case or matter, at any time or from time to time, order that . . . one or more questions of fact be tried before the others . . . and in all cases may order that one or more issues of fact be tried before any other or others." 200 F.R.D. 21, 25 (E. D.N.Y. 2001) (citing Rules of the English Supreme Court of Judicature (1883) order 36, rule 8.).

zero, must interpret the law reasonably, with some tolerance if it is to effectively serve its protective role; and (2) it is responding to a complex nationwide fraud allegedly created by defendants. The basic premise of law in this country remains that for every wrong there is a remedy, an effective and realistic remedy.[332]

Courts have discretion to manage their cases as they judge most efficient and fair. Those decisions are within a court's broad discretion and will not be disturbed absent an abuse of discretion.[333]

Bifurcation comes in many forms, from the straightforward bifurcation of liability from damages to "reverse trifurcation," such as that reviewed and advocated by Kathleen Strickland in California asbestos cases, where the first issues tried were medical causation and damages, the second issue was liability, and the third issue was punitive damages.[334] Strickland observes that mass tort cases are ideal examples where bifurcation can produce efficiency.

> Mass toxic tort litigation by its name denotes multi-party, multi-issues and therefore lengthy trials often resulting in, at minimum, court congestion and prevention of trials of criminal cases and other non-complex civil cases and, at worst, paralysis of the judicial system.... Bifurcation/trifurcation preserves each party's right to individually present his claim to a jury, shortens the trial (thereby saving costs to the litigants, judicial system and the taxpayers), facilitates jury understanding of the issues (thereby providing for a verdict that both parties can live with) and promotes resolution of the case by settlement after one or more initial stages. Bifurcation has long been used in anti-trust, patent, trademark and securities litigation and is therefore not a new solution to the problem of toxic tort litigation. However, the increasing—and overwhelming—number of toxic tort suits which are pending and which are waiting in the wings makes use of such management devices in such torts more important to the judicial system than ever before.[335]

As mentioned above, the concept of bifurcation has its critics. For example, Jennifer M. Granholm and William J. Richards refer to bifurcation and severance as "insidious" devices that "deconstruct" trials.[336] They probably would share Kanner's and Kanazawa's

---

332. *Simon*, 200 F.R.D. at 51.
333. *Id.* at 27; *see also In re* Master Key Antitrust Litig., 528 F.2d 5 (2d Cir. 1975); Parmer v. Nat'l Cash Register Co., 503 F.2d 275 (6th Cir. 1974).
334. Kathleen Strickland, *How to Structure a Mass Toxic Tort Trial—Bifurcation, Trifurcation, or Neither: Practical Considerations*, 406 P.L.I./Lit. 287 (Mar. 1991) (citing Meado v. Superior Court, 205 Cal. App. 3d 64 (Cal. App. 1 Dist. 1988)).
335. *Id.*
336. Granholm and Richards, *supra* note 330, at 542–43.

holistic view of the trial process. Indeed, they make analogies of the trial to concepts in Gestalt psychology:

> Gestalt psychology is the study of the perception of whole organisms. It may be summed up in one sentence: 'The whole is different from the sum of its parts.' Gestalt psychologists believe that nothing can be perceived or analyzed in a vacuum. It is a theory of interdependence and of wholes, not of artificially atomized components of the whole.... Studies of perception by Gestalt psychologists have demonstrated that people see parts of the whole, standing alone, differently than they view the whole in its entirety.[337]

You will find numerous sources analyzing empirical data on bifurcation, drawing conclusions on both sides of the question.[338]

Trifurcation

Punitive damages, where available, add to the potential complexity. Liability for punitive damages is arguably closely linked to the evidence to be presented concerning liability, while the quantum of punitive damages can involve evidence concerning such things as the wealth of the defendants. Courts have struggled with the best and most practical placement of the trials on these issues in cases where trial is divided into segments. Trifurcation of some sort is generally the result.[339] In *Hilao v. Estate of Marcos*, the trifurcation involved a trial of liability, then a trial of punitive damages, and finally a trial of compensatory damages. The court upheld that order of trial, noting the close link between evidence on punitive damages and evidence with regard to liability in the facts of that case (torture and murder).[340]

Test Plaintiffs

One option for the court and the parties is to use "bellwether trials." There are three principal issues here: (1) the use that will be made of the bellwether findings; (2) the means by which the bellwether plaintiffs will be selected; and (3) the manner in which the bellwether trials will be conducted.

---

337. Id.
338. See Meiring de Villiers, *A Legal and Policy Analysis of Bifurcated Litigation*, 2000 COLUM. BUS. L. REV. 153 (2000); Stephan Landsman, Shari Diamond, Linda Dimitropoulos & Michael J. Saks, *Be Careful What You Wish For: The Paradoxical Effects of Bifurcating Claims for Punitive Damages*, 1998 WIS. L. REV. 297 (1998) (providing a thorough and most interesting discussion of mock trial principles as applied in furtherance of the authors' experiment designed to produce data testing the conventional wisdom that bifurcation reduces trial time and favors the defendant, reviewing the data developed during their experiment and commenting on the nuances of the effect, if any, of bifurcation).
339. See, e.g., In re Bendectin Litig., 857 F.2d 290 (6th Cir. 1988), cert. denied, 488 U.S. 1006 (1989).
340. 103 F.3d 767 (9th Cir. 1996). Compare with comment regarding the danger of such early trial of punitive damages with respect to the rights of the defendants, D. Alan Rudlin, *Environmental and Toxic Tort Matters*, supra note 198; In re Simon II Litig., 211 F.R.D. 86, 187 (E.D.N.Y. 2002).

First is the issue of whether the findings will be extrapolated automatically across the balance of the plaintiffs. Absent agreement between the parties on this topic, there are substantial problems with extrapolation being required.[341] For example, if there are 200 individual plaintiffs, who have all allegedly sustained some sort of injury from a release of a chemical, trying the causation and damage issues with regard to 10 of them as individuals will not tell you what has happened to the other 190—on an individual basis. Causation as to each of them is likely to be based upon facts peculiar to the individuals, and people react differently under varying circumstances, making damages individualized. So, the first problem is the factual disconnect between what a court may decide as to the first 10, in this example, and the remaining 190. Second, if the case is tried to a jury, you run into the problem of parties' entitlement to have a jury make a decision as to each individual, a right that extrapolation would deny them. More commonly, bellwether plaintiffs are used for the purpose of benchmarking the value of the claim for settlement purposes. The parties and the court recognize that trying enough cases, if the plaintiffs are appropriately selected, will serve two related purposes. First, they will begin to give the parties enough information to value the cases for settlement. And, in the absence of settlement, the cases will have to be tried anyway—such small groupings perhaps being the only way that can be done.

Second, the court and the parties face the issue of how to select the bellwether plaintiffs. There are two principal paths that can be taken, either some form of party participation or some form of random selection. The problem with party participation in the selection process is that it normally results in the selection of extremes. The plaintiffs want their best claimants, and the defendants want precisely the opposite. If the objective is to foster settlement, such trials of extremes often achieve no purpose.

---

341. *See, e.g.*, Silivanch v. Celebrity Cruises, Inc., 333 F.3d 355, 359 (2d Cir. 2003), *cert. denied*, 540 U.S. 1105 (2004); Dodge v. Cotter Corp., 203 F.3d 1190 (10th Cir. 2000), *cert. denied*, 540 U.S. 1003 (2000) (another case where, in the absence of an agreed CMO or other order binding the balance of the plaintiffs to judgments concerning same, the court ruled that subsequent plaintiffs were not so bound. Multiple plaintiffs were involved in similar claims. The parties agreed to an initial bellwether trial of eight plaintiffs' claims. That trial resulted in a verdict for the defense when the jury determined plaintiffs failed to prove the defendant's negligence caused their exposure to hazardous materials. The Tenth Circuit held the second set of bellwether plaintiffs were not collaterally estopped from litigating defendant's liability); *In re* TMI Litig., 193 F.3d 613 (3d Cir. 1999), *cert. denied*, 530 U.S. 1225 (2000) (trial court's extension of findings adverse to test plaintiffs by summary judgment to the entire body of consolidated plaintiffs' claims overruled as an impermissible implication of the nontest plaintiffs' right to a jury trial); *In re* Chevron U.S.A., Inc., 109 F.3d 1016, 1021 (5th Cir. 1997) (results of a bellwether trial can be extrapolated to untried individual cases only if the court uses a "randomly selected, statistically significant sample" to ensure the test plaintiffs are representative of the group as a whole) (*see* § 6-2(b) for a more complete discussion of Chevron); *In re* Dow Corning Corp., 211 B.R. 545 (Bankr. E.D. Mich. 1997) (rejecting parties' proposal to choose test plaintiffs due to lack of showing of representativeness); MASS TORT LITIGATION § 16:26.

There are various ways to structure the participation of the parties in selection, though all, in the end, tend to suffer from this problem of extremes. Some alternatives include:

(a) Each side chooses some number of plaintiffs and the other party gets some smaller number of strikes;
(b) Each side selects a certain number of plaintiffs from across the full universe of plaintiffs;
(c) Each side selects a certain number of plaintiffs from each of several categories of plaintiffs;
(d) One party selects the category of plaintiffs from which the trial plaintiffs will be selected, and the other party selects the actual plaintiffs within that category (this presumes that all categories of plaintiffs will not furnish bellwethers for that particular round);
(e) Each side picks a certain number from each category (with strikes provided for if there are multiple selections from each category, and no strikes provided if each side only gets one per category).

There are undoubtedly many more ways to go about this, if active participation by the parties in the selection process is the approach adopted.

The other substantive alternative, regarded by many litigants and courts as being the superior option, is random selection. There are two principal paths to take here. One can simply select randomly from the entire population of plaintiffs, or one can categorize the plaintiffs and then select randomly within the categories. If one is trying to develop information that will be useful in settlement, the latter is generally considered to be the more effective method. It is generally referred to as "stratified random selection." The use of this method was endorsed by the Fifth Circuit Court of Appeals in *In re Chevron, USA* where the court stated:

> [t]he reasons for acceptance by bench and bar are apparent. If a representative group of claimants are tried to verdict, the results of such trials can be beneficial for litigants who desire to settle such claims by providing information on the value of the cases as reflected by the jury verdicts.[342]

---

342. 109 F.3d 1016 (5th Cir. 1997); *see also Hilao*, 103 F.3d at 782 (137 bellwether plaintiffs randomly selected from total 10,059 claims); *In re* Dow Corning Corp., 211 B.R. at 571–72 (suggesting a system of stratified random sampling in breast-implant bankruptcy litigation); Cimino v. Raymark Indus., Inc., 751 F. Supp. 649, 653 (E.D. Tex. 1990) (random selection of 160 trial plaintiffs in asbestos litigation involving 2,298 plaintiffs); Perez v. Wyeth Labs., Inc., 734 A.2d 1245, 1248–49 & n.2 (N.J. 1999) (discussing selection of five bellwether plaintiffs out of total of "approximately fifty" plaintiffs and referencing discussion in *Chevron* of representative sample of plaintiffs).

The mechanics of "stratified random selection" can vary. Typically, the court is called upon to randomly select plaintiffs from the various categories that have been agreed to previously by the parties and the court. Since discovery oftentimes has not been conducted on an individual level by the time this is done, discovery concerning the individual plaintiffs will take place between the time of this random selection and trial. In those circumstances, the parties may suggest to the court that its random selection in each category include more plaintiffs than ultimately would go to trial, then including a right on the part of the parties to strike a specified number of plaintiffs after the discovery is complete. The specific number of plaintiffs for the court to select and the specific numbers, if any, for the parties to have the right to strike would depend upon the nature of the litigation and the views of the parties. Obviously, the more the parties can participate in the selection process, the less "random" it ultimately becomes. Consequently, the more the parties participate, the less likely it is that a beneficial result will emerge.

Third, it is important to determine how the case will then be tried. There are two principal approaches that are taken: either trying all of the bellwethers together in a single consolidated proceeding or trying the bellwethers individually. If they are tried individually, the parties and the court must determine whether each bellwether trial will involve a completely separate jury or whether a single jury will hear more than one bellwether trial.

While trying a relatively modest number of bellwether plaintiffs' claims in a single trial has some practical attractiveness, the prejudice to the result (and to the utility of the result in settlement evaluations) is a notable consideration.[343] Trying cases involving too few bellwether plaintiffs will cost a great deal and not achieve much. If one were to use the illustration stated earlier in this section (200 individuals exposed in a chemical release) a trial involving only two of them could cost a great deal, but not really tell anyone very much about the likely range of findings (both as to causation and damages) a court or juries might come to if a substantially larger sampling went to trial. There is a balance, of course. You can have too few plaintiffs and not learn much— while spending a great deal. On the other hand, you can have so many plaintiffs that no one—judge or jury—can keep track of them and they all begin to look pretty much the same. All lawyers who try these cases have their own rules of thumb, oftentimes driven by the nature of the individual facts in their case and the number of plaintiffs. The point here, of course, is to think about it carefully once you get to that decision point in a case.

The number of bellwethers to use is also important—too many and the jury will not effectively differentiate between them, too few and little is learned. The right number is

---

343. *See* Malcolm v. Nat'l Gypsum Co., 995 F.2d 346, 351–352 (2d Cir. 1993); *In re* Repetitive Stress Injury Litig., 11 F.3d 368, 374 (2d Cir. 1993); Arnold v. E. Air Lines, Inc., 712 F.2d 899, 906 (4th Cir. 1983); Willging, *supra* note 34, at 354; Richard O. Faulk, et al., *Building a Better Mousetrap? A New Approach to Trying Mass Tort Cases*, 29 TEX. TECH. L. REV. 779, 794 (1998).

oftentimes a reflection of the type of case involved. The more individualized and complicated the types of damage to the plaintiffs, the smaller the number should be.

The decisions with respect to the use of bellwethers—how many, how selected, whether to consolidate for trial, and use that can be made of the results—are critical to how this process is employed by the parties and the court. The devil is truly in the details, and it is very important that those details be spelled out very carefully in the CMO.

Postinjury Evidence Concerning the Defendant's Culpability

The section heading[344] conjures up Federal Rule of Evidence 407, which concerns the admissibility of evidence of subsequent remedial measures.[345] Ellis and Case identified two circumstances where evidence of postinjury evidence concerning the defendant's culpability is admissible and does not run afoul of the policy reasons behind Rule 407:[346] (1) postinjury evidence probative of preinjury conduct for punitive damages purposes;[347] and (2) postinjury evidence of defendant's breach of continuing duty to warn of danger after exposure ceases.[348]

In *Dykes v. Raymark Industries*, at issue was the admissibility of documents created by the defendant after the last possible date on which the plaintiff was exposed to asbestos. The trial court admitted the documents "only to determine whether combined with other evidence in the case or standing alone they demonstrate that National Gypsum is liable for punitive damages for its activities before 1967."[349]

The plaintiff's theory in support of punitive damages was that National Gypsum suppressed information about asbestos dangers, and the letters at issue, from safety officials at National Gypsum, "imply opposition to printing safety labels and a desire to dilute the language in a pamphlet proposed by Johns-Manville. . . ."[350] The court conducted a straightforward relevance analysis[351] observing that "[i]t does not logically follow simply because the proffered evidence seeks to establish some act occurring after the injury that

---

344. *See* L. Neal Ellis, Jr. & Charles D. Case, *supra* note 90.
345. When, after an injury or harm allegedly caused by an event, measures are taken that, if taken previously, would have made the injury or harm less likely to occur, evidence of the subsequent measures is not admissible to prove negligence, culpable conduct, a defect in a product, a defect in a product's design, or a need for a warning or instruction. This rule does not require the exclusion of evidence of subsequent measures when offered for another purpose, such as proving ownership, control, or visibility of precautionary measures, if controverted, or impeachment. FED. R. EVID. 407.
346. "(1) [T]he conduct is not in fact an admission, since the conduct is equally consistent with injury by mere accident or through contributory negligence. . . . (2) [T]he other, more impressive ground for exclusion rests on a social policy of encouraging people to take, or at least not discouraging them from taking, steps in furtherance of added safety." FED. R. EVID. 407 advisory committee's note.
347. *See* Dykes v. Raymark Indus., Inc., 801 F.2d 810 (6th Cir. 1986).
348. *See* Lockwood v. A C & S, Inc., 744 P.2d 605 (Wash. 1987).
349. *Dykes*, 801 F.2d at 817–18.
350. *Id.*
351. *See* FED. R. EVID. 401.

the evidence cannot make the fact of the pre-injury conduct more probable than not."[352] The Court of Appeal quoted the trial court approvingly and affirmed the admission of the evidence:

> There was substantial circumstantial evidence that defendant knew or should have known that its asbestos-containing products constituted a significant potential health hazard during the period in which plaintiff's decedent used them. However, defendant took no steps to explore or cure that hazard during that period. However, *after the exposure period*, defendant generated a wealth of documents which demonstrate that it wished to avoid dealing with the problem, and which, we concluded in a document-by-document review, circumstantially demonstrated that defendant's attitude as reflected therein was *consistent with its position of non-activity during the period of plaintiffs' exposure*. Did, then, the fortuity of plaintiff's decedent's having stopped using National Gypsum products prevent the jury from considering whether the later-generated documents provided a basis for inferring that defendant acted willfully or recklessly during the exposure period?....[353]

This passage shows that the district court examined the postinjury documents and concluded that some foundation for their admission was established, that is, an attitude consistent with that which the plaintiffs claim existed prior to the injury.

In *Lockwood v. A C & S, Inc.*, an asbestotic plaintiff brought negligence and strict liability causes of action against the manufacturer of asbestos products to which he was exposed.[354] The trial court admitted evidence of knowledge of asbestos hazards that the defendant acquired after the plaintiff's last exposure to asbestos in the subject shipyards. The evidence was admitted as relevant to the continuing duty to warn claim. The documents were summarized by the Supreme Court as follows:

> The evidence at issue consists of three documents dated after 1972, when Lockwood retired. First, Lockwood introduced notes written in 1974 by John Marsh, Raymark's Director of Environmental Affairs. In these notes, Marsh describes his attempts to communicate with Raymark management about the seriousness of the asbestos health issue, and his assessment of that issue. The second document is a post-1974 review of literature on asbestos health from 1906 to 1974, which was prepared by Raymark officials. Finally, Lockwood introduced a 1977 paper by the

---

352. *Dykes*, 801 F.2d at 818.
353. *Id.*
354. 744 P.2d 605 (Wash. 1987).

Corporate Medical Director of Raymark on medical aspects of occupational exposure to asbestos.[355]

The defendants contended that any liability for failure to give a warning depended only on the extent of its knowledge of asbestos hazards when its product was manufactured or sold, or at the latest, when the plaintiff was last exposed. The defendant further argued that evidence of knowledge it acquired after the last exposure was irrelevant because there was no continuing duty to warn of the dangers after he was no longer exposed.

Plaintiff's position was summarized by the Court as follows:

> Lockwood argues that, because of the unique nature of asbestos exposure and disease, it is particularly appropriate to recognize a continuing duty to warn after such exposure ceases. Lockwood emphasizes that the health risks to persons exposed to asbestos continue after exposure. Hence, cases involving asbestos exposure are different from any other cases involving failure to warn of the dangers of a product, where the danger often ceases once the product is no longer being used. Specifically, Lockwood points out that after his exposure to asbestos ended, he permanently carried in his lungs the asbestos fibers he had inhaled. Lockwood argues that if he had been informed after he stopped working at the shipyards of the danger due to asbestos exposure and of the risk of smoking while asbestos fibers remained in his body, he could have reduced his disability by stopping smoking.[356]

The Court ruled as follows:

> We believe that where a person's susceptibility to the danger of a product continues after that person's direct exposure to the product has ceased, the manufacturer still has a duty after exposure to exercise reasonable care to warn the person of known dangers, if the warning could help to prevent or lessen the harm. Such a warning should be required to the extent practicable. Thus, it will depend on the circumstances if a warning to previous users of the product must be made by direct personal contact with such users. Alternative warning methods which may be reasonable in a given situation might include notices to physicians or advertisements.[357]

---

355. *Id.* at 618.
356. *Id.* at 619.
357. *Id.*; *see also* U.S. Gypsum Co. v. Mayor of Baltimore, 647 A.2d 405 (Md. 1994) (admitting postsale evidence of knowledge of asbestos manufacturer relevant pursuant to continuing duty to warn).

Although no case on point is found where this concept has been applied in a mass tort situation other than an asbestos products case, perhaps there will be circumstances where, after an occurrence such as a chemical release and the alleged tortfeasor generates documents indicating a postoccurrence recognition of a hazard, those documents might be admissible in a situation where there is a punitive damage claim and the evidence is consistent with preinjury conduct or where there is a continuing duty to warn.[358]

---

358. See Allan E. Corpela, *Failure to Warn as Basis of Liability under Doctrine of Strict Liability in Tort*, 53 A.L.R. 3d 239, § 5 (1973–2012).

CHAPTER 7

Settlement Considerations

Brendan K. Collins

By their nature, toxic tort cases are very difficult to try to a jury verdict. The factual and legal complexities presented by a typical case make jury response even more difficult to gauge. As trial nears, the plaintiffs and their counsel will have invested much more time and money to prepare the toxic tort case than a typical plaintiff's case would require, and the defendants will be forced to confront the risks of potentially enormous verdicts. These factors all create incentives for settlement. Paradoxically, while settlements are not uncommon, certain aspects of toxic tort cases may make it difficult to settle a case at an early point, or even a mid-point, in the proceedings. For example, because the viability and value of a plaintiff's case may be entirely dependent upon so-called novel scientific evidence, the defendant may not be willing to engage in serious settlement discussions until *Daubert* or *Frye* hearings take place. Also, given the long latency of some injuries that may result from exposures giving rise to toxic tort cases, a defendant may be uncertain as to the magnitude of the risk it faces until the case is several years old; the defendant may resist an early settlement to avoid establishing a precedent, should the injury claimed prove to be more widespread than anticipated. Finally, for cases involving an environmental exposure, the consequences of regulatory liability to the government play a role in determining whether and when the parties are able to reach a settlement.

Case Valuation: The First Step toward Settlement

Before the parties can make any progress toward settlement, each must have a clear sense of the risks involved in pursuing the case to verdict. Plaintiffs must know what they want or need, and defendants must know what they ought to be willing to pay to avoid the risk posed by trial. The parties must begin with a candid, unblinking examination of their own cases.

Assessing the Strengths and Vulnerabilities of Your Case

At bottom, toxic tort cases are no different from any other tort claims. The plaintiff must show that the defendant did something wrong, that the defendant's actions or omissions caused the plaintiff to be harmed in some way, and that the plaintiff's harm is sufficiently severe that a substantial award of money damages is appropriate. What separates toxic tort litigation from more common tort cases is that each of these components may be layered with enormous legal and factual complexity. This complexity means that each toxic tort claim is unique to some degree, making a formulaic approach to case valuation very difficult. There are a number of sound databases available through the major legal research providers and through more specialized providers that contain information about verdicts and settlements in toxic tort cases, but the idiosyncratic nature of these types of cases limits the specific usefulness of this information to some degree. It is much easier to identify the considerations that must be taken into account than it is to knit those considerations into a comprehensive case valuation approach. Accordingly, we offer here only a menu of considerations.

Wrongdoing

In toxic tort cases, theories of wrongdoing can range from ordinary negligence, to failure to comply with an environmental regulation, to strict liability for a defective product. The common thread is that the plaintiff needs to be able to display to the jury some conduct, or some omission, on the part of the defendant, that will rouse the jury to impose a verdict against the defendant. As a matter of law, a verdict might be sufficiently supported by conduct covering a broad spectrum, from an unintentional violation of an exceedingly complicated and technical regulatory scheme to knowing or reckless disregard for the health and safety of the public. Big verdicts tend to be associated with the latter end of that spectrum, not the former. The parties need to determine where on this continuum of culpability the defendant's conduct lies.

Causation

Causation is frequently the first hurdle a plaintiff must overcome by relying heavily on science. Expert testimony is indispensable to demonstrate causation, as toxic torts virtually always involve either personal injury or a risk of personal injury for which compensation is sought in the form of medical monitoring damages. In any case involving exposure to toxic substances, the plaintiff will need to present expert testimony that the plaintiff was exposed at or above a certain level, and that that exposure caused or can be expected to cause adverse changes in his or her health. In environmental cases, the fate and transport of contaminants in the environment through soil, soil vapor, groundwater, and air must be established by expert testimony. In this context, a case is only as good as the experts. While some exposure scenarios are simple for a jury to understand (e.g., ingesting a drug), others are much more complicated, and require a jury to absorb, or at least to accept, advanced scientific principles. Whether a jury reacts with skepticism or with credulity to complicated scientific theories may ultimately turn on the relative appeal of the parties and the expert witnesses they present.

The uncertainties with respect to causation are not only factual, but legal as well. Courts routinely conduct hearings to apply the *Daubert/Frye* standards to determine what expert testimony the jury will be permitted to hear. However, these hearings often take place shortly before trial, and therefore neither party can be confident of the expert testimony that it will be able to present to the jury until trial is nearly underway. Particularly in cases in which the defendant believes that it might succeed in excluding one of the plaintiff's critical experts, the timing of the *Daubert/Frye* hearing may affect the defendant's willingness to engage in serious settlement negotiations until trial is nearly at hand. The issue of causation and the use of experts in toxic tort cases is covered in detail in chapters 4, 5, and 9 through 12.

Damages

Toxic tort actions focus primarily on personal injury damages and potential personal injury damages, that is, medical monitoring damages. In certain types of toxic torts, for example, environmental contamination torts, other monetary damages may apply. The plaintiff may have lost property value or been unable to obtain financing or been required to replace a private water supply with public water supply. These damages may be substantial in a given case, particularly where many properties have been affected, and have the advantage of being liquidated, as they are generally supported by expert testimony. However, not all toxic torts involve property damage and the damages that receive the greatest attention tend to be personal injury damages and medical monitoring damages. Theories of liability and damages in toxic tort cases are discussed in chapter 2.

The evaluation of personal injury damages is conceptually routine, but practically less so. Rather than seeking damages for some orthopedic injury that may be well within the easy understanding of the jury, the toxic tort plaintiff might be seeking compensation for requiring surgery to replace a heart valve, or for sustaining some subtle neurological damage. Such damages are difficult to quantify; indeed, the value attached to such claims by a jury may depend as much on the persuasiveness of the plaintiff's liability case as it does on the evidence of damages.

In addition, a toxic tort case may include a claim for medical monitoring for the life of the affected plaintiff. The nature of the medical monitoring required adds, however, an additional level of complexity to the analysis. The defendant may argue that the plaintiff needs nothing more than a thorough annual physical, a practice typically recommended for the general population. The plaintiff's experts may opine as to the necessity of many advanced procedures, and other procedures that are routine (e.g., mammograms), but that should be performed more frequently as a result of the exposure. Medical monitoring claims, however, have one advantage—generally, they are liquidated by expert testimony, just as property damage and other economic claims are. Therefore, it is at least simple for a plaintiff to put a number on his claim, and for the defendant to put a number on its risk. It is far more difficult for counsel on both sides to evaluate the potential recovery of a plaintiff who has contracted leukemia and is in remission, but who may have lifetime impairments as a result of the leukemia and ensuing treatment.

Assessing Strengths and Vulnerabilities of Your Client

Once counsel develops an estimate of the range of potential recoveries in the case, he or she must evaluate the other factors that influence whether and when a case should be settled. Typically, defendants have a greater range of considerations to take into account, but plaintiffs, too, must look at factors beyond the strict merits of the claims. Ordinarily, timing is the most important factor to the plaintiffs. An elderly person who has been displaced from his home, or a child who has suffered neurological damage and requires special education and counseling, cannot wait indefinitely to get relief. With respect to the defendants, however, far more than timing must be taken into account. The defendants need to consider, at a minimum, the following factors: single verdict risk; repeatability; regulatory risk; and marketing/shareholder relations.

Single Verdict Risk

This refers to the ability of the client to absorb the largest verdict within any realistic range of probabilities. If defense counsel believes that there is a possibility, however small, of a company-threatening verdict, counsel must discuss that possibility thoroughly with the client and take it into account in forming recommendations. Of course, the realistic range of probabilities also is affected by the forum. Cases filed in courts with a history of pro-plaintiff rulings and large jury verdicts can make attractive settlement candidates, even when there is no genuine possibility of a company-threatening verdict.

Repeatability

This refers to the number of similar cases that are currently pending or are likely to be filed against the defendant. Litigation over environmental contamination at a particular facility is generally not repeatable, although a noteworthy exception to this rule is litigation against manufacturers of products with specific environmental impacts, such as methyl tertiary butyl ether (MTBE). Conversely, products liability litigation over pharmaceuticals is virtually always repeatable, so that one case, particularly a successful one, may beget thousands or tens of thousands of claims, singly or through consolidated class actions. When a claim is repeatable, a settlement may have implications for the defendant (and perhaps the defendant's industry) that go far beyond the case at hand. The defense must take these broader implications into account, as its approach to settlement will become part of its litigation strategy in other cases, and will influence the strategy of its opponents. Some defendants may choose to defend each claim vigorously, so as to discourage "copycat" litigation. However, in some cases it may be judicious to settle, even generously, strong claims until one is brought that the defense can use to alter the perceived value of all related claims. When a claim appears to be very weak, or is filed in a forum deemed more favorable to the defendants, the defense should exploit the opportunity provided not only to defeat that claim, but to discourage future litigation by undermining the viability of all such claims.

Regulatory Risk
This describes other exposure beyond civil damages that may be implicated should a defendant be found liable in a particular matter. Because the discharge of toxic substances to the environment is generally thoroughly regulated, the defendants in toxic tort cases typically have to consider not only litigation exposure to the plaintiffs, and similarly situated potential plaintiffs, but also a regulatory overlay. In the case of an environmental release (e.g., a release of gasoline from an underground storage tank system), the defendant is likely to be undertaking government-supervised remediation, or facing some other enforcement action. In the case of workplace releases, the defendant may be facing an Occupational Safety and Health Administration (OSHA) investigation, and may need to address risk issues on a facility-wide basis. Transportation incidents that result in civil claims may also result in enforcement action by the U.S. Department of Transportation. Pharmaceutical claims, of course, are often followed by action by the Food and Drug Administration (FDA). Toxic tort defendants must consider the impact that a settlement, or more important, the absence of a litigated result, would have on their ability to satisfy regulatory obligations, and vice versa. For example, if a plaintiff recovers on the theory that the defendant's defective product caused a release of contamination at one site, government agencies may seek to compel that defendant to undertake remedial action not only at that site, but at any other site at which the defendant's product may have been shown to have failed. In such a case, the precedential value of the civil verdict might result in ultimate liability for remediation far greater than any amount recovered by the plaintiff.

Marketing/Shareholder Relations
Finally, the defendant must consider the ongoing impact of the case on its reputation with the public, its shareholders, and with regulatory agencies that affect the defendant's business. Given the heightened attention accorded in recent years to disclosures to shareholders of publicly traded companies, companies have tended to adopt a more conservative approach to disclosing potential liabilities. Claims for damages that would be deemed

"material" must be disclosed, and the penalties for failing to disclose a claim that subsequently proves to be material may be very high, indeed.

Even beyond securities disclosure laws is the damage that certain types of claims can inflict on the carefully cultivated "brand" of a defendant. Many companies today make claims regarding ecological sensitivity, energy conservation, use of recycled products, and other types of claims lumped under the general heading of "sustainability." When a company ties its economic identity to such values, its investment in that brand image can be irreparably damaged by prolonged or widespread litigation claiming that the company exposed its neighbors, employees or, worst of all, customers to toxic substances.

Unique Considerations in Environmental Toxic Torts

While certain settlement considerations are common to all types of toxic tort claims, toxic tort claims arising from environmental contamination pose additional unique concerns. In addition to civil litigation, the defendants may confront regulatory compliance obligations and citizens' suits, each of which can be used as additional leverage in settlement negotiations by civil plaintiffs.

How Liability Claims Mesh with Cleanup Obligations

One question that arises whenever any remedial action is performed is what the end point should be, that is, "How clean is 'clean'?" Cleanup levels are often derived from an assessment of the health risk a site poses, and predictably there are often disputes between and among regulators, the responsible party, and the area residents as to an acceptable level of residual risk. A pending toxic tort action may provide a vehicle for a plaintiff to demand a more extensive cleanup from the defendant, and resolving the tort action may ease the pressure on the regulatory agency, resulting in a more rational approach to cleanup.

Noneconomic Relief Available to Plaintiff

Many state and federal statutes authorize private plaintiffs in environmental contamination cases to bring "citizens' suits" against violators of state statutes or regulations. The statutes authorize courts to award injunctive relief requiring the defendants to comply with provisions of environmental law, to abate nuisances, and to replace damaged water supplies, among other things. While these statutes typically do not provide for monetary damages to be paid to the plaintiffs directly, the plaintiffs are entitled to seek an assessment of civil penalties and restoration of environmental damage. Civil penalties are paid to the government, not the plaintiffs, but the recipient is less relevant than the fact that statutory civil penalties can reach into the millions of dollars. Likewise, environmental restoration can represent an enormous expense.

Statutory Claims for Attorneys' Fees

To the extent that plaintiffs pursue "citizens' suit" actions, the statutes that authorize such actions generally also authorize an award of attorney fees to the prevailing party. These fees are customarily calculated on a "lodestar" basis based on hours and rates. However, courts may take into account the size of the civil penalties recovered, or the environmental restoration ordered.[1]

Insurance Coverage Issues

Comprehensive General Liability insurance policies issued after 1986 generally do not cover environmental damages as a result of the "absolute pollution exclusion." Many companies, however, maintain separate insurance policies known as "Pollution Legal Liability" policies. Most of these are "claims made" policies, meaning that the policy in effect at the time the claim is presented to the insured is the policy applicable to the claim, assuming the claim is covered. Unfortunately, PLL policies also are ordinarily "diminishing" or "declining" policies, meaning that defense costs are deducted from policy limits. Unless the policy is quite large, the defendants' attorneys' fees and costs might entirely exhaust the coverage before any verdict or settlement can be paid.

Settlement Methods and Alternative Dispute Resolution

Once the parties evaluate the strength of their respective cases, the potential for recovery and the implications to both parties of a settlement or a verdict, the parties have a variety of options available to them under the general heading of "alternative dispute resolution" (ADR). The list below is not intended to be exhaustive, but rather to provide a sampling of the types of ADR processes that might be employed by motivated parties. In fact, one of the primary strengths of ADR as a means of resolution is that the ground rules applied and the legal effect of the outcome are entirely within the control of the parties, and limited only by their imaginations.

---

1. The "lodestar" analysis involves the calculation of the reasonable number of hours spent by the attorney multiplied by the reasonable hourly rate, but allows for upward/downward adjustment based upon the contingency of success, whether the fees were contingency-based, the quality of the attorney's work, and the results obtained. Pennsylvania v. Del. Valley Citizens Council for Clean Air, 478 U.S. 546, 553–54 (1986); Hensley v. Eckerhart, 461 U.S. 424, 435–36 (1983). In addition, courts have found that a "fee enhancement" in addition to lodestar-derived fees may be appropriate, but only when the lodestar amount would be insufficient to induce lawyers of comparable skill, judgment, professional representation, and experience to litigate the case. However, there is a strong presumption that the lodestar calculation is reasonable, and the fee applicant must present specific evidence that the lodestar fee would not have been "'adequate to attract competent counsel.'" Perdue v. Kenny A., 130 S. Ct. 1662, 1672 (2010) (quoting Blum v. Stenson, 465 U.S. 886, 897 (1984)).

Negotiation

Negotiation is not often discussed as a form of ADR, but it is, in fact, the original "alternative." In complex toxic tort cases, it is important that parties approach settlement negotiations with the same level of preparation that they might apply to more formal proceedings. Counsel should review all relevant expert reports, evaluate what testimony might be excluded based on a *Daubert/Frye* analysis, and become familiar with each detail of the plaintiff's claims, down to which tests the plaintiff seeks to have as part of a medical monitoring claim. In cases in which a trial date appears remote, it can be useful for the parties to agree to a conceptual deadline for concluding settlement negotiations. Although such deadlines are not binding, they can be effective in focusing the parties' attention and efforts on achieving a settlement while the window is open. The fact that the parties can agree at any time to resume negotiations is not fatal to the exercise. If the parties do, indeed, devote substantial time and attention to the settlement process, the deadline creates its own weight. If the deadline arrives and a settlement is not imminent, the parties will have a much better sense as to whether the discussions should be continued, or whether the parties should table the settlement issue until some time in the future.

Mediation

Mediation is a nonbinding process in which the parties are assisted in their negotiations by a neutral third party. The mediation process is entirely negotiable, although certain mediators prefer certain mediation styles, and it is essential that all of the participants and the mediator have a clear understanding of the manner in which the mediation will be conducted, and the mediator's role. Generally, mediation involves a presentation of some kind by each party to the mediator and to the other parties. The formality of such a presentation may range from a memorandum stating each party's case (similar to an opening statement) to the presentation of actual expert reports and deposition transcripts (though usually not live witnesses). The mediator, who is bound by the strictest rules of confidentiality, will then meet privately with each party to discuss its settlement position and opening offer. The mediator may conduct additional face-to-face meetings with the parties, or may engage in continuous shuttle diplomacy. Like a judge in a settlement conference, the mediator will prod the parties closer to a settlement by sharing his views of the strengths and weaknesses of each party's case and by general cajoling and wheedling. In all cases, the parties retain the ultimate decision-making authority, and aside from his persuasive powers, a mediator can do nothing to compel an unwilling party to settle the case.

Arbitration

Arbitration comes in many shapes and sizes, but it is generally a more formal process than mediation. Arbitration is patterned after the model of a bench trial, with the arbitrator, or panel of arbitrators, serving as both judge and finder of fact. Litigants ordinarily will present evidence at an arbitration hearing, and the nature of the evidence to be received and the conduct of the arbitration is generally conducted according to a set of written rules, most typically those published by the American Arbitration Association (hence the term "Triple-A Arbitration"). At the end of the proceeding, the arbitrator or panel will issue an award in favor of one party or another, accompanied by no written opinion or other explanation of the award. The effect of that award and a number of other features about the arbitration are subject to the agreement of the parties.

Most attorneys are familiar with the arbitration process through so-called court-annexed or compulsory arbitration. Many state and federal courts have local rules directing that all disputes of a certain size be diverted to a mandatory arbitration hearing. Most commonly, court-annexed arbitration involves a very brief hearing before a single arbitrator, who typically issues an award on the spot. Court-annexed arbitration is always nonbinding, and has been instituted by courts primarily to shorten their dockets by applying settlement pressure to smaller cases at an early stage.

Binding arbitration is a much more serious process in which the parties agree to submit their dispute to an arbitrator or a panel of arbitrators, and to be bound by the award without any right of appeal. Parties will ordinarily use either a single arbitrator, if they are able to agree on one, or each party will appoint an arbitrator, with the two arbitrators together picking a third arbitrator from an agreed-upon list of neutral arbitrators. Binding arbitration proceedings generally are conducted with a significant level of formality. However, it is important to remember that while the outcome of the process is nonconsensual, and will be enforced by any court, the decision to enter into the arbitration process is entirely voluntary.[2] Therefore, the parties can agree in advance to any set of rules that suits their needs, but once those rules are established and the proceeding is underway, the outcome can be modified only through the consent of all parties. Like mediation, the parties bear the cost of arbitration, with the exception of court-annexed arbitration, which is paid for typically by the court.

Because the outcome of arbitration is an award, arbitration lends itself to a number of interesting variations. For example, "baseball arbitration," named after the arbitration procedure described in the collective bargaining agreement governing major league baseball players, requires each party to submit its proposed award at the conclusion of the case, and the arbitrator must select either one proposed award or the other. "High-low arbitration" limits the arbitrator to an award within a certain range. As with all ADR methods, the variations in the structure are limited only by the parties' creativity, but it is important not to lose the ultimate purpose among the gimmickry. If parties devote too much time and energy to negotiating the terms of any arbitration, they may find that that time and energy might be better spent in direct settlement negotiations.

---

2. This assumes, of course, that the parties are not under a preexisting contractual obligation to arbitrate.

Summary Jury Trial

For cases destined for a jury trial, the parties may feel that one arbitrator, or even three, cannot adequately emulate the approach that a jury might bring to a case. The summary jury trial is designed to provide a means of answering the question, "What would a jury do?" The parties retain a neutral arbitrator (usually a retired trial judge) to serve as a judge, and empanel a private jury (usually of six), and sometimes two juries. The parties present scaled-down versions of their cases, typically with openings and closings, some live testimony, and videotaped expert testimony or expert reports. The scope of the presentation is determined by the parties, and the summary trial is ordinarily attended by representatives of the parties with decision-making authority. After the closings, the jury deliberates and renders a verdict.

Summary jury trial verdicts are not binding unless the parties agree in advance. The verdicts are advisory, and provide the parties with a "reality check" that may break down entrenched positions on one or both sides, paving the way to an accord. Advisory verdicts can be especially helpful when the parties and decisionmakers witness, or even participate in, the proceedings. Seeing even a mock-up of the trial process firsthand can educate clients about the risks of trial better than the most eloquent lecture in a lawyer's office. In this sense, summary jury trials are similar to the "bellwether plaintiff" approach to mass tort litigation, in which several representative cases are litigated to verdicts, and those verdicts used as a basis for settling remaining claims.

In crafting the parameters of a summary jury trial, the parties should keep two things in mind: cost and strategic exposure. The cost of the undertaking is substantial, but may vary widely. For example, the parties might hire a trial consultant to conduct telephone surveys and compile questionnaires to select a jury that most closely matches the jury likely to be empanelled by the court. Alternatively, the parties might wait around the courthouse until the jury pool is dismissed one day, and offer a random sample of jurors $100 to spend a few hours listening to the case. More important than the cost, however, is a party's risk of revealing too much about its case to the other side. For this reason, summary jury trials do not ordinarily provide an opportunity for cross-examination, and deposition testimony is often read aloud in lieu of truly "live" testimony.

Other Variations and Less Common Methods

The flexibility of ADR permits creative variations on the methods presented above. As noted, several variants of arbitration have developed, each with different strengths and weaknesses. Parties might agree to mediation that converts to arbitration after a certain period of time, with either the mediator or a new person serving as arbitrator. The possibilities of ADR are limited only by the imagination of the parties, but parties must avoid the temptation to allow the process to overwhelm the primary objective: resolving the outstanding claims.

Class Settlements under Federal Rule of Civil Procedure 23

Class action litigation, and the nuances of Federal Rule of Civil Procedure 23, are discussed in chapter 6, but a number of practical and legal issues arise when Rule 23 is used as a means of resolving a case rather than as a means of broadening one. Classes that are formed and ultimately certified solely for the purpose of implementing a settlement agreed to by the parties are known as "settlement classes." The degree to which proposed settlement classes must meet the criteria for class certification set forth in Rule 23, or more precisely, the vigor with which trial court judges apply those criteria, has engendered several disputes that ultimately have been resolved by the Supreme Court of the United States.

U.S. Supreme Court's Views

The two cases that define the Supreme Court's views on settlement classes are *Amchem Products, Inc. v. Windsor*[3] and *Ortiz v. Fibreboard Corp.*[4] Both *Amchem* and *Ortiz* considered settlement classes arising in the context of nationwide asbestos claims litigation.

Amchem Products, Inc. v. Windsor

In *Amchem*, the Supreme Court considered the use of settlement classes to consolidate asbestos claims throughout the nation and to settle them with respect to both present and future plaintiffs.[5] Committees representing the plaintiffs and the defendants conducted settlement negotiations and reached a global settlement agreement. The parties brought suit in federal court without any actual intention to litigate, seeking both certification of the class and approval of the global settlement agreement. The proposed class included all persons who had been exposed to asbestos attributable to any of the defendants, and the global settlement agreement set up administrative procedures to compensate current and future persons within the class.[6] The parties sought certification under Rule 23(b)(3), which provides an opportunity for class members to opt out of a settlement.

The Supreme Court's decision in *Amchem* addressed (1) the role that settlement plays in determining whether a class should be certified,[7] and (2) whether the fairness of the settlement is relevant to certification.[8] The Court first stated that "settlement is relevant

---

3. 521 U.S. 591 (1997).
4. 527 U.S. 815 (1999).
5. 521 U.S. at 597.
6. *Id.* at 600–02.
7. Prior to *Amchem*, courts were divided on whether the fact that a settlement had been reached should affect the certification determination. *See* Jennifer Dinham Henderson, *Protecting Rule 23 Class Members from Unfair Class Action Settlements: The Supreme Court's Amchem and Ortiz Decisions*, 27 Wm. Mitchell L. Rev. 489, 502 n.66 (*comparing* Georgine v. Amchem Prods., Inc., 83 F.3d 610, 617 (3d Cir. 1996), and In re Gen. Motors Corp. Pick-Up Truck Fuel Tank Prods. Liab. Litig., 55 F.3d 768, 799–800 (3d Cir. 1995), *with* In re Asbestos Litig., 90 F.3d 963, 975 (5th Cir. 1996), and White v. Nat'l Football League, 41 F.3d 402, 408 (8th Cir. 1994), *cert. denied*, 515 U.S. 1137 (1995)).
8. The *Amchem* court noted that some "courts have held that settlement obviates or reduces the need to measure a proposed class against the enumerated Rule 23 requirements." 521 U.S. at 618–19 (citing In

to a class certification" under Rule 23.[9] For example, "a district court need not inquire whether the case, if tried, would present intractable management problems . . . for the proposal is that there be no trial."[10] However, the Court urged that "other specifications of the rule—those designed to protect absentees by blocking unwarranted or overbroad class definitions—demand undiluted, even *heightened*, attention in the settlement context."[11] Furthermore, the Court stressed that in analyzing these requirements, a district court must reference only the claims or defenses raised in the pleadings and not those that may be covered by the settlement agreement.[12] The Supreme Court firmly directed lower courts not to consider the fairness of a settlement proposal until determining that the requirements for class certification were otherwise met. Ultimately, the Court's opinion in *Amchem* stands for the proposition that lower courts should more rigidly apply the certification requirements of Rule 23 with respect to settlement classes than was, perhaps, necessary in considering class certification without a contemporaneous settlement agreement.

The Supreme Court found that the adequate representation requirement under Rule 23(a)(4) was not satisfied in *Amchem* because the disparity of interests among class members who were presently injured and those who had only been exposed was too great. The presently injured plaintiffs were motivated by a desire for "generous immediate payments," while the plaintiffs who had only been exposed were seeking an "ample, inflation-protected fund for the future."[13]

Ortiz v. Fibreboard Corp.

As in *Amchem*, *Ortiz* involved a national settlement of asbestos claims with respect to both present and future plaintiffs.[14] Consequently, the Supreme Court reiterated the importance of heightened scrutiny of Rule 23's certification requirements with a focus on the claims and defenses in the pleadings as opposed to the settlement agreement.[15] However, unlike *Amchem*, the parties in *Ortiz* sought certification of a mandatory class under Rule 23(b)

---

re *Asbestos Litig.*, 90 F.3d at 975; *White*, 41 F.3d at 408; *In re* A.H. Robins Co., 880 F.2d 709, 740 (4th Cir. 1989), *cert. denied sub nom.* Anderson v. Aetna Cas. & Sur. Co., 493 U.S. 959 (1989); Malchman v. Davis, 761 F.2d 893, 900 (2d Cir. 1985), *cert. denied*, 475 U.S. 1143 (1986)).

9. *Amchem*, 521 U.S. at 619.
10. *Id.* at 620 (internal citation omitted).
11. *Id.* (emphasis added). In *Amchem*, the proposed certification was sought under Rule 23(b)(3), which requires "that the questions of law or fact common to class members predominate over any questions affecting only individual members, and that a class action is superior to other available methods for fairly and efficiently adjudicating the controversy." Fed. R. Civ. P. 23(b)(3). In addition, Rule 23(a)'s requirements of numerosity, commonality, typicality, and adequate representation must be satisfied for any class to be certified.
12. *Amchem*, 521 U.S. at 623.
13. *Id.* at 621–26.
14. *Ortiz*, 527 U.S. at 823–24.
15. *Id.* at 831–32.

(1)(B).[16] The defendants in *Ortiz* desired "total peace" from any future liability,[17] and certification under Rule 23(b)(1) "does not provide for absent class members to receive notice and to exclude themselves from class membership as a matter of right."[18] A Rule 23(b)(1)(B) certification may be appropriate where all potential plaintiffs must resort to a "limited fund" insufficient to satisfy all claims.[19] Under the settlement agreement, the *Ortiz* defendants were to create a trust fund that would be used to satisfy the claims of all current and future plaintiffs. This was the "limited fund" on which the proposed Rule 23(b)(1)(B) class certification was premised.[20]

The Supreme Court criticized this use of the limited fund model as contrary to the traditional concept of a limited fund, which had three defining characteristics. First, "the totals of the aggregated liquidated claims and the fund available for satisfying them, set definitely at their maximums, demonstrate[d] the inadequacy of the fund to pay all claims."[21] Second, "the whole of the inadequate fund was to be devoted to the overwhelming claims."[22] Third, "the claimants identified by a common theory of recovery were treated equitably among themselves."[23] The Court found that the fund in *Ortiz* was merely "limited . . . by the agreement of the parties" and "did not support the essential premises of mandatory limited fund actions."[24] To certify a mandatory class under the limited fund theory, the Court stated that under the heightened scrutiny required by *Amchem*, a district court must have evidence on which it "may ascertain the limit and the insufficiency of the fund, with support in findings of fact following a proceeding in which the evidence is subject to challenge."[25] Finally, the *Ortiz* Court cautioned that "any attempt to aggregate individual tort claims on a limited fund rationale" may compromise "the Seventh Amendment jury trial rights of absent class members,"[26] and that aggregation of monetary damage claims in such actions implicates the fundamental due process right of an individual not to be

---

16. Certification under Rule 23(b)(1)(B) requires that the "prosecuti[on] [of] separate actions by or against individual class members would create a risk of . . . adjudications with respect to individual class members that, as a practical matter, would be dispositive of the interests of the other members not parties to the individual adjudications or would substantially impair or impede their ability to protect their interests." FED. R. CIV. P. 23(b)(1)(B).
17. *Ortiz*, 527 U.S. at 823–24.
18. *Id.* at 832 n.13. It should be noted that Rule 23 was amended to provide that "[f]or any class certified under Rule 23(b)(1) or (b)(2), the court *may* direct appropriate notice to the class." FED. R. CIV. P. 23(c)(2)(A) (emphasis added). To some extent, this may ameliorate some of the *Ortiz* court's concerns with respect to notice to absent class members in mandatory class actions.
19. *See Ortiz*, 527 U.S. at 834–37.
20. *Id.* at 825–27.
21. *Id.* at 838.
22. *Id.* at 839.
23. *Id.*
24. *Id.* at 848.
25. *Id.* at 849.
26. *Id.* at 845–46.

"bound by a judgment *in personam* in a litigation in which he is not designated as a party or to which he has not been made a party by service of process."[27]

Lower Court Decisions

Amchem and *Ortiz* instruct district courts to place greater emphasis on the interests of absent class members in certifying settlement classes by a more rigorous analysis of Rule 23's certification requirements. While this instruction is often cited, lower courts frequently find distinguishing characteristics in the cases before them that permit settlement class certification.[28]

For example, in *Petrovic v. Amoco Oil Co.*,[29] the Eighth Circuit Court of Appeals stated that "the circumstances in *Amchem* and *Ortiz* that called for heightened attention to the requirements of [Rule 23]" were not present because the parties had engaged in years of extensive discovery and trial preparations and because the class was certified months before the parties reached the settlement.[30] Under the Eighth Circuit's view, *Amchem* and *Ortiz* are limited to those situations "in which the parties agree[] upon a class definition and a settlement before formally initiating litigation, and then present[] the district court with the complaint, proposed class, and proposed settlement" simultaneously.[31] Only where settlement and certification are proposed simultaneously does the court lack "'the opportunity, present when a case is litigated, to adjust the class, informed by the proceedings as they unfold.'"[32]

Numerous courts have recognized the heightened scrutiny required by *Amchem* and *Ortiz*, but have continued to certify settlement classes by distinguishing the Supreme Court cases factually. In *In re Pet Food Products Liability Litigation*,[33] the Third Circuit Court of Appeals approved certification of a settlement class composed of those who sought reimbursement for purchases of recalled pet food and those who sought other economic

---

27. *Id.* at 846 (quotation and citation omitted).
28. For a recent example of the cursory manner in which such settlement classes are sometimes certified, see *In re* IMAX Securities Litigation, No. 06-6128, 2012 U.S. Dist. LEXIS 86513 (S.D.N.Y. June 20, 2012) (holding that the heightened scrutiny under Rule 23(a) and (b) required in the settlement class certification context was satisfied in a case involving claims brought under the Securities Exchange Act). *See also* Hawkins v. Comm'r of the N.H. Dep't of Health & Human Servs., No. 99-143, 2004 U.S. Dist. LEXIS 807, at *5–13 (D.N.H. Jan. 23, 2004) (approving certification of a settlement class involving claims against the New Hampshire Department of Health and Human Services for failure to provide dental services for which the plaintiffs were eligible under the Social Security Act).
29. 200 F.3d 1140 (8th Cir. 1999).
30. *Id.* at 1145–46.
31. *Id.*; *see also* Joel A. v. Giuliani, 218 F.3d 132, 139 (2d Cir. 2000) (distinguishing *Amchem* because "the class was certified and the case intensively litigated for more than two years before settlement negotiations began"); *In re* Cendant Corp. Sec. Litig., 109 F. Supp. 2d 235, 252 (D.N.J. 2000) (distinguishing *Amchem* because the "composition of the class here was already scrutinized and certified for litigation" prior to settlement), *aff'd*, 264 F.3d 201 (3d Cir. 2001).
32. *Petrovic*, 200 F.3d at 1146 (quoting *Amchem*, 521 U.S. at 620).
33. 629 F.3d 333 (3d Cir. 2010).

damages for pets that became ill or died.[34] The Third Circuit rejected an objection to certification on the ground that an intraclass conflict prevented the named plaintiffs from adequately representing the class, distinguishing *Amchem* where some class members had only future claims. In *In re Pet Food Products*, all class members had present claims.[35] Many of the objectors' concerns were preserved for the fairness inquiry, to be reached by the court only after certifying the class.[36] Similarly, in *Hanlon v. Chrysler Corp.*,[37] the Ninth Circuit Court of Appeals stressed that the adequate representation problem in *Amchem* was that the "class was never divided into sub-classes and additional counsel was never appointed to represent the interests of plaintiffs with as yet undeveloped or undiagnosed injuries."[38] In *Hanlon*, the plaintiffs filed a series of state class actions seeking recovery from Chrysler on a variety of tort theories for an allegedly defective rear latchgate, which actions were consolidated in federal court. Settlement was reached quickly, and the parties sought certification of the nationwide class and approval of the settlement agreement. The only relief covered by the settlement agreement was repair or compensation for the "allegedly defective rear latchgate," which was essentially identical for all the plaintiffs.[39] Personal injury and wrongful death claims were excluded from the settlement agreement. Therefore, the *Hanlon* class presented no adequate representation problem.[40]

Some courts have focused on the predominance requirement of Rule 23(b)(3) in distinguishing a case from *Amchem*. In *Ingram v. Coca-Cola Co.*,[41] the district court addressed predominance in the context of a Title VII pattern or practice of discrimination claim against an employer. Focusing on *Amchem*'s directive to address the certification requirements "on the substantive aspects of class members' legal claims, rather than on the terms of a proposed settlement,"[42] the district court found predominance to exist because of "the 'significance' of common issues under the substantive law governing each class member's claim of discrimination."[43] Since proving the pattern or practice claim as to the class entitled all of the individual claims of discrimination to a presumption of validity, common issues predominated.[44] Some courts simply address the predominance issue by citing

---

34. *Id.* at 337–38, 344.
35. *Id.* at 344; *see also* Schneider v. Citicorp Mortg., Inc., 324 F. Supp. 2d 372, 375 (E.D.N.Y. 2004) (distinguishing *Amchem* because the class in question was "not split between groups of currently injured and potentially injured persons" presenting the potential for conflicting interests and inadequate representation).
36. *In re Pet Food Prods.*, 629 F.3d at 346 n.20, 353–56 (remanding for further Rule 23(e) proceedings on the allocation for certain claims). *See* "Fairness Hearings," *infra*.
37. 150 F.3d 1011 (9th Cir. 1998).
38. *Id.* at 1020.
39. *Id.* at 1018, 1021.
40. *Id.*
41. 200 F.R.D. 685 (N.D. Ga. 2001).
42. *Id.* at 700.
43. *Id.*
44. *Id.* at 701; *see also* Shaw v. Toshiba Am. Info. Sys., Inc., 91 F. Supp. 2d 942, 957 (E.D. Tex. 2000) (distinguishing *Amchem* because, unlike the asbestos claimants, the plaintiffs were not "exposed to different

to *Amchem* for the proposition that predominance "'is a test readily met in certain cases alleging consumer . . . fraud.'"[45]

In a recent *en banc* decision, the Third Circuit found that in the settlement context, variations in state law that may be outcome-determinative do not predominate over common issues.[46] The focus of the predominance inquiry is on "whether the defendant's conduct was common as to all of the class members, not on whether each plaintiff has a 'colorable' claim."[47] At issue was the certification of a class and settlement of antitrust claims brought by direct purchasers and indirect purchasers of diamonds, which the district court approved even though many states' antitrust statutes do not extend standing to indirect purchasers.[48] The *en banc* opinion noted that "concerns regarding variations in state law largely dissipate when a court is considering the certification of a settlement class" because the court "need not inquire whether the case 'would present intractable management problems,'" citing *Amchem*.[49]

There are, however, limits to the liberties lower courts will take to certify a settlement class, particularly when doing so implicates due process issues such as adequate representation. An intraclass conflict was found to exist in *Dewey v. Volkswagen AG*,[50] where the Third Circuit Court of Appeals reversed the district court's certification of a single-settlement class in a products liability and consumer fraud action, alleging that sunroofs on certain vehicle models allowed water to leak into the vehicle. The class was made up of the "reimbursement group" and the "residual group," and all representative plaintiffs were in the reimbursement group.[51] Residual group members could make claims on money remaining in a settlement fund but only after claims of members in the reimbursement group were satisfied by the fund.[52] The representative plaintiffs thus had an "incentive

---

products from different sources over different time periods," did not have varying levels of injury, and presented no conflict of law issues); *In re* Lorazepam & Clorazepate Antitrust Litig., 205 F.R.D. 369 (D.D.C. 2002) (finding that common issues predominate because the only individually unique issue was calculation of damages for each plaintiff and resolution of the case in one proceeding would be far more efficient than individualized litigation); Ramirez v. DeCoster, 203 F.R.D. 30 (D. Me. 2001) (common issues predominate in plaintiff workers' racial discrimination claims against defendant egg farmers because discriminatory practices making up the bulk of the case are common to all plaintiffs).

45. *See* Grove v. Principal Mut. Life Ins. Co., 200 F.R.D. 434, 440–41 (S.D. Iowa 2001) (quoting *Amchem*, 521 U.S. at 625) (holding that adequate representation and predominance requirements were met because plaintiffs were a class of readily identifiable consumers allegedly defrauded via the same or similar deceptive sales techniques who sought money damages that were subject to objective quantification via standardized formulas).
46. Sullivan v. DB Invs., Inc., 667 F.3d 273 (3d Cir. 2011), *cert. denied sub nom.* Murray v. Sullivan, 132 S. Ct. 1876 (2012).
47. *Id.* at 299–300 (citing Wal-Mart Stores, Inc. v. Dukes, 131 S. Ct. 2541, 2551 (2011)).
48. *Id.* at 304.
49. *Id.* at 297, 302–03 (quoting *Amchem*, 521 U.S. at 620). The Third Circuit likened the dissent's insistence that a district court assure itself that each class member has a valid claim to a Rule 12(b)(6) inquiry. *Id.* at 305. In the settlement context, however, a "merits inquiry is particularly unwarranted." *Id.* at 306.
50. 681 F.3d 170 (3d Cir. 2012).
51. *Id.* at 187.
52. *Id.* at 175–76.

to shift the dividing line between the residual and reimbursement groups in order to maximize their own recovery, at the expense of other members of the class who lacked a representative to protect their interests."[53] Focusing on whether any intraclass conflict was "fundamental" and thus violated Rule 23(a)(4), the Third Circuit found present "precisely the type of allocative conflict of interest that exacerbated the misalignment of interests in *Amchem*."[54] The court suggested that on remand the plaintiffs either eliminate the distinction between the reimbursement group and the residual group, or divide the groups into subclasses that would be certified separately.[55] Notably, the court rejected an objection that there is an intraclass conflict between class members who have already suffered leakage and those who have not, though all of the representative plaintiffs fell into the former category.[56]

State Court Settlement Class Certification

When considering the use of settlement classes, it is important to recognize that not all of the federal jurisprudence under Rule 23 is transferable to state court litigation. However, to the extent the federal jurisprudence is based on constitutional limitations, for example, the preservation of Seventh Amendment jury rights, these decisions will control. Also, as the Eighth Circuit noted in *Petrovic*, the "heightened scrutiny" required by *Amchem* and *Ortiz* is not necessary when the class has been certified prior to the settlement, and the issues relevant to class certification have been thoroughly vetted by the parties and the court.

Fairness Hearings

Whether as part of the certification process of a settlement class, or independently in the case of a settlement of a preexisting class action, the court must ultimately determine the "fairness" of any settlement binding upon class members.[57] This fairness evaluation, which the Supreme Court banished from the certification analysis for settlement classes, does not differ between settlement classes and classes certified before a settlement is reached. The parties must provide notice to all reasonably identifiable class members of the certification of the class and the terms of the settlement, and the court must hold a hearing to receive evidence from the parties and objections from class members and other affected parties before approving the settlement. As the Supreme Court points out in *Ortiz*, this hearing is especially important when the certification of a mandatory class is sought on the "limited fund" theory.

---

53. *Id.* at 187 n.15.
54. *Id.* at 188.
55. *Id.* at 189–90 (citing *Ortiz*, 527 U.S. at 856).
56. *Id.* at 185–87.
57. *See* FED. R. CIV. P. 23(e).

In a fairness hearing, the court must give comprehensive consideration to all relevant factors and yet the settlement hearing must not be turned into a trial.[58] These factors include (1) the complexity, expense and likely duration of the litigation; (2) the reaction of the class to the settlement; (3) the stage of the proceedings and the amount of discovery completed; (4) the risks of establishing liability; (5) the risks of establishing damages; (6) the risks of maintaining the class action throughout trial; (7) the ability of the defendant to withstand a greater judgment; (8) the range of reasonableness of the settlement fund in light of the best possible recovery; and (9) the range of reasonableness of the settlement fund to a possible recovery in light of all attendant risks of litigation.[59]

The court may approve a settlement only if it determines that it is "fair, reasonable and adequate" in light of all these factors.

Conclusion

The size and complexity of toxic tort cases makes the prospect of settlement at once more difficult and more urgent. If the parties approach the settlement table with equal parts preparation, motivation, and imagination, however, it is possible to reach an accord in even the most intractable case.

---

58. *See* UAW v. Gen. Motors Corp., 497 F.3d 615, 635 (6th Cir. 2007).
59. *Schneider*, 324 F. Supp. 2d at 376 (quotation and citation omitted).

CHAPTER 8

Emerging Areas of Litigation and Significant Legal Issues

Shawna Bligh and Chris Wendelbo

This chapter provides an overview of emerging areas of toxic tort litigation and significant legal issues related to such litigation. Evolving areas of toxic tort litigation include climate change–based nuisance actions, groundwater and subsurface contamination, hydraulic fracturing, and workplace exposure. This chapter also will address recent case law on issues relevant to the toxic tort litigator, including new developments and emerging patterns on issues such as class actions, damages, experts, medical monitoring, and the use of risk assessments to prove causation in toxic tort cases. One common theme is prevalent in all of these issues—toxic tort litigation remains a highly dynamic area of law requiring even the most skilled practitioner to stay abreast of the latest developments.

Emerging or Evolving Areas of Toxic Tort Litigation
Hydraulic Fracturing

As part of a renaissance of increased domestic oil and gas production, U.S. oil and gas producers are using improved techniques to access oil and gas reserves that were previously unavailable, as well as rejuvenating formerly diminished wells. One method for increasing production is through the use of hydraulic fracturing, also known as "fracking." During the fracturing process, engineered fluids containing chemical and natural additives are pumped under high pressure into a natural gas or oil well to create and hold open fractures in the oil or natural gas formation. These fractures, in turn, allow oil and gas to flow to the well by increasing the exposed surface area of the rock in the formation.[1]

---

1. *See* Mary Tiemann & Adam Vann, *Hydraulic Fracturing and Safe Drinking Water Act Issues*, Congressional Research Service 7-5700 (Apr. 10, 2012), *available at* http://www.crs.gov (citing American Petroleum Institute, *Hydraulic Fracturing*, http://www.api.org/policy/exploration/hydraulicfracturing).

As the use of hydraulic fracturing has increased, so too have concerns about perceived potential negative environmental and human health impacts. Many concerns about hydraulic fracturing center on potential risks to public health and the environment, including contamination of drinking water resources, increased groundwater withdrawal, creation of wastewater and contaminated waste, destruction of habitat, and even seismic activity.

The most significant recent developments in hydraulic fracking involve the unprecedented amount of state legislative and regulatory activity. In the absence of clear federal statutory or regulatory governance of fracking, various states have begun modifying existing or promulgating new statutory and regulatory guidance. Thus, the practitioner must closely examine the respective state regulatory structure for possible new regulatory schemes that make historic governance or case law potentially obsolete.

In addition to spawning increases in regulatory activity, increased hydraulic fracking has resulted in more traditional private tort lawsuits claiming personal injury, making medical monitoring claims, and asserting traditional property damage claims for contamination to surface or groundwater. In addition, fracking has prompted numerous claims for various forms of injunctive relief to prohibit fracking, including requests to impose moratoriums on fracking.

It appears from a survey of cases on file that plaintiffs have generally asserted claims involving traditional negligence, nuisance, trespass, and violation of state regulatory provisions. Several recent traditional tort cases bear mentioning. A representative case is *Fiorentino v. Cabot Oil & Gas Corp.*[2] In *Fiorentino*, the plaintiffs brought a claim alleging that the defendants negligently conducted hydraulic fracturing and other natural gas production activities, allegedly releasing methane, natural gas, and other toxins onto the plaintiffs' land and into their groundwater. Their causes of action included: (1) a claim pursuant to the Pennsylvania Hazardous Sites Cleanup Act (HSCA); (2) negligence; (3) private nuisance; (4) strict liability; and (5) medical monitoring.

Interestingly, the defendants had previously entered into a consent order and agreement (COA) with the Pennsylvania Department of Environmental Protection (PDEP) agreeing to implement corrective action to address some of the same environmental violations that form the basis of the plaintiffs' claims, including allegations that faulty gas well casings caused the alleged contamination of the plaintiffs' private water supplies. In response to the defendants motion to strike and motion to dismiss, the court ruled that the plaintiffs could proceed with the litigation.[3]

This ruling leaves unanswered whether operators will be required to defend both private causes of action and enforcement actions by a regulatory agency simultaneously for the same alleged activities or violations. A second unanswered issue was whether fracking

---

2. 750 F. Supp. 2d 506 (M.D. Pa. 2010).
3. *Id.* at 516.

was deemed to be an abnormally dangerous or ultrahazardous activity as a matter of law, subjecting the defendants to strict liability (without proof of fault) for harm caused by their activities.

When used in conjunction with a fracking case, strict liability encompasses several theories, but the operative one in natural gas litigation is probably the abnormally dangerous theory. Since liability is, however, limited to the type of harm that makes the activity abnormally dangerous, several factors influence whether an activity is considered abnormally dangerous: the existence of a high degree of risk of great harm; the inability to eliminate the risk through reasonable care; whether the activity is unusual; whether the activity is inappropriate for the area; and the extent to which the activity's dangerousness outweighs its value to the community.[4]

A good representative case regarding the assertion of strict liability claims against an oil and gas producer is *Berish v. Southwestern Energy Production Co.*[5] In *Berish*, the plaintiffs claimed that gas drilling is, by definition, abnormally dangerous. The court declined to dismiss the strict liability claim prior to discovery, suggesting that theoretically natural gas by definition may be an abnormally dangerous activity. The court noted, however, that the claim may be difficult to prove. A second representative case is *Tucker v. Southwestern Energy Co.*[6] In *Tucker*, the court addressed whether hydraulic fracking was an ultrahazardous activity for strict liability purposes and whether air contamination may be considered a trespass. In a consolidated case, one group of plaintiffs asserted that the defendants' fracking had contaminated their water well, while another group of plaintiffs asserted that the fracking had contaminated the air on their property. They alleged claims of nuisance, trespass, negligence, and strict liability, as well as injunctive relief in the form of monitoring.

The court denied the motion to dismiss prior to summary judgment, arguing that determination of whether hydraulic fracking was an ultrahazardous activity was a question of law, and such a fact-intensive determination would be decided on a full record at the summary judgment stage. The court stated that fracking would be considered an ultrahazardous activity if the companies' production activities (1) necessarily present a risk of serious harm that cannot be eliminated by the exercise of the utmost care, and (2) are not a matter of common usage.[7]

In *Evenson v. Antero Resources*, a Colorado district court ruled that declaratory relief claims to halt drilling operations, brought in anticipation of fracking that had not yet occurred, could not be supported.[8] The class action lawsuit sought to force the defendants

---

4. *Id.*
5. 763 F. Supp. 2d 702 (M.D. Pa. Feb 3, 2011).
6. 2012 U.S. Dist. LEXIS 20697 (E.D. Ark. Feb. 17, 2012).
7. *Id.* at 3.
8. Case No. 2011 CV 5118 (Dist. Ct., Denver Cnty.) (Aug. 12, 2012).

to establish a medical monitoring fund to cover research and treatment of any illnesses that can be linked to drilling activities, as well as use state-of-the-art safety measures to safeguard the health of those living near the drilling rigs. The initial complaint also sought compensation to homeowners for lost property values related to the presence of drilling nearby. In response to a motion to dismiss, the plaintiffs amended their complaint to a single claim of declaratory relief in the form of a permanent injunction prohibiting the plaintiffs from conducting oil or gas drilling activities near the retirement community of Battlement Mesa in Colorado. While not explicitly alleged as an anticipatory nuisance case, the plaintiffs in *Evenson* alleged acute health effects (burning eyes and throats) and regulatory violations largely based on potential future injuries and conditions such as water contamination, chemical exposures, and personal injuries as the basis for the suit.

The court ruled that it lacked jurisdiction to grant declaratory relief because Colorado's Oil and Gas Conservation Act and Administrative Procedures Act provided a statutory mechanism to seek judicial review of a drilling permit. Second, the claim was not ripe as no drilling had occurred and the plaintiffs could not support their tort claims until injuries began to occur.

An emerging area of litigation involving hydraulic fracturing involves the extent to which a municipality may regulate or govern hydraulic fracturing within its corporate boarders. *Anschutz Exploration Corp. v. Town of Dryden*,[9] a case of first impression in New York, could be a sentry case for many other cases that might arise throughout the United States as opponents of hydraulic fracturing attempt to stop the practice. In *Anschutz*, the New York state trial court was asked to determine whether a local municipality may use its power to regulate land use to prohibit exploration for, and production of, oil and natural gas by use of high-volume hydraulic fracturing. The court held that the town of Dryden's ban on gas drilling fell within the authority of local governments to regulate local land use, affirming the authority of towns to ban drilling—including fracturing—within their borders.[10] In reaching its decision, the court noted that Pennsylvania and Colorado courts have considered the issue of the use of the local zoning power to regulate the location of natural gas and reached the same conclusion.

Groundwater and Subsurface Contamination

While groundwater and subsurface contamination have long been issues of consequence to the toxic tort practitioner, state tort law claims and their interrelationship with state environmental laws are gaining prominence as the causes of action of choice for many claimants. The use of state tort law to address groundwater and subsurface contamination raises a myriad of ancillary issues, such as statutes of limitation and the interrelationship

---

9. 940 N.Y.S.2d 458 (Sup. Ct. 2012).
10. *Id*. at 457–69.

of these statutes on various common law doctrines, including the continuing tort doctrine. Other issues arising in litigation asserting state law claims for groundwater and subsurface contamination include recoverable costs under state environmental laws and preclusion of state tort law claims by state environmental laws.

In *Abnet v. Coca-Cola Co.*, neighboring property owners brought an action in Michigan federal court alleging that Coca-Cola's spraying of wastewater on its property contaminated groundwater in violation of Michigan law.[11] More specifically, the plaintiffs alleged that the spraying depleted oxygen in the affected soil, creating conditions that caused naturally occurring heavy metals such as manganese, iron, lead, and arsenic to leach into groundwater. The plaintiffs claimed a variety of harms resulting from the allegedly contaminated groundwater, including property damage, loss in property value, and physical ailments such as gastrointestinal problems, developmental disabilities, kidney dysfunction, and nausea. The plaintiffs asserted seven different causes of action, including negligence and/or gross negligence, negligence per se, nuisance, trespass, strict liability based on abnormally dangerous activity, Part 201 of Michigan's Natural Resources and Environmental Protection Act (NREPA), and the Michigan Environmental Protection Act (MEPA).[12]

Coca-Cola moved to dismiss four of the seven claims—namely, negligence per se, trespass, the plaintiffs' claims under 201 of NREPA, and the plaintiffs' claims brought pursuant to MEPA. With respect to negligence per se, Coca-Cola asserted that such a claim was not an independent cause of action under Michigan law. The federal district court agreed, holding that while negligence per se is a burden-shifting mechanism under a claim of negligence, the plaintiffs cannot maintain a separate claim of negligence per se.[13]

With respect to trespass, the district court stated that to recover in Michigan, a plaintiff must show "an unauthorized direct or immediate intrusion of a physical, tangible object onto land over which the plaintiff has a right of exclusive possession."[14] The court found persuasive dicta from prior Michigan cases that stated "one does not have ownership or exclusive possession over water beneath one's property."[15] Accordingly, the court held that Michigan law does not recognize claims of trespass where groundwater contamination is the only alleged injury.

---

11. 786 F. Supp. 2d 1341 (W.D. Mich. 2011).
12. *Id.* at 1343.
13. *Id.* at 1345 (citing Zeni v. Anderson, 243 N.W.2d 270 (Mich. 1976) ("While some Michigan cases seem to speak of negligence per se as a kind of strict liability . . . the negligence per se approach just does not work."); Klanseck v. Anderson Sales & Serv., Inc., 393 N.W.2d 356 (Mich. 1986) ("The fact that a person has violated a safety statute may be admitted as evidence bearing on the question of negligence . . . evidence of violation of a penal statute creates a rebuttable presumption of negligence.")).
14. *Id.* (citing Adams v. Cleveland Cliffs Iron Co., 602 N.W.2d 215 (Mich. Ct. App. 1999)).
15. *Id.* at 1346 (citing Postma v. Cnty. of Ottawa, 2004 Mich. App. LEXIS 2307, at *9 (Mich. Ct. App. Sept. 2, 2004)).

The federal district court also dismissed the plaintiffs' claims under Part 201 of NREPA. As noted by the court, NREPA defines "'costs of response activity'" to mean "'all costs incurred in taking or conducting a response activity, including enforcement costs.'"[16]

A "response activity" is, in turn, "evaluation, interim response activity, remedial action, demolition, or the taking of other actions necessary to protect the public health, safety, or welfare, or the environment or the natural resources. Response activity also includes health assessments or health effect studies carried out under the supervision, or with the approval of, the department of public health and enforcement actions related to any response activity."[17]

The plaintiffs sought to recover the cost of bottled water for drinking and cooking, and for the replacement or repair of plumbing fixtures and other personal property. The district court held that these costs were not recoverable under NREPA because "Part 201 allows recovery of costs for response activities, which are activities taken to identify and remedy environmental or health hazards" and "not reimbursement of private property damage."[18]

Finally, the district court considered Coca-Cola's motion to dismiss the plaintiffs' claims for injunctive and declarative relief under MEPA. Coca-Cola asserted that courts do not have subject matter jurisdiction to review an ongoing environmental response directed by Michigan Department of Natural Resources & Environment (MDNRE). The federal court noted that while decisions by MDNRE are ultimately subject to judicial review, Part 201 of NREPA states that a court "does not have jurisdiction to review challenges to a response activity selected or approved by the [MDNRE]" until "after the completion of the response activity."[19] The plaintiffs, however, stated that they were not challenging MDNRE decisions, but were merely seeking additional response activities under MEPA, which, they alleged, provided citizens with the right to seek declaratory and equitable relief "for the protection of the air, water, and other natural resources and the public trust in these resources from pollution, impairment, or destruction." The plaintiffs alleged that because they are not seeking to enjoin or directly interfere with the response activities mandated by MDNRE, the preenforcement bar to judicial review did not apply.

The federal court rejected this argument stating, "seeking injunctive relief requiring Defendants to perform additional response activities not required by MDNRE is tantamount to challenging the adequacy of MDNRE's decisions with respect to remedial action."[20] The court acknowledged that while MEPA provides an outlet for such a claim,

---

16. *Id.* (quoting MICH. COMP. LAWS § 324.20101(ff)).
17. *Id.* (quoting MICH. COMP. LAWS § 324.20101(ee)).
18. *Id.*
19. *Id.* at 1347 (citing MICH. COMP. LAWS § 324.20137(4)(d)).
20. *Id.*

the Michigan courts have held that MEPA is subject to the preenforcement rule. Accordingly, the court held that it lacked subject matter jurisdiction to review MDNRE decisions until the remedial activities deemed necessary by MDNRE have been completed and that this extended to petitions for injunctive relief, which would require additional remedial actions.

This case substantially limits the extent to which property owners in Michigan may rely upon state environmental laws to recover damages for contaminated groundwater. Similarly, property owners in New Jersey encountered difficulty with state law to recover damages related to alleged hazardous waste leachate. This time, however, the property owners did not rely on state environmental laws, but rather relied upon state common law. Importantly, the following case also discusses the interrelationship of common law claims to state doctrine regarding the applicable statute of limitations for such claims.

Haddonbrook Associates v. General Electric Co. arose out of hazardous waste discharges in Voorhees Township, New Jersey.[21] In the 1970s, hazardous waste was discarded into a landfill located on two different parcels of land, causing pollution to the surrounding environment. General Electric Company (GE) owned one such lot and Voorhees Township owned the other. The plaintiff owned land that was adjacent to the Voorhees Township lot.

In 1991, GE filed an action against the operator of the landfill and several other parties for costs that it incurred in remediating the environmental contamination at the landfill site. Three years later, Plantation Homes, Inc. (Plantation), the plaintiff's predecessor in title, moved to intervene in GE's action. In its proposed complaint, Plantation claimed that GE and Voorhees Township, along with the defendants, had illegally disposed of hazardous waste and contaminated the surrounding environment, thereby causing irreparable harm to Plantation. Joseph Samost, Plantation's president and a managing partner of the plaintiff, provided a supporting certification for the motion. Plantation asserted negligence and strict liability claims. In 1995, Plantation's motion to intervene was denied.[22]

In 2007, almost thirteen years after the denial of Plantation's motion to intervene, the plaintiff filed an action against GE in New Jersey state court, which GE removed to federal court. In the 2007 complaint, the plaintiff asserted that due to the disposal of hazardous waste on GE's property, its property had become contaminated and that it was undevelopable for any commercial or residential use. The plaintiff included negligence, strict liability, and nuisance claims in its complaint.

The federal district court granted summary judgment to GE on statute of limitations grounds. The district court reasoned that because Samost attested to his knowledge of the facts in Plantation's proposed 1994 complaint, and because his knowledge was imputed to the plaintiff, the plaintiff knew of its claims against GE at least thirteen years prior to its filing suit against GE. The district court rejected the plaintiff's continuing torts theory

---

21. 427 Fed. App'x 99 (3d Cir. 2011).
22. *Id.* at 100–01.

because the plaintiff "failed to allege any 'new injury' within the limitations period necessary to apply the continuing tort doctrine" and held the complaint was barred by New Jersey's six-year statute of limitations.[23]

The Third Circuit affirmed. The Third Circuit first reviewed the continuing tort doctrine, citing case law from the New Jersey Supreme Court that governed the doctrine's application.[24] The Third Circuit noted that the doctrine is more often implicated in nuisance claims. The Third Circuit cited the New Jersey Supreme Court's explanation in *Russo Farms, Inc. v. Vineland Board of Education*:

> When a court finds that a continuing nuisance has been committed, it implicitly holds that the defendant is committing a new tort, including a new breach of duty, each day, triggering a new statute of limitations. That new tort is an "alleged present failure" to remove the nuisance, and "[s]ince this failure occurs each day that [defendant] does not act, the [defendant's] alleged tortious inaction constitutes a continuous nuisance for which a cause of action accrues anew each day." . . . Essentially, courts in those cases impose a duty on the defendant to remove the nuisance . . . . Because the defendant has a duty to remove the nuisance, and because the defendant's failure to remove the nuisance is a breach of that duty, each injury is a new tort. The plaintiff is therefore able to collect damages for each injury suffered within the limitations period.[25]

The Third Circuit noted that a continuing tort must contain every element of a new tort, including a new breach of duty, and that the new injury must result from a new breach of duty. The district court had found that the plaintiff failed to allege any "new injury" within the limitations period, which was necessary to trigger the continuing tort doctrine, and the Third Circuit agreed with the district court's reasoning and conclusion that the plaintiff failed to allege a continuing nuisance.[26] The Third Circuit also agreed with the district court that the plaintiff could not establish its negligence and strict liability claims, and failed to allege any conduct within the limitations period to justify the application of the continuing tort doctrine. The Third Circuit concluded that because the plaintiff's "nuisance, negligence, and strict liability claims do not constitute continuing torts under *Russo Farms*, they are barred by the statute of limitations."[27]

These cases evidence the particular challenges property owners potentially face when relying on state laws to recover damages stemming from environmental contamination.

---

23. *Id.* at 102 (citing N.J.S.A. § 2A:14-1).
24. *Id.* at 101 (citing Russo Farms, Inc. v. Vineland Bd. of Educ., 675 A.2d 1077 (N.J. 1996)).
25. *Id.* (quoting *Russo Farms*, 675 A.2d at 1084).
26. *Id.* at 102.
27. *Id.* at 102–03.

Climate Change–Based Nuisance Actions

For those seeking to "fill the gap" in the absence of comprehensive federal legislation addressing climate change, common law nuisance was the cause of action of choice. The cases discussed in this section highlight the role that nuisance law has played in the climate change–based litigation area, and also addresses whether there exists insurance coverage to address the impacts of climate change.

The first significant climate change case was *Native Village of Kivalina v. ExxonMobil Corp.*[28] In that case, an Eskimo village brought an action against multiple oil, energy, and utility companies for federal common law nuisance, based on the emission of greenhouse gases that the village alleged contributed to global warming and caused erosion of Arctic sea ice. The defendants filed motions to dismiss for lack of subject matter jurisdiction. The United States District Court for the Eastern District of California held that the village's federal nuisance claim was barred by the political question doctrine and also was barred due to lack of standing under Article III of the U.S. Constitution.

In determining nuisance was barred by the political question doctrine, the district court examined the six independent factors set forth by the U.S. Supreme Court in *Baker v. Carr* that govern whether a nonjusticiable political question exists. The six independent *Baker* factors analyzed by the court are: "[1] a textually demonstrable constitutional commitment of the issue to a coordinate political department; [2] a lack of judicially discoverable and manageable standards for resolving it; [3] the impossibility of deciding without an initial policy determination of a kind clearly for nonjudicial discretion; [4] the impossibility of a court's undertaking independent resolution without expressing lack of the respect due coordinate branches of government; [5] an unusual need for unquestioning adherence to a political decision already made; or [6] the potentiality of embarrassment from multifarious pronouncements by various departments on one question."[29]

First, the district court examined "whether there is 'a textually demonstrable constitutional commitment of the issue to a coordinate political department.'"[30] The defendants argued that the village failed this first inquiry because allowing the village to proceed with its global warming claim would run afoul of the first *Baker* factor as "it would intrude upon the political branches'" constitutionally committed authority over foreign policy. However, the district court held that merely because global warming had an indisputable international dimension, this fact did not automatically render it a nonjusticiable controversy. As such, the court held that the first *Baker* factor was not implicated.

Second, the district court examined "whether there was 'a lack of judicially discoverable and manageable standards' and whether a decision is impossible 'without an initial

---
28. Native Vill. of Kivalina v. Exxon Mobil Corp., 663 F. Supp. 2d 863 (E.D. Cal. 2009).
29. Baker v. Carr, 369 U.S. 186 (1962).
30. *Native Vill. of Kivalina*, 663 F. Supp. 2d 871–72 (citing *Baker*, 369 U.S. at 217).

policy determination of a kind clearly for nonjudicial discretion.'"[31] The village asserted that "[t]he judicially discoverable and manageable standards here are the same as they are in all nuisance cases."[32] Rejecting this assertion, the district court held that the village's argument was flawed because it overlooked the fact that in evaluating a nuisance claim, the focus is not entirely on the unreasonableness of the harm, but also that courts must balance the utility and benefit of the alleged nuisance against the harm caused. The district court found that the village failed to articulate any particular judicially discoverable and manageable standards that would guide a fact-finder in rendering a decision that is principled, rational, and based upon reasoned distinctions.[33] The court concluded that the second *Baker* factor precluded judicial consideration of the nuisance claim.

Finally, the district court found the third *Baker* factor equally problematic. Specifically, whether the village's case would require the court to make an initial policy determination "of a kind clearly for nonjudicial discretion." The court noted, "[a] political question under this factor 'exists when, to resolve a dispute, the court must make a policy judgment of a legislative nature, rather than resolving the dispute through legal and factual analysis.'"[34] The plaintiffs alleged that there was no need for the court to delve into the task of retroactively determining what emission limits should have been imposed. The court found this argument flawed, holding the plaintiffs were in fact asking the court to make an initial policy decision in contravention of the political question doctrine.[35] As such, the court held that the plaintiffs' claims were barred by the political question doctrine.[36]

Having concluded its examination of the *Baker* factors and determining that the plaintiffs' claims were barred by the political question doctrine, the district court next turned to the defendants' allegation that the village lacked Article III standing. The district court pointed out that "[t]he standing dispute in this case centers on what the Supreme Court has defined as 'the causation requirement' of standing, i.e., fair traceability."[37] The court noted that to satisfy the causation requirement, the plaintiff must "demonstrate a causal connection between the injury and the conduct complained of—the injury has to be fairly traceable to the challenged action of the defendant, and not the result of the independent action of some third party not before the court."[38] The village conceded that it was not able to trace its alleged injuries to any particular defendant. It claimed, however, that it did not need to do so. Instead, the village argued it "need only allege that Defendants 'contributed' to their injuries." The village admitted that its version of Article III standing

---

31. *Id.* at 873 (citing Wang v. Masaitis, 416 F.3d 992, 996 (9th Cir. 2005)).
32. *Id.* at 874.
33. *Id.* at 875 (citing Alperin v. Vatican Bank, 410 F.3d 532, 552 (9th Cir. 2005)).
34. *Id.* at 876 (citing EEOC v. Peabody W. Coal Co., 400 F.3d 774, 784 (9th Cir. 2005)).
35. *Id.* at 877.
36. *Id.* at 883.
37. *Id.* at 877 (citing Bennett v. Spear, 520 U.S. 154, 167 (1997)).
38. *Id.* at 877–78 (citing Salmon Spawning & Recovery Alliance v. Gutierrez, 545 F.3d 1220, 1227 (9th Cir. 2008); Ecological Rights Found. v. Pacific Lumber Co., 230 F.3d 1141, 1152 (9th Cir. 2000)).

stemmed from cases brought under the Clean Water Act, which found "the 'fairly traceable' requirement 'is not equivalent to a requirement of tort causation,' and as such, the plaintiffs 'need only show that there is a *substantial likelihood*' that defendant's conduct caused plaintiffs' harm.'"[39] However, the district court contrasted these cases finding that there was a critical distinction between the Clean Water Act cases and a federal nuisance law claim and that the village therefore lacked standing. Significantly, in Clean Water Act cases, the court noted that when a plaintiff exceeds "Congressionally-prescribed federal limits" there arises a presumption that "there is a 'substantial likelihood' that defendant's conduct caused plaintiffs' harm."[40] The Court stated that only when this presumption exists, is "it permissible for the plaintiff to rely on the notion that the defendant 'contributed' to plaintiff's injury on the ground that it may not be possible to trace the injury to a particular entity."[41]

Two years later, the U.S. Supreme Court closed the door on the use of federal common law nuisance claims to address climate change in *American Electric Power Co. v. Connecticut*.[42] Asserting federal common law nuisance claims, eight states, New York City, and three land trusts separately sued four electric power plants seeking abatement of contributions to global warming. The United States District Court for the Southern District of New York dismissed the plaintiffs' federal common law nuisance claims as nonjusticiable under the political question doctrine.[43] The plaintiffs appealed. The Second Circuit vacated and remanded, but the Supreme Court granted *certiorari*.

The Supreme Court explained that the lawsuits at issue in the instant case began well before EPA initiated efforts to regulate greenhouse gases. In the instant case, the plaintiffs asserted that the defendants' emissions substantially and unreasonably interfered with public rights, in violation of the federal common law nuisance, or, in the alternative, of state tort law. The plaintiffs wanted the courts to place an initial cap on the carbon dioxide emissions from each defendant, to be further reduced annually. The Court held that the Clean Air Act and EPA's rulemaking actions displace any federal common-law right to seek abatement of carbon dioxide emissions from fossil-fuel fired power plants. According to the Court, Congress determined that EPA is the party best suited to serve as the regulator of emissions, and therefore empowered EPA to set greenhouse gas emissions limits; federal judges do not have concurrent jurisdiction to do so.[44] The Court, however, did not reach the issue of whether any state law nuisance claims that the plaintiffs could have asserted were preempted by the Clean Air Act.

---

39. *Native Vill. of Kivalina*, 663 F. Supp. 2d at 878.
40. *Id.* at 879.
41. *Id.* at 880.
42. 131 S. Ct. 2527 (2011).
43. Connecticut v. Am. Elec. Power Co., 406 F. Supp. 2d 265 (S.D.N.Y. 2005).
44. *Am. Elec. Co.*, 131 S. Ct. at 2535–40.

In *Comer v. Murphy*, it appeared that the Fifth Circuit was perfectly situated to address the issue of whether state nuisance law claims were preempted by the Clean Air Act.[45] Owners of real property along the Mississippi Gulf Coast brought a putative class action against oil and energy companies asserting a variety of claims, including private and public nuisance claims. The plaintiffs claimed that the operation of these oil and energy companies caused emissions of greenhouse gases that contributed to global warming and added to the ferocity of a hurricane that destroyed their property. The district court granted the defendants' motion to dismiss. The plaintiffs appealed.

Unlike *Kivalina*, the Fifth Circuit ruled that the plaintiffs had Article III standing to bring nuisance, trespass, and negligence claims because they satisfied the traceability requirement.[46] However, the Fifth Circuit held that the plaintiffs lacked Article III standing to bring claims for unjust enrichment, fraudulent misrepresentation, and civil conspiracy because they did not have federal prudential standing.[47] The Fifth Circuit defined "prudential standing" as standing, "which embodies 'judicially self-imposed limits on the exercise of federal jurisdiction . . .'"[48] With respect to the plaintiffs' unjust enrichment, fraudulent misrepresentation, and civil conspiracy claims, the circuit stated, "[e]ach of the plaintiffs' second set of claims presents a generalized grievance that is more properly dealt with by the representative branches and common to all consumers of petrochemicals and the American public."[49]

The Fifth Circuit also ruled, unlike *Kivalina*, that the plaintiffs' nuisance, trespass, and negligence claims did not present a nonjusticiable political question. The circuit noted, "[a] question, issue, case or controversy is 'justiciable' when it is constitutionally capable of being decided by a federal court."[50] "A 'nonjusticiable' question is also known as a 'political question,' denoting that it has been constitutionally entrusted exclusively to either or both the executive or the legislative branch, which are called the 'political' or 'elected' branches."[51] The Fifth Circuit stated that "[a] case or question that is 'political' only in the broad sense, i.e., that it has political implications or ramifications, is capable of being decided constitutionally by a federal court, so long as the question has not been committed by constitutional means exclusively to the elected or political branches." In holding that the plaintiffs' nuisance, trespass, and negligence claims did not present a nonjusticiable political question, the circuit held that "[t]he questions posed by this case . . . whether defendants are liable to plaintiffs in damages under Mississippi's common law torts of

---

45. Comer v. Murphy Oil, 607 F.3d 1049 (5th Cir. 2010).
46. Comer v. Murphy Oil, 585 F.3d 855, 867 (5th Cir. 2009).
47. *Id.* at 868.
48. *Id.* (citing Allen v. Wright, 468 U.S. 737, 751 (1984)).
49. *Id.*
50. *Id.* at 869.
51. *Id.*

nuisance, trespass or negligence, are justiciable because they plainly have not been committed by the Constitution or federal laws or regulations to Congress or the president."[52]

Appellee applied for *en banc* rehearing and a vote was taken. By six to three, the nine qualified judges voted to grant rehearing *en banc*. The grant of rehearing *en banc* "vacate[d] the panel opinion and judgment of the court."[53] However, shortly thereafter, one of the six judges who voted for an *en banc* rehearing recused herself thereby causing the circuit to lose its quorum. The Fifth Circuit ruled, "a court without a quorum cannot conduct judicial business."[54] There existed no rule allowing for reinstatement of the panel decision in the event there was a loss of quorum after a grant of rehearing *en banc*. As such, the holding of the district court, dismissing the plaintiffs' claims against the defendants, remains in effect.

These cases indicate that while federal nuisance law may not be an avenue for recovery of damages stemming from global climate change, state common law nuisance claims may still be a viable legal theory under which complainants may seek relief.

In *AES Corp. v. Steadfast Insurance Co.*, the Virginia Supreme Court addressed an issue tangentially related to the assertion of nuisance claims to abate the effects of climate change—the issue of insurance coverage for nuisance claims.[55] A commercial general liability (CGL) insurer (Steadfast) for an electric company (AES) brought a declaratory judgment action that it owed no duty to defend AES against the nuisance claims asserted by the Native Village of Kivalina against AES' alleged contribution global warming. The trial court entered judgment in Steadfast's favor. AES appealed to the Virginia Supreme Court.

The Virginia Supreme Court held that damage to the Alaskan island, which made the native village uninhabitable (allegedly as a result of global warming), was not caused by an "accident" and, thus, was not caused by "occurrence" within meaning of the CGL policy.[56]

In each of the CGL policies at issue, Steadfast agreed to defend AES against suits claiming damages for bodily injury or property damage, if such damages were "caused by an 'occurrence.'" The policies defined an "occurrence" as "an accident, including continuous or repeated exposure to substantially the same general harmful condition." The Virginia Supreme Court found that the terms "occurrence" and "accident" are "synonymous and . . . refer to an incident that was unexpected from the viewpoint of the insured."[57] The court, citing its previous holdings, stated, "an 'accident' is commonly understood to mean 'an event which creates an effect which is not the natural or probable consequence of the means employed and is not intended, designed, or reasonably anticipated.'"[58] The

---

52. *Id.* at 870.
53. *Comer*, 607 F.3d at 1053 (citing 5th Cir. R. 41.3; Thompson v. Connick, 578 F.3d 293 (5th Cir. 2009)).
54. *Id.* at 1055 (citing Nguyen v. United States, 539 U.S. 69, 82 n.14 (2003)).
55. 725 S.E.2d 532 (Va. 2012).
56. *Id.* at 537–38.
57. *Id.* at 536 (citing Utica Mut. Ins. Co. v. Travelers Indem. Co., 286 S.E.2d 225, 226 (Va. 1982)).
58. *Id.* (citing Lynchburg Foundry Co. v. Irvin, 16 S.E.2d 646, 648 (Va. 1941)).

dispositive issue with respect to whether or not an accidental injury occurred was not, in the court's opinion, whether the action undertaken by the insured was intended, but rather, "whether the resulting harm is alleged to have been reasonably anticipated or the natural or probable consequence of the insured's intentional act."[59] The court concluded that whether the underlying complaint alleges a covered "occurrence . . . turns on whether the Complaint can be construed as alleging that Kivalina's injuries, at least in the alternative, resulted from unforeseen consequences that were not natural or probable consequences of AES's deliberate act of emitting carbon dioxide and greenhouse gases."

AES asserted that the underlying complaint alleged that AES "[i]ntentionally or negligently" created the nuisance and global warming, and that the defendants' concerted action in causing the nuisance "constitutes a breach of duty." AES contended that this language shows that Kivalina alleged both intentional and negligent tortuous acts. AES asserted that an insured is entitled to a defense when negligence is alleged. AES further asserted that because the complaint alleged that AES "knew or should know" that its activities in generating electricity would result in the environmental harm suffered by Kivalina, Kivalina alleges, at least in the alternative, that the consequences of AES's intentional carbon dioxide and greenhouse gas emissions were unintended. AES reasoned that the damage alleged by Kivalina was therefore accidental from the viewpoint of AES and within the definition of an "occurrence" under the CGL policies. In essence, AES argued that the alleged damage to the village purportedly caused by AES's electricity-generating activities was accidental because such damage may have been unintentional. However, the Virginia Supreme Court rejected this argument. The court held that the policies at issue do not provide coverage or a defense for all suits against the insured alleging damages not caused intentionally. Likewise, the court held that the policies in this case do not provide coverage for all damages resulting from AES's negligent acts. According to the court, the relevant policies only require Steadfast to defend AES against claims for damages for bodily injury or property damage caused by an "occurrence" or "accident."[60] The court held:

> [u]nder the CGL policies, Steadfast would not be liable because AES's acts as alleged in the complaint were intentional and the consequences of those acts are alleged by Kivalina to be not merely foreseeable, but natural or probable. Where the harmful consequences of an act are alleged to have been not just possible, but the natural or probable consequences of an intentional act, choosing to perform the act deliberately, even if in ignorance of that fact, does not make the resulting injury an "accident" even when the complaint alleges that such action was negligent.[61]

---

59. *Id.* (citing Eric M. Holmes, *Appleman on Insurance 2d* § 129.2(I)(5) (2002 & Supp. 2009); Fidelity & Guar. Ins. v. Allied Realty Co., 238 Va. 458, 462, 384 S.E.2d 613, 615 (1989)).
60. *Id.* at 537.
61. *Id.* at 537–38.

The court reasoned that "[e]ven if AES were actually ignorant of the effect of its actions and/or did not intend for such damages to occur, Kivalina alleges its damages were the natural and probable consequence of AES's intentional actions." As such, the court found that Kivalina did not allege its damages were "the result of a fortuitous event or accident," and thus, were not covered under the relevant CGL policies.[62]

This case likely reflects the lack of coverage that will exist from damages allegedly stemming from effects of climate change.

Workplace Exposure

Workplace exposure remains a robust area of toxic tort litigation. One emerging or hot topic with respect to workplace exposure toxic tort litigation is "take home" exposure. "Take home" exposure extends an employer's potential liability to the employee's household members, usually a spouse or children. The case discussed below provides an in-depth analysis of this emerging liability theory wherein the concepts of "forseeability" and "duty" are quite significant. This liability theory opens up a new class of potential plaintiffs and leaves open the limits of employer liability for workplace exposure.

In *Simpkins v. CSX Corp.*, the Fifth District of the Appellate Court of Illinois concluded that an employer owes a duty of care to the family members of employees who bring home asbestos fibers on their work clothes.[63] In doing so, the court held that, while a duty still requires that the two parties stand in an applicable relationship to one another, "[t]he term 'relationship' does not necessarily mean a contractual, familial, or other particular special relationship. . . . As the Supreme Court has noted, 'the concept of duty in negligence cases is very involved, complex, and indeed nebulous.'" The court added, "every person owes every other person the duty to use ordinary care to prevent any injury that might naturally occur as the reasonably foreseeable consequence of his or her own actions."[64]

The issue, the court wrote, is not whether the employer "actually foresaw" the risk, but whether it "should have." "[W]e believe that it takes little imagination to presume that when an employee who is exposed to asbestos brings home his work clothes, members of his family are likely to be exposed as well."[65] Therefore, according to the appellate court, the harm was foreseeable. The court also found that preventing against take-home exposure through substitution of products, issuance of warnings, and updating of hygienic practices is not unduly burdensome.[66]

However, several other jurisdictions have found that the relationship present here is not substantial enough that a duty can be built upon it. Thus, for instance, in *Estate of*

---

62. *Id.* at 538.
63. 929 N.E.2d 1257, 1266 (5th Dist. 2010).
64. *Id.* at 1261–62.
65. *Id.* at 1264.
66. *Id.* at 1266.

Holmes v. Pneumo Abex, the estate of Jean Holmes, who died of peritoneal mesothelioma, brought an action to recover damages for wrongful death.[67] Mrs. Holmes's husband had worked at an asbestos plant from 1962 to 1963. Both Johns-Manville and Raybestos allegedly supplied asbestos to the plant during that time period. The action alleges that Mrs. Holmes's husband brought home asbestos fibers on his person and on his clothes, resulting in her exposure, illness, and death.

The estate argued that literature "going back as far as 1913 showed the potential for disease as a result of workers bringing home toxic substances. . . ."[68] However, this literature did not specifically address asbestos. The *Holmes* court noted that the U.S. States Court of Appeals for the Sixth Circuit had noted that "other courts have found there was no knowledge of bystander exposure in the asbestos industry in the 1950's," and found that the "first studies of bystander exposure were not published until 1965."[69] Likewise, the *Holmes* court also noted the Fourteenth District Court of Appeals of Texas, in a 2007 case, held that "the risk of 'take home' asbestos exposure was, in all likelihood, not foreseeable by defendant while [the plaintiff] was working at defendant's premises from 1954 to 1965."[70] Studies on nonoccupational asbestos exposure were also not first published until 1965.[71]

In *Holmes*, an industrial hygienist who testified on behalf of the defendants, said that he had found only a 1960 article that discussed mesothelioma that allegedly resulted from a worker bringing home asbestos fibers, resulting in his family's exposure. Even the plaintiff's own expert admitted at trial that the first epidemiological study "showing an association between disease and asbestos fibers brought home from the workplace" was presented and published in October 1964. The Illinois court's analysis, therefore, came to hinge upon what was known about the likelihood of injury from secondary, nonoccupational exposure to asbestos during the pertinent time.

The Illinois appellate court ultimately found that the defendants did not owe a duty to Jean Holmes.[72] The likelihood of injury from secondary exposure was simply too abstract of a theory at the time her husband worked with and around asbestos products for the defendants to have realistically anticipated the possibility of injury to a worker's immediate family. Even if the requisite relationship did exist between the defendants and Jean Holmes, the court said "we would find no duty existed because of the lack of foreseeability in this case."[73]

---

67. 955 N.E.2d 1173 (Ill. App. 2011).
68. *Id.* at 1178.
69. *Id.* at 1178 (citing Martin v. Cincinnati Gas & Elec. Co., 561 F.3d 439, 445 (6th Cir. 2009)).
70. *Id.* at 1179 (citing *In re* Certified Question from the Fourteenth District Court of Appeals of Texas, 740 N.W.2d 206, 218 (2007)).
71. *Id.* (citing Alcoa, Inc. v. Behringer, 235 S.W.3d 456, 461 (Tex. App. 2007)).
72. *Id.*
73. *Id.*

This Illinois court wanted something more in order to establish that the defendants owed a duty to the household family member. "To show the injury was reasonably foreseeable here, plaintiff had to establish that when decedent's husband worked at Unarco from 1962 to 1963, it was reasonably foreseeable asbestos affixed to a worker's clothes during work would be carried home and released at levels that would cause an asbestos-related disease in a household member."[74] In conclusion, whether the defendant owes a duty is based upon the reasonable forseeability of injury.

As evidenced by the cases discussed above, in the context of emerging toxic torts, courts are frequently asked to extend the boundaries of traditional tort law principles to new types of claims. This is particularly true in emerging areas for which there is an absence of comprehensive federal legislation. The result, oftentimes, is a patchwork of conflicting legal precedent, thus resulting in predictive uncertainty for the toxic tort practitioner.

Significant Legal Issues in Toxic Tort Litigation
Class Actions

Although personal injury classes have long been disfavored, class actions have sometimes been a vehicle for toxic tort litigation involving property damage claims. What has emerged recently, however, are more heightened restrictions with respect to class certification for such claims. The cases below discuss emerging case law in the area of toxic tort class litigation.

In *Benefield v. International Paper Co.*, the United States District Court for the Middle District of Alabama denied the plaintiffs' motion for class certification in a lawsuit alleging that International Paper's manufacturing facility contaminated neighboring residential properties.[75]

The plaintiffs proposed to define the class as everyone who "owned residential property within two miles of the outer boundary of the Facility . . . [and whose] property was contaminated by releases of various substances into the environment from the Facility, and [who] suffered in excess of $100 of diminution in value of the real property." The district court, however, rejected the plaintiffs' proposed class definition because the description was not sufficiently definite so that it would be administratively feasible for the court to determine whether a person was a member.[76]

First, the district court found that the plaintiffs had to do more than select a broad geographical region to identify potential class members. They failed to establish that all residential property owners within a two-mile radius of the facility actually owned "contaminated" property. Second, the court stated that it was not plausible to identify property

---

74. *Id.* at 1178–79.
75. 270 F.R.D. 640, 654 (M.D. Ala. 2010).
76. *Id.* at 644–45.

owners who have suffered a diminution in excess of $100 to their property's value simply by using the mass appraisal formula offered by the plaintiffs' expert.

The court also concluded that none of the named plaintiffs were adequate representatives for the putative class because (1) one named plaintiff did not own property in the area, and (2) the other named plaintiff's claims were not typical of the class because he owned a single-family home while others owned vacant lots, mobile homes, and multi-family residential properties.[77] Thus, the court held that redefinition would not cure the deficiencies identified above.

The Fourth Circuit also has heightened restrictions with respect to standing in class action suits. In *Rhodes v. E.I. Du Pont De Nemours & Co.*, the plaintiffs sued Du Pont alleging it discharged perfluorooctanoic acid (PFOA) into the public water supply.[78] The plaintiffs raised various claims, individually and on behalf of a class of customers of the water department in West Virginia.[79]

The plaintiffs sought damages and injunctive relief to obtain medical monitoring of any latent diseases that might arise from the contamination of the water. The district court denied class-certification and concluded that the "elements of a medical monitoring tort could not be proved on a class-wide basis using the type of evidence presented by the plaintiffs."[80]

In order to appeal the adverse ruling, the plaintiffs filed a stipulation of voluntary dismissal of their individual claims for medical monitoring. On appeal, the manufacturer argued that the Fourth Circuit lacked jurisdiction to address the district court's denial of class certification. Specifically, the manufacturer asserted, "plaintiffs no longer have standing to advance this argument on appeal because, by voluntarily dismissing their individual claims for medical monitoring, the plaintiffs abandoned their interest in litigating the certification question."[81]

The Fourth Circuit agreed with the manufacturer, holding "when a putative class plaintiff voluntarily dismisses the individual claims underlying a request for class certification . . . there is no longer a 'self-interested party advocating' for class treatment in the manner necessary to satisfy Article III standing requirements."[82] Without standing, the Fourth Circuit held that it lacked jurisdiction to address the district court's denial of class certification.

In *Westwood Apex v. Contreras*, the Ninth Circuit joined the Fourth and Seven Circuits in holding that third parties joined to a class action as additional counterclaim defendants are not "true defendants" within the definition of 28 U.S.C. §§ 1446 or 1453(b) and may

---

77. *Id.* at 646–47.
78. *Id.* at 92–93.
79. 636 F.3d 88, 92-93 (4th Cir. 2011).
80. *Id.* at 93.
81. *Id.* at 98.
82. *Id.* at 100.

not remove the class action to federal court under the Class Action Fairness Act (CAFA).[83] The Ninth Circuit held that CAFA did not amend the definition of "defendant" or "defendants" in the removal statute. As such, only traditional defendants, or those against whom the original plaintiff asserts claims, may seek removal under CAFA.[84] The right of removal under CAFA does not extend to counterclaim defendants, third-party defendants, or additional counterclaim defendants.

The Ninth Circuit stated, "[t]he plainness or ambiguity of statutory language is determined by reference to the language itself, the specific context in which that language is used, and the broader context of the statute as a whole."[85] "Where language is susceptible to varying interpretations, we will look to other sources to determine congressional intent, such as the canons of construction or a statute's legislative history."[86] In examining these factors, the Ninth Circuit found that the defendants' assertion gave too much weight to the "adjective—'any.'"[87] Furthermore, the circuit noted that the defendants' argument ran afoul of the established meaning of "defendant" in Chapter 89 of the Judicial Code. The circuit noted that it was well settled that the term "defendant" meant or referred only to "original" or "true defendants" and excluded "plaintiffs and non-plaintiff parties who become defendants through a counterclaim."[88] The circuit determined that Congress's intent when enacting CAFA did not change or alter this interpretation of "defendant."[89]

In *Gates v. Rohm & Haas Co.*, an opinion addressing several important questions of class action law, the Third Circuit affirmed a district court's decision denying certification of medical monitoring and property damage classes in a suit alleging environmental contamination.[90] The plaintiffs in *Gates* alleged that, by dumping wastewater, companies operating a nearby manufacturing facility released vinyl chloride into the air over the plaintiffs' residential community. The plaintiffs requested certification of a class of asymptomatic residents seeking medical monitoring for diseases associated with vinyl chloride exposure as well as a class seeking compensation for property damage. The district court denied class certification under Fed. R. Civ. P. 23, and the plaintiffs sought interlocutory review.

The Third Circuit held that the district court properly denied class certification under Rule 23(b)(2).[91] Citing the U.S. Supreme Court's recent inference that monetary relief may be unavailable in 23(b)(2) classes,[92] the Third Circuit also "question[ed]" whether medical

---

83. 644 F.3d 799, 807 (9th Cir. 2011).
84. *Id.* at 807.
85. *Id.* at 803 (citing Robinson v. Shell Oil Co., 519 U.S. 337, 341 (1997)).
86. *Id.* (citing Jonah R. v. Carmona, 446 F.3d 1000, 1005 (9th Cir. 2006)).
87. *Id.* at 804.
88. *Id.* (citing Shamrock Oil & Gas Corp. v. Sheets, 313 U.S. 100 (1941)).
89. *Id.* at 805–06.
90. 655 F.3d 255 (3d Cir. 2011).
91. *Id.* at 270.
92. *Id.* at 263–64 (citing Wal-Mart Stores, Inc. v. Dukes, 131 S. Ct. 2541, 2557, 2561 (2011)).

monitoring claims can ever be certified under (b)(2).[93] Even if they can, however, the Third Circuit held that the plaintiffs' claims lacked the requisite cohesion.

The Third Circuit explained that the plaintiffs failed to show how they could prove, on a class-wide basis, three of the elements of a medical monitoring claim under governing Pennsylvania law. First, expert evidence about average daily exposure to vinyl chloride in the plaintiffs' community did not "constitute common proof of exposure above background levels."[94] Levels of vinyl chloride in the air varied over the decades-long class period, the plaintiffs had differing susceptibilities to exposure, and the plaintiffs' varying work and recreational schedules resulted in different levels of exposure. Thus, "[a]verages . . . would not be probative of any individual's claim because any one class member may have an exposure level well above or below the average." According to the Third Circuit, the plaintiffs could not "substitute evidence of exposure of actual class members with evidence of hypothetical, composite persons in order to gain class certification."[95]

Second, the *Gates* plaintiffs did not establish a level of vinyl chloride exposure that "would create a significant risk of contracting a serious latent disease for all class members." EPA's regulatory threshold limit for vinyl chloride exposure "would not be the threshold for each class member who may be more or less susceptible to diseases from exposure to vinyl chloride."[96]

Third, the plaintiffs could not prove on a class-wide basis that the proposed medical monitoring regime was "reasonably medically necessary." The Third Circuit credited defense experts who testified that the negative effects of medical monitoring, such as dangers from the contrast agent used for MRIs to patients with kidney disease, might outweigh any benefits. Individual inquiries would be needed "to consider class members' individual characteristics and medical histories and to weigh the benefits and safety of a monitoring program."[97]

The Third Circuit also affirmed denial of a medical monitoring class under Rule 23(b)(3). Citing the same factors that prevented (b)(2) certification, the circuit held that individual issues predominated over common questions. While the plaintiffs suggested that their experts could provide evidence to overcome these individual issues, the circuit observed "[a] party's assurance to the court that it intends or plans to meet the requirements is insufficient."[98]

---

93. *Id.* at 268–69 (citing Barnes v. American Tobacco Co., 161 F.3d 127, 146 (3d Cir. 1998) ("Although the general public's monitoring program can be proved on a classwide basis, an individual's monitoring program by definition cannot."); *Principles of the Law of Aggregate Litigation* § 2.04 reporter's notes cmt. *b*, at 126 (2010) ("[A]fter *Barnes*, courts often have withheld class certification for medical monitoring due to the presence of individualized issues. . . .")).
94. *Id.* at 265.
95. *Id.* at 266.
96. *Id.* at 267–68.
97. *Id.* at 268–69.
98. *Id.* at 270.

The Third Circuit also rejected certification of a property damage class under Rule 23(b)(3). Distinguishing cases that have certified property damage classes, the circuit stated that "the potential difference in contamination on the properties" meant "common issues do not predominate."[99]

Finally, the Third Circuit rejected the plaintiffs' request for an "issues-only" class on liability under Rule 23(c)(4). Noting a circuit split concerning whether Rule 23(c)(4) permits issue certification when common questions do not predominate "for the cause of action as a whole," the circuit adopted a third approach, reciting a "non-exclusive list of factors" to consider.[100] Applying that standard, the circuit held that the district judge properly denied issue certification. A class trial would leave "significant and complex questions" concerning causation and damages "unanswered," and "common issues" were "not divisible from individual issues."

By holding that the plaintiffs may not use statistical averages or regulatory pronouncements to overcome differences in putative class members' risk factors, the Third Circuit's decision in *Gates* imposes a high bar on certifying medical monitoring classes. Thus, even in the minority of states that recognize medical monitoring as a claim or remedy for the plaintiffs who have not incurred physical injuries, application of the *Gates* standard substantially reduces the dangers posed by medical monitoring suits.

The difficulty of certifying a class is also demonstrated by *Kemblesville HHMO Center LLC v. Landhope Realty Co.*[101] In *Kemblesville*, the plaintiffs sued based on a theory that the presence of MTBE in sites surrounding a gas station diminished the value of property out to a 2,500-foot (roughly, half-mile) radius. The plaintiffs asked the Pennsylvania federal district court to certify a class of all property owners within that radius.

The district court began by noting the burden the plaintiffs carry in arguing for certification, and the fact that "[t]he requirements set out in Rule 23 are not mere pleading rules."[102] The court also articulated why overly broad class definitions are not a good idea, stating the class must be sufficiently identifiable without being overly broad. "Overbroad

---

99. *Id.* at 272.
100. *Id.* at 273. The factors considered by the Court were ". . . the type of claim(s) and issue(s) in question; the overall complexity of the case; the efficiencies to be gained by granting partial certification in light of realistic procedural alternatives; the substantive law underlying the claim(s), including any choice-of-law questions it may present and whether the substantive law separates the issue(s) from other issues concerning liability or remedy; the impact partial certification will have on the constitutional and statutory rights of both the class members and the defendant(s); the potential preclusive effect or lack thereof that resolution of the proposed issue class will have; the repercussions certification of an issue(s) class will have on the effectiveness and fairness of resolution of remaining issues; the impact individual proceedings may have upon one another, including whether remedies are indivisible such that granting or not granting relief to any claimant as a practical matter determines the claims of others; and the kind of evidence presented on the issue(s) certified and potentially presented on the remaining issues, including the risk subsequent triers of fact will need to reexamine evidence and findings from resolution of the common issue(s)." *Id.*
101. No. 08-2405, 2011 U.S. Dist. LEXIS 83324 (E.D. Pa. July 28, 2011).
102. *Id.* at *8 (citing *In re* Hydrogen Peroxide, 552 F.3d 305, 311 (3d Cir. 2008)).

class descriptions violate the definiteness requirement because they 'include individuals who are without standing to maintain the action on their own behalf.'"[103]

The plaintiffs tried to avoid any overbreadth by claiming that the relationship between the alleged contamination and the geographic boundary of their class was a "merits issue." Nevertheless, the district court disagreed, stating:

> Plaintiffs' proposed class includes properties simply because they exist, irrespective of any actual connection to Defendants' activities. The Court does not at this stage require Plaintiffs to adduce definitive evidence about the specific amount and effect of MTBE dispersion. However, to enable this Court to conclude that there is a reasonable relationship between the relevant MTBE release and the proposed class area, Plaintiffs need to adduce some evidence of dispersion that indicates MTBE may have traveled, or will ever travel, near a radius of 2,500 feet.[104]

The district court also found a numerosity problem that stemmed from the overbreadth of the class. The court stated:

> because this class definition is too overbroad, I cannot accept Plaintiffs' numerosity argument. Plaintiffs have failed to provide evidence that MTBE contamination is present throughout the class area . . . According to Plaintiffs, many properties are in contaminated or soon-to-be contaminated areas. However, that estimate is purely speculative, and conclusory allegations do not satisfy Rule 23(a)(1)'s numerosity requirement.[105]

Experts

Like class action certification, emerging toxic tort litigation demonstrates a trend toward heightened standards for the admissibility of expert testimony and the role of such testimony with respect to proving causation. The cases below illustrate this emerging pattern and discuss what may or may not meet the *Daubert* standard or equivalent state evidentiary laws with respect to utilizing expert testimony to prove causation in toxic tort cases.

In *Kuxhausen v. Tillman Partners, LP*, the Kansas Supreme Court rejected an expert's opinion that a plaintiff's medical symptoms were caused by chemical sensitivity stemming from exposure to paint fumes, finding that the testimony at issue lacked an evidentiary

---

103. *Id.* at *13–14 (citing Oshana v. Coca-Cola Bottling Co., 225 F.R.D. 575, 580 (N.D. Ill. 2005); Guillory v. American Tobacco Co., No. 97-C-8641, 2001 WL 290603 at *2 (N.D. Ill. Mar. 20, 2001) (stating that a well-recognized prerequisite to class certification is that the proposed class must be sufficiently definite and identifiable)).
104. *Id.* at *5.
105. *Id.* at *25–26.

basis sufficient to differentiate it from mere speculation.[106] Accordingly, the Kansas Supreme Court held that the expert opinion was inadmissible.

After working in the defendant's building and being exposed to fumes from epoxy-based paints for brief periods over three days, the plaintiff claimed a variety of medical ailments, including an "ongoing sensitivity to a variety of chemicals." The plaintiff filed suit and sought to introduce the expert testimony of three physicians to establish her chemical sensitivity diagnosis, however, only one expert testified that the plaintiff's symptoms were caused by her exposure to paint fumes at the defendant's building. That expert's physical examination of the plaintiff and other test results indicated no abnormalities and while he evaluated a material safety data sheet (MSDS) for the paint, he offered no information on whether there existed any relationship between the potential adverse health issues identified on the MSDS and the plaintiff's medical ailments.

The Kansas Supreme Court upheld the trial court's grant of summary judgment in favor of the defendant. Under Kansas law, the court noted, "[e]xpert witnesses should confine their opinions to relevant matters which are certain or probable, not those which are merely possible" when testifying to causation.[107] Here, the court found that the expert's causation opinion lacked factual support and therefore had to be stricken as mere speculation. Without the causation evidence, the court found the plaintiff could not maintain her claim and summary judgment was appropriate.[108]

Similarly, in *Pluck v. BP Oil Pipeline Co.*, the Sixth Circuit ruled that a causation expert's opinion was unreliable based on his inability to quantify the plaintiff's dose of benzene exposure.[109] The Sixth Circuit therefore upheld the dismissal of a benzene exposure suit alleging the plaintiff's non-Hodgkin's lymphoma was caused by benzene migrating to her drinking water from a pipeline.

The plaintiff and her family purchased a home in Franklin Township, Ohio, in 1996. They used well water to drink, wash, shower, and irrigate their yard and garden. BP, the prior owner, had purchased the home along with other homes as part of a settlement with local residents over groundwater contamination from an underground gasoline pipeline that passed through the town. In October 1996, benzene was detected in the well on their property. This time frame also coincided with the time the plaintiff noticed a gasoline odor in her home and water. EPA's maximum permissible contaminant level for benzene was 5 parts per billion (ppb). Even though the well's benzene level was measured at 3.6 ppb, BP made several attempts to remediate the area. However, samples continued to show trace amounts of benzene in the well water. In 2002, the plaintiff was diagnosed

---

106. 241 P.3d 75 (Kan. 2010).
107. *Id.* at 79 (citing State v. Struzik, 269 Kan. 95 (2000)).
108. *Id.* at 80–81.
109. 640 F.3d 671 (6th Cir. 2011).

with non-Hodgkin's lymphoma. In 2005, on the recommendation of her treating physician, the plaintiff moved out of the home.

The plaintiff filed suit for strict liability for hazardous activity, negligence, and loss of consortium based on alleged benzene exposure. To support her claims, the plaintiff retained two experts on causation to demonstrate that benzene is generally capable of causing non-Hodgkin's lymphoma and that benzene specifically caused the plaintiff's non-Hodgkin's lymphoma.

BP filed a motion *in limine* to exclude the testimony of the plaintiff's causation expert on the grounds that his testimony failed to satisfy the standard for reliability set forth in *Daubert*. BP argued the expert's testimony was unreliable "because he formulated a specific causation opinion without evidence of dose, and subsequently performed an unreliable dose reconstruction in an attempt to support his opinion."[110]

Approximately one month after BP filed its *Daubert* motions and motion for summary judgment, the challenged expert submitted a supplemental declaration in which he evaluated the plaintiff's illness now under a differential diagnosis methodology. The trial court agreed with BP, and concluded that the expert formulated his opinion on dose "without any exposure data, only having been told that [Pluck] had been 'heavily' exposed to benzene in her water"; he relied upon a "no safe dose" theory that had been discredited by other courts as a basis for establishing specific causation; he could not explain the "scribbles" used to calculate the plaintiff's dose of benzene; and he filed an untimely supplemental declaration that contradicted his previous testimony and employed "an entirely new differential diagnosis methodology that was not mentioned at any point prior to the submission of his declaration."[111] Without any expert opinion on specific causation, the trial court granted summary judgment in favor of BP.

On appeal, the plaintiff argued that the district court improperly demanded precise data regarding dose of benzene and ignored the expert's differential-diagnosis methodology. The plaintiff's appeal also challenged the district court's exclusion of the expert's supplemental declaration, which was filed five months after the deadline for expert reports. The plaintiff conceded that the expert did not establish dose, and instead argued that the expert used differential diagnosis to determine specific causation, and that the district court "ignore[d] the ability of a physician to apply causal and probabilistic reasoning to arrive at a differential diagnosis and offer an opinion on specific causation."[112]

In response, BP maintained that the expert did not apply differential diagnosis in either his expert opinion or his deposition, but did so only in an untimely supplemental declaration filed five months after the deadline for expert reports. The Sixth Circuit agreed with BP. The Sixth Circuit concluded that the expert's causation of proof failed under *Daubert*

---

110. *Id.* at 674–75.
111. *Id.* at 675–76.
112. *Id.* at 677–78.

because the expert "did not ascertain Mrs. Pluck's level of benzene exposure, nor did he determine whether she was exposed to quantities of benzene exceeding the EPA's safety regulations."[113] The circuit also explained that it is well settled that the mere existence of a toxin in the environment is insufficient to establish causation without proof that the level of exposure could cause the plaintiff's symptoms.

The plaintiff's expert offered no evidence of the level of exposure. Rather, in attempting to estimate exposure, the expert relied upon a gasoline-vapor-concentration study. The study discussed the correlation between benzene exposure and leukemia, but did not find a statistically significant association between residing near a gasoline spill and non-Hodgkin's lymphoma.

The Sixth Circuit noted that even if the expert had properly ruled that benzene exposure caused the illness, the expert failed to rule out alternative causes, "as is required under the differential-diagnosis methodology."[114] Due to her extensive smoking habit and her exposure to other organic solvents, the plaintiff was exposed to other sources of benzene, but the expert did not identify these other solvents and did not determine the potential level of exposure to them. Thus, the expert did not properly "rule out" alternative causes of the non-Hodgkin's lymphoma. The Sixth Circuit also concluded that the expert's supplemental declaration containing an alternative differential diagnosis, filed one month after BP filed its *Daubert* motions and motion for summary judgment and five months after the deadline for expert reports, was an untimely attempt to introduce a new causation methodology, and as such rejected it.[115]

The Third Circuit has also recently exhibited stringent requirements for the admissibility of expert opinions. In *Pritchard v. Dow Agro Sciences*, the Third Circuit affirmed the exclusion of expert testimony in a toxic tort suit in which the plaintiff alleged the defendants' insecticide products caused his non-Hodgkin's lymphoma.[116] His wife claimed to have suffered derivative injuries. The plaintiffs retained an expert who provided testimony stating that the pesticide caused the cancer. Although the trial court found the expert to be qualified, the court ruled that the expert's proposed testimony was unreliable and therefore inadmissible at trial under *Daubert*. The exclusion doomed the lawsuit, because the plaintiffs presented no other evidence of causation.

On appeal, the plaintiffs asserted that the trial court violated the doctrine set forth in *Erie v. Railroad Co. v. Tompkins*,[117] by applying substantive rules of federal common law in a diversity action that is properly governed by state law. The plaintiffs argued that the trial court erroneously relied on principles that were supposedly at odds with Pennsylvania

---

113. *Id.* at 679.
114. *Id.* at 680 (citing Tamraz v. Lincoln Elec. Co., 620 F.3d 665, 674 (6th Cir. 2010)).
115. *Id.* at 680–81.
116. 430 Fed. App'x 102 (3d Cir. 2011).
117. 304 U.S. 64 (1938).

state law governing the level of certainty required to establish causation related to idiopathic disease and epidemiological studies. In reaching the holding in the case, the trial court noted that the plaintiffs' expert did not rule out unknown or idiopathic causes and the epidemiological study on which the doctor wished to rely showed only a relative risk of 2.0.[118] The trial court also observed that the proposed testimony was not grounded in science as the expert did not present any statistically significant evidence showing an association between the chemical agent at issue and non-Hodgkin's lymphoma.

The trial court considered these factors among "a host of other deficiencies," in determining that the proffered testimony failed to satisfy the admissibility standard. The trial court did not adopt any bright-line rules, but instead evaluated the plaintiffs' proffer using a "flexible" approach.[119] The trial court never reached any substantive issues regarding causation, but merely addressed procedural issues related to the admissibility the expert's testimony. The Third Circuit explained that the trial court's decision was an evidentiary ruling and federal law governs such procedural issues. As such, the trial court did not violate the *Erie* doctrine.[120]

The plaintiffs also argued that the trial court "improperly 'invaded the province of the jury' by excluding [the expert's] testimony after weighing the plaintiffs' proffered evidence against the defendants'—the suggestion being that a jury should have been presented with both sides' testimony and allowed to decide which was more credible." The Third Circuit noted that the Federal Rules of Evidence "embody a strong preference for admitting any evidence that may assist the trier of fact" and "should not be excluded simply because a judge thinks its probative value is outweighed by other evidence." [121]

The Third Circuit found, however, that the trial court did not engage in any such balancing test. Instead, the Third noted that the trial court concluded the expert's proposed testimony was unreliable due to numerous cracks in its scientific foundation. As such, the trial court committed no error in excluding the testimony.

Medical Monitoring

In this section, we discuss emerging trends with respect to medical monitoring class actions.

In *Alsteen v. Wauleco, Inc.*, seventy plaintiffs appealed an order dismissing their personal injury claims against the defendant.[122] The plaintiffs alleged that they were exposed to carcinogenic chemicals, which the defendant purportedly released from a nearby window factory. The plaintiffs fell into three groups: (1) those that alleged that their exposure had caused various health problems; (2) those that alleged the defendant's release damaged

---

118. *Pritchard*, 430 Fed. App'x at 103–04.
119. *Id.* at 104 (citing Heller v. Shaw Indus., 167 F.3d 146 (3d Cir. 1999)).
120. *Id.*
121. *Id.* (citing Pineda v. Ford Motor Co., 520 F.3d 237, 243 (3d Cir. 2008)).
122. 335 Wis. 2d 473, 476 (Wis. Ct. App. 2011).

their property; and (3) those who did not allege any current adverse health effects but "alleged that their exposure . . . 'significantly increased their risk of contracting cancer' at some point in the future."[123] For damages, the risk of cancer group sought future expenses related to medical monitoring.

The defendant moved to dismiss the risk of cancer claims, arguing that Wisconsin law requires a plaintiff to allege actual injury in order to sustain a tort claim, rather than only an increased risk of future harm. The trial court granted the defendant's motion, concluding those plaintiffs failed to state a claim.

On appeal, the Wisconsin Appellate Court affirmed, noting that a plaintiff does not have a personal injury claim until he or she has suffered "actual" injury or damage. Increased risk of future harm is not an actual injury under Wisconsin law.[124]

In *Hirsch v. CSX Transportation Corp.*, the Sixth Circuit recently affirmed denial of class certification in a medical monitoring case where it found that the "alleged injuries consist solely of the increased risk of . . . certain diseases."[125] The *Hirsch* case arose from a train derailment in which cars carrying hazardous materials were overturned. A fire burned for three days, allegedly consuming more than 2,800 tons of combustibles, which the plaintiffs claimed resulted in the release of toxic materials into the atmosphere. As a result of these events, some 1,300 residents within a half-mile radius were forced to evacuate for three days.

The plaintiffs brought suit for negligence, nuisance, strict liability, trespass, and medical monitoring under Ohio law, but CSX obtained dismissal of all claims save negligence, under which the district court permitted the plaintiffs to seek medical monitoring as a remedy. The plaintiffs' own experts, however, placed the risk at one in one million exposed persons of additional risk of developing cancer. Accordingly, their alleged injuries consisted solely of the increased risk of—and corresponding cost of screening for—certain diseases that the plaintiffs claimed were likely to occur because of the train crash and fire. Stating that not every risk of disease warrants increased medical scrutiny, the Sixth Circuit emphasized that Ohio law required medical monitoring only if a "*reasonable*" physician would deem monitoring necessary. A mere "risk" was deemed insufficient to confer Article III standing.[126] The Sixth Circuit affirmed the district court's decision.

Risk Assessments to Prove Causation

Plaintiffs frequently seek to use risk assessments prepared in developing government regulations as the basis to prove causation in toxic tort litigation. However, as the following cases demonstrate, plaintiffs may do so at their peril.

---

123. *Id.*
124. *Id.* at 476.
125. 656 F.3d 359, 363 (6th Cir. 2011).
126. *Id.* at 364.

In addition to its significance in the emerging trends within the context of class actions, which is discussed in more detail above, *Gates v. Rohm and Haas Co.*, is equally significant with respect to the use of risk assessments to prove causation. In *Gates*, the Third Circuit held, "plaintiffs could not carry their burden of proof for a class of specific persons simply by citing regulatory standards for the population as a whole."[127]

Similarly, in *Baker v. Chevron USA Inc.*, a federal district court in Ohio held that "probably" in a regulatory context does not mean "more probable than not" in a tort context.[128] In *Baker*, residents of nearby villages sued the defendant asserting state law tort claims based on personal injuries and property damage they claimed were sustained as a result of air emissions from the defendant's refinery. The defendant moved to exclude the plaintiffs' expert opinions. The district court provided an in-depth analysis of the plaintiffs' expert's causation opinions, ultimately holding that the opinions were unreliable and consequently, inadmissible.

Specifically, the plaintiffs' expert found that the plaintiffs' illnesses occurred because they were exposed to benzene in excess of regulatory levels. However, the district court noted that "[t]he mere fact that Plaintiffs were exposed to benzene emissions in excess of mandated limits is insufficient to establish causation."[129] The court stated, "regulatory agencies are charged with protecting public health and thus reasonably employ a lower threshold of proof in promulgating their regulations than is used in tort cases."[130]

Furthermore, the court recognized that "an expert's opinion does not have to be unequivocally supported by epidemiological studies in order to be admissible under *Daubert*."[131] However, the court found that the "opinions expressed" by the plaintiffs' expert were based on "a scattershot of studies and articles which superficially touch on each of the illnesses at issue."[132] The court found that the expert provided "no depth of opinion . . . in any of the selected references as to any of Plaintiffs' illnesses."[133]

---

127. *Gates*, 655 F.3d at 268; *cf.* Wright v. Willamette Indus., Inc., 91 F.3d 1105, 1107 (8th Cir. 1996) ("Whatever may be the considerations that ought to guide a legislature in its determination of what the general good requires, courts and juries, in deciding cases, traditionally make more particularized inquiries into matters of cause and effect.").
128. 680 F. Supp. 2d 865, 884 (S.D. Ohio 2010).
129. *Id.* at 880 (citing 243 F.3d 244, 252–53 (6th Cir. 2001); David L. Eaton, *Scientific Judgment and Toxic Torts—A Primer in Toxicology for Judges and Lawyers*, 12 J.L. & POL'Y 5, 39 (2003) ("[R]egulatory levels are of substantial value to public health agencies charged with ensuring the protection of the public health, but are of limited value in judging whether a particular exposure was a substantial contributing factor to a particular individual's disease or illness.")).
130. *Id.* (citing Allen v. Penn. Eng'g Corp., 102 F.3d 194, 198 (5th Cir. 1996)).
131. *Id.* at 887 (citing Knight v. Kirby Inland Marine, Inc., 482 F.3d 347, 354 (5th Cir. 2007)).
132. *Id.*
133. *Id.*

PART TWO

Regional Standards for Causation

CHAPTER 9

Western States

*Karen R. Leviton, Michael G. Romey,
and R. Peter Durning Jr.*

This chapter discusses proof of causation in toxic tort cases in the Western states of Alaska, Arizona, California, Colorado, Hawaii, Idaho, Montana, Nevada, New Mexico, Oregon, Utah, Washington, and Wyoming.[1]

While some of these states have well-articulated bodies of law addressing the element of causation in toxic tort cases, there are also several states where toxic tort law, and the law of causation more generally, is not comprehensively developed.

In summary, although there are some important variations among the Western states' approaches to causation in the toxic tort context, there are several features of the law that are consistent throughout most of these jurisdictions. Most states require proof of both general and specific causation. Furthermore, most states apply a version of "but for" causation in the typical case and a version of "substantial factor" causation in a case involving independent concurring causes. Lastly, the standard of proof is generally a preponderance of the evidence, viewed in light of the reasonable probabilities afforded by expert medical, epidemiological, or statistical evidence. While not every state follows each of these principles in the same way, these broad outlines are common to the majority of the Western states.

The authors wish to thank Ashley N. Johndro of the law firm of Latham & Watkins LLP (San Diego) for her assistance in researching and writing this chapter.

1. This survey chapter focuses on a narrow but extremely significant aspect of any toxic tort case seeking damages for personal injury—namely, the criteria for establishing the elements of general and specific causation in the particular jurisdictions covered. For a more generalized discussion regarding causation in personal injury and other types of toxic tort actions, as well as a broader discussion regarding the claims, defenses, and general strategies in these cases, please refer to earlier chapters in this book.

Alaska

Overall Standard for Causation

Under Alaskan law, tort plaintiffs must prove that a defendant's negligent conduct was the "legal cause" of their injuries.[2] This requires a showing that the "negligent act was more likely than not a substantial factor in bringing about the injury."[3] "The substantial factor test [in Alaska] is satisfied by showing both that the [injury] would not have happened but for the defendant's negligence and that the negligent act was so important in bringing about the injury that reasonable men would regard it as a cause and attach responsibility to it."[4] That is, "[t]wo distinct prongs are encompassed in the concept of legal cause in negligence [in Alaska]: actual causation, and a more intangible legal policy element," which imposes foreseeability as a limit.[5] Alaskan law uses the terms "substantial factor" and "proximate cause" interchangeably.[6]

General and Specific Causation

In *John's Heating Service v. Lamb*,[7] the plaintiffs sued a heating service company, alleging that the company's failure to repair the furnace exposed them to toxic levels of carbon monoxide, causing them to suffer from carbon monoxide poisoning. On appeal, the defendant company unsuccessfully argued that the trial court erred in admitting the plaintiffs' expert testimony that chronic exposure to carbon monoxide has harmful effects. The importance of this evidence to the outcome of the case suggests that, under Alaskan law, general causation is a necessary component of a toxic tort claim, and expert testimony is an accepted (if not a required) method of proving general causation.[8]

The Supreme Court of Alaska characterized the testimony as an "extrapolation from the fact that short-term, high-level carbon monoxide exposures are harmful (and sometimes fatal) to the theory that long-term, low-level carbon monoxide exposures are also harmful."[9] Even though this testimony was based on an extrapolated relationship, and not a statistically proven one, the court found the testimony competent and upheld its admission. The court did so even though the testimony revealed that "the threshold level at which carbon monoxide becomes harmful is unknown."[10]

Alaska also requires a showing of specific causation. In *Lamb*, the plaintiffs offered differential diagnosis[11] expert testimony that the plaintiffs were harmed by the chronic

---

2. Dep't of Corr. v. Cowles, 151 P.3d 353, 365 (Alaska 2006) (quotation and citation omitted).
3. *Id.* (quotation and citation omitted); *see also* State v. Abbott, 498 P.2d 712, 726 (Alaska 1972) (same).
4. *Cowles*, 151 P.3d at 365 (alteration in original) (internal quotations omitted).
5. Staton *ex rel.* Vincent v. Fairbanks Mem'l Hosp., 862 P.2d 847, 851 (Alaska 1993).
6. *See, e.g.*, Winschel v. Brown, 171 P.3d 142, 149 (Alaska 2007).
7. 46 P.3d 1024, 1028 (Alaska 2002).
8. *See id.* at 1034.
9. *Id.* at 1035.
10. *Id.*
11. The court defined differential diagnosis as "'the determination of which of two or more diseases with

exposure, which the Supreme Court found admissible because it is a standard medical methodology.[12] No epidemiological studies were introduced. The implications from *Lamb* are twofold. First, toxic tort plaintiffs are required to prove specific causation. Second, differential diagnosis expert testimony may be admissible in Alaska even when plaintiffs fail to provide epidemiological studies in support of their theory of causation.

Similarly, in *Maines v. Kenworth Alaska, Inc.*, the court indicated that specific causation must be proven. In reversing summary judgment, the court found a material issue of fact with respect to causation regarding whether the plaintiff's "symptoms were of the type to occur in a person exposed to this type of toxic gas or whether they were due to his lifestyle."[13] Accordingly, proof of specific causation under Alaskan law seems to require that plaintiffs account for potential alternative causes.

Arizona
Overall Standard for Causation

Arizona law has no distinct doctrine dealing with mass torts, toxic torts, or environmental torts in particular, although there are some cases dealing with defective or toxic products, scenarios that Arizona has not treated as materially different from other tort litigation.[14]

Overall, the standard of proof for causation has been fairly low in Arizona, for several reasons. First, Arizona uses a relaxed standard of proof,[15] leaving the jury with broad discretion to decide if the plaintiff's injury was more likely than not caused by the defendant. Second, the courts have occasionally shown a willingness to accept minimal scientific evidence as sufficient, as long as it is corroborated by factors that the court deems reliable.[16] Third, the courts have historically set a very low bar for the admission of expert testimony, which compounds the effect of the already low standard of proof. However, recent amendments to the state's rules of evidence may lead to more rigorous admissibility standards.

General and Specific Causation

In an oft-cited passage from *Coca-Cola Bottling Co. of Tucson v. Fitzgerald*,[17] the Court of Appeals of Arizona stated:

> To establish the causal connection between an accident and injury ... medical testimony as to the *possibility* of such causal connection, without more, is insufficient. But if there

---

similar symptoms is the one from which the patient is suffering, by systematic comparison and contrasting of the clinical findings.'" *Lamb*, 46 P.3d at 1034 n.43 (citations omitted).
12. *Lamb*, 46 P.3d at 1035–36.
13. 155 P.3d 318, 329 (Alaska 2007).
14. *E.g.*, Baroldy v. Ortho Pharm. Corp., 760 P.2d 574, 580–83 (Ariz. Ct. App. 1988) (birth control device).
15. *See, e.g.*, Wisener v. State, 598 P.2d 511, 513–14 (Ariz. 1979); *see also* Kreisman v. Thomas, 469 P.2d 107, 110 (Ariz. Ct. App. 1970).
16. *See infra* note 22 and accompanying text.
17. 413 P.2d 869, 872 (Ariz. Ct. App. 1966).

is medical evidence of the possibility of the existence of the causal relationship together with other evidence or circumstances indicating such relationship, the finding that the accident caused the injury will be sustained.[18]

This articulates a requirement for both general and specific causation. In this context, "medical evidence of the possibility of the existence of the causal relationship" is akin to evidence of general causation.[19] Such evidence is probative of the causation element overall, but it does not constitute sufficient proof on its own. When coupled "with other evidence or circumstances indicating" causation, there is sufficient proof to uphold a finding on the element of proximate cause.[20]

The standard necessary to prove causation under Arizona law has not been consistently stated. In the typical case, proof must be made by a preponderance of the evidence: "causation must be shown to be *probable* and not merely *possible*, and generally expert medical testimony that a subsequent illness or disease 'could' or 'may' have been the cause of the injury is insufficient."[21] However, as in *Fitzgerald*, there are cases where the courts appear to be willing to accept something *less* than a preponderance, as long as "other evidence or circumstances" support a finding of causation.[22]

The combination of lax pre-amendment standards for the admissibility of expert testimony and few requirements dealing with the content of expert testimony historically has created a low standard of proof overall in Arizona.[23] For example, in *Baroldy v. Ortho Pharmaceutical Corp.*,[24] the court of appeals held that "plaintiffs need not provide an existing scientific study showing a statistical correlation between the product and the injury to establish a causal relation in a products liability action." Language such as this, combined with the possibility of making out sufficient expert proof with less than a preponderance of the evidence (as discussed above with *Fitzgerald*), shows that proof of causation might succeed in Arizona even when weak by general standards. This approach in determining issues of causation is captured both by the case law and by the generality of the relevant

---

18. *Id.* (emphasis in original); *see also* Ideal Food Prods. Co. v. Rupe, 261 P.2d 992, 994 (Ariz. 1953); Apache Powder Co. v. Bond, 145 P.2d 988, 990 (Ariz. 1944); *Kreisman*, 469 P.2d at 111; Montague v. Deagle, 462 P.2d 403, 405 (Ariz. Ct. App. 1969).
19. *Fitzgerald*, 413 P.2d at 872.
20. *Id.*
21. *Kreisman*, 469 P.2d at 110; *see also* Wisener v. State, 598 P.2d 511, 513–14 (Ariz. 1979).
22. *Fitzgerald*, 413 P.2d at 872. *See, e.g.*, Benkendorf v. Advanced Cardiac Specialists Chtd., 269 P.3d 704, 706 n.4 (Ct. App. 2012) (collecting cases).
23. In the words of an unpublished opinion, the Arizona "supreme court has interpreted [pre-amendment Rule 702] to set a relatively low threshold for qualification as an expert. . . ." State v. Cotten, No. 1 CA-CR 11-0433, 2012 WL 2476242, at *2 (Ariz. Ct. App. June 19, 2012) (unpublished opinion). Previous cases have held that "[t]he degree of qualification goes to the weight given the testimony, not its admissibility." State v. Davolt, 84 P.3d 456, 475 (Ariz. 2004).
24. 760 P.2d 574, 583 (Ariz. Ct. App. 1988).

pattern jury instruction: "Negligence causes an injury if it helps produce the injury and if the injury would not have happened without the negligence."[25]

However, the standards surrounding scientific testimony, its admissibility, and its weight in Arizona are currently undergoing a change. For decades, Arizona hewed to the "general acceptance" standard set by *Frye v. United States*[26] for the admissibility of scientific evidence. In *Logerquist v. McVey*,[27] the Arizona Supreme Court specifically rejected the United States Supreme Court's modern framework as expressed in *Daubert v. Merrell Dow Pharmaceuticals, Inc.*[28] However, in 2011, the Arizona Rules of Evidence were amended so that *Daubert*'s emphasis on methodology and reliability have now supplanted *Frye*'s "general acceptance" standard in Arizona.[29]

There are a limited number of cases that have applied the amended version of Rule 702 in Arizona, which became effective as recently as January 1, 2012. Courts appear to be looking to federal applications of *Daubert* and its progeny for guidance with the amended rule.[30]

Arizona Federal Cases

In *Cloud v. Pfizer, Inc.*,[31] the United States District Court for the District of Arizona applied Arizona law to a product liability claim involving a suicide allegedly caused by the prescription medication Zoloft. In its analysis of the case, the court broke out the issues of general and specific causation, treating them separately. However, the federal district court cited no Arizona authorities over the course of this discussion. Instead, the court cited Arizona authorities only for the proposition that "Arizona views causation liberally."[32]

Despite this liberal causation standard, the district court rejected the plaintiff's claim in *Cloud* because the evidence was insufficient on the issue of specific causation. The evidence on general causation showed a link between the medication and akathisia (restless leg syndrome), and a link between akathisia and suicide. However, the plaintiff did not offer any admissible evidence that the decedent had suffered from akathisia.[33]

---

25. REVISED ARIZ. JURY INSTRUCTIONS-CIVIL: FAULT INSTRUCTIONS 33 (4th ed. 2005).
26. 293 F. 1013, 1014 (D.C. Cir. 1923).
27. 1 P.3d 113, 132 (Ariz. 2000).
28. 509 U.S. 579, 592–95 (1993).
29. *See* ARIZ. R. EVID. 702 (newly amended Rule of Evidence 702 identifies four factors as relevant to the qualification of an expert: (1) whether the expert's specialized knowledge will help the trier of fact understand the evidence or determine a fact at issue; (2) whether the testimony is based on sufficient facts or data; (3) whether the testimony is the product of reliable principles and methods; and, (4) whether the expert has reliably applied the principles and methods to the facts of the case).
30. *E.g.*, State v. Sosnowicz, No. 1 CA-CR 10-0789, 2012 Ariz. App. LEXIS 133, at *24 n.12 (Ariz. Ct. App. Mar. 8, 2012); State v. Burke *ex rel.* Cnty. of La Paz, No. 1 CA-SA 12-0028, 2012 WL 1470103, at *2 (Ariz. Ct. App. Apr. 26, 2012) (unpublished opinion).
31. 198 F. Supp. 2d 1118, 1138–39 (D. Ariz. 2001).
32. *Id.* at 1132–38 (citing Stephens v. Bashas' Inc., 924 P.2d 117, 121 (Ariz. Ct. App. 1996), and Robertson v. Sixpence Inns of Am., Inc., 789 P.2d 1040, 1047 (Ariz. 1990)).
33. *Id.*

Similarly, in *Benshoof v. National Gypsum Co.*,[34] the U.S. Court of Appeals for the Ninth Circuit held that causation would not be proven under Arizona law where only one of several plaintiffs had any exposure to materials containing asbestos, and this exposure lasted for only one week. Rejecting the notion that Arizona law allowed for recovery where a defendant's conduct contributed "'only a little'" to the plaintiff's damages, the Ninth Circuit noted that "such minor causes" must be necessary causes, without which "'the damages would not have occurred.'"[35] In other words, the *Benshoof* court said, Arizona law requires "but for" causation. The Arizona state courts, which have not dealt with asbestos-related litigation, have not passed directly on this passage in *Benshoof*. However, in *Barret v. Harris*, the Arizona Court of Appeals held that Arizona state courts "follow the substantial-factor test set forth in [the Second] Restatement [of Torts] § 431 and referenced in § 435."[36]

California
Overall Standard for Causation
Under California law, causation is analyzed in two stages: "determining cause in fact and considering various policy factors that may preclude imposition of liability."[37] Furthermore, "'California has definitively adopted the substantial factor test of the Second Restatement of Torts for cause-in-fact determinations.'"[38]

This substantial factor test, in turn, consists of two parts. First, the test asks whether the cause was a necessary condition of the alleged injury—that is, it asks the question of "but for" causation.[39] Second, the test asks whether, in addition to being a necessary cause of the injury, the defendant's negligence was also a "substantial factor" in producing the injury.[40] However, the California Supreme Court has advised that undue emphasis should not be placed on the term "substantial," indicating that the second part of this test does not require robust proof.[41] Accordingly, in most cases, cause in fact is a matter of "but for" causation.[42]

---

34. 978 F.2d 475, 477 (9th Cir. 1992).
35. *Id.* at 477 (quoting *Sixpence Inns*, 789 P.2d at 1047).
36. 86 P.3d 954, 961 (Ariz. Ct. App. 2004).
37. Viner v. Sweet, 70 P.3d 1046, 1048 n.1 (Cal. 2003).
38. *Id.* at 1051 (quoting Rutherford v. Owens-Illinois, Inc., 941 P.2d 1203, 1214 (Cal. 1997)).
39. RESTATEMENT (SECOND) OF TORTS § 431 cmt. *a* (1965); *see also Viner*, 70 P.3d at 1051 ("[T]he 'substantial factor' test *subsumes* the 'but for' test." (emphasis in original) (quotation and citation omitted)).
40. The term "substantial factor" is "sufficiently intelligible to any layman to furnish an adequate guide to the jury, and it is neither possible nor desirable to reduce it to lower terms." Mitchell v. Gonzales, 819 P.2d 872, 878 (Cal. 1991) (quotation and citation omitted).
41. *See id.* ("[T]he 'substantial factor' test subsumes the 'but for' test. 'If the conduct which is claimed to have caused the injury had nothing at all to do with the injuries, it could not be said that the conduct was a factor, let alone a substantial factor, in the production of the injuries.'" (quoting Doupnik v. Gen. Motors Corp., 275 Cal. Rptr. 715, 721 (Cal. Ct. App. 1990))).
42. The exception is for cases with concurrent independent causes—in such cases a showing of "but for" causation is logically impossible and unnecessary under the law. *See* RESTATEMENT (SECOND) OF TORTS

General and Specific Causation

California law recognizes the importance of a plaintiff proving both general and specific causation in the toxic tort context. For example, many California cases have refused to find causation where the evidence fails to indicate both that the toxin at issue is capable of causing the disease alleged and that the defendant's conduct did in fact cause the disease in the injured party.[43] A plaintiff must prove both "exposure to [the] defendant's product and biological processes from the exposure which result in disease."[44] The standard for proving causation is a preponderance of the evidence, and such proof must include "competent expert testimony."[45] For example, in *Jones v. Ortho Pharmaceutical Corp.*, there was evidence linking the defendant's birth control drug with a certain type of cancer.[46] However, the plaintiff's cancer developed more quickly and after a shorter exposure than those documented in the scientific and medical studies.[47] Nevertheless, the plaintiff argued that "the drug accelerated the normal progression of the disease."[48] Finding the testimony of the plaintiff's medical experts to be "highly conjectural and ambiguous," the court granted the defendant's motion for a nonsuit.[49] In reviewing the issue of general causation, the *Jones* court relied heavily on the statistical and epidemiological literature.

California law also applies the basic principle of specific causation, namely, that a product's mere potential to cause harm is not enough, and it must have caused actual harm in order for an injury to be actionable. For example, in *Bockrath v. Aldrich Chemical Co.*, the court held that in addition to "identify[ing] each product that allegedly caused" the plaintiff's cancer, the plaintiff must also "allege that as a result of the exposure, the toxins entered his body," and "that he suffers from a specific illness, and that each toxin that entered his body was a substantial factor in bringing about, prolonging, or aggravating

---

§ 432(2) (1965); *see also Viner*, 70 P.3d at 1051 (citing *Mitchell*, 819 P.2d at 876). Related problems were adjudicated in *Rutherford*, 941 P.2d at 1219–20. In *Rutherford*, the question was how to apportion liability among asbestos manufacturers where the causal link between asbestos and the plaintiff's injury was established, but it was unclear which particular manufacturers had caused the injury.

43. *See, e.g.*, Lineaweaver v. Plant Insulation Co., 37 Cal. Rptr. 2d 902, 908–09 (Cal. Ct. App. 1995); Jones v. Ortho Pharm. Corp., 209 Cal. Rptr. 456, 458 (Cal. Ct. App. 1985); *see also* Jones v. United States, 933 F. Supp. 894, 900–01 (N.D. Cal. 1996) (applying California law and holding, in a wrongful birth action, that plaintiffs had to show that (1) there was a "scientifically validated interaction between Penicillin-VK and Triphasil-28 birth control pills that made it more likely that [plaintiff] would become pregnant while taking both drugs than if she were merely taking birth control pills alone"; and, (2) "the interaction between Penicillin-VK and Triphasil-28 birth control pills was the probable, not merely a possible, cause of [plaintiff's] pregnancy").

44. *Lineaweaver*, 37 Cal. Rptr. 2d at 906.

45. *Jones*, 209 Cal. Rptr. at 458; *see also* Sindell v. Abbott Labs., 607 P.2d 924, 940 (Cal. 1980) ("A mere possibility of causation is not enough; and when the matter remains one of pure speculation or conjecture, or the probabilities are at best evenly balanced, it becomes the duty of the court to direct a verdict for the defendant." (quotation, emphasis, and citation omitted)).

46. *Jones*, 209 Cal. Rptr. at 458.

47. *Id.*

48. *Id.*

49. *Id.*

that illness."[50] This holding sets forth the basic principle of specific causation, namely, that exposure to a toxin is not, in itself, sufficient proof of causation. Rather, there must be specific evidence linking the alleged injury to the toxic exposure.

Because of the "complicated and possibly esoteric medical causation issues" presented in mass toxic tort cases, California law requires the plaintiffs in such cases to provide expert medical testimony to establish causation. In particular, California requires plaintiffs to prove to "a reasonable medical probability based on competent expert testimony that the defendant's conduct contributed to [the] plaintiff's injury."[51] However, expert testimony must be based on facts rather than assumptions or conjecture,[52] and expert testimony must have "a reasonable basis."[53] In California, an expert "does not possess a carte blanche to express any opinion."[54] For these reasons, expert testimony on specific causation requires a certain degree of definiteness, such as the ability to quantify the dose of toxic exposure that is necessary to cause injury, and some factual basis for alleging that a plaintiff received the type and quantity of exposure necessary to cause him harm.[55]

Colorado
Overall Standard for Causation

Under Colorado law, a defendant's negligent conduct constitutes the proximate cause of an injury if the plaintiff can prove, with reasonable "probability" (or that it is more likely than not) that the defendant's conduct was a substantial contributing cause.[56] In turn, negligent conduct is a substantial contributing cause if "the injury would not have occurred in the absence of the defendant's negligence."[57] In this sense, the "substantial contributing cause" test is the same as "but for" causation—"[t]o prove causation in a negligence case, the plaintiff must show by a preponderance of the evidence the injury would not have occurred but for the defendant's negligent conduct."[58] Colorado courts treat the issue of causation as the same basic inquiry in both negligence and strict liability cases.[59]

---

50. 980 P.2d 398, 404 (Cal. 1999).
51. *Id.* at 403 (quotation and citation omitted).
52. Lopez v. City of Los Angeles, 126 Cal. Rptr. 3d 706, 717 (Cal. Ct. App. 2011); *see also* Pac. Gas & Elec. v. Zuckerman, 234 Cal. Rptr. 630, 642–44 (Cal. Ct. App. 1987).
53. Lockheed Litig. Cases, 10 Cal. Rptr. 3d 34, 35 (Cal. Ct. App. 2004).
54. Jennings v. Palomar Pomerado Health Sys., Inc., 8 Cal. Rptr. 3d 363, 368 (Cal. Ct. App. 2003).
55. *See* Geffcken v. D'Andrea, 41 Cal. Rptr. 3d 80, 90–91 (Cal. Ct. App. 2006) (excluding expert testimony that assumed exposure without evidence of actual exposure); *see also* Lineaweaver v. Plant Insulation Co., 37 Cal. Rptr. 2d 902, 906 (Cal. Ct. App. 1995) (determinations of specific causation require examination of the "[f]requency of exposure, regularity of exposure, and proximity of the [chemical] to plaintiff").
56. Vento v. Colo. Nat'l Bank-Pueblo, 907 P.2d 642, 646 (Colo. Ct. App. 1995); *see also* Widefield Homes, Inc. v. Griego, 416 P.2d 365, 366 (Colo. 1966) (plaintiff must offer evidence "showing a probability of proximate cause[;] . . . mere possibility and speculation" are insufficient).
57. Graven v. Vail Assocs., 909 P.2d 514, 520 (Colo. 1995); *see also* Rupert v. Clayton Brokerage Co., 737 P.2d 1106, 1112 (Colo. 1987) (citing Thropp v. Bache Halsey Stuart Shields, Inc., 650 F.2d 817, 821 (6th Cir. 1981)).
58. Kaiser Found. Health Plan of Colo. v. Sharp, 741 P.2d 714, 719 (Colo. 1987).
59. *See, e.g.*, States v. R.D. Werner Co., 799 P.2d 427, 430 (Colo. Ct. App. 1990) (holding that where

In *Merkley v. Pittsburgh Corning Corp.*,[60] the defendant won summary judgment against the plaintiff's claim that the defendant's products caused her husband's asbestos-related cancer. The court of appeals affirmed, finding that the plaintiff had failed to prove that her husband had been exposed to the defendant's product. The court held that without such evidence of exposure, the plaintiff could not prove that the "defendant's product was a substantial contributing cause of his injury" under Colorado law.[61] The court borrowed this "substantial contributing cause" test from general tort cases in Colorado.[62]

Colorado Federal Cases

In *June v. Union Carbide Corp.*,[63] the plaintiffs alleged that the defendant's milling operations exposed them to various radioactive materials, which caused or increased the risk of radiation-related illness. The trial court granted summary judgment in the defendant's favor, finding that the plaintiffs had failed to provide any evidence of "but for" causation. The plaintiffs appealed, arguing that "when there 'are potential multiple or concurring causes' for an injury, Colorado applies a 'substantial factor test' for causation, not the more stringent but-for test."[64] In particular, the plaintiffs contended that "an actor's conduct can be deemed causal 'where it is of sufficient significance in producing the harm as to lead reasonable persons to regard it as a cause and to attach responsibility.'"[65] The U.S. Court of Appeals for the Tenth Circuit rejected this argument, ruling that Colorado would not likely part from the approach of the *Restatement (Second) of Torts*, which provides that a defendant cannot be liable "unless its conduct is either (a) a but-for cause of the plaintiff's injury or (b) a necessary component of a causal set that (probably) would have caused the injury in the absence of other causes."[66]

The federal cases in Colorado require plaintiffs to prove both general and specific causation.[67] In *Watson v. Dillon Cos.*, the district court framed the general causation inquiry as whether "the toxic substance at issue has been demonstrated to cause in humans the disease or illness suffered by the plaintiff."[68] This formulation of the question appears to contemplate some form of epidemiological or statistical evidence.[69]

---

plaintiff's strict liability claim failed to show causation, his negligence claim must be rejected on the same basis). *But see id.* at 429 (discussing the special situation of "enterprise liability" in product liability actions).
60. 910 P.2d 58, 59 (Colo. Ct. App. 1995).
61. *Id.*
62. *Id.*
63. 577 F.3d 1234, 1237 (10th Cir. 2009).
64. *Id.* at 1239.
65. *Id.*
66. *Id.* at 1244.
67. *See, e.g.*, Norris v. Baxter Healthcare Corp., 397 F.3d 878, 881 (10th Cir. 2005) ("[P]laintiffs must show both general and specific causation."); Watson v. Dillon Cos., 797 F. Supp. 2d 1138, 1149 (D. Colo. 2011) (citing *Norris*, 397 F.3d at 881).
68. *Watson*, 797 F. Supp. 2d at 1149.
69. *See Norris*, 397 F.3d at 882 ("[E]pidemiology is the best evidence of general causation in a toxic tort

As for specific causation, the district court in *Watson* discussed a number of factors, including whether the relevant toxic exposure was sufficient in quantity to cause the claimed injury, whether the chronological relationship between exposure and the alleged injury is biologically plausible, and the likelihood that the exposure, and not some other known cause, is responsible for the injury.[70] "Of particular concern," the court noted, "is the 'dose-response' relationship, *i.e.*, 'the relationship in which a change in amount, intensity, or duration of exposure to a chemical is associated with a change in risk of disease' and the amount of the plaintiff's alleged exposure."[71] The federal cases also demonstrate that, when dealing with specific causation, if epidemiological evidence is available but the plaintiffs do not offer it, evidence of differential diagnosis is reliable and admissible only if general causation already has been established.[72]

Hawaii
Overall Standard for Causation
Because there is no body of Hawaiian law that deals specifically with the particular problems raised by toxic tort litigation, the relevant causation standards derive from the more general field of Hawaiian product liability and tort law.[73] Hawaii defines causation as that which forms a "substantial factor" in bringing about the plaintiff's injury. The courts decline to further explain the meaning of the "substantial factor" test, leaving it to the jury to determine whether the defendant's conduct was more likely than not a "substantial factor" in producing the injury. The jury has broad discretion in weighing the evidence.[74]

General and Specific Causation
Hawaiian cases do not treat the issues of general and specific causation as discrete analytical tasks. Instead, proximate cause is discussed more generally through language taken from the *Restatement (Second) of Torts*: "The actor's negligent conduct is a legal cause of harm to another if . . . his conduct is a substantial factor in bringing about the harm."[75] Under the substantial factor test, the defendant's conduct "need not have been the whole cause or the only factor" in bringing about the plaintiff's injury—it need only have been a "substantial factor."[76]

---

      case. . . . While the presence of epidemiology does not necessarily end the inquiry, where epidemiology is available, it cannot be ignored. As the best evidence of general causation, it must be addressed.").
70. *Watson*, 797 F. Supp. 2d at 1149.
71. *Id.* (quotation and citation omitted).
72. *See Norris*, 397 F.3d at 885 (finding that "differential diagnosis without supporting epidemiological evidence" is inadmissible because "[d]ifferential diagnosis *assumes* that general causation has been proven" (quotation and citation omitted)); *see also In re* Breast Implant Litig., 11 F. Supp. 2d 1217, 1229–30 (D. Colo. 1998).
73. Knodle v. Waikiki Gateway Hotel, Inc., 742 P.2d 377, 386 (Haw. 1987) (quotation and citation omitted).
74. *Id.* at 384–386.
75. *Id.* at 386 (quotation and citation omitted); *see also* Mitchell v. Branch, 363 P.2d 969, 973 (Haw. 1961).
76. *Knodle*, 742 P.2d at 386 (quotation and citation omitted).

Although they acknowledge that the phrase "substantial factor" can be viewed as "too general," the Hawaiian courts have stood by it as "the touchstone when the issue of causal relation must be submitted to the jury."[77] This is because the phrase is "sufficiently intelligible to furnish an adequate guide in instructions to the jury, and . . . it is neither possible nor desirable to reduce it to any lower terms."[78] Accordingly, the state pattern jury instruction provides simply that "[a]n act or omission is a legal cause of an injury/damage if it was a substantial factor in bringing about the injury/damage."[79]

As for the standard of proof, the Supreme Court of Hawaii has held that "the test contemplates a factual determination that the negligence of the defendant was more likely than not a substantial factor in bringing about the result complained of."[80] In other words, the substantial factor test is evaluated according to a preponderance of the evidence standard.

In applying the "substantial factor" test, courts leave the bulk of the task to the jury. Taking into account "the whole evidence relating to a particular issue," the judge may decide "whether more than one reasonable inference can be drawn," but the actual drawing of inferences—which is to say, the weighing of evidence—is the province of the jury.[81]

For most cases, there is no indication that the courts impose any presumptions or preferences on the jury with respect to certain kinds of evidence. The exception is medical malpractice, where "the plaintiff must prove both breach and causation through expert testimony."[82] In a typical product liability case, however, "[p]roof of defect and causation may be provided by expert testimony or by circumstantial evidence."[83]

For example, in *Cho v. State*, the trial judge made detailed findings of fact in favor of the defendant.[84] The court noted that the defense experts were more credible than the plaintiffs' experts, that the plaintiffs' claim suffered from narrative inconsistencies, and that the plaintiffs' own medical records undermined their theory of causation.[85] However, the court notably did not treat any one of these factors, such as the expert testimony, as more important, authoritative, or reliable than any other category of evidence. Thus, as a general rule, "expert 'testimony is not conclusive and like any testimony, the jury may accept or reject it.'"[86]

---

77. *Id.* (citing Bidar v. Amfac, Inc., 669 P.2d 154, 159 (Haw. 1983)).
78. *Id.* (quotation and citation omitted).
79. Hawai'i Civil Jury Instructions § 7.1 (1999).
80. Taylor-Rice v. State, 979 P.2d 1086, 1100–01 (Haw. 1999) (quoting McKenna v. Volkswagenwerk Aktiengesellschaft, 558 P.2d 1018, 1022 (Haw. 1977)).
81. *Knodle*, 742 P.2d at 384.
82. Todd v. Shankel, 83 F. App'x 952, 953–54 (9th Cir. 2003).
83. Acoba v. Gen. Tire, Inc., 986 P.2d 288, 304 (Haw. 1999).
84. 168 P.3d 17, 35–38 (Haw. 2007).
85. *Id.*
86. Ray v. Kapiolani Med. Specialists, 259 P.3d 569, 578 (Haw. 2011) (quoting Bachran v. Morishige, 469 P.2d 808, 812 (Haw. 1970)).

Hawaii Federal Cases

As for federal litigation, the opinion of the U.S. Court of Appeals for the Ninth Circuit, *In re Asbestos Cases*, found no error in the district court's lengthy jury instruction on proximate causation.[87] Applying Hawaiian law, this instruction informed the jury that "many factors or things . . . may be a proximate cause of the injury, if it is a substantial factor in bringing about the injury."[88]

Idaho
Overall Standard for Causation

Idaho treats general and specific causation as distinct inquiries. Both inquiries are resolved under a preponderance of the evidence standard, although the courts have hinted at policy concerns that might motivate the application of a more lenient standard. In Idaho, *Daubert v. Merrell Dow Pharmaceuticals*[89] provides guidance for the admissibility of expert testimony touching on causation. Idaho's formulation of specific causation maintains that toxic exposure need not have been the primary cause of a plaintiff's injury, as long as it is one of several causes that were more likely than not to have been sufficient to cause the plaintiff's injury.

General and Specific Causation

The leading case in Idaho is *Earl v. Cryovac*.[90] *Earl* was a toxic tort case arising from the plaintiff's exposure to vapors emitted from a plastic film that was manufactured at his workplace. In vacating an order of summary judgment for the defendant, the Court of Appeals of Idaho engaged in a thorough discussion of "the elements of a toxic tort action, the requirement of proximate cause, and the use of expert testimony to establish causation."[91]

The court identified the issues of general and specific causation as two independent parts of the causation analysis. "[T]he causation issue turns upon two subsidiary questions: (a) Did the product, or a substance in the product, have the capacity to cause the type of harm claimed by the plaintiff? (b) Was the plaintiff's exposure sufficient to produce a toxic effect?"[92]

In evaluating these questions, Idaho employs "a preponderance of the evidence" standard: "the plaintiff's claim of causation [must be] 'more probably true than not true.'"[93] In a footnote, the court acknowledged that "[s]ome scholars have questioned the applicability

---

87. 847 F.2d 523, 526 & n.3 (9th Cir. 1988).
88. *Id.*
89. 509 U.S. 579, 592–95 (1993).
90. 772 P.2d 725 (Idaho Ct. App. 1989).
91. *Id.* at 726.
92. *Id.*
93. *Id.* at 727.

of the probability standard to mass toxic tort cases," based on the "unique problems [of these cases] such as indeterminate plaintiffs . . . or indeterminate defendants."[94] Noting that the case before it did not present any of these problems, the court pressed on with the preponderance standard, noting that it "strikes a balance between plaintiffs' and defendants' rights. It avoids compelling a plaintiff to meet the virtually impossible burden of proving causation with certainty . . . [and it] also avoids compelling a defendant to pay damages when his connection with the plaintiff's injury is nothing more than a mere possibility."[95] The preponderance standard has also been recognized by a federal court applying Idaho law.[96]

In addressing the issue of general causation, the *Earl* court urged caution to the fact finder. An expert's conclusion, or the lack of one, does not end the inquiry. Rather, the trial court

> [M]ay not assume that a causal relationship is probable merely because a physician deems it significant in his diagnosis and treatment of a patient's condition. Neither may they assume that a causal relationship is improbable merely because it has not been documented in a body of research literature where a high degree of certainty is demanded.[97]

The court went on to discuss the criteria for the admissibility of expert testimony. However, it should be recognized that *Earl* predates the United States Supreme Court's decision in *Daubert v. Merrell Dow Pharmaceuticals*.[98] Since the advent of that case, Idaho has endorsed the "guidance" of the *Daubert* standard.[99]

The *Earl* court used the term "particular evidence" to refer to specific causation.[100] Proof may be made by circumstantial evidence, or by circumstantial evidence supplemented with expert testimony, including diagnostic and toxicological testimony. In addition, the *Earl* court's formulation of specific causation allows for a finding of independent concurring causes: "a proximate cause need not be the sole or primary cause in fact. It may be concurrent with other causes which, in combination, cause the harm."[101]

---

94. *Id.* at 727 n.1 (internal citations omitted). The court quoted several authorities, including Note, *Trans-Science in Torts*, 96 YALE L.J. 428, 429 (1986) (discussing "the inherent problems with a causation standard that requires that the hazardous nature of a substance be quantified in the general population before granting recovery," and "propos[ing] a causation standard that circumvents problems whose solutions are scientifically indeterminate by combining a qualitative showing of causation with proof that the manufacturer acted negligently in introducing an 'abnormally dangerous' product").
95. *Id.* at 727.
96. Longmore v. Merrell Dow Pharm., Inc., 737 F. Supp. 1117, 1119–20 (D. Idaho 1990) (Bendectin litigation).
97. *Earl*, 772 P.2d at 727–28.
98. 509 U.S. 579, 592–95 (1993).
99. State v. Parkinson, 909 P.2d 647, 652 (Idaho Ct. App. 1996).
100. *Earl*, 772 P.2d at 726 ("The issue may be addressed by general or particular evidence.").
101. *Id.* at 727, 732.

Montana

Overall Standard for Causation

In Montana, to prevail on a claim of negligence, a plaintiff must prove causation in fact.[102] There are two means of proving causation in fact. The typical case employs the "but for" causation test.[103] However, where there are independent concurring causes, Montana courts use the "substantial factor" test.[104] In such cases, each act must be considered a "substantial factor" in bringing about the injury where "the conduct of each is a cause in fact of the event."[105] In this regard, Montana follows the rule set out in the *Restatement (Second) of Torts*.[106]

Significantly, Montana used to require evidence of "proximate or legal causation" in addition to causation in fact.[107] However, Montana now "limit[s] the analysis of foreseeability to a determination of whether there is negligence in the first place, and then deal[s] with cause as simply cause-in-fact."[108]

General and Specific Causation

In *Meyer v. Creative Nail Design, Inc.*, the Supreme Court of Montana affirmed that plaintiffs can establish a prima facie claim of product liability by offering evidence of exposure to specific products, and expert testimony as to general and specific causation.[109] The court held that the plaintiffs had established a prima facie case with respect to causation by offering "scientific and medical authorities regarding the causal connection between the [specific] chemical exposure [at issue] and injury," and expert testimony that "the seven chemical injuries [experienced by the plaintiff] were directly and proximately caused" by the chemical exposure.[110]

In *Hagen v. Dow Chemical Co.*, the Supreme Court of Montana held that circumstantial evidence is sufficient to "establish[] causation in chemical poisoning cases because of

---

102. U.S. Fid. & Guar. Co. v. Camp, 831 P.2d 586, 589 (Mont. 1992).
103. *Id.* ("Under the 'but for' test . . . the defendant's conduct is a cause of an event if the event would not have occurred but for that conduct; conversely, the defendant's conduct is not a cause of the event if the event would have occurred without it." (quotation and citation omitted)).
104. Rudeck v. Wright, 709 P.2d 621, 628 (Mont. 1985) ("When the conduct of two or more actors is so related to an event that their combined conduct, viewed as a whole, is a 'but for' cause of event [*sic*], and application of the 'but for' rule to them individually would absolve all of them, the conduct of each is a cause in fact of the event.").
105. *Id.*
106. *See* RESTATEMENT (SECOND) OF TORTS § 432(2) (1965).
107. *See Camp*, 831 P.2d at 589 ("This Court has separated the element of causation into two separate components, causation in fact, and proximate or legal causation, both of which must be proven to prevail in an action for negligence. . . . Proximate cause is analyzed in terms of foreseeability. 'A defendant is liable for his wrongful conduct if it is reasonably foreseeable that plaintiff's injury may be the natural and probable consequence of that conduct.'" (quoting Thayer v. Hicks, 793 P.2d 784, 795 (Mont. 1990))).
108. Busta v. Columbus Hosp. Corp., 916 P.2d 122, 138 (Mont. 1996).
109. 975 P.2d 1264, 1271 (Mont. 1999).
110. *Id.* at 1268–70.

the inherent difficulty in offering direct proof in these situations."[111] In *Hagen*, a stock of fish died shortly after herbicide was sprayed near their water supply, and the fish farmers brought suit against the herbicide's manufacturer. The trial court granted summary judgment in favor of the defendants. On appeal, the defendants argued that because the plaintiffs failed to offer admissible expert testimony, and because they provided no direct evidence that the fish had been exposed to the herbicide, summary judgment should be affirmed.

The Supreme Court of Montana disagreed, finding that Montana "has adopted a flexible standard of proof on causation which may be met by circumstantial, as well as direct, evidence."[112] The court explained:

> Although a plaintiff does not meet his burden of proof by merely establishing that an incident occurred, it is well established that in actions dealing with product liability, sufficient evidence to make a prima facie case may consist of establishing the circumstances of the incident, similar occurrences under similar circumstances, and elimination of alternative causes.[113]

Accordingly, the court found that the plaintiffs had put on sufficient proof of causation by showing: (1) the fish died shortly after the weed poison was washed into water tanks; (2) test fish died when exposed to a similar herbicide mixture and exhibited the same symptoms prior to death; and, (3) no alternative causes had been proven.[114]

Nevada
Overall Standard for Causation

Under Nevada law, causation is assessed in terms of actual cause and proximate cause.[115] Actual cause is a matter of "but for" causation, and proximate cause "'is essentially a policy consideration that limits a defendant's liability to foreseeable consequences that have a reasonably close connection with both the defendant's conduct and the harm which that conduct created.'"[116] In other words, "proximate cause" in Nevada "is any cause which in natural and continuous sequence, unbroken by any efficient intervening cause, produces the injury complained of and without which the result would not have occurred."[117]

---

111. 863 P.2d 413, 417 (Mont. 1993).
112. *Id.*
113. *Id.*
114. *Id.* at 418.
115. Goodrich & Pennington Mortgage Fund, Inc. v. J.R. Woolard, Inc., 101 P.3d 792, 797 (Nev. 2004).
116. *Id.* (quoting Dow Chem. Co. v. Mahlum, 970 P.2d 98, 107 (Nev. 1998), *overruled in part on other grounds by* GES, Inc. v. Corbitt, 117 Nev. 265, 271 (Nev. 2001)).
117. Taylor v. Silva, 615 P.2d 970, 971 (Nev. 1980) (quotation and citation omitted).

Nevada law provides for two different causation tests: one where "each party argued its own theory of causation, mutually exclusive of the other," and another where a party seeks to prove independent concurring causes.[118] Cases involving distinct, mutually exclusive causation arguments require a "but for" causation instruction.[119] With respect to independent concurring causes, Nevada courts have employed the "substantial factor" standard in strict product liability actions. In this context, the Supreme Court of Nevada has held that while

> [A] but-for causation instruction applies when each party argued its own theory of causation, the two theories were presented as mutually exclusive, and the cause of the plaintiff's injuries could only be the result of one of those theories, but not both .... A substantial-factor causation instruction is appropriate when "an injury may have had two causes, either of which, operating alone, would have been sufficient to cause the injury."[120]

In this regard, Nevada follows the rule set out in the *Restatement (Second) of Torts*.[121] Yet while this remains the causation standard in strict product liability cases, "whether the substantial-factor instruction applies in negligence cases" is still an open question in Nevada.[122]

In *Dow Chemical Co. v. Mahlum*, plaintiffs brought negligence and strict liability actions against a manufacturer of allegedly defective breast implants. Assessing the causation evidence in terms of "actual cause" and "proximate cause," the court found "substantial evidence" and upheld the jury's finding of causation.[123] The court noted that "[d]emonstrating causation in cases involving medical products often requires expert medical testimony."[124] Citing statutory authority, the court observed that "[e]xpert testimony is admissible if scientific, technical, or other specialized knowledge will assist the trier of fact to understand the evidence or determine a fact in issue."[125] In a footnote, the court refused to fully adopt the federal standard for the admissibility of expert testimony, *Daubert v. Merrell Dow Pharmaceuticals*,[126] though it deemed the *Daubert* standard "persuasive."[127]

---

118. Wyeth v. Rowatt, 244 P.3d 765, 769 (Nev. 2010).
119. *Id.*
120. *Id.* at 778 (Nev. 2010) (citations omitted).
121. *See* RESTATEMENT (SECOND) OF TORTS § 432(2) (1965).
122. *Wyeth*, 244 P.3d at 778 n.8.
123. Dow Chem. Co. v. Mahlum, 970 P.2d 98, 107 (Nev. 1998), *overruled in part on other grounds by* GES, Inc. v. Corbitt, 117 Nev. 265, 271 (Nev. 2001).
124. *Id.* at 107–08 (citation omitted).
125. *Id.* at 107 (citing NEV. REV. STAT. § 50.275 (1971) ("If scientific, technical or other specialized knowledge will assist the trier of fact to understand the evidence or to determine a fact in issue, a witness qualified as an expert by special knowledge, skill, experience, training or education may testify to matters within the scope of such knowledge.")).
126. 509 U.S. 579, 592–95 (1993).
127. *Mahlum*, 970 P.2d at 108 n.3.

In *Higgs v. State*, the Supreme Court of Nevada reaffirmed that *Daubert* is not controlling law in Nevada.[128]

Nevada Federal Cases

The Nevada federal cases also shed some insight on the overall causation standard, and standards for expert testimony in toxic tort cases, at least in federal litigation. Generally, the federal courts have set the standard of proof at a preponderance of the evidence.[129] Furthermore, such proof must be made to a "reasonable medical probability" and "based upon competent expert testimony."[130] Expert competency requires not just medical training in general but some expertise in toxicology, epidemiology, risk-assessment, or environmental medicine.[131]

New Mexico

Overall Standard for Causation

Under New Mexico law, to establish liability in a tort case, "there must be a chain of causation initiated by some negligent act or omission of the defendant, which in legal terms is the cause in fact."[132] The standard of proof is a preponderance of the evidence: "the plaintiff must introduce evidence that the injury more likely than not was proximately caused by the act of negligence in question."[133] Whether an act or omission constitutes a proximate cause depends on whether "it contributes to bringing about the injury, if the injury would not have occurred without it, and if it is reasonably connected as a significant link to the injury."[134]

In requiring a reasonable connection to the injury, New Mexico "superimposes considerations of foreseeability on causation in fact. . . . New Mexico follows the rule that 'any harm which is in itself foreseeable, as to which the actor has created or increased the recognizable risk, is always 'proximate,' no matter how it is brought about.'"[135] In applying New Mexico law to the toxic tort context, federal decisions have suggested that the New Mexico Supreme Court would apply the "but for" causation test to this category of cases.[136]

---

128. 222 P.3d 648, 658 (2010).
129. Layton v. Yankee Caithness Joint Venture, 774 F. Supp. 576, 580 (D. Nev. 1991) ("[A] plaintiff bears the burden of proving causation by a preponderance of the evidence.").
130. *Id.*
131. *See* Morin v. United States, 534 F. Supp. 2d 1179, 1185 (D. Nev. 2005).
132. Talbott v. Roswell Hosp. Corp., 118 P.3d 194, 201 (N.M. Ct. App. 2005) (quotation and citation omitted).
133. *Id.* at 202–03 (quotation and citation omitted); *see also* Alberts v. Schultz, 975 P.2d 1279, 1286 (N.M. 1999) ("[T]he evidence . . . must show to a reasonable degree of medical probability that the defendant's negligence caused the [harm].").
134. *Talbott*, 118 P.3d at 201.
135. Andrews v. Saylor, 80 P.3d 482, 489 (N.M. Ct. App. 2003) (citations omitted).
136. *See, e.g.*, Wilcox v. Homestake Mining Co., 619 F.3d 1165, 1169 (10th Cir. 2010) ("[A]s we interpret New Mexico law, a toxic tort plaintiff must demonstrate only to a reasonable degree of medical probability—not as a certainty—that exposure to a substance was a but-for cause of the injury or would have been a but-for cause in the absence of another sufficient cause.").

General and Specific Causation

New Mexico law deploys the analytical framework of general and specific causation in the toxic tort context.[137] To prove general causation under New Mexico law, expert evidence is required: "[s]cientific knowledge of the harmful level of exposure to a chemical, plus knowledge that the plaintiff was exposed to such quantities, are minimal facts necessary to sustain the plaintiffs' burden in a toxic tort case."[138]

With respect to specific causation, the standard in toxic tort cases is proof to a reasonable degree of medical probability (or that it is more likely than not) that the plaintiff's injury was caused by the defendant's negligent act.[139] Under New Mexico law, differential diagnosis is itself insufficient evidence of specific causation.[140]

In *Parkhill v. Alderman-Cave Milling & Grain Co.*, the plaintiff horse owners brought a toxic tort action against horse feed manufactures seeking to recover damages for personal injuries allegedly sustained while handling feed. Applying *Daubert v. Merrell Dow Pharmaceuticals, Inc.*,[141] the trial court excluded the plaintiffs' proffered expert testimony on causation. The court of appeals affirmed, stating that expert opinion relating to causation must offer proof "to a reasonable degree of medical probability, [that] the [plaintiffs'] health symptoms were caused by their exposure" to chemicals in defendants' feed.[142] The court distinguished between internal causation—meaning the plaintiffs' personal health information and risk factors that may have contributed to their alleged injuries—and external causation, or the probability that their injuries were caused by a toxic exposure. Applying this framework, the court held that differential diagnosis alone is an insufficient method for proving external causation in toxic tort cases, and is inadmissible without testimony regarding "differential etiology."[143] The court further held that "testimony as to external causation, or etiology, was beyond the expertise of the average treating physician and .... required specific scientific knowledge."[144] Lastly, the court added that circumstantial evidence of causation, such as the temporal relationship between exposure and injury, is inadmissible to establish causation when "direct evidence of dosage [can] be obtained."[145]

---

137. Andrews v. U.S. Steel Corp., 250 P.3d 887, 890 (N.M. Ct. App. 2011) ("[T]o establish cause in a toxic tort case, the evidence must show both 'general causation' and 'specific causation.'" (citing Norris v. Baxter Healthcare Corp., 397 F.3d 878, 881 (10th Cir. 2005))).
138. *Id.* (quoting Allen v. Pa. Eng'g Corp., 102 F.3d 194, 199 (5th Cir. 1996)).
139. Parkhill v. Alderman-Cave Milling & Grain Co., 245 P.3d 585, 589 (N.M. Ct. App. 2010).
140. *Id.* at 589–90.
141. 509 U.S. 579, 592–95 (1993).
142. *Parkhill*, 245 P.3d at 592.
143. *Id.* at 589–90 (quotation and citation omitted). "Differential etiology" is "'a term used on occasion by expert witnesses or courts to describe the investigation and reasoning that leads to the determination of external causation.... Differential diagnosis refers to the clinical process by which doctors determine the internal disease that is causing the patient's suffering; differential etiology is used for determining the external causes of the problems.'" *Id.* (quotation omitted).
144. *Id.* at 589.
145. *Id.* at 593–94.

Oregon

Overall Standard for Causation

Oregon courts have discarded the notion of "proximate cause" and require proof of cause in fact only:

> Causation in Oregon law refers to causation in fact, that is to say, whether someone examining the event without regard to legal consequences would conclude that the allegedly faulty conduct or condition in fact played a role in its occurrence. "'Causation in fact' is unrelated to 'proximate' or 'legal' cause, concepts which have been discarded by this court."[146]

In *Joshi v. Providence Health System of Oregon*, the court of appeals described the test for cause in fact as "generally requir[ing] evidence of a reasonable probability that, but for the defendant's negligence, the plaintiff would not have been harmed."[147] The court went on to discuss the language of "substantial factor" causation, noting that "'substantial factor' generally does not eliminate the concept of 'but-for' causation. Rather, the substantial factor standard is an alternate description of the cause-in-fact test and requires a showing of 'but-for' causation in all but a few cases."[148] These "few cases" are those with concurrent independent causes, where either cause, "operating alone, probably would have brought about the harm . . . . In that situation, both forces are substantial factors in causing the harm, although neither was a necessary cause."[149] For example, in *McEwen v. Ortho Pharmaceutical Corp.*,[150] the Supreme Court of Oregon laid out the substantial factor test as follows:

> The respective liability of multiple defendants depends upon whether the negligence of each was a substantial factor in producing the complained of harm. If both [defendants] were negligent and their negligence combined to produce plaintiff's injuries, then the negligence of [one] was concurrent with that of [the other] and does not insulate [the other] from liability. This is true although the negligent omissions of each defendant occurred at different times and without concerted action. Nor is it essential to [a defendant's] liability that its negligence be sufficient to bring about plaintiff's harm by itself[;] it is enough that [the defendant] substantially contributed to the injuries eventually suffered by [the plaintiff].[151]

---

146. Sandford v. Chevrolet Div. of Gen. Motors, 642 P.2d 624, 633 (Or. 1982) (quoting McEwen v. Ortho Pharm. Corp., 528 P.2d 522, 528 n.7 (Or. 1974)).
147. 108 P.3d 1195, 1197 (Or. Ct. App. 2005).
148. *Id.* at 1198.
149. *Id.* at 1198–99 (internal citation omitted).
150. *McEwen*, 528 P.2d at 543.
151. *Id.* (citations omitted); *see also* Purcell v. Asbestos Corp., 959 P.2d 89, 93, 94 (Or. Ct. App. 1998) (quoting *id.*).

The overall standard of proof for causation in Oregon is a preponderance of the evidence.[152]

Standard of Proof and Expert Testimony

Oregon state toxic tort cases have established that expert testimony is required to prove causation. For example, in *Hudjohn v. S&G Machinery Co.*, the Court of Appeals of Oregon held that because the alleged injury was "a result of a single exposure to toxic fumes . . . the issue of causation . . . involved a complex medical question." Such questions, "as a matter of law," require the plaintiff to "present[] expert testimony that there is a reasonable medical probability that the alleged negligence caused plaintiff's injuries."[153]

In addition, decisions from the medical malpractice context in Oregon suggest that expert testimony based on differential diagnosis alone would be insufficient to establish causation in toxic tort cases. In *Marcum v. Adventist Health System/West*,[154] the Supreme Court of Oregon admitted differential diagnosis testimony, distinguishing the medical malpractice allegations in that case from the typical toxic tort case. Specifically, the court held that in a "typical toxic tort case, there may be 'a complicated causal chain, a long latency period, or low levels of exposure. . . .' In those circumstances, reliable testimony on causation may require 'extremely accurate data and methods,' peer-reviewed studies, and small and controlled error rates to 'rule in' a possible cause."[155]

Utah

Overall Standard for Causation

Under Utah law, the standard of proof generally is a preponderance of the evidence.[156] Utah allows for weak inferential evidence to establish "but for" causation as a prima facie matter, but this can be rebutted if the defendant offers evidence sufficient to negate the "but for" inference. As the Supreme Court of Utah explained in *Alder v. Bayer Corp.*:

> Individuals routinely feel the effects of a wide array of common phenomena whose mechanisms remain unexplained by science, including, for example, the law of gravity . . . . If

---

152. Griffin v. K.E. McKay's Mkt. of Coos Bay, Inc., 865 P.2d 1320, 1322 (Or. Ct. App. 1993) ("[A plaintiff] must introduce evidence which affords a reasonable basis for the conclusion that it is more likely than not that the conduct of the defendant was a substantial factor in the result. A mere possibility of such causation is not enough; and when the matter remains one of pure speculation or conjecture, or the probabilities are at best evenly balanced, it becomes the duty of the court to direct a verdict for the defendant." (citations omitted)); *see also* Harris v. Kissling, 721 P.2d 838, 841 (Or. Ct. App. 1985).
153. 114 P.3d 1141, 1148 (Or. Ct. App. 2005) (quoting Baughman v. Pina, 113 P.3d 459, 460 (Or. Ct. App. 2005)).
154. 193 P.3d 1, 6–7 (Or. 2008).
155. *Id.* (citations omitted); *see also* McClellan v. I-Flow Corp., 710 F. Supp. 2d 1092, 1098 (D. Or. 2010) (framing the issue in terms of "general" causation).
156. *See, e.g.*, Lindsay v. Gibbons & Reed, 497 P.2d 28, 31 (Utah 1972) (plaintiff must prove "that there is a greater probability that the conduct relied upon was the proximate cause of the injury than there is that it was not").

a bicyclist falls and breaks his arm, causation is assumed without argument because of the temporal relationship between the accident and the injury. The law does not object that no one measured the exact magnitude and angle of the forces applied to the bone. Courts do not exclude all testimony regarding the fall because the mechanism of gravity remains undiscovered. Legally, an observable sequence of condition[,] event[,] altered condition, has been found sufficient to establish causation even when the exact mechanism is unknown.[157]

Accordingly, Utah law allows certain plaintiffs to establish causation where the temporal relationship between cause and effect is manifest, and the proof of causation is otherwise clear. The precise standard of such proof in "clear" cases, and which factors are important, remain uncertain. However, once causation has been established in this manner, the defendant has an opportunity to prevail by proving the lack of causation under the "but for" test.[158]

General and Specific Causation

In *Alder*, the court held that to admit circumstantial evidence probative of causation (such as the amount of time between toxic exposure and injury), some scientific literature or expert medical testimony also must be offered to prove the same.[159] However, the *Alder* court also held that the expert medical testimony need not provide direct proof through medical studies, or quantify the level of exposure necessary to produce the alleged harm. The court stated that "if all chemicals are harmful and the poison is in the dose, then wherever chemicals are part of the environment, victims' toxic symptoms are themselves evidence of harmful levels, at least as an issue of triable fact."[160] A plaintiff can establish causation through the use of differential diagnosis if the type of exposure alleged is proven sufficient to have caused the type of injury at issue.[161] In addition, in *Gunn Hill Dairy Properties, LLC v. Los Angeles Department of Water & Power*, the Court of Appeals of Utah held that "epidemiological studies can provide 'powerful evidence of causation.'"[162]

Washington
Overall Standard for Causation
Washington defines proximate cause "as a cause which, in a direct sequence, unbroken by any new, independent cause, produces the injury complained of and without which

---

157. Alder v. Bayer Corp., 61 P.3d 1068, 1090 (Utah 2002).
158. *See* Scott v. HK Contractors, 196 P.3d 635, 640 (Utah Ct. App. 2008).
159. 61 P.3d at 1087, 1089.
160. *Id.* at 1088.
161. *Id.* at 1090.
162. 269 P.3d 980, 994 (Utah Ct. App. 2012) (citation omitted).

the injury would not have occurred."[163] This definition is embodied both in the case law and in the relevant pattern jury instruction on causation. Washington law further breaks down proximate cause into elements of "cause in fact" and "legal causation."[164] "Cause in fact" is an inquiry into "but for" causation, whereas "legal causation 'rests on policy considerations as to how far the consequences of a defendant's acts should extend.'"[165]

As for cause in fact, Washington courts have rejected attempts to substitute the lesser "substantial factor" causation standard for the more robust standard of "but for" causation.[166] There are three exceptions in which the substantial factor standard is appropriate: (1) where there are independent concurring causes, both of which "played so important a part in producing the result that responsibility should be imposed on it"; (2) where a similar, but not identical, result would have followed without the defendant's act; and, (3) where one defendant has made "a clearly proven but quite insignificant contribution to the result."[167] The courts have also applied the substantial factor test in toxic tort cases involving multiple suppliers of an allegedly toxic product—such cases are in the nature of the "independent concurring cause" exception.[168]

General and Specific Causation

Washington law requires proof of both general and specific causation in the toxic tort context. In assessing this proof, "[t]rial courts should consider a number of factors" before allowing the jury to make a finding of causation.[169] Factors probative of general causation include "the types of . . . products to which the plaintiff was exposed" and "the amounts and percentages" of toxic agents within those products.[170] "In addition, trial courts must consider the evidence presented as to medical causation of the plaintiff's particular disease," including "expert testimony on the effects of [the toxic exposure] on human health in general and on the plaintiff in particular."[171]

In addition to this expert medical testimony, Washington courts are directed to look to other factors probative of specific causation. These factors include "the ways in which [toxic] products were handled and used," as well as "any other substances that could have

---

163. Fabrique v. Choice Hotels Int'l, Inc., 183 P.3d 1118, 1121 (Wash. Ct. App. 2008) (citing Stoneman v. Wick Constr. Co., 349 P.2d 215, 218 (Wash. 1960)).
164. Id.
165. Id. (quoting Hartley v. State, 698 P.2d 77, 83 (Wash. 1985)).
166. Id. at 1122 (citing Blasick v. City of Yakima, 274 P.2d 122, 126 (Wash. 1954)).
167. Id. (quoting Daugert v. Pappas, 704 P.2d 600, 605–06 (Wash. 1985)).
168. See id. (citing Sharbono v. Universal Underwriters Ins. Co., 161 P.3d 406, 426 (Wash. Ct. App. 2007)); see also Hue v. Farmboy Spray Co., 896 P.2d 682, 684 (Wash. 1995); Mavroudis v. Pittsburgh Corning Corp., 935 P.2d 684, 689 (Wash. Ct. App. 1997).
169. Lockwood v. AC & S, Inc., 744 P.2d 605, 613 (Wash. 1987).
170. Id.
171. Id.

contributed to the plaintiff's disease."[172] In conducting this inquiry into other possible causes of the plaintiff's injury, expert testimony is necessary.[173]

Wyoming
Overall Standard for Causation
Under Wyoming law, proof of causation requires that "the injury producing event be the natural and probable consequence of the act of negligence."[174] The Supreme Court of Wyoming consistently has held that merely showing "but for" causation is not alone sufficient proof, and that the existence of proximate cause, defined as a "natural and continuous sequence, unbroken by any efficient intervening cause," is the key to the analysis of causation.[175]

Moreover, the "ultimate test" in assessing proximate cause "is foreseeability of injury. To qualify as a legal cause, the conduct must be a substantial factor in bringing about plaintiff's injuries."[176] Conduct that "created only a condition or occasion for the harm to occur" does not constitute proximate cause.[177] Proximate cause is generally a question of fact.[178]

General and Specific Causation
The Supreme Court of Wyoming has required "both general and specific causation" in a "general tort" claim.[179] In *Easum v. Miller*, the plaintiff sued a local electric company after his alleged exposure to ungrounded electrical current, which he claimed caused him neurological and other personal injuries.[180] The court explained that "product liability [and] toxic tort actions prosecuted in federal courts . . . require that proof of causation be produced for two components, general and specific."[181] The court held that, because the plaintiff's injury was allegedly caused by electricity, which under the court's precedents was "not a product," the "case [did] not involve toxic tort allegations."[182] Nevertheless, and even though the case rested on no more than "a general tort claim," the court stated that findings as to "both general and specific causation" were required.[183]

---

172. Id.
173. Id.
174. Downen v. Sinclair Oil Corp., 887 P.2d 515, 520 (Wyo. 1994); *see also* Lynch v. Norton Constr., 861 P.2d 1095, 1099 (Wyo. 1993).
175. Collings v. Lords, 218 P.3d 654, 656–57 (Wyo. 2009) (quotation and citation omitted); Black v. William Insulation Co., 141 P.3d 123, 128–29 (Wyo. 2006) (quotation and citation omitted); Lemos v. Madden, 200 P. 791, 794 (Wyo. 1921).
176. *Collings*, 218 P.3d at 656.
177. Id. at 657.
178. Id.
179. Easum v. Miller, 92 P.3d 794, 803 (Wyo. 2004).
180. Id. at 796.
181. Id. at 803.
182. Id.
183. Id.

CHAPTER 10

Midwestern States

Andrew Holly and Colin Wicker

This chapter discusses proof of toxic tort causation in the Midwestern states of Illinois, Indiana, Iowa, Kansas, Michigan, Minnesota, Missouri, Nebraska, North Dakota, Ohio, Oklahoma, and South Dakota.[1] These states vary greatly both in the amount of experience they have with toxic tort cases and in the degree of scientific rigor they require to prove causation. Standards for the admission of expert testimony also differ between states. North Dakota and South Dakota's appellate courts have had little to say regarding toxic torts, while more populous states such as Illinois and Ohio have substantial bodies of relevant case law. Nebraska stands out for having several relatively recent cases that establish criteria for the scientific evidence necessary to prove causation.

Illinois
Overall Standard for Causation
In Illinois, plaintiffs in toxic tort actions must present evidence of proximate causation, which includes both cause in fact and legal (or proximate) cause.[2] A plaintiff may show causation in fact by satisfying the substantial factor test. That is, the plaintiff can show that the defendant's conduct was a material element and substantial factor in bringing about the alleged injury.[3] Legal causation is determined by looking to the foreseeability

---

1. This survey chapter focuses on a narrow but extremely significant aspect of any toxic tort case seeking damages for personal injury—namely, the criteria for establishing the elements of general and specific causation in the particular jurisdictions covered. For a more generalized discussion regarding causation in personal injury and other types of toxic tort actions, as well as a broader discussion regarding the claims, defenses, and general strategies at play in these cases, please refer to earlier chapters in this book.
2. Donaldson v. Cent. Ill. Pub. Serv. Co., 767 N.E.2d 314, 331 (Ill. 2002), *abrogated on other grounds by In re* Commitment of Simons, 821 N.E.2d 1184 (Ill. 2004); Thacker v. UNR Indus., Inc., 603 N.E.2d 449, 455 (Ill. 1992).
3. *Thacker*, 603 N.E.2d at 455.

of the injury. Unlike other states, Illinois does not characterize causation in terms of general and specific causation.[4]

Illinois follows a version of the *Frye* test in determining whether to admit expert testimony.[5] Illinois courts look to whether the "methodology or scientific principle upon which the opinion is based is 'sufficiently established to have gained general acceptance in the particular field in which it belongs.'"[6] Two important limitations on the Illinois *Frye* test allow for expert testimony that might not be accepted under the tests applied in some other jurisdictions. First, the "general acceptance" test applies to methodology, not conclusions. In *Donaldson v. Central Illinois Public Service Co.*, the Illinois Supreme Court explained that "[i]f the underlying method used to generate an expert's opinion are reasonably relied upon by experts in the field, the fact finder may consider the opinion—despite the novelty of the conclusion rendered by the expert."[7] Questions regarding the reliability of the data used and the application of the generally accepted methodology go to weight, not admissibility. So, an expert testifying that his or her conclusions are based on a methodology commonly used in the field may well be allowed to testify even if the conclusions reached by the expert are not supported by the medical literature. Even the issues regarding the specific application of the methodology used by the expert may be left for cross-examination and testimony from a rebuttal expert. Second, "general acceptance" does not mean universal acceptance. A methodology can be acceptable under the Illinois *Frye* test even if it is not accepted by a majority of experts in the field.[8]

In *Donaldson*, the plaintiffs' experts did not have specific studies showing a causal relationship. Instead, they relied on studies showing similar, though not identical, cause-and-effect relationships and extrapolated based on those studies. The Illinois Supreme Court concluded that such an approach is admissible, at least in instances in which there is not a well-developed scientific literature on the specific causal relationship, and that the objections go to the weight of the evidence. In considering this aspect of Illinois law, it is important to remember that Illinois courts are not expected to serve a gatekeeper function. Further, the Illinois Supreme Court has expressed an interest in allowing legal remedies even in those instances in which there is not a well-developed scientific understanding, stating in *Donaldson* that "extrapolation offers those with rare diseases the opportunity to seek a remedy for the wrong they have suffered."[9] Illinois law regarding the admissibility

---

4. *Donaldson*, 767 N.E.2d at 331 (quoting Lee v. Chicago Transit Auth., 605 N.E.2d 493, 503 (Ill. 1992)).
5. Frye v. United States, 293 F. 1013, 1014 (D.C. Cir. 1923), used to be the leading federal case on the admissibility of expert testimony. The *Frye* standard was adopted by many state courts and still remains the law in many of those states. *Daubert v. Merrell Dow Pharm.*, Inc., 509 U.S. 579 (1993) overruled *Frye* at the federal level and has been adopted in several states. For a further discussion of the two cases and the admissibility of expert testimony, please see chapter 5.
6. *Donaldson*, 767 N.E.2d at 323–24 (quoting *Frye*, 293 F. at 1014).
7. *Id.* at 324.
8. *Id.* at 326, 324.
9. *Id.* at 328.

of expert testimony and the evidence sufficient to prove causation is perhaps best understood in light of that stated concern with providing a remedy for the injured.

General and Specific Causation

As stated above, Illinois does not analyze causation in terms of general and specific causation.[10] Instead, causation in toxic tort cases is analyzed in terms of cause in fact and legal cause. Under these standards, a plaintiff does have the burden to prove that the substance in question was a substantial factor in bringing about the injury in question. However, the evidence required to make such a showing can be circumstantial and the standards for the admissibility of expert testimony regarding causation are low. Even evidence that the substance in question is capable of causing the injury in question can also be quite imprecise. In the *Donaldson* matter, there were no studies indicating that the coal tar at issue could cause neuroblastoma (a peripheral nervous system cancer), but the plaintiffs' experts were allowed to testify regarding their extrapolation from studies documenting other causal relationships that they believed were similar.[11]

A plaintiff can satisfy the burden of proof on cause in fact using circumstantial evidence from which a jury may infer other connected facts that usually and reasonably follow according to common experience. In other words, Illinois law does not require unequivocal or unqualified evidence of causation—especially when there exists limited medical knowledge of the injury at issue.[12] To that end, a risk assessment that identifies—among other factors—the temporal relationship between the injury and exposure, the statistical strength of the association, the dose-response relationship, and the alternative causes of the injury can provide valuable evidence of causation. In addition, even though animal studies rarely offer direct evidence that an injury to any one individual was caused by exposure to a toxic substance, they are accepted in Illinois in order to rule out other risk factors known to cause the injury.[13]

A plaintiff is required to establish that he or she came into contact with the allegedly toxic substance. In the asbestos context, Illinois follows the "frequency, regularity and proximity" test.[14] The "frequency, regularity and proximity" test requires more than a mere showing that the plaintiff and an asbestos product were present at the same time. Instead, the test requires a showing that there was "exposure to a specific product on a regular basis over some extended period of time in proximity to where the plaintiff actually worked."[15] In other toxic tort cases, however, plaintiffs are not required to show the

---

10. *Donaldson*, 767 N.E.2d at 331.
11. *Id.* at 328.
12. *Id.* at 331–32 (citing Thacker v. UNR Indus., Inc., 603 N.E.2d 449, 456 (Ill. 1992), and Nat'l Castings Div. of Midland-Ross Corp. v. Indus. Comm'n, 302 N.E.2d 330, 333 (Ill. 1973)).
13. *See id.* at 333–35.
14. *Thacker*, 603 N.E.2d at 457.
15. Lohrmann v. Pittsburgh Corning Corp., 782 F.2d 1156, 1162–63 (4th Cir. 1986); *accord Thacker*, 603

exact amount of exposure to the toxic substance because the Illinois Supreme Court has held that such exact information regarding when or where the exposure occurred is usually unavailable.[16] Evidence of community exposure to a toxic substance may be enough to satisfy the exposure requirement in environmental exposure cases under Illinois law.[17]

Indiana
Overall Standard for Causation
Indiana has relatively limited law on the subject of causation of toxic torts. The state follows the general rule that plaintiffs must establish both general and specific causation to prevail on a toxic tort cause of action.[18] In toxic tort litigation, Indiana generally requires that causation be established by expert testimony.[19]

General and Specific Causation
Consistent with the rule in other circuits, Indiana courts have made clear that expert testimony regarding general causation must be well grounded in scientific fact, and must offer more than "only the experts' qualifications, their conclusions and their assurances of reliability."[20] Where an expert's assertions of "general causation" do not meet this standard, they will not be credited.

The *Hannan v. Pest Control Services, Inc.* case offers the most clarification regarding the specific causation standard in Indiana. In that case, the plaintiffs allegedly suffered from pesticide poisoning after their residence had been sprayed with pesticides.[21] When considering the link between the plaintiffs' injuries and the pesticide, the *Hannan* court stated that a plaintiff must rule out alternative causes—including preexisting conditions—when establishing specific causation in Indiana.[22] Further, a plaintiff must present credible evidence of exposure to the toxic substance at issue.[23] A failure to produce quantitative measurements of exposure level or dose through modeling studies when such studies are possible may prove fatal to a plaintiff's causation argument. Depending on the context, a physical examination, full blood work-up, and a pulmonary function test likely strengthen

---

N.E.2d at 458–59 (noting that even lay evidence of fiber drift is relevant to the proximate cause prong of the "frequency, regularity and proximity" test).
16. *Donaldson*, 767 N.E.2d at 332; La Salle Nat'l Bank v. Malik, 705 N.E.2d 938, 944 (Ill. 1999).
17. See *Donaldson*, 767 N.E.2d at 332–33.
18. See 7-Eleven, Inc. v. Bowens, 857 N.E.2d 382, 389 (Ind. Ct. App. 2006).
19. See Hannan v. Pest Control Servs., Inc., 734 N.E.2d 674, 679 (Ind. Ct. App. 2000) ("[Q]uestions of medical causation of a particular injury are questions of science necessarily dependent on the testimony of physicians and surgeons learned in such matters." (citing Brown v. Terre Haute Reg'l Hosp., 537 N.E.2d 54, 61 (Ind. Ct. App. 1989))).
20. Aurand v. Norfolk S. Ry., 802 F. Supp. 2d 950, 959 (N.D. Ind. 2011).
21. See *Hannan*, 734 N.E.2d at 676–77.
22. See id. at 682 ("'[D]ifferential diagnosis' testing is important in toxic tort cases so that other causes may be negated.").
23. See id. at 682–83 (criticizing the plaintiffs' experts for their failure to analyze the exposure levels or the dose of the pesticides received by the plaintiffs).

a specific causation conclusion. Finally, a mere temporal relationship between an injury and an alleged exposure to a toxic substance will not sustain a specific causation claim.[24]

It is worth noting that in Indiana, in order to recover damages for emotional distress from an alleged exposure to a toxic substance, a plaintiff must prove with "some certainty" that he or she was actually exposed to the toxic substance.[25] In *Adams v. Clean Air Systems, Inc.*, the court determined that the plaintiff was not entitled to recover damages for emotional distress unless he could prove that he actually inhaled asbestos.

Iowa
Overall Standard for Causation

In 2010, the Supreme Court of Iowa in *Ranes v. Adams Laboratories, Inc.* recognized that many courts bifurcate the toxic tort causation analysis into general causation and specific causation.[26] Prior to *Ranes*, this bifurcated analysis had not been explicitly used as the standard in Iowa. However, due to the widespread acceptance of the general causation and specific causation standard among scholars and courts in other jurisdictions, the *Ranes* court determined that the bifurcated standard was the appropriate standard for Iowa courts. Therefore, in Iowa, both general causation and specific causation must be proven in toxic tort cases, and "expert medical and toxicological testimony is unquestionably required to assist the jury."[27]

Iowa does not require a plaintiff to demonstrate either element of causation with absolute certainty. Rather, a plaintiff need only prove that the toxic substance at issue *probably caused* the injury claimed.[28]

General Causation

In order to prove general causation in Iowa, a qualified expert must establish that the toxic substance at issue is capable of causing the alleged injury. To do so, an expert may rely—at least in part—on medical and scientific literature that supports the conclusion that a toxic substance is capable of causing the relevant injury.[29] And although clinical trials (in which participants are divided into two groups and one group is exposed to the substance under study while the other group, the control group, is left unexposed) are the "gold standard" for determining the relationship between a substance and a health outcome, Iowa does not require them.[30]

---

24. *See id.* at 682.
25. Adams v. Clean Air Sys., Inc., 586 N.E.2d 940, 942 (Ind. Ct. App. 1992).
26. 778 N.W.2d 677, 687–88 (Iowa 2010).
27. *Id.*; *see* Junk v. Terminix Int'l Co., 628 F.3d 439, 450 (8th Cir. 2010) (applying Iowa toxic tort law).
28. *See Ranes*, 778 N.W.2d at 688; *see also* Johnson v. Knoxville Cmty. Sch. Dist., 570 N.W.2d 633, 637 (Iowa 1997) (noting that there is no requirement that an expert be able to express an opinion regarding causation with absolute certainty).
29. *See Ranes*, 778 N.W.2d at 691.
30. *Id.* at 692.

As an alternative to clinical trials, Iowa allows an expert to consider case-control studies in formulating an opinion about general causation. According to the *Ranes* court, case-control studies measure and compare the frequency of exposure in the group with the disease and the group without the disease.[31] Case-control studies must be directly relevant to the injuries alleged in the toxic tort claim in order for an expert to use them to form a conclusion regarding general causation.

Finally, in limited circumstances, case reports may also be used to prove general causation.[32] "Case reports are reports in medical journals describing clinical events involving one individual or a few individuals."[33] Because case reports often lack control groups, they are less useful for evaluating causation compared to controlled epidemiological studies. And while Iowa does not require that a medical expert cite published epidemiological studies on general causation before making a conclusion, "the methodology used by the expert becomes suspect when it is only supported by case reports."[34] Only if reasonable medical experts would rely upon the anecdotal information from a case report may such a case report be used to prove general causation.[35]

Specific Causation

In order to prove specific causation in Iowa, a qualified expert must apply a scientifically valid methodology to the facts of the case that indicates that the toxic substance at issue caused the plaintiff's specific injuries.[36] A differential diagnosis is one such scientific method found to be valid for proving specific causation.[37] A differential diagnosis involves "ruling in" specific causes, followed by a process of elimination through which other potential causes are "ruled out," resulting in a final suspected cause.[38] Of course, this final suspected cause must be capable of causing the alleged injury. Although the process of differential diagnosis is not an exact science, Iowa does require experts testifying about specific causation to combine their knowledge of the probability of injury from a toxic substance with their understanding of the signs and symptoms of a given injury to progressively modify and ultimately arrive at their view of the likelihood of the injury under consideration.[39]

For toxic tort claims that involve asbestos, Iowa follows a version of the "frequency, regularity and proximity" test for specific causation.[40] However, in Iowa, the "frequency,

---

31. *See id.*
32. *See id.* at 692–93.
33. *Id.* at 693.
34. *Id.*; *see* Kosmacek v. Farm Serv. Co-op of Persia, 485 N.W.2d 99, 104 (Iowa Ct. App. 1992).
35. *See Ranes*, 778 N.W.2d at 694.
36. *See Ranes*, 778 N.W.2d at 689.
37. *See id.* at 695.
38. *See* Cavallo v. Star Enter., 892 F. Supp. 756, 771 (E.D. Va. 1995), *aff'd in relevant part*, 100 F.3d 1150, 1159 (4th Cir. 1996).
39. *See Ranes*, 778 N.W.2d at 695–96.
40. *See* Spaur v. Owens-Corning Fiberglas Corp., 510 N.W.2d 854, 859 (Iowa 1994).

regularity and proximity" test is only used to analyze whether a plaintiff's evidence sufficiently demonstrates that the defendant's product, combined with the plaintiff's exposure to that product, was a substantial factor in bringing about the plaintiff's injury. Importantly, it is not necessary to establish exactly how much the defendant's asbestos product contributed to the resulting injury so long as the defendant's product was a substantial contributing cause to the plaintiff's injury.[41]

Kansas
Overall Standard for Causation

Under Kansas law, plaintiffs have the burden of proving that their injuries arose as a direct and proximate cause of the defendant's conduct. To do so, they must present evidence that affords a reasonable basis on which to conclude that the injuries in question were caused by the defendant.[42] In Kansas, there is no general requirement that plaintiffs in toxic tort cases satisfy a two-step general and specific causation test.[43]

The general rule in Kansas is that expert testimony is required with respect to questions ordinary persons are not equipped by common knowledge and skill to judge.[44] Accordingly, expert testimony should be required in most or all toxic tort cases. The basic standard for admission of expert testimony is provided in Section 6/1–/256(b) of the Kansas Statutes, which states:

> If the witness is testifying as an expert, testimony of the witness in the form of opinions or inferences is limited to such opinions as the judge finds are (1) based on facts or data perceived by or personally known or made known to the witness at the hearing and (2) within the scope of the special knowledge, skill, experience or training possessed by the witness.[45]

In addition to that basic standard, Kansas courts have added the *Frye* standard as a "qualification."[46] The *Frye* standard is to be applied by Kansas courts when they are faced with new or experimental scientific techniques. If a new technique is not generally accepted, testimony based on that technique is not admissible. The Kansas *Frye* standard is focused on techniques and methodologies, not conclusions. Consequently, a "lack of popularity" with regard to an expert's conclusion is not a barrier to the admissibility of the expert's

---

41. *See id.* at 859–61.
42. Kuxhausen v. Tillman Partners L.P., 241 P.3d 75, 81 (Kan. 2010).
43. Kuhn v. Sandoz Pharm. Corp., 14 P.3d 1170, 1184–85 (Kan. 2000).
44. Bowman v. Doherty, 686 P.2d 112, 120 (Kan. 1984); McConwell v. FMG of Kan. City, Inc., 861 P.2d 830, 838 (Kan. Ct. App. 1993) (citing *Bowman*, 686 P.2d at 120); Knowles v. Burlington N. R.R., 856 P.2d 1352, 1355 (Kan. Ct. App. 1993).
45. Kan. Stat. Ann. § 60-456(b) (West, Westlaw through 2012 legislation).
46. *Kuhn*, 14 P.3d at 1178.

testimony.[47] For example, in *Douglas v. Lombardino*, defense experts in a medical malpractice case were allowed to testify that a particular medicine was "cardiotoxic" even though the theory was not generally accepted in the field.[48] The experts appear to have based their opinions on animal studies and anecdotal evidence.[49]

Another important qualification on the Kansas *Frye* standard is that it is not applied to so-called pure opinion. That is, an expert's inductions based on the expert's own experience, observation, and research are not subject to *Frye*.[50] Such opinions are to be tested with cross-examination; instead, *Frye* is used to keep out seemingly definitive tests and conclusions. In *Kuhn v. Sandoz Pharmaceuticals Corp.*, the Kansas Supreme Court determined that differential diagnoses conducted by three expert physicians were not, therefore, subject to the *Frye* test.[51]

Kuhn should not, however, be taken as an indication that all medical testimony couched as opinion based on personal observation will be admitted in Kansas. In *Kuxhausen v. Tillman Partners L.P.*, the plaintiff attempted to offer testimony of a doctor in support of her claim that exposure to paint fumes had caused multiple chemical sensitivity.[52] The doctor spent an hour with her and reviewed reports from other physicians and the material safety data sheet for the paint in question. However, the doctor did not obtain any information regarding the plaintiff's actual exposure to paint fumes and whether the paint fumes were capable of causing her symptoms. The Kansas Supreme Court upheld the trial court's decision to exclude the testimony. The court cited Section 60–456(b) of the Kansas Statutes and concluded that the testimony in question was insufficiently based in fact and was not, therefore, admissible.[53]

General and Specific Causation

In *Kuhn*, the defendant claimed that the plaintiff should have to separately prove both general and specific causation. The court declined to impose this requirement, stating, "The cases on which [the defendant] relies to establish the need for both general and specific causation are distinguishable based upon the different legal standards employed in their respective jurisdictions."[54] The court held that independent proof of general causation is not necessarily required in product liability matters.

Nonetheless, the Kansas Supreme Court did hold open the possibility that in a future case with "appropriate facts" toxic tort plaintiffs might be required to separately prove

---

47. *Id.* at 1183.
48. 693 P.2d 1138, 1149–50 (Kan. 1985).
49. *See id.* at 1143–44.
50. *Kuhn*, 14 P.3d at 1179.
51. *Id.* at 1179–82.
52. Kuxhausen v. Tillman Partners L.P., 241 P.3d 75, 79 (Kan. 2010).
53. *See id.* at 79–81.
54. Kuhn v. Sandoz Pharm. Corp., 14 P.3d 1170, 1184 (Kan. 2000).

general and specific causation. The court provided some guidance as to when proof of general causation might be required in Kansas by describing the factors that would make a general causation requirement more appropriate. First, the court noted that a general causation requirement is typically applied in cases involving mass exposure to a substance. The court was concerned that requiring rigorous proof of general causation would unduly prejudice individual plaintiffs or small groups of plaintiffs who have been exposed to a substance that has not been the subject of extensive study. Second, the court claimed that a general causation requirement is typically imposed in instances in which there is a well-developed body of epidemiological research.[55]

It appears, therefore, that a plaintiff in Kansas who was not the subject of a mass exposure, and whose claimed exposure has not been the subject of extensive study, can provide sufficient evidence of causation using a differential diagnosis, perhaps supplemented with toxicological evidence.[56] However, plaintiffs in mass exposure cases or those involving extensively studied substances could be required to prove general causation, presumably using epidemiological evidence.

As for specific causation, Kansas plaintiffs are required to prove that exposure to toxic substance was the substantial cause of their injuries.[57] Simply showing that symptoms appeared following exposure is not sufficient.[58] Differential diagnoses are accepted.[59] However, it appears that Kansas does not require that all possible alternative causes be ruled out.[60]

Michigan
Overall Standard for Causation
As in most states, in Michigan a plaintiff must demonstrate both "but for" and "proximate" causation to establish causation.[61] Michigan courts have not explicitly adopted the requirement that plaintiffs prove both general and specific causation, but, nonetheless, do seem to expect at least some evidence of both general and specific causation.[62]

---

55. *Id.* at 1184–85.
56. *Id.*
57. *See* Lyons v. Garlock, Inc., 12 F. Supp. 2d 1226, 1228–29 (D. Kan. 1998).
58. *See* Kuxhausen v. Tillman Partners L.P., 241 P.3d 75, 81 (Kan. 2010).
59. *See Kuhn*, 14 P.3d at 1177, 1184–85.
60. *See id.* at 1183–84.
61. Genna v. Jackson, 781 N.W.2d 124, 128 (Mich. Ct. App. 2009).
62. *See id.* at 1128–1130 (declining to adopt requirement that both specific and general causation be shown, but later noting that there was expert testimony establishing that mold could cause the types of symptoms suffered by plaintiffs and facts from which it could be inferred that the mold had caused the medical problems at issue); *see also* Gass v. Marriott Hotel Servs., Inc., 501 F. Supp. 2d 1011, 1023–24 (W.D. Mich. 2007) (requiring proof of specific and general causation), *rev'd on other grounds*, 558 F.3d 419 (6th Cir. 2009).

Under Michigan law, while a toxic tort plaintiff will usually rely upon expert testimony to establish these elements of causation, that is not required.[63] For example, in *Gass v. Marriott Hotel Services, Inc.*, two plaintiffs alleged they suffered chemical poisoning and ongoing ill effects after the defendants applied pesticides to the plaintiffs' hotel room.[64] Although the plaintiffs offered no expert testimony demonstrating that these pesticides actually caused their injuries, the Sixth Circuit ruled (overturning the district court) that the plaintiffs' (and treating physician's) testimony regarding their symptoms was sufficient.[65] This testimony established a triable issue of fact that the plaintiffs got sick following the application of the pesticides, with symptoms similar to those caused by exposure to one of those pesticides as described in its material safety data sheet. Under those circumstances, no exert testimony was necessary.[66]

Similarly, in *Genna v. Jackson*, the Michigan Court of Appeals also affirmed that expert testimony is not always needed to prove causation in toxic tort cases.[67] In *Genna* a condo flooded, causing a variety of toxic molds to flourish. Over several months, children in a neighboring condo became acutely ill and required several trips to the emergency room. The court found that where toxic mold was readily apparent and the injured children's symptoms improved when they left the mold-filled condo, the jury did not need an expert to "facilitate reasonable inferences" and avoid wild speculation regarding specific causation.[68] (Expert testimony did establish general causation in that case.)

While cases such as *Gass* and *Genna* make clear that expert testimony is not always necessary to demonstrate causation, in most toxic tort cases, where the inquiry into causation is more technical, an expert's testimony will most likely be necessary to show causation.[69]

When expert testimony is introduced, it must satisfy the *Daubert* standard. Until 2004, Michigan used the *Frye* test for evaluating expert testimony. In 2004, however, Michigan amended its rules of evidence to more closely track the federal rules.[70] These changes made *Daubert* and its progeny the appropriate standard for evaluating expert testimony.[71]

---

63. *See Gass*, 501 F. Supp. 2d at 1023; *Genna*, 781 N.W.2d at 128–30. *But see* Kalamazoo River Study Grp. v. Rockwell Int'l Corp., 171 F.3d 1065, 1069–73 (6th Cir. 1999) (arguing that where causation requires a complex and technical scientific inquiry about the ability of chemicals to seep into the ground and eventually reach a river, expert testimony is required to furnish appropriate proofs).
64. *See Gass*, 501 F. Supp. 2d at 1013–15.
65. *See* Gass v. Marriott Hotel Servs., Inc., 558 F.3d 419, 429 (6th Cir. 2009).
66. *Id.* at 430–32 (citation omitted) (quoting Lince v. Monson, 108 N.W.2d 845, 848 (Mich. 1961)).
67. *See Genna*, 781 N.W.2d at 128–30.
68. *See id.* at 130 (quoting Skinner v. Square D. Co., 516 N.W.2d 475, 480 (Mich. 1994)) (internal quotation marks omitted).
69. *See* Kalamazoo River Study Grp. v. Rockwell Int'l Corp., 171 F.3d 1065, 1069–73 (6th Cir. 1999) (arguing that where causation requires a complex and technical scientific inquiry about the ability of chemicals to seep into the ground and eventually reach a river, expert testimony is required to furnish appropriate proofs).
70. *See* Cynthia Lynne Pike, *The Impact of Revised MRE 702 and 703 in Response to Daubert*, 52 WAYNE L. REV. 285, 285–87 (2006).
71. Gilbert v. DaimlerChrysler Corp., 685 N.W.2d 391, 408–09 (Mich. 2004).

Accordingly, an expert's opinion testimony must be based on sufficient facts or data, must be the product of reliable principles and methods, and the witness must have applied the principles and methods reliably to the facts of the case.[72]

General Causation

In order to prove causation, plaintiffs must first prove general causation—that the substance they were exposed to is capable of producing the kind of injury they allege. Most often, plaintiffs use expert testimony to meet this element of causation.[73] For example, in *Genna*, where two children were made gravely ill by toxic mold growing in a neighbor's condo, both the plaintiffs' and the defendant's experts confirmed that mold can be toxic to humans and cause deleterious health effects.[74] This consensus established general causation. Similarly, in *Brisboy v. Fibreboard Corp.*, where an asbestos worker at an insulation plant sued the manufacturer of certain insulation after acquiring lung cancer, the plaintiff furnished an epidemiologist who testified that adenocarcinoma is generally associated with asbestos.[75]

In *Stites v. Sundstrand Heat Transfer, Inc.*, more elaborate evidence was offered. In *Stites*, workers at a manufacturing plant were exposed to a variety of chemicals including a degreasing agent, trichloroethylene (TCE).[76] The plaintiffs argued the exposure had caused damage to their health and created a fear of cancer. (Enhanced risk of future cancer is a compensable injury under Michigan law where injury is "reasonably certain.")[77] To support general causation, the plaintiffs offered several pieces of expert testimony (including epidemiological studies and animal studies) to suggest that TCE is a carcinogen.[78]

Physician testimony is not the only way, however, to prove general causation. In some cases, plaintiffs use documentation.[79] For example, in *Gass*, the plaintiffs were exposed to a cloud of unknown pesticides in their hotel room by exterminators.[80] The plaintiffs introduced the material safety data sheets required by federal regulation for at least two of the three chemicals used by the defendants; these sheets identified various health risks the chemicals posed and accompanying symptoms (including the symptoms that the plain-

---

72. *Id.* at 408 (quoting Rule 702 of the Michigan Rules of Evidence).
73. *See* Stites v. Sundstrand Heat Transfer, Inc., 660 F. Supp. 1516, 1518–22 (W.D. Mich. 1987); Brisboy v. Fibreboard Corp., 418 N.W.2d 650, 652–54 (Mich. 1988); Genna v. Jackson, 781 N.W.2d 124, 130 (Mich. Ct. App. 2009).
74. *See Genna*, 781 N.W.2d at 130.
75. *Brisboy*, 418 N.W.2d at 652.
76. *Stites*, 660 F. Supp. at 1517.
77. *See id.* at 1519.
78. *See id.* at 1524–26 (listing the proofs offered and concluding they were insufficient as to proximate cause).
79. *See, e.g.*, Gass v. Marriott Hotel Servs., Inc., 558 F.3d 419, 430–33 (6th Cir. 2009); *see also* Newson v. Monsanto Co., 869 F. Supp. 1255, 1257 (E.D. Mich. 1994) (using the defendants' material safety data sheets to establish the risks and necessary precautions for using polyvinyl butyryl).
80. *See Gass*, 558 F.3d at 422–23.

tiffs ultimately suffered). The court held this evidence was sufficient to create a triable issue as to general causation.[81]

The existence of a regulatory standard is not sufficient to establish general causation.[82] In *Stites*, the fact that regulatory standards limited the concentration of TCE to 1 ppm did not automatically establish the chemical posed a health risk at higher concentrations. The *Stites* court distinguished between the prophylactic goals of regulation and a plaintiff's obligation to prove causation: "While this risk may be unacceptable in a regulatory setting, it does not demonstrate a reasonable certainty that the affected plaintiff will get cancer."[83]

Epidemiological studies are not necessary to prove general causation, as long as an expert's underlying rationale is sound.[84] However, an expert must have a reasonable basis to conclude a substance can cause the type of injuries a plaintiff alleges before the expert can give an opinion as to specific causation.[85] General causation is a necessary building block for specific causation.

Specific Causation

After establishing general causation, a plaintiff must prove that the particular toxic exposure actually caused his or her symptoms. This is known as "specific" causation.

In order to prevail in a toxic tort claim, a plaintiff must prove that the defendant exposed him or her to a toxic substance.[86] In *Kalamazoo River Study Group v. Rockwell International Corp.*, the court granted summary judgment for the defendant because the plaintiff's expert failed to show that the defendant was responsible for creating the polychlorinated biphenyl exposure.[87] Similarly, in *Roberts v. Owens-Corning Fiberglass Corp.*, the district court observed that Michigan offers no presumption of liability where a toxic chemical is found in a workplace; a plaintiff must prove that he or she was exposed to the defendant's product and it caused harm.[88]

Where there are multiple possible causes, a plaintiff doesn't need to show that the exposure was the sole or predominant cause of his or her condition, only that the exposure was a proximate cause of the plaintiff's injury.[89] However, where there are multiple factors, the exposure "will not be considered a proximate cause of the harm unless it

---

81. *See id.* at 430–31.
82. *See Stites*, 660 F. Supp. at 1521, 1525.
83. *Id.* at 1525.
84. *See* Gass v. Marriott Hotel Servs., Inc., 501 F. Supp. 2d 1011, 1019 (W.D. Mich. 2007) (citing Benedi v. McNeil-P.P.C., Inc., 66 F.2d 1378, 1384 (4th Cir. 1995)), *rev'd on other grounds*, 558 F.3d 419 (6th Cir. 2009).
85. *See Gass*, 501 F. Supp. 2d at 1019–21.
86. *See* Kalamazoo River Study Grp. v. Rockwell Int'l Corp., 171 F.3d 1065, 1068–73 (6th Cir. 1999); Roberts v. Owens-Corning Fiberglas Corp., 726 F. Supp. 172, 174 (W.D. Mich. 1989).
87. *See Kalamazoo River Study Grp.*, 171 F.3d at 1068–73.
88. *See Roberts*, 726 F. Supp. at 174.
89. *See* Brisboy v. Fibreboard Corp., 418 N.W.2d 650, 653 (Mich. 1988).

was a substantial factor in producing the injury."[90] For example, in *Brisboy*, an asbestos manufacturer could be held liable for the decedent's lung cancer even though the decedent's smoking habit could have been a contributing factor. The doctor who performed the decedent's autopsy testified that he had found "a massive amount of asbestos material" in the lungs of the deceased; while cigarette smoking could have caused the lung cancer, the doctor testified there was stronger evidence it was asbestos.[91]

In Michigan, plaintiffs do not need to prove the exact dosage or precise chemical composition of the toxins they received.[92] For example, in *Gass*, the federal district court noted that Michigan "case law does not always require evidence of the precise level of a toxic substance"; however, the court concluded that "'[s]cientific knowledge of the harmful level of exposure to a chemical, plus knowledge that the plaintiffs were exposed to such quantities, are minimal facts necessary to sustain the plaintiffs' burden in a toxic tort case.'"[93] The district court found that because the plaintiffs could not connect their ailments to a particular pesticide they could not show proximate cause. On appeal, the Sixth Circuit disagreed, saying that a reasonable jury could deduce from the cloud of chemicals and the "thick, horrid, acrid putrid odor" that there had been a significant exposure to a harmful chemical that caused the plaintiffs' injuries.[94] Similarly in *Genna*, while the pediatricians were unable to quantify the children's exposure to toxic mold, environmental testing in the condominiums showing high levels of airborne mold toxins helped substantiate specific causation.[95]

Differential diagnosis is a valid way to demonstrate specific causation.[96] Differential diagnosis is a method of determining the cause of a patient's symptoms; "[t]he physician considers all relevant potential causes of the symptoms and then eliminates alternative causes based on a physical examination, clinical tests, and a thorough case history."[97] Mere temporal links are insufficient to prove causation; alternate causes must be ruled out.[98]

For example, in *Genna*, two children displayed a variety of symptoms including nosebleeds, diarrhea, and respiratory distress over a period of months.[99] Doctors ruled out prior health problems, viruses, and bacterial infections. When the children's symptoms

---

90. *Id.*
91. *Id.* at 652–53.
92. *See* Gass v. Marriott Hotel Servs., Inc., 558 F.3d 419, 431 (6th Cir. 2009); Gass v. Marriott Hotel Servs., Inc., 501 F. Supp. 2d 1011, 1024 (W.D. Mich. 2007), *rev'd on other grounds*, 558 F.3d 419 (6th Cir. 2009); Genna v. Jackson, 781 N.W.2d 124, 129–30 (Mich. Ct. App. 2009).
93. *Gass*, 501 F. Supp. 2d at 1024 (quoting Curtis v. M&S Petroleum, Inc., 174 F.3d 661, 670 (5th Cir. 1999)).
94. *Gass*, 558 F.3d at 429, 433 (internal quotation marks omitted).
95. *See Genna*, 781 N.W.2d at 129–30.
96. *See Gass*, 501 F. Supp. 2d at 1020; *Genna*, 781 N.W.2d at 129–30.
97. *Gass*, 501 F. Supp. 2d at 1021 (quoting Hardyman v. Norfolk & W. Ry., 243 F.3d 255, 260 (6th Cir. 2001)).
98. *See id.* at 1019–20.
99. *See Genna*, 781 N.W.2d at 127.

subsided after moving out of the mold-infested condominium, the cause of their ailments was apparent because the other sources of illness had been eliminated. This, the court ruled, was sufficient to establish a triable issue regarding specific causation.[100]

Minnesota
Overall Standard for Causation

In Minnesota, toxic torts plaintiffs must produce evidence to show that the defendant's product was a substantial factor in the plaintiff's injury.[101] In *Souder v. Owens-Corning Fiberglas Corp.*, the Eighth Circuit noted that the Minnesota Court of Appeals had rejected the *Summers v. Tice* alternative liability doctrine[102] and instead used the substantial factor test.[103] The court found the *Souder* plaintiff failed to establish causation when the evidence did not show that the decedent was exposed to asbestos made by the defendants rather than by a different manufacturer.[104]

General Causation

Minnesota toxic torts plaintiffs must establish general causation, but they do not need to rely on epidemiological studies.[105] Where a plaintiff's experts rely on animal studies and peer-reviewed studies, "[t]he issue of whether the toxic substances ingested by plaintiffs are capable of harming humans is a disputed factual issue which will be resolved by the trier of fact."[106]

Specific Causation

The Minnesota Supreme Court has acknowledged the challenges in setting a standard for establishing causation in toxic torts cases, but has not decided what methodology the court will require. In *Goeb v. Theraldson*, the plaintiffs argued it would be "an impossible burden of proof in toxic tort actions" to require plaintiffs to show dose and dose-response data, since in most toxic torts cases the plaintiffs have no way of measuring exposure.[107] The plaintiffs suggested instead that considerations such as temporal proximity, differential diagnoses, and studies of the relationship between exposure and symptoms should be

---

100. *See id.* at 129–30.
101. Souder v. Owens-Corning Fiberglas Corp., 939 F.2d 647, 650 (8th Cir. 1991).
102. Under this doctrine, first established in *Summers v. Tice*, 199 P.2d 1 (Cal. 1948), if there is more than one defendant who is culpable and it is difficult to determine which particular defendant actually harmed the plaintiff, the burden of proof shifts so that defendants have the burden of proving that they are not liable.
103. *See Souder*, 939 F.2d at 650.
104. *Id.* at 651.
105. Werlein v. United States, 746 F. Supp. 887, 900 (D. Minn. 1990), *vacated in part on other grounds*, 793 F. Supp. 898 (D. Minn. 1992).
106. *See id.* at 900–01.
107. *See* Goeb v. Tharaldson, 615 N.W.2d 800, 815 (Minn. 2000). *Goeb* involved a family that suffered a range of symptoms after use of an insecticide to control an ant infestation in their rental home.

sufficient for establishing causation. One of the defendants pointed to the principle that "the dose makes the poison," and that even water, in large quantities, can be toxic. While noting that the Fifth, Eighth, and Tenth Circuits have all required plaintiffs to prove dose in order to establish causation, the Minnesota Supreme Court explicitly declined to set such a rule in *Goeb* and resolved the case on other grounds.[108]

In concluding that the lower court did not abuse its discretion in excluding expert testimony, the *Goeb* court implied that medical testimony on causation must include a differential diagnosis.[109] The lower court excluded as unreliable the testimony of one physician who claimed to have conducted a differential diagnosis, but who did not review the plaintiffs' full pre-exposure medical records and did not explain postexposure medical tests that showed neurological and blood test results. The court also excluded as unreliable the testimony of a physician who relied solely on the plaintiffs' self-reporting in his or her differential diagnosis. The *Goeb* court noted that "self-reporting of a plaintiff's medical history in preparation for litigation, without additional independent confirmation, is inherently unreliable."[110]

In *Goeb*, the plaintiffs were unable to establish causation without expert medical testimony, but the court did not explain whether medical testimony is always required in toxic torts cases.[111] After the exclusion of their medical experts, the *Goeb* plaintiffs' remaining evidence included (1) a memorandum from the county health department stating that the plaintiffs' house probably contained a concentration of a toxin that exceeded the National Academy of Sciences recommended maximum; (2) the temporal proximity of the plaintiffs' exposure and their symptoms; (3) deposition testimony of others who experienced symptoms after entering the plaintiffs' home; and (4) air samples collected from the plaintiffs' home showing the presence of the toxin.[112] The court held that, without expert testimony linking this evidence to the plaintiffs' symptoms, the plaintiffs failed to establish causation.

Missouri
Overall Standard for Causation
In Missouri, a toxic torts plaintiff must prove that "the conduct of the defendant was a substantial cause of the injury."[113] In this context, "substantial" means that "the defendant's conduct had such an effect that reasonable people would regard it as the cause of the harm."[114] Although the law in Missouri is not expressed in terms of general and specific causation, the Missouri Court of Appeals has explained that there are five elements

---

108. *See id.*
109. *See id.* at 815–16.
110. *Id.*
111. *Id.* at 817.
112. *See id.* at 804–05, 817.
113. Elam v. Alcolac, Inc., 765 S.W.2d 42, 178 (Mo. Ct. App. 1989).
114. Ray v. Upjohn Co., 851 S.W.2d 646, 654 (Mo. Ct. App. 1993).

for establishing causation in a toxic torts case: (1) "an exposure to an identified harmful substance significant enough to activate disease"; (2) "a demonstrable relationship between the substance and biologic disease"; (3) the "diagnosis of such disease in the plaintiff"; (4) an "expert opinion that the disease found in plaintiff is consistent with exposure to the harmful substance"; and (5) that the "defendant was responsible for the etiologic agent of the disease diagnosed in plaintiff."[115] Notably, element four specifically contemplates the use of expert testimony. Because the diagnosis of a plaintiff's condition "is essentially a scientific undertaking," the plaintiff is required to produce evidence that would meet scientific standards for establishing causation.[116]

The admissibility of expert evidence is governed by Section 490.065.3 of the Missouri Revised Statutes, which provides:

> The facts or data in a particular case upon which an expert bases an opinion or inference may be those perceived by or made known to him at or before the hearing and must be of a type reasonably relied upon by experts in the field in forming opinions or inferences upon the subject and must be otherwise reasonably reliable.[117]

The Missouri Supreme Court has explained that this provision requires (1) a showing that the facts and data used by the expert are of a type reasonably relied upon by experts in the field and (2) an independent assessment as to the reliability of the facts and data relied upon by the expert.[118] Missouri's statutory standard is similar to the *Daubert* standard, but not identical. In Missouri, the relevant scientific community must be specifically identified in order to determine whether the facts and data relied upon by the expert are of the sort relied upon by experts in that community.[119]

General Causation

A toxic tort plaintiff in Missouri must show that the substance "can be demonstrated to cause the type of harm the plaintiff reports."[120] In *Elam v. Alcolac, Inc.*, the court explained that "[t]he relationship between toxicants and biological disease is a subject of toxicology, pharmacology and epidemiology."[121] The *Elam* court further explained that the usual

---

115. *Elam*, 765 S.W.2d at 178.
116. *Id.*
117. Mo. Rev. Stat. § 490.065.3 (2011).
118. State Bd. of Registration for the Healing Arts v. McDonagh, 123 S.W.3d 146, 156 (Mo. 2003).
119. *See id.* at 156–57.
120. *See Elam*, 765 S.W.2d at 178. However, in *Bonner v. ISP Technologies, Inc.*, the Eighth Circuit quoted from *Turner v. Iowa Fire Equipment Co.* for the proposition that "[t]he first several victims of a new toxic tort should not be barred from having their day in court simply because the medical literature, which will eventually show the connection between the victims' condition and the toxic substance, has not yet been completed." Bonner v. ISP Techs., Inc., 259 F.3d 924, 928 (8th Cir. 2001) (quoting Turner v. Iowa Fire Equip. Co., 229 F.3d 1202, 1208–09 (8th Cir. 2000)) (internal quotation marks omitted).
121. 765 S.W.2d at 185.

methods for demonstrating "a biologically plausible relationship between a chemical toxin and disease" are "epidemiologic studies, animal bioassays and short-term assays."[122] However, the defendants in that case did not dispute that the plaintiffs' experts clearly had established that the toxins at issue were capable of causing many of the maladies suffered by the plaintiffs. Consequently, the leading Missouri toxic tort case addressed the topic in general terms and did not have to specifically determine what sort of evidence would be sufficient to carry the burden of proof on this issue. Other cases have not provided more illumination. In *Ray v. Upjohn Co.*, the plaintiff was able to introduce a key piece of nonexpert evidence relevant to general causation: one of the defendant's own publications stated that persons sensitized to the chemical in question could have severe "asthma-like attacks," like those experienced by the plaintiff, whenever re-exposed to even minute traces of the chemical.[123]

Specific Causation

Lack of precise information with regard to dose and exposure levels is not necessarily fatal to a plaintiff's toxic tort claim in Missouri.[124] In *Elam*, the plaintiffs were unable to show direct proof of the identity or quantities of chemicals emitted by the defendant because the defendant did not keep records and otherwise obscured its conduct.[125] Because of overwhelming circumstantial evidence that the defendant's chemicals were the cause of the plaintiffs' injuries, the court concluded that "[t]here is simply no color of validity to the contention that no incident of [the defendant's] emission of a substance that could impinge harmfully on any plaintiff was proven."[126] The evidence in *Elam* showed that the defendant emitted toxic agents from its smokestacks, incinerators, and bioponds over the course of more than seven years. The court reasoned that exact measurements of the toxins were unnecessary, particularly when the reason for the lack of measurements was the defendant's own failure to comply with government orders.[127] Moreover, the court concluded that the defendant "was the only reasonably possible point source of the pollution to which the plaintiffs were exposed."[128]

More generally, in *Lewis v. FAG Bearings Corp.*, the court explained:

Even where the evidence does not identify the particular chemical at a particular exposure, the particular concentration of the chemical, the particular dosage of the chemical

---

122. *Id.* at 187 n.63.
123. *See* Ray v. Upjohn Co., 851 S.W.2d 646, 651 (Mo. Ct. App. 1993).
124. *See* Lewis v. FAG Bearings Corp., 5 S.W.3d 579, 585 (Mo. Ct. App. 1999).
125. 765 S.W.2d at 178–79.
126. *Id.* at 181.
127. *See id.* at 179–80.
128. *Id.* at 182.

taken in bodily, or the particular duration of the exposures, the identity of the toxic substances to which the harm is attributed may be shown by circumstantial evidence.[129]

Many of the facts relevant to specific causation may, therefore, be proved using circumstantial evidence.

Differential diagnosis is recognized as a valid form of proof with regard to specific causation. In *Elam*, the plaintiffs' experts conducted differential diagnoses, which were accepted by the court.[130] The court noted that the expert did consider alternative causes for the maladies. It is not clear, however, whether the consideration and rejection of such alternative causes is a requirement in Missouri.

Nebraska
Overall Standard for Causation

In Nebraska, the plaintiff in a toxic tort case must show evidence sufficient for a reasonable person to "conclude that the plaintiff's exposure probably caused her injuries."[131] Expert testimony is required in Nebraska in cases in which symptoms of an injury are subjective.[132] The admissibility of expert evidence in Nebraska is to be determined using the *Daubert* standard.[133] The Nebraska Supreme Court has explained that, while the court is to ensure that expert witnesses employ the same level of intellectual rigor that characterizes the practice of experts in the field, reasonable differences in scientific evaluation are not a basis for excluding expert testimony.[134]

The plaintiff has the burden of establishing both general causation—that a substance is capable of causing a particular injury—and specific causation—that the substance caused the plaintiff's injury.[135] The court should consider evidence of general causation before reaching the question of specific causation.

General Causation

In Nebraska, "[p]laintiffs do not always need epidemiological studies to prove causation."[136] However, "frequently, plaintiffs find epidemiological studies indispensable in toxic tort cases when direct proof of causation is lacking." The studies themselves do not "prove"

---

129. 5 S.W.3d. at 585.
130. *See* 765 S.W.2d at 195.
131. King v. Burlington N. Santa Fe Ry., 762 N.W.2d 24, 41 (Neb. 2009).
132. *See* McNeel v. Union Pac. R.R., 753 N.W.2d 321, 329 (Neb. 2008) (holding that expert testimony was necessary to establish that the plaintiff's injury was caused by inhaling fumes attributable to the defendant's negligence); *see also* Golden v. Union Pac. R.R., 804 N.W.2d 31 (Neb. 2011) (involving facts similar to *McNeel v. Union Pacific Railroad* and applying the same standard).
133. Schafersman v. Agland Coop, 631 N.W.2d 862, 876–77 (Neb. 2001).
134. *King*, 762 N.W.2d at 43.
135. *Id.* at 34.
136. *King*, 762 N.W.2d at 35.

general causation but can provide a basis for an expert to opine that a certain agent can cause a disease.[137] Three factors are to be considered when considering epidemiological evidence: (1) whether the study reveals an association between the disease and the agent; (2) whether any errors in the study contributed to an inaccurate result; and (3) whether the relationship between the agent and the disease is causal.

With regard to association, Nebraska allows experts to consider and rely upon epidemiological studies showing a relative risk of greater than 1.0, meaning that a group exposed to a toxin is more likely to exhibit symptoms than a group not exposed to the toxin.[138] The significance of studies with weak positive associations is a question of weight, not admissibility. There is no "statistical significance" requirement for studies relied upon by the expert, so long as the expert can show that others in the field would rely on the study to support a causation opinion and "the probability of chance causing the study's results is low."[139] Likewise, although courts should normally require an expert to rely upon more than one study, there is no set minimum number of studies showing a positive association, particularly if the expert has other nonepidemiological studies supporting the general causation opinion. Any meta-analysis relied upon by the expert should be performed using a generally accepted methodology.[140]

A plaintiff's expert opining on general causation may rely on epidemiological studies in reaching that opinion; however, the studies themselves "need not draw definitive conclusions on causation."[141] The Nebraska Supreme Court has recognized that determining general causation requires subjective judgment. "While the drawing of causal inference is informed by scientific expertise, it is not a determination that is made by using scientific methodology."[142] Some factors relevant to that determination are the strength of the association between the toxin and the disease, replication of findings, and biological plausibility. An expert's inability to explain the progression or pathology of a disease will go to weight, not admissibility.[143]

Specific Causation

To establish specific causation in Nebraska, an expert must perform a reliable differential etiology, determining all of the possible explanations for a plaintiff's injury and then ruling out the least likely possibilities.[144] "At the ruling-in stage . . . , an expert's opinion

---

137. *Id.* at 36.
138. *Id.* at 46–47.
139. *Id.* at 47.
140. *Id.* at 48.
141. *Id.*
142. *Id.* at 39.
143. *Id.* at 39–42.
144. *See King*, 762 N.W.2d at 50; *see also* Boren v. Burlington N. & Santa Fe Ry., 637 N.W.2d 910, 920–21 (Neb. Ct. App. 2002) (holding that a medical expert's use of differential etiology is sufficient to meet the standards for admissibility).

is not reliable if the expert considers a suspected agent that cannot cause the patient's disease. Nor is the opinion reliable if the expert 'completely fails to consider a cause that could explain the patient's symptoms.'"[145] When ruling out hypotheses, the expert must have "a reasonable basis for concluding that one of the plausible causative agents was the most likely culprit for the patient's symptoms." The ruling-out process is necessarily case-specific. However, "[u]nsupported speculation will not suffice."[146] Not surprisingly, given the foregoing standards, experts have not been permitted to opine that symptoms must have been caused by the toxin merely because they arose after the exposure.[147]

A plaintiff does have to identify the toxic agent that is alleged to have caused the injury.[148] However, in *Boren v. Burlington Northern & Santa Fe Railway*, the Nebraska Court of Appeals considered a plaintiff who had been "unable to present any specific information concerning the dose or level of any of the chemicals to which he was exposed."[149] The defendant argued that the plaintiff had to present the specific level or dose of exposure. The court rejected that argument, concluding the plaintiff "needed only to present evidence from which a reasonable person could conclude that his exposure probably caused his injuries."[150] The plaintiff had established that he was exposed to a variety of chemicals over thirty years of employment and had established in general terms the length of time during which he worked with various chemicals. When considered with the other evidence of causation, including evidence of general causation and evidence ruling out other possible causes for his condition, the court held that was sufficient.

North Dakota
Overall Standard for Causation

There is a dearth of toxic tort cases applying North Dakota law.[151] In *Anderson v. Hess*, discussed below, the federal district court for the District of North Dakota exclusively relied upon Eighth Circuit law from other states in a motion for summary judgment based upon an inadequate showing of causation.[152]

To establish causation in a toxic tort case, previous Eighth Circuit case law required a plaintiff to show evidence from which a reasonable person could conclude that the plaintiff's exposure to the defendant's substance probably caused the plaintiff's injury.[153] "The

---

145. *King*, 762 N.W.2d at 50 (footnotes omitted) (quoting Carlson v. Okerstrom, 675 N.W.2d 89, 105 (Neb. 2004)).
146. *Id.*
147. *See* McNeel v. Union Pac. R.R., 753 N.W.2d 321, 332 (Neb. 2008).
148. *See id.*
149. 637 N.W.2d at 922.
150. *Id.* at 922–23.
151. Due to the general lack of case law from North Dakota, this section will largely rely upon Eighth Circuit cases taken from various jurisdictions.
152. *See* 592 F. Supp. 2d 1174, 1184 (D. N.D. 2009).
153. Bonner v. ISP Techs., Inc., 259 F.3d 924, 928 (8th Cir. 2001); Bednar v. Bassett Furniture Mfg. Co., 147 F.3d 737, 740 (8th Cir. 1998); Wright v. Willamette Indus., Inc., 91 F.3d 1105, 1107 (8th Cir. 1996).

plaintiff in a toxic tort strict liability case needs to establish causation through expert testimony," showing both that the toxic exposure was capable of causing the plaintiff's injuries and that the plaintiff was exposed to a sufficient quantity of the toxin to cause his or her injuries.[154] A plaintiff need not produce "a mathematically precise table equating levels of exposure with levels of harm," but must show that he or she "was exposed to a quantity of the toxin that exceeded safe levels."[155]

General Causation

Although a plaintiff usually must establish general causation, the Eighth Circuit sometimes waives this requirement, especially for new toxic torts for which the scientific literature has not yet been developed.[156] "The first several victims of a new toxic tort should not be barred from having their day in court simply because the medical literature, which will eventually show the connection between the victims' condition and the toxic substance, has not yet been completed."[157]

Specific Causation

A plaintiff may establish specific causation through an expert's reliable differential diagnosis, in which the expert both rules in all possible causes for the plaintiff's symptoms and rules out the less likely causes.[158] The *Anderson* court found expert testimony admissible when a doctor had performed a differential diagnosis that involved both ruling-in and ruling-out analyses, but the court did not allow testimony of other medical experts who did not perform differential diagnoses.[159] In *Turner v. Iowa Fire Equipment Co.*, the plaintiff's expert did not pass *Daubert* admissibility standards because, rather than performing a differential diagnosis for the purpose of determining the cause of the plaintiff's injury, the expert only examined the plaintiff to diagnose her condition.[160]

When differential diagnoses are not available, courts sometimes allow plaintiffs to show specific causation based on the temporal connection between exposure and injury. Temporal proximity without an additional "established scientific connection between exposure and illness," however, "is entitled to little weight in determining causation."[161]

---

154. *See* Barrett v. Rhodia, Inc., 606 F.3d 975, 980–81 (8th Cir. 2010). *But see* Turner v. Iowa Fire Equip. Co., 229 F.3d 1202, 1210 (8th Cir. 2000) ("If [the plaintiff] suffered 'visible' injuries as a result of the exposure, her proof of causation does not necessarily depend on expert medical testimony.").
155. Bonner, 259 F.3d at 928 (quoting Bednar, 147 F.3d at 740) (internal quotation marks omitted).
156. Turner, 229 F.3d at 1208–09.
157. Id. at 1209.
158. *See* Turner, 229 F.3d at 1209.
159. Anderson, 592 F. Supp. 2d 1174, 1180–84 (D. N.D. 2009).
160. *See* Turner, 229 F.3d at 1208 (clarifying the two meanings attached to the term "differential diagnosis" and explaining that only a diagnosis of causation, not a diagnosis of condition, can be used to establish causation in a toxic torts case).
161. Bland v. Verizon Wireless, (VAW) L.L.C., 538 F.3d 893, 898–99 (8th Cir. 2008) (quoting Moore v. Ashland Chem. Inc., 151 F.3d 269, 278 (5th Cir. 1998)). In *Bland*, temporal proximity was insufficient to

When temporal proximity plays a role in establishing causation, courts may restrict the subject matter on which a treating physician is allowed to testify.[162] In *Bonner v. ISP Technologies, Inc.*, the Eighth Circuit affirmed the district court's decision to allow the treating physician to testify that the plaintiff suffered acute symptoms after exposure but preclude the doctor from testifying about cause of the plaintiff's ongoing injuries.[163] The doctor relied heavily on the temporal connection between the plaintiff's exposure and her symptoms, and the court found this a reasonable basis for testifying about causation of the initial symptoms, but not strong enough to show causation of the plaintiff's long-term injuries. Similarly, in *Metcalf v. Lowe's Home Centers, Inc.*, the court allowed the treating physician to testify on causation when there was close temporal proximity between the plaintiff's exposure and her injuries, but the court found that without a differential diagnosis, the doctor's opinion on the plaintiff's long-term prognosis was not sufficiently reliable.[164]

Ohio
Overall Standard for Causation

"Under Ohio law, plaintiffs must establish a causal relationship between the tort alleged and the claimed physical injury by the opinion of medical witnesses competent to express such opinions."[165] In *Terry v. Caputo*, the Ohio Supreme Court stated that "[e]stablishing general causation and specific causation in cases involving exposure to mold or other toxic substances involves a scientific inquiry, and thus causation must be established by the testimony of a medical expert."[166]

Expert testimony in Ohio must satisfy the *Daubert* standard.[167] "*Daubert* attempts to strike a balance between a liberal admissibility standard for relevant evidence on the one hand and the need to exclude misleading 'junk science' on the other."[168] Under the *Daubert* standard, Ohio courts are expected to serve as gatekeepers and assess the reliability of expert methodology and the relevance of any testimony before allowing an

---

establish causation when the plaintiff suffered exercise-induced asthma after taking a few drinks from a water bottle filled with freon. *Id.* at 894–96, 899.

162. *See* Bonner v. ISP Techs., Inc., 259 F.3d 924, 930–31 (8th Cir. 2001); Metcalf v. Lowe's Home Ctrs., Inc., No. 4:09-CV-14 CAS, 2010 WL 1657424, at *4 (E.D. Mo. Apr. 26, 2010).
163. 259 F.3d at 930–31.
164. 2010 WL 1657424, at *4–6.
165. Conde v. Velsicol Chem. Corp., 804 F. Supp. 972, 994 (S.D. Ohio 1992) (applying Ohio law).
166. 875 N.E.2d 72, 77 (Ohio 2007); *see also* Pluck v. BP Oil Pipeline Co., 640 F.3d 671, 677 (6th Cir. 2011) (citing *Terry*); Baker v. Chevron USA, Inc., 680 F. Supp. 2d 865, 874 (S.D. Ohio 2010) (same); Darnell v. Eastman, 261 N.E.2d 114, 116 (Ohio 1970) (observing in a traditional tort case that "[e]xcept as to questions of cause and effect which are so apparent as to be matters of common knowledge, the issue of causal connection between an injury and a specific subsequent physical disability involves a scientific inquiry and must be established by the opinion of medical witnesses competent to express such opinion").
167. *See Terry*, 875 N.E.2d at 77–78; Valentine v. Conrad, 850 N.E.2d 683, 686–87 (Ohio 2006); *see also* Daubert v. Merrell Dow Pharm., Inc., 509 U.S. 579, 587–95 (1993).
168. *Baker*, 680 F. Supp. 2d at 875 (applying Ohio toxic tort law).

expert to testify.[169] Ohio courts require that scientific or expert testimony "have a traceable, analytical basis in objective fact before it may be considered on summary judgment."[170]

In *Terry*, the plaintiffs had offered expert testimony in support of their claim that exposure to toxic mold in the workplace had caused them injury.[171] The expert in question had opined that the plaintiffs had "experienced clinical symptoms consistent with building-related illness that was the result of multiple problems including water incursion leading to mold and mildew growth, poor ventilation and poor filtration."[172] The trial court excluded the expert's opinion regarding specific causation, and the intermediate appellate court and Ohio Supreme Court upheld that decision because the expert's opinion was not supported on sufficient facts or data, wasn't the product of reliable principles and methods, and the methods were not reliably applied to the facts of the case.[173] The expert in question was familiar with the plaintiffs' symptoms but had not examined the plaintiffs or taken steps to consider other possible causes of the symptoms in question. Likewise, in *Valentine v. Conrad*, the Ohio Supreme Court upheld the exclusion of the plaintiff's experts because, although both experts were highly qualified, the opinions of the experts were "based on unscientific principles and methodology."[174] According to the court, none of the experts had been able to show that the injury suffered by the decedent could be caused by the chemicals to which he had been exposed. Thus, the experts failed to prove general causation.

General Causation

The Ohio Supreme Court has adopted the familiar two-step method of proving toxic tort causation. The first step, general causation, requires that the plaintiff prove that the substance in question is capable of causing the injury alleged.[175] The preferred method of establishing general causation in Ohio is epidemiological evidence.[176] Epidemiologists "compare rates of disease in various populations to determine whether there is an increased risk of disease in those who used a particular substance in comparison to non-users."[177]

Where it is used, epidemiological evidence must be linked to the substances and injuries alleged.[178] In *Baker v. Chevron USA, Inc.*, residents sued a nearby refinery for illnesses

---

169. *Terry*, 875 N.E.2d at 77–78.
170. Valentine v. PPG Indus., Inc., 821 N.E.2d 580, 591 (Ohio Ct. App. 2004) (quoting Bragdon v. Abbott, 524 U.S. 624, 653 (1998)), *aff'd sub nom.* Valentine v. Conrad, 850 N.E.2d 683 (Ohio 2006).
171. *See Terry*, 875 N.E.2d at 75.
172. *Id.* (internal quotation marks omitted).
173. *See id.* at 75, 79.
174. *See* 850 N.E.2d at 688.
175. *Terry*, 875 N.E.2d at 76.
176. *See* Baker v. Chevron USA, Inc., 680 F. Supp. 2d 865, 875–78 (S.D. Ohio 2010); *In re* Meridia Prods. Liab. Litig., 328 F. Supp. 2d 791, 800–01 (N.D. Ohio 2004).
177. *In re Meridia*, 328 F. Supp. 2d at 800 (quoting *In re* Diet Drugs Prods. Liab. Litig., MDL No. 1203, 2000 U.S. Dist. LEXIS 9661, *21 (E.D. Pa. June 28, 2000)).
178. *See Baker*, 680 F. Supp. 2d at 875–78; *In re Meridia*, 328 F. Supp. 2d at 800–01; *Valentine*, 850 N.E.2d at 687.

allegedly caused by the refinery's emissions. The plaintiffs provided an expert to support their allegations. When the expert's failure to prove general causation drew a critique, the expert filed a supplemental report, which drew upon a variety of epidemiological studies including studies of refinery workers and some animal studies. The court rejected the expert testimony because it was produced late and was "based on a scattershot of studies and articles which superficially touch on each of the illnesses at issue."[179]

In order for epidemiological evidence to be a valid proof of general causation in Ohio, an expert must explain how epidemiological evidence reliably bears upon the relevant controversy.[180] In *Valentine*, the court rejected the expert's epidemiological evidence because it lacked sufficient connection to the controversy.[181] The proffered epidemiological evidence studied workers in a different occupation and failed to identify a particular group of chemicals linked to the type of brain tumor the decedent presented.[182]

However, while epidemiological evidence can be persuasive and is looked upon favorably, it is not required to prove general causation.[183] Other methods are valid. For example, an expert can testify based on animal studies or other proofs as long as sufficient foundation is laid to draw inferences. However, nonepidemiological proofs still are required to have valid scientific underpinnings.[184]

If there is not reliable and relevant expert testimony supporting general causation, Ohio courts are likely to exclude an expert's assertion of specific causation as unfounded. For example, in *Valentine* the Ohio Supreme Court discounted expert testimony that the plaintiff's brain tumor was directly and proximately caused by exposure to workplace toxins because the experts in question had failed to first establish general causation.[185]

Specific Causation

After establishing general causation, the successful toxic tort plaintiff must prove by a preponderance of the evidence that the toxic exposure in question caused his or her injury.[186] In Ohio, specific causation must be established "through medical expert testimony" made "by probability"; opinions offered on mere possibility "must be excluded as speculative."[187]

---

179. See *Baker*, 680 F. Supp. 2d at 887–88.
180. See *id.* at 881–82 (rejecting expert's epidemiological evidence regarding benzene exposure because there was "simply too great an analytical gap between the data and the opinion proffered" (quoting Gen. Elec. Co. v. Joiner, 522 U.S. 136, 146 (1997)); see also *Valentine*, 850 N.E.2d at 687.
181. See *Valentine*, 850 N.E.2d at 687.
182. See *id.*; see also Valentine v. PPG Indus., Inc., 821 N.E.2d 580, 591 (Ohio Ct. App. 2004) ("In addition to being scientifically or technically reliable, expert testimony also must 'fit' the case at hand.... '[A]dmissibility depends in part on "the proffered connection between the scientific research or test result to be presented and particular disputed factual issues in the case."'" (quoting *In re* Paoli R.R. Yard PCB Litig., 35 F.3d 717, 743 (3d Cir. 1994))), *aff'd sub nom. Valentine*, 850 N.E.2d 683.
183. See *In re Meridia*, 328 F. Supp. 2d at 800–01.
184. See, e.g., *id.* at 805–06.
185. See *Valentine*, 850 N.E.2d at 686–87.
186. See Terry v. Caputo, 875 N.E.2d 72, 77 (Ohio 2007).
187. See Shumaker v. Oliver B. Cannon & Sons, Inc., 504 N.E.2d 44, 46 (Ohio 1986). *But see* State v.

Federal courts applying Ohio law have indicated that dose is an important consideration in proving specific causation.[188] For example, in *Baker* the court was very skeptical of the expert's calculation of dose.[189] The court expressed dissatisfaction with the expert's efforts to link scholarship with the plaintiffs' injuries, observing that the selected studies were conducted at benzene exposure levels much greater than those experienced by the plaintiffs.[190] Similarly in *Bartel v. John Crane, Inc.*, the court rejected expert opinion resting on the "theory that exposure to any asbestos fiber no matter how small can cause mesothelioma"; the court indicated dose was an important consideration.[191] Finally, in *Pluck v. BP Oil Pipeline Co.*, the Sixth Circuit declared an expert's causation analysis flawed because the expert failed to determine whether the plaintiff's benzene exposure was sufficient to create health problems.[192]

Merely showing the plaintiff was exposed to a toxin in concentrations higher than a regulatory standard does not prove specific causation. In *Baker*, the court rejected expert testimony that relied upon the fact the plaintiffs' benzene exposure exceeded regulatory levels to establish specific causation.[193] The court observed that regulatory levels are set to protect public health "but are of limited value in judging whether a particular exposure was a substantial contributing factor to a particular individual's disease or illness."[194]

Differential diagnosis is used in Ohio to establish specific causation.[195] However, in order to be valid, the technique must adhere to accepted methods.[196] The Ohio Supreme Court has explained that differential diagnosis "is performed after 'physical examination, the taking of medical histories, and the review of clinical tests, including laboratory tests,' and generally is accomplished by determining the possible causes for the patient's symptoms and then eliminating each of these potential causes until reaching one that cannot be ruled out or determining which of those that cannot be excluded is most likely."[197] This

---

D'Ambrosio, 616 N.E.2d 909, 915 (Ohio 1993) ("While several decisions from this court indicate that speculative opinions by medical experts are inadmissible since they are based on possibilities and not probabilities, we believe that the better practice, especially in criminal cases, is to let experts testify in terms of possibility." (citation omitted) (citing *Shumaker*, 504 N.E.2d 44)).

188. See Pluck v. BP Oil Pipeline Co., 640 F.3d 671, 677–78 (6th Cir. 2011); Baker v. Chevron USA, Inc., 680 F. Supp. 2d 865, 875–81 (S.D. Ohio 2010); Bartel v. John Crane, Inc., 316 F. Supp. 2d 603, 611 (N.D. Ohio 2004).
189. See *Baker*, 680 F. Supp. 2d at 875–78.
190. See id. at 887–88.
191. *Bartel*, 316 F. Supp. 2d at 611.
192. *Pluck*, 640 F.3d at 679.
193. See *Baker*, 680 F. Supp. 2d at 880.
194. *Id*.
195. See Valentine v. PPG Indus., Inc., 821 N.E.2d 580, 598–99 (Ohio Ct. App. 2004), *aff'd sub nom.* Valentine v. Conrad, 850 N.E.2d 683 (Ohio 2006); Terry v. Ottawa Cnty. Bd. of Mental Retardation & Developmental Delay, 847 N.E.2d 1246, 1255–57 (Ohio Ct. App. 2006), *aff'd in relevant part sub nom.* Terry v. Caputo, 875 N.E.2d 72 (Ohio 2007).
196. See *Terry*, 847 N.E.2d at 1255–57; see also *Pluck*, 640 F.3d at 678 (rejecting differential diagnosis where the expert failed to rule out other viable causes of the plaintiff's condition).
197. See *Valentine*, 821 N.E.2d at 598–99 (quoting Westberry v. Gislaved Gummi AB, 178 F.3d 257, 262 (4th Cir. 1999)).

interest in the specific manner in which a differential diagnosis is conducted can also be seen in *Terry*. In that matter, the expert in question "did not conduct a reliable differential diagnosis because he relied too heavily upon the temporal relationship between exposure and symptoms and . . . failed to rule out other causes of the symptoms exhibited by the claimants."[198]

In addition to having the burden of proving causation generally required of all toxic tort plaintiffs, asbestos plaintiffs are required under Ohio law to satisfy supplemental procedural and substantive requirements.[199] In particular, an asbestos plaintiff must provide medical testimony documenting his or her physical impairment and furnish competent written authority testifying that the asbestos exposure was a "substantial contributing factor" to his or her illness.[200] Ohio statute defines "substantial contributing factor" as a toxic exposure (1) that is the "predominate cause" of the illness and (2) without which the injury would not have occurred.[201] To avoid finding the asbestos legislation unconstitutional under the Ohio State Constitution, the Ohio Supreme Court has narrowly interpreted the requirement of predominance.[202] The court has read the two requirements together as requiring that the asbestos be a "significant, direct" and "but for" cause of a plaintiff's illness.[203]

Oklahoma
Overall Standard for Causation

While Oklahoma's toxic tort case law is not as well developed as other states, as with other states, Oklahoma separates the causation inquiry into two components: general and specific causation.[204]

Expert testimony may be useful in showing exposure to a toxin but is not always necessary.[205] This follows the rule for general negligence torts, which provides that expert medical testimony is not needed if "the common knowledge or experience of laymen is extensive enough to recognize or infer negligence from the facts."[206] Consistent with this rule, however, Oklahoma law requires a plaintiff introduce expert testimony "if 'the fact in issue is not within the realm of ordinary experience of mankind.'"[207] Generally speaking,

---

198. Terry v. Caputo, 875 N.E.2d 72, 77 (Ohio 2007).
199. *See* OHIO REV. CODE ANN. § 2307.91-.98 (West 2012).
200. *See* Ackison v. Anchor Packing Co., 897 N.E.2d 1118, 1122 (Ohio 2008).
201. OHIO REV. CODE ANN. § 2307.91(FF).
202. *See Ackison*, 897 N.E.2d at 1127–28. The plaintiff in Ackison had claimed that the legislation had resulted in a retroactive change in substantive law. The interpretation given by the Ohio Supreme Court made the statute's requirements consistent with prior law.
203. *Id.* at 1128.
204. *See* Christian v. Gray, 65 P.3d 591, 602 (Okla. 2003).
205. *See id.* at 607.
206. *See* Boxberger v. Martin, 552 P.2d 370, 373 (Okla. 1976).
207. Hollander v. Sandoz Pharm. Corp., 289 F.3d 1193, 1214 (10th Cir. 2002) (quoting Strubhart v. Perry Mem'l Hosp. Trust Auth., 903 P.2d 263, 274 (Okla. 1995)).

assessing the potential effects of a toxin is not generally thought to be within the realm of ordinary experience.[208] For example, in *Twyman v. GHK Corp.*, the court concluded an expert would be needed to help the jury evaluate the effects an oilfield's contamination of a nearby well would have on local cattle.[209]

Oklahoma has explicitly adopted the *Daubert* standard for evaluating expert testimony.[210] Under this standard, where expert testimony is offered, the plaintiff bears the burden of showing by a preponderance of the evidence that the evidence is reliable.[211]

General Causation

The first step for a toxic tort plaintiff in Oklahoma is proving general causation—"whether a substance is capable of causing a particular injury or condition in the general population."[212]

Case reports are not always an effective scientific basis for establishing general causation. In *Hollander v. Sandoz Pharmaceuticals Corp.*, the court was very critical of case studies purporting to link a drug with strokes.[213] In particular, the court expressed concern about the small sample of case studies and the potential for bias, as well as the danger that "they simply describe reported phenomena without comparison to the rate at which the phenomena occur in the general population"; they "do not isolate and exclude potentially alternative causes."[214]

Studies can be a useful way to demonstrate general causation. However, the studies must offer evidence that is analogous to the circumstances alleged to be a valid form of proof. For example, in *Hollander*, the court was skeptical of the plaintiffs' epidemiological data because the data examined only the drug's relationship to hypertension, not stroke, and it was not clear how the data could be extrapolated to people "who took the drug as a postpartum lactation suppressant," as did one of the plaintiffs.[215] The court also rejected the plaintiffs' animal studies because, unlike the plaintiff in question had been, the animals were neither pregnant nor postpartum. Accordingly, the court found that the similarities were not readily apparent and causation seemed too attenuated. Similarly the court rejected human studies as a method for showing specific causation in a case involving injury to cattle after an oilfield contamination because the experts failed to establish that animals would have a similar reaction.[216]

---

208. *See Hollander*, 289 F.3d at 1214; Twyman v. GHK Corp., 93 P.3d 51, 56–57 (Okla. Ct. App. 2004).
209. *See Twyman*, 93 P.3d at 56–57.
210. *See Christian*, 65 P.3d at 599–600; *see also* Daubert v. Merrell Dow Pharm., Inc., 509 U.S. 579, 587–95 (1993).
211. *See Christian*, 65 P.3d at 603.
212. *Id.* at 602.
213. *See Hollander*, 289 F.3d at 1210–11.
214. *Id.* at 1210 (quoting Casey v. Ohio Med. Prods., 877 F. Supp. 1380, 1385 (N.D. Cal. 1995)).
215. *See id.* at 1208–09.
216. *See* Twyman v. GHK Corp., 93 P.3d 51, 60 (Okla. Ct. App. 2004).

Specific Causation

After establishing general causation, a toxic tort plaintiff must prove specific causation—"whether that substance caused the particular individual's injury."[217]

Differential diagnosis is a valid way of proving specific causation in Oklahoma, provided there is independently reliable evidence establishing general causation.[218] An expert typically conducts differential diagnosis by performing a physical exam, taking a medical history, and conducting various clinical tests and then eliminating the likely causes of a particular ailment until only the most likely remains. It is important that before an expert conducts differential diagnosis general causation is established, to make sure that the remaining cause is a viable one.[219]

While dose is an important factor in specific causation, Oklahoma does not require a plaintiff to prove the exact quantity of his or her toxic exposure.[220] It is sufficient to prove (1) that the plaintiff was exposed to a toxin and (2) the exposure caused injury. For example, in *Christian v. Gray*, several individuals experienced respiratory problems after being exposed to airborne lime at a circus.[221] There was no expert on hand during the exposure to measure the precise concentration of lime in the air, and thus plaintiffs were not able to prove their exact exposure. While the Oklahoma Supreme Court said it was unnecessary for the expert to prove the exact quantity of the exposure, it concluded that the expert's testimony was deficient because the expert failed to provide a basis (lay observation or otherwise) for believing there was a sufficient quantity of airborne lime present to cause the plaintiffs' injuries.[222] The court concluded that some indication of dosing is needed to show specific causation.

South Dakota
Overall Standard for Causation

There is a very limited body of toxic tort case law in South Dakota. The most instructive and relevant cases are from the federal district court, not the South Dakota state courts. The federal decisions cite and discuss decisions from the Eighth Circuit and other federal courts, even with regard to issues of substantive law. The federal district court has concluded that South Dakota requires a toxic tort plaintiff prove by a preponderance of the evidence that exposure to a toxic substance caused his or her injury. This causal inquiry

---

217. Christian v. Gray, 65 P.3d 591, 602 (Okla. 2003). In asbestos cases, a plaintiff must show by a preponderance that there is a significant probability the defendant's acts were related to the plaintiff's injury. See Dillon v. Fireboard Corp., 919 F.2d 1488, 1491 (10th Cir. 1990).
218. See *Christian*, 65 P.3d at 604–05.
219. See Hollander v. Sandoz Pharm. Corp., 289 F.3d 1193, 1210–11 (10th Cir. 2002).
220. See *Christian*, 65 P.3d at 605–06; see also Mid-Continent Petroleum Corp. v. Epley, 250 P.2d 861 (Okla. 1952) (allowing the plaintiff to recover for injuries sustained from exposure to natural gas even though she offered no exact figure quantifying her exposure).
221. See *Christian*, 65 P.3d at 594, 601.
222. See *id.* at 606–07.

is split into two proofs: general and specific causation.[223] To meet these prongs "a plaintiff must show both that the alleged toxin is capable of causing injuries like that suffered by the plaintiff in human beings subjected to the same level of exposure as the plaintiff, and that the toxin was the cause of the plaintiff's injury."[224]

When expert testimony is introduced in the South Dakota courts, it must comply with the *Daubert* standard.[225] Under the familiar *Daubert* requirements, the trial judge serves as a gatekeeper and is charged with making sure that the expert's testimony "rests on a reliable foundation and is relevant to the task at hand."[226]

General Causation

In order to prevail in a toxic tort action, a plaintiff must first show the toxic substance is capable of causing the injury alleged. In state and federal court, a product's label can be used to establish its hazardousness.[227] For example, in *Fryer v. Kantz*, a workers' compensation case, the plaintiff cited the product label, which warned that the vapors are harmful, to show that the substance was capable of causing her injuries.[228] Similarly, in *Mattis v. Carlon Electrical Products*, the plaintiffs used the material safety data sheet to prove that the substance in question was capable of creating harmful vapors.[229]

Scientific studies are also recognized by the federal district court as a persuasive way to establish general causation. In *Mattis*, the expert drew on scientific literature describing reactive airways dysfunction syndrome (RADS).[230] While the literature did not connect the particular substance at issue in that case to RADS, the plaintiffs' expert was allowed to extrapolate based on the similarities between that substance and several other irritating chemicals known to cause RADS.[231] The court accepted that extrapolation as valid scientific testimony under the *Daubert* standard.

Specific Causation

In addition to proving general causation, a plaintiff must show that the toxic exposure in question caused the plaintiff's ailments. Differential diagnosis is a valid way of establishing

---

223. Mattis v. Carlon Elec. Prods., 295 F.3d 856, 860 (8th Cir. 2002).
224. *Id.* (quoting Bonner v. ISP Techs., Inc., 259 F.3d 924, 928 (8th Cir. 2001)).
225. *See* Boomsma v. Dakota, Minn., & E. R.R., 651 N.W.2d 238, 247 (S.D. 2002), *overruled on other grounds by* State v. Martin, 683 N.W.2d 399 (S.D. 2004); State v. Hofer, 512 N.W.2d 482, 484 (S.D. 1994); *see also* Daubert v. Merrell Dow Pharm., Inc., 509 U.S. 579, 587–95 (1993).
226. *See Boomsma*, 651 N.W.2d at 247 (quoting *In re Dokken*, 604 N.W.2d 487, 498 (S.D. 2000)).
227. *See* Mattis v. Carlon Elec. Prods., 114 F. Supp. 2d 888, 891 (D.S.D. 2000), *aff'd*, 295 F.3d 856 (8th Cir. 2002); Fryer v. Kranz, 616 N.W.2d 102, 103 (S.D. 2000); *see also* Olson-Roti v. Kilcoin, 653 N.W.2d 254 (S.D. 2002) (involving a claim for lead poisoning from paint labeled as containing lead, but this issue was not reached on the merits).
228. *See Fryer*, 616 N.W.2d at 103.
229. *See Mattis*, 114 F. Supp. 2d at 891–92.
230. *See id.* at 890–91.
231. *See id.* at 890–91, 894–95.

specific causation. For example, in *Mattis*, a plaintiff experienced serious respiratory distress after working with a particular cement.[232] At trial, the plaintiff offered the expert testimony of a pulmonologist who had performed a physical exam, taken a medical history, taken a series of laboratory tests, and ruled out a variety of alternate causes and preexisting conditions. The physician concluded the plaintiff's respiratory disease was caused by exposure to the cement fumes.

While it is generally important to show a plaintiff was exposed to some critical threshold of a toxin, it is not necessary to show an exact level of exposure.[233] "[A] plaintiff need only make a threshold showing that he or she was exposed to toxic levels known to cause the type of injuries he or she suffered."[234] In *Mattis*, an expert's experiments approximating the exposure setting provided a sufficient showing that solvent vapors would have exceeded safe levels.

---

232. *See Mattis*, 114 F. Supp. 2d at 889.
233. *See* Mattis v. Carlon Elec. Prods., 295 F.3d 856, 860–61 (8th Cir. 2002).
234. *Id.* at 860–61.

CHAPTER 11

Southern States

Lisa Horvath Shub

The Southern states include Alabama, Arkansas, Florida, Georgia, Kentucky, Louisiana, Mississippi, North Carolina, South Carolina, Tennessee, Texas, Virginia, and West Virginia. These states, especially Texas, have had a great deal of experience addressing toxic tort claims in both individual and mass tort cases. Of all of the states, Texas has most specifically clarified the criteria for scientific evidence that must exist to meet the causation element required for all causes of action arising from exposure claims. This chapter summarizes each of the Southern states' causation standards with respect to toxic tort litigation.[1]

Alabama
Overall Standard for Causation
To recover damages under Alabama law, the plaintiff must establish that the defendant's breach of a duty of care was a proximate cause of the damages that the plaintiff incurred.[2] Proximate cause has been defined by Alabama courts as "an act or omission that in a natural and continuous sequence, unbroken by any new and independent causes, produces the injury and without which the injury would not have occurred."[3] Proximate cause also

---

The author would like to thank the following individuals who assisted with this chapter: Kathy Grant, Emilie Baine, Rose Kanusky, Lauren Valkenaar, Tim Fischer, and Arnold Cantu.

1. This survey chapter focuses on a narrow but extremely significant aspect of any toxic tort case seeking damages for personal injury—namely, the criteria for establishing the elements of general and specific causation in the particular jurisdictions covered. For a more generalized discussion regarding causation in personal injury and other types of toxic tort actions, as well as a broader discussion regarding the claims, defenses, and general strategies at play in these cases, please refer to earlier chapters in this book.
2. *See* Byrd v. Commercial Credit Corp., 675 So. 2d 392, 393 (Ala. 1996).
3. *Id.*; Nance v. Southerland, 79 So. 3d 612, 624 (Ala. Civ. App. 2010).

has been defined as the precipitating or immediate cause, as opposed to a remote cause.[4] It requires the elements of cause-in-fact and foreseeability.[5] Proximate cause is generally a question of fact for a jury, but becomes a question of law where there is a total lack of evidence from which a fact finder can reasonably infer a direct causal relationship between the defendant's conduct and the plaintiff's injury.[6]

In a toxic tort case that involves matters not within the common knowledge or experience of lay jurors, expert medical testimony is required to support the element of causation.[7] For example, in *Whately v. Cardinal Pest Control*, the plaintiff alleged that he sustained urticaria (hives) as a result of exposure to the defendant's pesticides. In attempting to defend a summary judgment motion on causation, the plaintiff presented factual arguments, without expert testimony, that the plaintiff's urticaria did not exist before the exposure, that the condition started immediately after the exposure, that the pesticide was poisonous when inhaled or absorbed through the skin or eyes, that the plaintiff inhaled the pesticide, and that other individuals suffered the same symptoms at the same time and place. However, the defendant's expert stated at deposition that the pesticide unequivocally did not cause the plaintiff's condition. The court held that the question of whether the pesticide could cause urticaria was not a matter within the common knowledge or experience of lay jurors. Because the plaintiff offered no expert testimony, the defendant's uncontradicted expert testimony negating causation was sufficient to sustain summary judgment.[8]

Importantly, Alabama has recognized that "product identification is one element of causation."[9] Alabama plaintiffs must identify the alleged "injury-causing product and its manufacturer."[10] Further, after the alleged injury-causing product has been identified, the plaintiff must establish that the product manufactured by the defendant "was a substantial factor" in producing his injury.[11] "A mere possibility of such causation is not enough. . . ."[12]

Older Alabama cases did not always analyze the reliability underlying the basis of the expert testimony. Accordingly, when conflicting expert testimony on causation was presented, the question of cause automatically became a question of fact for the jury.[13] As early as 1997, the Alabama Supreme Court cited *Daubert v. Merrell Dow Pharmaceu-*

---

4. Nix v. Goodyear Tire & Rubber Co., 624 So. 2d 641, 643 (Ala. Civ. App. 1993).
5. Springer v. Jefferson Cnty., 595 So. 2d 1381, 1384 (Ala. 1982).
6. *See* Cooper v. Diversy Corp., 742 So. 2d 1244, 1247 (Ala. Civ. App. 1998) (discussing causation in case alleging injury from exposure to dry cleaning chemicals) (citing Lyon v. Volkswagon of Am., Inc., 676 So. 2d 356 (Ala. Civ. App. 1996)).
7. *See* Whately v. Cardinal Pest Control, 388 So. 2d 529, 531–32 (Ala. 1980).
8. *Id.* at 530–31.
9. Sheffield v. Owens-Corning Fiberglass, 595 So. 2d 443, 450 (Ala. 1992) (maritime law exposure case applying the "general law of torts") (quoting Dillon v. Fibreboard Corp., 919 F.2d 1488, 1491 n.4 (10th Cir. 1990) (noting that all products liability cases require identification of product causing injury)).
10. *Id.*
11. *Id.* (citing RESTATEMENT (SECOND) OF TORTS § 433B, cmt. *a* (emphasis added)).
12. *Id.*
13. *See Cooper*, 742 So. 2d at 1248 (finding entire case hinged on conflicting expert testimony required to be submitted to a jury).

ticals, Inc.[14] and rejected conclusive and speculative expert testimony lacking a proper foundation, deeming such testimony insufficient to create a fact issue on causation.[15] But in 2000, Alabama courts nonetheless held that the *Daubert* standard only applied to admission of DNA evidence.[16]

Pursuant to recent legislation, however, Alabama now has made clear that the *Daubert* reliability standard is required for the admission of scientific expert testimony in all civil state court actions.[17] Further, Alabama has amended Alabama Rule of Evidence 702 to make it consistent with Federal Rule of Evidence 702.

Accordingly, for civil state court actions commenced on or after January 1, 2012, in addition to requiring that the evidence be from a qualified witness, expert testimony on causation is only admissible in Alabama state courts if:

- The testimony is based on sufficient facts or data;
- The testimony is the product of reliable principles and methods; and
- The witness has applied the principles and methods reliably to the facts of the case.[18]

General and Specific Causation

Because the specific *Daubert* evidentiary criteria have only recently been adopted, it is reasonable to expect that the Alabama courts soon will develop case law interpreting the requirement of scientific evidence to support claims of general and specific causation. However, Alabama courts already have signaled a recognition that general and specific causation must be proven for any claimant to be successful in a toxic tort case, even mass toxic tort cases. For instance in the mandamus action *Ex parte Flexible Products Co.*,[19] more than 1,500 coal miners claimed that they had been injured by exposure to isocyanate used during the mining process. The plaintiffs sued eleven defendants allegedly involved in the manufacture, use, and distribution of isocynate.[20] The trial court entered a case management order that required a "consolidated common issues trial," and trials on

---

14. 509 U.S. 579 (1993).
15. Becton v. Rhone-Poulenc, Inc., 706 So. 2d 1134, 1142 (Ala. 1997) (citing *Daubert* and noting conclusory affidavit by medical expert claiming that the plaintiff's exposure to carbon disulfide contributed to disease was insufficient to create a fact issue on causation).
16. S. Energy Homes, Inc. v. Washington, 774 So. 2d 505, 517 n.5 (Ala. 2000) (explaining that *Daubert* only applied to DNA evidence); Barber v. State, 952 So. 2d 393, 407 (Ala. Crim. App. 2005)(stating that in 2005 *Daubert* only applied to DNA evidence in Alabama courts) *cert. denied*, 549 U.S. 1306 (2007); Turner v. State, 746 So. 2d 355, 359–61 (Ala. 1998) (holding that if admissibility of DNA evidence is contested court should hold a *Daubert* hearing outside presence of jury) *on remand*, 746 So. 2d 363 (Ala. Crim. App. 1998); *see also* 1994 amendments to Ala. Code §36-18-20 (1975) (legislative adoption of *Daubert* in DNA testing). *But see* Cooper, 742 So. 2d at 1248 (Crawley, J., dissenting) (finding basis for expert's conclusions that exposure caused injury should be analyzed under *Daubert*.)
17. ALA. CODE §12-21-160.
18. *See id.*
19. 915 So. 2d 34 (Ala. 2005).
20. *Id.* at 37.

specific causation and damages for a limited number of plaintiffs. The CMO also noted that issues of specific causation and damages for the remaining plaintiffs would be the subject of later trials. Although the Supreme Court of Alabama held that mandamus on a common issues trial was premature because the issues to be addressed at the common trial were as yet undefined, the court explained that the trial court must avoid prejudice to all the parties, citing as instructive the considerations presented by the Supreme Court of Texas in *In re Van Waters & Rogers, Inc.*, a mass toxic tort case involving allegations of a wide array of injuries from an undefined toxic soup.[21] Although the court was silent on the standard by which general causation would be judged, the court's recognition that each plaintiff's causation and damages would be tried in separate proceedings suggests that Alabama courts require a showing of specific cause for each plaintiff before liability may be imposed against a defendant.[22]

Although little case law yet examines the causation standard under the new admissibility rules, given the explicit legislative enactment of Rule 702, it is likely the Alabama courts will be persuaded by federal pronouncements regarding the level of reliability for opinion testimony on general and specific causation under *Daubert*.[23]

Arkansas

Overall Standard for Causation

Arkansas tort law has traditionally required plaintiffs to prove proximate causation whether they are proceeding under a negligence or strict liability theory.[24] Arkansas courts have defined proximate cause as a "cause which, in a natural and continuous sequence, produces damage and without which the damage would not have occurred."[25] Where several defendants' negligent acts may have produced the plaintiff's injury, to be considered a proximate cause, an individual defendant's tortious conduct must constitute a substantial contributing factor in bringing about the plaintiff's damages.[26] Arkansas has not adopted alternative or market share liability, but has retained the traditional requirement

---

21. *Id.* at 38, 43–45 (citing *In re* Van Waters & Rogers, Inc., 145 S.W.3d 203 (Tex. 2004)).
22. *Id.*; *see also Ex parte* Monsanto, 794 So. 2d 350, 359 (Ala. 2001) (noting specific causation requirement for each of 2,700 plaintiffs alleging injuries from alleged exposure to PCBs around manufacturing plant).
23. *See* McLain v. Metabolife Int'l, Inc., 401 F.3d 1233, 1244 (11th Cir. 2005) (holding expert testimony failing to establish a link between the product and the injuries, a sufficient level of exposure to cause medical problems, and evidence of increased incidence of strokes and heart attacks from the product's use over the background risk, was unreliable and inadmissible).
24. *See, e.g.*, ARK. CODE ANN. §§ 4-86-102(a), 16-116-102(5) (Michie 1991 & 1987) (strict products liability); Ellsworth Bros. Truck Lines, Inc. v. Canady, 245 Ark. 1055, 437 S.W.2d 243, 244 (1969) (negligence).
25. Rogers v. Armstrong World Indus., 744 F. Supp. 901, 904 (E.D. Ark. 1990) (citing *e.g.*, Ark. Model Jury Instr. Civil 3d Ed. 501).
26. *Id.* at 905.

of proximate cause in all tort cases.[27] Exposure to a defendant's specific product must be a "substantial factor" in producing the injuries.[28]

In *Farm Bureau Mutual Insurance Co. of Arkansas, Inc. v. Foote*,[29] the Arkansas Supreme Court adopted the reliability requirements for the admissibility of expert testimony on causation set forth in *Daubert*.

General Causation

A toxic tort plaintiff must adduce evidence of both general and specific causation.[30] General causation addresses whether a particular agent can cause a particular illness. In *Richardson v. Union Pacific Railroad Co.*, discussed further in the section addressing specific causation in Arkansas courts below, the Court of Appeals of Arkansas provided an extensive review of Arkansas cases addressing causation questions.[31]

Efforts to impose liability upon a defendant for a plaintiff's unknown exposure level to an undefined toxic soup have failed because a reliable opinion on general causation cannot be established in such circumstances.[32] In *Savage v. Union Pacific Railroad Co.*, the plaintiff claimed that his exposure to petroleum products, including but not limited to products allegedly found in creosote, caused his skin cancer. Although the case involved a lower causation standard because the case was brought under the Federal Employers' Liability Act (FELA), the court held that even under FELA's lower burden of proof,[33] the "plaintiff still bears the burden for presenting evidence from which a jury could conclude a 'probable' or 'likely' causal relationship as opposed to merely a 'possible' one."[34] The plaintiff's experts failed to identify the hazardous level of exposure for any specified substance. The plaintiff's experts also failed to identify any dose or exposure data for the plaintiff, and instead provided only subjective beliefs that the plaintiff's exposure was substantial. Further, one plaintiff's expert failed to examine the plaintiff's exposure to products other than creosote, and analyzed causation with regard to petroleum products generally without identifying the product that allegedly caused the illness at issue. Finally, literature relied upon by the plaintiff's experts dealt with a type of skin cancer that the plaintiff did not have. Therefore, the expert's opinions on general causation were unreliable because the

---

27. See Chavers v. Gen. Motors Corp., 349 Ark. 550, 560, 79 S.W.3d 361 (2002) (citing Jackson v. Anchor Packing Co., 994 F.2d 1295 (8th Cir. 1993)).
28. *Id.*
29. 341 Ark. 105, 14 S.W.3d 512 (2000).
30. Richardson v. Union Pac. R.R. Co., 2011 Ark. App. 562 at *3–4, 2011 Ark. App. LEXIS 602 (Ark. Ct. App. 2011).
31. *Id.* at *3–10.
32. See Savage v. Union Pac. R.R. Co., 67 F. Supp. 2d 1021, 1030–34 (E.D. Ark. 1999).
33. Under the FELA causation standard, the plaintiff must provide a reasonable basis for a jury to conclude that an employer's negligence played any part, even the slightest, in producing the injury for which damages are sought. *Savage*, 67 F. Supp. at 1027.
34. *Id.* at 1027.

expert failed to identify reliable and direct scientific information that the specified substance caused the particular form of cancer at issue.[35]

Specific Causation

Specific causation addresses whether the substance at issue caused the particular plaintiff's illness.[36] Arkansas has adopted the *Lohrmann* "frequency, regularity, and proximity test"[37] in asbestos cases to establish that the dose the plaintiff received from a specific defendant's product was sufficient to support the element of causation.[38] Although originally applied in the context of asbestos cases only, the Supreme Court of Arkansas later applied the *Lohrmann* test to exposures other than asbestos.[39] The test has been described as a method for establishing specific causation using circumstantial evidence.[40] Under the test, the plaintiff must establish that the defendant's particular substance was used with sufficient frequency and regularity, and in proximity to where the plaintiff actually worked, such that it is probable that exposure to the defendant's products caused the plaintiff's injuries.[41]

Although it may not be necessary to establish a plaintiff's exposure or dose levels with precision, to establish specific causation, an Arkansas plaintiff must demonstrate that he or she was exposed to or received a dose of the substance at issue at levels that meet or exceed the doses made the subject of any epidemiological studies relied upon by the plaintiff's experts.[42] In *Richardson v. Union Pacific Railroad Co.*, the plaintiff alleged he contracted multiple myeloma from exposure to diesel fuel, diesel exhaust, creosote, and pesticides during his employment as a brakeman for Union Pacific Railroad. The court excluded the plaintiff's expert witness, holding that causation requires more than proof that the plaintiff was exposed to the allegedly offending substance above ambient levels; instead to establish specific causation, the plaintiff must first present evidence of the levels of the exposure that are hazardous to human beings generally, and then evidence of the plaintiff's actual level of exposure. The plaintiff argued that the trial court erred in requiring him to prove with a precise parts-per-million measurement, his exact exposure level, and further argued that by requiring more, the trial court exceeded the *Daubert*

---

35. *Id.* at 1029–40.
36. Richardson, 2011 Ark. App. 562 at *4 (citing Aurand v. Norfolk S. Ry. Co., 2011 WL 2938447 (N.D. Ind. 2011)).
37. The "frequency, regularity, and proximity test" was derived from the Court's language in Lohrmann v. Pittsburgh Corning Corp., 782 F.2d 1156 (4th Cir. 1986) ("Whether a plaintiff could get to a jury or defeat a motion for summary judgment . . . would depend upon the frequency of the use of the product and the regularity and of the plaintiff's employment in proximity thereto.").
38. *Chavers*, 79 S.W.3d at 368–69.
39. Green v. Alpharma, Inc., 373 Ark. 378, 284 S.W.3d 29 (Ark. 2008) (*Green I*).
40. Baxter D. Drennon, *Toxic Exposure in Arkansas: The "Chicken" Littered Case of Green v. Alpharma, Inc.*, 63 Ark. L. Rev. 391, 414 (2010).
41. *Chavers*, 79 S.W.3d at 368–69.
42. *Richardson*, 2011 Ark. App. 562 (2011).

gatekeeper role. The plaintiff's expert characterized the plaintiff's exposure to benzene as "excessive exposure" because it was above ambient levels. However, the court held that the trial court had not abused its discretion and that the plaintiff provided no reliable data on the plaintiff's actual exposure to either diesel exhaust or benzene.[43] The court rejected as unreliable the opinion of the plaintiff's experts' that any dose above background levels can cause multiple myeloma, and upheld the exclusion of the causation testimony.

In two appeals arising from the same case (*Green I* and *Green II*), the Supreme Court of Arkansas provided guidance on the standards of evidence necessary to support a fact question on causation.[44] In *Green I* and *II*, the plaintiff alleged that his exposure to arsenic-containing chicken litter caused his chronic myelogenous leukemia (CML).[45] The arsenic in the litter was alleged to have come from a chicken feed additive that contained an organic arsenical compound that allegedly passed through the chickens and accumulated in the litter. The litter was alleged to also contain viruses, bacteria, and fungi. The litter was then used as fertilizer in fields surrounding the plaintiff's home and school.

The poultry producers, who allegedly fed their chickens the arsenic-containing feed, moved for summary judgment arguing that the plaintiff did not have an illness that the scientific community had recognized as having a causal connection with poultry litter and/or arsenic.[46] They further argued that exposure to trace amounts of arsenic could not have caused the illness. One of the plaintiff's experts purported to opine on environmental conditions in the area, sources of contamination, and the levels of the plaintiff's arsenic exposure through a table known as Table 9. Table 9 reflected the expert's purported conversion values of measurements of arsenic in dust to arsenic in air. The Table 9 conversion formula was developed by the EPA to examine lead exposure, not arsenic. Two additional experts for the plaintiffs relied upon Table 9 in rendering their conclusions on causation. A fourth expert used the raw data from Table 9 to calculate the amount of the plaintiff's alleged arsenic ingestion, any alleged corresponding cancer risk, and as the foundation for his causation opinion. The circuit court deemed the methodology used to create Table 9 unreliable under *Daubert*, and also excluded testimony from all four plaintiff experts that relied upon Table 9. The circuit court also excluded the testimony relying upon the source data contained in Table 9.[47]

Noting that Arkansas did not adopt market share liability, the circuit court granted the poultry producers' motions for summary judgment on the ground that the plaintiff could not establish exposure to any particular defendant's chicken litter. However, the circuit court denied the motion as to the feed-additive supplier, the case was tried, and a

---

43. *Id.* at *28, 34.
44. Compare *Green I*, 284 S.W.3d 29, *with* Green v. George's Farms, Inc., 2011 Ark. 70, 2011 Ark. LEXIS 65 (2011) (*Green II*).
45. *Green I*, 284 S.W.3d at 33–34; *Green II*, 2011 Ark. 70 at *2–3.
46. *Green I*, 284 S.W.3d at 34.
47. *Id.* at 34–35, 41.

jury rendered a verdict in favor of the defendant supplier. The plaintiff appealed both the exclusion of the plaintiff's experts' testimony, as well as the summary judgments granted in favor of the poultry producers.[48]

The Supreme Court of Arkansas applied the frequency, regularity, and proximity test, and determined that sufficient evidence, in the form of expert affidavits and deposition testimony from spreaders, property owners, teachers and medical personnel, had been presented by the plaintiff to at least create a fact issue as to whether the plaintiff had been exposed to the individual poultry-producers' chicken litter. The court also held that the plaintiff had produced ample scientific and medical evidence suggesting that "there *may be* a causal link" between the litter and the plaintiff's injury.[49] Further, Arkansas case law generally holds that causation is almost always a fact question, and not appropriate for summary judgment. However, the court noted that the plaintiff had presented expert testimony that "there was no safe level of arsenic exposure,"[50] and that "the medical literature contains numerous studies detailing the causative links between inorganic arsenic exposure in humans and the development of lymphohemotopoietic diseases, including leukemia."[51] The Supreme Court did not appear to examine the reliability of the underlying literature supporting these expert opinions, and viewing this testimony in the light most favorable to the plaintiff, held that the trial court should not decide the probative strength of conflicting evidence, and held summary judgment for the poultry producers was inappropriate.

The Supreme Court of Arkansas also examined the plaintiff expert's methodology relating to the calculations set forth in Table 9, and held that the circuit court correctly concluded that any testimony based thereon was properly excluded under *Foote*, *Daubert*, and Arkansas Rule of Evidence 702. The validity of his formula had not been tested, had not been subjected to peer review and publication, included a conversion factor that he had not used in previous cases, used assumptions he admitted could be incorrect, excluded nondetect values when calculating sampling averages, and his methods had not been generally accepted in the scientific community. However, one of the plaintiff's experts was permitted to use raw data reflected in Table 9 to perform dose calculations and testify thereto because the raw data did not suffer the same failings as the calculated values.[52]

The verdict in favor of the defendant feed-additive producer was upheld, but the case against the defendant poultry producers was remanded for trial. On remand, the jury rendered a verdict in favor of the defendant poultry producers. In *Green II*, the plaintiff sought reconsideration of the court's exclusion of expert testimony related to Table 9,

---

48. *Id.*
49. *Id.* at 39 (emphasis added).
50. *Id.* at 39.
51. *Id.* at 38–42.
52. *Id.* at 38–56.

and challenged the court's decision to exclude evidence of "other cancers" to support the plaintiff's causation claims. The court upheld its prior exclusion of Table 9, despite the fact that the formula was later published in a peer-reviewed journal, because the plaintiff's expert altered calculations without explanation, and disregarded dust samples that were below detectable limits. The post-trial judgment, pre-appeal publication of a peer-reviewed article using the formula did not render the methodology reliable because it was based on unreasonable assumptions and unsound mathematical extrapolations, and had not been tested by any other scientist.[53] The court excluded the plaintiff expert's testimony because his methodology remained scientifically unreliable, and therefore, an inappropriate means of establishing the plaintiff's exposure levels.

Opinion testimony on causation should be based upon the specific illness or disease alleged by the plaintiff. In *Green II*, the plaintiff alleged that he should be permitted to introduce evidence of "other cancers" that were not lymphohematopoietic cancers. Citing a post–*Green I* published article that suggested that the feed additive promoted cancer, the plaintiff argued that evidence of other cancers in the area should have been admitted at trial. The Supreme Court of Arkansas held that evidence that the substance promoted cancer generally was irrelevant to whether the substance caused leukemia, so that evidence of other cancers was properly excluded.[54] It is unclear whether the plaintiff experts examined, the defendants raised, and/or the court considered analysis of leukemias other than CML, but the court's holding suggests that the basis for expert testimony must be based on science that is specific to the plaintiff's disease or illness.

Florida
Overall Standard for Causation

Products liability cases in Florida, whether arising out of negligence or strict liability, require proof of proximate cause.[55] Florida courts have historically followed a "but for" causation standard.[56] However, the courts have also stated that where there is "concurrent cause," the more appropriate standard is "substantial factor."[57]

The United States District Court for the Middle District of Florida explained that Florida law is unsettled regarding proper use of the substantial factor test when examining allegations of concurrent cause.[58] Specifically, the court noted that it is unclear whether

---

53. *Green II*, 2011 Ark. 70 at *6.
54. *Id.* at *11–12.
55. *See* West v. Caterpillar Tractor Co., Inc., 336 So. 2d 80, 83, 87 (Fla. 1976) *aff'd*, 547 F.2d. 885 (5th Cir. 1977).
56. Jones v. Utica Mut. Ins. Co., 463 So. 2d 1153, 1155 (Fla. 1985); Stahl v. Metro. Dade Cnty., 438 So. 2d 14, 17 (Fla. Dist. Ct. App. 1983); Pope v. Pinkerton-Hays Lumber Co., 120 So. 2d 227, 230 (Fla. Dist. Ct. App. 1960), *cert. denied*, 127 So. 2d 441 (Fla.1961).
57. *Stahl*, 438 So. 2d at 18; *see also* Asgrow-Kilgore Co. v. Mulford Hickerson Corp., 301 So. 2d 441, 444–45 (Fla. 1974); Loftin v. Wilson, 67 So. 2d 185, 191 (Fla.1953).
58. Guinn v. Astrazeneca Pharm., 598 F. Supp. 2d 1239, 1246 (M.D. Fla. 2009).

the substantial factor test applies only where each of the concurrent causes alone could have caused the injury, or whether it also applies where the plaintiff can show that the defendant's negligence substantially contributed to the injury, even though it was just one of the concurring causes that "acted in combination to cause the injury."[59] However, despite this lack of clarity, a court may still find expert opinion unreliable under *Daubert* and therefore insufficient to support the element of causation in Florida federal courts.[60]

Expert testimony is necessary to establish causation only where the issue is beyond the knowledge of a layperson.[61] However, even if the issue of causation does not require expert testimony, this does not negate the requirement that the claimant demonstrate causation by some competent evidence.[62]

Until recently, Florida's evidentiary rule on admissibility of expert testimony was similar to Federal Rule 702, yet Florida was in the minority of states that continued to use the *Frye* standard.[63] In 1995, the Florida Supreme Court explained the burdens imposed by the *Frye* test as follows:

> [T]he burden is on the proponent of the evidence to prove the general acceptance of both the underlying scientific principle and the testing procedures used to apply that principle to the facts of the case at hand . . . . The general acceptance under the *Frye* test must be established by a preponderance of the evidence.[64]

The court later stated:

> [I]t is well-settled in Florida that in the arena of determining the admissibility of novel expert opinion testimony, it is of paramount importance that the court "not permit cases to be resolved on the basis of evidence for which a predicate of reliability has not been established. Reliability is fundamental to issues involved in the admissibility of evidence."[65]

---

59. *Id.*
60. *Id.* (holding that no evidence supported claim that Seroquel contributed to diabetes under *Daubert* analysis).
61. Benitez v. Joseph Trucking, Inc., 68 So. 3d 428, 431 (Fla. Dist. Ct. App. 2011) (finding that it was not beyond the common knowledge of laymen that deterioration of a wooden truck bed would reduce its load-bearing capacity); Greene v. Flewelling, 366 So. 2d 777, 780 (Fla. Dist. Ct. App. 1978) *cert. denied*, 374 So. 2d 99 (Fla. 1979).
62. *Flewelling*, 366 So. 2d at 780.
63. Fla. H.B. 7015 (2013), http://myfloridahouse.gov/Sections/Bills/bills.aspx.
64. Ramirez v. State, 651 So. 2d 1164, 1168 (Fla. 1995).
65. U.S. Sugar Corp. v. Henson, 823 So. 2d 104 (Fla. 2002) (quoting Hadden v. State, 690 So. 2d 573, 578 (Fla. 1997)).

Appellate review of *Frye* determinations was *de novo*.[66] The *Frye* standard was also applied in worker's compensation cases alleging toxic injuries.[67]

However, effective July 1, 2013, Florida state courts shall no longer follow *Frye*. Florida is amending rule section 90.702 because "the Florida Legislature intends to adopt the standards for expert testimony in the courts of this state as provided in *Daubert* . . . and to no longer apply the standard in *Frye*. . . ." The new rule shall read as follows:

> 90.702. Testimony by experts.—If scientific, technical, or other specialized knowledge will assist the trier of fact in understanding the evidence or in determining a fact in issue, a witness qualified as an expert by knowledge, skill, experience, training, or education may testify about it in the form of an opinion or otherwise, if:
>
> (1) The testimony is based upon sufficient facts or data;
>
> (2) The testimony is the product of reliable principles and methods; and
>
> (3) The witness has applied the principles and methods reliably to the facts of the case. . . .

General Causation

The question of general causation focuses on whether a substance is capable of causing a disease.[68] The federal courts have held that plaintiffs in toxic tort cases must present evidence of general and specific causation.[69] Florida state court cases have not stated these requirements explicitly, but imply the same requirements.

Pure opinion testimony shall no longer be sufficient to establish causation. The Florida legislature specifically stated that it "intends to prohibit in this state pure opinion testimony as provided in *Marsh v. Valyou*. . . ."[70] The previous rule led to inconsistent rulings in state and federal courts. For instance, in *Hood v. Matrixx Initiatives*, a case following *Marsh*, an appellate court held that *Frye*-testing was not required for an expert's opinions on general causation because they were considered "pure opinion" testimony. The plaintiff alleged that a nasal spray containing zinc gluconate caused the plaintiff to lose his sense of smell. The defendants moved to exclude the plaintiff's expert on general causation as unreliable and inadmissible under *Frye* because the opinions of the plaintiff's expert were based upon improper experiments regarding whether the nasal spray actually reached the

---

66. *U.S. Sugar Corp.*, 823 So. 2d at 109.
67. *Id.* (finding that an expert's opinion that worker's exposure to organophosphates as a pesticide sprayer caused his neurological complaints satisfied *Frye* because opinions were based upon a differential diagnosis, which is a generally accepted scientific methodology).
68. Berry v. CSX Transp., Inc., 709 So. 2d 552, 557 (Fla. Dist. Ct. App. 1998).
69. Hood v. Matrixx Initiatives, 50 So. 3d 1166, 1172 n.4 (Fla. Ct. App. 2011) (citing *Berry*, 709 So. 2d at 557).
70. Fla. H.B. 7015 (2013), *available at* http://myfloridahouse.gov/Sections/Bills/bills.aspx.

relevant nasal tissue, relied on literature relating to zinc sulfate instead of zinc gluconate, and improperly determined the amount of an allegedly harmful dose. The trial court found the plaintiff expert's opinions on general causation unreliable and not generally accepted, struck the expert, and granted summary judgment for the defendant.[71]

The appellate court held it was unnecessary for the plaintiff to conclusively demonstrate a causal link or demonstrate a precise etiology of the injury. Instead, it reasoned that a medical expert was permitted to render a causation opinion based upon a review of the plaintiff's medical records, a clinical examination, his impressions of the strong temporal association between the alleged exposure and the acute nature of the smell loss, published scientific literature showing an "association or possible etiology" between a predicate event and illness, and a differential diagnosis.[72] While the appellate court recognized that the plaintiff expert's opinion had been uniformly deemed inadmissible by federal courts, it held that the testimony would be admissible in Florida state court under *Marsh*, which allows "a 'battle-of-the-experts approach' to the admissibility of expert testimony."[73] The appellate court held that both parties should be permitted to present dueling expert testimony.[74] Given the appellate court's recognition that its holding would likely have been different under the federal standard, the recent change in Florida Statute 90.702 suggests litigants can expect a more consistent evaluation of scientific causation claims after July 13, 2013.

A causation expert's use of epidemiological studies likely will readdressed. For instance, the Florida Supreme Court applying the former *Frye* standard found that epidemiological studies need not establish that exposure to a particular substance results in a particular injury if the injury is a very rare birth defect.[75] In *Castillo v. E. I. DuPont de Nemours*, the Florida Supreme Court considered whether the plaintiff's expert properly testified that a pregnant woman's exposure to Benlate caused her child's rare birth defect microphthalmia, a condition involving severely underdeveloped eyes. The plaintiff's expert testified that fetal exposure to benomyl, a component in Benlate, at a concentration of 20 ppb in the maternal bloodstream would cause microphthalmia. He based these opinions on rat gavage studies, lab experiments on human and rat cells, and dermal exposure testing. The defendant argued that the plaintiff's expert failed to use epidemiological studies, improperly used a differential diagnosis, failed to consider a lack of other malformations, and improperly extrapolated from *in vitro* cell tests and animal studies to determine the dosage at which benomyl becomes a human teratogen. Although the defendant's expert explained that the plaintiff's expert had failed to rule out other causes, such as genetic

---

71. *Id.* at 1170–75.
72. *Id.*
73. *Id.* at 1174–75 (citing Marsh v. Valyou, 977 So. 2d 543 (Fla. 2007)).
74. *Id.* at 1175.
75. Castillo v. E. I. DuPont de Nemours & Co., 854 So. 2d 1264 (Fla. 2003).

causes, the plaintiff's expert stated that genetic causes had been ruled out as there were no known causes for this defect.[76] However, the opinion does not address whether the defendant's or the plaintiff's expert addressed, or the court considered, how a differential diagnosis can be valid when causes of a particular birth defect are unknown.

The court acknowledged that epidemiology is generally accepted in the scientific community as a way of studying causal links between disease and chemicals, but also stated that epidemiology was not necessarily required because exposure was rare. Although the defendant attempted to point to epidemiological studies negating a causation claim, the plaintiff cited flaws in those studies and the court deemed them inconclusive.[77]

The Florida Supreme Court further ruled that the plaintiff's expert's method of extrapolating dose from an *in vitro* study, though new, could still pass *Frye* if it could be shown that it was not "junk science."[78] Because the court determined that *in vitro* testing would be necessary to establish dose, and that it was used with other certain (albeit unnamed) reliable data, the *in vitro* study was an acceptable basis for establishing general causation. Determining whether dose extrapolations are not "junk science" will also be subject to the new rules, and the reasoning of *Castillo* will likely be revisited in future cases.

Specific Causation

As set out previously, specific causation is whether an exposure actually caused the disease in question in a specific individual.[79] The Supreme Court of Florida has held that a "differential diagnosis" is a "generally accepted method for determining specific causation."[80] However, the court was silent as to the requirements of the courts in other states that have recognized that even differential diagnosis must be based on scientifically valid decisions as to which potential causes should be ruled in and ruled out.[81]

Although it is unclear under Florida law whether a plaintiff *must* rule out alternative causes to establish specific causation, a defendant may present evidence about alternative causes, even though the defendant's expert has not determined whether the alternative causes in fact caused the plaintiff's illness.[82] In *R.J. Reynolds Tobacco Co. v. Mack*, the plaintiff averred that his addiction to cigarette smoking caused his laryngeal cancer and chronic obstructive pulmonary disease (COPD). At trial, the defendant's expert was precluded from offering his opinion that the plaintiff's strong family history of cancer, and significant asbestos exposure played a more significant role in the development of the

---

76. *Id.* at 1267–71.
77. *Id.* at 1267–70 (discounting studies comparing hospital birth records to general statistics).
78. *Id.* at 1273.
79. *Berry*, 709 So. 2d at 557.
80. *Marsh*, 977 So. 2d at 549.
81. *See, e.g.*, Mason v. Home Depot U.S.A., Inc., 658 S.E.2d 603, 610–11 (Ga. 2008) (citing Ervin v. Johnson & Johnson, Inc., 492 F.3d 901, 904 (7th Cir. 2007)).
82. *See* R.J. Reynolds Tobacco Co. v. Mack, No. 1D11-2448, 2012 WL 2122305, at *3, *reh'g denied* (Fla. Dist. Ct. App. June 13, 2012).

plaintiff's diseases than his cigarette smoking that had ceased more than sixteen years prior to his diagnoses. The trial court had excluded the testimony of the defendant's expert regarding the plaintiff's family history and other occupational exposures because he was unwilling to state that these factors caused the plaintiff's cancer to a reasonable degree of medical probability. On appeal, the defendant contended that the trial court should not have excluded the testimony on alternative causation, and the appellate court agreed. By requiring evidence from a defense expert to address only alternative cause if the expert was willing to testify that the alternative cause was the cause-in-fact of the plaintiff's injury to a reasonable degree of medical probability, the trial court had improperly shifted the burden of proof to the defendant. Instead, the defendant's expert may properly introduce evidence of other possible causes, even though the defense expert has not reached a conclusion to a reasonable degree of medical probability about what actually caused the plaintiff's illness.[83]

Georgia
Overall Standard for Causation
In a negligence case, proximate cause testimony should not be based only on "possibilities," but on whether there was a determination that there was a "reasonable probability" that the negligent act caused the injury.[84] However, medical testimony regarding "possibilities" may be sufficient if supplemented by probative nonexpert testimony on causation.[85]

Under Georgia law, a defendant may be held liable if the defendant's "conduct or defective product was a proximate cause of the condition, i.e., a substantial factor in bringing the condition about."[86] Proximate cause differs from "cause-in-fact" in that proximate cause entails an analysis of the defendant's duties,[87] intervening cause, and foreseeability.[88] However, Georgia toxic tort cases addressing causation tend to focus on the question of cause-in-fact, though negligence actions using a "proximate cause" standard are often cited.[89]

Under Georgia law, causation is an essential element in a toxic tort case, and generally requires reliable expert testimony.[90] Georgia recognizes that determining whether a defen-

---

83. Id.
84. Rodrigues v. Georgia-Pacific Corp., 661 S.E.2d 141, 143 (Ga. Ct. App. 2008).
85. Id. (finding that deposition testimony stating the possibility that chlorine exposure caused pneumonia was supplemented by an affidavit noting probability of causation, as well as nonexpert evidence of temporal association and other cases of chlorine inhalation injuries).
86. Fulmore v. CSX Transp., Inc., 557 S.E.2d 64, 74 (Ga. Ct. App. 2001) (quoting Grassis v. Johns-Mansville Corp., 248 N.J. Super. 446, 591 A.2d 671 (App. Div. 1991)).
87. Peterson v. Reeves, 727 S.E.2d 171, 176 (Ga. Ct. App. 2012).
88. Knight v. Roberts, 2012 WL 2579256, at *16–17 (Ga. Ct. App. Jul. 3, 2012).
89. See Union Carbide Corp. v. Fields, 726 S.E.2d 521, 526, 529 (Ga. Ct. App. 2012).
90. See Butler v. Union Carbide Corp., 712 S.E.2d 537, 544 (Ga. Ct. App. 2011); Allstate Ins. Co. v. Sutton, 658 S.E.2d 909, 915 (Ga. Ct. App. 2008) (finding a causal link between exposure to a substance and a medical condition to be a medical question established by physicians as expert witnesses and not by lay persons).

dant's actions in a toxic tort case caused a plaintiff's injury is beyond common knowledge and experience and will require expert testimony.[91] The admissibility of expert testimony rests in the trial court and cannot be overruled absent an abuse of discretion.[92]

In 2005, the Georgia Legislature passed OCGA Section 24-9-67.1,[93] which states that when evaluating expert testimony in civil cases, the trial court *may* draw from the holdings in *Daubert* and its progeny.[94] Further, *Daubert*'s reliability components were expressly adopted in OCGA Section 24-9-67.1(b). That section was slightly amended effective January 1, 2013, as noted below:

> (b) If scientific, technical, or other specialized knowledge will assist the trier of fact in any cause of action to understand the evidence or to determine a fact in issue, a witness qualified as an expert by knowledge, skill, experience, training, or education may testify thereto in the form of an opinion or otherwise, if:
>
> (1) The testimony is based upon sufficient facts or data which are or will be admitted into evidence at the hearing or trial;
>
> (2) The testimony is the product of reliable principles and methods; and
>
> (3) The witness has applied the principles and methods reliably to the facts of the case *which have been or will be admitted into evidence before the trier of fact*.[95]

Even given the amendments above, the Georgia rules still provide that an expert may rely upon facts or data that are not admissible in evidence "[i]f of a type reasonably relied upon by experts in the particular field in forming opinions or inferences upon the subject."[96]

Under Georgia law, in asbestos cases, the threshold for every theory of causation is that an injured plaintiff was exposed to a product or substance for which the defendant is responsible.[97] "[T]he plaintiff must present evidence 'that a particular defendant's asbestos-containing product was used at the job site and that the plaintiff was in proximity

---

91. *See* Cowart v. Widener, 697 S.E.2d 779, 785 (Ga. 2010).
92. *Butler*, 712 S.E.2d at 541; Cotten v. Phillips, 633 S.E.2d 655, 657–58 (Ga. Ct. App. 2006).
93. The Code reads in subsection (f) that, "It is the intent of the legislature that, in all civil cases, the courts of the State of Georgia not be viewed as open to expert evidence that would not be admissible in other states. Therefore, in interpreting and applying this code section, the courts of this state may draw from the opinions of the United States Supreme Court in Daubert v. Merrell Dow Pharms., Inc., 509 U.S. 579 (1993); Gen. Elec. Co. v. Joiner, 522 U.S. 136 (1997); Kumho Tire Co. Ltd. v. Carmichael, 526 U.S. 137 (1999); and other cases in federal courts applying the standards announced by the United States Supreme Court in these cases."
94. *Mason*, 658 S.E.2d603 (where state standards for the qualification of expert witnesses are based on *Daubert*, it is proper to exclude the testimony of purported expert witnesses where there is apparent lack of scientific support for methods used and/or evidence of unreliability of methods).
95. *Compare* OCGA § 24-9-67.1(b), *with* OCGA § 24-7-702 (effective Jan. 1, 2013).
96. *Compare* OCGA § 24-9-67.1(a), *with* OCGA § 24-7-703 (effective Jan. 1, 2013).
97. Union Carbide Corp. v. Fields, 726 S.E.2d 521, 526 (Ga. Ct. App. 2012) (citing Hoffman v. AC & S, Inc., 548 S.E.2d 379 (2001)).

to that product at the time it was being used.'"[98] Beyond this threshold requirement, a plaintiff must also make a showing that the defendant's substance caused a particular individual's injury.[99] Absent reliable expert testimony that exposure to a defendant's product contributed to a disease or condition, there is insufficient evidence to create a jury issue as to causation.[100]

Objections to the scientific reliability of an expert's theories must be raised at the trial court level.[101]

General and Specific Causation

General causation addresses whether a substance is capable of causing a particular injury or condition in the general population.[102] For instance, whether diesel fumes can cause respiratory problems in the human population generally is a question of general causation.[103] Whether diesel fumes actually did cause a particular plaintiff's respiratory problems is a question of specific causation.

Two methods exist by which a plaintiff may establish specific causation "(1) 'dose/response relationship' or 'threshold phenomenon'; and (2) 'differential diagnosis.'"[104] In Georgia, if a differential diagnosis is used to serve as a component of a specific causation opinion, the opinion "must be based on scientifically valid decisions as to which potential causes should be 'ruled in' and 'ruled out.'"[105] Opinions based only on the witness's own experience, without any support in published scientific journals or use of reliable techniques for discerning the effects of chemicals used in a product, are insufficiently reliable to be admissible.[106] An opinion based solely on the temporal complaints between the onset of symptoms and exposure is insufficient.[107] The witness must consider all relevant potential causes, and use a complete medical history.[108]

Further, a plaintiff must present reliable defendant-specific evidence that a particular defendant's product contributed to causing the injury.[109] In *Butler v. Union Carbide Corp.*,

---

98. *Id.*; Hoffman v. AC&S, Inc., 548 S.E.2d 379, 382 (Ga. Ct. App. 2001); *accord* Adamson v. Gen. Elec. Co., 694 S.E.2d 363, 367 (Ga. Ct. App. 2010) ("To survive summary judgment, the appellant needed to present evidence that the manufacturer defendants' asbestos-containing product was used at the location of [the plaintiff's] employment and that he was in proximity to that product at the time it was being used.") (citation and punctuation omitted).
99. *Butler*, 712 S.E.2d at 540–41, 545.
100. *Id.* at 544.
101. *Union Carbide Corp.*, 726 S.E.2d at 530 (finding that failure to object to "mixed exposure" theory as unreliable could not be raised for first time on appeal).
102. *Butler*, 712 S.E.2d at 540–41.
103. *See* Shiver v. Georgia & Florida Railnet, 652 S.E.2d 819, 821 (Ga. Ct. App. 2007).
104. *Id.* at 820.
105. *Mason*, 658 S.E.2d at 610–11 (citing *Ervin*, 492 F.3d at 904).
106. *Id.*
107. *See Shiver*, 652 S.E.2d at 820.
108. *Id.* at 821.
109. *Butler*, 712 S.E.2d at 544.

the trial court considered an expert's opinion that chrysotile asbestos from a particular molding compound contributed to the decedent's mesothelioma. The expert opined that the substance was "genotoxic," so that there was no safe exposure threshold; and further opined that the defendant's product had to be considered a causative factor.[110] However, the trial court found the plaintiff's expert's testimony on specific causation scientifically unreliable, excluded the testimony, and granted summary judgment for the defendant. The court of appeals noted that the OCGA provides the trial courts with substantial discretion to decide how to test an expert's reliability.[111] Although the plaintiff's expert argued that his specific causation opinion was based upon a literature review in accordance with generally accepted principles, the court ruled that the scientific literature upon which he relied did not support his opinion. The appellate court further rejected the plaintiff's claims that "any exposure to asbestos above background" was a principle generally accepted in the scientific community, explaining that other courts had determined this theory was scientifically unreliable. Although the plaintiff also complained about the trial court's determination that the plaintiff's expert was a "quintessential expert for hire," the appellate court cited evidence in the record that the plaintiff's expert did not attempt to provide an empirical basis for his opinion until *after* his opinion had been provided in sworn testimony.[112] The appellate court determined that the trial court's comments about the expert being "for hire" did not constitute an improper attack on the expert's credibility, but was instead an evaluation of whether the expert had properly used the scientific method. Improper credibility determinations result when the court attempts to weigh testimony of conflicting experts, which did not happen here.[113] Simply providing evidence that a harmful substance was used at the job site and that the plaintiff was in proximity to that product at the time it was being used is insufficient, and does not result in a presumption that the plaintiff was exposed to or harmed by the *defendant's* products.[114] Without evidence of specific causation, a plaintiff cannot establish a case, and summary judgment in favor of the defendant was proper.

---

110. *Id.* at 539–41.
111. *Id.* at 541 (relying on OCGA § 24-9-67.1).
112. *Id.* at 543.
113. *Id.* at 541–43.
114. *See* Hoffman v. AC&S, Inc., 548 S.E.2d 379 (Ga. Ct. App. 2001); *accord* Adamson v. Gen. Elec. Co., 694 S.E.2d 363, 367 (Ga. Ct. App. 2010) ("To survive summary judgment, the appellant 'needed to present evidence that [the manufacturer defendants'] asbestos-containing product was used at [the location of Adamson's employment] and that [he] was in proximity to that product at the time it was being used.'" (Citations and punctuation omitted.); Blackston v. Shook & Fletcher Insulation Co., 764 F.2d 1480, 1481 (11th Cir. 1985) ("the threshold for every theory is proof that an injured plaintiff was exposed to asbestos-containing products for which the defendant is responsible").

Kentucky

Overall Standard for Causation

Kentucky "adopted the substantial factor test for causation set forth in Section 431 of the *Restatement (Second) of Torts*. . . . ."[115] Under the *Restatement*, an "actor's negligent conduct is a legal cause of harm to another if his conduct is a substantial factor in bringing about the harm."[116] Comment (a) to Section 431 explains that "but for" causation is necessary, but not sufficient. Comment (a) defines "substantial" as "used to denote the fact that the defendant's conduct has such an effect in producing the harm as to lead reasonable men to regard it as a cause, using that word in the popular sense, in which there always lurks the idea of responsibility . . . ."[117]

General Causation

In *Burton v. CSX Transportation, Inc.*, the Supreme Court of Kentucky defined general causation as "whether exposure to [the toxin] had been proven to cause [the alleged injury]."[118] Kentucky has explicitly adopted the *Daubert* analysis for admissibility of expert evidence.[119]

More than expert qualifications are required to express an opinion on general causation.[120] The Supreme Court of Kentucky held that "a medical degree, standing alone, would not be sufficient . . . without some showing of expertise in relevant specific areas of study."[121]

Specific Causation

Specific causation requires proving "a causative link [exists] between th[e] defendant's specific tortious acts and the plaintiff's injuries."[122] The Supreme Court of Kentucky recently examined the exposure evidence necessary for causation in *CertainTeed Corp. v. Dexter*, an asbestos case:

> Though evidence of exposure may be related to causation (e.g., testimony about the length and intensity of exposure), it is not exactly what we mean [by] . . . causation. Instead, the primary evidence of causation . . . was from the medical experts, who discussed generally

---

115. Pathways, Inc. v. Hammons, 113 S.W.3d 85, 91–92 (Ky. 2003) (citing Deutsch v. Shein, 597 S.W.2d 141, 143–44 (Ky. 1980)).
116. RESTATEMENT (SECOND) OF TORTS § 431 (1965).
117. Id.
118. 269 S.W.3d 1, 8, n.19 (Ky. 2008) (General causation is shown "by demonstrating that exposure to a substance can cause a particular disease.") (internal citation omitted).
119. Mitchell v. Com., 908 S.W.2d 100, 101 (Ky. 1995), *overruled in part on other grounds by* Fugate v. Com., 993 S.W.2d 931, 937 (Ky. 1999).
120. Burton, 269 S.W.3d at 8.
121. Id.
122. Cardinal Indus. Insulation Co., Inc. v. Norris, 2004-CA-000525-MR, 2009 WL 562614, at *8 (Ky. Ct. App. Mar. 6, 2009) (citing Estes v. Gibson, 257 S.W.2d 604, 607 (Ky. 1953)).

how much exposure to asbestos was necessary to cause injury and specifically whether Dexter's various exposures caused his cancer.[123]

The *Dexter* court found that plaintiff's expert evidence, in conjunction with high asbestos levels in the victim's lungs, sufficiently demonstrated specific causation. Both an asbestos expert and the victim's physician testified that every instance of asbestos exposure was a substantial contributing factor to his asbestosis and lung cancer.[124] Another plaintiff expert testified that causation depended on "the intensity, [and] the duration that they were exposed to it."[125] However, the court found the intensity and duration testimony consistent with the others because the defense expert did not set a cap for intensity or duration, and agreed that the risk of disease increases with exposure.[126]

Bailey v. North American Refractories Co. discussed other states' use of the "frequency-regularity-proximity" and "fiber drift" tests for asbestos causation, but declined to adopt exclusive use of either.[127] Proof of specific causation in *Bailey* proceeded in three stages. First, the plaintiffs introduced evidence that asbestos was released.[128] Second, they used expert evidence regarding the ability of asbestos to travel far enough to reach the plaintiffs. Third, an expert "opined that the asbestos-containing materials were a substantial contributing factor to [plaintiffs'] diseases."[129] This evidence, viewed together, presented material issues of fact as to causation.[130]

In *Cardinal Industrial Insulation Co. v. Norris*, the court held that the fiber drift expert's failure to establish specific causation "is not necessarily fatal to plaintiff's claims."[131] The plaintiffs could still meet the substantial factor test if they produced evidence permitting a reasonable inference that the victim was so close to the defendant's asbestos that exposure probably, not merely possibly, caused the injury. A co-workers' testimony may be sufficient for this purpose.[132]

The Supreme Court of Kentucky recently approved the use of differential diagnosis with additional scientific evidence in *Hyman & Armstrong, P.S.C. v. Gunderson*, a medical products liability case for the drug Parlodel.[133] "[D]ifferential diagnosis calls for the

---

123. 330 S.W.3d 64, 77 (Ky. 2010).
124. *Id.* at 68, 78. The experts found asbestos exposure a substantial factor of the victim's fatal lung cancer notwithstanding the fact that the victim was a long-term smoker.
125. *Id.* at 78.
126. *Id.*
127. 95 S.W.3d 868, 873 (Ky. App. 2001). A subsequent Court of Appeals of Kentucky decision, Cardinal Indus. Insulation Co. v. Norris, interpreted *Bailey* as affirming that "substantial factor" is the correct test for determining specific causation. 2004-CA-000525-MR, 2009 WL 562614, at *5.
128. *Bailey*, 95 S.W.3d at 873.
129. *Id.*
130. *Id.* (reversing the defendant's summary judgment).
131. 2004-CA-000525-MR, 2009 WL 562614, at *4, 7.
132. *See id.* at *7, 8. (However, the court found the co-worker testimony at hand insufficient.)
133. 279 S.W.3d 93, 107 (Ky. 2008) (alleging Parlodel caused birth mother's death).

physician to list the known possible causes of a disease or condition .... Then, utilizing diagnostic tests, the physician attempts to eliminate causes from the list until he is left with the most likely cause."[134]

All of the *Gunderson* plaintiff's experts used differential diagnosis to determine specific causation. First, they examined the plaintiff's medical history and death reports to eliminate all possible causes of death except sudden death syndrome. Then, they eliminated the possibility that another drug was the cause of her sudden death. Last, they concluded that the plaintiff's headache prior to her death, and the proximity to childbirth, indicated an adverse reaction to Parlodel.[135]

Louisiana
Overall Standard for Causation

Louisiana courts generally use "but for" causation, but apply a "substantial factor" test where multiple causes exist.[136] Additionally, several Louisiana Courts of Appeal have adopted a substantial factor test for asbestos cases, requiring evidence of defendant-specific exposure. Under that test, "the exposure has to be a substantial contributing factor to the plaintiff's disease."[137]

In *Watters v. Department of Social Services*,[138] a mold exposure case, the court of appeal identified five elements it considered for causation:

> (i) the presence of mold, (ii) the cause of the mold and the relationship of that cause to a specific defendant, (iii) actual exposure to the mold, (iv) the exposure was a dose sufficient to cause health effects (general causation), and (v) a sufficient causative link between the alleged health problems and the specific type of mold found (specific causation).[139]

The *Watters* plaintiffs proved the first element through expert and lay witnesses, as well as hard evidence such as photographs and samples. The plaintiffs' testimony regarding their whereabouts in the building in relation to continuous water intrusions satisfied the second component. The court found plaintiffs' expert evidence regarding mold levels throughout the building sufficient to meet the exposure component.[140] Elements four and five are discussed in the sections addressing general and specific causation below.

---

134. *Id.*
135. *Id.* at 107–09.
136. Simmons v. CTL Distrib., 2003-1301, p. 10 (La. App. 5 Cir. 2/23/04); 868 So. 2d 918, 925.
137. Zimko v. Am. Cyanamid, 2003-0658, p. 26 (La. App. 4 Cir. 6/8/05); 905 So. 2d 465, 485; Vodanovich v. A.P. Green Indus., Inc., 2003-1079, pp. 3–4 (La. App. 4 Cir. 3/3/04); 869 So. 2d 930, 932–33; Egan v. Kaiser Aluminum & Chemical Corp., 94-1939, p. 11 (La. App. 4 Cir. 5/22/96); 677 So. 2d 1027, 1034–35 (citing Quick v. Murphy Oil Co., 1993-2267 (La. App. 4 Cir. 9/20/94); 643 So. 2d 1291).
138. 15 So. 3d 1128 (La. App. 4 Cir.), *writ denied*, 21 So. 3d 291 (La. 2009).
139. *Id.* at 1143 (citing *Zimko*, 905 So. 2d at 485–86).
140. *Id.* at 1143–46.

General Causation

Louisiana defines general causation as "proving exposure in a dose sufficient to cause health effects—that exposure to [the toxin] can cause disease."[141] Louisiana courts use expert evidence to determine both general and specific causation,[142] and to determine the admissibility of expert evidence under *Daubert*.[143]

The *Watters* court found that expert testimony proved general causation.[144] The plaintiffs' microbiologist cited various scientific publications, and opined that the plaintiffs' "Sick Building Syndrome" symptoms "were consistent with mold exposure."[145] He also testified that "it is possible to determine unsafe levels of mold exposure," but did not specify what exact level is unsafe.[146] Instead, he testified that a "strong correlation" exists between the type and levels of mold present in the building, and the plaintiffs' disease.[147]

Although expert evidence is "sometimes essential" to showing general causation, Louisiana courts are careful to indicate it is not always required.[148] In *Lasha v. Olin Corp.*, the Supreme Court of Louisiana held that expert evidence is not required for "medical matters within common knowledge" that "may be proved by other direct or circumstantial evidence."[149] Further, the fact finder "is required to assess the credibility of both expert and lay witnesses to determine the most credible evidence."[150]

Nonetheless, the *Lasha* plaintiff's physicians testified that exposure to chlorine gas caused aggravation of his asthma and depression.[151] The trial court had found that the plaintiff failed to prove causation to a "reasonable medical certainty."[152] Reversing for the plaintiff, the Supreme Court held that "reasonable medical certainty" implies a burden of proof higher than "by a preponderance of the evidence," the correct standard.[153] The court also criticized "reasonable medical certainty" as incorrectly implying that expert evidence is necessary.[154]

---

141. *Id.* at 1143 n.18.
142. See *Zimko*, 2003-0658, at 26–30; 905 So. 2d at 485–86 (discussing the use of expert testimony to show both general and specific causation related to asbestos exposure).
143. State v. Foret, 628 So. 2d 1116, 1123 (La. 1993).
144. *Watters*, 2008-0977, at 23–27; 15 So. 3d at 1146–49.
145. *Id.* at 23–24; 1146–47 ("By consistent, [the expert] explained that he meant the reported symptoms were what he would expect to see—and what the literature says we would expect to see—in individuals [exposed to mold].")
146. *Id.* at 24; 1147.
147. *Id.* (more specifically, the expert testified that "a strong correlation has been shown between any Stachybotrys growing on building materials, high levels of Penicillium in the air, and Sick Building Syndrome.")
148. Lasha v. Olin Corp., 625 So. 2d 1002, 1005 (La. 1993) (holding it "self-evident" that expert medical witnesses may not be required).
149. *Id.* (referencing Jordan v. Travelers Ins. Co., 245 So. 2d 151, 155 (La. 1971)).
150. Johnson v. E.I. DuPont de Nemours & Co., Inc., 08-628, pp. 7–9 (La. App. 5 Cir. 1/13/09); 7 So. 3d 734, 740–741.
151. *Lasha*, 625 So. 2d at 1004.
152. *Id.* at 1003.
153. *Id.* at 1005.
154. *Id.*

Specific Causation

Louisiana defines specific causation as "proving a sufficient causative link between the [injury] and the specific type of [exposure]."[155] In the *Watters* mold case, the court defined specific causation as proving "a sufficient causative link between the alleged health problems and the specific type of mold found."[156] While *Lasha* explicitly held that expert testimony is not required to show general causation, *Watters* interpreted *Lasha* as requiring medical testimony to prove specific causation.[157]

Watters used "but for" causation to analyze "whether 'but for' the defendant's alleged breach of duty the plaintiffs would have sustained injuries."[158] The court reviewed the plaintiffs' medical history and their testimony regarding the timing of their symptoms. Expert testimony then linked the plaintiffs' health problems to their exposure to mold on the defendant's premises. Specifically, the plaintiffs' expert examined the plaintiffs and their symptoms, and concluded several of their symptoms "were consistent with their exposure to mold."[159]

The *Watters* plaintiffs' expert limited her opinion to an examination of the class representatives and findings in a book from the Institute of Medicine of the National Academies that discussed studies associating upper respiratory tract symptoms with mold exposure.[160] The defendant's expert argued that this association did not show causation.[161] He also pointed out that the plaintiffs' expert did not diagnose the plaintiffs with a specific disease or run any objective tests. Despite the defendant's objections, *Watters* upheld the trial court's holding, in which the trial court sided with the plaintiffs' expert after noting that her conclusions were supported by various organizations, including the EPA.[162]

In another *Watters* decision, the Louisiana Court of Appeals held that expert testimony was not required to establish specific causation for each class member of a mold exposure class action.[163] The court considered the "finding of specific causation by the class representatives . . . significant of the remaining class members."[164]

---

155. *Watters*, 2008-0977, at p. 17 n.18; 15 So. 3d at 1143 n.18 (citing *Zimko*, 2003–0658, at p. 28 (La. App. 4 Cir. 6/8/05); 905 So. 2d at 485–86).
156. *Id.*
157. *Id.* at 31; 1152 ("The test for determining the causal relationship between the tortious conduct and subsequent injuries is whether the plaintiff proved *through medical testimony*. . . ." (citing *Lasha*, 625 So. 2d at 1005) (emphasis added)).
158. *Id.* at 25 n.22; 1147 n.22.
159. *Id.* at 25–32; 1147–52.
160. *Id.* at 27; 1149.
161. *Id.* at 29–30; 1150–51.
162. *Id.* at 30–32; 1151–52.
163. Watters v. Dep't of Soc. Servs., 2011-1174, pp. 4–6 (La. App. 4 Cir. 3/14/12); 2012 WL 860386, *4–7 (unreleased opinion).
164. *Id.*

Mississippi
Overall Standard for Causation

Under Mississippi substantive law, to prove that a defendant is liable in tort for injuries resulting from exposure to toxins, the plaintiff must introduce evidence that affords a reasonable basis for the conclusion that the defendant's conduct was, more likely than not, the proximate cause of the damage that the plaintiff suffered.[165] A mere possibility of such causation is not enough.[166]

Mississippi defines "proximate cause" as the "cause which in natural and continuous sequence unbroken by any efficient intervening cause produces the injury and without which the result would not have occurred."[167] Proximate cause has two separate and distinct concepts: (1) cause in fact; and (2) foreseeability.[168] "Cause in fact" means "that the act or omission was a substantial factor in bringing about the injury, and without it the harm would not have occurred."[169] Foreseeability means "that a person of ordinary intelligence should have anticipated the dangers" that his act created for others.[170]

A plaintiff in a toxic tort action must establish by expert testimony a causal connection between her illness and the exposure to chemicals.[171] In 2003, Mississippi abandoned the general acceptance test set forth in *Frye*[172] and adopted the standards found in *Daubert*,[173] as modified in *Kumho Tire Co. v. Carmichael*,[174] as the analytical framework for evaluating

---

165. Glover v. Jackson State Univ., 968 So. 2d 1267, 1277 (Miss. 2007); *see also* MISS. CODE ANN. § 11-1-63 (requiring a plaintiff in a product liability action to prove, among other things, that "the defective and unreasonably dangerous condition of the defendant's product proximately caused the damages for which recovery is sought"); Monsanto Co. v. Hall, 912 So. 2d 134, 136 (Miss. 2005) (Mississippi law on products liability in asbestos cases requires proof of product identification, exposure, and proximate cause); Moore v. Miss. Valley Gas Co., 863 So. 2d 43, 46 (Miss. 2003) ("[I]t is incumbent upon the plaintiff in any products liability action to show that the defendant's product was the cause of the plaintiff's injuries.")
166. Burnham v. Tabb, 508 So. 2d 1072, 1074 (Miss. 1987) (quoting W. KEETON, PROSSER & KEETON ON TORTS, § 41 (5th ed. 1984)).
167. Titus v. Williams, 844 So. 2d 459, 466 (Miss. 2003); McIntosh v. Victoria Corp., 877 So. 2d 519 (Miss. Ct. App.), *cert. denied*, 878 So. 2d 67 (Miss. 2004).
168. Davis v. Christian Brotherhood Homes of Jackson, MS, Inc., 957 So. 2d 390, 404 (Miss. Ct. App. 2007) (quoting Johnson v. Alcorn State Univ., 929 So. 2d 398, 411 (Miss. App. 2006)).
169. *Id.*
170. *Id.*
171. *See* Collins v. Koppers, Inc., 59 So. 3d 582, 584 (Miss. 2011) (affirming trial court's dismissal with prejudice when the plaintiff failed to provide expert opinions that causally linked her injuries to alleged exposure to contaminates from a wood treatment plant); Cole v. Superior Coach Corp., 106 So. 2d 71, 72 (Miss. 1958) (in a worker's compensation case, "[t]he issues with reference to an alleged injury [] are properly within the province of medical experts. In all but the simple and routine cases, it is necessary to establish medical causation by expert testimony."); *see also* Hammond v. Coleman Co., Inc., 61 F. Supp. 2d 533, 541 (S.D. Miss. 1999) (in products liability action, to prove causation, a potential plaintiff must offer expert testimony that the product was defective.)
172. Frye v. United States, 293 F. 1013, 1014 (D.C. Cir. 1923).
173. 509 U.S. 579 (1992).
174. 526 U.S. 137 (1999).

the reliability and admissibility of expert witness testimony.[175] The focus of this analysis "must be solely on principles and methodology, not on the conclusions they generate."[176]

General and Specific Causation

Courts in Mississippi have acknowledged that a plaintiff in a chemical exposure case has a duty to prove both general and specific causation, that is, that the chemical substance at issue *can* cause the injury at issue, and that the defendant's specific product did cause the plaintiff's specific injury.[177] In other words, the plaintiff must establish (1) that at least one of the subject chemical agents (or one of their constituents) can cause the plaintiff's injury; (2) the minimum amount of the given chemical agent necessary to cause the plaintiff's injury; (3) the amount of the given chemical agent to which the plaintiff was exposed; and (4) that the plaintiff was exposed to the requisite amount of at least one of the subject agents to cause his injury.[178]

In suits alleging harm caused by exposure to asbestos products in Mississippi, the Mississippi Supreme Court has adopted the "frequency-regularity-proximity" test.[179] This test requires that an asbestos plaintiff must prove more than casual or minimal contact with the defendant's product, and instead must show that the defendant's asbestos products were used with sufficient frequency and regularity in locations from which asbestos fibers could have traveled to the plaintiff's work areas, and that it is probable that the plaintiff actually breathed asbestos fibers originating from the defendant's products.[180] In *E.I. DuPont de Nemours & Co. v. Strong*,[181] the Mississippi Supreme Court declined the invitation to extend this "frequency, regularity, proximity" standard outside the context of asbestos litigation to cases alleging injury due to exposure to other environmental contaminents.[182]

The Mississippi Supreme Court has at times stated that evidence of a dose-response ratio is required to demonstrate specific causation between exposure to a toxin and an injury.[183] In the workers' compensation context, the Supreme Court has been willing to waive this requirement in cases alleging exposure to new or novel chemical substances.

---

175. Mississippi Transp. Comm'n v. McLemore, 863 So. 2d 31, 35, 39–40 (Miss. 2003) (abandoning the general acceptance test set forth in *Frye* and adopting the standards found in *Daubert*, as modified in *Kumho Tire Co.*, as the analytical framework for evaluating the reliability and admissibility of expert witness testimony.)
176. *McLemore*, 863 So. 2d at 36–37 (quoting *Daubert*, 509 U.S. at 595, 113 S. Ct. 2786).
177. Hill *ex rel.* Hill v. Koppers, 2009 WL 4908836, at *7 (N.D. Miss. Dec. 11, 2009) (the plaintiff carries burden to show general causation and specific causation); Watts v. Radiator Specialty Co., 990 So. 2d 143, 146 (Miss. 2008) (testimony that "benzene causes non-Hodgkin's lymphoma" addresses "general causation," whereas testimony that "benzene-containing Liquid Wrench caused Mr. Watt's non-Hodgkin's lymphoma" addresses "specific causation.")
178. *Hill*, 2009 WL 4908836, at * 8.
179. *See Lohrmann*, 782 F.2d at 1163.
180. *See* Gorman-Rupp Co. v. Hall, 908 So. 2d 749, 755–57 (Miss. 2005); *Monsanto*, 912 So. 2d at 137.
181. 968 So. 2d 410 (Miss. 2007).
182. *Id.* at 418–19.
183. Sherwin-Williams Co. v. Gaines, 75 So. 3d 41, 45–46 (Miss. 2011); Watts, 990 So. 2d at 147 n.9.

For example, in *Franklin Corp. v. Tedford*,[184] the plaintiffs alleged that they had suffered injury from exposure to a relatively unstudied neurotoxin while at work, and the Mississippi Supreme Court upheld the trial court's admission of four expert witnesses who testified as to the effect the toxin had on the plaintiffs. On appeal, the defendants argued that the trial court had erred in allowing the expert testimony because "[n]one knew of the [neurotoxin] exposure level at which injury occurs in humans," and "[n]one knew of the exposure experienced by the . . . [p]laintiffs."[185] However, the court did have data that exposures to at least some workers exceeded the recommended limits set forth in the MSDSs.[186] In its review, the court noted that the impact of the specific toxin at issue on humans was a new field of study, and that ethical constraints have limited scientists' studies on the exact lower level of exposure that caused neurologic injury. In this instance, the court found that "the absence of data on the exact exposure level at which humans suffer neurologic injury ought not preclude the Plaintiffs' experts from testifying. . . ."[187]

North Carolina
Overall Standard for Causation
Under the common law of North Carolina, the essential elements of a claim of negligence are duty, breach of duty, proximate cause, and damages.[188]

North Carolina courts have defined proximate cause as:

> that cause, unbroken by any new or independent cause, which produces the result in continuous sequence and without which it would not have occurred, and one from which any man of ordinary prudence could have foreseen that such a result was probable under all of the facts then existing. Foreseeability is thus a requisite of proximate cause, which is, in turn, a requisite for actionable negligence.[189]

Where the exact nature and probable genesis of a particular injury involves complicated medical questions far removed from the ordinary experience and knowledge of laypersons, only an expert can give competent opinion evidence as to the cause of the injury.[190] Where medical opinion testimony is required, "medical certainty is not required, [but] an expert's 'speculation' is insufficient to establish causation."[191] Furthermore, the causal

---
184. 18 So. 3d 215, 238 (Miss. 2009).
185. *Id.* at 237.
186. *Id.* at 223.
187. *Id.* at 237.
188. Cameron v. Merisel Props., 187 N.C. App. 40, 44, 652 S.E.2d 660, 664 (N.C. Ct. App. 2007).
189. Clodfelter v. Leonard, 630 S.E.2d 742 (N.C. Ct. App. 2006) (quoting Williams v. Smith, 68 N.C. App. 71, 73, *cert. denied*, 311 N.C. 769, 321 S.E.2d 158 (1984)).
190. Peagler v. Tyson Foods, Inc., 532 S.E.2d 207, 211 (N.C. Ct. App. 2000) (quoting Click v. Pilot Freight Carriers, 265 S.E.2d 389 (1980)).
191. Holley v. ACTS, Inc., 581 S.E.2d 750, 754 (N.C. 2003).

relationship must be established by evidence "such as to take the case out of the realm of conjecture and remote possibility."[192]

In North Carolina, trial courts must decide preliminary questions concerning the qualifications of experts to testify and the admissibility of expert testimony.[193] Trial courts are afforded "wide latitude of discretion when making a determination about the admissibility of expert testimony."[194]

Although North Carolina has not adopted the standard articulated by the U.S. Supreme Court in *Daubert*,[195] its approach to determining the admissibility of expert testimony shares similarities with the *Daubert* standard.[196] This approach was defined by the North Carolina's Supreme Court in *State v. Goode*, where the court set out a three-part analysis for determining whether to permit expert testimony.[197]

The first step evaluates whether the reasoning or methodology underlying the testimony is sufficiently valid and whether that reasoning or methodology can be properly applied to the facts in issue.[198] To determine whether an expert's area of testimony is considered sufficiently reliable, "a court may look to testimony by an expert specifically relating to the reliability, may take judicial notice, or may use a combination of the two."[199] Initially, the trial court should look to precedent for guidance in determining whether the theoretical or technical methodology underlying an expert's opinion is reliable.[200] Although North Carolina does not exclusively adhere to the *Frye* "general acceptance" test,[201] when specific precedent justifies recognition of an established scientific theory or technique advanced by an expert, the trial court should favor its admissibility, provided the other requirements of admissibility are likewise satisfied.[202] Where, however, the trial court is without precedential guidance or faced with novel scientific theories, unestablished techniques, or compelling new perspectives on otherwise settled theories or techniques, the trial court should generally focus on the following nonexclusive "indices of reliability" to determine whether the expert's proffered scientific or technical method of proof is sufficiently reliable, including

---

192. *Id.* at 753.
193. Howerton v. Arai Helmet, Ltd., 597 S.E.2d 674, 686 (N.C. 2004) (citing N.C.G.S. § 8C-1, Rule 104(a)).
194. Lane v. Am. Nat'l Can Co., 640 S.E.2d 732, 735 (N.C. Ct. App. 2007) (quoting State v. Bullard, 322 S.E.2d 370, 376 (N.C. 1984)).
195. 509 U.S. at 579.
196. *Howarton*, 597 S.E.2d at 689 (explaining that while North Carolina shares obvious similarities with the principles underlying *Daubert*, "application of the North Carolina approach is decidedly less mechanistic and rigorous than the 'exacting standards of reliability' demanded by the federal approach.").
197. 461 S.E.2d 631 (N.C. 1995).
198. *Id.* at 639 (citing Daubert v. Merrell Dow Pharms., Inc., 509 U.S. 579 (1993).
199. *Id.* at 641.
200. *Howarton*, 597 S.E.2d at 686–87.
201. *See* State v. Cardwell, 516 S.E.2d 388, 395 (N.C. Ct. App. 1999) (noting that "[t]he general acceptance of a particular method by the scientific community may be one indicator of its reliability; however, a lack of general acceptance is not dispositive.").
202. *Id.* (citations omitted).

(1) the expert's professional background; (2) independent research conducted by the expert; (3) the use of established techniques; and (4) explanatory testimony (including, for example, the "use of visual aids before the jury so that the jury is not asked 'to sacrifice its independence by accepting [the] scientific hypotheses on faith'").[203]

The second step determines whether the witness testifying at trial is qualified as an expert to apply this method to the specific facts of the case.[204] As the *Goode* court explained,

> It is not necessary that an expert be experienced with the identical subject matter at issue or be a specialist, licensed, or even engaged in a specific profession. It is enough that the expert witness "because of his expertise is in a better position to have an opinion on the subject than is the trier of fact."[205]

As the court later explained, the trial court must be satisfied that the expert possesses "scientific, technical or other specialized knowledge [that] will assist the trier of fact to understand the evidence or to determine a fact in issue."[206]

The third step asks whether the expert's testimony is relevant.[207] The court defined relevant evidence as evidence having "any tendency to make the existence of any fact that is of consequence to the determination of the action more probable or less probable than it would be without the evidence."[208] In judging relevance, the court stated that expert testimony is properly admissible when such testimony can assist the jury to draw certain inferences from facts because the expert is better qualified than the jury to draw such inferences.[209]

Once the trial court makes a preliminary determination that the scientific or technical area underlying a qualified expert's opinion is sufficiently reliable and relevant, any lingering questions or controversy concerning the quality of the expert's conclusions go to the weight of the testimony rather than its admissibility.[210]

General and Specific Causation

Federal courts in North Carolina draw a distinction between "general causation" and "specific causation."[211] General causation "is established by demonstrating . . . that exposure to

---

203. *Id.*
204. State v. Goode, 461 S.E.2d 631, 640 (citing N.C.G.S. § 8C-1, Rule 702).
205. *Id.* at 641 (citations and quotations omitted).
206. *Howarton*, 597 S.E.2d at 688 (citing N.C.G.S. § 8C-1, Rule 702(a); 2 KENNETH S. BROUN, BRANDIS & BROUN ON NORTH CAROLINA EVIDENCE § 184, at 44–45 (6th ed. 2004)).
207. *Goode*, 461 S.E.2d at 641.
208. *Id.* (citing N.C.G.S. § 8C-1, Rule 401).
209. *Id.*
210. *Howarton*, 597 S.E.2d at 688 (citations omitted).
211. Dunn v. Sandoz Pharms. Corp., 275 F. Supp. 2d 672, 676 (M.D.N.C. 2003) (citing REFERENCE MANUAL ON SCIENTIFIC EVIDENCE 444 (2d ed. 2000)).

a substance can cause a particular disease."[212] Specific, "or individual, causation, however is established by demonstrating that a given exposure is the cause" of a particular individual's disease.[213] If a plaintiff is not able to establish general causation, it is unnecessary to consider whether the plaintiff can establish specific causation.[214]

The requirement for claimants to show both "general causation" and "specific causation" is incorporated into North Carolina's Workers' Compensation Act, albeit using somewhat different terminology. Under the act, to prove that a claimant has contracted a compensable occupational disease, the claimant must establish both "increased risk" and "causation."[215] "Increased risk" is akin to "general causation" and is proved by showing: (1) that the disease is "characteristic of" and "peculiar to" individuals engaged in the claimant's particular trade or occupation; and (2) that their disease is not one to which the general public is equally amenable.[216] "A disease is 'characteristic' of a profession when there is a 'recognizable link' between the nature of the job and an increased risk of contracting the disease in question."[217] A disease is "peculiar to the occupation" when the conditions of the employment result in a hazard that distinguishes it in character from employment generally.[218] "Causation" in this context is analogous to "specific causation"; the claimant must show that his or her employment significantly contributed to, or was a significant causal factor in, the disease's development.[219] "Causation" may be demonstrated using circumstantial evidence that can include consideration of (1) the extent of claimant's exposure to the disease or disease-causing agents during employment, (2) the claimant's extent of exposure outside employment, and (3) the claimant's absence of the disease prior to his or her work-related exposure, as shown by the claimant's medical history.[220] In this specific context, a plaintiff is not required to prove that he was exposed to a specific quantity of toxic material or chemicals.[221]

In suits alleging harm from exposure to asbestos products in North Carolina, the North Carolina federal courts apply the "frequency-regularity-proximity" test first announced in

---

212. *Id.* (citations omitted).
213. *Id.* (citations omitted).
214. *Id.*
215. *See* Rutledge v. Tultex Corp., 301 S.E.2d 359 (N.C. 1983).
216. Booker v. Duke Med. Ctr., 256 S.E.2d 189, 196 (N.C. 1979).
217. *Id.* at 198.
218. *Id.* at 199.
219. Hardin v. Motor Panels, Inc., 524 S.E.2d 368, 371 (N.C. Ct. App. 2000).
220. *Booker*, 256 S.E.2d at 200. *But see* Young v. Hickory Bus. Furniture, 538 S.E.2d 912, 916 (N.C. 2000) (holding in a case where the threshold question was the cause of a controversial medical condition, evidence that a disease did not exist before an event or exposure, but did exist afterward was not competent evidence of causation).
221. *See* Keel v. H&V Inc., 421 S.E.2d 362, 366 (N.C. Ct. App. 1992) (noting that "[o]ur Supreme Court rejected the requirement that an employee quantify the degree of exposure to the harmful agent during his employment") (citing McCuiston v. Addressograph-Multigraph Corp., 303 S.E.2d 795, 797 (N.C. 1983)).

Lohrmann v. Pittsburgh Corning Corp.[222] This test requires that an asbestos plaintiff must prove more than casual or minimal contact with the defendant's product, and instead must present "evidence of exposure to a specific product [of the defendant] on a regular basis over some extended period of time in proximity to where the plaintiff actually worked."[223]

South Carolina
Overall Standard for Causation

South Carolina requires both cause-in-fact and legal cause to establish causation.[224] Cause-in-fact is proved by establishing that the injury would not have occurred "but for" the defendant's negligence.[225] Legal cause is proved by establishing foreseeability.[226]

"Foreseeability of some injury from an act or omission is a prerequisite to its being a proximate cause of the injury for which recovery is sought."[227] Foreseeability is determined by looking to the natural and probable consequences of the complained act.[228] Foreseeability is judged from the perspective of the defendant at the time of the negligent act, not after the injury has occurred.[229]

South Carolina applies a "substantial factor" test to determine proximate cause, and a defendant may be liable for anything that appears to have been a probable consequence of his negligence. "If the actor's conduct is a substantial factor in the harm to another, the fact that he neither foresaw nor should have foreseen the *extent* of harm or the *manner* in which it occurred does not negative [sic] his liability."[230] Negligence is deemed a "substantial factor" where the defendant's negligence is a concurring or a contributing proximate cause of the injury. "[C]oncurring causes operate contemporaneously to produce the injury, so that it would not have happened in the absence of either."[231] In determining whether asbestos exposure is actionable, South Carolina courts adopt the frequency, regularity, and proximity test set forth in *Lohrmann*.[232]

---

222. 782 F.2d 1156 (4th Cir. 1986). For examples of North Carolina federal court cases applying this standard, *see* Agner v. Daniel Int'l Corp., 2007 WL 57769 (W.D.N.C. Jan. 5, 2007), and Mills v. AC&S, Inc., 2005 WL 2989639 (W.D.N.C. Nov. 7, 2005).
223. *Lohrmann*, 782 F.2d at 1162–63.
224. Oliver v. South Carolina Dep't of Highways & Pub. Transp., 422 S.E.2d 128, 130–31 (S.C. 1992).
225. *Id.* at 131; *see also* Whitlaw v. Kroger Co., 410 S.E.2d 251, 253 (S.C. 1991) ("Causation in fact is proved by establishing the injury would not have occurred 'but for' the defendant's negligence"); Bramlette v. Charter Medical-Columbia, 393 S.E.2d 914, 916 (S.C. 1990).
226. *Bramlette*, S.E.2d at 916.
227. Young v. Tide Craft, Inc., 242 S.E.2d 671, 675 (S.C. 1978) (quoting Kennedy v. Carter, 249 S.C. 168 (1967)).
228. *Id.* (internal quotations omitted).
229. Crolley v. Hutchins, 387 S.E.2d 716, 717 (S.C. Ct. App. 1989).
230. *See* Childers v. Gas Lines, Inc., 149 S.E.2d 761, 765 (S.C. 1966) (emphasis added).
231. Baggerly v. CSX Transp., Inc., 635 S.E.2d 97, 101 (S.C. 2006) (quoting Player v. Thompson, 193 S.E.2d 531, 534 (S.C. 1972)).
232. Henderson v. Allied Signal, Inc., 644 S.E.2d 724, 727 (S.C. 2007); *see* Lohrmann v. Pittsburgh Corning Corp., 782 F.2d 1156, 1162 (4th Cir. 1986).

South Carolina determines the admissibility of scientific evidence pursuant to South Carolina Rule of Evidence Rule 702, which is identical to its federal counterpart.[233] To admit scientific evidence, a trial court must find: (1) the evidence will assist the trier of fact; (2) the expert witness is qualified; and (3) the underlying science is reliable.[234]

The South Carolina Supreme Court has not adopted the standard announced in *Daubert* to determine reliability, but trial courts are instructed to consider, *inter alia*, (1) the publications and peer review of the technique; (2) prior application of the method to the type of evidence involved in the case; (3) quality control procedures used to ensure reliability; and (4) the consistency of the method with recognized scientific laws and procedures.[235]

If a claimant attempts to establish the cause of a medically complex condition, expert medical testimony is required.[236] In *Armstrong v. Weiland*,[237] the Supreme Court of South Carolina succinctly stated the standard for expert testimony:

> When the testimony of an expert witness is not relied upon to establish proximate cause, it is sufficient for plaintiff to put forth some evidence that rises above mere speculation or conjecture; however, when the opinions of medical experts are relied upon to establish causal connection of negligence to injury, the proper test to be applied is that the expert must, with reasonable certainty, state that in his professional opinion the injuries complained of most probably resulted from the alleged negligence of the defendant.[238]

General and Specific Causation

Very little case law addressing the standards for causation in toxic tort cases exist in South Carolina state court. Pre-*Daubert* opinions make clear that it is not necessary that the expert actually use the words "most probably," but only that he show, in his professional opinion, that the defendant's negligence is the most likely cause of injury among the possible causes.[239] Expert testimony that concludes only that there was a "possibility" or "considerable evidence" that the defendant caused the harm is insufficient.[240] Further, in asbestos cases South Carolina has expressly adopted the *Lohrmann* "frequency, regularity and proximity test."[241]

The Fourth Circuit, applying *Daubert*, found that a differential diagnosis, in the absence of epidemiology to support opinions on general causation, was adequately reliable to

---

233. State v. Council, 515 S.E.2d 508, 518 (S.C. 1999).
234. Id.
235. Id. at 517–18.
236. Smith v. Michelin Tire Corp., 465 S.E.2d 96, 97 (S.C. Ct. App. 1995), *reh'g and cert. denied* (1996).
237. 225 S.E.2d 851 (S.C. 1976).
238. Armstrong v. Weiland, 225 S.E.2d 851, 853 (S.C. 1976).
239. Baughman v. Am. Tel. & Tel. Co., 410 S.E.2d 537, 543 (S.C. 1991).
240. Id. at 544.
241. Henderson, 644 S.E.2d at 727.

support the element of proximate cause.[242] In *Westberry v. Gislaved*, the plaintiff claimed that his employer was liable for damages suffered as a result of the company's failure to warn him of the dangers of a talcum powder lubricant used for the manufacture of gaskets. The plaintiff claimed the lubricant caused aggravation of his preexisting sinus problems requiring hospitalization. The defendant complained that the expert's causation testimony was inadmissible because the claim of causation was not supported by epidemiological studies, peer-reviewed publications, lab samples, animal data, or tissue samples, but instead relied only on a differential diagnosis supported by a temporal relationship between exposure and symptoms. On general causation, the court noted that "while precise information concerning the exposure necessary to cause specific harm to humans and exact details pertaining to the plaintiff's exposure are beneficial, such evidence is not always available, or necessary, to demonstrate that a substance is toxic to humans."[243] Citing a talc material safety data sheet, the court noted that it was undisputed that talc irritates the mucous membranes. Further, although the plaintiff lacked specific dose information, the court suggested that enough evidence indicated that the exposure was significant. The court acknowledged that while a temporal association can be coincidental, a strong temporal relationship still could be compelling evidence of causation "depending on the circumstances."[244] Citing cases from the Second, Third, Ninth, and D.C. Circuits, the court held that "a reliable differential diagnosis provides a valid foundation for an expert opinion" and affirmed judgment for the plaintiff.[245]

Tennessee
Overall Standard for Causation

Tennessee requires both cause-in-fact and proximate cause (often called legal cause), the latter being the "'ultimate issue' in negligence cases."[246] "Causation and proximate cause are distinct elements of negligence, and both must be proven by the plaintiff by a preponderance of the evidence."[247]

---

242. Westberry v. Gislaved Gummi AB, 178 F.3d 257, 262 (4th Cir. 1999).
243. *Id.* at 259, 262, 264.
244. *Id.* at 263–65.
245. *Id.* at 263 (citing Heller v. Shaw Indus., Inc., 167 F.3d at 154, 156–57 (3d Cir. 1999) (concluding that a proper differential diagnosis is adequate to support expert medical opinion on causation); Kennedy v. Collagen Corp., 161 F.3d 1226, 1228–30 (9th Cir. 1998) (holding district court abused its discretion in excluding an expert opinion on causation based upon a reliable differential diagnosis), *cert. denied*, 67 U.S.L.W. 3570 (U.S. May 3, 1999) (No. 98-1424); Baker, 156 F.3d at 252–53 (determining that a differential diagnosis rendered expert opinion on causation sufficiently reliable for admission); Zuchowicz v. United States, 140 F.3d 381, 385–87 (2d Cir. 1998) (upholding determination that expert opinion was reliable in part based on differential diagnosis); and Ambrosini v. Labarraque, 322 U.S. App. D.C. 19, 101 F.3d 129, 140–41 (D.C. Cir. 1996) (holding that because expert opinion was based on differential diagnosis, district court abused its discretion in refusing to admit it).
246. McClenahan v. Cooley, 806 S.W.2d 767, 774 (Tenn. 1991).
247. Kilpatrick v. Bryant, 868 S.W.2d 594, 598 (Tenn. 1993).

Cause-in-fact means that the injury or harm would not have occurred "but for" the defendant's negligent conduct.[248] In *McClenahan v. Cooley*, the court set forth a three-part test for proximate cause: (1) the tortfeasor's conduct must be a "substantial factor" in bringing about the alleged harm;[249] (2) no rule or policy exists that would relieve the tortfeasor of liability; and (3) the harm giving rise to the action could be reasonably foreseen by a person of ordinary intelligence or prudence.[250]

Although the Tennessee Supreme Court has not expressly adopted the *Daubert* standard in determining the reliability of scientific evidence, it has held that Tennessee Rules of Evidence 702 and 703 supersede the *Frye* test and explained that the *Daubert* test is useful to the analysis of admitting expert testimony.[251] In fact, the court determined that Tennessee Rules of Evidence 702 and 703 actually require that the probative force of the proffered expert testimony must be stronger in Tennessee state courts than in federal courts. For instance, Tennessee Rule of Evidence 702 requires that expert testimony "substantially assist" the trier when its federal counterpart omits the word "substantially," so that it need only "assist" the trier of fact. Tennessee Rule of Evidence 703 requires the trial court to examine whether the underlying facts or data lack trustworthiness, and no similar language exists in the federal rule. The Supreme Court of Tennessee in *McDaniel v. CSX Transportation, Inc.* clarified that the standards for determining the admissibility of scientific evidence in Tennessee state courts are consistent with the *Daubert* factors. More specifically, under the *McDaniel* factors a trial court may consider:

> (1) whether scientific evidence has been tested and the methodology with which it has been tested; (2) whether the evidence has been subjected to peer review or publication; (3) whether a potential rate of error is known; (4) whether, as formally required by *Frye*, the evidence is generally accepted in the scientific community; and (5) whether the expert's research in the field has been conducted independent of litigation.[252]

In *McDaniel*, the Supreme Court of Tennessee examined the admissibility of occupational physician testimony that chronic low-level exposure to four particular organic solvents—trichloroethane, trichloroethylene, perchloroethylene, and mineral spirits—caused a form of brain damage known as toxic encephalopathy.[253] The plaintiff's experts' testimony was founded upon epidemiological studies and a differential diagnosis because "[t]he experts

---

248. *Id.*
249. It seems as though the court is actually referring to cause-in-fact in the first prong, which would put its line of reasoning at odds with the decision in *Kilpatrick*, which favored the "but for" test in determining cause-in-fact. Considering the court has recently cited *McClenahan* with approval, it may be unclear which rule the Tennessee Supreme Court follows.
250. *McClenahan*, 806 S.W.2d at 776.
251. McDaniel v. CSX Transp., Inc., 955 S.W.2d 257, 265 (Tenn. 1997), *cert. denied*, 524 U.S. 915 (1998).
252. *Id.*
253. *Id.* at 257–59.

agreed that there is no objective diagnostic tool, (such as an MRI, CT Scan, or X-Ray), that will support a diagnosis...."[254] The defendants objected to the admissibility of the experts' testimony because the epidemiological studies upon which the opinions were based failed to find that exposure to the solvents more than doubled the risk of the alleged illness. Further, the studies lacked dose-response information and failed to control for confounding factors. The defendants provided expert testimony that the medical community had not generally accepted the conclusion that low-dose solvent exposure caused encephalopathy. Finally, the defendants identified epidemiological studies that did not support the plaintiff's experts conclusions, arguing that the epidemiological studies relied upon by the plaintiff's experts were inconsistent. The *McDaniel* court examined the criticisms of the epidemiological studies and found that a diagnosis of solvent-induced encephalopathy was recognized by textbooks, journals, and national and world health organizations. The court declined to hold that, as a matter of law, an epidemiological study must show a relative risk or odds ratio greater than 2.0, instead holding that the strength of the risk was relevant and could be the subject of cross-examination. The court considered that the studies were conducted independent of litigation, peer-reviewed, published in leading journals, and stated that the trial court "should allow the jury to consider legitimate but conflicting views about the scientific proof."[255]

More recently, in *Brown v. Crown Equipment Corp.*,[256] the Supreme Court of Tennessee confirmed that the trial court should also consider two additional factors: (1) the expert's qualifications, and (2) the connection between those qualifications and the basis for the expert's opinion.[257] The court warned that focusing on qualifications alone would be inappropriate, however, as to do so would suggest that the mere ipse dixit of an expert is admissible when it is not.[258] The court may consider whether the opinion testimony is offered by "'the marginally-qualified full-time expert witness who is testifying about a methodology that she has not employed in real life' and 'the highly credentialed expert who has devoted her life's work to the actual exercise of the methodology upon which her testimony is based.'"[259] Finally, the court instructed that a trial court should consider the connection between the expert's knowledge and the basis for the expert's opinion to ensure that an "analytical gap" does not exist between the data relied upon and the opinion being rendered.[260] The trial court has great latitude in assessing the reliability of expert testimony. "The reasonableness of the *McDaniel* factors in assessing reliability

---

254. *Id.* at 259.
255. *Id.* at 255–66.
256. 181 S.W.3d 268 (Tenn. 2005) (discussing *McDaniel* factors in examining reliability of engineering testimony).
257. Brown v. Crown Equip. Corp., 181 S.W.3d 268, 274–75 (Tenn. 2005).
258. *Id.* at 274.
259. *Id.* (quoting Sarah Brew, *Where the Rubber Hits the Road: Steering the Trial Court through a Post-Kumho Tire Evaluation of Expert Testimony*, 27 Wm. Mitchell L. Rev. 467, 486 (2000)).
260. *Id.* at 275.

depends upon the nature of the issue, the witness's particular expertise, and the subject of the expert's testimony."[261]

Texas
Overall Standard for Causation

Under Texas law, causation in a toxic tort case must be supported by expert testimony.[262] "When an expert's opinion is based on assumed facts that vary materially from the actual, undisputed facts, the opinion is without probative value and cannot support a verdict or judgment."[263]

In *E.I. du Pont de Nemours & Co. v. Robinson*,[264] the Texas Supreme Court adopted the four *Daubert* factors[265] for reliability of expert testimony and endorsed two more: (1) the extent to which the technique relies upon the subjective interpretation of the expert; and (2) the nonjudicial uses that have been made of the theory or technique. It further clarified that causation has both a general and specific element.

In *Merrill Dow Pharmaceuticals, Inc. v. Havner*,[266] the Texas Supreme Court further clarified that epidemiological studies must meet certain baseline criteria to form a basis of an admissible expert opinion on causation. Testimony that relies upon epidemiology failing to meet the criteria set forth in *Havner* is not competent.[267] Moreover, testimony based on science that does not meet *Havner*'s criteria constitutes no evidence of causation as a matter of Texas law.[268] Testimony that constitutes no evidence is irrelevant, and should not be admitted.[269]

General Causation

To establish general causation, the plaintiff must show that exposure to the substance at issue can cause the alleged injury in the general population, and as support, the plaintiff

---

261. *Id.* (citing State v. Stevens, 78 S.W.3d 817, 833 (Tenn. 2002), and Kumho Tire Co. v. Carmichael, 526 U.S. 137, 150 (1999)).
262. Burroughs Wellcome Co. v. Crye, 907 S.W.2d 497, 499 (Tex. 1995) (finding expert testimony necessary to establish a claim that exposure to medicinal spray caused a frostbite injury); *see also* Coastal Tankships, U.S.A., Inc. v. Anderson, 87 S.W.3d 591, 603 (Tex. App.—Houston [1st Dist.] 2002), *rev. denied* (stating that expert testimony required in toxic exposure case where "general experience and common sense simply do not enable a fair understanding of causation").
263. *Id.* at 499–500.
264. 923 S.W.2d 549, 556–57 (Tex. 1995).
265. The four *Daubert* factors include (1) whether theory or technique can be tested, (2) whether it has been subjected to peer review and publication, (3) the known potential rate of error, and (4) whether the theory or technique has attained general acceptance in the scientific community.
266. 953 S.W.2d 706, 715–17 (Tex. 1997).
267. *See* City of San Antonio v. Pollock, 284 S.W.3d 809, 816 (Tex. 2009) (citing Coastal Transp. Co. v. Crown Cent. Petroleum Corp., 136 S.W.3d 227, 232 (Tex. 2004)) (explaining that opinion testimony lacking a sufficient basis is incompetent).
268. *See id.* at 820.
269. *See* TEX. R. EVID. 702; *see also* Wells v. Smithkline Beecham Corp., 601 F.3d 375, 380 (5th Cir. 2010) (addressing interplay between reliability and admissibility).

may offer properly designed and executed epidemiological studies.[270] Such studies must show that exposure to the substances at issue result in at least a doubling of the relative risk of the alleged injury at issue. In other words, the studies must show that the incidence of an injury or condition in the exposed population was more than double the incidence in the unexposed or control population.[271]

Additionally, under *Havner*, the doubling of the relative risk must be statistically significant.[272] If the confidence interval includes a relative risk of 1.0, the study is not statistically significant or, said another way, is inconclusive. This is because the confidence interval includes relative risk values that are both less than and greater than the null hypothesis (1.0), leaving the researcher with results that suggest that there may be an association, or that there may not be an association. Under *Havner*, the confidence level must be 95%, meaning that if the study was repeated numerous times, the confidence interval would indicate the range of relative risk values that would result 95% of the time.[273] Arguments that the *Havner* requirements of a statistically significant doubling of the risk may not be necessary if the expert can point to multiple studies showing an increase, but not doubling, of the risk, have been rejected, even when arguments suggest that these studies must be viewed in light of the "totality of the evidence."[274] Instead, the totality of the evidence is examined only after a plaintiff passes the primary reliability inquiry required by *Havner*.[275]

Isolated case reports, random experience, and reports lacking the details to permit scientific evaluation cannot be considered as supporting evidence.[276] A single, properly designed and executed study finding a statistically significant doubling of the risk is, without replication, no evidence of causation.[277]

Finally, even if the plaintiff is able to produce statistically significant studies showing a doubling of the risk of a particular outcome, "that association does not equate to causation."[278] By way of example, the court in *Havner* repeated, "there is a demonstrable association between summertime and death by drowning, but summertime does not cause drowning."[279]

---

270. *See Havner*, 953 S.W.2d at 715, 719.
271. *Id.* at 716–22; *see also* Bic Pen Corp. v. Carter, 346 S.W.3d 533 (Tex. 2011) (explaining basis for requiring a doubling of the risk requirement).
272. *Havner*, 953 S.W.2d at 723.
273. *Id.*; *see also* Brock v. Merrell Dow Pharm., Inc., 874 F.2d 307, 312 (5th Cir. 1989) (discussing relative risk and confidence level in pre-*Daubert* decision that found no sufficient evidence that Bendectin caused birth defects), *as modified by* 884 F.2d 166, 167 (5th Cir. 1989).
274. Merck & Co., Inc. v. Garza, 347 S.W.3d 256, 265–66 (Tex. 2011).
275. *Id.* at 266.
276. *Havner*, 953 S.W.2d at 720 (citing 21 C.F.R. § 314.126(e)).
277. *Id.* at 727.
278. *Id.* at 724.
279. *Id.* at 724.

Specific Causation

Specific causation questions whether a substance has caused a particular individual's injury or condition.[280] A defendant is entitled to know, through discovery, if a medical determination has been made on whether a specific chemical or substance caused the plaintiff's alleged injury.[281]

A plaintiff must do more than show a substantially elevated risk between exposure and injury.[282] To satisfy specific causation, the plaintiff must also show that he or she is similar to the individuals constituting the exposed population in the studies. This similarity includes proof that the injured person (1) was exposed to the *same substance* as those in the studies; (2) received comparable or higher *dose levels* to those in the studies; and (3) had *temporally consistent* onsets of injury after exposure. Finally, the plaintiff must rule out other plausible causes of the alleged injury or condition, and must do so with reasonable certainty.[283] Without proof of these various elements, the plaintiff's claim fails for lack of specific causation.[284]

In order to support a specific causation claim, Texas also requires a plaintiff to establish defendant-specific evidence of the dose received. Although often advanced in asbestos cases, Texas courts do not assume that causative dose has been received if the plaintiff spent time in proximity to a particular product or substance with frequency and regularity, often called the "frequency, regularity, and proximity test."[285] While the Texas Supreme Court agreed with *Lohrmann* that a "frequency, regularity, and proximity" test can be *part* of an exposure analysis, it held that such a test was insufficient evidence of dose necessary to support the element of causation. Instead, defendant-specific evidence relating to the approximate dose to which the plaintiff was exposed, coupled with evidence that the dose was a substantial factor in causing the asbestos-related disease, is necessary.[286] In products cases, therefore, the plaintiff must establish that a dose received from the defendant's particular product was a substantial factor in bringing about the injury.[287]

Finally, even if a defendant-specific dose is established, the plaintiff must establish that the dose of the defendant-specific product was a "producing cause" of the injury. That is, the plaintiff must establish the essential elements of producing cause: (1) the conduct/product must be a substantial factor in bringing about the injury at issue, and (2) "but

---

280. *Id.* at 714.
281. See *In re* Allied Chem. Corp., 227 S.W.3d 652, 656 (Tex. 2007); *In re* Van Waters & Rogers, Inc., 62 S.W.3d 197, 200 (Tex. 2001) (citing Able Supply v. Moye, 898 S.W.2d 766, 770 (Tex. 1995), *In re* Colonial Pipeline, 968 S.W.2d 938, 942 (Tex. 1998)).
282. *Havner*, 953 S.W.3d at 720.
283. *Id.*
284. See *Pollock*, 284 S.W.3d at 819–20.
285. *Compare Lohrmann*, 782 F.2d 1156, *with* Borg-Warner v. Flores, 232 S.W.3d 765 (Tex. 2007).
286. *Borg-Warner*, 232 S.W.3d at 769–70.
287. *Id.* at 7734.

for" exposure to the defendant's product (or on the defendant's premises or worksite), the alleged injury at issue would not have occurred.[288]

Virginia
Overall Standard for Causation

Establishing causation in a Virginia tort suit requires proving both cause-in-fact and proximate causation, although both are simply referred to by Virginia courts as "proximate cause."[289] Proximate cause is the action "without which that event would not have occurred," and is typically proven by a "but for" test—but for the alleged defect, the injury would not have occurred.[290] While the cause does not have to be the only or most significant factor involved in the injury, the plaintiff has the burden to prove by preponderance of the evidence the exposure caused the harm,[291] because "the law of products liability in Virginia does not permit recovery where responsibility is conjectural."[292]

Proximate cause requires the ultimate harm be foreseeable.[293] Although the issue of proximate causation is typically determined by a jury, a Virginia judge may determine whether proximate cause existed if reasonable minds could not differ under the facts.[294]

Although tort cases in Virginia are not required to prove causation by expert testimony, the complexity of causation in many toxic tort suits often makes experts necessary.[295] Virginia has neither adopted nor rejected the *Daubert* test for admissibility of expert witness testimony; however, some Virginia courts have found *Daubert* instructive.[296] The Virginia

---

288. Ford Motor Co. v. Ledesma, 242 S.W.3d 32, 46 (Tex. 2007).
289. See Banks v. City of Richmond, 348 S.E.2d 280, 282–83 (Va. 1986) (examining the various definitions of proximate cause in Virginia courts); Wells v. Whitaker, 151 S.E.2d 422, 429 (Va. 1966) (finding proximate cause encompasses cause-in-fact stating "the element of proximate cause under consideration in the instant case is the initial one of causation in fact").
290. Banks, 348 S.E.2d at 282–83; see Wells, 151 S.E.2d at 429 (finding manufacturer not liable for effects when negligence was not the "but for" cause of the injury).
291. See Sanders v. UDR, Inc., No. 3:10-CV-459, 2011 WL 2669977, at *11 (E.D. Va. June 30, 2011) (diversity case where court rejected causation argument because the plaintiff failed to rule out the injury might have resulted from exposure to mold *outside* the plaintiff's home); Sneed v. Sneed, 244 S.E.2d 754, 755 (Va. 1978) ("The plaintiff must show why and how the accident happened. And if the cause of the accident is left to conjecture, guess, or random judgment, the plaintiff cannot recover.").
292. Stokes v. L. Geismar, S.A., 815 F. Supp. 904, 908 (E.D. Va. 1993).
293. See Jappell v. Am. Ass'n of Blood Banks, 162 F. Supp. 2d 476, 483 (E.D. Va. 2001) (applying Virginia substantive law and finding reasonable minds could differ on the establishment of proximate cause when patients contracting AIDS from contaminated blood was clearly foreseeable, but there was no direct evidence that screening would have excluded all infected samples).
294. Id. at 483.
295. See McCauley v. Purdue Pharma L.P., 331 F. Supp. 2d 449, 464 (W.D. Va. 2004) (commenting the conflicting factors of pain, dependence, substance abuse, and tolerance required medical professionals to testify on the overlap of these issues in product liability suit against drug manufacturers).
296. See, e.g., John v. Im, 559 S.E.2d 694, 697–98 n.3 (Va. 2002) (avoiding deciding whether to adopt *Daubert*, but commenting "[p]rior to *Daubert*, . . . we discussed the trial court's role in making a threshold finding of scientific reliability when unfamiliar scientific evidence is offered"); Hasson v. Com., No. 0403-05-4, 2006 WL 1387974, at *9 (Va. Ct. App. May 23, 2006) (acknowledging that while *Daubert* is not dispositive in Virginia courts, its guidance on scientific reliability is helpful to admissibility analysis); Com. v. Isse, 80 Va. Cir. 493 (2010) (evaluating the *Daubert* standard in light of the case's facts).

standard for admissibility of expert opinions only rejects "inherently unreliable" testimony, setting a slightly lower threshold than *Daubert*, by which courts may only admit testimony verified by reliable principles and methods.[297]

In the context of workers' compensation laws, toxic tort cases must rise to the level of "injurious exposure," which means "reasonably calculated to bring on the disease in question."[298] The statute relieves some of the burden on the plaintiffs to establish specific causation when direct linkage is difficult, allowing proof of causation by showing "aggravation of the disease or . . . that the exposure was of such duration and intensity that it generally causes the disease in question."[299] The Supreme Court of Virginia found a plaintiff suffered injurious exposure in *Caudle-Hyatt, Inc. v. Mixon*, when the plaintiff's expert testified that asbestos exposure for only one month could cause mesothelioma, and that the plaintiff was exposed to asbestos for four months.[300]

General Causation

A Virginia federal court applying state law described general causation as "whether X *can* cause Y."[301] While the potential for a toxin to produce certain injuries must be established, general causation has not been addressed in detail by Virginia state courts.[302] However, discussion by Virginia federal courts in toxic tort cases provides guidance for evidentiary standards of general causation.[303]

Specific Causation7

Specific causation considers whether "X *did* cause Y in a given case."[304] Specific causation is provable if more than one potential intervening cause exists; however, to recover damages a plaintiff must directly attribute the injury to the toxin at issue,[305] as indicated in *McCauley v. Purdue Pharma L.P.*:

---

297. *See* Commonwealth v. Isse, 80 Va. Cir. 493 (comparing *Daubert*, which requires testimony to be the product of reliable principles, with Virginia law excluding only "inherently unreliable" testimony).
298. VA. CODE ANN. § 65.2-404.
299. Caudle-Hyatt, Inc. v. Mixon, 260 S.E.2d 193, 196 (Va. 1979).
300. *Id.*
301. Sanders, 2011 WL 2669977, at *10.
302. *But see Caudle-Hyatt, Inc.*, 260 S.E.2d at 196 (requiring plaintiff to prove that a short period of exposure could cause the illness under workers' compensation law, although failing to discuss specific requirements of general causation).
303. *See, e.g.*, Benedi v. McNeil-P.P.C., Inc., 66 F.3d 1378, 1384 (4th Cir. 1995) (finding epidemiological studies not required to prove that acetaminophen caused liver damage because *Daubert* only requires methodology be reliable); Ellis v. Int'l Playtex, Inc., 745 F.2d 292, 302–04 (4th Cir. 1984) (admitting epidemiological study establishing the link between Toxic Shock Syndrome and menstruation to the jury); *Jappell*, 162 F. Supp. 2d at 483–84 (allowing the plaintiff to present an expert to establish failure to test donated blood for HIV causes patients to contract the virus).
304. Sanders, 2011 WL 2669977, at *10.
305. *See* Roche v. Lincoln Prop. Co., 278 F. Supp. 2d 744, 750–51 (E.D. Va. 2003) (applying Virginia state law and holding expert did not establish causation because he failed to distinguish between mold and other common allergens).

When there is substantial evidence introduced which tends to prove that plaintiff's injuries may have resulted from one of two causes, for one of which the defendant is responsible and for the other of which he is not responsible, . . . the plaintiff must fail if his evidence does not prove that his damages were produced by the negligence of the defendant; and he must also fail if it appears from the evidence just as probable that damages were caused by one as by the other because the plaintiff must make out his case by a preponderance of the evidence.[306]

A plaintiff must establish a direct causal link between the toxin and his injuries, which includes identifying the amount and length of exposure.[307] Under Virginia law, exposure to a toxin can be established by circumstantial evidence, as stated in the asbestos litigation case *Owens-Corning Fiberglas Corp. v. Watson*:

Although the fact-finder is not authorized to indulge in speculation or guesswork, this does not destroy the weight of circumstantial evidence in fixing civil liability. "Proof of facts from which it can be reasonably inferred that an act or circumstance sought to be established occurred or existed is sufficient to authorize submission of the issue to the jury." But such circumstantial evidence must be sufficient to establish that the result alleged is a probability rather than a mere possibility.[308]

However, "[w]hen a verdict is based on circumstantial evidence, 'all that is required is that a jury be satisfied with proof which leads to a conclusion with probable certainty where absolute logical certainty is impossible.'"[309] The court in *Owens-Corning* held that the following circumstantial evidence was sufficient to establish proximate cause between the manufacturer's product and the individual's death: (1) the death of plaintiff's deceased was caused by asbestos exposure, (2) very limited exposure can result in the development of mesothelioma, (3) the defendant was the predominant supplier of the type of asbestos product used by the plaintiff's deceased to the workplace at issue, and (4) the deceased handled asbestos products of the type supplied by the defendant during his employment.[310]

---

306. *McCauley*, 331 F. Supp. 2d at 463 (applying Virginia substantive law).
307. *See id.* at 465 (applying Virginia law, the court rejected the plaintiff's claims against manufactures of OxyContin for lack of causation since no link was established between the drug and the plaintiff's medical injuries).
308. Owens-Corning Fiberglas Corp. v. Watson, 413 S.E.2d 630, 639 (Va. 1992).
309. *Id.* at 639 (quoting Chase v. Breitt, 306 S.E.2d 877, 878 (Va. 1983)); *see also* Bussey v. E.S.C. Rests. Inc., 620 S.E.2d 764, 536 (Va. 2005) (holding even though the plaintiff did not prove the existence of staphylococcal bacteria in the plaintiff, the expert testimony regarding the laboratory testing that excluded other illnesses, the doctor's expertise in dealing with food poisoning, and the emphasis on the last meal eaten for diagnosis, was sufficient to establish the bacteria in the defendant's beef caused the plaintiff's injury).
310. *Owens-Corning Fiberglas Corp.*, 413 S.E.2d at 639.

West Virginia

Overall Standard for Causation

A plaintiff in toxic tort litigation must "establish by a preponderance of evidence (1) the presence of the injury-causing substance, (2) that he or she has been exposed to the substance, and (3) that the exposure has caused certain injuries."[311] To succeed in a tort claim, a plaintiff must establish the defendant's actions or products proximately caused the plaintiff's injury.[312] According to the West Virginia Supreme Court of Appeals, proximate causation is the "cause which in actual sequence, unbroken by any independent cause, produces the event and without which the event would not have occurred."[313]

In exposure cases, a plaintiff must clearly identify the actual cause of his injuries; the mere fact a plaintiff had the "opportunity" for exposure is insufficient.[314] If causation is challenged by summary judgment, "the plaintiff must identify evidence which amounts to a probability of causation, rather than a mere possibility of it, to guard against 'raw speculation' by the fact finder."[315] For instance, in toxic tort cases based on inadequate labeling, proximate cause is established by the plaintiff proving had the manufacturer used a different label the plaintiff's actions would not only be changed, but they would be changed in such a manner that the injury would not have occurred.[316]

Expert testimony is required in toxic tort cases to analyze and present the jury with the causal link necessary for proximate cause.[317] Therefore, the admissibility of an expert witness's statements is crucial for plaintiffs to establish a prima facie case.[318] West Virginia courts rejected the *Frye* test as a standard for admissibility of expert scientific testimony,

---

311. White v. Dow Chem. Co., No. 2:05-CV-00247, 2007 WL 6948824, at *2 (S.D.W. Va. Nov. 29, 2007) (applying West Virginia substantive law).
312. *See, e.g.,* Aikens v. Debow, 541 S.E.2d 576, 581 (W. Va. 2000) (requiring the plaintiff establish proximate cause in negligence suit); City Nat'l Bank of Charleston v. Wells, 384 S.E.2d 374, 382–84 (W. Va. 1989) (requiring the plaintiff establish proximate cause in breach of warranty suit); Morningstar v. Black & Decker Mfg. Co., 253 S.E.2d 666, 680 (W. Va. 1979) (requiring the plaintiff establish proximate cause in strict liability suit).
313. Johnson v. Mays, 447 S.E.2d 563, 568 (W. Va. 1994).
314. *See* Tolley v. ACF Indus. Inc., 575 S.E.2d 158, 168 (W. Va. 2002) (finding the plaintiff failed to prove causation when their expert could not identify the chemical that aggravated plaintiff's asthma by testifying the injury had "three potential causes"); White v. Dow Chem. Co., No. 2:05-CV-00247, 2007 WL 6948824, at *3 (S.D.W. Va. Nov. 29, 2007) (finding under West Virginia law, the lack of proof that the plaintiff was exposed to diesel fuel mixed with the defendant's herbicide products on a "particular day, on a particular job site," failed to show causation).
315. *White*, 2007 WL 6948824, at *5 (applying West Virginia substantive law).
316. *See* Meade v. Parsley, No. 2:09-CV-00388, 2010 WL 4909435, at *9–10 (S.D.W. Va. Nov. 24, 2010) (finding that the plaintiff failed to prove proximate causation because plaintiff testified that she did not read the label and the doctor stated he failed to review the warning).
317. *Id.* at *7 (finding the argument that the manufacturer's warning, which stated their product could cause the plaintiff's illness, did not satisfy the causation element, because medical testimony is generally required to prove a direct linkage between the plaintiff and the product).
318. *See* Tolley v. Carboline Co., 617 S.E.2d 508, 512 (W. Va. 2005) (holding that without evidence presented showing the plaintiff had the chemical from the defendant's paint in his blood "there is no basis from which a jury could begin to conclude that Mr. Tolley's breathing condition resulted from exposure to isocyanates.").

saying the standard "was inconsistent with the *liberal* thrust of the Federal and West Virginia Rules of Evidence."[319] In the early 1990s, West Virginia adopted the *Daubert* standard that requires a court to conduct a two-part analysis when considering expert testimony:

First, the circuit court must determine whether the expert's testimony reflects "scientific knowledge," whether the findings are derived by "scientific method," and whether the work product amounts to "good science." Second, the circuit court must ensure that the scientific testimony is "relevant to the task at hand."[320]

In West Virginia, an expert's opinion on causation must be stated in terms of "reasonable probability."[321] The West Virginia Supreme Court of Appeals has stated "the law is clear that a mere possibility of causation, and more specially, 'indeterminate expert testimony on causation that is based solely on possibility' . . . is not sufficient to allow a reasonable juror to find causation."[322]

General and Specific Causation

Although West Virginia courts have presently failed to discuss in detail standards for general and specific causation, federal district courts interpreting West Virginia state law acknowledge the plaintiff's duty to prove these two factors.[323] General causation is "whether a substance is capable of causing a particular injury or condition in the general population, while specific causation is whether a substance caused a particular individual's injury."[324]

General Causation

The plaintiffs must prove the toxin is capable of producing the alleged injury in the general population. It is a basic principle that causation evidence in toxic tort cases must be in the form of expert scientific testimony.[325] Thus, in West Virginia, general causation is "established by demonstrating, often through a review of scientific and medical literature, that exposure to a substance can cause a particular disease."[326] Further, an expert

---

319. Gentry v. Mangum, 466 S.E.2d 171, 179 (W. Va. 1995).
320. *Id.* at 182.
321. Hovermale v. Berkely Spring Moose Lodge No. 1483, 271 S.E.2d 335, 340 (W. Va. 1980).
322. *Meade*, 2010 WL 4909435, at *7 (quoting Tolley v. ACF Indus., Inc., 575 S.E.2d 158, 168 (W. Va. 2002)); *see also* Casdorph v. West Virginia Office Ins. Com'r, 690 S.E.2d 102, 105 (W. Va. 2009) (finding in the context of worker's compensation claims, where the Rules of Evidence and Procedure do not strictly apply "[a]lthough the Appellees assert that the case studies cited by Appellant showing a causal connection between benzene exposure and CML have not been able to get peer reviewed textbooks to acknowledge and print them as common or accepted consensus medical opinion, we find that these case studies, although small, are valid studies that have been peer reviewed and published").
323. *See Meade*, 2010 WL 4909435, at *5 n.5 ("Although the West Virginia Supreme Court of Appeals has not addressed the issue, it is well-settled that a plaintiff in a toxic tort case must prove both general and specific causation."); Bourne *ex rel.* Bourne v. E.I. DuPont de Nemours & Co., 189 F. Supp. 2d 482, 485 (S.D.W. Va. 2002) ("In a toxic tort case, a plaintiff must generally establish both general and specific causation for his injuries.").
324. *Meade*, 2010 WL 4909435, at *5.
325. *Id.* at *5–7.
326. *Id.* at *5.

cannot focus solely on specific causation in an effort to establish general causation by inference—each must be independently proven by expert testimony.[327]

In a failure-to-warn case, a West Virginia district court failed to find that general causation was established by the manufacturer's own warning label because "without explaining the scientific basis for the warning, [the label] is no substitute for expert testimony that establishes causation in terms of reasonable probability."[328] The court further rejected the argument that a Food and Drug Administration (FDA) directive requiring drug manufactures to issue a warning was sufficient to establish the drug's potential to cause illness in others because the FDA cost-benefit standard differs from the causation standard in tort cases.[329]

Specific Causation

In proving whether a particular substance caused injury, the plaintiff must first show he was exposed to the toxin. "Critical to establishing exposure to a toxic chemical is knowledge of the dose or exposure amount and the duration of the exposure."[330] Once the level of actual exposure is ascertained, the "plaintiff must demonstrate 'the levels of exposure that are hazardous to human beings generally as well as the plaintiff's actual level of exposure.'"[331]

However, in one case involving toxic exposure to bacteria in an undercooked hamburger, the West Virginia Supreme Court allowed an expert to prove causation through "differential diagnosis."[332] The process of differential diagnosis identifies the medical problem by eliminating likely causes until the expert isolates the most probable cause. In finding a doctor's causation testimony reliable and admissible, the court stated the process "has been subjected to peer review/publication, does not frequently lead to incorrect results, and is generally accepted in the medical community."[333] Even though the testimony did not rule out all possible causes of the illness, the court found a causal conclusion from the methodology admissible, because the jury determines the weight that it should give the expert's testimony.[334] A differential diagnosis must be analyzed on a case-by-case basis.[335]

---

327. *Id.* at *6 (S.D.W. Va. Nov. 24, 2010) ("[I]n opining on specific causation, [the expert] necessarily assumed the existence of general causation. . . . But this mere assumption does not establish general causation.").
328. *Id.* at *7.
329. *Id.* at *8.
330. Tolley v. ACF Indus., Inc., 575 S.E.2d 158, 169 (W. Va. 2002).
331. *White*, No. 2:05-CV-00247, 2007 WL 6948824, at *5 (applying West Virginia substantive law).
332. San Francisco v. Wendy's Int'l Inc., 656 S.E.2d 485, 497–99 (W. Va. 2007).
333. *Id.* at 497–99.
334. *Id.* at 499–500.
335. *Id.* at 499.

CHAPTER 12

Eastern States

Libretta Stennes

This chapter discusses proof of causation in toxic tort cases in the Eastern states of Connecticut, Delaware, the District of Columbia, Maine, Maryland, Massachusetts, New Hampshire, New Jersey, New York, Pennsylvania, Rhode Island and Vermont.[1] The body of law specific to toxic tort causation varies across these jurisdictions, and some of the Eastern states such as New York, New Jersey, Pennsylvania, and Maryland have more extensively developed law. Many of the Eastern states decline to adopt bright-line rules of the type of evidence permissible to establish causation. There are common themes across these states; however, each requires proof of general and specific causation.

Connecticut

Overall Standard for Causation

Under Connecticut law, a plaintiff[2] must demonstrate that a defendant's conduct was both the cause in fact and the proximate cause of the plaintiff's harm.[3] Connecticut applies a substantial factor test to determine proximate cause.[4] "This substantial factor test reflects the inquiry fundamental to all proximate cause questions, namely, whether

---

1. This survey chapter focuses on a narrow but extremely significant aspect of any toxic tort case seeking damages for personal injury—namely, the criteria for establishing the elements of general and specific causation in the particular jurisdictions covered. For a more generalized discussion regarding causation in personal injury and other types of toxic tort actions, as well as a broader discussion regarding the claims, defenses, and general strategies at play in these cases, please refer to earlier chapters in this book.
2. In Martin v. Shell Oil Co., 180 F. Supp. 2d 313 (D. Conn. 2002), a plaintiff tried unsuccessfully to shift the burden to defendant on causation because, as she alleged, defendant had failed to perform adequate product testing. *Id.* at 320.
3. Stewart v. Federated Dep't Stores, Inc., 662 A.2d 753, 758 (Conn. 1995).
4. *Id.*; Paige v. St. Andrew's Roman Catholic Church Corp., 734 A.2d 85, 91 (1999) ("[T]he test of proximate cause is whether the defendant's conduct is a substantial factor in bringing about the plaintiff's injuries.") (quotations omitted).

the harm which occurred was of the same general nature as the foreseeable risk created by the defendant's negligence...."[5]

The Connecticut Superior Court has addressed a plaintiff's burden to demonstrate causation in toxic tort cases.[6] The court found that no settled law existed in Connecticut on how a plaintiff must establish that exposure to defendant's products was a substantial factor in his or her injury. Citing the frequency, regularity, and proximity test applied in other jurisdictions, the court concluded that a plaintiff must offer some evidence that the defendant's product contained asbestos and that it was either used at the worksite during the plaintiff's tenure or that the plaintiff was otherwise exposed.

General and Specific Causation

Connecticut courts have accepted differential diagnosis as the basis for both general *and* specific causation opinions.[7] However, the federal district court of Connecticut recognizes that specific causation may be based upon other grounds such as temporal association.[8] In *Perkins v. Origin Medsystems Inc.*, the federal district court, citing authority from various federal jurisdictions, set out the following standard for reliable differential diagnosis:

> [D]ifferential diagnosis requires the expert to "take serious account of other potential causes."... Although an expert is not required to eliminate every potential cause in order for his or her opinion to be admissible under *Daubert*, the expert is required to employ either standard diagnostic techniques to eliminate obvious alternative causes or, if the defendant suggests some likely alternative cause of the plaintiff's condition, the expert is required to offer a reasonable explanation why he or she still believes that the defendant's action or product was a substantial factor in bringing about the plaintiff's condition.... A strong temporal relationship between the patient's symptoms and exposure to the defendant's product can certainly assist a physician in offering a reasonable explanation.... Moreover, the court affords great weight to the testimony of treating physicians.[9]

Baker v. Metro-North Railroad accepted as reliable a differential diagnosis of a treating orthopedic surgeon after the expert testified that he followed his routine out-of-court

---

5. Shegog v. Zabrecky, 654 A.2d 771, 745 (Conn. App. 1995) (quotations omitted).
6. Splendorio v. ACMAT Corp., No. CV030407882S, 2005 WL 589957, at *2 (Conn. Super. Ct. Feb. 2, 2005) ("[P]laintiff must show that a particular defendant's product was used at the job site and that the plaintiff was in proximity to that product at the time it was being used."); Cormier v. 3M Corp., No. CV040409253S, 2005 WL 288824, at *2 (Conn. Super. Ct. Jan. 11, 2005).
7. *See, e.g.*, Zuchowicz v. United States, 140 F.3d 381, 385 (2d Cir. 1998) (accepting differential diagnosis when lack of available human studies was explained and temporal association found between drug overdose and cause of death).
8. Martin v. Shell Oil Co., 180 F. Supp. 2d 313, 320 (D. Conn. 2002).
9. 299 F. Supp. 2d 45, 61 (D. Conn. 2004) (citations omitted).

diagnostic process.[10] The district court rejected the defendant's challenge that the expert failed to rule out alternative causes, noting that the defendant had not actually identified any such possible causes.[11]

Connecticut often requires expert testimony to establish the existence, extent, or cause of an injury or disease "because the medical effect on the human system of the infliction of injuries is generally not within the sphere of common knowledge of the lay person."[12] The Connecticut Supreme Court, however, has allowed for the possibility that a plaintiff may demonstrate causation for medical injuries solely through lay testimony. In *Asipazu v. Orgera*, the court noted that when a condition is so obvious or common, especially if the lay witness is describing her own physical condition, expert testimony may not be required.[13] Additionally, the court stated: "[e]xpert testimony may also not be necessary to establish causation if the plaintiff's evidence creates a probability so strong that a jury can form a reasonable belief without the aid of any expert opinion."[14]

The Connecticut Supreme Court has explained that an expert testifying on medical causation can present her testimony in multiple ways, including direct opinion of a physician, deduction by a physician eliminating causes other than the alleged cause (i.e., differential diagnosis), or by opinion based upon hypothetical question.[15] The expert must present sufficient evidence upon which a jury could find probable, not possible, cause. "An expert, however, need not use 'talismanic words' to show reasonable probability."[16]

In one case involving acute occupation exposure, the defendant moved for summary judgment based in large part on the plaintiff's failure to submit expert testimony to support causation.[17] When a pipe burst, the plaintiff was exposed to toxic fumes and experienced acute effects (dizziness, breathing trouble, chest pains). The plaintiff submitted evidence that the defendant acknowledged the accident and that the plaintiff received medical treatment. The court denied the defendant's motion, reasoning that this fell under the type of cases from *Asipazu* in which a plaintiff need not support his claim with expert testimony. Accordingly, the court found that the defendant had failed to demonstrate the absence of a material disputed fact on proximate causation. However, proving causation without expert testimony is still the exception, not the rule.

---

10. No. 3:98CV1073, 2003 WL 22439730, at *2 (D. Conn. Oct. 23, 2003).
11. Id.
12. Shegog v. Zabrecky, 654 A.2d 771, 745–46 (Conn. App. Ct. 1995); Asipazu v. Orgera, 535 A.2d 338, 342 (Conn. 1987); Collette v. Collette, 418 A.2d 891, 894 (Conn. 1979) (finding expert testimony required to establish cause of miscarriage).
13. 535 A.2d 338, 342 (Conn. 1987).
14. Id.
15. Boland v. Vanderbilt, 102 A.2d 362, 365 (Conn. 1953); Shegog, 654 A.2d at 776–77.
16. *Shegog*, 654 A.2d at 776.
17. Case v. Upjohn Co., No. 308420, 1992 WL 259203, at *2 (Conn. Super. Ct. Sept. 16 1992).

Delaware

Overall Standard for Causation

Delaware follows a "but for" standard to determine causation. In *Culver v. Bennett*, the Delaware Supreme Court discussed the history of Delaware common law on causation:

> Delaware has long recognized that there may be more than one proximate cause of an injury.... Nevertheless, "our time-honored definition of proximate cause" has been the "but for" rule.... "Most simply stated, proximate cause is [defined in Delaware as] that direct cause without which the accident would not have occurred."[18]

The *Culver* court observed that Delaware's comparative fault statute did not demonstrate any legislative intent to modify Delaware's common law determination of proximate cause. "Consequently, Delaware continues to adhere to its common law 'but for' rule of proximate cause."[19]

General Causation

Unlike some jurisdictions, in Delaware, epidemiology is not required as a matter of law to demonstrate general causation. Nothing in Delaware law requires that evidence to take the form of, or comprise (even in part), epidemiological evidence. This is true regardless of whether plaintiff is able to exclude all other potential causes beyond the toxic substance at issue.[20]

In *Long v. Weider Nutrition Group, Inc.*, basing its conclusion, in part, on public policy, the Delaware Superior Court held:

> [I]f a properly qualified medical expert performs a reliable differential diagnosis through which, to a reasonable degree of medical certainty, all other possible causes of the victims' condition can be eliminated, leaving only the toxic substance as the cause, a causation opinion based on that differential diagnosis should be admitted.[21]

In a subsequent case, the Delaware Superior Court again examined the role of epidemiology to establish general causation. After noting that jurisdictions vary on whether epidemiology is required, the court concluded: "[u]nder the circumstances presented here, the Court is satisfied that the jurisdictions that have declined to adopt a hard and fast rule have endorsed the better and more practical view on the subject."[22]

---

18. Culver v. Bennett, 588 A.2d 1094, 1096–97 (Del. 1991).
19. *Id.* at 1098.
20. *See In re* Asbestos Litig., 900 A.2d 120, 154 (Del. Super. Ct. 2006) (citations omitted).
21. Long v. Weider Nutrition Grp., Inc., Civ.A.00C-12-249MMJ, 2004 WL 1543226, at *6 (Del. Super. Ct. June 25, 2004) (citation omitted).
22. *Asbestos Litig.*, 900 A.2d at 151.

Specific Causation

For specific causation, the Delaware Superior Court has held that a medical doctor must provide testimony to establish specific causation; epidemiology cannot address specific causation.[23]

The Delaware Supreme Court has not squarely addressed the "single fiber" or "no threshold" theory. In one decision, however, the court indicated that if the issue was subsequently before it on appeal, the court would carefully scrutinize such testimony.[24] A Delaware federal bankruptcy court has rejected the single molecule theory in asbestos litigation. The court noted that the experts acknowledged that some level of exposure presents no risk.[25]

District of Columbia
Overall Standard for Causation

The District of Columbia defines proximate cause as "that cause which, in natural and continual sequence, unbroken by any efficient intervening cause, produces the injury, and without which the result would not have occurred."[26] Proximate cause is divided into cause in fact and policy considerations that limit the liability of persons who have, in fact, caused the injury "where the chain of events appears highly extraordinary in retrospect."[27] The District of Columbia requires plaintiff to demonstrate that defendant's conduct was a substantial factor in causing plaintiff's injury.[28] The D.C. Court of Appeals expressly declined to adopt Maryland's *Lohrmann* decision (discussed *infra*) as the law of D.C.[29] The *Lorhmann* test calls for evidence of exposure to a specific product on a regular basis over some extended period of time in proximity to where a plaintiff actually worked.[30] The D.C. Court of Appeals considered Maryland's test "too exacting," especially where the plaintiff testified not merely that he worked in an area with asbestos products but that he worked on the boilers containing the products.[31]

---

23. Lee v. A.C. & S. Co., Inc., 542 A.2d 352, 356 (Del. Super. Ct. 1987).
24. *Asbestos Litig.*, 900 A.2d at 154 n.202 (citing a case rejecting "single fiber" or "no threshold" theory as inconsistent with prevailing science).
25. *In re* W. R. Grace & Co., 355 B.R. 462, 476 (Bankr. D. Del. 2006) (finding the use of a no safe level model to demonstrate unreasonable risk contradicts the principles of dose response).
26. McKethean v. Washington Metro. Area Transit Auth., 588 A.2d 708, 716 (D.C. 1991) (quotations omitted).
27. Ferrell v. Rosenbaum, 691 A.2d 641, 650 (D.C. 1997) (citations omitted).
28. Weakley v. Burnham Corp., 871 A.2d 1167, 1173 (D.C. 2005).
29. *Id.* at 1176–77 (recognizing earlier trial courts had followed the frequency, regularity, and proximity test).
30. Lohrmann v. Pittsburgh Corning Corp., 782 F.2d 1156, 1162–63 (4th Cir. 1986).
31. *Weakley*, 871 A.2d at 1177.

General and Specific Causation

When epidemiology evidence is available to evaluate general causation, or whether an exposure to a substance is capable of causing an injury, courts applying D.C. law have excluded or found insufficient expert proof that fails to consider the available scientific evidence appropriately. For example, when plaintiff offered only epidemiology studies with results that were not statistically significant, the D.C. Superior Court has found that plaintiff did not sustain its burden on general causation.[32] However, where epidemiological evidence is available and presented, the D.C. Circuit has held that an opposing expert cannot rely solely on case reports or other evidence.[33] To support a general causation opinion, the expert must evaluate the available studies using sound epidemiological methods.[34]

The D.C. Circuit has held that a plaintiff may present expert testimony in support of a causal relationship even when it may not yet be clearly established by animal or epidemiological studies.[35] The court has placed emphasis on the reliability of the expert's methodology as opposed to whether a body of statistically significant studies exist to support the conclusion.[36] Reaching this conclusion, the court noted the difference between the legal standard for general causation and the scientific standard to establish causation. The court also emphasized that a lack of epidemiology should not preclude a plaintiff's case from reaching a jury.

However, where epidemiology is already developed, the D.C. Circuit has repeatedly held that chemical *in vitro* and *in vivo* toxicology studies are not sufficient to demonstrate causation in humans "in the face of the overwhelming body of contradictory epidemiological evidence."[37] Indeed, the court has noted one issue with reliance on animal toxicology studies: "Humans are not rats, and it is far from clear how readily one may generalize from one mammalian species to another."[38]

Young v. Burton illustrates an example of problems of proof plaintiffs may face when science is emerging.[39] In a sick building syndrome case, the plaintiff's expert relied upon visible mold, musty smells, and other circumstantial evidence of mold in the building to support his opinion that the plaintiff was exposed to mold. He presented no environmental

---

32. Oxendine v. Merrell Dow Pharm., Inc., No. 82-1245, 1996 WL 680992 (D.C. Super. Oct. 24, 1996).
33. Meister v. Medical Eng'g Corp., 267 F.3d 1123, 1132 (D.C. Cir. 2001).
34. *Id.*
35. Ferebee v. Chevron Chem. Co., 736 F.2d 1529, 1535 (D.C. Cir. 1984) (finding sufficient causation evidence to support the jury verdict for plaintiff); *see* Ethyl Corp. v. Envtl. Prot. Agency, 541 F.2d 1, 26 (D.C. Cir. 1976), *cert. denied*, 426 U.S. 941 (1976) (noting a range of scientific methods for investigating questions of causation—for example, toxicology and animal studies, clinical research, and epidemiology—which all have distinct advantages and disadvantages). *Ferebee* applied Maryland law to the substantive tort claims in this federal wrongful death suit. However, the discussion as to causation was not specific to Maryland law.
36. *Ferebee*, 736 F.2d at 1535–36.
37. Richardson v. Richardson-Merrell, Inc., 857 F.2d 823, 830 (D.C. Cir. 1988); Raynor v. Merrell Pharms. Inc., 104 F.3d 1371, 1376 (D.C. Cir. 1997).
38. Int'l Union v. Pendergrass, 878 F.2d 389, 394 (D.C. Cir. 1989).
39. 567 F. Supp. 2d 121 (D.D.C. 2008).

testing to show mycotoxins or other toxins in the air, though. Further, the expert opined that diagnosis of the disease demonstrates actual exposure; circular logic viewed with skepticism by the court. Finally, the expert contended that it was unnecessary to determine the dose of concentration of exposure because dose response is invalid when, as in this case, it was his opinion that the plaintiff had a genetic susceptibility to mold exposure. The court noted that scientific studies did not yet exist to demonstrate whether and at what level water-damaged buildings cause injury to humans. Without such studies, the court found the plaintiff's expert's opinions to be nothing other than conjecture. Even if such studies existed, the court noted the expert would be unable to show what substances existed and at what levels. "Thus, there is no basis upon which to conclude that plaintiffs' exposures were sufficient to account for the variety of symptoms they have experienced."[40] As discussed later under the Maryland section of this chapter, a Maryland trial court considering the same evidence from the same expert admitted the opinion as basis for both general and specific causation.

Maine
Overall Standard for Causation
Maine applies a two-part inquiry for causation: (1) whether the negligent act plays a substantial part to cause the injury, and (2) if so, whether the injury was reasonably foreseeable as a result of the act.[41] "[D]efendants' conduct must be shown to have been a 'substantial factor' in producing each plaintiff's injury."[42] The Maine Supreme Court has cautioned against jury instructions that invoke "but for" causation.[43]

The Supreme Judicial Court of Maine has held that "[a]llowing a jury to infer causation" in cases involving complex medical facts, without the aid of expert testimony and without some evidence the defendant's conduct was more likely than not the cause of plaintiff's injury, "stretches the jury's role beyond its capacity."[44] Although not a toxic tort case, *Merriam* illustrates that simply putting on the stand an expert able to convince a jury may not be sufficient to sustain a burden. On appeal, the Supreme Judicial Court of Maine set aside the jury verdict because neither expert testified that the plaintiff's damages would have been avoided if the defendant had acted properly.[45] Although the court found the jury was properly instructed on proximate cause, it found no evidence in the record upon which the jury could have reasonably found proximate cause.

---

40. *Id.* at 133.
41. Crowe v. Shaw, 755 A.2d 509, 512 (Me. 2000).
42. Millett v. Atl. Richfield Co., No. CV-98-555, 2000 WL 359979, at *13 (Me. Super. Mar. 2, 2000), *appeal dismissed*, 760 A.2d 250 (Me. 2000).
43. Wheeler v. White, 714 A.2d 125, 127–28 (Me. 1998).
44. Merriam v. Wanger, 757 A.2d 778, 782 (Me. 2000); *see also* Tolliver v. Dep't of Transp., 948 A.2d 1223 (Me. 2008).
45. *Merriam*, 757 A.2d at 782.

General and Specific Causation

Applying Maine law, the First Circuit observed: "[e]xperts may present epidemiological statistics in different ways to indicate causation."[46] Although affirming exclusion of the expert testimony at issue, the First Circuit did not apply rigid rules to the nature of epidemiological support necessary (e.g., whether relative risk is greater than 2). In fact, the court noted that odds ratios in some cases may be proper basis for a causation opinion.[47] However, the First Circuit affirmed that in this particular case, the expert had improperly used odds ratios. "When a person's chances of a better outcome are 50% greater with treatment (relative to the chances of those who were not treated), that is not the same as a person having a greater than 50% chance of experiencing the better outcome with treatment. The latter meets the required standard for causation; the former does not."[48]

Maryland
Overall Standard for Causation

Maryland follows a substantial factor test for causation in complex toxic tort matters.[49] In order to determine whether an act or omission was a substantial factor in bringing about harm, Maryland courts look to three things:

(a) the number of other factors which contribute in producing the harm and the extent of the effect which they have in producing it;

(b) whether the actor's conduct has created a force or series of forces which are in continuous and active operation up to the time of the harm, or has created a situation harmless unless acted upon by other forces for which the actor is not responsible;

(c) lapse of time.[50]

Foreseeability is also a factor in determining causation. A Maryland appellate court vacated judgment after finding error with jury instructions that stated the defendant's negligence must be "the" cause of injury, suggesting the jury must find it was the sole cause.[51] The plaintiff must offer expert testimony to support causation when the cause of an injury is a complicated medical question.[52]

---

46. Samaan v. St. Joseph Hosp., 670 F.3d 21, 34 (1st Cir. 2012).
47. Id. (noting an example of reversal of an exclusion of specific causation testimony based in part on an odds ratio).
48. Id. at 33.
49. Pittway Corp. v. Collins, 973 A.2d 771, 787 (Md. 2009). Maryland courts have followed a "but for" causation test when an injury is allegedly caused by only one cause. Yonce v. Smithkline Beecham Clinical Labs., 680 A.2d 569, 575–76 (Md. Ct. Spec. App. 1996).
50. Yonce, 680 A.2d at 576.
51. Stickley v. Chisholm, 765 A.2d 662, 667 (Md. Ct. Spec. App. 2001).
52. Aventis Pasteur, Inc. v. Skevofilax, 914 A.2d 113, 135 (Md. 2007).

The Fourth Circuit, applying Maryland law, set forth a test, often referred to as the *Lohrmann* test, that calls for evidence of exposure to a specific product on a regular basis over some extended period of time in proximity to where the plaintiff actually worked.[53] The Maryland Court of Appeals has found that substantial cause may be determined by examining the frequency, regularity, and proximity of exposure to asbestos products.[54] The test is fact-specific and calls for an understanding of the physical characteristics of the workplace and the relationship between activities of direct users and bystander plaintiffs.[55]

In *Aldridge v. Goodyear Tire & Rubber Co.*, the plaintiff alleged exposure to multiple chemicals, and the court concluded that the plaintiff must demonstrate that each "be an independently sufficient cause of harm before it can be a substantial contributing factor."[56] Because of the "host of different chemicals interacting with each other, some supplied by [defendant] and some not," and because of the "complicating effects" of other potential causes of plaintiff's cancer and heart disease (e.g., genetics, lifestyle choices), the court found that a reasonable fact-finder would not be able to conclude that any one chemical supplied by the defendant caused the plaintiff's cancer or heart disease.[57]

General and Specific Causation

In Maryland, epidemiology is the primary generally accepted methodology to prove general causation.[58] However, as the District Court of Maryland has observed: "There is a range of scientific methods for investigating questions of causation—for example, toxicology and animal studies, clinical research, and epidemiology—which all have distinct advantages and disadvantages."[59] When an expert chooses between conflicting epidemiology studies, the expert must articulate the weighing process and how he or she accepted or rejected the studies.

Maryland courts generally accept a properly performed differential diagnosis to establish specific causation. "A reliable differential diagnosis typically, though not invariably, is performed after 'physical examinations, the taking of medical histories, and the review of clinical tests, including laboratory tests,'" and generally is accomplished by determining

---

53. Lohrmann v. Pittsburgh Corning Corp., 782 F.2d 1156, 1162–63 (4th Cir. 1986).
54. Eagle-Picher Indus., Inc. v. Balbos, 604 A.2d 445, 460 (Md. 1992).
55. Owens-Corning Fiberglas Corp. v. Garrett, 682 A.2d 1143, 1156 (Md. 1996) (citing Eagle-Picher v. Balbos, 604 A.2d 445, 460 (Md. 1992)).
56. 34 F. Supp. 2d 1010, 1020 (D. Md. 1999), *vacated on other grounds and remanded*, 223 F.3d 263 (4th Cir. 2000); *see also* McClelland v. Goodyear Tire & Rubber Co., 735 F. Supp. 172, 174 (D. Md. 1990) (plaintiff workers allege injury from multiple chemicals referred to as "toxic soup," failed to produce sufficient evidence "that would allow a reasonable fact-finder to conclude that it was more likely than not that any particular, identifiable negligent or intentional conduct by [defendant] was the cause of any of the plaintiffs' particular illnesses").
57. *Aldridge*, 34 F. Supp. 2d at 1019.
58. Culpepper v. Dae Corp., No. 24C09006364LP, 2011 WL 7063620, at *3 (Md. Cir. Ct. July 6, 2011).
59. Marder v. G.D. Searle & Co., 630 F. Supp. 1087, 1094 (D. Md. 1986), *aff'd sub nom.* Wheelahan v. G.D. Searle & Co., 814 F.2d 655 (4th Cir. 1987).

the possible causes for the patient's symptoms and then eliminating each of these potential causes until reaching one that cannot be ruled out or determining which of those that cannot be excluded is the most likely.[60] The Maryland Court of Appeals has expressly adopted the view that an expert must not only rule in the contaminant at issue, but must also rule out possible causes including that plaintiff's disease developed idiopathically.[61]

In *Chesson v. Baltimore Washington Conference*, a Maryland trial court found a differential diagnosis in a moldy building case to be admissible to establish both general and specific causation.[62] The court discussed the clinical-medical approach and a trend in courts to relax or even reject the necessity of certain rigid toxicological concepts. The trial court found that "precise information concerning the exposure necessary to cause specific harm to humans and exact details pertaining to the plaintiff's exposure are beneficial, [but] such evidence is not always available, or necessary, to demonstrate that a substance is toxic to humans. . . ."[63] The trial court explained the clinical-medical approach as follows:

> Although the clinical-medical approach does not demand scientific studies to isolate or identify the pollutant or rigid scientific certitude as [defendant's expert] urges, it does not abandon or deemphasize the requirement that the expert's underlying methodology be reliable. Rather, the clinical-medical approach acknowledges that a clinical physician who employs the tried and true practice of differential diagnosis may have an opinion on causation that is equally valid to that of a toxicologist. While differential diagnosis, the foundation of the clinical-medical approach, may not produce the kind of scientific certitude that is required in the research laboratory, simply put, scientific certainty is not the degree of certitude required here. A medical opinion, to be admissible, must be to a reasonable degree of medical certainty.[64]

The court cautioned that labeling something a differential diagnosis will not automatically render it admissible and discussed several factors for courts to employ to evaluate reliability of the underlying methodology, including whether the expert actually performed an examination, the method of examination used, and whether the ruled in cause is plausible.

Massachusetts
Overall Standard for Causation
Massachusetts applies a substantial factor test to determine causation in toxic tort cases. The Supreme Judicial Court of Massachusetts upheld the following jury instruction:

---

60. *Culpepper*, 2011 WL 7063620, at *4.
61. *Id.* at *5–6 (citing Blackwell v. Wyeth, 971 A.2d 235 (Md. 2009)).
62. No. 13-C-03-056903, 2009 WL 7450518, at *13 (Md. Cir. Ct. Nov. 10, 2009).
63. *Id.* at *10 (quoting Westberry v. Gislaved Gummi AB, 178 F.3d 257, 264 (4th Cir. 1999)).
64. *Id.* at *11.

For you to answer yes to [whether exposure was a substantial factor], you have to find that the asbestos contained in this defendant's products was a substantial contributing cause of his illness and death. It doesn't have to be the only cause, but it has to be a substantial contributing cause.... *It means something that makes a difference in the result.* There can be and often are more than one cause present to produce an injury, and more than one person legally responsible for an injury or disease, so here, even if other manufacturers of asbestos-containing products were at fault, and their products contributed to [plaintiff's] disease, [defendant] is not thereby relieved from liability if you should find ... that its ... products were ... a substantial contributing factor to his disease and ... death. So you look to see ... how much asbestos he was exposed to, whether he inhaled or retained any fibers from the asbestos, consider the medical evidence, how mesothelioma and asbestos are related, consider the evidence as to the effects on the body of different types of asbestos fibers, and then determine whether [defendant's] fibers, if you find he was exposed to them, did cause his mesothelioma or contribute substantially to that disease.[65]

On appeal, the plaintiff challenged the court's substantial factor instruction, specifically the statement that the product need not be the only cause, but it must be something that makes a difference in the result. Plaintiff argued that the instruction amounted to a "but for" causation standard and improperly called for her to separate out the effects from all defendant's products. The appellate court upheld the instruction, but noted that this particular decision was a close call.[66]

In *Welch v. Keene Corp.*, defendants argued that the evidence was insufficient to demonstrate causation as a matter of law.[67] Specifically, the defendants contended that the plaintiff failed to demonstrate that the alleged exposure was substantial enough to cause injury. The court noted, however, that the plaintiff did not need to prove that "but for" exposure to products from each manufacturer, he would not have been harmed.[68]

General Causation

Epidemiology is not always necessary to demonstrate causation.[69] The absence of scientific or epidemiological studies does not compel a finding that an expert's theory is unreliable. Rather, a party seeking to introduce scientific evidence may lay an adequate foundation by showing that the evidence is reliable or valid through alternate means.[70] In *Stewart v.*

---

65. O'Connor v. Raymark Indus., Inc., 518 N.E.2d 510, 511–12 (Mass. 1988) (emphasis added).
66. *Id.* at 513.
67. 575 N.E.2d 766, 769 (Mass. App. Ct. 1991).
68. *Id.* at 769–70.
69. Vassallo v. Baxter Healthcare Corp., 696 N.E.2d 909, 915–16 (1998) (lack of epidemiological testing not enough, by itself, to exclude testimony on causation of disease).
70. *Id.*; Commonwealth v. Sands, 675 N.E.2d 370, 371 (Mass. 1997); Stewart v. F.W. Woolworth Co., No. 87-5552, 1993 WL 327782, at *7 (Mass. Super. May 6, 1997).

F.W. Woolworth Co., the court admitted the causation opinion of the plaintiff's treating physician, finding the doctor had followed an acceptable scientific method to rule out other causes, examined the plaintiff, and observed him in a follow-up evaluation.[71] Additionally, as with many Eastern states, Massachusetts has permitted a plaintiff's general causation opinions based upon what the defendant claims to be statistically insignificant data to reach the jury.[72]

In 2011, the First Circuit reversed exclusion of an opinion on general causation in a benzene exposure case.[73] The expert at issue followed a "weight of the evidence" approach to opine that benzene exposure is capable of causing a very rare leukemia. Much of the First Circuit opinion addresses the appropriate boundaries of the gatekeeper role under *Daubert*; however, in one section, the First Circuit addresses the type of epidemiological evidence necessary to support causation. The First Circuit found legal error with the lower court's holding that "'[Plaintiff's expert's] attempt to support his conclusion with data that concededly lacks statistical significance' was 'a deviation from sound practice of the scientific method' that provided grounds for exclusion."[74] The First Circuit contrasted the instant case from situations in which available epidemiological studies found no causal link or where no cases of the disease are found among occupationally exposed workers:

> Rather, this is a case in which there is a lack of statistically significant epidemiological evidence, and in which the rarity of APL and difficulties of data collection in the United States make it very difficult to perform an epidemiological study of the causes of APL that would yield statistically significant results.[75]

In *Sutera v. Perrier Group of America, Inc.*, the plaintiff sought to rely upon the EPA goal for benzene of zero parts per billion in drinking water.[76] The court held that in the absence of further evidence such as epidemiological studies or other reliable methodologies used to demonstrate causation, a regulatory standard was not an appropriate measure of causation.

Specific Causation

A plaintiff must offer proof of exposure and that the exposure is a sufficient dose to cause harm. Citing the *Reference Manual on Scientific Evidence*, the Federal District Court of Massachusetts has explained that a plaintiff's expert may prove exposure through direct measurement, through mathematical modeling, or through biological monitoring.[77]

---

71. 1993 WL 327782, at *7.
72. Linnen v. A.H. Robins Co., Inc., No. 972307, 2000 WL 145758, at *5 (Mass. Super. Jan. 4, 2000).
73. Milward v. Acuity Specialty Prods. Grp., Inc., 639 F.3d 11, 23–25 (1st Cir. 2011).
74. *Id.* at 25.
75. *Id.* at 24.
76. 986 F. Supp. 655 (D. Mass 1997).
77. Polaino v. Bayer Corp., 122 F. Supp. 2d 63, 70 (D. Mass. 2000).

However, the First Circuit concluded that an expert may not rely solely on a temporal relationship between a potential source of exposure and plaintiff's illness, even when the expert cites literature finding association between the chemicals and illness.[78] Massachusetts applies a Maryland *Lohrmann*-like test in cases where causation is established through circumstantial evidence.[79]

The District of Massachusetts allowed expert testimony from an industrial hygienist on exposure to solvents even though the expert was not able to determine whether the exposure to any particular chemical exceeded guideline limits.[80] The court accepted the testimony that when an individual is exposed to "multiple chemicals that target the same systems in the human body, the industrial hygienist considers the exposure to the entire mixture of chemicals."[81] The court found the defendant's objection that the expert report lacked specific measurements as to the concentration of solvents or duration of dose went more to credibility as opposed to admissibility.

New Hampshire
Overall Standard for Causation

In New Hampshire, a plaintiff must establish that the negligent conduct was a substantial factor in leading to the alleged harm.[82] The negligent conduct need not be the sole cause of injury, but in order to establish proximate cause, the plaintiff must prove that defendant's conduct caused or contributed to cause the harm.[83] In *Grimes v. Hoffman-La Roche, Inc.*, the Federal District Court of New Hampshire considered a general causation opinion that was not based upon epidemiology.[84] The *Grimes* court excluded the opinion, but not because of a requirement that general causation must be based upon epidemiological data. Instead, the court found fault with the expert's failure to provide a reliable basis for drawing conclusions about one drug based upon studies of another. The court also based its decision on the expert's failure to address dose necessary to cause the plaintiff's injury.[85] In *Baker Valley Lumber, Inc. v. Ingersoll Rand Co.*, the New Hampshire

---

78. *Id.*
79. O'Connor v. Raymark Indus., Inc., 518 N.E.2d 510, 511 (Mass. 1988) (approving jury instruction stating that proof of causation required "evidence of some exposure . . . on a regular basis over some period of time where [the plaintiff] was actually working with the product himself or in proximity to where others were working with the product").
80. Allen v. Martin Surfacing, 263 F.R.D. 47, 54, 57 (D. Mass. 2009).
81. *Id.* at 56.
82. Carignan v. New Hampshire Int'l Speedway, Inc., 858 A.2d 536, 541–42 (N.H. 2004).
83. *Id.* ("Legal cause requires the plaintiff to establish that the negligent conduct was a substantial factor in bringing about the harm," but it "need not be the *sole* cause of the injury"; "to establish proximate cause, the plaintiff must prove that the defendant's conduct caused or contributed to cause the harm."); Peterson v. Gray, 628 A.2d 244, 246 (N.H. 1993).
84. 907 F. Supp. 33, 38 (D. N.H. 1995).
85. *Id.*

Supreme Court acknowledged that differential diagnosis is generally accepted to demonstrate medical causation.[86]

New Jersey
Overall Standard for Causation

New Jersey applies a substantial factor test to determine causation in toxic tort cases.[87] To demonstrate negligence, "a plaintiff must show that the defendant's actions were the proximate cause of his or her injury." As one New Jersey court has explained: "To prove medical causation, a plaintiff must show that exposure was a substantial factor in causing or exacerbating the disease."[88] Moreover, "[e]xpert medical testimony is often used. . . ."[89] Proof that a defendant's conduct caused a plaintiff's injuries is "more subtle and sophisticated" in toxic tort cases.[90] And, "the task of proving causation is invariably made more complex because of the long latency period of illnesses caused by carcinogens or other toxic chemicals."[91] The New Jersey Supreme Court has described its approach to toxic tort causation as striking a balance "with regard to proof of causation that is fair to both plaintiffs and defendants in view of the almost certain lack of direct scientific proof in such cases."[92]

New Jersey has applied a "frequency, regularity and proximity" medical causation test in asbestos cases.[93] The frequency, regularity, and proximity test "is not a rigid test with an absolute threshold level necessary to support a jury verdict."[94] "The phraseology should not supply 'catch words' [and] the underlying concept should not be lost."[95] Tailoring causation to the facts and circumstances of the case, "the frequency and regularity prongs become less cumbersome when dealing with cases involving diseases, like mesothelioma, which can develop after only minor exposures to asbestos fibers."[96]

---

86. 813 A.2d 409, 416–17 (N.H. 2002) (remanding to determine whether fire investigators attempting to determine the cause of a sawmill fire by differential etiology was reliable).
87. James v. Bessemer Processing Co., Inc., 714 A.2d 898, 908–09 (N.J. 1998). ("To prove medical causation, a plaintiff must show 'that the exposure [to each defendant's product] was a substantial factor in causing or exacerbating the disease.'") (quoting Sholtis v. Am. Cyanamid Co., 568 A.2d 1196, 1208 (N.J. Super. 1989)).
88. Buttitta v. Allied Signal, Inc., 2010 WL 1427273, at *7 (N.J. Super. Ct. A.D. Jan. 4, 2010); *see also* James v. Bessemer Processing Co., 714 A.2d 898, 908–09 (N.J. 1998); Sholtis v. Am. Cyanamid Co., 568 A.2d 1196, 1208 (N.J. Super. Ct. A.D. 1989).
89. Creanga v. Jardal, 886 A.2d 633, 638 (N.J. 2005).
90. Landrigan v. Celotex Corp., 605 A.2d 1079, 1084 (N.J. 1992).
91. Ayers v. Jackson, 525 A.2d 287, 301 (N.J. 1987).
92. *James*, 714 A.2d at 909.
93. Sholtis v. Am. Cyanamid Co., 568 A.2d 1196, 1207 (N.J. Super. Ct. A.D. 1989).
94. *James*, 714 A.2d at 910 (quoting Tragarz v. Keene Corp., 980 F.2d 411, 420 (7th Cir. 1992)).
95. *Sholtis*, 568 A.2d at 1207.
96. *Tragarz*, 980 F.2d at 420.

In *James v. Bessemer Processing Co.*, the New Jersey Supreme Court extended the "frequency, regularity and proximity" test to an occupational nonasbestos tort exposure. Reversing an award of summary judgment to all defendants, the appellate held:

> at least for summary judgment purposes, we are convinced that the *Sholtis* analysis is relevant to the "medical causation" issue in a toxic-tort case, such as this, involving occupational exposure to cancer-causing substances manufactured by a determinant number of defendants, all of whom, it is alleged, acted tortiously by failing to warn of the dangerous propensities of their products.

The court further explained:

> We recognize that the dynamics and causative effects of exposure to asbestos dust may differ from the disease process resulting from exposure to chemicals containing known carcinogens. However, these differences should not cause rejection of the "frequency, regularity and proximity" model. Based on circumstantial evidence, the jury may find in any toxic-tort case, that a plaintiff in the workplace was exposed to the cancer-causing products of defendant-manufacturers on many occasions, and that the exposures were a substantial factor in causing plaintiff's cancer. Application of the "frequency, regularity and proximity" test necessarily focuses on the cumulative effects of exposure to the carcinogen over a prolonged period of time, the dosage of exposure and mode of absorption into the human body.[97]

The New Jersey Supreme Court agreed and held that "plaintiff in an occupational-exposure, toxic-tort case may demonstrate medical causation by establishing: (1) factual proof of the plaintiff's frequent, regular and proximate exposure to a defendant's products; and (2) medical and/or scientific proof of a nexus between the exposure and the plaintiff's condition."[98]

The New Jersey Supreme Court in *James* also distinguished its earlier holding in *Becker v. Baron Brothers*, which was relied upon by the trial court to grant summary judgment.[99] The New Jersey Supreme Court in *Becker* reversed and remanded a case in which a dispute existed as to whether chrysotile-asbestos fibers caused the plaintiff's cancer. Rather than permit the jury to resolve the disputed issue of fact as to the specific type of asbestos product, the trial court instructed the jury that it had found as a matter of law that all asbestos-containing friction products without a warning are defective. The New Jersey

---

97. 714 A.2d at 911; *see also* James v. Chevron U.S.A., Inc., 694 A.2d 270, 278–79 (N.J. Super. Ct. A.D. 1997).
98. *James*, 714 A.2d at 911.
99. *Id.* at 914 (citing Becker v. Baron Bros., 138 N.J. 145 (1994)).

Supreme Court explained that not all asbestos products are uniformly harmful and "thus should not be treated by courts as a monolithic group." But, the New Jersey Supreme Court contrasted the circumstances in *James* under which the decedent was exposed to a variety of products:

> Plaintiff's toxicologist's report indicates that all of those products contain benzene and PAHs, and that any exposure to those chemicals would have contributed, cumulatively, to James's cancer. Plaintiff is not seeking to impose, and our holding today does not invoke, market-share or alternative theories of liability. . . . Liability will attach only with respect to defendants to whose products plaintiff can prove James was frequently, regularly and proximately exposed. Furthermore, this appeal arose from an order granting summary judgment. We do not hold as a matter of law that every petroleum-based product to which James was exposed was defective, required a warning, or was capable of causing James's stomach and liver cancer. We hold only that plaintiff's proofs on those questions present disputed issues of material fact and therefore preclude a determination on motion for summary judgment that the petroleum defendants are not liable for failure to warn of the potential hazards of exposure to their products as a matter of law.[100]

However, in a lead paint case, *Baker v. Peoples*, the New Jersey Superior Court affirmed summary judgment for the defendants in a case in which the plaintiffs did not offer medical testimony to support causation.[101] The *Baker* court distinguished *Sholtis* and *James*, both involving exposures to multiple products over multiple decades from *Baker*'s case involving exposure to lead from chipped paint in one apartment for about nine months.[102]

General Causation

Rather than draw bright-line rules for what type of data may form the basis of causation opinions, New Jersey courts focus on the scientific reliability of the expert's methodology. The New Jersey Supreme Court in *Rubanick v. Witco Chemical Corp.* also relaxed the standard for admissibility of novel scientific evidence relating to causation in toxic tort litigation.[103] Under the relaxed standard, "a scientific theory of causation that has not yet reached general acceptance may be found to be sufficiently reliable if it is based on a sound, adequately-founded scientific methodology involving data and information of the type reasonably relied on by experts in the scientific field." "[I]t is not essential that there be general agreement with the opinions drawn from the methodology used. There must merely be some expert consensus that the methodology and the underlying data are

---

100. *Id.*
101. No. L-2044-09, 2012 WL 360283 (N.J. Super. Ct. A.D. Feb. 6, 2012).
102. *Id.* at *4.
103. 593 A.2d 733, 747–48 (N.J. 1991).

generally followed by experts in the field."[104] Thus, "*Rubanick* changed the focus of the inquiry from the scientific community's acceptance of the substance of the opinion to its acceptance of the methodology and reasoning underlying it."[105]

New Jersey courts recognize the utility of epidemiology to establish causation in toxic tort cases but do not require epidemiological evidence as the sole basis to establish causation.[106] Under certain factual circumstances, New Jersey courts are willing to accept reliance on epidemiological studies with relative risk less than 2.0.[107]

Animal studies can be an acceptable basis for an expert causation opinion.[108] The District of New Jersey, though, has recognized potential limitations on reliance on animal data to demonstrate causation in humans.[109]

New Jersey courts have permitted causation testimony based at least in part on case studies. In *Harris v. Peridot Chemical (N.J.), Inc.*, the appellate court found no error in admission of testimony based upon case reports from an expert in occupational and environmental medicine.[110] In *McCarrell v. Hoffman-La Roche, Inc.*, the appellate division declined to hold that case studies are per se excludable from an expert's conclusion.[111]

Specific Causation

A plaintiff may rely upon differential diagnosis to demonstrate specific causation.[112] As in other jurisdictions, though, New Jersey has recognized that the label "differential diagno-

---

104. *Id.*
105. Clark v. Safety-Kleen Corp., 845 A.2d 587, 599 (N.J. 2004).
106. McCarrell v. Hoffman-La Roche, Inc., 2009 WL 614484, at *22–23 (N.J. Super. Ct. A.D. Mar. 12, 2009), citing cases from other jurisdictions: In re Paoli R.R. Yard PCB Litig., 35 F.3d 717, 743 (3d Cir. 1994) (animal studies are admissible to prove causation in humans if good grounds are shown for extrapolating from animals to humans); Ferebee v. Chevron Chem. Co., 736 F.2d 1529, 1535 (D.C. Cir. 1984) (cause-effect relationship need not be established with epidemiological studies so long as the expert's opinion is otherwise based on sound methodology); *see also* DeLuca v. Merrell Dow Pharm., Inc., 911 F.2d 941, 954 (3d Cir. 1990) ("The reliability of expert testimony founded on reasoning from epidemiological data is generally a fit subject for judicial notice; epidemiology is a well-established branch of science and medicine, and epidemiological evidence has been accepted in numerous cases.").
107. Magistrini v. One Hour Martinizing Dry Cleaning, 180 F. Supp. 2d 584, 606 (D. N.J. 2002) ("[A] relative risk of 2.0 is not so much a password to a finding of causation as one piece of evidence, among others for the court to consider in determining whether an expert has employed a sound methodology in reaching his or her conclusion."); Landrigan v. Celotex Corp., 605 A.2d 1079, 1087 (N.J. 1992) (relative risk greater than 2.0 "could support an inference that the exposure was the probable cause of the disease in a specific member of the exposed population"); Grassis v. Johns-Manville Corp., 591 A.2d 671, 675 (N.J. Super. Ct. App. Div. 1991) ("The physician or other such qualified expert may view the epidemiological studies and factor out other known risk factors such as family history, diet, alcohol consumption, smoking . . . or other factors which might enhance the remaining recognized risks, even though the risk in the study fell short of the 2.0 correlation.").
108. Rubanick v. Witco Chem. Corp., 593 A.2d 733, 747–48 (N.J. 1991).
109. Magistrini v. One Hour Martinizing Dry Cleaning, 180 F. Supp. 2d 584, 593 (D. N.J. 2002) (calling for careful assessment of methodological validity and power of the available epidemiology as well as the quality of the toxicological studies and noting questions of interspecies extrapolation and dose-response).
110. 712 A.2d 1181 (N.J. Super. Ct. A.D. 1998).
111. 2009 WL 614484, at *41 (N.J. Super. Ct. A.D. Mar. 12, 2009).
112. Lapka v. Porter Hayden Co., 745 A.2d 525 (N.J. 2000); Rubanick v. Witco Chem. Corp., 593 A.2d 733 (N.J. 1991).

sis" does not automatically create an admissible opinion.[113] The Supreme Court of New Jersey has held that under certain circumstances, an expert who is not a physician may offer testimony to support specific causation.[114] However, the New Jersey District Court has excluded expert testimony purporting to demonstrate causation of one substance by claiming that similar substances are known to cause harm.[115]

New Jersey has not squarely addressed whether regulatory risk assessment may be used as a surrogate for dose response as part of specific causation. However, in *Rowe v. E. I. DuPont de Nemours & Co.*, the federal district court of New Jersey rejected the plaintiff's reliance on regulatory risk assessment techniques as a measure of harm in a proposed medical monitoring class.[116] The district court observed that a risk assessment does not identify a "danger point" above which people are at a distinctive increased risk. "Rather, the risk assessment serves to identify the 'safe' level that will protect the most sensitive members of the population."[117] The court's skepticism of the probative value of exposure over a risk assessment value suggests that absent additional proof, the court would not find such evidence sufficient.

New York
Overall Standard for Causation

In New York, a plaintiff must demonstrate that defendant's conduct was a substantial factor causing his or her injury.[118] New York Pattern Jury Instructions explain "substantial factor" as follows:

> An act or omission is regarded as a cause of an injury if it was a substantial factor in bringing about the injury, that is, if it had such an effect in producing the injury that reasonable people would regard it as a cause of the injury. There may be more than one cause of an injury, but to be substantial, it cannot be slight or trivial. You may, however, decide that a cause is substantial even if you assign a relatively small percentage to it.[119]

---

113. Creanga v. Jardal, 886 A.2d 633, 640 (N.J. 2005) ("To be admitted, the expert witness must demonstrate what he or she did and that the proper diagnostic procedures were followed when performing the diagnosis").
114. Rubanick v. Witco Chem. Corp., 593 A.2d 733 (N.J. 1991) (affirming ruling by Appellate Division that a biochemist, who was not a physician, could testify that exposure to PCBs had caused colon cancer in the individual plaintiffs); Landrigan v. Celotex Corp., 605 A.2d 1079 (N.J. 1992) (reversing lower court's exclusion of specific causation testimony because the proffering expert was not a medical doctor and had never treated patients).
115. DeLuca v. Merrell Dow Pharm., Inc., 791 F. Supp. 1042, 1054 (D. N.J. 1992), *aff'd*, 6 F.3d 778 (3d Cir. 1993) (concluding that the fact that drugs with similar structures are known to cause birth defects is not sufficient to demonstrate that Bendectin is capable of causing birth defects).
116. No. 06-1810, 2008 WL 5412912 (D. N.J. Dec. 23, 2008).
117. *Id.* at *18.
118. *In re* New York City Asbestos Litig., 860 N.Y.S.2d 506, 507 (N.Y. App. Div. 2008).
119. N.Y. PJI 2:70 (3d ed. 2001). Courts interpreting the standard in nontoxic tort cases have affirmed that a slight cause of an injury may be sufficient to satisfy the substantial factor test. *See, e.g.*, Stewart v. New

In order to establish causation in a toxic tort case, a plaintiff must offer admissible expert proof to establish that the plaintiff has been exposed to a toxin, that the toxin is capable of causing the plaintiff's injury, and that the plaintiff was exposed to sufficient levels of the toxin to cause the illness.[120] An expert opinion that a plaintiff's injuries could have been caused by one or more of the defendant's products, possibly by themselves or possibly in combination, is not sufficient to demonstrate proximate cause.[121]

Earlier New York state decisions do not apply any relaxed standard of proof for causation simply because a matter involves a latent disease, underdeveloped science, or complex exposure patterns. "The law does not intend that the less that is known about a disease the greater shall be the opportunity of recovery in court."[122] Some later opinions permit slightly relaxed evidence to reach a jury. For instance, the New York Court of Appeals has held that a plaintiff need not always "quantify exposure levels precisely or use the dose-response relationship."[123] The court recognized multiple ways in which an expert might demonstrate causation that do not require precise mathematical calculation of plaintiff's exposure. However, the court affirmed exclusion of a subjective exposure opinion that failed to state the level of exposure in underlying epidemiology studies and provide some reasonable basis for a jury to conclude that the plaintiff's exposure exceeded that level.[124]

General Causation

New York recognizes epidemiology as an appropriate and acceptable methodology to assess general causation.[125] The Second Circuit recognizes broad discretion of the district court to determine what type of evidence is admissible to support general causation expert opinions. In *Ruggiero v. Warner-Lambert Co.*, the Second Circuit found no error in the district court's exclusion of a general causation opinion based upon differential diagnosis and no epidemiology.[126] The Second Circuit noted that in the instant case, although the

---

York City Health & Hosps. Corp., 616 N.Y.S.2d 499, 499 (N.Y. App. Div. 1994); Lewis v. AMTRAK, 675 N.Y.S.2d 504, 506 (N.Y. Civ. Ct. 1998).

120. Parker v. Mobil Oil Corp., 857 N.E.2d 1114, 1120–21 (N.Y. 2006). The Second Circuit has found expert evidence necessary when injury has multiple potential etiologies even in claims under the Jones Act where plaintiffs burden of proof to establish causation is reduced. *See* Wills v. Amerada Hess Corp., 379 F.3d 32, 46 (2d Cir. 2004).
121. Carlin v. RFE Indus., Inc., No. 88-CV-842, 1995 WL 760739, at *4 (N.D.N.Y. Nov. 27, 1995).
122. Miller v. Nat'l Cabinet Co., 168 N.E.2d 811, 818 (N.Y. 1960) (finding plaintiff failed to demonstrate a direct cause-in-fact between benzol and leukemia).
123. *Parker*, 857 N.E.2d at 1121; *see also* Jackson v. Nutmeg Techs., Inc., 43 A.D.3d 599, 602 (N.Y. App. Div. 2007) (affirming denial of summary judgment based upon expert causation opinion that created material disputed fact).
124. *Parker*, 857 N.E.2d at 1121–22.
125. *Jackson*, 43 A.D.3d at 601 (citing Nonnon v. City of New York, 32 A.D.3d 91, 104–05 (N.Y. App. Div. 2006), *aff'd*, 874 N.E.2d 720 (N.Y. 2007)).
126. Ruggiero v. Warner-Lambert Co., 424 F.3d 249, 254–55 (2d Cir. 2005). New York state courts follow the *Frye* standard of general acceptance in the scientific community to determine whether expert opinions are admissible.

expert ruled out other potential causes of plaintiff's injury, the expert provided no basis upon which he ruled in the drug at issue.

However, the court clarified that it was not holding that a differential diagnosis could never be the basis for a general causation opinion. "There may be instances where, because of the rigor of differential diagnosis performed, the expert's training and experience, the type of illness or injury at issue, or some other case-specific circumstance, a differential diagnosis is sufficient to support an expert's opinion in support of both general and specific causation."[127] The Second Circuit cited to a previous decision that found no error admitting an opinion based upon care and treatment of plaintiff, medical history, pathological studies, material safety data sheets for products at issue, reference to scientific and medical treatises, the expert's training and experience, and differential diagnosis.

The Southern District of New York, perhaps in deference to commentary from the Second Circuit, has evolved its approach to whether epidemiology studies must be statistically significant in order to support a causation opinion. In 1993, the court stated: "[N]o matter how many studies yield a positive but statistically insignificant SMR for colorectal cancer, the results remain statistically insignificant. Just as adding a series of zeros together yields yet another zero as the product, adding a series of positive but statistically insignificant SMRs together does not produce a statistically significant pattern."[128] On other grounds, the Second Circuit reversed the entry of judgment as a matter of law and reinstated the jury verdict. Commenting specifically on the Southern District's conclusions as to statistical significance, the Second Circuit stated:

> The district court [] cited no authority for the bold assertion that SMRs of less than 1.50 are statistically insignificant and cannot be relied upon by a jury to support a finding of causation. Although perhaps a floor can be set as a matter of law, we are reluctant to adopt such an approach. We believe that it would be far preferable for the district court to *instruct* the jury on statistical significance and then let the jury decide whether many studies over the 1.0 mark have any significance in combination.[129]

Over a decade later, the Southern District declined to exclude expert testimony on the grounds that plaintiffs' expert failed to produce statistically significant results to support the causation opinion. In *In re Ephedra Products Liability Litigation*, the district court explained that the more probable than not standard does not necessarily equate to the scientific convention of statistical significance.[130]

---

127. *Id.* (citing McCullock v. H.B. Fuller Co., 61 F.3d 1038, 1043–44 (2d Cir. 1995)).
128. *In re* Joint E. & S. Dist. Asbestos Litig., 827 F. Supp. 1014, 1042 (S.D.N.Y. 1993).
129. *In re* Joint E. & S. Dist. Asbestos Litig., 52 F.3d 1124, 1134 (2d Cir. 1995).
130. 393 F. Supp. 2d 181, 193 (S.D.N.Y. 2005).

Specific Causation

Jackson v. Nutmeg Technologies, Inc. provides an example of plaintiffs surviving a motion *in limine* on the adequacy of foundation of proof of exposure.[131] In *Jackson*, the defendants did not dispute general causation, but challenged the foundation of the specific causation opinion because the plaintiff's expert did not establish exposure to an established dangerous level of the toxin. The court affirmed denial of summary judgment by the trial court, noting that the plaintiffs had proffered evidence explaining the low levels of toxin measured in the air shortly after the leak and submitted a published investigation report detailing the epidemiological methods used by the expert.[132]

However, in *Fraser v. 301-52 Townhouse Corp.*, the majority affirmed exclusion of a causation opinion based upon differential diagnosis that was not supported by published studies that demonstrate that dampness and mold are capable of causing the plaintiff's injuries.[133] The dissent characterized an "association" in epidemiology as "a continuum, which spans from [coincidence] to unquestionable causation."[134] The dissent considered the plaintiff's proffered evidence sufficient to be closer to the causal side of the continuum; and, thus, the dissent would have found materially disputed facts sufficient to reverse summary judgment. The majority responded:

> We have no argument with the dissent's statement that "'[a]ssociation'. . . is a continuum . . . span[ning] from . . . coincidence . . . to causation." This observation is of little help to plaintiffs, however, because the dissent points to nothing in the record, other than [the expert's] unsupported assertions, that justifies the conclusion that the observed association between the conditions and ailments in question is strong enough to constitute evidence of causation.[135]

The majority also rejected the plaintiff's specific causation opinion because the plaintiff offered no threshold level of mold necessary to cause the plaintiff's injuries. Acknowledging prior precedent regarding exposure quantification, the court concluded: "we do not believe that, under the circumstances, plaintiffs' reliance on the method of differential diagnosis was an adequate substitute for quantitative proof."[136]

New York courts have also addressed the probative value of regulatory standards to establish causation. For example, the New York Court of Appeals rejected reliance on

---

131. 43 A.D.3d 599 (N.Y. App. Div. 2007).
132. *Id.* at 601–02; *see also* B.T.N. v. Auburn Enlarged City Sch. Dist., 45 A.D.3d 1339 (N.Y. App. Div. 2007) (upholding denial of summary judgment when plaintiff's expert relied upon differential diagnosis to demonstrate specific causation with no precise quantification of exposure or establishment of dose response).
133. 57 A.D.3d 416 (N.Y. App. Div. 2008).
134. *Id.* at 432.
135. *Id.* at 419 n.4.
136. *Id.* at 419–20.

regulatory standards as a basis for causation opinions, stating: "[S]tandards promulgated by regulatory agencies as protective measures are inadequate to demonstrate legal causation."[137] The Eastern District of New York's often-cited opinion, *In re Agent Orange Product Liability Litigation*, also distinguished regulatory risk assessment from the necessary proof of causation:

> The distinction between avoidance of risk through regulation and compensation for injuries after the fact is a fundamental one. In the former, risk assessments may lead to control of a toxic substance even though the probability of harm to any individual is small and the studies necessary to assess the risk are incomplete; society as a whole is willing to pay the price as a matter of policy. In the latter, a far higher probability (greater than 50%) is required since the law believes it unfair to require an individual to pay for another's tragedy unless it is shown that it is more likely than not that he caused it.[138]

In one case, the plaintiffs' expert conceded that he had not determined the level of exposure, but instead relied solely upon potential deleterious health effects listed in various regulatory documents.[139] The court pointed out that the regulatory sheets were written as cleanup guides for either substations or spills. The court also noted the only exposure limits in the document were for exposure pathways that were not at issue in the instant case. Finally, the court explained that the regulatory documents, "regardless of the deleterious health effects they recite," could not be "accepted in lieu of statistically sound, scientific, medical studies linking exposures to toxins to particular illnesses in living creatures.... Thus, such recommended or prescribed precautionary standards cannot provide legal causation here."[140]

On the other hand, New York has also rejected the argument by a defendant that contaminant levels below a maximum contaminant level (MCL) present no injury.[141]

---

137. Parker v. Mobil Oil Corp., 857 N.E.2d 1114, 1122 (N.Y. 2006).
138. 597 F. Supp. 740, 781 (E.D.N.Y. 1984), *aff'd*, 818 F.2d 145 (2d Cir. 1987), *cert. denied sub nom.* Pinkney v. Dow Chem. Co., 484 U.S. 1004 (1988).
139. Mancuso v. Consol. Edison Co. of N.Y., 967 F. Supp. 1437, 1448–49 (S.D.N.Y. 1997).
140. *Id.* at 1448.
141. Suffolk Cnty. Water Auth. v. Dow Chem. Co., 942 N.Y.S.2d 765, 770 (N.Y. Sup. Ct. 2012) ("[C]ourts throughout the country have specifically rejected the use of the bright line MCL test as a measure of when injury occurs."); *In re* MTBE Prods. Liab. Litig., 458 F. Supp. 2d 149, 157–59 (S.D.N.Y. 2006) ("[W]hile the MCL may serve as a convenient guidepost in determining that a particular level of contamination has likely caused an injury, the MCL does not define *whether* an injury has occurred."); German v. Fed. Home Loan Mortgage Corp., 885 F. Supp. 537, 559 (S.D.N.Y. 1995) (denying summary judgment where contamination was below MCL because factual issue of whether plaintiff was injured at lower levels of exposure was disputed).

Pennsylvania

Overall Standard for Causation

In toxic tort litigation, one Pennsylvania court set forth a plaintiff's burden to demonstrate causation as follows:

> In order to meet their burden plaintiffs must offer evidence, (presumably in the form of expert medical testimony), from which a jury can reasonably find or infer, that *the specific plaintiff involved in this case* was, *in fact*, proximately caused to develop an asbestos-related disease as a result of the plaintiff's inhalation of fibers shed from a specific friction product of the defendant.[142]

The court recognized practical restrictions on human capacities render it impossible to directly observe a single fiber from a defendant's product into the body of a plaintiff. Instead, Pennsylvania law requires medical expert proof to demonstrate causation in complex cases.[143]

Pennsylvania courts apply a "regularity, frequency, and proximity" test. In *Robertson*, the Third Circuit rejected the plaintiff's argument that Pennsylvania courts would abandon the "regularity, frequency, and proximity" test in cases that involved expert testimony as opposed to relying solely on circumstantial evidence.[144] After examining relevant authority, the Third Circuit predicted that the Pennsylvania Supreme Court would find the elements apply with equal force. "Under Pennsylvania law, the fiber drift theory, as defined by the plaintiffs, is insufficient to create a jury question on the issue of causation."[145]

The Pennsylvania Supreme Court has affirmed exclusions of a plaintiff's expert testimony concluding that every exposure to asbestos is a substantial contributing factor to cause a plaintiff's harm.[146] In *Gregg v. V-J Auto Parts, Co.*, the trial court rejected that a single fiber of asbestos could be a substantial factor, stating that would be the same as "if one took a bucket of water and dumped it into the ocean, [finding that the bucket of water] was a substantial contributing factor to the size of the ocean."[147] In *Betz v. Pneumo Abex, LLC*, the Pennsylvania Supreme Court noted that the plaintiff's expert conceded there

---

142. *In re* Toxic Substances Cases, No. A.D. 03-319, 2006 WL 2404008, at *4 (Pa. Com. Pl. Aug. 17, 2006).
143. *In re* Dobrowsky, 735 F.2d 90, 92 (3d Cir. 1984) ("Under Pennsylvania law ... when an injury is not the 'obvious, natural or probable result' of an accident, the plaintiff has the preliminary burden of demonstrating causation by introducing expert medical testimony."); Kemmerer v. State Farm Ins. Co., No. 01-5445, 2004 WL 87017, at *3 (E.D. Pa. Jan. 19, 2004).
144. Robertson v. Allied Signal Inc., 914 F.2d 360, 382 (3d Cir. 1990).
145. *Id.*
146. Betz v. Pneumo Abex, LLC, 44 A.3d 27, 57–58 (Pa. 2012); Gregg v. V-J Auto Parts, Co., 943 A.2d 216, 223 (Pa. 2007).
147. 943 A.2d at 223 (quotations omitted).

is a dose response with asbestos exposure that contradicted the same expert's testimony that exposure to a single fiber among millions was substantially causative.[148]

General Causation

Whether an expert will be required to cite epidemiological evidence to support a general causation opinion is driven to some degree by the body of available science. In *Gannon v. United States*, the district court examined competing causation analysis and concluded that plaintiffs failed to meet their burden to show general and specific causation.[149] The court cited the following key factors in excluding plaintiffs' expert: (1) the expert relied solely upon biological evidence despite statements in the cited reports that biological data on their own cannot show causality; (2) the expert did not consider more recent available epidemiological studies; and (3) the expert relied upon animal toxicology data but admits that animals form tumors in a different way from humans.[150]

By contrast, in *Heller v. Shaw Industries*, the Third Circuit held that a properly conducted analysis underlying an expert's opinion could be admissible to demonstrate causation even in the absence of published literature supporting the opinion.[151] The court concluded that a bright-line test requiring that an expert cite published studies would be improper, especially in situations where the state of research is in its early stages. Although *Heller* held that epidemiology studies are not per se required to support general causation, the court did not address a situation in which the expert (as in *Gannon*) ignores available epidemiological studies.[152]

The Pennsylvania Supreme Court has stated that case reports, animal studies, and regulatory standards are "ineffectual in terms of substantial-factor causation, since the most these can do is suggest that there is underlying risk from the defendant's products. . . ."[153] In *Blum v. Merrell Dow Pharmaceuticals, Inc.*, the court stated that animal studies, although possibly suggestive of causation, are not sufficient in the absence of epidemiology to establish causation.[154] The *Blum* court found the causal proof insufficient because "no

---

148. 44 A.3d at 36–37.
149. 571 F. Supp. 2d 615 (E.D. Pa. 2007).
150. *Id.* at 203; *see also* Pritchard v. Dow Agro Scis., 705 F. Supp. 2d 471, 484–85 (W.D. Pa. 2010); *aff'd*, No. 10-2168, 2011 WL 2160456 (3d Cir. June 2, 2011) (In evaluating general causation opinions, courts should examine "whether the expert relied on epidemiology studies; whether the expert ignored or sufficiently addressed epidemiological studies which contradicted his hypothesis, explaining the discrepancy between his hypothesis and that of the authors; and, whether the findings set forth in the studies are statistically significant.").
151. 167 F.3d 146, 155 (3d Cir. 1999).
152. *Pritchard*, 705 F. Supp. 2d at 485.
153. Betz v. Pneumo Abex, LLC, 44 A.3d 27, 55 (Pa. 2012).
154. 705 A.2d 1314, 1323 (Pa. Super. Ct. 1997) (distinguishing both the dose provided in animal studies from human exposures and the mechanism of action in animals as compared to humans). *But see In re* Paoli R.R. Yard PCB Litig., 35 F.3d 717, 781 (3d Cir. 1994) (district court abused its discretion in excluding animal studies relied upon by the EPA), *cert. denied sub nom.* Gen. Elec. Co. v. Ingram, 513 U.S. 1190 (1995).

epidemiological study of Bendectin concludes that there is a statistically significant relative risk high enough to support a claim of general causation. . . ."[155] In *Perry v. Novartis Pharmaceuticals Corp.*, the Eastern District of Pennsylvania recognized that "while an expert's conclusions reached on the basis of other studies could be sufficiently reliable where no epidemiological studies have been conducted, no reliable scientific approach can simply ignore the epidemiology that exists."[156] Expert testimony relying solely upon case reports has been excluded as not meeting "the most basic standards of scientific validity."[157]

Keeping with the Third Circuit's more flexible approach to *Daubert* evaluations, the Western District of Pennsylvania favored a more flexible interpretation of the relative risk. The *Pritchard* court concluded that a relative risk of 2.0 is not dispositive of causation but is one factor to consider, along with confidence intervals, range of relative risk values set forth in the study, and whether the authors found the association to be statistically significant.[158]

Specific Causation

Under Pennsylvania law, a plaintiff may rely upon differential diagnosis to prove specific causation. The Eastern District of Pennsylvania has determined that differential diagnosis, while it may be the basis for a specific causation opinion, is not a proper basis to demonstrate general causation.[159] The Third Circuit found error with a district court's requirement that an expert rule out all possible causes of plaintiff's injury in order to be an admissible differential diagnosis.[160]

In order to establish exposure sufficient to cause harm (dose/response), one Pennsylvania court permitted an expert to extrapolate that acute high doses known to cause harm may also cause harm at chronic low doses;[161] however, subsequent decisions place limitations on permissible extrapolation.[162] One Pennsylvania court rejected the "single molecule" exposure theory, stating:

> Generally accepted scientific methodology may well establish that certain "high dose" asbestos exposure causes, or contributes to, a specific hypothetical plaintiff's disease, but the plaintiffs have not proffered any generally accepted methodology to support the contention that a single exposure or an otherwise vanishingly small exposure has,

---

155. *Blum*, 705 A.2d at 1323.
156. 564 F. Supp. 2d 452, 465 (E.D. Pa. 2008).
157. *In re* TMI Litig., 911 F. Supp. 775, 801 (M.D. Pa. 1996), *aff'd*, 193 F.3d 613 (3d Cir. 1999).
158. Pritchard v. Dow Agro Scis., 705 F. Supp. 2d 471, 486 (W.D. Pa. 2010).
159. Leake v. United States, No. 09-4564, 2011 WL 6934057, at *7 (E.D. Pa. Dec. 29, 2011).
160. Heller v. Shaw Indus., 167 F.3d 146, 156 (3d Cir. 1999).
161. Trach v. Fellin, 817 A.2d 1102, 1119–20 (Pa. Super. Ct. 2003) (relying heavily on Ferebee v. Chevron Chem. Co., 736 F.2d 1529, 1535–36 (D.C. Cir. 1984) discussed under District of Columbia).
162. *In re* Toxic Substances Cases, No. A.D. 03-319, 2006 WL 2404008, at *7–8 (Pa. Com. Pl. Aug. 17, 2006); Vinitski v. Adler, No. 2533, 2004 WL 2579288, at *5 (Pa. Com. Pl. Sept. 17, 2004).

in fact, in any case, ever caused or contributed to any specific individual's disease, or even less so, that in this case such a small exposure did, in fact, contribute to this specific plaintiff's disease.[163]

The court illustrated the fundamental toxicological principle that the dose makes the poison as follows:

> The fallacy of the "extrapolation down" argument is plainly illustrated by common sense and common experience. Large amounts of alcohol can intoxicate, larger amounts can kill; a very small amount, however, can do neither. Large amounts of nitroglycerine or arsenic can injure, larger amounts can kill; small amounts, however, are medicinal. Great volumes of water may be harmful, greater volumes or an extended absence of water can be lethal; moderate amounts of water, however, are healthful. In short, the poison is in the dose.[164]

The Eastern District of Pennsylvania rejected plaintiff's reliance on a regulatory risk screening level as a surrogate to establish that a proposed class was exposed to a sufficient dose to cause harm.[165] The court noted that the screening level reflects a level below which the public health agency believes the "mixed" population is safe. The court further explained that exposure above such a prophylactic safety marker does not equate to significant harm or even predict actual risk to the entire population.

Rhode Island
Overall Standard for Causation

Rhode Island requires that a plaintiff demonstrate that "but for" defendant's conduct the plaintiff's injury would not have occurred, and that the defendant's conduct produced the event in an unbroken and natural sequence. "Proximate cause is a more exacting standard than simple 'but for' causation."[166]

In *DiPetrillo v. Dow Chemical Co.*,[167] Dow challenged the trial court's jury instruction on proximate cause. The trial judge instructed: "under Rhode Island law in order to prove proximate cause, plaintiff must prove by a preponderance of the evidence that but for the breach of the implied warranty, the injury complained of would not have occurred." The trial court also instructed that "an injury is proximately caused by an act or a failure to act whenever it appears from the preponderance of the evidence that act or omission in

---

163. *In re* Toxic Substances Cases, 2006 WL 2404008, at *9.
164. *Id.* at *7.
165. Gates v. Rohm and Haas Co., 265 F.R.D. 208, 226–27 (E.D. Pa. 2010), *aff'd*, 655 F.3d 255 (3d Cir. 2011).
166. State v. Lead Indus. Ass'n, Inc., 951 A.2d 428, 451 (R.I. 2008) (citing Tavares v. Aramark Corp., 841 A.2d 1124, 1128 (R.I. 2004)).
167. 729 A.2d 677 (R.I. 1999).

natural, unbroken and continuous sequence produced the event about which complaint is made." The trial court also responded to two jury requests for additional instruction on proximate cause as follows:

> Before plaintiff can recover damages, he has the burden of proving by a preponderance of the evidence that his injuries were proximately caused by exposure to the chemical. Plaintiff must show that his multiple myeloma *would not have occurred in the absence of the exposure* to the chemical.[168]

Next, the trial court instructed: "Proximately pertains to that which in an *ordinary, natural sequence* produces a specific result." The Supreme Court of Rhode Island found no error with the instructions, because it concluded the trial court properly and adequately instructed the jury that it must find "but for" causation and that defendant's act or omission produced the event in a natural, unbroken, and continuous sequence.

The plaintiff bears the burden to demonstrate that defendant caused the harm that is the subject of the litigation. A plaintiff may do this, in some instances, through circumstantial evidence. But, the plaintiff must produce sufficient evidence to establish that it is probable, not merely possible, that defendant is the source of the product or contaminant.[169] Expert testimony is required to support causation if the underlying facts and inferences are not obvious to a layperson and lie beyond common knowledge.[170] Epidemiology evidence, while perhaps not sufficient to demonstrate specific causation, is relevant in general causation for nuisance.[171]

Rhode Island has an extensive history with lead paint litigation. In 1999, the Rhode Island Attorney General filed suit against various former lead paint manufacturers and a national trade association. The first trial ended as a mistrial. The second trial took four months and resulted in the first jury verdict imposing liability on lead pigment manufacturers for creating a public nuisance. Ultimately, the Supreme Court of Rhode Island reversed the judgment for abatement. Along the way, however, the trial court considered causation in context of a public nuisance. The defendants argued that the state should be required to identify the specific defendant responsible for the injury. The trial court distinguished the instant case from one in which it is alleged that one defendant out of a number of defendants made a product causing a single injury to a plaintiff. Rather, the plaintiff alleged that each defendant's own separate actions substantially contributed to the cumulative effect of lead pigment in buildings throughout the state. Thus, in order

---

168. *Id.* at 692–93.
169. *See* Clift v. Vose Hardware, 848 A.2d 1130, 1132 (R.I. 2004).
170. Mills v. State Sales, Inc., 824 A.2d 461, 468 (R.I. 2003); *see also* Evans v. Liguori, 374 A.2d 774, 777 (R.I. 1977) (recognizing expert testimony not always required in wrongful death action but necessary when causation is not obvious to layperson).
171. State v. Lead Indus. Ass'n, Inc., No. PC 99-5226, 2007 WL 711824, at *48 (R.I. Sup. Ct. Feb. 26, 2007).

to prove causation, the court held that the plaintiff must establish that each defendant's conduct was a substantial cause of the public nuisance *and* that the public nuisance was a substantial factor in causing the injuries to the public.

Vermont
Overall Standard for Causation
Vermont applies a "but for" causation standard in most tort cases; however, in cases involving more than one proximate cause of injury, Vermont has employed a substantial factor analysis.[172] The Vermont Supreme Court has explained, though, that the standard to demonstrate substantial factor is no less rigorous than the standard to demonstrate "but for" causation.[173] Rather, it simply recognizes the potential for more than one proximate cause of harm.

In toxic tort cases, the Vermont Supreme Court has held that the plaintiff must establish by probability, not merely possibility, both exposure to a chemical at a level that could cause his physical condition and exposure to the chemical did in fact cause the condition.[174] Expert testimony is considered essential to establish causation in toxic tort cases because the connection between chemical exposure and plaintiff's injury "is not at all obvious."[175] Experts in toxic tort cases must testify to a reasonable degree of scientific certainty.[176]

General Causation
The Vermont Supreme Court has stated that a relative risk of greater than 2.0 is a useful benchmark in evaluating epidemiologic evidence underlying causation opinions.[177] However, an expert's reliance upon studies with relative risks greater than 2.0 does not automatically create a jury question on causation. In *Blanchard v. Goodyear Tire & Rubber Co.*, where the plaintiff's own expert admitted "no-one will ever know if there was benzene on the field and [] plaintiff's statements as to the amount of time he played on the field say nothing about his level of exposure," the court concluded that epidemiology studies linking benzene to plaintiff's illness "cannot overcome these shortcomings."[178]

Specific Causation
The Vermont Supreme Court recognizes differential diagnosis as an accepted method to prove specific causation.[179] However, the court notes circumstances such as weak circum-

---

172. Wilkins v. Lamoille Cnty. Mental Health Servs., Inc., 889 A.2d 245, 251 & n.3 (Vt. 2005).
173. *Id.* at 251.
174. Blanchard v. Goodyear Tire & Rubber Co., 30 A.3d 1271, 1274–75 (Vt. 2011).
175. Soutiere v. Betzdearborn, Inc., 189 F. Supp. 2d 183, 190 (D. Vt. 2002).
176. Graham v. Canadian Nat'l Ry., Co., 749 F. Supp. 1300, 1318 (D. Vt. 1990).
177. George v. Vermont League of Cities & Towns, 993 A.2d 367, 375 (Vt. 2010).
178. *Blanchard*, 30 A.3d at 1278.
179. *Blanchard*, 30 A.3d at 1275–76.

stantial evidence of exposure or failure to rule out idiopathic origin for disease may call for more than just a differential diagnosis to sustain a plaintiff's burden of proof.

The Vermont Supreme Court recognizes, though, that "in many, if not most, toxic tort cases it is impossible 'to quantify with hard proof—such as the presence of the alleged toxic substance in the plaintiff's blood or tissue—the precise amount of the toxic substance to which an individual plaintiff was exposed.'"[180] A plaintiff's experts may establish exposure levels through circumstantial evidence and mathematical modeling. However, the Vermont Supreme Court observed that while precise quantification of exposure may not be necessary, courts generally exclude expert testimony lacking in any measure of a plaintiff's exposure to the allegedly harmful substance.

In *Graham v. Canadian National Railway Co.*, the federal district court concluded that the dose of herbicide reaching the plaintiffs' homes was insufficient to cause harm to humans, plants, or animals.[181] The court found the defendant's expert, a medical toxicologist, persuasive. The expert testified that the plaintiffs' injuries could not have been caused by herbicides, since their exposure was well below the reference dose, which he calculated by taking the no observable adverse effect level from toxicology studies and decreasing it by a safety factor to ensure no human effect.[182] Accordingly, the court found no proximate cause of the alleged injuries from spraying the herbicide. The court further explained that shortage of proof of proximate cause "is not cured by reliance on the doctrine of *res ipsa loquitur*." "In order for an occurrence to provide sufficient evidence of the cause of harm, the underlying proof must tend to eliminate other possible sources of harm in such a way that the inference is clear the injury is causally attributed to the conduct of the defendant."[183]

In contrast, the District of Vermont found sufficient evidence to reach a jury in a circumstantial evidence exposure case.[184] In *McCullock v. H.B. Fuller Co.*, the plaintiff offered testimony from a consulting engineer that plaintiff was within the "breathing zone" of a hot-melt glue pot. The plaintiff's expert based his testimony on interviews of the plaintiff, review of material safety data sheets, review of safety material on ventilation, and his practical experience with fumes. Defendants argued that the expert did not know the constituents of the glue and could not determine the concentration level of any fumes. The Second Circuit affirmed, finding the exposure testimony, coupled with a differential diagnosis, provided sufficient basis to reach the jury.[185]

---

180. *Blanchard*, 30 A.3d at 1275 (quoting Plourde v. Gladstone, 150 F. Supp. 2d 708, 721 (D. Vt. 2002)).
181. 749 F. Supp. 1300 (D. Vt. 1990).
182. *Id.* at 1311–12 & n.11.
183. *Id.* at 1319.
184. McCullock v. H.B. Fuller Co., 61 F.3d 1038 (2d Cir. 1995).
185. *Id.* at 1045.

TABLE OF CASES

A

Abarca v. Franklin County Water Dist., 761 F. Supp. 2d 1007 (E.D. Cal. 2011), 120n33, 127n23, 157n86, 211n186

Abbatiello v. Monsanto Co., 522 F. Supp. 2d 524 (S.D.N.Y. 2007), 17n48

ABB Indus. Sys., Inc. v. Prime Tech., Inc., 120 F.3d 351 (2d Cir. 1997), 64n43

Abbott, State v., 498 P.2d 712 (Alaska 1972), 310n3

Able Supply Co. v. Moye, 898 S.W.2d 766 (Tex. 1995), 227n233, 398n281

Abnet v. Coca-Cola Co., 786 F. Supp. 2d 1341 (W.D. Mich. 2011), 283

Abrams v. CIBA Specialty Chems. Corp., 659 F. Supp. 2d 1225 (S.D. Ala. 2009), 71n83

Abrams v. CIBA Specialty Chems. Corp., No. 08-0068-WSB, 2009 WL 3254443 (S.D. Ala. Oct. 1, 2009), 96n246

Acceleron, LLC v. Egenera, Inc., 634 F. Supp. 2d 758 (E.D. Tex. 2009), 230n250

Acevedo v. Consol. Edison Co. of N.Y., 596 N.Y.S.2d 68 (N.Y. App. Div. 1993), 118n387

Ackermann v. Wyeth Pharm., 526 F.3d 203 (5th Cir. 2008), 106n310, 112n347, 112n349

Ackison v. Anchor Packing Co., 897 N.E.2d 1118 (Ohio 2008), 16n41, 17n48, 358n200, 358n202

Acoba v. General Tire, Inc., 986 P.2d 288 (Haw. 1999), 319n83

Acosta Orellana v. CropLife Int'l, 711 F. Supp. 2d 81 (D.D.C. 2010), 16n40

Actiesselskabet Ingrid v. Cent. R.R. Co. of N.J., 216 F. 72 (2d Cir. 1912), 23n79

Acuna v. Brown and Root, Inc., 200 F.3d 335 (5th Cir. 2000), 227n234

Acushnet River & New Bedford Harbor: Proceedings re Alleged PCB Pollution, *In re*, 716 F. Supp. 676 (D. Mass. 1989), 50n251

Adams v. A.J. Ballard, Jr. Tire & Oil Co., Nos. 01 CVS 1271, 03 CVS 912 & 03 CVS 1124, 2006 WL 1875965 (N.C. Super. Ct. June 30, 2006), 88n208

Adams v. Clean Air Sys., Inc., 586 N.E.2d 940 (Ind. Ct. App. 1992), 337

Adams v. Cleveland Cliffs Iron Co., 602 N.W.2d 215 (Mich. Ct. App. 1999), 283n14

Adams v. NVR Homes, Inc., 135 F. Supp. 2d 675 (D. Md. 2001), 29n119

Adams v. Union Carbide Corp., 737 F.2d 1453 (6th Cir. 1984), 107n315

Adams-Arapahoe Sch. Dist. No. 28-J v. U.S. Gypsum Co., 958 F.2d 381, 1992 WL 58963 (10th Cir. Mar. 23, 1992), 89n212

Adamson v. General Elec. Co., 694 S.E.2d 363 (Ga. Ct. App. 2010), 378n98, 379n114

Adkins v. Thomas Solvent Co., 487 N.W.2d 715 (Mich. 1992), 19n61, 100n273

AES Corp. v. Steadfast Ins. Co., 725 S.E.2d 532 (Va. 2012), 291n55

Agent Orange Prod. Liab. Litig., *In re*, 821 F.2d 139 (2d Cir. 1987), 199n143, 201n154

Agent Orange Prod. Liab. Litig., *In re*, 517 F.3d 76 (2d Cir. 2008), 117

Agent Orange Prod. Liab. Litig., *In re*, 597 F. Supp. 740 (E.D.N.Y. 1984), *aff'd*, 818 F.2d 145 (2d Cir. 1987), *cert. denied sub nom.* Pinkney v. Dow Chem. Co., 484 U.S. 1004 (1988), 426

Agent Orange Prod. Liab. Litig., *In re*, 611 F. Supp. 1223 (E.D.N.Y. 1985), *aff'd*, 818 F.2d 187 (2d Cir. 1987), 36n168, 134n69

Agner v. Daniel Int'l Corp., 2007 WL 57769 (W.D.N.C. Jan. 5, 2007), 391n222

Aguilar v. Citgo Refining & Chems. Co., No. C-97-279 (S.D. Tex. Nov. 3, 1998), reported in 13 Tox. L. Rptr. 810 (BNA) (Nov. 25, 1998), 152

A.H. Robins Co., *In re*, 880 F.2d 709 (4th Cir. 1989), *cert. denied sub nom.* Anderson v. Aetna Cas. & Sur. Co., 493 U.S. 959 (1989), 272n8

Aikens v. Debow, 541 S.E.2d 576 (W. Va. 2000), 402n312

Air Crash Disaster at New Orleans, La., *In re*, 795 F.2d 1230 (5th Cir. 1986), 158n93

Alamo Nat'l Bank v. Kraus, 616 S.W.2d 908 (Tex. 1981), 51n261

Alberts v. Schultz, 975 P.2d 1279 (N.M. 1999), 325n133

Alcoa, Inc. v. Behringer, 235 S.W.3d 456 (Tex. App. 2007), 294nn71–73

Alder v. Bayer Corp., 61 P.3d 1068 (Utah 2002), 328, 329

Aldridge v. Goodyear Tire & Rubber Co., 34 F. Supp. 2d 1010 (D. Md. 1999), *vacated & remanded*, 223 F.3d 263 (4th Cir. 2000), 413

Alexander v. Hulsey Envtl. Servs., Inc., 702 S.E.2d 435 (Ga. Ct. App. 2010), 97n251

Alexander v. Bozeman Motors, Inc., 234 P.3d 880 (Mont. 2010), 119

Alexander Grant & Co. Litig., *In re*, 820 F.2d 352 (11th Cir. 1987), 199n140

Alfred L. Snapp & Son, Inc. v. Puerto Rico *ex rel.* Barez, 458 U.S. 592 (1982), 34nn154–155

Allen v. International Bus. Machs. Corp., 128 F. App'x 311 (4th Cir. 2005), 118nn385–386

Allen v. Martin Surfacing, 263 F.R.D. 47 (D. Mass. 2009), 417nn80–81

Allen v. Pennsylvania Eng'g Corp., 102 F.3d 194 (5th Cir. 1996), 146, 157, 306n130, 326n138

Allen v. Uni-First Corp., 558 A.2d 961 (Vt. 1988), 19n60

Allgood v. General Motors Corp., No. 1:02-cv-1077-DFH-TAB, 2006 WL 2669337, U.S. Dist. LEXIS 70764 (S.D. Ind. Sept. 18, 2006), 45n224, 88

Allied Chem. Corp., *In re*, 227 S.W.3d 652 (Tex. 2007), 398n281

Allison v. McGhan Med. Corp., 184 F.3d 1300 (11th Cir. 1999), 71n78, 132n60

Allstate Ins. Co. v. Sutton, 658 S.E.2d 909 (Ga. Ct. App. 2008), 376n90

Alperin v. Vatican Bank, 410 F.3d 532 (9th Cir. 2005), 288n33

Alsteen v. Wauleco, Inc., 335 Wis. 2d 473 (Wis. Ct. App. 2011), 37n180, 304

Alston v. Hormel Foods, Corp., 730 N.W.2d 376 (Neb. 2007), 66n54, 68nn59–60, 68nn62–63

Ambling Mgmt. Co. v. Purdy, 640 S.E.2d 620 (Ga. Ct. App. 2006), 68n61

Ambrosini v. Labarraque, 322 U.S. App. D.C. 19, 101 F.3d 129 (D.C. Cir. 1996), 393n245

Amchem Prods., Inc. v. Windsor 3, 521 U.S. 591 (1997), 271, 272, 274, 275, 276, 277

American Auto. Mfrs. Ass'n v. Massachusetts Dep't of Envtl. Prot., 163 F.3d 74 (1st Cir. 1998), 75n112

American Cyanamid Co. v. Capuano, 381 F.3d 6 (1st Cir. 2004), 27n106

American Elec. Power Co. v. Connecticut, 131 S. Ct. 2527 (2011), 99nn265–266, 289

American Tobacco Co., *In re*, 880 F.2d 1520 (2d Cir. 1989), 192n109

Amland Props. Corp. v. Aluminum Co. of Am., 711 F. Supp. 784 (D.N.J. 1989), 100N272

Andel v. Getz Servs., Inc., 399 S.E.2d 226 (Ga. Ct. App. 1990), 58n2

Anderson v. Aetna Cas. & Sur. Co., 493 U.S. 959 (1989), 272n8

Anderson v. Airco, Inc., No. 03-123-SLR, 2003 WL 21842085 (D. Del. July 28, 2003), 86n193, 353

Anderson v. Hackett, 646 F. Supp. 2d 1041 (S.D. Ill. 2009), 118n384

Anderson v. Hess, 592 F. Supp. 2d 1174 (D.N.D. 2009), 352

Anderson v. Owens-Corning Fiberglas Corp., 810 P.2d 549 (Cal. 1991), 25n92, 26n95, 115n364

Anderson v. Sybron Corp., 353 S.E.2d 816 (Ga. Ct. App. 1983), 62n24

Andrade v. Chase Home Fin., LLC, No. 04 C 8229, 2005 WL 3436400 (N.D. Ill. Dec. 12, 2005), 230n248

Andrews v. Goodyear Tire & Rubber Co., 191 F.R.D. 59 (D.N.J. 2000), 196n130

Andrews v. Saylor, 80 P.3d 482 (N.M. Ct. App. 2003), 325n135

Andrews v. U.S. Steel Corp., 250 P.3d 887 (N.M. Ct. App. 2011), 326n137

Andritz Sprout-Bauer, Inc. v. Beazer E., Inc., 174 F.R.D. 609 (M.D. Pa. 1997), 189n97

Anglado v. Leaf River Forest Prods., Inc., 716 So. 2d 543 (Miss. 1998), 151

Angle v. Koppers, Inc., 42 So. 3d 1 (Miss. 2010), 59, 64n40, 64n42

Anker v. G.D. Searle Co., 126 F.R.D. 515 (M.D.N.C. 1989), 191n104, 192nn105–106, 192n110

Anschutz Exploration Corp. v. Town of Dryden, 940 N.Y.S.2d 458 (Sup. Ct. 2012), 282

Anthony v. Small Tube Mfg. Corp., 535 Fed. Supp. 2d 506 (E.D. Pa. 2007), 181N65

Apache Powder Co. v. Bond, 145 P.2d 988 (Ariz. 1944), 312n18

Apodaca v. AAA Gas Co., 73 P.3d 215 (N.M. Ct. App. 2003), 22n76, 23n83

Arkansas *ex rel.* Bryan v. Dow Chem. Co., 981 F. Supp. 1170 (E.D. Ark. 1997), 49n245

Arlandson v. Hartz Mountain Corp., 792 F. Supp. 2d 691 (D.N.J. 2011), 85n183

Arlington Forest Assoc. v. Exxon Corp., 774 F. Supp. 387 (E.D. Va. 1991), 23n83

Armstrong v. City of N.Y., Inc., No. 111725/04, 2005 WL 742432 (N.Y. Sup. Ct. Feb. 22, 2005), 102

Armstrong v. Weiland, 225 S.E.2d 851 (S.C. 1976), 392

Arness v. Boeing N. Am., Inc., 997 F. Supp. 1268 (C.D. Cal. 1998), 118n384

Arnold v. Eastern Air Lines, Inc., 712 F.2d 899 (4th Cir. 1983), 255n343

Arvayo v. United States, 766 F.2d 1416 (10th Cir. 1985), 59n8

Asbestos Cases, *In re*, 847 F.2d 523 (9th Cir. 1988), 320

Asbestos Litig., *In re*, 90 F.3d 963 (5th Cir. 1996), 271nn7–8

Asbestos Litig., *In re*, 900 A.2d 120 (Del. Super. Ct. 2006), 408n20, 408n22, 409n24

Asbestos Prods. Liab. Litig., *In re*, (No. VI), MDL 875, 2011 WL 3925419 (E.D. Pa. July 27, 2011), 193n115

Asbury v. A.W. Chesterton Co., 2010 WL 1280470 (R.I. Super. Mar. 29, 2010), 230n250

Asgrow-Kilgore Co. v. Mulford Hickerson Corp., 301 So. 2d 441 (Fla. 1974), 371n57

Asher v. Unarco Material Handling, Inc., 596 F.3d 313 (6th Cir. 2010), 59n6, 59n7

Asipazu v. Orgera, 535 A.2d 338 (Conn. 1987), 407

Askey v. Occidental Chem. Corp., 477 N.Y.S.2d 242 (N.Y. App. Div. 1984), 36n163

Atlantic States Legal Found., Inc. v. Tyson Foods, Inc., 897 F.2d 1128 (11th Cir. 1990), 55n283

Atlas Minerals & Chems., Inc., United States v., No. 91-5118, 1995 U.S. Dist. LEXIS 13097, 41 ERC 1417 (E.D. Pa. 1995), 28n112, 212n188

Atwood v. Warner Elec. Brake & Clutch Co., 605 N.E.2d 1032 (Ill. App. Ct. 1992), 228n236

Aurand v. Norfolk S. Ry. Co., 2011 WL 2938447, 802 F. Supp. 2d 950 (N.D. Ind. 2011), 110n339, 336n20, 368n36

Aventis Pasteur, Inc. v. Skevofilax, 914 A.2d 113 (Md. 2007), 412n52

Avila v. Willits Envtl. Remediation Trust, 633 F.3d 828 (9th Cir. 2001), 60n14, 61n20, 63n30

AVX Corp. v. Horry Land Co., 686 F. Supp. 2d 621 (D.S.C. 2010), 46n227, 211n185

Axel Johnson, Inc. v. Carroll Carolina Oil Co., 191 F.3d 409 (4th Cir. 1999), 27n106, 30n125

Ayers v. Jackson, 525 A.2d 287 (N.J. 1987), 36n167, 37n173, 37n176, 42n204, 45n221, 46n225, 418n91

Ayers v. United States, 67 Fed. Cl. 776 (2005), 74n106

B

Bachran v. Morishige, 469 P.2d 808 (Haw. 1970), 319n86

Badillo v. American Brands, Inc., 16 P.3d 435 (Nev. 2001), 42n203

Baggerly v. CSX Transp., Inc., 635 S.E.2d 97 (S.C. 2006), 391n231

Bahrle v. Exxon Corp., 652 A.2d 178 (N.J. Super. 1995), 12n16, 13n19

Bahura v. S.E.W. Investors, 754 A.2d 928 (D.C. Ct. App. 2000), 37n174

Bailey v. North Am. Refractories Co., 95 S.W.3d 868 (Ky. App. 2001), 381

Baker v. Carr, 369 U.S. 186 (1962), 287, 288, 356n179, 357, 420

Baker v. Chevron USA, Inc., 680 F. Supp. 2d 865 (S.D. Ohio 2010), 39n185, 306, 354n166, 355, 357

Baker v. Dalkon Shield Claimants Trust, 156 F.3d 248 (1st Cir. 1998), 110N339

Baker v. Liggett Grp., Inc., 132 F.R.D. 123 (D. Mass. 1990), 198n137

Baker v. Metro-N. R.R., No. 3:98CV1073, 2003 WL 22439730 (D. Conn. Oct. 23, 2003), 406

Baker v. Peoples, No. L-2044-09, 2012 WL 360283 (N.J. Super. Ct. A.D. Feb. 6, 2012), 420

Baker Valley Lumber, Inc. v. Ingersoll Rand Co., 813 A.2d 409 (N.H. 2002), 417

Ball v. Union Carbide Corp., 385 F.3d 713 (6th Cir. 2004), 62n25, 69n67

Ballenger v. Grand Saline, 276 S.W.2d 874 (Tex. Civ. App. 1955), 18n59

Bankers Life & Cas. Co. v. Case, No. 05 C 6532, 2005 WL 3542523 (N.D. Ill. Dec. 23, 2005), 230n248

Bankhead v. Arvinmeritor, Inc., 139 Cal. Rptr. 3d 849 (Cal. Ct. App. 2012), 52n267, 53

Banks v. City of Richmond, 348 S.E.2d 280 (Va. 1986), 399nn289–290

Barber v. Pittsburgh Corning Corp., 529 A.2d 491 (Pa. Super. Ct. 1987), rev'd, 555 A.2d 766 (Pa. 1989), 33n146

Barber v. State, 952 So. 2d 393 (Ala. Crim. App. 2005), 365n16

Barlow v. General Motors Corp., 595 F. Supp. 2d 929 (S.D. Ind. 2009), 44n212, 46n225

Barnes v. American Tobacco Co., 161 F.3d 127 (3d Cir. 1998), 298n93

Barnes v. Century Aluminum Co., No. 05-62, 2012 U.S. Dist. LEXIS 73120 (D.V.I. May 24, 2012), 48n236, 49n248

Barnes v. Koppers, Inc., 534 F.3d 357 (5th Cir. 2008), 60n12, 63n32, 64nn37–40

Baroldy v. Ortho Pharm. Corp., 760 P.2d 574 (Ariz. Ct. App. 1988), 311n14, 312

Barret v. Harris, 86 P.3d 954 (Ariz. Ct. App. 2004), 314

Barrett v. Rhodia, Inc., 606 F.3d 975 (8th Cir. 2010), 353n154

Barrous v. BP P.L.C., No. 10-CV-02944-LHK, 2011 U.S. Dist. LEXIS 113597 (N.D. Cal. 2011), 51n256

Bartel v. John Crane, Inc., 316 F. Supp. 2d 603 (N.D. Ohio 2004), 357

Bartlett v. Mutual Pharm. Co., 742 F. Supp. 2d 182 (D.N.H. 2010), 193n114

Bass v. Air Prods. & Chems., Inc., No. A-4542-03T3, 2006 WL 1419375 (N.J. Super. Ct. App. Div. 2006), 86n194

Bass v. Planned Mgmt. Servs., 761 P.2d 566 (Utah 1988), 14n29

Bates v. Dow Agroscis., LLC, 544 U.S. 431 (2005), 84, 85n183

Bauer v. Bayer A.G., 564 F. Supp. 2d 365 (M.D. Pa. 2008), 124n9, 126n18

Baughman v. Am. Tel. & Tel. Co., 410 S.E.2d 53 (S.C. 1991), 392nn239–240

Baughman v. Pina, 113 P.3d 459 (Or. Ct. App. 2005), 328n153

Bayless v. United States, No. 2:09CV495DAK, 2012 WL 1802390 (D. Utah May 17, 2012), 60n17

Bazley v. Tortorich, 397 So. 2d 475 (La. 1981), 119n389

BB In Tech. Co. v. JAF, LLC, 242 F.R.D. 632 (S.D. Fla. 2007), 231n252

Beal v. West Farmers Elec. Coop., 228 P.3d 538 (Okla. Civ. App. 2009), 97n255

Beatty v. Washington Metro. Area Transit Auth., 860 F.2d 1117 (D.C. Cir. 1988), 67n55

Becker v. Baron Bros., 138 N.J. 145 (1994), 419

Becton v. Rhone-Poulenc, Inc., 706 So. 2d 1134 (Ala. 1997), 65n45, 150, 365n15

Bednar v. Bassett Furniture Mfg. Co., 147 F.3d 737 (8th Cir. 1998), 352n153

Beeman v. Manville Corp. Asbestos Disease Comp. Fund, 496 N.W.2d 247 (Iowa 1993), 149n38

Bell v. Swift Adhesives, Inc., 804 F. Supp. 1577 (S.D. Ga. 1992), 109n332

Bella v. Aurora Air, Inc., 566 P.2d 489 (Or. 1977), 23n81

Bendectin Litig., *In re*, 857 F.2d 290 (6th Cir. 1988), *cert. denied*, 488 U.S. 1006 (1989), 220n212, 252n339

Benedi v. McNeil-PPC, Inc., 66 F.3d 1378 (4th Cir. 1995), 400n303

Benefield v. International Paper Co., 270 F.R.D. 640 (M.D. Ala. 2010), 295nn75–76

Benitez v. Joseph Trucking, Inc., 68 So. 3d 428 (Fla. Dist. Ct. App. 2011), 372n61

Benjamin Moore & Co., *In re*, 309 F.3d 296 (5th Cir. 2002), 228n240

Benkendorf v. Advanced Cardiac Specialists Chtd., 269 P.3d 704 (Ct. App. 2012), 312n22

Bennett v. MIS Corp., 607 F.3d 1076 (6th Cir. 2010), 117n376, 117n377

Bennett v. Spear, 520 U.S. 154 (1997), 288n37

Benshoof v. National Gypsum Co., 978 F.2d 475 (9th Cir. 1992), 314

Bentley v. Honeywell Int'l, Inc., 223 F.R.D. 471 (N.D. Ohio 2004), 39n186

Berg v. Popham, 113 P.3d 604 (Alaska 2005), 28n109

Bergfeld v. Unimin Corp., 319 F.3d 350 (8th Cir. 2003), 104

Berish v. Southwest Energy Prod. Co., 763 F. Supp. 2d 702 (M.D. Pa. 2011), 22n76, 24n86, 43n210, 281

Bernbach v. Timex Corp., 989 F. Supp. 403 (D. Conn. 1996), 250n325

Berry v. CSX Transp., Inc., 709 So. 2d 552 (Fla. Dist. Ct. App. 1998), 373n68, 375n79

Beshada v. Johns-Manville Prods. Corp., 447 A.2d 539 (N.J. 1982), 116n367

Best v. Lowe's Home Ctrs., Inc., 563 F.3d 171 (6th Cir. 2009), 154nn69–70

Bestfoods, United States v., 524 U.S. 51 (1998), 168n3, 171n20, 172

Betts v. Manville Personal Injury Settlement Trust, 588 N.E.2d 1193 (Ill. App. Ct. 1992), 37n179

Betz v. Pneumo Abex, LLC, 44 A.3d 27 (Pa. 2012), 427, 428n153

B.F. Goodrich v. Betkoski, 99 F.3d 505 (2d Cir. 1996), 171n21

Bic Pen Corp. v. Carter, 346 S.W.3d 533 (Tex. 2011), 397n271

Bidar v. Amfac, Inc., 669 P.2d 154 (Haw. 1983), 319n77

Biniek v. Exxon Mobil Corp., 818 A.2d 330 (N.J. Super. Ct. Law Div. 2002), 23n81

Bisphenol-A (BPA) Polycarbonate Plastic Prods. Liab. Litig., *In re*, 687 F. Supp. 2d 897 (W.D. Mo. 2009), 31nn129–130

Bittner v. Huth, 876 A.2d 157 (Md. Ct. Spec. App. 2005), 13n21

Bixby v. KBR, Inc., 748 F. Supp. 2d 1224 (D. Or. 2010), 118n383

Black v. William Insulation Co., 141 P.3d 123 (Wyo. 2006), 331n175

Blackston v. Shook & Fletcher Insulation Co., 764 F.2d 1480 (11th Cir. 1985), 379n114

Blanchard v. Goodyear Tire & Rubber Co., 30 A.3d 1271 (Vt. 2011), 432, 433n180

Bland v. Verizon Wireless, (VAW) LLC, 538 F.3d 893 (8th Cir. 2008), 353n161

Blane v. American Inventors Corp., 934 F. Supp. 903 (M.D. Tenn. 1996), 230n249

Blanton v. Cooper Indus., Inc., 99 F. Supp. 2d 797 (E.D. Ky. 2000), 6n12

Blasick v. City of Yakima, 274 P.2d 122 (Wash. 1954), 330n166

Blasland, Bouck & Lee, Inc. v. City of N. Miami, 283 F.3d 1286 (11th Cir. 2002), 73n89

Bloomington v. Westinghouse Elec. Corp., 891 F.2d 611 (7th Cir. 1989), 23n83

Blue Circle Cement, Inc. v. Board of County Comm'rs, 27 F.3d 1499 (10th Cir. 1994), 80n149

Blum v. Merrell Dow Pharms., Inc., 705 A.2d 1314 (Pa. Super. Ct. 1997), 428, 429n155

Blum v. Stenson, 465 U.S. 886 (1984), 267n1

Blumenshine v. Baptiste, 869 P.2d 470 (Alaska 1994), 37n179

BMW of North Am. v. Gore, 517 U.S. 559 (1996), 51

BNT Co. v. Baker Precythe Dev. Co., 564 S.E.2d 891 (N.C. Ct. App. 2002), 100n271

Board of County Comm'rs of La Plata v. Brown Grp. Retail, Inc., 598 F. Supp. 2d 1185 (D. Colo. 2009), 30n127

Bockrath v. Aldrich Chem. Co., 21 Cal. 4th 71, 980 P.2d 398 (Cal. 1999), 111, 315

Bohus v. Beloff, 950 F.2d 919 (3d Cir. 1991), 69n67, 70nn68–69

Boland v. Vanderbilt, 102 A.2d 362 (Conn. 1953), 407n15

Bolin v. Cessna Aircraft Co., 759 F. Supp. 692 (N.D. Kan. 1991), 65n46

Bolinder Real Estate, LLC v. United States, No. 2:97-cv- 0912C, 2002 WL 732155 (D. Utah Apr. 24, 2002), 115n366

Bond v. Utreras, 585 F.3d 1061 (7th Cir. 2009), 198n139

Bonner v. ISP Techs., Inc., 259 F.3d 924 (8th Cir. 2001), 146n21, 153, 348n120, 352n153, 353n155, 354, 361n224

Bonnie Blue, Inc. v. Reichenstein, 127 S.W.3d 366 (Tex. App. 2004), 30n126

Booker v. Duke Med. Ctr., 256 S.E.2d 189 (N.C. 1979), 390nn217–218, 390n220

Boomsma v. Dakota, Minn. & E. R.R., 651 N.W.2d 238 (S.D. 2002), *overruled,* State v. Martin, 683 N.W.2d 399 (S.D. 2004), 361n225

Borel v. Fibreboard Paper Prods. Corp., 493 F.2d 1076 (5th Cir. 1973), 25n94

Boren v. Burlington N. & Santa Fe Ry., 637 N.W.2d 910 (Neb. Ct. App. 2002), 36n166, 36n171, 351n144, 352

Borg-Warner Corp. v. Flores, 232 S.W.3d. 765 (Tex. 2007), 151, 398nn285–287

Borland v. Sanders Lead Co., 369 So. 2d 523 (Ala. 1979), 39n185

Bormann v. Board of Supervisors, 584 N.W.2d 309 (Iowa 1998), 97n251

Bosch v. Secretary of Dep't of Health & Human Servs., No. 95-0313V, 1997 WL 254218 (Fed. Cl. Apr. 25, 1997), 133n64

Boughton v. Cotter Corp., 65 F.3d 823 (10th Cir. 1995), 46n225

Bourne *ex rel.* Bourne v. E.I. DuPont de Nemours & Co., 189 F. Supp. 2d 482 (S.D.W. Va. 2002), 403n323

Bower v. Westinghouse Elec. Corp., 522 S.E.2d 424 (W. Va. 1999), 42n205

Bowman v. Doherty, 686 P.2d 112 (Kan. 1984), 339n44

Boxberger v. Martin, 552 P.2d 370 (Okla. 1976), 358

Boyd v. Allied Signal, Inc., 898 So. 2d 450 (La. Ct. App. 2004), 129n34

Boyd v. Lincoln Elec. Co., 902 N.E.2d 1023 (Ohio Ct. App. 2008), 112n346

Boyes v. Shell Oil Prods. Co., 199 F.3d 1260 (11th Cir. 2000), 75n107, 81

Boyette v. L.W. Looney & Son, 932 F. Supp. 1344 (D. Utah 1996), 51n262

Boyle v. United Techs. Corp., 487 U.S. 500 (1988), 116

Bradley v. American Smelting & Ref. Co., 709 P.2d 782 (Wash. 1985), 19n63

Bradley v. Armstrong Rubber Co., 130 F.3d 168 (5th Cir. 1997), 47n232

Brady v. Ralph M. Parsons Co., 572 A.2d 1115 (Md. Ct. Spec. App. 1990), 11n10

Brafford v. Susquehanna Corp., 586 F. Supp. 14 (D. Colo. 1984), 39n187

Bragdon v. Abbott, 524 U.S. 624 (1998), 355n170

Bramlette v. Charter Med.-Columbia, 393 S.E.2d 914 (S.C. 1990), 391n225

Branch v. Western Petroleum, Inc., 657 P.2d 267 (Utah 1982), 24n85, 89n212, 100n270

Breast Implant Litig., *In re*, 11 F. Supp. 2d 1217 (D. Colo. 1998), 109n330, 134n69, 134n71

Breiggar Props., LLC v. H.E. Davis & Sons, Inc., 52 P.3d 1133 (Utah 2002), 66n54

Brenner v. American Cyanamid Co., 263 A.D.2d 165 (N.Y. App. Div. 1999), 170n10, 170n13, 170n16, 171n18

Bridgestone/Firestone, Inc. Tires Prods. Liab. Litig., *In re*, 333 F.3d 763 (7th Cir. 2003), 183n71

Brisboy v. Fibreboard Corp., 418 N.W.2d 650 (Mich. 1988), 343–345

Briscoe v. Harper Oil Co., 702 P.2d 33 (Okla. 1985), 18n56

Bristol, City of v. Tilcon Minerals, Inc., 931 A.2d 237 (Conn. 2007), 18

Brock v. Merrell Dow Pharm., Inc., 874 F.2d 307, *amended*, 884 F.2d 167 (5th Cir. 1989), 109n328, 109n332, 397n273

Brod v. Omya, Inc., 653 F.3d 156 (2d Cir. 2011), 74nn98–99

Brooks v. E. I. du Pont de Nemours & Co., 944 F. Supp. 448 (E.D.N.C. 1996), 38n183, 88, 106n308, 156

Brooks v. Medtronic, Inc., 750 F.2d 1227 (4th Cir. 1984), 105n307

Broward Gardens Tenants Ass'n v. EPA, 311 F.3d 1066 (11th Cir. 2002), 79n136

Brown v. Crown Equip. Corp., 181 S.W.3d 268 (Tenn. 2005), 395

Brown v. Dow Chem. Co., 875 F.2d 197 (8th Cir. 1989), 6n12

Brown v. National Football League, 219 F. Supp. 2d 372 (S.D.N.Y. 2002), 249n317

Brown v. Petrolane, Inc., 162 Cal. Rptr. 551 (Cal. Ct. App. 1980), 18n57

Brown v. Superior Court, 751 P.2d 470 (Cal. 1988), 115n364

Brown v. Terre Haute Reg'l Hosp., 537 N.E.2d 54 (Ind. Ct. App. 1989), 336n19

Bruce v. Martin-Marietta Corp., 544 F.2d 442 (10th Cir. 1976), 114n363

Bryant v. Yorktowne Cabinetry, Inc., 538 F. Supp. 2d 948 (W.D. Va. 2008), 197n135

B.T.N. v. Auburn Enlarged City Sch. Dist., 45 A.D.3d 1339 (N.Y. App. Div. 2007), 425n132

Buchanan v. American Motors Corp., 697 F.2d 151 (6th Cir. 1983), 191n105

Buckman Co. v. Plaintiffs' Legal Comm., 531 U.S. 341 (2001), 87n199

Bullard, State v., 322 S.E.2d 370 (N.C. 1984), 388n194

Bulot v. Intracoastal Tubular Servs., Inc., 888 So. 2d 1017 (La. Ct. App. 2004), 127n24

Bunger v. Hartman, 851 F. Supp. 461 (S.D. Fla. 1994), 27n102

Burka v. U.S. Health & Human Servs., 87 F.3d 508 (D.C. Cir. 1996), 192n107

Burke *ex rel.* County of La Paz, State v., No. 1 CA-SA 12-0028, 2012 WL 1470103 (Ariz. Ct. App. Apr. 26, 2012), 313n30

Burleson v. Texas Dep't of Criminal Justice, 393 F.3d 577 (5th Cir. 2004), 145

Burley v. Burlington N. & Santa Fe Ry. Co., 273 P.3d 825 (Mont. 2012), 65n50, 66n52, 66n54, 67n55

Burlington, City of v. Dague, 505 U.S. 557 (1992), 56n287

Burlington N. & Santa Fe Ry. Co. v. Grant, 505 F.3d 1013 (10th Cir. 2007), 68n63

Burlington N. & Santa Fe Ry. Co. v. Poole Chem. Co., 419 F.3d 355 (5th Cir. 2005), 71n82

Burlington N. & Santa Fe Ry. Co. v. United States, 556 U.S. 599 (2009), 27n101, 27n103

Burnham v. Tabb, 508 So. 2d 1072 (Miss. 1987), 385N16

Burroughs Wellcome Co. v. Crye, 907 S.W.2d 497 (Tex. 1995), 396n262

Burt v. Fumigation Serv. & Supply, Inc., 926 F. Supp. 624 (W.D. Mich. 1996), 31n130

Burton v. CSX Transp., Inc., 269 S.W.3d 1 (Ky. 2008), 380

Bussey v. E.S.C. Rests. Inc., 620 S.E.2d 764 (Va. 2005), 401n309

Busta v. Columbus Hosp. Corp., 916 P.2d 122 (Mont. 1996), 322n108

Butler v. Advanced Drainage Sys., 717 N.W.2d 760 (Wis. 2006), 18n57, 19n62, 377n92, 378nn99–100

Butler v. Union Carbide Corp., 712 S.E.2d 537 (Ga. Ct. App. 2011), 376n90, 378

Buttitta v. Allied Signal, Inc., 2010 WL 1427273 (N.J. Super. Ct. A.D. Jan. 4, 2010), 418n88

Byers v. Lincoln Elec. Co., 607 F. Supp. 2d 840 (N.D. Ohio 2009), 111

Byrd v. Commercial Credit Corp., 675 So. 2d 392 (Ala. 1996), 363n2

C

California Fed. Sav. & Loan Ass'n v. Guerra, 479 U.S. 272 (1987), 77n123

Callano v. Oakwood Park Homes Corp., 219 A.2d 332 (N.J. Super. Ct. App. Div. 1966), 34n152
Cameron v. Merisel, Inc., 593 S.E.2d 416 (N.C. Ct. App. 2004), 118n385
Cameron v. Merisel Props., 187 N.C. App. 40, 652 S.E.2d 660 (N.C. Ct. App. 2007), 387n188
C&A Carbone, Inc. v. Town of Clarkstown, 511 U.S. 383 (1994), 80n147
Cannon v. Gates, 538 F.3d 1328 (10th Cir. 2008), 78n131, 79nn136–137, 298
Cannon v. United States, 338 F.3d 1183 (10th Cir. 2003), 59nn6–7, 60n14, 66n51
Capricorn Power Co. v. Siemens Westinghouse Power Corp., 220 F.R.D. 429 (W.D. Pa. 2004), 219n207
Cardinal Indus. Insulation Co. v. Norris, 2004-CA-000525-MR, 2009 WL 562614 (Ky. Ct. App. Mar. 6, 2009), 380n122, 381
Cardwell, State v., 516 S.E.2d 388 (N.C. Ct. App. 1999), 388nn201–202
Carignan v. New Hampshire Int'l Speedway, Inc., 858 A.2d 536 (N.H. 2004), 417nn82–83
Carlin v. RFE Indus., Inc., No. 88-CV-842, 1995 WL 760739 (N.D.N.Y. Nov. 27, 1995), 423n121
Carlough v. Amchem Prods., Inc., 834 F. Supp. 1437 (E.D. Pa. 1993), 51n260
Carlson v. Okerstrom, 675 N.W.2d 89 (Neb. 2004), 352

Carmichael v. Samyang Tire, Inc., 131 F.3d 1433 (11th Cir. 1997), 162n118
Carrecter v. Colson Equip. Co., 499 A.2d 326 (Pa. Super. Ct. 1985), 113n354
Carroll v. Litton Sys., No. B-C-88-253, 1990 WL 312969 (W.D.N.C. Oct. 29, 1990), 221n214
Carson Harbor Vill., Ltd. v. Unocal Corp., 270 F.3d 863 (9th Cir. 2001), 97n255
Carson Harbor Vill., Ltd. v. Unocal Corp., 287 F. Supp. 2d 1118 (C.D. Cal. 2003), 45n222
Carter v. Monsanto Co., 575 S.E.2d 342 (W. Va. 2002), 19n62
Casdorph v. West Va. Off. Ins. Comm'r, 690 S.E.2d 102 (W. Va. 2009), 403n322
Case v. Upjohn Co., No. 308420, 1992 WL 259203 (Conn. Super. Ct. Sept. 16 1992), 407n17
Casey v. Ohio Med. Prods., 877 F. Supp. 1380 (N.D. Cal. 1995), 140n1, 359n214
Castano v. American Tobacco Co., 84 F.3d 734 (5th Cir. 1996), 177n42
Castillo v. E. I. DuPont de Nemours & Co., 854 So. 2d 1264 (Fla. 2003), 374, 375
Caudle-Hyatt, Inc. v. Mixon, 260 S.E.2d 193 (Va. 1979), 400
Cavallo v. Star Enter., 892 F. Supp. 756 (E.D. Va. 1995), aff'd, 100 F.3d 1150 (4th Cir. 1996), 110n339, 140n1, 338n38
Cavanaugh v. Looney, 248 U.S. 453 (1919), 54n276

Cavanaugh v. Skil Corp., 751 A.2d 518 (N.J. 2000), 115n364
Caves v. Yarbrough, 991 So. 2d 142 (Miss. 2008), 60n12
C.C. Carlton Indus., Ltd. v. Blanchard, 311 S.W.3d 654 (Tex. Ct. App. 2010), 99n267
Celebrezze, State *ex rel.* v. CECOS Int'l Inc., 583 N.E.2d 1118 (Ohio Ct. App. 12 Dist. 1990), 189n97
Cendant Corp. Sec. Litig., *In re*, 109 F. Supp. 2d 235 (D.N.J. 2000), *aff'd*, 264 F.3d 201 (3d Cir. 2001), 274n31
Cendant Corp. Sec. Litig., *In re*, 343 F.3d 658 (3d Cir. 2003), 240n292
Certified Question from Fourteenth Dist. Court of Appeals of Tex., *In re*, 740 N.W.2d 206 (Mich. 2007), 101n278, 294n70
Chambers v. Capital Cities/ABC, 159 F.R.D. 441 (S.D.N.Y. 1995), 196n127
Chappell v. SCA Servs., Inc., 540 F. Supp. 1087 (C.D. Ill. 1982), 82
Chase v. Breitt, 306 S.E.2d 877 (Va. 1983), 401n309
Chatham v. CSX Transp., Inc., 613 So. 2d 341 (Ala. 1993), 69n64
Chavers v. General Motors Corp., 79 S.W.3d 361 (Ark. 2002), 149n39, 368n38, 368n41
Chavez v. South Pac. Transp. Co., 413 F. Supp. 1203 (E.D. Cal. 1976), 23n80
Chemical Waste Mgmt., Inc. v. Armstrong World Indus., Inc., 669 F. Supp. 1285 (E.D. Pa. 1987), 28n114

Chesapeake, City of v. Sutton Enters., Inc., 138 F.R.D. 468 (E.D. Va. 1990), 82n162, 82n164
Chesson v. Baltimore Wash. Conference, No. 13-C-03-056903, 2009 WL 7450518 (Md. Cir. Ct. Nov. 10, 2009), 414n62
Chevron USA, *In re*, 109 F.3d 1016 (5th Cir. 1997), 175n37, 253n341, 254
Chevron USA, Inc., United States v., Civ. A. No. 88-6681, 1989 WL 121616 (E.D. Pa. Oct. 16, 1989), 190
Chiarella v. United States, 445 U.S. 222 (1980), 70n69
Chicago v. Environmental Def. Fund, 511 U.S. 328 (1994), 80n147
Chicago Tribune Co. v. Bridgestone/Firestone, Inc., 263 F.3d 1304 (11th Cir. 2001), 198n139, 199n145, 200n152
Chico Serv. Station, Inc. v. Sol P.R. Ltd., 633 F.3d 20 (1st Cir. 2011), 75n111
Childers v. Gas Lines, Inc., 149 S.E.2d 761 (S.C. 1966), 391n230
Chism v. W.R. Grace Co., 158 F.3d 988 (8th Cir. 1998), 152
Cho v. State, 168 P.3d 17 (Haw. 2007), 319
Christ Church Parish v. Cadet Chem. Corp., 199 A.2d 707 (Conn. Super. Ct. 1964), 23n79
Christian v. Gray, 65 P.3d 591 (Okla. 2003), 358nn204–205, 359nn210–212, 360
Christiansburg v. EEOC, 434 U.S. 412 (1978), 56n285
Christopher v. Cutter Labs., 53 F.3d 1184 (11th Cir. 1995), 111n344

Church of Christ in Hollywood v. Superior Court, 121 Cal. Rptr. 2d 810 (Cal. Ct. App. 2002), 15n34
Church of Scientology v. IRS, 792 F.2d 146 (D.C. Cir. 1986), 185n78
Cicogna v. City of N.Y., 801 N.Y.S.2d 231 (N.Y. Sup. Ct. 2005), 118n387
Cimino v. Raymark Indus., Inc., 151 F.3d 297 (5th Cir. 1998), 105n306
Cimino v. Raymark Indus., Inc., 751 F. Supp. 649 (E.D. Tex. 1990), 254n342
Cipollone v. Liggett Grp., Inc., 505 U.S. 504 (1992), 77n122, 77n125
Cipollone v. Liggett Grp., Inc., 113 F.R.D. 86 (D.N.J. 1986), 198n138, 199n147, 200n150
Citizens Against Pollution v. Ohio Power Co., 484 F. Supp. 2d 800 (S.D. Ohio 2007), 56n286
City Nat'l Bank of Charleston v. Wells, 384 S.E.2d 374 (W. Va. 1989), 402n312
City of _____. See name of city
C.L. Ritter Lumber Co. v. Consolidation Coal Co., No. 1:11cv00019, 2011 WL 3793320 (W.D. Va. Aug. 25, 2011), 64n40
Clark v. Baxter Healthcare Corp., 100 Cal. Rptr. 2d 223 (Cal. Ct. App. 2000), 61n19
Clark v. Greenville County, 437 S.E.2d 117 (S.C. 1993), 18n58
Clark v. Safety-Kleen Corp., 845 A.2d 587 (N.J. 2004), 421n105
Clausen v. M/V New Carissa, 339 F.3d 1049 (9th Cir. 2003), 147

Cleveland v. Johns-Manville Corp., 690 A.2d 1146 (Pa. 1997), 37n175
Click v. Pilot Freight Carriers, 265 S.E.2d 389 (1980), 387n190
Clift v. Vose Hardware, 848 A.2d 1130 (R.I. 2004), 431n169
Clodfelter v. Leonard, 630 S.E.2d 742 (N.C. Ct. App. 2006), 387n189
Coastal Envtl. Specialists, Inc. v. Chem-Lig Int'l, Inc., 818 So. 2d 12 (La. Ct. App. 2001), 33nn147–148, 34n152
Coastal Tankships, U.S.A., Inc. v. Anderson, 87 S.W.3d 591 (Tex. App. Houston 1st Dist. 2002), 396n262
Coastal Transp. Co. v. Crown Cent. Petroleum Corp., 136 S.W.3d 227 (Tex. 2004), 396n267
Coca-Cola Bottling Co. of Tucson v. Fitzgerald, 413 P.2d 869 (Ariz. Ct. App. 1966), 311, 312
Coeur d'Alene Tribe v. Asarco, Inc., 280 F. Supp. 2d 1094 (D. Idaho 2003), 50n251
Coffman v. Keene Corp., 628 A.2d 710 (N.J. 1993), 113n342
Colbert v. U.S. Postal Serv., 831 F. Supp. 2d 2403 (D.D.C. 2011), 74n106
Coldwell Banker Residential Brokerage Co. v. Superior Court, 11 Cal. Rptr. 3d 564 (Cal. Ct. App. 2004), 30n124
Cole v. Appalachian Power Co., 903 F. Supp. 975 (S.D. W.Va. 1995), 196n132
Cole v. Superior Coach Corp., 106 So. 2d 71 (Miss. 1958), 385n171
Collette v. Collette, 418 A.2d 891 (Conn. 1979), 407n12

Collings v. Lords, 218 P.3d 654 (Wyo. 2009), 331n175

Collins v. Koppers, Inc., 59 So. 3d 582 (Miss. 2011), 385n171

Colonial Pipeline, *In re*, 968 S.W.2d 938 (Tex. 1998), 398n281

Comer v. Murphy Oil, 585 F.3d 855 (5th Cir. 2009), 290nn46–51

Comer v. Murphy Oil, 607 F.3d 1049 (5th Cir. 2010), 290, 291n53

Commissioner of the Dep't of Planning & Natural Res. v. Century Aluminum Co., No. 05-62, 2012 U.S. Dist. LEXIS 77128 (D.V.I. June 4, 2012), 35n156

Commitment of Simons, *In re*, 821 N.E.2d 1184 (Ill. 2004), 333n2

Commonwealth v. _____. *See name of opposing party*

Community Org. v. Honeywell Int'l, Inc., 263 F. Supp. 2d 796 (D.N.J. 2003), 66n53

Complaint of Weeks Marine, Inc., *In re*, No. 04-494, 2005 U.S. Dist. LEXIS 30196 (D.N.J. 2005), 22n76

Conde v. Velsicol Chem. Corp., 804 F. Supp. 972 (S.D. Ohio 1992), 354n165

Connecticut v. American Elec. Power Co., 406 F. Supp. 2d 265 (S.D.N.Y. 2005), 289n43

Connecticut v. Cahill, 217 F.3d 93 (2d Cir. 2000), 34n154

Consolidated Canal Co. v. Mesa Canal Co., 177 U.S. 296 (1900), 54n275

Consumer Def. Grp. v. Rental Housing Indus. Members, 40 Cal. Rptr. 3d 832 (Cal. Ct. App. 2006), 55n284

Continental Title Co. v. Peoples Gas Light & Coke Co., No. 96 C 3257, 1999 U.S. Dist. LEXIS 22206 (N.D. Ill. Mar. 18, 1999), 33n149

Cook v. Rockwell Int'l Corp., 273 F. Supp. 2d 1175 (D. Colo. 2003), 84n176

Cooper v. Diversy Corp., 742 So. 2d 1244 (Ala. Civ. App. 1998), 364n6

Cooper Indus., LLC v. City of South Bend, 899 N.E.2d 1274 (Ind. 2009), 59n10

Copart Indus., Inc. v. Consolidated Edison Co. of N.Y., Inc., 362 N.E.2d 968 (N.Y. 1977), 100n270

Cordis Corp. Pacemaker Prod. Liab. Litig., *In re*, No. MDL 850, C-3-86-543, 1992 WL 754061 (S.D. Ohio Dec. 23, 1992), 114n357

Cormier v. 3M Corp., No. CV040409253S, 2005 WL 288824 (Conn. Super. Ct. Jan. 11, 2005), 406n6

Cornell v. E.I. DuPont deNemours & Co., 841 F.2d 23 (1st Cir. 1988), 6n12

Cotten v. Phillips, 633 S.E.2d 655 (Ga. Ct. App. 2006), 377n92

Cotten, State v., No. 1 CA-CR 11-0433, 2012 WL 2476242 (Ariz. Ct. App. June 19, 2012), 312n23

Cottle v. Superior Court, 3 Cal. App. 4th 1367 (Cal. App. 2d Dist. 1992), 228n

Council, State v., 515 S.E.2d 508 (S.C. 1999), 392nn233–235

Country Classics at Morgan Hill Homeowners' Ass'n v. Country Classics at Morgan Hill, LLC,

780 F. Supp. 2d 367 (E.D. Pa. 2011), 231n252
County of _____. *See name of county*
Covell v. Bell Sports, Inc., 651 F.3d 357 (3d Cir. 2011), 114n359
Covington v. Jefferson County, 358 F.3d 626 (9th Cir. 2004), 92
Cowart v. Widener, 697 S.E.2d 779 (Ga. 2010), 377n91
Coyne v. American Tobacco Co., 183 F.3d 488 (6th Cir. 1999), 182n69
CPC Int'l, Inc. v. Hartford Accident & Indem. Co., 262 N.J. Super. 191, 620 A.2d 462 (N.J. Super. 1992), 189n97
Crane-McNab v. County of Merced, 773 F. Supp. 2d 861 (E.D. Cal. 2011), 124n11, 125n16
Creanga v. Jardal, 886 A.2d 633 (N.J. 2005), 418n89, 422n113
Crolley v. Hutchins, 387 S.E.2d 716 (S.C. Ct. App. 1989), 391n229
Crook v. Kaneb Pipe Line Operating P'ship, 231 F.3d 1098 (8th Cir. 2000), 111n345
Crowe v. Shaw, 755 A.2d 509 (Me. 2000), 411n41
Culpepper v. Dae Corp., No. 24C09006364LP, 2011 WL 7063620 (Md. Cir. Ct. July 6, 2011), 413n58, 414nn60–61
Culver v. Bennett, 588 A.2d 1094 (Del. 1991), 408
Curd v. Mosaic Fertilizer, LLC, 39 So. 3d 1216 (Fla. 2010), 102
Curley v. Cumberland Farms, Inc., 134 F.R.D. 77 (D.N.J 1991), 197n135

Curtis v. M&S Petroleum, Inc., 174 F.3d 661 (5th Cir. 1999), 104n296, 345n93
Cutting Underwater Techs. USA, Inc. v. Eni United States Operating Co., 671 F.3d 512 (5th Cir. 2012), 249n316

D

D'Ambrosio, State v., 616 N.E.2d 909 (Ohio 1993), 356n187
D&J Co. v. Stuart, 765 N.E.2d 368 (Ohio Ct. App. 2001), 89n212
Daniels v. Lyondell-Citgo Refining Co., 99 S.W.3d 722 (Tex. App. Hous. 1st Dist. 2003), 145, 146n14
Darnell v. Eastman, 261 N.E.2d 114 (Ohio 1970), 354n166
Darney v. Dragon Prods. Co., 771 F. Supp. 2d 91 (D. Me. 2011), 97n250, 97n252, 99
Dart v. Wiebe Mfg., 709 P.2d 876 (Ariz. 1985), 25n94
Daubert v. Merrell Dow Pharms., Inc., 509 U.S. 579 (1993), 39n185, 133n63, 150, 155, 158–165, 173, 192, 193, 225, 229n243, 248, 263, 268, 300, 302, 303, 306, 313, 320, 321, 334n5, 342, 350, 354, 359n210, 361, 364, 365, 367–370, 372n60, 373, 377, 380, 383, 385, 386, 388, 392, 394, 396, 397n273, 399, 400, 403, 416
Daubert v. Merrell Dow Pharms., Inc., 43 F.3d 1311 (9th Cir. 1995), 109n330, 136n83
Daugert v. Pappas, 704 P.2d 600 (Wash. 1985), 330n167

Davel Commc'ns, Inc. v. Qwest Corp., 460 F.3d 1075 (9th Cir. 2006), 75n112

David v. Velsicol Chem. Corp., 49 So. 3d 997 (La. Ct. App. 2010), 91n226

Davis v. Christian Brotherhood Homes of Jackson, MS, Inc., 957 So. 2d 390 (Miss. Ct. App. 2007), 385n168

Davis Bros., Inc. v. Thornton Oil Co., 12 F. Supp. 2d 1333 (M.D. Ga. 1998), 66n54

Davolt, State v., 84 P.3d 456 (Ariz. 2004), 312n23

Dayton Newspapers, Inc. v. Department of the Air Force, 35 F. Supp. 2d 1033 (S.D. Ohio 1998), *on reconsideration*, 107 F. Supp. 2d 912 (S.D. Ohio 1999), 185n84

Debiec v. Cabot Corp., 352 F.3d 117 (3d Cir. 2003), 62n24

Debusscher v. Sam's East, Inc., 505 F.3d 475 (6th Cir. 2007), 13n17

Deford v. Schmid Prod. Co., Div. of Schmid Labs., Inc., 120 F.R.D. 648 (D. Md. 1987), 200nn148–151

Deitchman v. E.R. Squibb & Sons, Inc., 740 F.2d 556 (7th Cir. 1984), 191n105, 192n107

deJesus v. Seaboard Coastline R.R. Co., 281 So. 2d 198 (Fla. 1973), 11n9

Delta/AirTran Baggage Fee Antitrust Litig., *In re*, 846 F. Supp. 2d 1335 (N.D. Ga. 2012), 217n203

DeLuca v. Merrell Dow Pharm., Inc., 911 F.2d 941 (3d Cir. 1990), 134n71, 135n83, 421n106

DeLuca v. Merrell Dow Pharm., Inc., 791 F. Supp. 1042 (D.N.J. 1992), *aff'd*, 6 F.3d 778 (3d Cir. 1993), 422n115

Demmler v. SmithKline Beecham Corp., 671 A.2d 1151 (Pa. Super. Ct. 1996), 112n346, 112n349

Demos v. Ferris-Shell Oil Co., 740 N.E.2d 9 (Ill. App. Ct. 2000), 249n317

Dennis v. ICL, Inc., 957 F. Supp. 376 (D. Conn. 1997), 61n19

Denver, City & County of, United States v., 100 F.3d 1509 (10th Cir. 1996), 78n131

Department of Corr. v. Cowles, 151 P.3d 353 (Alaska 2006), 310n2, 310n4

Department of Fish & Game v. Superior Court, 129 Cal Rptr. 3d 719 (Cal. Ct. App. 2011), 101n275

Derailment Cases, *In re*, 416 F.3d 787 (8th Cir. 2005), 22n75

Deutsch v. Shein, 597 S.W.2d 141 (Ky. 1980), 380n115

Dewey v. Volkswagen AG, 681 F.3d 170 (3d Cir. 2012), 276

Dexter Corp., United States v., 132 F.R.D. 8 (D. Conn. 1990), 189n97

Dickens v. Oxy Vinyls, LP, 631 F. Supp. 2d 859 (W.D. Ky. 2009), 16n47, 18n56, 23n82, 45n222

Dietz v. SmithKline Beecham Corp., 598 F.3d 812 (11th Cir. 2010), 112n347

Dillon v. Fibreboard Corp., 919 F.2d 1488 (10th Cir. 1990), 216n199, 360n217, 364n9

DiPetrillo v. Dow Chem. Co., 729 A.2d 677 (R.I. 1999), 430

Di Viaio v. Kelley, 571 F.2d 538 (10th Cir. 1978), 185n81

Doane v. Givaudan Flavors Corp., 919 N.E.2d 290 (Ohio Ct. App. 2009), 104n296

Dobrowsky, *In re*, 735 F.2d 90 (3d Cir. 1984), 427n143

Dodge v. Cotter Corp., 328 F.3d 1212 (10th Cir. 2003), 128n27

Dodge v. Cotter Corp., 203 F.3d 1190 (10th Cir.), *cert. denied*, 540 U.S. 1003 (2000), 253n341

Dokken, *In re*, 604 N.W.2d 487 (S.D. 2000), 361n226

Domingues v. FBI., 229 F.3d 1151, 2000 WL 1140594 (6th Cir. 2000), 185n78

Donahue v. Phillips Petroleum Co., 866 F.2d 1008 (8th Cir. 1989), 104n294, 106n313

Donaldson v. Cent. Ill. Pub. Serv. Co., 767 N.E.2d 314 (Ill. 2002), *abrogated*, *In re* Commitment of Simons, 821 N.E.2d 1184 (Ill. 2004), 113n356, 333n2, 334, 335, 336nn16–17

Doner, State *ex rel.* v. Zody, 958 N.E.2d 1235 (Ohio 2011), 66n51

Douglas v. Lombardino, 693 P.2d 1138 (Kan. 1985), 340

Doupnik v. General Motors Corp., 275 Cal. Rptr. 715 (Cal. Ct. App. 1990), 314n41

Dow Chem. Co. v. Allen, 672 F.2d 1262 (7th Cir. 1982), 191n105, 192n108

Dow Chem. Co. v. Mahlum, 970 P.2d 98 (Nev. 1998), *overruled*, GES, Inc. v. Corbitt, 117 Nev. 265 (Nev. 2001), 323n116, 324n123

Dow Corning Corp., *In re*, 211 B.R. 545 (Bankr. E.D. Mich. 1997), 253nn341–342

Downen v. Sinclair Oil Corp., 887 P.2d 515 (Wyo. 1994), 331n174

Dravo Corp. v. Liberty Mut. Ins. Co., Civ. A. No. 95-MC-229-GTV, 1995 WL 519959 (D. Kan. Aug. 21, 1995), 209n179

Drayton v. Jiffee Chem. Corp., 395 F. Supp. 1081 (N.D. Ohio 1975), 10

Dunn v. Sandoz Pharm. Corp., 275 F. Supp. 2d 672 (M.D.N.C. 2003), 109n328, 389n211

Dykes v. Raymark Indus., Inc., 801 F.2d 810 (6th Cir. 1986), 256

E

Eagle-Picher Indus., Inc. v. Balbos, 604 A.2d 445 (Md. 1992), 413nn54–55

Eagle-Pitcher Indus., Inc. v. U.S. EPA, 822 F.2d 132 (D.C. Cir. 1987), 221n215

Earl v. Cryovac, 772 P.2d 725 (Idaho Ct. App. 1989), 320, 321

Easum v. Miller, 92 P.3d 794 (Wyo. 2004), 331

Eaton v. Cormier, 748 A.2d 1006 (Me. 2000), 97n250, 97n252

eBay Inc. v. MercExchange, LLC, 547 U.S. 388 (2006), 54n277

Ebel v. Eli Lilly & Co., 321 F. App'x 350 (5th Cir. 2009), 106n310

Eck v. Parke, Davis & Co., 256 F.3d 1013 (10th Cir. 2001), 111n345, 112nn349–350

Ecological Rights Found. v. Pacific Lumber Co., 230 F.3d 1141 (9th Cir. 2000), 288n38

EEOC v. _____. *See name of opposing party*

Egan v. Kaiser Aluminum & Chem. Corp., 94-1939 (La. App. 4 Cir. May 22, 1996), 382n137

Eggar v. Burlington N. R.R., Nos. CV 89-159-BLG-JFB, CV 89-170-BLG-JFB, CV 89-179-BLG-JFB, CV 89-181-BLG-JFB, CV 89-236-BLG-JFB, & CV 89-291-BLG-JFB, 1991 WL 315487 (D. Mont. Dec. 18 1991), 228n236

Ehlis v. Shire Richwood, Inc., 367 F.3d 1013 (8th Cir. 2004), 106n309, 111n345

E.I. DuPont de Nemours & Co. v. Robinson, 923 S.W.2d 549 (Tex. 1995), 396

E.I. DuPont de Nemours & Co. v. Strong, 968 So. 2d 410 (Miss. 2007), 386

E.I. DuPont de Nemours & Co. v. United States, 460 F.3d 515 (3d Cir. 2006), 78n131

E.I. DuPont de Nemours & Co., United States v., 432 F.3d 161 (3d Cir. 2005), 28n114

E.I. DuPont de Nemours & Co.–Benlate Litig., *In re*, 99 F.3d 363 (11th Cir. 1996), 203n165

Elam v. Alcolac, Inc., 765 S.W.2d 42 (Mo. Ct. App. 1989), 347n113, 348–350

Eli Lilly & Co., *In re*, 142 F.R.D. 454 (S.D. Ind. 1992), 199n144, 200nn148–149

Elledge v. Richland/Lexington Sch. Dist. Five, 573 S.E.2d 789 (S.C. 2002), 249n317

Ellis v. C.R. Bard, Inc., 311 F.3d 1272 (11th Cir. 2002), 106n309, 106n312

Ellis v. International Playtex, Inc., 745 F.2d 292 (4th Cir. 1984), 400n303

Ellsworth Bros. Truck Lines, Inc. v. Canady, 245 Ark. 1055, 437 S.W.2d 243 (1969), 366n24

Elmore v. Owens-Illinois, Inc., 673 S.W.2d 434 (Mo. 1984), 25

Emerald Coast Utils. Auth. v. 3M Co., 746 F. Supp. 2d 1216 (N.D. Fla. 2010), 90n219

Emery v. Owens-Corp., 813 So. 2d 441 (La. Ct. App. 2001), *cert. denied*, 815 So. 2d 84 (La. 2002), 37n175

English v. General Elec. Co., 496 U.S. 72 (1990), 77nn122–123, 77n125

ENSCO, Inc. v. Dumas, 807 F.2d 743 (8th Cir. 1986), 81

Ephedra Prods. Liab. Litig., *In re*, 393 F. Supp. 2d 181 (S.D.N.Y. 2005), 109n329, 424

Erbrich Prods. Co. v. Wills, 509 N.E.2d 850 (Ind. Ct. App. 1987), 23n83

Erie v. R.R. Co. v. Tompkins, 304 U.S. 64 (1938), 303, 304

Ervin v. Johnson & Johnson, Inc., 492 F.3d 901 (7th Cir. 2007), 375n81

Eskenazi v. Mackoul, 905 N.Y.S.2d 169 (N.Y. App. Div. 2010), 96n246

Estados Unidos Mexicanos v. DeCoster, 229 F.3d 332 (1st Cir. 2000), 34n154

Estes v. Gibson, 257 S.W.2d 604 (Ky. 1953), 380n122

Ethyl Corp. v. Environmental Prot. Agency, 541 F.2d 1 (D.C. Cir.), cert. denied, 426 U.S. 941 (1976),   410n35
Ethylene Propylene Diene Monomer (EPDM) Antitrust Litig., In re, 255 F.R.D. 308 (D. Conn. 2009),   201n154
Evans v. Liguori, 374 A.2d 774 (R.I. 1977),   431n170
Evenson v. Antero Resources, Case No. 2011 CV 5118 (Dist. Ct., Denver County Aug. 12, 2012),   281
Everhart v. Rich's, Inc., 229 Ga. 798, 194 S.E.2d 425 (1972),   65n49
Ex parte _____. See name of party
Exxon Corp. v. Makofski, 116 S.W.3d 176 (Tex. Ct. App. 2003),   129n35, 134n74
Exxon Mobil Corp. v. Allapattah Servs., 545 U.S. 546 (2005),   45n223
Exxon Mobil Corp. v. Ford, 40 A.3d 514 (Md. Ct. App. 2012),   36n170

F

Fabrique v. Choice Hotels Int'l, Inc., 183 P.3d 1118 (Wash. Ct. App. 2008),   330nn163–168
Fair Auto. Repair, Inc. v. Car-X Serv. Sys., 471 N.E.2d 554 (Ill. App. Ct. 1984),   196n129
Falada v. Trinity Indus., Inc., 642 N.W.2d 247 (Iowa 2002),   115n364
Far East Conference v. United States, 342 U.S. 570 (1952),   75n107
Farm Bureau Mut. Ins. Co. of Ark., Inc. v. Foote, 341 Ark. 105, 14 S.W.3d 512 (2000),   367

Farmland Indus., Inc. v. Morrison-Quirk Grain Corp., 54 F.3d 478 (8th Cir. 1995),   27n107
Farnsworth v. Proctor & Gamble Co., 758 F.2d 1545 (11th Cir. 1985),   190n105, 199n144
Federal Deposit Ins. Corp. v. Laidlaw Transit, Inc., 21 P.3d 344 (Alaska 2001),   66n54
Feikema v. Texaco, Inc., 16 F.3d 1408 (4th Cir. 1994),   78n130, 81
Feldman v. Lederle Labs., 479 A.2d 374 (N.J. 1984),   116n367
FEMA Trailer Formaldehyde Prods. Liab. Litig., In re, No. 07-1873, 2010 U.S. Dist. LEXIS 35976 (E.D. La. Apr. 12, 2010),   31n129
Ferebee v. Chevron Chem. Co., 736 F.2d 1529 (D.C. Cir. 1984),   410nn35–36, 421n106, 429n161
Fermenta ASC Corp., State v., 656 N.Y.S.2d 342 (N.Y. App. Div. 1997),   17n49
Ferrell v. Rosenbaum, 691 A.2d 641 (D.C. 1997),   409n27
Fibreboard Corp. v. Fenton, 845 P.2d 1168 (Colo. 1993),   26n95
Fibreboard Corp. v. Hartford Accident & Indem. Co., 20 Cal. Rptr. 2d 376 (Cal. Ct. App. 1993),   15n35
Fidelity & Guar. Ins. v. Allied Realty Co., 238 Va. 458, 384 S.E.2d 613 (1989),   292n59
Field v. Philadelphia Elec. Co., 565 A.2d 1170 (Pa. Super. Ct. 1989),   33n145
Fillingane v. Siemens Energy & Auto., Inc., 809 So. 2d 737 (Miss. Ct. App. 2002),   193n113

Fiorentino v. Cabot Oil & Gas Corp., 750 F. Supp. 2d 506 (M.D. Pa. 2010), 280

First Nat'l Bank v. Langley, 314 So. 2d 324 (Miss. 1975), 41n211

First Nat'l Bank & Trust Corp. v. American Eurocopter Corp., 378 F.3d 682 (7th Cir. 2004), 104nn296–297

First United Methodist Church of Hyattsville v. U.S. Gypsum Co., 882 F.2d 862 (4th Cir. 1989), 71n82

Fisher v. CIBA Specialty Chems. Corp., 238 F.R.D. 273 (S.D. Ala. 2006), 92n232

Fisher v. Monsanto Co., 863 F. Supp. 285 (W.D. Va. 1994), 31

Flagg *ex rel.* Bond v. City of Detroit, 268 F.R.D. 279 (E.D. Mich. 2010), *reconsideration denied* (June 24, 2010), 200n152

Flemings v. State, 19 So. 3d 1220 (La. Ct. App. 2009), 96n249

Flexible Prods. Co., *Ex parte*, 915 So. 2d 34 (Ala. 2005), 365

Florida v. Liquid Air Corp. (*In re* Carbon Dioxide Indus. Antitrust Litig.), 229 F.3d 1321 (11th Cir. 2000), *cert. denied*, 532 U.S. 920 (2001), 173n26

Florida Lime & Avocado Growers, Inc. v. Paul, 373 U.S. 132 (1963), 77n124

Flo-Sun, Inc. v. Kirk, 783 So. 2d 1029 (Fla. 2001), 76n117

Folsom v. Sears, Roebuck & Co., 329 S.E.2d 217 (Ga. App. 1985), 25

Foltz v. State Farm Mut. Auto. Ins. Co., 331 F.3d 1122 (9th Cir. 2003), 200n150

Ford Motor Co. v. Ledesma, 242 S.W.3d 32 (Tex. 2007), 25, 399n288

Forest Park Nat'l Bank & Trust v. Ditchfield, 881 F. Supp. 2d 949 (N.D. Ill. 2012), 91n220

Foret, State v., 628 So. 2d 1116 (La. 1993), 383n143

Fortier v. Dona Anna Plaza Partners, 747 F.2d 1324 (10th Cir. 1984), 248n312

Fosamax Prods. Liab. Litig., *In re*, MDL 1789, 2009 WL 2395899 (S.D.N.Y. Aug. 4, 2009), 191n105, 192n107

Fosamax Prods. Liab. Litig., *In re*, No. 06 MD 1789 (JFK), 2011 WL 2566074 (S.D.N.Y. June 29, 2011), 115n364

Fraley v. American Cyanamid Co., 589 F. Supp. 826 (D. Colo. 1984), 112n348

Frank v. Shell Oil Co., 828 F. Supp. 2d 835 (E.D. La. 2011), 118nn385–386, 119n389

Frankl, Estate of v. Goodyear Tire & Rubber Co., 853 A.2d 880 (2004), 201, 202

Franklin Corp. v. Tedford, 18 So. 3d 215 (Miss. 2009), 387

Fraser v. 301-52 Townhouse Corp., 57 A.D.3d 416 (N.Y. App. Div. 2008), 425

Frazier v. Pioneer Am. LLC, 445 F.3d 542 (5th Cir. 2006), 181n64

Frederick v. Koziol, 727 F. Supp. 1019 (E.D. Va. 1990), 228n237

Freier v. Westinghouse Elec. Corp., 303 F.3d 176 (2d Cir. 2002), 64n41, 65n44, 65n46

Freightliner Corp. v. Myrick, 514 U.S. 280 (1995), 77n124

Frey v. EPA, 270 F.3d 1129 (7th Cir. 2001), 74n104

Frey v. EPA, 403 F.3d 828 (7th Cir. 2005), 79n137

Frias v. Atl. Richfield Co., 999 S.W.2d 97 (Tex. App. Houston 14th Dist. 1999), 12n12

Friends of Santa Fe County v. Lac Minerals, Inc., 892 F. Supp. 1333 (D.N.M. 1995), 75n110, 76n114, 76n117

Frye v. United States, 293 F. 1013 (D.C. Cir. 1923), 157, 159n98, 263, 268, 313, 334, 339, 342, 372–375, 385, 388, 394, 402, 423n126

Fryer v. Kranz, 616 N.W.2d 102 (S.D. 2000), 361

Fugate v. Com., 993 S.W.2d 931 (Ky. 1999), 380n119

Fullen v. Philips Elecs. N. Am. Corp., 266 F. Supp. 2d 471 (N.D. W. Va. 2002), 86n193

Fulmore v. CSX Transp., Inc., 557 S.E.2d 64 (Ga. Ct. App. 2001), 376n86

Furrer v. Brown, 62 F.3d 1092 (8th Cir. 1995), 28n114

G

Gabel v. IRS., 1998 WL 817758 (N.D. Cal. June 25, 1998), 185n78

Gacke v. Pork Xtra, LLC, 684 N.W.2d 168 (Iowa 2004), 20n66

Gade v. National Solid Wastes Mgmt. Ass'n, 505 U.S. 88 (1992), 77n125

GAF Corp. v. United States, 818 F.2d 901 (D.C. Cir. 1987), 74n104

Gannon v. United States, 571 F. Supp. 2d 615 (E.D. Pa. 2007), 428

Gass v. Marriott Hotel Servs., Inc., 501 F. Supp. 2d 1011 (W.D. Mich. 2007), rev'd, 558 F.3d 419 (6th Cir. 2009), 157n87, 341n62, 342, 343nn79–80, 345

Gates v. Rohm & Haas Co., 265 F.R.D. 208 (E.D. Pa. 2010), aff'd, 655 F.3d 255 (3d Cir. 2011), 156, 179, 297, 306, 430n165

Gates ex rel. Triumph Mortgage, Inc. v. Sprint Spectrum, L.P., 349 F. App'x 257 (10th Cir. 2009), 91n222

Geffcken v. D'Andrea, 41 Cal. Rptr. 3d 80 (Cal. Ct. App. 2006), 316n55

Geier v. American Honda Motor Co., 529 U.S. 861 (2000), 77n124

General Cas. Co. v. Hills, 561 N.W.2d 718 (Wis. 1997), 35n161

General Dynamics Corp. v. Brottem, 53 So. 3d 334 (Fla. Dist. Ct. App. 2010), 118n385

General Elec. Co. v. Ingram, 513 U.S. 1190 (1995), 428n154

General Elec. Co. v. Joiner, 522 U.S. 136 (1997), 109n328, 133n63, 158, 161nn111–113, 356n180, 377n93

General Elec. Co. v. Litton Indus. Automation Sys., Inc., 920 F.2d 1415 (8th Cir. 1990), abrogated, Key Tronic Corp. v. United States, 511 U.S. 809 (1994), 26n100, 73n89

General Motors Corp. Pick-Up Truck Fuel Tank Prods. Liab. Litig., In re, 55 F.3d 768 (3d Cir. 1995), 271n7

General Tel. Co. v. Bi-Co Pavers, Inc., 514 S.W.2d 168 (Tex. App. 1974), 16n40

General Tel. Co. of Sw. v. Falcon, 457 U.S. 147, 102 S. Ct. 2364 (1982), 178nn48–49

Genereux v. American Beryllia Corp., 577 F.3d 350 (1st Cir. 2009), 104n299

Genna v. Jackson, 781 N.W.2d 124 (Mich. Ct. App. 2009), 341n61, 342–345

Gentry v. Mangum, 466 S.E.2d 171 (W. Va. 1995), 403nn319–320

George v. Celotex Corp., 914 F.2d 26 (2d Cir. 1990), 113n355

George v. Reisdorf Bros., 410 Fed. App'x 382 (2d Cir. 2011), 56n285

George v. Vermont League of Cities & Towns, 993 A.2d 367 (Vt. 2010), 432n177

George, Estate of v. Vermont League of Cities & Towns, 993 A.2d 367 (Vt. 2010), 109n330

Georgia v. Tenn. Copper Co., 206 U.S. 230 (1907), 35n156

Georgine v. Amchem Prods., Inc., 83 F.3d 610 (3d Cir. 1996), 271n7

German v. Federal Home Loan Mortgage Corp., 885 F. Supp. 537 (S.D.N.Y. 1995), 426n141

Gerzeski v. State, 268 N.W.2d 525 (Mich. 1978), 100n271

GES, Inc. v. Corbitt, 117 Nev. 265 (Nev. 2001), 323n116, 324n123

Getty Petroleum Mktg., Inc., v. Capital Terminal Co., 391 F.3d 312 (1st Cir. 2004), 114n358, 114n361

Getz v. Boeing Co., 654 F.3d 852 (9th Cir. 2011), 116nn373–374

Gilbert v. DaimlerChrysler Corp., 685 N.W.2d 391 (Mich. 2004), 342n71

Gill v. LDI, 19 F. Supp. 2d 1188 (W.D. Wash. 1998), 249n325

Glastetter v. Novartis Pharm. Corp., 252 F.3d 986 (8th Cir. 2001), 157n86

Glover v. Jackson State Univ., 968 So. 2d 1267 (Miss. 2007), 385n165

Goeb v. Tharaldson, 615 N.W.2d 800 (Minn. 2000), 346, 347

Goewey v. United States, 886 F. Supp. 1268 (D.S.C. 1995), 132n55

Goffman v. Gross, 59 F.3d 668 (7th Cir. 1995), 157n87

Golden v. Union Pac. R.R., 804 N.W.2d 31 (Neb. 2011), 350n132

Good v. Fluor Daniel Corp., 222 F. Supp. 2d 1236 (E.D. Wash. 2002), 109n328

Goode, State v., 461 S.E.2d 631 (N.C. 1995), 388, 389

Goodrich & Pennington Mortgage Fund, Inc. v. J.R. Woolard, Inc., 101 P.3d 792 (Nev. 2004), 323n115

Gore v. People's Sav. Bank, 665 A.2d 1341 (Conn. 1995), 11n9, 52, 53

Gorman-Rupp Co. v. Hall, 908 So. 2d 749 (Miss. 2005), 386n180

Gourdine v. Crews, 955 A.2d 769 (Md. Ct. App. 2008), 115n367

Gracyalny v. Westinghouse Elec. Corp., 723 F.2d 1311 (7th Cir. 1983), 106n313

Graham v. Canadian Nat'l R.R. Co., 749 F. Supp. 1300 (D. Vt. 1990), 432n176, 433

Grand Pier Ctr. LLC v. Tronox, LLC, No. 03 C 7767 U.S. Dist. LEXIS 88201 (N.D. Ill. 2008), 22n74

Granfield v. CSX Transp., Inc., 597 F.3d 474 (1st Cir. 2010), 60n44

Grant v. E.I. DuPont de Nemours & Co., Civ. A. No. 91-55-CIV-4H, 1993 WL 146634 (E.D.N.C. 1993), 227n233, 228n236

Grassis v. Johns-Mansville Corp., 248 N.J. Super. 446, 591 A.2d 671 (App. Div. 1991), 376n86

Grassis v. Johns-Mansville Corp., 591 A.2d 671 (N.J. Super. Ct. App. Div. 1991), 421n107

Graven v. Vail Assocs., 909 P.2d 514 (Colo. 1995), 316n57

Gray v. Badger Mining Corp., 676 N.W.2d 268 (Minn. 2004), 103n288, 103n290, 103n293, 104n296, 105nn304–305, 106n311, 106n313, 107n315

Green v. Alpharma, Inc., 373 Ark. 378 S.W.3d 29 (Ark. 2008) (Green I), 368n39, 369nn44–47, 370nn48–52, 371

Green v. George's Farms, Inc., 2011 Ark. 70, 2011 Ark. LEXIS 65 (2011) (Green II), 151n51, 369nn44–45, 370, 371

Green, United States v., 33 F. Supp. 2d 203 (W.D.N.Y. 1998), 74n106, 135nn75–77, 135nn79–83, 136n85, 137n88

Greene v. Flewelling, 366 So. 2d 777 (Fla. Dist. Ct. App. 1978) *cert. denied*, 374 So. 2d 99 (Fla. 1979), 372nn61–62

Greenville, City of v. Syngenta Crop Prot., Inc., 756 F. Supp. 2d 1001 (S.D. Ill. 2010), 38n183, 91n219

Greenville, City of v. W.R. Grace & Co., 827 F.2d 975 (4th Cir. 1987), 39n185, 50n254

Gregg v. V-J Auto Parts, Co., 943 A.2d 216 (Pa. 2007), 148, 427

Griffin v. K.E. McKay's Mkt. of Coos Bay, Inc., 865 P.2d 1320 (Or. Ct. App. 1993), 328n152

Griffin v. Unocal Corp., 990 So. 2d 291 Ala. (2008), 58nn1–2

Grimes v. Hoffman-La Roche, Inc., 907 F. Supp. 33 (D.N.H. 1995), 417

Grine v. Coombs, 214 F.R.D. 312 (W.D. Pa. 2003), *aff'd*, 2004 WL 1179349 (3d Cir. 2004), 248n315

Grove v. Principal Mut. Life Ins. Co., 200 F.R.D. 434 (S.D. Iowa 2001), 276n45

Guaranty-First Trust Co. v. Textron, Inc., 622 N.E.2d 597 (Mass. 1993), 95n243

Guevara v. Ferrer, 247 S.W.3d 662 (Tex. 2007), 110n337

Guillory v. American Tobacco Co., No. 97-C-8641, 2001 WL 290603 (N.D. Ill. Mar. 20, 2001), 300n103

Guinn v. Astrazeneca Pharm., 598 F. Supp. 2d 1239 (M.D. Fla. 2009), 154n71, 371n58

Gulden v. Crown Zellerbach Corp., 890 F.2d 195 (9th Cir. 1989), 32n140, 119n390

Gunn Hill Dairy Props., LLC v. Los Angeles Dep't of Water & Power, 269 P.3d 980 (Utah Ct. App. 2012), 329

Gussack Realty Co. v. Xerox Corp., 224 F.3d 85 (2d Cir. 2000), 55n282

Gustavson v. United States, 655 F.2d 1034 (10th Cir. 1981), 59n7

H

Habecker v. Clark Equip. Co., 36 F.3d 278 (3d Cir. 1994), 114n357

Hackwell v. United States, No. 04-CV-00827-EWN, 2008 U.S. Dist. LEXIS 56641 (D. Colo. 2008), 54n277

Hadden v. State, 690 So. 2d 573 (Fla. 1997), 372n65

Haddix v. Playtex Family Prods. Corp., 138 F.3d 681 (7th Cir. 1998), 25n88

Haddonbrook Assocs. v. General Elec. Co., 427 Fed. App'x 99 (3d Cir. 2011), 285

Hagan v. Coca-Cola Bottling Co., 804 So. 2d 1234 (Fla. 2001), 43n209

Hagen v. Dow Chem. Co., 863 P.2d 413 (Mont. 1993), 322, 323

Hagerty v. L&L Marine Servs., Inc., 788 F.2d 315 (5th Cir. 1986), 37n173

Hall v. Ashland Oil Co., 625 F. Supp. 1515 (D. Conn. 1986), 106n313

Hall v. Babcock & Wilcox, 69 F. Supp. 2d 716 (W.D. Pa. 1999), 135n74, 154

Hall v. Baxter Healthcare Corp., 947 F. Supp. 1387 (D. Or. 1996), 133n64

Hallstrom v. Tillamook County, 493 U.S. 20 (1989), 73n94, 74n95, 74n97

Hamilton v. Beretta U.S.A. Corp., 222 F.2d 36 (2d Cir. 2000), 170n13

Hamilton v. Beretta U.S.A. Corp., 750 N.E.2d 1055 (N.Y. 2001), 170n13

Hanford Nuclear Reservation Litig., *In re*, 534 F.3d 986 (9th Cir. 2008), 84n175, 117n382

Hanford Nuclear Reservation Litig., *In re*, 350 F. Supp. 2d 871 (E.D. Wash. 2004), 23n83

Hanlon v. Chrysler Corp., 150 F.3d 1011 (9th Cir. 1998), 275

Hanna v. Motiva Enters., LLC, 839 F. Supp. 2d 654 (S.D.N.Y. 2012), 99

Hannan v. Pest Control Servs., 734 N.E.2d 674 (Ind. Ct. App. 2000), 227n233, 336

Hanover Shoe, Inc. v. United Shoe Mach. Corp., 392 U.S. 481 (1968), 69n63

Hansen v. Baxter Healthcare Corp., 764 N.E.2d 35 (Ill. 2002), 106n312

Hansen v. Mountain Fuel Supply Co., 858 P.2d 970 (Utah 1993), 42n205

Hardin v. Motor Panels, Inc., 524 S.E.2d 368 (N.C. Ct. App. 2000), 390n219

Harduvel v. General Dynamics Corp., 878 F.2d 1311 (11th Cir. 1989), 116n372

Hardyman v. Norfolk & W. Ry., 243 F.3d 255 (6th Cir. 2001), 345n97

Harper v. Regency Dev. Co., 399 So. 2d 248 (Ala. 1981), 22n77

Harrington v. Chavez, 196 P. 320 (N.M. 1921), 14n29

Harris v. Kissling, 721 P.2d 838 (Or. Ct. App. 1985), 328n152

Harris v. Peridot Chem. (N.J.), Inc., 712 A.2d 1181 (N.J. Super. Ct. A.D. 1998), 421

Harrison v. Digital Equip. Corp., 465 S.E.2d 494 (Ga. Ct. App. 1995), 61n21

Harrison v. Fed. Bureau of Prisons, 681 F. Supp. 2d 76 (D.D.C. 2010), 185n81

Harrisonville v. W.S. Dickey Clay Mfg. Co., 289 U.S. 334 (1933), 67n55

Hartley v. State, 698 P.2d 77 (Wash. 1985), 330n165

Hasson v. Com., No. 0403-05-4, 2006 WL 1387974 (Va. Ct. App. May 23, 2006), 399n296

Hatco Corp. v. W.R. Grace & Co., 836 F. Supp. 1049 (D.N.J. 1993), 127n25, 128n6

Hauenstein v. Loctite Corp., 347 N.W.2d 272 (Minn. 1984), 25nn92–93

Hawaii Fed. Asbestos Cases, *In re*, 734 F. Supp. 1563 (D. Haw. 1990), 36n162, 36n164, 36n170, 39n190

Hawkins v. Commissioner of the N.H. Dep't of Health & Human Servs., No. 99-143, 2004 U.S. Dist. LEXIS 807 (D.N.H. Jan. 23, 2004), 274n28

Healey v. Firestone Tire & Rubber Co., 87 N.Y.2d 596 (N.Y. 1996), 170n10

Heard v. Sheahan, 253 F.3d 316 (7th Cir. 2001), 68n61

Hedgepath v. AT&T Co., 559 S.E.2d 327 (S.C. Ct. App. 2001), 67n57

Heller v. Shaw Indus., 167 F.3d 146 (3d Cir. 1999), 304n119, 393n245, 428, 429n160

Henderson v. Allied Signal, Inc., 644 S.E.2d 724 (S.C. 2007), 391n232, 392n241

Henke v. Arco Midcon, LLC, 750 F. Supp. 2d 1052 (E.D. Mo. 2010), 24n85

Hennessy v. Committee Edison Co., 764 F. Supp. 495 (N.D. Ill. 1991), 32n142

Henry v. Dow Chem. Co., 701 N.W.2d 684 (Mich. 2005), 37n180, 38n181, 41n202, 42n205

Hensley v. Eckerhart, 461 U.S. 424 (1983), 267n1

Heparin Prods. Liab. Litig., *In re*, No. 1:08HC60000, MDL No. 1953, 2011 WL 2971918 (N.D. Ohio July 21, 2011), 109n333

Hermes Consol., Inc. v. People, 849 P.2d 1302 (Wyo. 1993), 81n151

Hess v. A.I. DuPont Hosp. for Children, No. 08-0229, 2009 U.S. Dist. LEXIS 19492 (E.D. Pa. Mar. 5, 2009), 51n259

Hickman v. Thomas C. Thompson Co., 644 F. Supp. 1531 (D. Colo. 1986), 248n311

Hicks v. Humble Oil & Ref. Co., 970 S.W.2d 90 (Tex. App. 1998), 22n75

Higgs v. State, 222 P.3d 648 (2010), 325

Highland Indus. Park, Inc. v. BEI Def. Sys. Co., 357 F.3d 794 (8th Cir. 2004), 65n47, 66n54

Hilao v. Estate of Marcos, 103 F.3d 767 (9th Cir. 1996), 252, 254

Hildebrandt v. Allied Corp., 839 F.2d 396 (8th Cir. 1987), 6n12

Hill v. Metropolitan Dist. Comm'n, 787 N.E.2d 526 (Mass. 2003), 95n243

Hill v. Wilmington Chem. Corp., 156 N.W.2d 898 (Minn. 1968), 103n293

Hill *ex rel.* Hill v. Koppers, 2009 WL 4908836 (N.D. Miss. Dec. 11, 2009), 386n177

Hillsborough County v. Automated Med. Lab., Inc., 471 U.S. 707 (1985), 77n120, 77n122, 77n127

Hines v. Davidowitz, 312 U.S. 52 (1941), 77n124

Hinton v. Monsanto Co., 813 So. 2d 827 (Ala. 2001), 37n178

Hirsch v. CSX Transp. Corp., 656 F.3d 359 (6th Cir. 2011), 305

Hodge v. Harkey, 631 S.E.2d 143 (N.C. Ct. App. 2006), 70, 71

Hoery v. United States, 324 F.3d 1220 (10th Cir. 2003), 68n63

Hoery v. United States, 64 P.3d 214 (Colo. 2003), 17nn50–51, 19n62, 66nn53–54

Hoffman v. AC&S, Inc., 548 S.E.2d 379 (2001), 377n97, 378n98, 379n114

Hoffman v. Houghton Chem. Corp., 751 N.E.2d 848 (Mass. 2001), 105n304

Hogg v. Chevron USA, Inc., 45 So. 3d 991 (La. 2010), 66n51

Holder v. Enbridge Energy, L.P., No. 1:10-CV-752, 2011 U.S. Dist. LEXIS 99220 (W.D. Mich. Sept. 2, 2011), 22n76, 24n86

Hollander v. Sandoz Pharm. Corp., 289 F.3d 1193 (10th Cir. 2002), 109n328, 358n207, 359, 360n219

Holley v. ACTS, Inc., 581 S.E.2d 750 (N.C. 2003), 387n191

Holmes, Estate of v. Pneumo Abex, 955 N.E.2d 1173 (Ill. App. 2011), 293

Holstine v. Texaco Corp., No. CJ-97-221, 2001 WL 605137 (Okla. Dist. Ct. Apr. 16, 2001), 149n41

Hood v. Matrixx Initiatives, 50 So. 3d 1166 (Fla. Ct. App. 2011), 373

Hooker Chems. & Plastics Corp., United States v., 850 F. Supp. 993 (W.D.N.Y. 1994), 113n356

Horvath v. Delida, 540 N.W.2d 760 (Mich. Ct. App. 1995), 66n54

Hostetler v. Ward, 704 P.2d 1193 (Wash. Ct. App. 1985), 19n62

Hovermale v. Berkely Spring Moose Lodge No. 1483, 271 S.E.2d 335 (W. Va. 1980), 403n321

Howerton v. Arai Helmet, Ltd., 597 S.E.2d 674 (N.C. 2004), 388n193, 388n196, 388n200, 389n206

Hubbard-Hall Chem. Co. v. Silverman, 340 F.2d 402 (1st Cir. 1965), 10

Hudjohn v. S&G Mach. Co., 114 P.3d 1141 (Or. Ct. App. 2005), 328

Hudson v. Peavey Oil Co., 566 P.2d 175 (Or. 1977), 16n47

Hue v. Farmboy Spray Co., 896 P.2d 682 (Wash. 1995), 330n168

Huffman v. United States, 82 F.3d 703 (6th Cir. 1996), 68n63

Humboldt Baykeeper v. Union Pac. R.R., 244 F.R.D. 560 (N.D. Cal. 2007), 200n148

Hunt v. Chemical Waste Mgmt., Inc., 584 So. 2d 1367 (Ala. 1991), *rev'd*, 504 U.S. 334 (1992), 81n153

Hydrogen Peroxide, *In re*, 552 F.3d 305 (3d Cir. 2008), 299n102

Hyman & Armstrong, P.S.C. v. Gunderson, 279 S.W.3d 93 (Ky. 2008), 381, 382

I

Iberville Parish Waterworks District No. 3 v. Novartis Crop Prot., Inc., 45 F. Supp. 2d 934 (S.D. Ala.), *aff'd*, 204 F.3d 1122 (11th Cir. 1999), 38n183, 90n218

Idaho v. Bunker Hill Co., 635 F. Supp. 665 (D. Idaho 1986), 50n252

Idaho Rural Council v. Bosma, 143 F. Supp. 2d 1169 (D. Idaho 2001), 72n87

Ideal Food Prods. Co. v. Rupe, 261 P.2d 992 (Ariz. 1953), 312n18

IMAX Secs. Litig., *In re*, No. 06-6128, 2012 U.S. Dist. LEXIS 86513 (S.D.N.Y. June 20, 2012), 274n28

Indian Brand Farms, Inc. v. Novartis Crop Prot. Inc., 617 F.3d 207 (3d Cir. 2010), 85n183

Indiana Harbor Belt R.R. Co. v. American Cyanamid Co., 916 F.2d 1174 (7th Cir. 1990), 23n84

Ingram v. Coca-Cola Co., 200 F.R.D. 685 (N.D. Ga. 2001), 275

Inland Steel v. Pequignot, 608 N.E.2d 1378 (Ind. Ct. App. 1993), 12n14

In re _____. *See name of party*

Interfaith Cmty. Org. v. Honeywell Int'l, Inc., 263 F. Supp. 2d 796 (D.N.J. 2003), 23n84, 130n37, 130n41

Interfaith Cmty. Org. v. PPG Indus., Inc., 702 F. Supp. 2d 295 (D.N.J. 2010), 75n111

International Paper Co. v. Ouellette, 479 U.S. 481 (1987), 99n263

International Union v. Pendergrass, 878 F.2d 389 (D.C. Cir. 1989), 410n38

Irrer v. Milacron, Inc., 484 F. Supp. 2d 677 (E.D. Mich. 2007), 104

Isaacson v. Dow Chem. Co., 517 F.3d 129 (2d Cir. 2008), 117n376

Isabel v. Velsicol Chem. Co., 327 F. Supp. 2d 915 (W.D. Tenn. 2004), 37n177

Isse, Commonwealth v., 80 Va. Cir. 493 (2010), 399n296, 400n297

Italiano v. Jones Chems., Inc., 908 F. Supp. 904 (M.D. Fla. 1995), 36nn168–169

J

Jackson v. Johns-Manville Sales Corp., 781 F.2d 394 (5th Cir. 1986), 37n174

Jackson v. Nutmeg Techs., Inc., 43 A.D.3d 599 (N.Y. App. Div. 2007), 425

Jackson v. Target Corp., No. 09-10867, 2011 WL 533600 (E.D. Mich. Feb. 15, 2011), 96n249

Jacksonville v. Arkansas Dep't of Pollution Control & Ecology, 824 S.W.2d 840 (Ark. 1992), 81n151

Jacobs Farm/Del Cabo, Inc. v. Western Farm Serv., Inc., 119 Cal. Rptr. 3d 529 (Cal. Ct. App. 2010), 99

Jacques v. Pioneer Plastics, Inc., 676 A.2d 504 (Me. 1996), 97n252

James v. Bessemer Processing Co., 714
A.2d 898 (N.J. 1998), 169n9,
418nn87–88, 418n92, 418n94, 419
James v. Chevron U.S.A., Inc., 694
A.2d 270 (N.J. Super. Ct. A.D.
1997), 419n97, 420
Jandrt v. Jerome Foods, Inc., 601 N.W.2d
650 (Wis. 1999), 153
Jappell v. American Ass'n of Blood Banks,
162 F. Supp. 2d 476 (E.D. Va.
2001), 399n293, 400n303
Jarvill v. Porky's Equip., Inc., 189 P.3d
335 (Alaska 2008), 37n178
JBG/Twinbrook Metro. Ltd. P'ship
v. Wheeler, 697 A.2d 898 (Md.
1997), 16n46
Jefferson County v. Acker, 527 U.S. 423
(1999), 117n376
Jennings v. Palomar Pomerado Health
Sys., Inc., 8 Cal. Rptr. 3d 363 (Cal.
Ct. App. 2003), 316n54
Jensen v. General Elec. Co., 623 N.E.2d
547 (N.Y. 1993), 58n1
Jerry Harmon Motors, Inc. v. Farmers
Union Grain Terminal Ass'n, 337
N.W.2d 427 (N.D. 1983), 18n59
Jessup v. Luther, 277 F.3d 926 (7th Cir.
2006), 201n157, 201n159
J.M. Taylor, United States v., 166 F.R.D.
356 (M.D. N.C. 1996), 194
Joel A. v. Giuliani, 218 F.3d 132 (2d Cir.
2000), 274n31
Joffer v. Cargill, Inc., No. 08-4198,
2010 WL 1409444 (D.S.D. Apr. 1,
2010), 97n255
Johansen v. Combustion Eng'g, Inc.,
834 F. Supp. 404 (S.D. Ga.
1993), *vacated*, 517 U.S. 1217
(1996), 45n224

John v. Im, 559 S.E.2d 694 (Va.
2002), 399n296
John Does I-VI v. Yogi, 110 F.R.D. 629
(D.D.C. 1986), 199n140, 199n142
John's Heating Serv. v. Lamb, 46 P.3d
1024 (Alaska 2002), 310
Johnson v. Alcorn State Univ., 929 So. 2d
398 (Miss. App. 2006), 385n168
Johnson v. American Standard,
Inc., 179 P.3d 905 (Cal.
2008), 103nn289–290
Johnson v. E.I. DuPont de Nemours &
Co., No. 08-628 (La. App. 5 Cir.
Jan. 13, 2009), 383n150
Johnson v. Honeywell Int'l Inc., 179
Cal. App. 4th 549 (Cal. Ct. App.
2009), 103nn291–292
Johnson v. James Langley Operating
Co., 226 F.3d 957 (8th Cir.
2000), 73n89
Johnson v. Knox County P'ship, 728
N.W.2d 101 (Neb. 2007), 21n70
Johnson v. Knoxville Cmty. Sch.
Dist., 570 N.W.2d 633 (Iowa
1997), 337n28
Johnson v. Mays, 447 S.E.2d 563 (W. Va.
1994), 402n313
Johnson v. Paynesville Farmers Union
Co-op. Oil Co., 817 N.W.2d 693
(Minn. 2012), 13n21, 14n22
Johnson v. Philip Morris, Inc., 159
F. Supp. 2d 950 (S.D. Tex.
2001), 31n130
Johnson v. Raybestos-Manhattan, Inc.,
740 P.2d 548 (Haw. 1987), 25n92
Johnson & Johnson Corp., State *ex rel.*
v. Karl, 647 S.E.2d 899 (W. Va.
2007), 106n307

Johnston v. Maine Energy Recovery Co., 997 A.2d 741 (Me. 2010), 99n267

Joiner v. General Elec. Co., 78 F.3d 524 (11th Cir. 1996), 161nn109–110, 165

Joiner v. General Elec. Co., 864 F. Supp. 1310 (N.D. Ga. 1994), 160

Joint E. & S. Dist. Asbestos Litig., *In re*, 52 F.3d 1124 (2d Cir. 1995), 136n83, 424n129

Joint E. & S. Dist. Asbestos Litig., *In re*, 827 F. Supp. 1014 (S.D.N.Y. 1993), 424n128

Jolly v. Eli Lilly & Co., 751 P.2d 923 (Cal. 1988), 61nn19–20

Jonah R. v. Carmona, 446 F.3d 1000 (9th Cir. 2006), 297n86

Jones v. Chemetron Corp., 212 F.3d 199 (3d Cir. 2000), 59n2, 60n13

Jones v. Ortho Pharm. Corp., 209 Cal. Rptr. 456 (Cal. Ct. App. 1985), 315

Jones v. United States, 933 F. Supp. 894 (N.D. Cal. 1996), 315n43

Jones v. United States, 751 F. Supp. 2d 835 (E.D.N.C. 2010), 71

Jones v. Utica Mut. Ins. Co., 463 So. 2d 1153 (Fla. 1985), 371n56

Jordan v. Travelers Ins. Co., 245 So. 2d 151 (La. 1971), 383n149

Joseph v. Hess Oil, 867 F.2d 179 (3d Cir. 1989), 6n12

Joshi v. Providence Health Sys. of Or., 108 P.3d 1195 (Or. Ct. App. 2005), 327

June v. Union Carbide Corp., 577 F.3d 1234 (10th Cir. 2009), 317

Junk v. Terminix Int'l Co., 628 F.3d 439 (8th Cir. 2010), 337n27

K

Kaiser Found. Health Plan of Colo. v. Sharp, 741 P.2d 714 (Colo. 1987), 316n58

Kalamazoo River Study Grp. v. Eaton Corp., 258 F. Supp. 2d 736 (W.D. Mich. 2002), 128n26, 344

Kalamazoo River Study Grp. v. Rockwell Int'l Corp., 171 F.3d 1065 (6th Cir. 1999), 342n63, 342n69

Kallok v. Medtronic, Inc., 573 N.W.2d 356 (Minn. 1998), 54n280

Kaminski v. Metal & Wire Prods. Co., 927 N.E.2d 1066 (Ohio 2010), 118n386

Kansas v. Marion County Landfill, Inc., 76 P.3d 1000 (Kan. 2003), 89n212

Karuk Tribe of N. Cal. v. California Reg'l Water Quality Control Bd., 108 Cal. Rptr. 3d 40 (Cal. Ct. App. 2010), 55n284

Keel v. H&V Inc., 421 S.E.2d 362 (N.C. Ct. App. 1992), 390n221

Kelley v. American Heyer-Schulte Corp., 957 F. Supp. 873 (W.D. Tex. 1997), *appeal dismissed*, 139 F.3d 899 (5th Cir. 1998), 140n1

Kelley v. Cowesett Hills Assocs., 768 A.2d 425 (R.I. 2001), 32n141

Kemblesville HHMO Ctr. LLC v. Landhope Realty Co., No. 08-2405, 2011 U.S. Dist. LEXIS 83324 (E.D. Pa. July 28, 2011), 299

Kemmerer v. State Farm Ins. Co., No. 01-5445, 2004 WL 87017 (E.D. Pa. Jan. 19, 2004), 427n143

Kennedy v. Carter, 249 S.C. 168 (1967), 391n227

Kennedy v. Collagen Corp., 161 F.3d 1226 (9th Cir. 1998), *cert. denied*, 67 U.S.L.W. 3570 (U.S. May 3, 1999) (No. 98-1424), 393n245

Kennedy v. Southern Cal. Edison Co., 268 F.3d 763 (9th Cir. 2001), 151

Kennedy Bldg. Assocs. v. Viacom, Inc., 375 F.3d 731 (8th Cir. 2004), 29n117, 54n279, 56n286

Kentucky, United States v., 252 F.3d 816 (6th Cir. 2001), 83n169

Key Tronic Corp. v. United States, 511 U.S. 809 (1994), 26n100, 54n280, 55n282, 73n89

Keywell Corp. v. Weinstein, 33 F.3d 159 (2d Cir. 1994), 29n119

Kichline v. Consolidated Rail Corp., 800 F.2d 356 (3d Cir. 1986), 60n14

Kilpatrick v. Bryant, 868 S.W.2d 594 (Tenn. 1993), 393n247, 394n249

King v. Burlington N. Santa Fe Ry. Corp., 762 N.W.2d 24 (Neb. 2009), 133n64, 350n131, 350nn134–136, 351nn137–144, 352nn145–146

Kis v. Amerigas Propane L.P., No. DV 98-359, 2000 Mont. Dist. LEXIS 1835 (Mont. Dist.Ct. 2000), 23n83

Kivalina, Native Vill. of v. Exxon Mobil Corp., 663 F. Supp. 2d 863 (E.D. Cal. 2009), 287, 290

Klanseck v. Anderson Sales & Serv., Inc., 393 N.W.2d 356 (Mich. 1986), 283n13

Klasch v. Walgreen Co., 264 P.3d 1155 (Nev. 2011), 105n307

Klier v. Sordoni Skanska Constr. Co., 766 A.2d 761 (N.J. 2001), 196n126

Kling Realty Co. v. Chevron USA, Inc., 575 F.3d 510 (5th Cir. 2009), 66n54

Knight v. Kirby Inland Marine, Inc., 482 F.3d 347 (5th Cir. 2007), 134n73, 137n89, 146n24, 306n131

Knight v. Roberts, 2012 WL 25792567 (Ga. Ct. App. July 3, 2012), 376n88

Knodle v. Waikiki Gateway Hotel, Inc., 742 P.2d 377 (Haw. 1987), 318n73, 318n76

Knowles v. Burlington N. R.R., 856 P.2d 1352 (Kan. Ct. App. 1993), 339n44

Knox v. AC&S, Inc., 690 F. Supp. 752 (S.D. Ind. 1998), 63n33–34

Kocher v. Getz, 824 N.E.2d 671 (Ind. 2005), 95n244

Kolesar v. United Agri Prods., Inc., 412 F. Supp. 2d 686 (W.D. Mich. 2006), 94

Koronthaly v. L'Oreal USA, Inc., 374 F. App'x 257 (3d Cir. Mar. 26, 2010), 89n212

Korte v. ExxonMobil Coal USA, Inc., 164 Fed. App'x 553 (7th Cir. 2006), 157n87

Kosmacek v. Farm Serv. Co-op of Persia, 485 N.W.2d 99 (Iowa Ct. App. 1992), 338n34

Krebs v. United Ref. Co., 893 A.2d 776 (Pa. Super. Ct. 2006), 56n288

Kreisman v. Thomas, 469 P.2d 107 (Ariz. Ct. App. 1970), 311n15, 312n18

Kroll v. Lieberman, 244 F. Supp. 2d 100 (E.D.N.Y. 2003), 230n250

Kubrick, United States v., 444 U.S. 111 (1979), 59n9, 61n19

Kuhn v. Sandoz Pharm. Corp., 14 P.3d 1170 (Kan. 2000), 339n43, 339n46, 340nn50–51, 340n54, 341nn55–56, 341nn59–60

Kumho Tire Co. v. Carmichael, 526 U.S. 137 (1999), 158, 162–165, 192n112, 193n13, 377n93, 385, 386, 396n261

Kurer v. Parke, Davis & Co., 679 N.W.2d 867 (Wis. Ct. App. 2004), 112n349

Kuxhausen v. Tillman Partners L.P., 241 P.3d 75 (Kan. 2010), 300, 339n42, 340nn52–53, 341n58

L

Lamb v. IRS, 871 F. Supp. 301 (E.D. Mich. 1994), 185n81

Lamb v. Martin Marietta Energy Sys., Inc., 835 F. Supp. 959 (W.D. Ky. 1993), 89n212

Landgraf v. McDonnell Douglas Helicopter Co., 993 F.2d 558 (6th Cir. 1993), 116N372

Landrigan v. Celotex Corp., 605 A.2d 1079 (N.J. 1992), 418n90, 421n107, 422n114

Lane v. American Nat'l Can Co., 640 S.E.2d 732 (N.C. Ct. App. 2007), 388n194

Lapka v. Porter Hayden Co., 745 A.2d 525 (N.J. 2000), 421n112

Larkin v. Pfizer, Inc., 153 S.W.3d 758 (Ky. 2004), 106n308, 106n312

Lasha v. Olin Corp., 625 So. 2d 1002 (La. 1993), 383, 384

Lauria v. Donahue, 438 F. Supp. 2d 131 (E.D.N.Y. 2006), 118n388

Layton v. Yankee Caithness Joint Venture, 774 F. Supp. 576 (D. Nev. 1991), 325nn129–130

lcoa, Inc. v. Behringer, 235 S.W.3d 456 (Tex. Ct. App. 2007), 115n366

Lead Indus. Ass'n, Inc., State v., 951 A.2d 428 (R.I. 2008), 430n166

Lead Indus. Ass'n, Inc., State v., No. PC 99-5226, 2007 WL 711824 (R.I. Super. Feb. 26, 2007), 431n171

Leaf River Forest Prods. v. Ferguson, 662 So. 2d 648 (Miss. 1995), 47n230

Leahy, People v., 882 P.2d 321 (Cal. 1994), 158n91

Leake v. United States, No. 09-4564, 2011 WL 6934057 (E.D. Pa. Dec. 29, 2011), 429n159

Lebanon, City of v. Georgia-Pac. Corp., No. 02-6351-AA, 2004 WL 1078982 (D. Or. May 11, 2004), 97n250

Lechliter v. Department of Def., 371 F. Supp. 2d 589 (D. Del. 2005), 185n80

Lee v. A.C.&S. Co., 542 A.2d 352 (Del. Super. Ct. 1987), 409n23

Lee v. Chicago Transit Auth., 605 N.E.2d 493 (Ill. 1992), 334n4

Lee v. CSX Transp., Inc., 958 So. 2d 578 (Fl. Ct. App. 2007), 64n41

Lee v. Stewart, 10 S.E.2d 804 (N.C. 1940), 16n41

LeFarge Corp. v. Campbell, 813 F. Supp. 501 (W.D. Tex. 1993), 81

Leite v. Crane Co., 868 F. Supp. 2d 1023 (D. Haw. 2012), 117n376

Lenox Inc. v. Reuben Smith Rubbish Removal, 91 F. Supp. 2d 743 (D.N.J. 2000), 33n149

Leo v. Kerr-McGee Chem. Corp., 37 F.3d 96 (3d Cir. 1994),   171n22

Leo, United States v., 941 F.2d 181 (3d Cir. 1991),   192n111

Leucadia, Inc. v. Applied Extrusion Tech., Inc., 998 F.2d 157 (3d Cir. 1993),   199n141, 199nn146–147, 201n153, 201nn157–158

Levy v. Remington Arms Co., 836 F.2d 1104 (8th Cir. 1988),   218n205

Lewis v. AMTRAK, 675 N.Y.S.2d 504 (N.Y. Civ. Ct. 1998),   423n119

Lewis v. Babcock Indus., Inc., 985 F.2d 83 (2d Cir. 1993),   117n381

Lewis v. FAG Bearings Corp., 5 S.W.3d 579 (Mo. Ct. App. 1999),   349

Lewis v. General Elec. Co., 37 F. Supp. 2d 55 (D. Mass. 1999),   46n229

Lewis v. Kinder Morgan Se. Terminals, LLC, No. 2:07CV47ks-MTP, 2008 U.S. Dist. LEXIS 61060 (S.D. Miss. Aug. 6, 2008),   13n20

Lexecon, Inc. v. Milberg Weiss Bershad Hynes & Lerach, 523 U.S. 26 (1998),   173

LG Display Co. v. Madigan, 665 F.3d 768 (7th Cir. 2011),   34n154

Liberty Nat'l Life Ins. Co., *Ex parte*, 825 So. 2d 758 (Ala. 2002),   70n72

Lince v. Monson, 108 N.W.2d 845 (Mich. 1961),   342n66

Lincoln Elec. Co. v. McLemore, 54 So. 3d 833 (Miss. 2010),   60n12, 61

Lindsay v. Gibbons & Reed, 497 P.2d 28 (Utah 1972),   328n156

Lindsay v. Public Serv. Co., 725 F. Supp. 278 (W.D.N.C. 1989),   71n78

Lineaweaver v. Plant Insulation Co., 37 Cal. Rptr. 2d 902 (Cal. Ct. App. 1995),   315n43, 316n55

Linerboard Antitrust Litig., *In re*, 333 F. Supp. 2d 333 (E.D. Pa. 2004),   201n154

Linnen v. A.H. Robins Co., No. 972307, 2000 WL 145758 (Mass. Super. Jan. 4, 2000),   416n72

Linthicum v. Nationwide Life Ins. Co., 723 P.2d 675 (Ariz. 1986),   50n255

Liquid Carbonic Truck Drivers Chem. Poisoning Litig., *In re*, 423 F. Supp. 937 (J.P.M.L. 1976),   174n28

Liss v. Milford Partners, Inc., No. X07CV440251235, 2008 Conn. Super. LEXIS 2490 (Conn. Super. Ct. Sept. 29, 2008),   22n76

Little v. Liquid Air Corp., 952 F.2d 841 (5th Cir. 1992), *rev'd en banc*, 37 F.3d 1069 (5th Cir. 1994),   103n294

Lockheed Litig. Cases, *In re*, 23 Cal. Rptr. 3d 762 (Cal. Ct. App. 2005),   136n83, 316n53

Lockwood v. AC&S, Inc., 744 P.2d 605 (Wash. 1987),   257, 330nn169–171, 331nn172–173

Loftin v. Wilson, 67 So. 2d 185 (Fla. 1953),   371n57

Logerquist v. McVey, 1 P.3d 113 (Ariz. 2000),   313

Lohrmann v. Pittsburgh Corning Corp., 782 F.2d 1156 (4th Cir. 1986),   149, 151, 335n15, 368, 386n179, 391, 392, 398, 409, 413, 417

Long v. Weider Nutrition Grp., Inc., Civ.A.00C-12-249MMJ, 2004 WL 1543226 (Del. Super. Ct. June 25, 2004), 408

Longmore v. Merrell Dow Pharm., Inc., 737 F. Supp. 1117 (D. Idaho 1990), 321n96

Lopez v. City of Los Angeles, 126 Cal. Rptr. 3d 706 (Cal. Ct. App. 2011), 316n52

Lopez, United States v., 514 U.S. 549 (1995), 65

Lorazepam & Clorazepate Antitrust Litig., In re, 205 F.R.D. 369 (D.D.C. 2002), 276n44

Lore v. Lone Pine, Inc., No. L-33606-85, 1986 WL 637507 (N.J. Super. Ct. Nov. 18, 1986), 227, 228

Love Canal Actions, In re, 547 N.Y.S. 2d 174 (N.Y. Sup. Ct. 1989), *modified*, 555 N.Y.S. 2d 519 (N.Y. App. Div. 4th Dep't 1990), 228n236

Lowe v. Philip Morris USA, Inc., 183 P.3d 181 (Or. 2008), 42n202

Lowe v. Sporicidin Int'l, 47 F.3d 124 (4th Cir. 1995), 31n131

L.S. v. Scarano, 2011 WL 4948099 (S.D. Ohio Oct. 18, 2011), 193n113

Lujan v. National Wildlife Fed'n, 497 U.S. 871 (1990), 92

Lynch v. Norton Constr., 861 P.2d 1095 (Wyo. 1993), 331n174

Lynchburg Foundry Co. v. Irvin, 16 S.E.2d 646 (Va. 1941), 291n58

Lyon v. Volkswagon of Am., Inc., 676 So. 2d 356 (Ala. Civ. App. 1996), 364n6

Lyons v. Garlock, Inc., 12 F. Supp. 2d 1226 (D. Kan. 1998), 143n5, 149, 341n57

M

MacBride v. Pishvaian, 937 A.2d 233 (Md. 2007), 66n54

Maddy v. Vulcan Materials Co., 737 F. Supp. 1528 (D. Kan. 1990), 15n36, 15n38

Magistrini v. One Hour Martinizing Dry Cleaning, 180 F. Supp. 2d 584 (D. N.J. 2002), 134n73, 135n78, 421n107, 421n109

Magnolia Coal Terminal v. Phillips Oil Co., 576 So. 2d 475 (La. 1991), 221n213

Mailloux v. Town of Londonderry, 864 A.2d 335 (N.H. 2004), 72n86, 72n88

Maine People's Alliance v. Mallinckrodt, Inc., 471 F.3d 277 (1st Cir. 2006), 92n232

Maines v. Kenworth Alaska, Inc., 155 P.3d 318 (Alaska 2007), 311

Malchman v. Davis, 761 F.2d 893 (2d Cir. 1985), *cert. denied*, 475 U.S. 1143 (1986), 272n8

Malcolm v. Evenflo Co., 217 P.3d 514 (Mont. 2009), 115n363

Malcolm v. National Gypsum Co., 995 F.2d 346 (2d Cir. 1993), 175n34, 255n343

Mancuso v. Consolidated Edison Co. of N.Y., 967 F. Supp. 1437 (S.D.N.Y. 1997), 426nn139–140

Mangini v. Aerojet-Gen. Corp., 282 Cal. Rptr. 827 (Cal. Ct. App. 1991), 29n118, 67n57

Manhattanville Coll. v. James John Romeo Consulting Eng'g, P.C., 774 N.Y.S.2d 542 (N.Y. App. Div. 2004), 59n6

Manning, United States v., 527 F.3d 828 (9th Cir. 2008), 83n169

Marcum v. Adventist Health Sys./W., 193 P.3d 1 (Or. 2008), 328

Mardan Corp. v. C.G.C. Music, Ltd., 600 F. Supp. 1049 (D. Ariz. 1984), *aff'd*, 804 F.2d 1454 (9th Cir. 1986), 28n114

Marder v. G.D. Searle & Co., 630 F. Supp. 1087 (D. Md. 1986), *aff'd sub nom.* Wheelahan v. G.D. Searle & Co., 814 F.2d 655 (4th Cir. 1987), 413n59

Marin v. Exxon Mobil Corp., 48 So. 3d 234 (La. 2010), 66n54

Marine Asbestos Cases, *In re*, 265 F.3d 861 (9th Cir. 2001), 32n141

Marlin v. Bill Rich Constr., 482 S.E.2d 620 (W. Va. 1996), 44n213

Marmo v. IBP, Inc., No. 8:00 CV 527, 2005 WL 675810 (D. Neb. Feb. 4, 2005), 129n30

Marsh v. Valyou, 977 So. 2d 543 (Fla. 2007), 373n70, 374nn73–74, 375n80

Martin v. Cincinnati Gas & Elec. Co., 561 F.3d 439 (6th Cir. 2009), 294n69

Martin v. Reynolds Metals Co., 342 P.2d 790 (Or. 1959), 14nn23–24, 16n39

Martin v. Shell Oil Co., 180 F. Supp. 2d 313 (D. Conn. 2002), 11n8, 16n42, 24n85, 405n2, 406n8

Martin, State v., 683 N.W.2d 399 (S.D. 2004), 361n225

Maryland v. Louisiana, 451 U.S. 725 (1981), 77n126

Masaki v. General Motors Corp., 780 P.2d 566 (Haw. 1989), 50n255

Mason v. Home Depot U.S.A., Inc., 658 S.E.2d 603 (Ga. 2008), 375n81, 377n94, 378nn105–106

Massachusetts v. Blackstone Valley Elec. Co., 67 F.3d 981 (1st Cir. 1995), 75n107

Master Key Antitrust Litig., *In re*, 528 F.2d 5 (2d Cir. 1975), 251n333

Matomco Oil Co. v. Arctic Mech., Inc., 796 P.2d 1336 (Alaska 1999), 22n78

Matthews v. Ashland Chem. Inc., 770 F.2d 1303 (5th Cir. 1985), 249n322

Mattis v. Carlon Elec. Prods., 114 F. Supp. 2d 888 (D.S.D. 2000), *aff'd*, 295 F.3d 856 (8th Cir. 2002), 108n322, 143n5, 361, 362

Mauro v. Raymark Indus., Inc., 561 A.2d 257 (N.J. 1989), 36n163

Mavroudis v. Pittsburgh Corning Corp., 935 P.2d 684 (Wash. Ct. App. 1997), 330n168

McCarrell v. Hoffman-La Roche, Inc., 2009 WL 614484 (N.J. Super. Ct. A.D. Mar. 12, 2009), 421

McCauley v. Purdue Pharma L.P., 331 F. Supp. 2d 449 (W.D. Va. 2004), 399n295, 400, 401n306

McClain v. Metabolife Int'l, Inc., 401 F.3d 1233 (11th Cir. 2005), 108n323, 108n326, 110nn336–337, 131n45, 133n61

Table of Cases   469

McClellan v. I-Flow Corp., 710 F. Supp. 2d 1092 (D. Or. 2010),   109n331, 328n155

McClellan Ecological Seepage Situation v. Perry, 47 F.3d 325 (9th Cir. 1995),   79n136

McClelland v. Goodyear Tire & Rubber Co., 735 F. Supp. 172 (D. Md. 1990),   413n56

McClenahan v. Cooley, 806 S.W.2d 767 (Tenn. 1991),   393n246, 394

McClenathan v. Rhone-Poulenc, Inc., 926 F. Supp. 1272 (S.D. W. Va. 1996),   32n142

McCombs v. Synthes, 587 S.E.2d 594 (Ga. 2003),   106n307

McConwell v. FMG of Kan. City, Inc., 861 P.2d 830 (Kan. Ct. App. 1993),   339n44

McCormack v. Hankscraft Co., 154 N.W.2d 488 (Minn. 1967),   31n135

McCracken v. Exxon/Mobil Co., No. 08-2932, 2009 U.S. Dist. LEXIS 106930 (E.D. Pa. Nov. 12, 2009),   31n134

McCuiston v. Addressograph-Multigraph Corp., 303 S.E.2d 795 (N.C. 1983),   390n221

McCullock v. H.B. Fuller Co., 61 F.3d 1038 (2d Cir. 1995),   424n127, 433

McDaniel v. CSX Transp., Inc., 955 S.W.2d 257 (Tenn. 1997), *cert. denied*, 524 U.S. 915 (1998),   394, 395

McDonald v. Sun Oil Co., 548 F.3d 774 (9th Cir. 2008),   70n71, 70n73, 71nn83–84

McDonnell v. Falco, 784 A.2d 1051 (Conn. App. Ct. 2001),   36n169, 37n172

McEwen v. Ortho Pharm. Corp., 528 P.2d 522 (Or. 1974),   327

McGee v. AC&S, Inc., 933 So. 2d 770 (La. 2006),   35n161, 36n165, 37n176

McGowan v. Cooper Indus., 863 F.2d 1266 (6th Cir. 1988),   193n114

McGuire v. Kenoma, LLC, 375 S.W.3d 157 (Mo. Ct. App. 2012),   100n269

McIntosh v. Victoria Corp., 877 So. 2d 519 (Miss. Ct. App.), *cert. denied*, 878 So. 2d 67 (Miss. 2004),   385N167

McKenna v. Volkswagenwerk Aktiengesellschaft, 558 P.2d 1018 (Haw. 1977),   319n80

McKethean v. Washington Metro. Area Transit Auth., 588 A.2d 708 (D.C. 1991),   409n26

McLain v. Metabolife Int'l, Inc., 401 F.3d 1233 (11th Cir. 2005),   366n23

McNeel v. Union Pac. R.R., 753 N.W.2d 321 (Neb. 2008),   350n132, 352nn147–148

McNeil v. Wyeth, 462 F.3d 364 (5th Cir. 2006),   111n343

Meade v. Parsley, No. 2:09-CV-00388, 2010 WL 4909435 (S.D.W. Va. Nov. 24, 2010),   402n316, 403nn322–326, 404nn327–329

Meado v. Superior Court, 205 Cal. App. 3d 64 (Cal. App. 1 Dist. 1988),   251nn334–335

Meadows v. Union Carbide Corp., 710 F. Supp. 1163 (N.D. Ill. 1989), 68n61

Medtronic, Inc. v. Lohr, 518 U.S. 470 (1996), 77nn126–127

Meghrig v. KFC W., Inc., 516 U.S. 479 (1996), 73n94, 74n96, 80n147

Meister v. Medical Eng'g Corp., 267 F.3d 1123 (D.C. Cir. 2001), 410nn33–34

Mejdrech v. Lockformer Co., No. 01 C 6107, 2003 U.S. Dist. LEXIS 15598 (N.D. Ill. Sept. 4, 2003), 130n37

Mercer v. Rockwell Int'l Corp., 24 F. Supp. 2d 735 (W.D. Ky. 1998), 65n49, 90

Mercer Univ., Corporation of v. National Gypsum Co., 368 S.E.2d 732 (Ga. 1988), 58n2, 65n49

Merck & Co. v. Garza, 347 S.W.3d 256 (Tex. 2011), 397nn274–275

Meridia Prods. Liab. Litig., *In re*, 328 F. Supp. 2d 791 (N.D. Ohio 2004), 107n318, 355nn176–178, 356n183

Merkley v. Pittsburgh Corning Corp., 910 P.2d 58 (Colo. Ct. App. 1995), 317

Merrell Dow Pharm., Inc. v. Havner, 953 S.W.2d 706 (Tex. 1997), 108n327, 109n330, 110n335, 110n338, 136n83, 137n88, 145, 151, 396, 397, 398nn282–283

Merriam v. Wanger, 757 A.2d 778 (Me. 2000), 411

Mesa v. California, 489 U.S. 121 (1989), 117n376

Mest v. Cabot Corp., 449 F.3d 502 (3d Cir. 2006), 60n13, 62n24, 69nn66–67

Metabolife Int'l, Inc. v. Wornick, 264 F.3d 832 (9th Cir. 2001), 109n333

Metcalf v. Lowe's Home Ctrs., Inc., No. 4:09-CV-14 CAS, 2010 WL 1657424 (E.D. Mo. Apr. 26, 2010), 354

Methyl Tertiary Butyl Ether (MTBE) Prods. Liab. Litig., *In re*, 458 F. Supp. 2d 149 (S.D.N.Y. 2006), 38n184, 89, 426n141

Methyl Tertiary Butyl Ether (MTBE) Prods., *In re*, 739 F. Supp. 2d 576 (S.D.N.Y. 2010), 128n29

Metro-N. Commuter R.R. Co. v. Buckley, 521 U.S. 424 (1997), 40, 41, 43, 44

Meyer v. Creative Nail Design, Inc., 975 P.2d 1264 (Mont. 1999), 322

M.F. *ex rel.* Flowers v. Delaney, 830 N.Y.S.2d 412 (N.Y. App. Div. 2007), 95n243

M.H.D. v. Westminster Sch., 172 F.3d 797 (11th Cir. 1999), 65n48

Michals v. Baxter Healthcare Corp., 289 F.3d 402 (6th Cir. 2002), 60n18

Mid-Continent Petroleum Corp. v. Epley, 250 P.2d 861 (Okla. 1952), 360n220

Migliori v. Boeing N. Am., Inc., 114 F. Supp. 2d 976 (C.D. Cal. 2000), 133n64

Milford, Village of v. K-H Holding Corp., 390 F.3d 926 (6th Cir. 2004), 66n51

Miller v. Batesville Casket Co., 219 F.R.D. 56 (E.D.N.Y. 2003), 230n248

Miller v. Kingsley, 230 N.W.2d 472 (Neb. 1975), 51n258

Miller v. National Broad. Co., 232 Cal. Rptr. 668 (Cal. Ct. App. 1986), 16n40

Miller v. National Cabinet Co., 168 N.E.2d 811 (N.Y. 1960), 423n122

Miller v. Pfizer Inc., 196 F. Supp. 2d 1062 (D. Kan. 2002), *aff'd*, 356 F.3d 1326 (10th Cir. 2004), 109n328

Miller v. Rohling, 720 N.W.2d 562 (Iowa 2006), 20n65, 20n68

Millett v. Atlantic Richfield Co., No. CV-98-555, 2000 WL 359979 (Me. Super. Mar. 2, 2000), *appeal dismissed*, 760 A.2d 250 (Me. 2000), 411n42

Millison v. E.I. du Pont de Nemours & Co., 501 A.2d 505 (N.J. 1985), 118n385

Mills v. AC&S, Inc., 2005 WL 2989639 (W.D.N.C. Nov. 7, 2005), 391n222

Mills v. State Sales, Inc., 824 A.2d 461 (R.I. 2003), 431n170

Milward v. Acuity Specialty Prods. Grp., Inc., 639 F.3d 11 (1st Cir. 2011), 109n329, 416nn73–75

Minnesota *ex rel.* N. Pac. Ctr., Inc. v. BNSF Ry. Co., 686 F.3d 567 (8th Cir. 2012), 28n110

Mississippi Power & Light Co. v. United Gas Pipe Line Co., 532 F.2d 412 (5th Cir. 1976), 75n107

Mississippi Transp. Comm'n v. McLemore, 863 So. 2d 31 (Miss. 2003), 386

Mississippi Valley Silica Co. v. Eastman, 92 So. 3d 666 (Miss. 2012), 103n288

Mitchell v. Baltimore Sun Co., 883 A.2d 1008 (Md. Ct. Spec. App. 2005), 15n34

Mitchell v. Branch, 363 P.2d 969 (Haw. 1961), 318n75

Mitchell v. Com., 908 S.W.2d 100 (Ky. 1995), *overruled*, Fugate v. Com., 993 S.W.2d 931 (Ky. 1999), 380n119

Mitchell v. Contractors Specialty Supply, Inc., 544 S.E.2d 533 (Ga. Ct. App. 2001), 58n2

Mitchell v. E-Z Way Towers, Inc., 269 F.2d 126 (5th Cir. 1959), 231n252

Mitchell v. Gonzales, 819 P.2d 872 (Cal. 1991), 314n40, 315n42

Moayedi v. U.S. Customs & Border Prot., 510 F. Supp. 2d 73 (D.D.C. 2007), 185n78

Moeller v. Garlock Sealing Techs., LLC, No. 09-5670, 2011 U.S. App. LEXIS 19987 (6th Cir. Sept. 28, 2011), 148

Monsanto, *Ex parte*, 794 So. 2d 350 (Ala. 2001), 366n22

Monsanto Co. v. Hall, 912 So. 2d 134 (Miss. 2005), 149n39, 385n165, 386n180

Montague v. Deagle, 462 P.2d 403 (Ariz. Ct. App. 1969), 312n18

Montega Corp. v. Hazelrigs, 189 S.E.2d 421 (Ga. 1972), 44n211

Montgomery Ward & Co. v. Gregg, 554 N.E.2d 1145 (Ind. Ct. App. 1990), 115n364

Moody v. Cummings, 37 So. 3d 1054 (La. Ct. App. 2010), 96
Moore v. Ashland Chem. Inc., 151 F.3d 269 (5th Cir. 1998), 110n337, 353n161
Moore v. Ford Motor Co., 332 S.W.3d 749 (Mo. 2011), 113n342
Moore v. Memorial Hosp. of Gulfport, 825 So. 2d 658 (Miss. 2002), 106n312
Moore v. Mississippi Valley Gas Co., 863 So. 2d 43 (Miss. 2003), 385n165
Morgan v. Ford Motor Co., Civ. A. No. 06-1080, 2007 WL 1456154 (D.N.J. May 17, 2007), 228
Morin v. United States, 534 F. Supp. 2d 1179 (D. Nev. 2005), 325n131
Morningstar v. Black & Decker Mfg. Co., 253 S.E.2d 666 (W. Va. 1979), 402n312
Morrison v. Brandeis Univ., 125 F.R.D. 14 (D. Mass. 1989), 196n128
Moses Lake, City of v. United States, 430 F. Supp. 2d 1164 (E.D. Wash. 2006), 89
Moss v. Ole South Real Estate, Inc., 933 F.2d 1300 (5th Cir. 1991), 249n323
Motus v. Pfizer Inc., 358 F.3d 659 (9th Cir. 2004), 112n346
Mozeke v. International Paper Co., 933 F.2d 1293 (5th Cir. 1991), 32n138
Muncie Aviation Corp. v. Party Doll Fleet, Inc., 519 F.2d 1178 (5th Cir. 1975), 249n318
Munster, Town of v. Sherwin-Williams Co., 27 F.3d 1268 (7th Cir. 1994), 73n89
Muralo Co. v. Employers Ins. of Wausau, 759 A.2d 348 (N.J. Super. Ct. App. Div. 2000), 89n212
Murray v. Sullivan, 132 S. Ct. 1876 (2012), 276n46
Muzzey v. Kerr-McGee Chem. Corp., 921 F. Supp. 511 (N.D. Ill. 1996), 123n5

N

N.A.A.C.P. v. AcuSport, Inc., 271 F. Supp. 2d 435 (E.D.N.Y. 2003), 100n273
Nacco Materials Handling Grp., Inc. v. Lilly Co., 278 F.R.D. 395 (W.D. Tenn. 2011), 217n203
Nance v. Southerland, 79 So. 3d 612 (Ala. Civ. App. 2010), 363n3
National Ass'n of Mfrs. v. U.S. Dep't of the Interior, 134 F.3d 1095 (D.C. Cir. 1998), 49n246
National Bank of Commerce v. Dow Chem. Corp., 965 F. Supp. 1490 (E.D. Ark. 1996), 210n184
National Castings Div. of Midland-Ross Corp. v. Industrial Comm'n, 302 N.E.2d 330 (Ill. 1973), 335n12
National Steel Serv. Ctr. v. Gibbons, 319 N.W.2d 269 (Iowa 1982), 23n80
National Tel. Co-Op. Ass'n v. Exxon Corp., 38 F. Supp. 2d 1 (D.D.C. 1998), 16
Natural Res. Def. Council, Inc. v. Texaco Ref. & Mktg., Inc., 20 F. Supp. 2d 700 (D. Del. 1998), 130n42
Nature Conservancy v. Wilder Corp. of Del., 656 F.3d 646 (7th Cir. 2011), 72n86
Nautilus Motor Tanker Co., *In re*, 85 F.3d 105 (3d Cir. 1996), 249n321

Neal v. Darby, 318 S.E.2d 18 (S.C. 1984), 54n278
Neal v. Farmers Ins. Exch., 148 Cal. Rptr. 389 (Cal. 1978), 52n267
Nelson v. Tennessee Gas Pipeline Co., 243 F.3d 244 (6th Cir. 2001), 134n74, 135n75
Neodesha, City of v. BP Corp. N. Am., 287 P.3d 214 (Kan. 2012), 22n7
Neuse River Found., Inc. v. Smithfield Foods, Inc., 574 S.E.2d 48 (N.C. Ct. App. 2002), 98n255
Newburgh, City of v. Sarna, 690 F. Supp. 2d 136 (S.D.N.Y. 2010), 72n87
New England Legal Found. v. Costle, 666 F.2d 30 (1st Cir. 1981), 97n255
New Jersey Dep't of Envtl. Prot. & Energy v. Gloucester Envtl. Mgmt. Servs., 821 F. Supp. 999 (D.N.J. 1993), 28n112
New Jersey v. Ventron Corp., 468 A.2d 150 (N.J. 1983), 23n82
Newkirk v. ConAgra Foods, Inc., 727 F. Supp. 2d 1006 (E.D. Wash. 2010), 147n29
New Mexico v. General Elec. Co., 335 F. Supp. 2d 1185 (D.N.M. 2004), aff'd, 467 F.3d 1223 (10th Cir. 2006), 15n32, 35, 78n131, 79n136, 80nn144–145, 89n212, 130n40
Newson v. Monsanto Co., 869 F. Supp. 1255 (E.D. Mich. 1994), 343n79
New York v. Solvent Chem. Co., 685 F. Supp. 2d 357 (W.D.N.Y. 2010), 127n25, 128n29, 129n33
New York City Asbestos Litig., In re, 860 N.Y.S.2d 506 (N.Y. App. Div. 2008), 422n118

New York State Energy Research & Dev. Auth. v. Nuclear Fuel Servs., Inc., 561 F. Supp. 954 (W.D.N.Y. 1983), 14n26, 16n41
Nguyen v. United States, 539 U.S. 69 (2003), 291n54
Niagara Mohawk Power Corp. v. Chevron U.S.A., Inc., 596 F.3d 112 (2d Cir. 2010), 80nn140–141
Nielsen v. Sioux Tools, Inc., 870 F. Supp. 435 (D. Conn. 1994), 29n118
Nieman v. NLO, Inc., 108 F.3d 1546 (6th Cir. 1997), 68n6, 84n175
Niesig v. Team I, 558 N.E.2d 1030 (N.Y. 1990), 196n132
Nigh v. Dow Chem. Co., 634 F. Supp. 1513 (W.D. Wis. 1986), 51n262
Nix v. Goodyear Tire & Rubber Co., 624 So. 2d 641 (Ala. Civ. App. 1993), 364n4
NLRB v. _____. See name of opposing party
Nnadili v. Chevron U.S.A., Inc., 435 F. Supp. 2d 93 (D.D.C. 2006), 24n85, 44n212
Nobrega v. Edison Glen Assocs., 772 A.2d 368 (N.J. 2001), 29n121
Nolan v. Weil-McClain, 910 N.E.2d 549 (Ill. 2009), 149n39
Nonnon v. City of New York, 32 A.D.3d 91 (N.Y. App. Div. 2006), aff'd, 874 N.E.2d 720 (N.Y. 2007), 423n125
Norfolk & W. Ry. v. Ayers, 538 U.S. 135 (2003), 37n175
Norris v. Baxter Healthcare Corp., 397 F.3d 878 (10th Cir. 2005), 109n328, 109n334, 146, 155n75, 317n67, 318, 326n137

North Am. Refractory Co. v. Easter, 988 S.W.2d 904 (Tex. App. 1999), 51n261

North Carolina v. Tennessee Valley Auth., 615 F.3d 291 (4th Cir. 2010), 98, 99

North Haven Planning & Zoning Comm'n v. Upjohn Co., 753 F. Supp. 423 (D. Conn.), *aff'd*, 921 F.2d 27 (2d Cir. 1990), 81

Norton v. Snapper Power Equip., 806 F.2d 1545 (11th Cir. 1987), 114n357

NTL, Inc. Sec. Litig., *In re*, 244 F.R.D. 179 (S.D.N.Y. 2007), 217n203

NutraSweet Co. v. X-L Eng'g Corp., 926 F. Supp. 767 (N.D. Ill. 1997), 250n328

Nutting v. Northern Energy, 874 P.2d 482 (Colo. App. 1994), 12n17

Nye v. Bayer Cropsci., Inc., 347 S.W.3d 686 (Tenn. 2011), 103n288, 107n314

O

O'Brien v. O'Fallon, 400 N.E.2d 456 (Ill. Ct. App. 1980), 20n68

Ocean Advocates v. U.S. Army Corps of Eng'rs, 402 F.3d 846 (9th Cir. 2005), 72n87

O'Conner v. Commonwealth Edison Co., 13 F.3d 1090 (7th Cir. 1994), 83n171, 84n175

O'Connor v. Boeing N. Am., Inc., 311 F.3d 1139 (9th Cir. 2002), 58n4, 61n20, 63n30, 63n34

O'Connor v. Raymark Indus., Inc., 518 N.E.2d 510 (Mass. 1988), 415nn65–66, 417n79

Odabashian, United States v., 1999 WL 33944059 (W.D. Tenn. May 18, 1999), 212n188

Odom v. G. D. Searle & Co., 979 F.2d 1001 (4th Cir. 1992), 112n347

Ogden Envtl. Servs. v. City of San Diego, 687 F. Supp. 1436 (S.D. Cal. 1988), 81n151

Ohio v. U.S. Dep't of the Interior, 880 F.2d 432 (D.C. Cir. 1989), 49n246

Ohio Mfrs. Ass'n v. City of Akron, 801 F.2d 824 (6th Cir. 1986), 85n184

Oklahoma v. Tyson Foods, Inc., 258 F.R.D. 472 (N.D. Okla. 2009), 49n245

Old Bridge Chems., Inc. v. New Jersey Dep't of Envtl. Prot., 965 F.2d 1287 (3d Cir. 1992), 81n153

Olden v. LaFarge Corp., 383 F.3d 495 (6th Cir. 2004), 177n42

Olen Props. Corp. v. Sheldahl, Inc., 1994 U.S. Dist. LEXIS 7125 (C.D. Cal. 1994), 189, 190

Oliver v. Oshkosh Truck Corp., 96 F.3d 992 (7th Cir. 1996), 116n373, 117n374

Oliver v. South Carolina Dep't of Highways & Pub. Transp., 422 S.E.2d 128 (S.C. 1992), 391n224

Olivo v. Owens-Illinois, Inc., 895 A.2d 1143 (N.J. 2006), 101n278

Olson v. Prosoco, Inc., 522 N.W.2d 284 (Iowa 1994), 115n367

Olson v. Snap Prods., Inc., 183 F.R.D. 539 (D. Minn. 1998), 207n174

Olson-Roti v. Kilcoin, 653 N.W.2d 254 (S.D. 2002), 361n227

O'Neal v. Department of the Army, 852 F. Supp. 327 (M.D. Pa. 1994), 113n356

O'Neil v. Novartis Consumer Health, Inc., 147 Cal. App. 4th 1388 (Cal. Ct. App. 2007), 114n363

Open Am. v. Watergate Special Prosecution Force, 547 F.2d 605 (D.C. Cir. 1976), 186

Oresta v. Romano Bros., 73 S.E.2d 622 (W. Va. 1952), 96n246

Orthopedic Bone Screw Prods. Liab. Litig., *In re*, No. 1014, 1997 WL 230818 (E.D. Pa. May 5, 1997), 134n74

Ortiz v. Fibreboard Corp, 527 U.S. 815 (1999), 271–274, 277n55

Oshana v. Coca-Cola Bottling Co., 225 F.R.D. 575 (N.D. Ill. 2005), 300n103

Oullette v. International Paper Co., 96 F.R.D. 476 (D. Vt. 1980), 179

Outdoor Sys., Inc. v. Wood, 543 S.E.2d 414 (2000), 91n225

Owens-Corning Fiberglas Corp. v. Garrett, 682 A.2d 1143 (Md. 1996), 413n55

Owens-Corning Fiberglas Corp. v. Watson, 413 S.E.2d 630 (Va. 1992), 401

Owens-Ill., Inc. v. Zenobia, 601 A.2d 633 (Md. 1992), 25n92

Oxendine v. Merrell Dow Pharm., Inc., No. 82-1245, 1996 WL 680992 (D.C. Super. Oct. 24, 1996), 410n32

Oxygenated Fuels Ass'n Inc. v. Davis, 331 F.3d 665 (9th Cir. 2003), 77n127

P

Pacific Gas & Elec. Co. v. State Energy Res. Conservation & Dev. Comm'n, 461 U.S. 190 (1983), 83nn167–168

Pacific Gas & Elec. Co. v. Zuckerman, 234 Cal. Rptr. 630 (Cal. Ct. App. 1987), 316n52

Page v. United States, 729 F.2d 818 (D.C. Cir. 1984), 68n61

Paige v. St. Andrew's Roman Catholic Church Corp., 734 A.2d 85 (1999), 405n4

Palmer v. Pioneer Inn Assocs., Ltd., 59 P.3d 1237 (Nev. 2002), 196n125

Palsgraf v. Long Island R.R. Co., 162 N.E. 99 (1928), 101n276

Paoli R.R. Yard PCB Litig., *In re*, 916 F.2d 829 (3d Cir. 1990), 42n204

Paoli R.R. Yard PCB Litig., *In re*, 35 F.3d 717 (3d Cir. 1994), 46n228, 155n72, 356n182, 421n106, 428n154

Parker v. Brush Wellman, 230 Fed. App'x 878 (11th Cir. 2007), *partially vacated*, 2008 U.S. Dist. LEXIS 51751 (N.D. Ga. July 7, 2008), 39

Parker v. Mobil Oil Corp., 857 N.E.2d 1114 (N.Y. 2006), 423n120, 423nn123–124, 426n137

Parker v. Schmiede Mach. & Tool Corp., 445 F. App'x 231 (11th Cir. 2011), 103n290

Parkhill v. Alderman-Cave Milling & Grain Co., 245 P.3d 585 (N.M. Ct. App. 2010), 326

Parkinson, State v., 909 P.2d 647 (Idaho Ct. App. 1996), 321n99

Parks Hiway Enters., LLC v. CEM
  Leasing, Inc., 995 P.2d 657 (Alaska
  2000), 22n78, 24n85
Parmalat Sec. Litig., *In re*, 258 F.R.D. 236
  (S.D.N.Y. 2009), 199n142
Parmer v. National Cash Register
  Co., 503 F.2d 275 (6th Cir.
  1974), 251n333
Patel v. City of Everman, 179 S.W.3d 1
  (Tex. App. 2004), 14n27
Pathways, Inc. v. Hammons, 113 S.W.3d
  85 (Ky. 2003), 380n115
Patton v. General Signal Corp.,
  984 F. Supp. 666 (W.D.N.Y.
  1997), 37n179
Paz v. Brush Engineered Materials,
  Inc., 949 So. 2d 1 (Miss.
  2007), 37n178, 42n202, 43n210
Peabody W. Coal Co., EEOC v. 400 F.3d
  774 (9th Cir. 2005), 288n34
Peagler v. Tyson Foods, Inc., 532
  S.E.2d 207 (N.C. Ct. App.
  2000), 387n190
Pennsylvania v. Delaware Valley Citizens
  Council for Clean Air, 478 U.S. 546
  (1986), 56n287, 267n1
Pennsylvania Dep't of Envtl. Prot.
  v. Lockheed Martin Corp.,
  684 F. Supp. 2d 564 (M.D Pa.
  2010), 83n171
People v. _____. *See name of opposing
  party*
People for Am. Way Found. v. U.S. Dep't
  of Justice, 451 F. Supp. 2d 6 (D.D.C.
  2006), 185n83
Perdue v. Kenny A., 130 S. Ct. 1662
  (2010), 267n1

Pereira v. St. Joseph's Cemetery, 864
  N.Y.S.2d 491 (N.Y. App. Div.
  2008), 118n387
Perez v. Metabolife Int'l, Inc., 218 F.R.D.
  262 (S.D. Fla. 2003), 179N53
Perez v. Wyeth Labs., Inc., 734 A.2d 1245
  (N.J. 1999), 254n342
Perkins v. Madison County Livestock &
  Fair Ass'n, 613 N.W.2d 264 (Iowa
  2000), 20n67
Perkins v. Origin Medsys., Inc., 299 F.
  Supp. 2d 45 (D. Conn. 2004), 406
Perrine v. E.I. Du Pont de Nemours
  & Co., 694 S.E.2d 815 (W. Va.
  2010), 51n259
Perry v. Novartis Pharms. Corp., 564 F.
  Supp. 2d 452 (E.D. Pa. 2008), 429
Peteet v. Dow Chem. Co., 868 F.2d 1428
  (5th Cir. 1989), 39n185
Peter & John's Pump House, Inc., People
  v., 914 F. Supp. 809 (N.D.N.Y.
  1996), 34n154
Peterson v. Gray, 628 A.2d 244 (N.H.
  1993), 417n83
Peterson v. Instapak Corp., 690 F. Supp.
  697 (N.D. Ill. 1988), 6n12
Peterson v. Reeves, 727 S.E.2d 171 (Ga.
  Ct. App. 2012), 376n87
Pet Food Prods. Liab. Litig., *In re*, 629
  F.3d 333 (3d Cir. 2010), 274, 275
Petrovic v. Amoco Oil Co., 200 F.3d
  1140 (8th Cir. 1999), 274, 277
Pfohl Bros. Landfill Site Steering Comm.
  v. Allied Waste Sys., 255 F. Supp.
  2d 134 (W.D.N.Y. 2003), 168n2,
  171n19, 171n21
Philadelphia, City of v. Lead Indus.
  Ass'n., 994 F.2d 112 (3d Cir.

1993), 168n4, 170nn11–12, 170n15, 170n17

Philip Morris, Inc. v. Emerson, 368 S.E.2d 268 (Va. 1988), 52, 53nn269–270

Phillips v. Sun Oil Co., 121 N.E.2d 249 (N.Y. 1954), 16n42

Phillips Ranch, Inc. v. Banta, 543 P.2d 1035 (Or. 1975), 19n62

Pichowicz v. Atlantic Richfield Co, 37 F. Supp. 2d 98 (D.N.H. 1997), 156n80

Pineda v. Ford Motor Co., 520 F.3d 237 (3d Cir. 2008), 304n121

Pinkney v. Dow Chem. Co., 484 U.S. 1004 (1988), 426

Pipiton v. Biomatrix, Inc., 288 F.3d 239 (5th Cir. 2002), 146

Pitts, State *ex rel.* v. Roberts, 857 S.W.2d 200 (Mo. 1993), 197n133

Pittway Corp. v. Collins, 973 A.2d 771 (Md. 2009), 412n49

Player v. Motiva Enters. LLC, No. 02-3216 (RBK), 2006 WL 166452 (D.N.J. Jan. 20, 2006), 89

Player v. Thompson, 193 S.E.2d 531 (S.C. 1972), 391n231

Plaza Speedway Inc. v. United States, 311 F.3d 1262 (10th Cir. 2002), 59n6, 59nn8–9, 60

Plourde v. Gladstone, 69 Fed. App'x 485 (2d Cir. 2003), 32

Plourde v. Gladstone, 150 F. Supp. 2d 708 (D. Vt. 2002), 433n180

Pluck v. BP Oil Pipeline Co., 640 F.3d 671 (6th Cir. 2011), 155n74, 301, 354n166, 357

Pluid v. B.K., 948 P.2d 981 (Alaska 1997), 37n180

Plummer v. Lederle Labs., 819 F.2d 349 (2d Cir. 1987), 112n346

PMC, Inc. v. Sherwin-Williams Co., 151 F.3d 610 (7th Cir. 1998), 80n141

Polaino v. Bayer Corp., 122 F. Supp. 2d 63 (D. Mass. 2000), 416n77, 417n78

Polcha v. AT&T Nassau Metals Corp., 837 F. Supp. 94 (M.D. Pa. 1993), 27n105

Pollack v. United States Dep't of Justice, 577 F.3d 736 (7th Cir. 2009), 79n136, 92, 398n284

Pope v. Pinkerton-Hays Lumber Co., 120 So. 2d 227 (Fla. Dist. Ct. App. 1960), *cert. denied*, 127 So. 2d 441 (Fla. 1961), 371n56

Porterfield v. Ethicon, Inc., 183 F.3d 464 (5th Cir. 1999), 106n310

Postma v. County of Ottawa, 2004 Mich. App. LEXIS 2307 (Mich. Ct. App. Sept. 2, 2004), 283n15

Potter v. Chicago Pneumatic Tool Co., 694 A.2d 1319 (Conn. 1997), 113n343

Potter v. Firestone Tire & Rubber Co., 863 P.2d 795 (Cal. 1993), 36n167, 37n177, 42n205, 44

Pound v. Airosol Co., 498 F.3d 1089 (10th Cir. 2007), 55n283

Powers v. Taser Int'l, Inc., 174 P.3d 777 (Ariz. Ct. App. 2008), 115n367

Preferred Mut. Ins. Co. v. Gordon, No. 02-3147, 2003 Mass. Super. LEXIS 155 (Mass. Super. Ct. May 13, 2003), 130n37

Premcor Refining Grp., Inc., *In re*, 233 S.W.3d 904 (Tex. Ct. App. 2007) (Premcor I), 91

Premcor Refining Grp., Inc., *In re*, 262 S.W.3d 475 (Tex. Ct. App. 2008) (Premcor II), 91n222

Prempro Prods. Liab. Litig., *In re*, 514 F.3d 825 (8th Cir. 2008), 106n309, 111n345

Price v. E.I. DuPont de Nemours & Co., 26 A.3d 162 (Del. Super. Ct. 2011), 101n275

Price v. Martin, 79 So. 3d 960 (La. 2011), 178n50

Pritchard v. Dow Agro Scis., 705 F. Supp. 2d 471 (W.D. Pa. 2010), *aff'd*, 430 Fed. App'x 102, No. 10-2168, 2011 WL 2160456 (3d Cir. June 2, 2011), 303, 428n150, 428n152, 429n158

Public Serv. Elec. & Gas Co. v. Associate Elec. & Gas Ins. Servs., Ltd., 745 F. Supp. 1037 (D.N.J. 1990), 196n126

Purcell v. Asbestos Corp., 959 P.2d 89 (Or. Ct. App. 1998), 327n151

Pustejovsky v. PLIVA, Inc., 623 F.3d 271 (5th Cir. 2010), 105n307, 111n343, 112n347

Pyle v. Dow Chem. Co., 728 F.2d 1129 (8th Cir. 1984), 118n386

Q

Quate v. American Standard, Inc., 818 A.2d 510 (Pa. Super. Ct. 2003), 144n5

Quick v. Murphy Oil Co., 1993-2267 (La. App. 4 Cir. Sept. 20, 1994), 382n137

R

Rader v. Teva Parental Medicines, Inc., 795 F. Supp. 2d 1143 (D. Nev. 2011), 114n363

Radiation Incident at Wash., *In re*, 400 F. Supp. 1404 (J.P.M.L. 1975), 174n28

Ramirez v. Amsted Indus., Inc., 431 A.2d 811 (N.J. 1981), 171n22

Ramirez v. DeCoster, 203 F.R.D. 30 (D. Me. 2001), 276n44

Ramirez v. State, 651 So. 2d 1164 (Fla. 1995), 372n64

Ranes v. Adams Labs., Inc., 778 N.W.2d 677 (Iowa 2010), 337nn28–30, 338

Raritan Baykeeper, Inc. v. NL Indus., Inc., 660 F.3d 686 (3d Cir. 2011), 75n111, 76n113

Ray v. Kapiolani Med. Specialists, 259 P.3d 569 (Haw. 2011), 319n86

Ray v. Upjohn Co., 851 S.W.2d 646 (Mo. Ct. App. 1993), 347n114, 349

Raymond v. Eli Lilly & Co., 371 A.2d 170 (N.H. 1977), 6n12

Raynor v. Merrell Pharms. Inc., 104 F.3d 1371 (D.C. Cir. 1997), 410n37

Razore v. Tulalip Tribes of Wash., 66 F.3d 236 (9th Cir. 1995), 79n136

R.D. Werner Co., State v., 799 P.2d 427 (Colo. Ct. App. 1990), 316n59

Reading Co., *In re*, 115 F.3d 1111 (3d Cir. 1997), 33n149

Reading Co., *In re*, 115 F.3d 1111 (3d Cir. 1997), *abrogated,* E.I. DuPont de Nemours & Co. v. United States, 460 F.3d 515 (3d Cir. 2006), 78n131

Reasoner v. Chicago, R.I.&P. R. Co., 101 N.W.2d 739 (Iowa 1960), 15n33

Redland Soccer Club, Inc. v. Department of the Army, 696 A.2d 137 (Pa. 1997), 42n204

Reece v. Good Samaritan Hosp., 953 P.2d 117 (Wash. Ct. App. 1998), 31n130

Reich v. Hercules, Inc., 857 F. Supp. 367 (D.N.J. 1994), 189n97

Reichhold Chems. v. Textron, 157 F.R.D. 522 (N.D. Fla. 1994), 188–189

Reighard v. Yates, 285 P.3d 1168 (Utah 2012), 110n337

Reiter v. Cooper, 507 U.S. 258 (1993), 75n112

Renaud v. Martin Marietta Corp., 749 F. Supp. 1545 (D. Colo. 1990), aff'd, 972 F.2d 304 (10th Cir. 1992), 124n11, 127n23, 227n233, 248n314

Rentclub, Inc. v. Transamerica Rental Fin. Corp., 811 F. Supp. 651 (M.D. Fla. 1992), 197n134

Repetitive Stress Injury Litig., In re, 11 F.3d 368 (2d Cir. 1993), 255n343

Reyes v. Wyeth Labs., 498 F.2d 1264 (5th Cir. 1974), 112n349

Rezulin Prods. Liab. Litig., In re, 369 F. Supp. 2d 398 (S.D.N.Y. 2005), 210n184

Rhodes v. E.I. Du Pont De Nemours & Co., 636 F.3d 88 (4th Cir. 2011), 296

Rhodes v. E.I. DuPont de Nemours & Co., 253 F.R.D. 365 (S.D. W. Va. 2008), 157n86

Rhodes v. E.I. Du Pont de Nemours & Co., 657 F. Supp. 2d 751 (S.D. W. Va. 2009), 32n142

Rhodes, State ex rel. v. Simpson, 385 S.E.2d 329 (N.C. 1989), 14n27

Rice v. Santa Fe Elevator Corp., 331 U.S. 218 (1947), 77n123, 83n168

Richardson v. Richardson-Merrell, Inc., 857 F.2d 823 (D.C. Cir. 1988), 109n332, 410n37

Richardson v. Union Pac. R.R. Co., 2011 Ark. App. 562, 2011 Ark. App. LEXIS 602 (Ark. Ct. App. 2011), 367

Richardson-Merrell "Bendectin" Prods. Liab. Litig., In re, 624 F. Supp. 1212 (S.D. Ohio 1985), aff'd sub nom. In re Bendectin Litig., 857 F.2d 290 (6th Cir. 1988), 220n212

Rider v. Sandoz Pharm. Corp., 295 F.3d 1194 (11th Cir. 2002), 108n327

Riegel v. Medtronic, Inc., 552 U.S. 312 (2008), 77n121, 87n200

Riley v. Dow Chem. Co., 123 F.R.D. 639 (N.D. Cal. 1989), 204n170

Rimkus Consulting Grp., Inc. v. Cammarata, 688 F. Supp. 2d 598 (S.D. Tex. 2010), 217n203

Rite Aid Corp. v. Levy-Gray, 894 A.2d 563 (Md. 2006), 105n307

Rivera v. Fairbank Mgmt. Props., Inc., 703 A.2d 808 (Conn. Super. Ct. 1997), 12n13

Rivera v. Philip Morris, Inc., 209 P.3d 271 (Nev. 2009), 113n352

Rivera v. United Gas Pipeline Co., 697 So. 2d 327 (La. Ct. App. 1997), 50n254

R.J. Reynolds Tobacco Co. v. Mack, No. 1D11-2448, 2012 WL 2122305, *reh'g denied* (Fla. Dist. Ct. App. June 13, 2012),   375

Roberts v. Florida Power & Light Co., 146 F.3d 1305 (11th Cir. 1998),   84n175

Roberts v. Owens-Corning Fiberglas Corp., 726 F. Supp. 172 (W.D. Mich. 1989),   344

Robertson v. Allied Signal Inc., 914 F.2d 360 (3d Cir. 1990),   427

Robertson v. Sixpence Inns of Am., Inc., 789 P.2d 1040 (Ariz. 1990),   313n32, 314n35

Robinson v. Audi NSU Auto Union Aktiengesellschaft, 739 F.2d 1481 (10th Cir. 1984),   114n357

Robinson v. Shell Oil Co., 519 U.S. 337 (1997),   297n85

Robinson v. United States, 330 F. Supp. 2d 261 (W.D.N.Y. 2004),   96n249

Roche v. Lincoln Prop. Co., 278 F. Supp. 2d 744 (E.D. Va. 2003),   400n305

Rockwell Int'l Corp. v. Wilhite, 143 S.W.2d 604 (Ky. Ct. App. 2003),   14n24, 17n50, 20n66, 91n219

Rodrigues v. Georgia-Pac. Corp., 661 S.E.2d 141 (Ga. Ct. App. 2008),   376n84

Roes v. FHP, Inc., 985 P.2d 661 (Haw. 1999),   44n214

Rogers v. Armstrong World Indus., 744 F. Supp. 901 (E.D. Ark. 1990),   366n25

Rohm & Haas Co., United States v., 2 F.3d 1265 (3d Cir. 1993),   28n114

Rollins Envtl. Servs. (FS), Inc. v. Parish of St. James, 775 F.2d 627 (5th Cir. 1985),   82

Rollins Envtl. Servs. of La. v. Iberville Parish Police Jury, 371 So. 2d 1127 (La. 1979),   81n151

Rome Kraft Co. v. J.L. Davis, 102 S.E.2d 571 (Ga. 1958),   91n225

Romeo v. Sherry, 308 F. Supp. 2d 128 (E.D.N.Y. 2004),   95

Ronald Holland's A-Plus Transmission & Auto., Inc. v. E-Z Mart Stores, Inc., 184 S.W.3d 749 (Tex. Ct. App. 2005),   89n212

Roney v. Gencorp, 431 F. Supp. 2d 622 (S.D. W. Va. 2006),   118n385, 118n386

Rosato v. 2550 Corp., 894 N.Y.S.2d 513 (N.Y. App. Div. 2010),   130n37

Rose v. Union Oil Co. of Cal., No. C 97-3808 FMS, 1999 WL 51819 (N.D. Cal. Feb. 1, 1999),   89n212

Ross v. Conoco, Inc., 828 So. 2d 546 (La. 2002),   50n254

Rowe v. E. I. DuPont de Nemours & Co., No. 06-1810, 2008 WL 5412912 (D. N.J. Dec. 23, 2008),   422

Rubanick v. Witco Chem. Corp., 593 A.2d 733 (N.J. 1991),   420n103, 421

Ruble v. Alcoa, Inc., No. 1:07CV3521, 2012 WL 774958 (N.D. Ohio Mar. 7, 2012),   118n386

Ruckelshaus v. Sierra Club, 463 U.S. 680 (1983),   55n283

Rudd v. Electrolux Corp., 982 F. Supp. 355 (M.D.N.C. 1997),   11n8, 47n232, 130n39

Rudeck v. Wright, 709 P.2d 621 (Mont. 1985),   322n104
Ruff v. Ensign-Bickford Indus., Inc., 168 F. Supp. 2d 1271 (D. Utah 2011),   109n333
Ruggiero v. Warner-Lambert Co., 424 F.3d 249 (2d Cir. 2005),   155, 423
Runyon v. McCrary, 427 U.S. 160 (1986),   54n280
Rupert v. Clayton Brokerage Co., 737 P.2d 1106 (Colo. 1987),   316n57
Rushing v. Kansas City S. Ry., 185 F.3d 496 (5th Cir. 1999), cert. denied, 528 U.S. 1160, (2000),   249n316
Russell-Stanley Corp. v. Plant Indus., Inc., 595 A.2d 534 (N.J. Super. Ct. Ch. Div. 1991),   33, 34n152
Russo Farms, Inc. v. Vineland Bd. of Educ., 675 A.2d 1077 (N.J. 1996),   286
Rust v. Guinn, 429 N.E.2d 299 (Ind. Ct. App. 1981),   46
Rutherford v. Owens-Ill., Inc., 941 P.2d 1203 (Cal. 1997),   151n54, 314n38, 315n42
Rutledge v. Tultex Corp., 301 S.E.2d 359 (N.C. 1983),   390n215
Ruud v. United States, 256 F.2d 460 (9th Cir.), cert. denied, 358 U.S. 817 (1958),   204n170
Rylands v. Fletcher, 3 L.R. 330 (H.L. 1868),   4, 21, 24n85, 29

S

Safety-Kleen, Inc. v. Wyche, 274 F.3d 846 (4th Cir. 2001),   28n115
St. John's Organic Farm v. Gem County Mosquito Abatement Dist., 574 F.3d 1054 (9th Cir. 2009),   55n283
Saline River Props., LLC v. Johnson Controls, Inc., 823 F. Supp. 2d 670 (E.D. Mich. 2011),   101n275
Salmon Spawning & Recovery Alliance v. Gutierrez, 545 F.3d 1220 (9th Cir. 2008),   288n38
Samaan v. St. Joseph Hosp., 670 F.3d 21 (1st Cir. 2012),   412nn46–48
San Antonio, City of v. Pollock, 284 S.W.3d 809 (Tex. 2009),   396n267
Sanchez v. Esso Standard Oil Co., No. 08-2151, 2010 U.S. Dist. LEXIS 9942 (D.P.R. Feb. 5, 2010),   123n8
Sanders v. UDR, Inc., No. 3:10-CV-459, 2011 WL 2669977 (E.D. Va. June 30, 2011),   399n291, 400n301, 400n304
Sandford v. Chevrolet Div. of Gen. Motors, 642 P.2d 624 (Or. 1982),   327n146
Sandifer Motors, Inc. v. City of Roeland Park, 628 P.2d 239 (Kan. Ct. App. 1981),   100n271
Sandoz Pharm. Corp. v. Richardson-Vicks, Inc., 902 F.2d 222 (3d Cir. 1990),   87n199
Sands, Commonwealth v., 675 N.E.2d 370 (Mass. 1997),   415n70
Sanford St. Local Dev. v. Textron, Inc., 768 F. Supp. 1218 (W.D. Mich., 1991),   12n11
San Francisco Baykeeper v. Cargill Salt Div., No. C 96-2161 SI, 2003 U.S. Dist. LEXIS 8247 (N.D. Cal. Apr. 29, 2003),   129n35
San Francisco v. Wendy's Int'l Inc., 656 S.E.2d 485 (W. Va. 2007),   404nn332–335

Table of Cases

Santa Clara, County of v. Atlantic Richfield Co., 40 Cal. Rptr. 3d 313 (Cal. Ct. App. 2006), 15n35, 18n58

Santa Fe P'ship v. Arco Prods. Co., 54 Cal. Rptr. 2d 214 (Cal. Ct. App. 1996), 47n232

Santiago v. Lykes Bros. S.S. Co., 986 F.2d 423 (11th Cir. 1993), 68n63

Savage v. Union Pac. R.R. Co., 67 F. Supp. 2d 1021 (E.D. Ark. 1999), 367nn32–34

Save the Peaks Coalition v. U.S. Forest Serv., 669 F.3d 1025 (9th Cir. 2012), 72nn86–87

Scarlett & Assocs. v. Briarcliff Ctr. Partners, LLC, No. 1:05-CV-0145-CC, 2009 U.S. Dist. LEXIS 90483 (N.D. Ga. 2009), 30n127

Schafersman v. Agland Coop, 631 N.W.2d 862 (Neb. 2001), 350n133

Scheg v. Agway, Inc., 645 N.Y.S.2d 687 (N.Y. App. Div. 1996), 46n229

Schenk v. HNA Holdings, Inc., 613 S.E.2d 503 (N.C. Ct. App. 2005), 51n256

Schiff, United States v., 538 F. Supp. 2d 818 (D.N.J. 2008), aff'd, 602 F.3d 152 (3d Cir. 2010), 192n111, 193n116

Schiro v. American Tobacco Co., 611 So. 2d 962 (Miss. 1992), 6n12

Schladetsch v. United States HUD., No. 99-0175, 2000 WL 33372125 (D.D.C. Apr. 4, 2000), 185nn83–84

Schlagenhauf v. Holder, 379 U.S. 104 (1964), 216n196

Schneider v. Citicorp Mortg., Inc., 324 F. Supp. 2d 372 (E.D.N.Y. 2004), 275n35

Schneider Nat'l Carriers, Inc. v. Bates, 147 S.W.3d 264 (Tex. 2004), 59n6, 67n58, 278n59

Schwartzman, Inc. v. Atchison, Topeka & Santa Fe Ry. Co., 857 F. Supp. 838 (D.N.M. 1994), 76

Scott v. HK Contractors, 196 P.3d 635 (Utah Ct. App. 2008), 329n158

Scribner v. Summers, 84 F.3d 554 (2d Cir. 1996), 17

Sealy Conn., Inc. v. Litton Indus., Inc., 9 F. Supp. 2d 105 (D. Conn. 1998), 27n106

Sears, Roebuck & Co., NLRB v., 421 U.S. 132 (1975), 184n75

Seattle Times Co. v. Rhinehart, 467 U.S. 20 (1984), 200n152

SED, Inc. v. Dayton, 519 F. Supp. 979 (S.D. Ohio 1981), 82

Sellers v. Breaux, 422 So. 2d 1231 (La. Ct. App. 1982), 36n165, 36n167, 36n171

Sexton v. City of Mason, 883 N.E.2d 1013 (Ohio 2008), 66n51, 66n54

Shaffer v. RWP Grp., 169 F.R.D. 19 (E.D.N.Y. 1996), 216n199

Shamrock Oil & Gas Corp. v. Sheets, 313 U.S. 100 (1941), 297n88

Sharbono v. Universal Underwriters Ins. Co., 161 P.3d 406 (Wash. Ct. App. 2007), 330n168

Sharp ex rel. Gordon v. Case Corp., 595 N.W.2d 380 (Wis. 1999), 71n78

Sharpnack v. Secretary of the Dep't of Health & Human Servs., No. 90-983V, 1992 WL 167255 (Cl. Ct. June 29, 1992),   135n75

Shaw v. Toshiba Am. Info. Sys., Inc., 91 F. Supp. 2d 942 (E.D. Tex. 2000),   275n44

Sheffield v. Owens-Corning Fiberglass, 595 So. 2d 443 (Ala. 1992),   364n9

Shegog v. Zabrecky, 654 A.2d 771 (Conn. App. 1995),   406n5, 407n12, 407nn15–16

Shepherd v. American Broad. Co., 62 F.3d 1469 (D.C. Cir. 1995),   216n199

Sherwin-Williams Co. v. Gaines, 75 So. 3d 41 (Miss. 2011),   386n183

Shiver v. Georgia & Fla. Railnet, 652 S.E.2d 819 (Ga. Ct. App. 2007),   378nn107–108

Sholtis v. American Cyanamid Co., 568 A.2d 1196 (N.J. Super. Ct. A.D. 1989),   418nn87–88, 418n93, 418n95, 419, 420

Shumaker v. Oliver B. Cannon & Sons, Inc., 504 N.E.2d 44 (Ohio 1986),   356n187

Shutt v. Kaufman's, Inc., 438 P.2d 501 (Colo. 1968),   12nn17–18

Sierra Pac. Indus., United States v., 879 F. Supp. 2d 1128 (E.D. Cal. 2012),   95n244

Siharath v. Sandoz Pharm. Corp., 131 F. Supp. 2d 1347 (N.D. Ga. 2001),   132n57

Silicone Gel Breast Implant Litig., *In re*, MDL No. 926 (N.D. Ala. Nov. 30, 1998),   164n133

Silivanch v. Celebrity Cruises, Inc., 333 F.3d 355 (2d Cir. 2003), *cert. denied*, 540 U.S. 1105 (2004),   253n341

Silkwood v. Kerr-McGee Corp., 464 U.S. 238 (1984),   77n128, 83n166, 83nn170–171

Simmons v. CTL Distrib., No. 2003-1301 (La. App. 5 Cir. Feb. 23, 2004),   382n136

Simmons v. Pacor, Inc., 674 A.2d 232 (Pa. 1996),   43n209

Simon v. Philip Morris, 200 F.R.D. 21 (E.D.N.Y. 2001),   250n331

Simon II Litig., *In re*, 211 F.R.D. 86 (E.D.N.Y. 2002),   252n340

Simpkins v. CSX Corp., 929 N.E.2d 1257 (5th Dist. 2010),   293

Simsbury-Avon Pres. Soc'y, LLC v. Metacon Gun Club, Inc., No. 3:04cv803, 2010 U.S. Dist. LEXIS 30159 (D. Conn. Mar. 29, 2010),   56n285

Sindell v. Abbott Labs., 607 P.2d 924 (Cal. 1980),   315n45

Singleton v. Haywood Elec. Membership Corp., 588 S.E.2d 871 (N.C. 2003),   13n21

Skinner v. Square D. Co., 516 N.W.2d 475 (Mich. 1994),   342n68

Slaughter v. S. Talc Co., 949 F.2d 167 (5th Cir. 1991),   149n39

Smith v. Branch, 487 S.E.2d 35 (Ga. Ct. App. 1997),   65n49, 66n52

Smith v. Hughes Aircraft Co., 22 F.3d 1432 (9th Cir. 1994),   115n366

Smith v. Kansas Gas Serv. Co., 169 P.3d 1052 (Kan. 2007),   47n230

Smith v. Michelin Tire Corp., 465 S.E.2d 96 (S.C. Ct. App. 1995), *reh'g & cert. denied* (1996), 392n236

Smith v. Minster Mach. Co., 669 F.2d 628 (10th Cir. 1982), 113n355

Smith Land & Improvement Corp. v. Celotex Corp., 851 F.2d 86 (3d Cir. 1998), 73n89, 114

Sneed v. Sneed, 244 S.E.2d 754 (Va. 1978), 399n291

Snyder, *In re*, 115 F.R.D. 211 (D. Ariz. 1987), 191n103, 192n105

Snyman v. W.A. Baum Co., 360 F. App'x 251, 253 (2d Cir. 2010), 62n24

Sosna v. Am. Home Prods., 748 N.Y.S.2d 548 (N.Y. App. Div. 2002), 112n349

Sosnowicz, State v., No. 1 CA-CR 10-0789, 2012 Ariz. App. LEXIS 133 (Ariz. Ct. App. Mar. 8, 2012), 313n30

Souder v. Owens-Corning Fiberglas Corp., 939 F.2d 647 (8th Cir. 1991), 346

South Alaska Carpenters Health & Sec. Trust Fund v. Jones, 177 P.3d 844 (Alaska 2008), 41n200

South Carolina v. North Carolina, 558 U.S. 256 (2010), 35n156

South Dakota v. Ubbelohde, 330 F.3d 1014 (8th Cir. 2003), *cert. denied*, 541 U.S. 987 (2004), 34n153

Southeast Milk Antitrust Litig., *In re*, 666 F. Supp. 2d 908 (E.D. Tenn. 2009), 198n139

South Energy Homes, Inc. v. Washington, 774 So. 2d 505 (Ala. 2000), 365n16

South Lake Worth Inlet Dist. v. Town of Ocean Ridge, 633 So. 2d 79 (Fla. Ct. App. 1994), 98n255

Southwest Ctr. for Biological Diversity v. USDA, 170 F. Supp. 2d 931 (D. Ariz. 2000), 192n109

Soutiere v. Betzdearborn, Inc., 189 F. Supp. 2d 183 (D. Vt. 2002), 432n175

Spaur v. Owens-Corning Fiberglas Corp., 510 N.W.2d 854 (Iowa 1994), 149n38, 338n40

Spence v. Glock, 227 F.3d 308 (5th Cir. 2000), 179N54

Sperry v. Florida, 373 U.S. 379 (1963), 77n121

Splendorio v. ACMAT Corp., No. CV030407882S, 2005 WL 589957 (Conn. Super. Ct. Feb. 2, 2005), 406n6

Sprietsma v. Mercury Marine, 537 U.S. 51 (2002), 77N124

Springer v. Jefferson County, 595 So. 2d 1381 (Ala. 1982), 364n5

Stafford v. Wyeth, 411 F. Supp. 2d 1318 (W.D. Okla. 2006), 112n347

Stahl v. Metro. Dade County, 438 So. 2d 14 (Fla. Dist. Ct. App. 1983), 371nn56–57

Standard Guar. Ins. Co. v. Quanstrom, 555 So. 2d 828 (Fla. 1990), 56n288

Standard Quimica De Venez. v. Central Hispano Int'l, Inc., 189 F.R.D. 202 (D.P.R. 1999), 233n259

Stanley v. Amalithone Realty, Inc., 921 N.Y.S.2d 491 (N.Y. Sup. Ct. 2011), 97n255

State v. _____ *See name of opposing party*

State Bd. of Registration for the Healing Arts v. McDonagh, 123 S.W.3d 146 (Mo. 2003), 348nn118–119

State Farm Mut. Auto. Ins. Co. v. Campbell, 538 U.S. 408 (2003), 52nn265–266

Staton *ex rel.* Vincent v. Fairbanks Mem'l Hosp., 862 P.2d 847 (Alaska 1993), 310n5

Stebbins v. Doncasters, Inc., 819 A.2d 287 (Conn. 2003), 118n385

Stenger v. Hope Natural Gas Co., 80 S.E.2d 889 (W.V. 1954), 45n220, 45n223

Stephens v. Bashas' Inc., 924 P.2d 117 (Ariz. Ct. App. 1996), 313n32

Sternhagen v. Dow Chem. Co., 935 P.2d 1139 (Mont. 1997), 26n96, 116n367

Stevens, State v., 78 S.W.3d 817 (Tenn. 2002), 396n261

Stewart v. Bader, 907 A.2d 931 (N.H. 2006), 51n258

Stewart v. Federated Dep't Stores, Inc., 662 A.2d 753 (Conn. 1995), 405nn3–4

Stewart v. F.W. Woolworth Co., No. 87-5552, 1993 WL 327782 (Mass. Super. May 6, 1997), 415

Stewart v. New York City Health & Hosps. Corp., 616 N.Y.S.2d 499 (N.Y. App. Div. 1994), 422n119

Stickley v. Chisholm, 765 A.2d 662 (Md. Ct. Spec. App. 2001), 412n51

Stinson v. E.I. DuPont De Nemours & Co., 904 S.W.2d 428 (Mo. App. 1995), 25n89

Stites v. Sundstrand Heat Transfer, Inc., 660 F. Supp. 1516 (W.D. Mich. 1987), 343, 344

Stoddard v. West Carolina Reg'l Sewer Auth., 784 F.2d 1200 (4th Cir. 1986), 55n283

Stokes v. L. Geismar, S.A., 815 F. Supp. 904 (E.D. Va. 1993), 399n292

Stoneman v. Wick Constr. Co., 349 P.2d 215 (Wash. 1960), 330n163

Strawbridge v. Curtiss, 7 U.S. (3 Cranch) 267 (1806), 180N57

Strawn v. Canuso, 657 A.2d 420 (N.J. 1995), 29n120

Strubhart v. Perry Mem'l Hosp. Trust Auth., 903 P.2d 263 (Okla. 1995), 358n207

Struzik, State v., 269 Kan. 95 (2000), 301n107

Stuler v. IRS., 216 F. App'x 240, 242 (3d Cir. 2007), 185n81

Sturm, Ruger & Co. v. Day, 594 P.2d 38 (Alaska 1979), 113n355

Suarez v. City of Tampa, 987 So. 2d 681 (Fla. Ct. App. 2008), 66n54

Suffolk, County of v. Long Island Lighting Co., 907 F.2d 1295 (2d Cir. 1990), 75n107

Suffolk County Water Auth. v. Dow Chem. Co., 942 N.Y.S.2d 765 (N.Y. Sup. Ct. 2012), 91n219, 426n141

Sullivan v. DB Invs., Inc., 667 F.3d 273 (3d Cir. 2011), *cert. denied sub nom.* Murray v. Sullivan, 132 S. Ct. 1876 (2012), 276n46

Summar v. Secretary of the Dep't of Health & Human Servs., No. 90-415V, 1991 WL 133607 (Cl. Ct. July 3, 1991), 135n75

Summers v. Tice, 199 P.2d 1 (Cal. 1948), 346

Sunburst Sch. Dist. No. 2 v. Texaco, Inc., 165 P.3d 1079 (Mont. 2007), 45n224

Suter v. San Angelo Foundry & Mach. Co., 406 A.2d 140 (N.J. 1979), 113n355

Sutera v. Perrier Grp. of Am. Inc., 986 F. Supp. 655 (D. Mass. 1997), 157n86, 416

Swearingen v. Long, 889 F. Supp. 587 (N.D.N.Y. 1995), 14n25

Swedenberg v. Phillips, 562 So. 2d 170 (Ala. 1990), 21n71

Syms v. Olin Corp., 408 F.3d 95 (2d Cir. 2005), 58n1, 65n47

T

Talavera v. Shah, 638 F.3d 303 (D.C. Cir. 2011), 218n205

Talbott v. Roswell Hosp. Corp., 118 P.3d 194 (N.M. Ct. App. 2005), 325n132, 325n134

Tamraz v. Lincoln Elec. Co., 620 F.3d 665 (6th Cir. 2010), 303n114

T&E Indus., Inc. v. Safety Light Corp., 587 A.2d 1249 (N.J. 1991), 29n116

Tanoh v. Dow Chem. Co., 561 F.3d 945 (9th Cir. 2009), 180

Tapscott v. MS Dealer Serv. Corp., 77 F.3d 1353 (11th Cir. 1996), 228n240

Tarazi v. Exxon Corp., 703 N.Y.S.2d 205 (N.Y. App. Div. 2000), 7n12

Tate v. Boeing Helicopters, 55 F.3d 1150 (6th Cir. 1995), 116n372, 117n374

Tate v. Boeing Helicopters, 140 F.3d 654 (6th Cir. 1998), 116n373

Tate v. Eli Lilly & Co., 522 F. Supp. 1048 (M.D. Tenn. 1981), 70n70

Tavares v. Aramark Corp., 841 A.2d 1124 (R.I. 2004), 430n166

Taygeta Corp. v. Varia Assocs., Inc., 763 N.E.2d 1053 (Mass. 2002), 66n52, 66n54

Taylor v. American Chemistry Council, 576 F.3d 16 (1st Cir. 2009), 103n290, 104

Taylor v. Meirick, 712 F.2d 1112 (7th Cir. 1983), 68n61

Taylor v. Monsanto Co., 150 F.3d 806 (7th Cir. 1998), 104n295

Taylor v. Silva, 615 P.2d 970 (Nev. 1980), 323n117

Taylor-Rice v. State, 979 P.2d 1086 (Haw. 1999), 319n80

TDM Farms, Inc. of N.C. v. Wilhoite Family Farm, LLC, 969 N.E.2d 97 (Ind. Ct. App. 2012), 97n251

Temple-Inland Prods. Corp. v. Carter, 993 S.W.2d 88 (Tex. 1999), 43n210

Terrorist Attacks on September 11, 2001, *In re*, 454 F. Supp. 2d 220 (S.D.N.Y. 2006), 199n143

Terry v. Caputo, 875 N.E.2d 72 (Ohio 2007), 354, 355, 356n186, 357n195, 358

Terry v. Ottawa County Bd. of Mental Retardation & Dev. Delay, 847 N.E.2d 1246 (Ohio Ct. App. 2006), *aff'd sub nom.* Terry v. Caputo, 875 N.E.2d 72 (Ohio 2007), 357n195

Texas & Pac. Ry. Co. v. Abilene Cotton Oil Co., 204 U.S. 426 (1907), 76n115

Textron, Inc. v. Aetna Cas. & Sur. Co., 754 A.2d 742 (R.I. 2000), 113n356

Textron, Inc. v. Barber-Colman Co., 903 F. Supp. 1546 (W.D.N.C. 1995), 124n11

T.H. Agric. & Nutrition, LLC v. U.S. Envtl. Prot. Agency, 119 F. Supp. 2d 1367 (M.D. Ga. 2000), 130n40

Thacker v. UNR Indus., Inc., 603 N.E.2d 449 (Ill. 1992), 333nn2–3, 335n12, 335nn14–15

Thayer v. Hicks, 793 P.2d 784 (Mont. 1990), 322n107

Thing v. La Chusa, 48 Cal. 3d 644 (Cal. 1989), 101n277

Thomas v. FAG Bearings Corp., 846 F. Supp. 1400 (W.D. Mo. 1994), 37n179

Thomas v. Hoffman-LaRoche, Inc., 949 F.2d 806 (5th Cir. 1992), 111n344

Thomas *ex rel.* Gramling v. Mallett, 285 Wis. 2d 236 (2005), 170n14

Thompson v. Connick, 578 F.3d 293 (5th Cir. 2009), 291n53

Thompson v. Southern Pac. Transp. Co., 809 F.2d 1167 (5th Cir.), *cert. denied*, 484 U.S. 819 (1987), 155

325–343 E. 56th Street Corp. v. Mobile Oil Corp., 906 F. Supp. 669 (D.D.C. 1995), 250n327

Thropp v. Bache Halsey Stuart Shields, Inc., 650 F.2d 817 (6th Cir. 1981), 316n57

Tinman v. Blue Cross & Blue Shield, 176 F. Supp. 2d 743 (E.D. Mich. 2001), 200n150

Titus v. Williams, 844 So. 2d 459 (Miss. 2003), 385N167

TMI Litig., *In re*, 911 F. Supp. 775 (M.D. Pa. 1996), *aff'd*, 193 F.3d 613 (3d Cir. 1999), *cert. denied*, 530 U.S. 1225 (2000), 253n341, 429n157

TMI Litig. Cases Consol. II, *In re*, 940 F.2d 832 (3d Cir. 1991), 84n173, 84n175

TMJ Implants Prods. Liab. Litig., *In re*, 872 F. Supp. 1019 (D. Minn. 1995), 105n306

Todd v. Shankel, 83 F. App'x 952 (9th Cir. 2003), 319n82

Tolley v. ACF Indus. Inc., 575 S.E.2d 158 (W. Va. 2002), 402n314, 403n322, 404n330

Tolley v. Carboline Co., 617 S.E.2d 508 (W. Va. 2005), 402n318

Tolliver v. Department of Transp., 948 A.2d 1223 (Me. 2008), 411n44

Tota v. United States, 2000 WL 1160477 (W.D.N.Y. July 31, 2000), 185n80

Townley v. Norfolk & W. Ry. Co., 887 F.2d 498 (4th Cir. 1989), 60n14

Toxic Substances Cases, *In re*, No. A.D. 03-319, 2006 WL 2404008 (Pa. Com. Pl. Aug. 17, 2006), 427n142, 429n162, 430nn163–164

Trach v. Fellin, 817 A.2d 1102 (Pa. Super. Ct. 2003), 429n161

Tragarz v. Keene Corp., 980 F.2d 411 (7th Cir. 1992), 418n94, 418n96

Trimble v. Asarco, Inc., 232 F.3d 946 (8th Cir. 2000), *overruled*, Exxon Mobil Corp. v. Allapattah Servs., 545 U.S. 546 (2005), 45n223

Triplett v. Minnesota Mining & Mfg. Co., 422 F. Supp. 2d 779 (W.D. Ky. 2006), 105

Troy v. Soo Line R.R. Co., 409 F. Supp. 326 (E.D. Wis. 1976), 23n79

Troy Corp. v. Browner, 129 F.3d 1290 (D.C. Cir. 1997), 133n62

Tucker v. Southwestern Energy Co., 2012 U.S. Dist. LEXIS 20697 (E.D. Ark. Feb. 17, 2012), 281

Tucker v. South Wood Piedmont Co., 28 F.3d 1089 (11th Cir. 1994), 63n31, 63nn35–36, 68n63

Turner v. Iowa Fire Equip. Co., 229 F.3d 1202 (8th Cir. 2000), 348n120, 353

Turner v. State, 746 So. 2d 355 (Ala. 1998), 365n16

Turpin v. Merrell Dow Pharm., Inc., 959 F.2d 1349 (6th Cir. 1992), 109n329

Tuttle v. Raymond, 494 A.2d 1353 (Me. 1985), 50n255

Twyman v. GHK Corp., 93 P.3d 51 (Okla. Ct. App. 2004), 359

U

UAW v. General Motors Corp., 497 F.3d 615 (6th Cir. 2007), 278n58

Underwood Cotton Co. v. Hyundai, 288 F.3d 405 (9th Cir 2002), 70n73

Union Carbide Corp. v. Fields, 726 S.E.2d 521 (Ga. Ct. App. 2012), 376n89, 377n97, 378n101

Union Carbide Corp. Gas Plant, In re, 601 F. Supp. 1035 (J.P.M.L. 1985), 174n28

Union Carbide Corp. Gas Plant Disaster at Bhopal, In re, 634 F. Supp. 842 (S.D.N.Y. 1986), order aff'd as modified, 809 F.2d 195 (2d Cir. 1987), 174n28

United States v. _____. See name of opposing party

United States Fid. & Guar. Co. v. Camp, 831 P.2d 586 (Mont. 1992), 322n102

United States Fid. Guar. Co. v. Sulco, Inc., 171 F.R.D. 305 (D. Kan. 1997), 193n113

United States Gypsum Co. v. Mayor of Baltimore, 647 A.2d 405 (Md. 1994), 258n357

United States Postal Serv. v. Phelps Dodge Refining Corp., 852 F. Supp. 156 (E.D.N.Y. 1994), 190

United States Pub. Interest Research Grp. v. Atlantic Salmon of Me., 339 F.3d 34 (1st Cir. 2003), 75n111, 76n113

United States Sugar Corp. v. Henson, 823 So. 2d 104 (Fla. 2002), 372n65

Urie v. Thompson, 337 U.S. 163 (1949), 58n3, 59n5

Utica Mut. Ins. Co. v. Travelers Indem. Co., 286 S.E.2d 225 (Va. 1982), 291n57

V

Vaccariello v. Smith & Nephew Richards, Inc., 763 N.E.2d 160 (Ohio 2002), 106n312

Vaillancourt v. Town of Southington, No. X03CV010510816S, 2002 WL 1293053 (Conn. Super. Ct. May 7, 2002), 102

Valencia v. Shell Oil Co., 147 P.2d 558 (Cal. 1944), 95n244

Valentine v. PPG Indus., Inc., 821 N.E.2d 580 (Ohio Ct. App. 2004), aff'd sub nom. Valentine v. Conrad, 850

N.E.2d 683 (Ohio 2006), 355, 356, 357n195, 357n197

Van Waters & Rogers, Inc., *In re*, 62 S.W.3d 197 (Tex. 2001), 398n281

Van Waters & Rogers, Inc., *In re*, 145 S.W.3d 203 (Tex. 2004), 175nn35–36, 366

Vargas v. Lee, 317 F.3d 498 (5th Cir. 2003), 146

Vassallo v. American Coding & Marking Ink Co., 784 A.2d 734 (N.J. Super. Ct. App. Div. 2001), 107n318

Vassallo v. Baxter Healthcare Corp., 696 N.E.2d 909 (Mass. 1998), 116n367, 415nn69–70

Vector-Springfield Props., Ltd. v. Central Ill. Light Co., 108 F.3d 806 (7th Cir. 1997), 60n13, 61n21

Velsicol Chem. Corp. v. Enenco, Inc., 9 F.3d 524 (6th Cir. 1993), 73n89

Vento v. Colorado Nat'l Bank-Pueblo, 907 P.2d 642 (Colo. Ct. App. 1995), 316n56

Vermett v. Fred Christen & Sons Co., 741 N.E.2d 954 (Ohio Ct. App. 2000), 114n359

Vermont Gas Sys. v. United States Fid. & Guar. Co., 151 F.R.D. 268 (D. Vt. 1993), 190n102, 220n211

Vertac Chem. Corp., United States v., 966 F. Supp. 1491 (E.D. Ark. 1997), 212n188

Vettrus v. Ashland, No. C9-04-817 (Minn. 3d Jud. Dist. 2008), 86n194

Viagra Prods. Liab. Litig., *In re*, 572 F. Supp. 2d 1071 (D. Minn. 2008), 109n329

Victor Stanley, Inc. v. Creative Pipe, Inc., 269 F.R.D. 497 (D. Md. 2010), 216n199

Vicwood Meridian P'ship v. Skagit Sand & Gravel, 98 P.3d 1277 (Wash. Ct. App. 2004), 97n251

Viner v. Sweet, 70 P.3d 1046 (Cal. 2003), 314n37, 314n39

Vinitski v. Adler, No. 2533, 2004 WL 2579288 (Pa. Com. Pl. Sept. 17, 2004), 429n162

Vitanza v. Upjohn Co., 778 A.2d 829 (Conn. 2001), 106n307, 107n317

Vodanovich v. A.P. Green Indus., Inc., 2003-1079 (La. App. 4 Cir. Mar. 3, 2004), 382n137

Vogel v. Grant-Lafayette Elec. Co-op., 548 N.W.2d 829 (Wis. 1996), 100n270

W

Wade-Greaux v. Whitehall Labs., Inc., 874 F. Supp. 1441 (D.V.I. 1994), 132n57

Waldburger v. CTS Corp., No.1:11CV39, 2012 WL 380053 (W.D.N.C. Feb. 6, 2012), 71n82

Walker v. Consumers Power Co., 1990 U.S. App. LEXIS 2575 (6th Cir.), *cert. denied*, 498 U.S. 815 (1990), 230n249

Walker Drug Co. v. La Sal Oil Co., 972 P.2d 1238 (Utah 1998), 46n227, 46n229, 47n232, 67n55

Wall v. Sunoco, Inc., 211 F.R.D. 272 (M.D. Pa. 2002), 179n53

Wallace v. Lewis County, 137 P.3d 101 (Wash. Ct. App. 2006), 14n24

Wal-Mart Stores, Inc. v. Dukes, 131 S. Ct. 2541 (2011),   178, 276n47
Walter v. Cessna Aircraft Co., 358 N.W.2d 816 (Wis. Ct. App. 1984),   51n262
Walters v. Prairie Oil & Gas Co., 204 P. 906 (Okla. 1922),   15n34
Wang v. Masaitis, 416 F.3d 992 (9th Cir. 2005),   288n31
Warren v. Legg Mason Wood Walker, Inc., 896 F. Supp. 540 (E.D.N.C. 1995),   189n97
Waterkeeper Alliance, Inc. v. Alan & Kristin Hudson Farm, 278 F.R.D. 136 (D. Md. 2011),   200n150
Watson v. Dillon Cos., 797 F. Supp. 2d 1138 (D. Colo. 2011),   317, 318
Watters v. Department of Soc. Servs., No. 2011-1174 (La. App. 4 Cir. Mar. 14, 2012),   382, 383nn144–147, 384
Watters v. General Elec. Co., No. 4:98-cv-0195-HLM (N.D. Ga. April 2, 2001),   91
Watts v. Radiator Specialty Co., 990 So. 2d 143 (Miss. 2008),   386n177, 386n183
Weakley v. Burnham Corp., 871 A.2d 1167 (D.C. 2005),   409nn28–29, 409n31
Weinberger v. Romero-Barcelo, 456 U.S. 305 (1982),   54nn275–276
Weinhold v. Wolff, 555 N.W.2d 454 (Iowa 1996),   20n66, 54nn276–277
Weisburg v. U.S. Dep't of Justice, 705 F.2d 1344 (D.C. Cir. 1983),   185n80
Weiss v. Axler, 328 P.2d 88 (Colo. 1958),   13n20

Welch v. Keene Corp., 575 N.E.2d 766 (Mass. App. Ct. 1991),   415
Welding Fume Prods. Liab. Litig., *In re*, 364 F. Supp. 2d 669 (N.D. Ohio 2005),   86n188, 86nn190–192
Welding Fume Prods. Liab. Litig., *In re*, 526 F. Supp. 2d 775 (N.D. Ohio 2007),   111n341
Welding Fume Prods. Liab. Litig., *In re*, No. 1:03-CV-17000, MDL No. 1535, 2010 WL 7699456 (N.D. Ohio June 4, 2010),   103n288
Wellesley Hills Realty Trust v. Mobil Oil Corp., 747 F. Supp. 93 (D. Mass. 1990),   29n117
Wells v. Smithkline Beecham Corp., 601 F.3d 375 (5th Cir. 2010),   396n269
Wells v. Whitaker, 151 S.E.2d 422 (Va. 1966),   399nn289–290
Wendinger v. Forst Farms, Inc., 662 N.W.2d 546 (Minn. Ct. App. 2003),   15n37
Wendland v. Ridgefield Constr. Servs., Inc., 439 A.2d 954 (1981),   11n9
Werlein v. United States, 746 F. Supp. 887 (D. Minn. 1990), *vacated*, 793 F. Supp. 898 (D. Minn. 1992),   39, 346nn105–106
West v. Caterpillar Tractor Co., 336 So. 2d 80 (Fla. 1976) *aff'd*, 547 F.2d. 885 (5th Cir. 1977),   371n55
West Va. *ex rel.* Smith v. Kermit Lumber Pressure Treating Co., 488 S.E.2d 901 (W. Va. 1997),   67n56
Westberry v. Gislaved Gummi AB, 178 F.3d 257 (4th Cir. 1999),   110n337, 155n72, 357n197, 393, 393nn242–245, 414n63

Western Greenhouses v. United States, 878 F. Supp. 917 (N.D. Tex. 1995), 10, 115nn365–366

Western Pac. R.R. Co., United States v., 352 U.S. 59 (1956), 75nn108–109, 76n118

Western Props. Serv. Corp. v. Shell Oil Co., 358 F.3d 678 (9th Cir. 2004), *abrogated*, Cooper Indus., Inc. v. Aviall Servs., Inc., 543 U.S. 157 (2004), 73nn89–90

Westwood Apex v. Contreras, 644 F.3d 799 (9th Cir. 2011), 296

W.G. Duncan Coal Co. v. Jones, 254 S.W.2d 720 (Ky. Ct. App. 1953), 20n67

Whately v. Cardinal Pest Control, 388 So. 2d 529 (Ala. 1980), 364

Wheaton Indus. v. EPA, 781 F.2d 354 (3d Cir. 1986), 79n136

Wheelahan v. G.D. Searle & Co., 814 F.2d 655 (4th Cir. 1987), 413n59

Wheeler v. White, 714 A.2d 125 (Me. 1998), 411n43

White v. Dow Chem. Co., No. 2:05-CV-00247, 2007 WL 6948824 (S.D.W. Va. Nov. 29, 2007), 272n8, 402n311, 402n314, 404n331

White v. Mercury Marine, Div. of Brunswick, Inc., 129 F.3d 1428 (11th Cir. 1997), 68n60, 68n62

White v. National Football League, 41 F.3d 402 (8th Cir. 1994), *cert. denied*, 515 U.S. 1137 (1995), 271n7

Whiting v. Boston Edison Co., 891 F. Supp. 12 (D. Mass. 1995), 110n340

Whitlaw v. Kroger Co., 410 S.E.2d 251 (S.C. 1991), 391n225

Wichita, Kansas v. Trustees of the Apco Oil Corp. Liquidating Trust, 306 F. Supp. 2d 1040 (D. Kan. 2003), 125n12, 127n22, 128n28, 129n31, 129n36, 130n38, 212n187

Widefield Homes, Inc. v. Griego, 416 P.2d 365 (Colo. 1966), 316n56

Wilcox v. Homestake Mining Co., 401 F. Supp. 2d 1196 (D.N.M. 2005), 84n176

Wilcox v. Homestake Mining Co., 619 F.3d 1165 (10th Cir. 2010), 325n136

Wildewood Litig., *In re*, 52 F.3d 499 (4th Cir. 1995), 38n183

Wilhelm v. City of Great Falls, 732 P.2d 1315 (Mont. 1987), 100n270

Wilkins v. Lamoille County Mental Health Servs., Inc., 889 A.2d 245 (Vt. 2005), 432nn172–173

Williams v. Smith, 68 N.C. App. 71 *cert. denied*, 311 N.C. 769, 321 S.E.2d 158 (1984), 387n189

Williamson v. Mazda Motor of Am., Inc., 131 S. Ct. 1131 (2011), 77n124

Willingham v. Morgan, 395 U.S. 402 (1969), 117n377

Wills v. Amerada Hess Corp., 379 F.3d 32 (2d Cir. 2004), 423n120

Wilson v. Amoco Corp., 33 F. Supp. 2d 981 (D. Wyo. 1998), 47

Wilson v. Dake Corp., 497 F. Supp. 1339 (E.D. Tenn. 1980), 71n78

Wilson v. McLeod Oil Co., 398 S.E.2d 586 (N.C. 1990), 70n75

Wilson v. Stilwill, 309 N.W.2d 898 (Mich. 1981), 12n17

Wilsonville v. SCA Servs., Inc., 426 N.E.2d 824 (Ill. 1981), 54n275, 54n278

Winschel v. Brown, 171 P.3d 142 (Alaska 2007), 310n6

Winter v. Natural Res. Def. Council, Inc., 555 U.S. 7 (2008), 54n277

Wisener v. State, 598 P.2d 511 (Ariz. 1979), 311n15, 312n21

Wisner v. Illinois Cent. Gulf R.R., 537 So. 2d 740 (La. Ct. App. 1988), 36n166

Wolf by Wolf v. Procter & Gamble Co., 555 F. Supp. 613 (D.N.J. 1982), 114n360

Womack v. Stevens Transp., Inc., 205 F.R.D. 445 (E.D. Pa. 2001), 216n197

Wood v. Phillips Petroleum Co., 119 S.W.3d 870 (Tex. App. 2003), 25n94, 42n202

Wood v. Picillo, 443 A.2d 1244 (R.I. 1982), 129n35

Wood v. Wyeth-Ayerst Labs., 82 S.W.3d 849 (Ky. 2002), 41n199

Woodbury v. CH2M Hill, Inc., 76 P.3d 131 (Or. Ct. App. 2003), 249n319

W.R. Grace & Co., *In re*, 355 B.R. 462 (Bankr. D. Del. 2006), 409n25

Wright v. Group Health Hosp., 691 P.2d 564 (Wash. 1984), 196n131

Wright v. Jeep Corp., 547 F. Supp. 871 (E.D. Mich. 1982), 192n107

Wright v. Willamette Indus., Inc., 91 F.3d 1105 (8th Cir. 1996), 143n5, 150, 306n127, 352n153

Wyeth-Ayerst Labs. Co. v. Medrano, 28 S.W.3d 87 (Tex. Ct. App. 2000), 106n309

Wyeth v. Levine, 555 U.S. 555 (2009), 77nn125–126, 87n200

X

Xavier v. Philip Morris USA Inc., 787 F. Supp. 2d 1075 (N.D. Cal. 2011), 61n21

Y

Yasmin & Yaz (Drospirenone) Mktg., Sales Practices & Prods. Liab. Litig., *In re*, MDL, 2100 WL 5547133 (S.D. Ill. Nov. 15, 2011), 191n105, 192n108

Yommer v. McKenzie, 257 A.2d 138 (Md. 1969), 24n85

Yonce v. Smithkline Beecham Clinical Labs., 680 A.2d 569 (Md. Ct. Spec. App. 1996), 412nn49–50

York v. Union Carbide Corp., 586 N.E.2d 861 (Ind. Ct. App. 1992), 86n193

Young v. Burton, 567 F. Supp. 2d 121 (D.D.C. 2008), 410

Young v. Hickory Bus. Furniture, 538 S.E.2d 912 (N.C. 2000), 390n220

Young v. Tide Craft, Inc., 242 S.E.2d 671 (S.C. 1978), 391n227

Young v. United States, 181 F.R.D. 344 (W.D. Tex. 1997), 209n182

Z

Zamstein v. Marvasti, 692 A.2d 781 (Conn. 1997), 102n280

Zemansky v. U.S. EPA, 767 F.2d 569 (9th Cir. 1985), 185n81

Zeni v. Anderson, 243 N.W.2d 270 (Mich. 1976), 283n13

Zenith Radio Corp. v. Matsushita Elec. Indus. Co., 529 F. Supp. 866 (E.D. Pa. 1981), 200n149

Zicam Cold Remedy Mktg., Sales Practices, & Prods. Liab. Litig., *In re*, 797 F. Supp. 2d 940 (D. Ariz. 2011), 210n184

Zimko v. Am. Cyanamid, No. 2003-0658 (La. App. 4 Cir. June 8, 2005), 382n137, 382n139, 383n142, 384n155

Zubulake v. UBS Warburg, LLC, 220 F.R.D. 212 (S.D.N.Y. 2003), 218

Zuchowicz v. United States, 140 F.3d 381 (2d Cir. 1998), 110n339, 393n245, 406n7

INDEX

A

Abnormally dangerous activities, 21–22
　former landowner liability, 29
　fracking, 280–282
　unintentional trespass liability, 16
Absolute liability for product defects, 26
Absolute pollution exclusion, 267
Actual damages, 35
Actual data vs. modeling of exposure routes, 211–212
Adequacy requirement, 177, 272
Administrative remedies, exhaustion of, 73–75
Admissibility. *See* Evidence
AEA (Atomic Energy Act), preemption by, 82–84
Alabama
　causation standards, 363–365
Alaska
　causation standards, 310–311
Alternative dispute resolution methods, 267–268
　additional options, 270
　arbitration, 268–270
　mediation, 268
　negotiation, 268
　overview, 267
　summary jury trials, 270–271
American Arbitration Association, 268
American Bar Association Section of Environment, Energy and Resources, 184
American National Standards Institute (ANSI), 113
American Society for Testing and Materials (ASTM), 113
American Society of Mechanical Engineers (ASME), 113
Analytical testing, 203–204
　data as evidence, 203–205
　overview, 203
　sharing data, 205–206
　waste stream identification and reconstruction, 213–214
Animal studies, 132
ANSI (American National Standards Institute), 113
Arbitration, 268–270
Areas of emerging litigation, 279–280. *See also* Emerging legal issues
　climate change–based nuisance actions, 287–288
　groundwater and subsurface contamination, 282–284

Areas of emerging litigation (*continued*)
  hydraulic fracturing, 279–280
  workplace exposure, 293–294
Arizona
  causation standards, 311–312
Arkansas
  causation standards, 366–368
ASME (American Society of Mechanical Engineers), 113
Assault, 32–34
Association, 135
  consistency of, 141
  specificity of, 141
  strength of, 141
Assumption of the risk, 93
ASTM (American Society for Testing and Materials), 113
Atomic Energy Act (AEA)
  preemption by, 82–84
Attorney-client privilege, 189–191
  former employees, 197
Attorneys' fee awards, 54–56
  statutory availability effect on case valuation, 267

B

Baker factors, 287–289
Balancing of interests approach, protective orders, 199
Battery, 32–34
Bellwether plaintiffs, 176–177, 253–254
  selection process, 253–254
  summary jury trials compared, 270
Bias, 136
Bifurcation, 250–251
Biologic plausibility, 137, 142
Blue-ribbon juries, 223
Bradford Hill, Austin, 140

Bradford Hill criteria, 109, 136–137, 140–141
Breach of warranty, 30–33
Bulk raw materials supplier defense, 105
But-for causation. *See* Causation

C

CAA (Clean Air Act)
  climate change nuisance action preemption, 289–291
  permitted activity nuisance defense, 97–99
  standing, 92
CAFA (Class Action Fairness Act), 180–181
  counterclaim defendants, 296–298
Calibration, 126–127
California
  causation standards, 314–316
  fear of disease actions, 44
  punitive damages standard, 52
Case, Charles D., 186
Case-control studies, 134–136
Case management orders, 224–226
Case strategy and management, 167–168
  alignment of parties and forums, 172–173
    class actions, 177
    joinder of plaintiffs, 174–175
    multidistrict litigation, 172–174
    overview, 172
  case management orders, 224–226
  discovery and investigation issues, 183–185. *See also* Discovery and investigation issues
  motion practice, 229–230. *See also* Motion practice
  overview, 167–168

parallel regulatory proceedings
coordination, 219–221
information management, 222–223
party selection, 168–169. *See also* Party selection
trial issues, 234. *See also* Trial issues
Case valuation. *See* Valuation of case
Causation. *See also* Evidence
bellwether trials, 253
challenges to, 107–109
failure-to-warn theory causation defenses, 111–113
general and specific causation, 108–109
overview, 107
product identification, 111
general causation, 140–141. *See also* General causation
latency periods, 6
medical evidence, 143–144
general causation, 144
overview, 143–144
specific causation, 146–147. *See also* Specific causation
overriding significance in toxic torts, 4
Restatement (Third) of Torts approach, 4
risk assessments as evidence, 305–306
specific causation, 142–143. *See also* Specific causation
state-by-state standards, 309–310. *See also individual states*
Eastern states, 405–406
Midwestern states, 333–334
Western states, 309–310
valuation of case, 262–263
CERCLA (Comprehensive Environmental Response, Compensation, and Liability Act), 26–27
discovery rule, 62–63
Eckardt reports, 213
former landowner liability, 30
natural resources damage, 47–49
preemption by, 78–79
statutes of repose, 71
veil piercing, 172
Check samples, 125
Chemistry, 130
Circumstantial evidence, 152–154
Citizens' suits, 267
Class Action Fairness Act (CAFA), 180–181
counterclaim defendants, 296–298
Class actions, 177
additional counterclaim defendants, 296–298
emerging legal issues, 295–296
heightened certification standards, 295–296
medical monitoring remedy availability, 179, 297–298
settlements, 271
fairness hearings, 277–278
heightened scrutiny for certification, 271–273, 274–277
limited fund theory, 272–274
lower court decisions, 274–276
overview, 271
state court decisions, 277
Supreme Court views, 271–272
Clean Air Act (CAA)
climate change nuisance action preemption, 289–291
permitted activity nuisance defense, 97–99
standing, 92
Cleanup. *See also* Remediation of sites
emphasis in jury presentation, 246–247

Cleanup (*continued*)
  equitable remedies for costs, 33
  obligation relationship to liability in case valuation, 266
Climate change–based nuisance actions, 287–288
Closing arguments, 247–248
Coherence of association, 137
Cohort studies, 134–136
Colorado
  causation standards, 316–318
    federal cases, 317–318
  fracking, 281–283
Coming to the nuisance, 97
Commerce Clause, 64
Commerce, U.S. Secretary of, 48
Committees of counsel, 226
Commonality requirement, 177, 276
Common carrier exception, dangerous materials transport, 23
Common law fraud, 29
Comparative fault, 93–94, 408
  nuisance claims, 100–101
  party selection considerations, 168–170
Compensatory damages, 35–39
Comprehensive Environmental Response, Compensation, and Liability Act (CERCLA). *See* CERCLA (Comprehensive Environmental Response, Compensation, and Liability Act)
Comprehensive General Liability insurance, 267
  duty to defend, climate change actions, 291–293
Concealment actions, former landowners, 29
Confidence intervals, 141
Confounding factors, 136

Connecticut
  causation standards, 405–406
  expert testimony, 407–408
  trespass, 18
Consequential damages, 46
Consistency of association, 136, 141
Consolidation, 175
Consulting experts, 204
  remediation, 222–223
Continuing torts
  groundwater contamination, 285
  limitations period, 65–67
  trespass, 17
Contribution actions, 27, 105
Contributory negligence, 93–94
  nuisance claims, 100–101
Control groups, 141
Corporate depositions, 194–196
Counterclaim defendants, 296–298
Covered persons, 48

D

Damages, 35–38
  attorneys' fee awards, 54–56
  expansion of traditional approach, 6
  failure to mitigate, 95–97
  fear of disease, 43–44
  injunctive relief, 53–55
  limitations period, 67–70
  medical monitoring, 40–41
  natural resources damage, 47–49
  overview, 35–38
  present injury requirement, 37–40
  property damage, 45–47
  punitive damages, 50–52
  valuation of case, 263–264
Data as evidence, 203–205
  admissibility, 248
  sharing data, 205–206

validation of data, 222
Daubert trilogy, 159–160. *See also* Expert testimony
   expert reliability factors, 159
   federal rules and state codification, 164–165
   gatekeeper role, 416
   impact on civil litigation, 158–159
   medical evidence primacy following, 164–165
   multidistrict litigation combined hearings, 172–174
Defective condition unreasonably dangerous standard, 24
Defective-design theory, 25
Defective products liability, 24
Defenses to toxic tort suits, 57–58
   attacking causation, 107–109
      failure-to-warn theory causation defenses, 111–113
      general and specific causation, 108–109
      overview, 107
      product identification, 111
   contributory negligence, 93–94
   exhaustion of administrative remedies, 73–75
   failure to mitigate damages, 95–97
   government contractor defense, 116–118
   laches, 72–73
   lack of duty, 101–102. *See also* Lack of duty
   nuisance claim defenses, 97–99
      coming to the nuisance, 97
      contributory negligence, 100–101
      government authorization, 97–99
   overview, 57
   preemption, 76–78. *See also* Preemption
   primary jurisdiction doctrine, 75–76
   regulatory safe levels, 88–90
   standing, 90–93
   state of the art, 113–116
   statutes of limitations, 57–59. *See also* Statutes of limitations
   statutes of repose, 70–72
   workers' compensation bar, 118–119
Definition of toxic torts, 3–4
Delaware
   causation standards, 408
   comparative fault, 408
Demonstrative evidence, 246–247
Department of Transportation, U.S.
   investigation by, litigation risk, 265
Depositions
   government employees, 207–208
      nonparty agency, 208
      overview, 207–208
      party agency, 208
      special testimonial issues, 209–210
   30(b)(6) depositions, 194–196
DES (Diethylstilbestrol), 170
Designated person depositions, 194–196
Design defect theory, 25
Deviation from design specifications requirement, 25
Diethylstilbestrol (DES), 170
Differential diagnosis, 109, 154–155
Diminished earning capacity, 35
Diminution in value, 3, 45
Disability of plaintiff, tolling for, 70
Disclosures in property sales, 29
Discovery and investigation issues, 183–185
   analytical testing, 203–204. *See also* Analytical testing

Discovery and investigation issues (*continued*)
   case management order treatment, 227
   electronic data discovery and preservation, 217–219
   employee witnesses, 193–194
   environmental audit discoverability, 186–187
   exposure routes, 210–211
   FOIA and government information, 184–186
   government employee depositions, 207–208. *See also* Government employee depositions
   independent researchers, 191–192
   industry experts, 192–194
   modeling vs. actual data, 211–212
   motion practice, 232–233
   overview, 183
   preservation of evidence, 214–215. *See also* Preservation of evidence
   protective orders, 198–199. *See also* Protective orders
   site access, 206–208
   waste stream identification and reconstruction, 212–213. *See also* Waste stream identification and reconstruction

Discovery rule, 58–61
   CERCLA, 62–63

Disease, fear of, 43–44

District of Columbia
   causation standards, 409–410

Diversity jurisdiction, employee named to defeat, 194

DNA, changes to, 39

Dose evidence, 140–141

Dose of toxic substances, 131

Dose response, 131, 137, 142

Duplicate samples, 125

Duration of toxic substance exposure, 131

Duty, lack of. *See* Lack of duty

Duty of reasonable care
   defined, 9
   examples of breach, 10
   failure to prove breach, 101–103
   negligence per se as proof of breach, 11–12, 250
   products liability application, 25
   res ipsa loquitur inference of breach, 12

Duty to defend, climate change actions, 291–293

Duty to warn, 103

E

Early detection benefits, 42–43

Eastern U.S. state causation standards, 405–406. *See also individual states*
   overview, 405

Eckardt reports, 213

Electronic data discovery and preservation, 217–219

Electronic Freedom of Information Act Amendments (EFOIA), 185

Ellis, L. Neal, Jr., 186

Emerging legal issues, 295–296. *See also* Areas of emerging litigation
   class actions, 295–296
   experts, 300–301
   medical monitoring, 304–305
   risk assessments to prove causation, 305–306

Emotional distress, 36

Employee witnesses, 193–194

designated person depositions, 194–196
diversity, employee named to defeat, 194
ex parte contact, 195–198
former employees, 197–198
Environmental and Toxic Tort Matters: Updates and Trends, Case Management and Health Claims in Toxic Tort Litigation (Rudlin et al.), 225
Environmental and Toxic Tort Trials (Kanner), 235, 242
Environmental audits, discoverability, 186–187
   attorney-client privilege, 189–191
   EPA enforcement actions, 186–187
   self-critical analysis privilege, 188–190
Environmental Protection Agency (EPA)
   climate change nuisance action preemption, 289–291
   concentrations below recommended maximum contaminant level, 155
   depositions of agency employees, 207–208
   environmental audit use in enforcement actions, 186–187
   failure to discharge duties suits, 73
   field blanks recommendation, 124
   primary jurisdiction doctrine, 76
   standard testing methodologies, 123
   TSCA preemption of listed substances, 81
Epidemiology, 108, 133–135
   "gold standard" for general causation, 144–145
Equitable remedies
   injunctions, 53–55
   unjust enrichment and restitution, 33

Erie doctrine, 303
Error rate of technique, 159
Evidence. *See also* Causation
   analytical testing, 203–204. *See also* Analytical testing
   circumstantial evidence, 152–154
   data as, 203–205
      admissibility, 248
      sharing data, 205–206
      validation of data, 222
   demonstrative evidence, 246–247
   discovery and investigation. *See* Discovery and investigation issues
   expert testimony. *See Daubert* trilogy; Expert testimony
   industry codes, 249
   industry experts discovery standard, 192–194
   medical evidence. *See* Medical evidence
   postinjury evidence of culpability, 256–257
   preservation. *See* Preservation of evidence
   public records and reports, 249
   risk assessments, 305–306
   scientific evidence. *See* Scientific evidence
   violations of statutes and regulations, 250
Evidentiary motions, 232–234
Exclusive possession requirement, 14–15
Exhaustion of administrative remedies, 73–75
Ex parte contact with employee witnesses, 195–198
   former employees, 197
Experimental evidence support, 137

Expert testimony, 157–158
  data quality experts, 223
  Daubert trilogy, 159–160. *See also Daubert* trilogy
  Frye standard, 157–159
  heightened admissibility standard trend, 300–301
  historical background, 159, 159–160
  overview, 157–158
  reliability factors, 159
  remediation consultants, coordination with, 222–223
  scientific evidence. *See* Scientific evidence
Explosives handling, 23
Exposure evidence, 140–141
Exposure or occurrence rule, 58
Exposure routes, 210–211
  modeling vs. actual data, 211–212

F

Facility requirement, 27, 79
Failure to mitigate damages, 95–97
Failure to state claim motions, 231–232
Failure-to-warn theory
  causation defenses, 111–113
  lack of duty defenses, 103–105. *See also* Lack of duty
Fairness hearings, 277–278
Farming rights statutes, 21
Fate and transport, 127–128
Fear of disease, 43–44
Federal Employers Liability Act (FELA), 43–45
Federal Insecticide, Fungicide, and Rodenticide Act (FIFRA)
  preemption by, 84–86
Federal Officer Removal Statute, 117
Federal preemption. *See* Preemption

Federal Tort Claims Act (FTCA)
  exhaustion of administrative remedies, 74
  statute of repose application, 71
Fiber drift theory, 381–382, 427
Field blanks, 124
FIFRA (Federal Insecticide, Fungicide, and Rodenticide Act)
  preemption by, 84–86
Filing under seal, 201
Florida
  causation standards, 371–372
Food and Drug Administration (FDA), 87–88
  investigation by, litigation risk, 265
Food, Drug, and Cosmetic Act (FDCA)
  preemption by, 87–88
Former employee witnesses, 197–198
Former landowner liability, 28–30
Fracking, 279–280
  declaratory relief claims, 281–283
  municipal regulation, 282
  strict liability, 280–282
Fraud, 29
Fraudulent concealment, 69
Freedom of Information Act (FOIA), 184–186
Frequency of toxic substance exposure, 131
Frequency, regularity, and proximity test, 335, 338, 386, 390, 418. *See also* Lohrmann test
Frye standard, 157–159
Fuel handling, 23

G

Gatekeeping function of judges, 159, 161
General acceptance test, 157–159
General causation, 140–141

biologic plausibility, 142
challenges to, 108–109
consistency of association, 141
dose response, 142
medical evidence, 144
overview, 140–141
specificity of association, 141
state-by-state standards. *See individual states*
strength of association, 141
temporal relationship, 142
General damages, 36
Geology, 128
Georgia
causation standards, 376–377
Good cause requirement, protective orders, 199–200
Government authorization nuisance defense, 97–99
Government contractor defense, 116–118
Government employee depositions, 207–208
nonparty agency, 208
overview, 207–208
party agency, 208
special testimonial issues, 209–210
Government standards and risk assessments, 155–157
Granholm, Jennifer M., 252
Groundwater contamination, 282–284

H
Hawaii
causation standards, 318–319
federal cases, 320
Hazardous waste
RCRA regulation of, 28
HazCom Standard (OSHA Hazard Communication Standard)
bulk supplier defense, 105
preemption by, 85–87
Hearings, *Daubert*. *See Daubert* trilogy; Expert testimony
Hedonic damages, 36
Heeding presumption, 112
High-low arbitration, 269
Hindsight test for products liability, 25
Home State Exception, 180, 183
Hydraulic fracturing, 279–280
declaratory relief claims, 281–283
municipal regulation, 282
strict liability, 280–282
Hydrology, 129

I
Idaho
causation standards, 320–321
Illinois
causation standards, 333–335
frequency, regularity, and proximity test, 335
take-home workplace exposure, 293–294
Impact rule, 43
Implied warranties, 31
Independent medical examinations, 215–216
Independent researcher discovery, 191–192
Indiana
causation standards, 336–337
Industry experts discovery, 192–194
Information management, 222–223
Injunctive relief, 53–55
Insurance coverage issues, 267
duty to defend climate change actions, 291–293
Intangible physical invasions, 16

Intentional invasion standard for trespass, 19
Intent requirement for trespass, 16–17
Interior, U.S. Secretary of, 48
Investigations. *See* Discovery and investigation issues
Iowa
   causation standards, 337–338
   frequency, regularity, and proximity test, 338
   nuisance statute, 19

J
Joinder of plaintiffs, 174–175
Joint and several liability, 168–170
   CERCLA response costs, 27
Judicial Panel on Multidistrict Litigation (JPML), 173–174
Juries, 234
   blue-ribbon juries, 223
   cleanup emphasis, 246–247
   closing argument, 247–248
   consultants, 235–237
   defining the central issue, 234
   demonizing vs. personalizing, 245–246
   demonstrative evidence, 246–247
   getting sting out early, 245
   hyperbole vs. explanation, 242–243
   picking spots, 244–245
   selection strategy, 235
   simplification, 235
   voir dire, 240–241
Jury instructions, 312, 319, 320, 329, 411, 412, 414, 430
   New York Pattern Jury Instructions, 422–423

K
Kansas
   causation standards, 339–340
   expert witness qualification, 300–302
Kentucky
   causation standards, 379–380
   fiber drift theory, 381–382
Keynote software, 246

L
Lab data admissibility, 248
Laches, 72–73
Lack of duty, 101–102
   bulk raw materials supplier defense, 105
   duty of care, 101–103
   duty to warn, 103
   learned intermediary doctrine, 105–108
   overview, 101
   sophisticated user or intermediary doctrine, 103–105
Lack of procedural capacity motions, 231–232
Landowner liability. *See generally* CERCLA (Comprehensive Environmental Response, Compensation, and Liability Act); RCRA (Resource Conservation and Recovery Act)
   former landowners, 28–30
Last clear chance doctrine, 93
Latency periods, 6
Lay opinion giver testimony, 209
Lead counsel, 226
Learned intermediary doctrine, 105–108
Legacy of major mass events, 4–5
Liability theories, 9–10
   absolute liability, 26
   former landowner liability, 28–30
   imported theories for toxic tort context, 30–32

battery and assault, 32–34
breach of warranty, 30–33
overview, 30
parens patriae, 34–35
unjust enrichment and restitution, 33
negligence, 9–10. *See also* Negligence
nuisance, 18–19. *See also* Nuisance claims
overview, 18–19
statutory nuisance, 19
statutory liability, 26–27
strict liability, 21–22. *See also* Strict liability
trespass, 13–14. *See also* Trespass
Liaison counsel, 226
Limitations period for damages, 67–70
Limited fund theory, 272–274
fairness hearings, 277
Local Controversy Exception, 180–181
Lodestar calculation of fees, 56, 267
Lohrmann test, 148–150, 151, 368, 390, 391, 392, 398, 409, 413, 416
Lone Pine orders, 227
Loss of consortium, 36
Loss of enjoyment of life, 36
Lost earning capacity, 35
Louisiana
causation standards, 382
mitigation of damages, 96

M

Maine
causation standards, 411–412
Manual for Complex Litigation, Fourth (Federal Judicial Center), 225–227
Manufacturing defect theory, 25
Marketing, impact on case valuation, 265–266
Market share liability, 170–171
Maryland
causation standards, 405, 412–413
foreseeability, 412
Lohrmann test, 413
Massachusetts
causation standards, 414–415
Mass actions, 180
Mass torts definition, 4–5
Material safety data sheet (MSDS), 85
listed symptoms as causation evidence, 153
Maximum contaminant level (MCL), 89
MDL (multidistrict litigation), 172–174
Mediation, 268
Medical evidence, 139–140. *See also* Scientific evidence
expert testimony, 157–158. *See also* Expert testimony
exposure and dose, 140–141
general causation, 140–141. *See also* General causation
independent medical examinations, 215–216
post-*Daubert* primacy, 164–165
proving or disputing causation with, 143–144
general causation, 144
overview, 143–144
specific causation, 146–147. *See also* Specific causation
specific causation, 142–143. *See also* Specific causation
Medical examinations, independent, 215–216
Medical expenses, 35

Medical monitoring, 40–41
  class action remedy, 179, 297–298
  litigation trends, 304–305
Meteorology, 129
Michigan
  causation standards, 341–343
  groundwater contamination, 283–284
Midwestern U.S. state causation standards, 333–334. *See also individual states*
  overview, 333
Minnesota
  causation standards, 346–347
Mississippi
  causation standards, 385–386
  discovery rule, 59, 61
  frequency, regularity, and proximity test, 386
Missouri
  causation standards, 347–348
Mitigation of damages, 95–97
Modeling of exposure routes vs. actual data, 211–212
Montana
  causation standards, 322–323
More definite statement motions, 230–231
Motion practice, 229–230
  discovery motions, 232–233
  evidentiary motions, 232–234
  failure to state claim, 231–232
  more definite statement, 230–231
  overview, 229
  reconsideration motions, 233–234
  vagueness, 230–231
  venue, 229–231
Motions *in limine*, 232–234
MSDS (material safety data sheet), 85
Multidistrict litigation (MDL), 172–174

Multiplaintiff trials, 250–251
  bifurcation and reverse bifurcation, 250–251
  test plaintiffs, 253–254
  trifurcation, 252
Multiple causative agents, 151–152
Multiple laboratories in sampling and analysis, 126

N

Named parties. *See* Party selection
Natural resources damage, 47–49
Nature of neighborhood, 21
Nebraska
  causation standards, 350–351
Negligence, 9–10
  elements, 9–10
  overview, 9–10
  per se, 11–12
  res ipsa loquitur, 12
Negligence per se, 11–12
  state-of-the-art design, 114
  violations of statutes and regulations as evidence, 11, 250
Negotiation as ADR, 268
Nevada
  causation standards, 323–325
    federal cases, 325
New Hampshire
  causation standards, 417
New Jersey
  causation standards, 405, 418–419
  frequency, regularity, and proximity test, 418
  groundwater contamination, 285–286
  punitive damages standard, 52
New Mexico
  causation standards, 325–326
  parens patriae standing, 34

New York
  causation standards, 405, 422–423
  fracking, 282
  Pattern Jury Instructions, 422–423
No cause or right of action motions, 231–232
Noneconomic relief availability, 266
Nonjusticiability, 287–289
Nonparty rights, 201–202
North Carolina
  causation standards, 387–388
  groundwater quality standards, 88
  statute of repose, 70
North Dakota
  causation standards, 352–353
Nuclear energy regulation, 82–84
Nuisance claims, 18–19
  climate change–based nuisance actions, 287–288
  defenses, 97–99
    coming to the nuisance, 97
    contributory negligence, 100–101
    government authorization, 97–99
  former landowner liability, 29
  intentional invasion standard, 19
  overview, 18–19
  statutory nuisance, 19
Numerosity requirement, 177, 300–301

O

Occupational Safety and Health Administration (OSHA)
  HazCom standard preemption, 85–87
  investigation by, litigation risk, 265
Ohio
  causation standards, 354–355
Oil Pollution Act (OPA), 47–49
Oklahoma
  causation standards, 358–359

Open America Stay of Proceedings, 186
Oregon
  causation standards, 327–328
    expert testimony requirement, 328
OSHA (Occupational Safety and Health Administration)
  HazCom standard preemption, 85–87
  investigation by, litigation risk, 265
Out of control checks, 126
Out-of-pocket expenses, 35

P

PAA (Price-Anderson Act)
  preemption by, 82–84
Pain and suffering, 36
Parallel regulatory proceedings
  coordination, 219–221
  information management, 222–223
  overview, 219–221
Parens patriae, 34–35
Parent liability, 171–172
Particularized protective orders, 200–201
Party selection, 168–169
  comparative fault, 168–170
  joint and several liability, 168–170
  market share liability, 170–171
  overview, 168–169
  parent/successor liability, 171–172
Pecuniary damages, 35
Peer review of technique, 159
Pennsylvania
  causation standards, 405, 427–428
  fiber drift theory, 427
  fracking, 280–281
Permissive joinder, 174
Pesticides, 84–86
Petroleum handling, 23
  OPA natural resources damage liability, 47–49

Pharmaceutical safety, 87–88
　DES market share liability, 170
　FDA investigations as litigation risk, 265
　learned intermediary doctrine, 105–108
Physical invasion requirement, 15–17
Piercing the corporate veil, 172
Plausibility of association, 137, 142
Political question doctrine, 287–289
Pollution Legal Liability insurance policies, 267
Postinjury evidence of culpability, 256–257
Potentially responsible parties, 26–27
PowerPoint, 246
Predominance requirement, 177, 275–277
Preemption, 76–78
　AEA and PAA, 82–84
　CERCLA, 78–79
　　discovery rule, 63
　　statutes of repose, 71
　FDCA, 87–88
　FIFRA, 84–86
　OSHA HazCom Standard, 85–87
　overview, 76–78
　RCRA, 80–82
　TSCA, 81–83
Present injury requirement, 37–40
Preservation of evidence, 214–215
　court orders, 219
　credibility of litigant, basis, 219
　evidence examples, 215–216
　overview, 214–215
　spoliation, 216–218
Price-Anderson Act (PAA)
　preemption by, 82–84
Primary jurisdiction doctrine, 75–76
Priority of location, 20
Priority of occupation, 97

Prior nuisance or trespass doctrine, 91
Product defects liability, 24
Product identification, 111
Product line liability theory, 171
Property damages, 45–47
Protective orders, 198–199
　balancing of interests approach, 199
　good cause requirement, 199–200
　nonparty rights, 201–202
　overview, 198–199
　particularized orders, 200–201
　umbrella orders, 198–200
Proximate causation. *See* Causation
Public property, trespass on, 14
Public records and reports, 249
Punitive damages, 50–52

Q
Quality control in sampling and analysis, 125
　check samples, 125
　duplicate samples, 125
　multiple laboratories, 126
　overview, 125
　surrogate spikes, 125

R
Radiological exposure, 82–84
RCRA (Resource Conservation and Recovery Act), 26, 28
　exhaustion of administrative remedies, 73
　former landowner liability, 30
　preemption by, 80–82
　standing, 92
　waste management responsibility documentation, 212
Reasonable care. *See* Duty of reasonable care

Reasonably foreseeable users limitation, 25
Reconsideration motions, 233–234
Reference Manual on Scientific Evidence, 144–145, 156, 416
Regulatory risk, impact on case valuation, 265
Regulatory safe levels defense, 88–90
Relative risk, 135, 141
Remediation of sites, 26–27. *See also* CERCLA (Comprehensive Environmental Response, Compensation, and Liability Act); Cleanup
    attorneys' fees, 54–56
    civil penalties, condition of reduction, 188
    consultants, 222–223
    fate and transport role in determining scope, 130
Repeatability, impact on case valuation, 264
Residential disclosures, 29
Res ipsa loquitur, 12
Resource Conservation and Recovery Act (RCRA). *See* RCRA (Resource Conservation and Recovery Act)
Restatement (Second) of Torts
    abnormally dangerous activity doctrine, 21–22
    coming to the nuisance, 97
    mitigation of damages, 95
    negligence per se doctrine, 11–12, 250
    strict products liability standard, 24
    trespass doctrine, 5
Restatement (Third) of Torts
    causation approach, 4
    comparative fault, 168
    epidemiological evidence, 144–145
    learned intermediary doctrine, 107
    raw materials suppliers, 105
Restitution, 33
Reverse bifurcation, 250–251
Rhode Island
    causation standards, 430–431
Richards, William J., 252
Right of enjoyment, 18
Right to farm statutes, 21
Risk assessments to prove causation, 305–306, 425
Route of toxic substance ingestion, 131
Rudlin, D. Alan, 225
Rules of Procedure, Panel on Multi-District Litigation, 174

S
Sampling and analysis, 121–123
    calibration, 126–127
    overview, 121–123
    preservation, 126–127
        court orders, 219
    procedures, 123–125
    quality control, 125
    splitting samples, 219
SARA (Superfund Amendments and Reauthorization Act), 62
Scientific evidence, 121–123. *See also* Medical evidence
    Bradford Hill criteria, 136–137
    epidemiology, 133–135
    fate and transport, 127–128
    overview, 121–123
    sampling and analysis, 121–123. *See also* Sampling and analysis
    toxicology, 131
Seal, filing under, 201
Secretary of Commerce, U.S., 48
Secretary of Interior, U.S., 48

Self-critical analysis privilege, 188–190
Settlement considerations, 261–262
   alternative dispute resolution methods, 267–268. *See also* Alternative dispute resolution methods
   class settlements, 271
      fairness hearings, 277–278
      heightened scrutiny for certification, 271–273, 274–277
      limited fund theory, 272–274
      lower court decisions, 274–276
      overview, 271
      state court decisions, 277
      Supreme Court views, 271–272
   overview, 261
   valuation of case, 261–262. *See also* Valuation of case
Shareholder relations, impact on case valuation, 265–266
Sharing data, 205–206
Sick Building Syndrome, 383
Single verdict risk, 264
Site access, 206–208
Slight/gross system of comparative fault, 93
Sophisticated user or intermediary doctrine, 103–105
South Carolina
   causation standards, 391–392
South Dakota
   causation standards, 361–362
Southern U.S. state causation standards. *See also individual states*
   overview, 363
Special damages, 35
Specific causation, 142–143
   challenges to, 108–109
   medical evidence, 148–149
      circumstantial evidence, 152–154

      differential diagnosis, 154–155
      government standards and risk assessments, 155–157
      multiple causative agents, 151–152
      overview, 148
      substantial factor tests, 148–150
   state-by-state standards. *See individual states*
Specificity of association, 137, 141
Spiking, 125
Splitting samples, 219
Spoliation, 216–218
Standing, 90–93
   climate change nuisance actions, 289, 290
   natural resources damage, 48–50
   parens patriae, 34–35
State-by-state causation standards, 309–310. *See also individual states*
State of the art, 113–116
Statistical significance, 136
Statistics, use in fate and transport modeling, 129
Statutes of limitations, 57–59
   continuing torts, 65–67
   damages period, 67–70
   disability of plaintiff, 70
   discovery rule, 58–61
      CERCLA, 62–63
   fraudulent concealment theory, 69
   overview, 57–59
Statutes of repose, 70–72
Statutory liability theories, 26–27
Statutory nuisance, 19
Stratified random selection, 254–256
Strength of association, 136, 141
Strict liability, 21–22
   abnormally dangerous activities, 21–22
   absolute liability distinguished, 26

fracking, 280–282
product defects, 24
state-of-the-art design, 113–116
Study group, 141
Study size, 136
Subclinical impacts, 39
Substantial factor tests, 148–149, 151
Subsurface contamination, 282–284
Successor liability, 171–172
Summary jury trials, 270–271
Superfund Amendments and Reauthorization Act (SARA), 62
Superfund sites. *See* CERCLA (Comprehensive Environmental Response, Compensation, and Liability Act)
Superiority requirement, 177
Supremacy Clause, 76
Surrogate spikes, 125

T

Tagalong cases, 174
Take-home exposure, 293–294
Tangible physical invasions, 15
Temporal relationship, 137, 142
Tennessee
    causation standards, 393–395
    frequency, regularity, and proximity test, 390
Tennessee Valley Authority (TVA), 97
Tenth Amendment, 64
Testability of scientific theory or technique, 159
Test plaintiffs, 253–254
Texas
    causation standards, 396–397
    fear of disease actions, 43
    punitive damages standard, 51
Third party rights, 201–202

30(b)(6) depositions, 194–196
Threshold of toxic substance exposure, 132
Tolling
    laches, 72–73
    statutes of limitations, 57–59. *See also* Statutes of limitations
    statutes of repose, 70–72
Toxicology, 109, 131
    exposure routes, 210–212
Toxic Substances Control Act (TSCA)
    preemption by, 81–83
Toxic Torts Litigation Guide (Cetrulo), 235, 236–237, 242
Transportation, U.S. Department of
    investigation by, litigation risk, 265
Transport, fate and, 127–128
Transporting abnormally dangerous materials, 23
Trespass, 13–14
    abnormally dangerous activities, unintentional trespass liability, 16
    continuing trespass, 17
    elements, 13–14
    evolution of doctrine, 5
    exclusive possession requirement, 14–15
    groundwater contamination as, 283
    illustrative cases, 17–19
    intent requirement, 16–17
    overview, 13–14
    physical invasion requirement, 15–17
    public property, 14
    wrongful entry, 15
Trial counsel, 226
Trial issues, 234
    industry codes, 249
    jurors, shaping case for, 234. *See also* Juries

Trial issues (*continued*)
  lab data admissibility, 248
  multiplaintiff trial structuring, 250–251. *See also* Multiplaintiff trials
  postinjury evidence of culpability, 256–257
  public records and reports, 249
  violations of statutes and regulations, 250
Trifurcation, 252
Triple-A Arbitration, 268
TSCA (Toxic Substances Control Act)
  preemption by, 81–83
TVA (Tennessee Valley Authority), 97
Typicality requirement, 177

U

Ultrahazardous activities, 21–22
  former landowner liability, 29
  fracking, 280–282
  unintentional trespass liability, 16
Umbrella protective orders, 198–200
Under seal filing, 201
Uniform Commercial Code
  warranties, 30–33
Unjust enrichment, 33
Unknowns, testing standards for, 123
Utah
  causation standards, 328–329
Utilities supplier duties limitation, 102

V

Vagueness motions, 230–231
Validation of data, 222
Valuation of case, 261–262
  case strengths and vulnerabilities, 262–263
    causation, 262–263
    damages, 263–264
    wrongdoing, 262
  client strengths and vulnerabilities, 264–265
    marketing and shareholder relations, 265–266
    regulatory risk, 265
    repeatability, 264
    single verdict risk, 264
  overview, 261
  unique considerations for environmental toxic torts, 266–267
    cleanup obligation relationship to liability, 266
    insurance coverage issues, 267
    noneconomic relief availability, 266
    statutory attorneys' fees claims, 267
Veil piercing, 172
Venue motions, 229–231
Vermont
  causation standards, 432
Virginia
  causation standards, 399–400
  duty to defend, climate change actions, 291–293
Voir dire, 240–241

W

Wage loss, 35
Warranty breach, 30–33
Washington
  causation standards, 329–331
Waste stream identification and reconstruction, 212–213
  analytical data, 213–214
  pre-regulatory vs. post-regulatory scenarios, 212–213

Western U.S. state causation standards, 309–310. *See also individual states*
West Virginia
    causation standards, 402–403
    fear of disease actions, 44
Wisconsin
    medical monitoring, 304–305
    punitive damages standard, 51
Workers' compensation bar, 118–119
Workplace exposure, 293–294
Wrongdoing, impact on case valuation, 262
Wrongful entry, 15
Wyoming
    causation standards, 331